Prentice Hall

Writing and Grammar

Communication in Action

Copper Level

Featuring: iText
Interactive text online and on CD-ROM

Copper Level

PEARSON
Prentice Hall

Upper Saddle River, New Jersey
Needham, Massachusetts

Program Authors

The program authors guided the direction and philosophy of *Prentice Hall Writing and Grammar: Communication in Action*. Working with the development team, they contributed to the pedagogical integrity of the program and to its relevance to today's teachers and students.

Joyce Armstrong Carroll

In her forty-year career, Joyce Armstrong Carroll, Ed.D., has taught on every grade level from primary to graduate school. In the past twenty years, she has trained teachers in the teaching of writing. A nationally known consultant, she has served as president of TCTE and on NCTE's Commission on Composition. More than fifty of her articles have appeared in journals such as *Curriculum Review, English Journal, Media & Methods, Southwest Philosophical Studies, Ohio English Journal, English in Texas,* and the *Florida English Journal.* With Edward E. Wilson, Dr. Carroll co-authored *Acts of Teaching: How to Teach Writing* and co-edited *Poetry After Lunch: Poems to Read Aloud.* Beyond her direct involvement with the writing pedagogy presented in this series, Dr. Carroll guided the development of the Hands-on Grammar feature. She co-directs the New Jersey Writing Project in Texas.

Edward E. Wilson

A former editor of *English in Texas,* Edward E. Wilson has served as a high-school English teacher and a writing consultant in school districts nationwide. Wilson has served on the Texas Teacher Professional Practices Commission and on NCTE's Commission on Composition. With Dr. Carroll, he co-wrote *Acts of Teaching: How to Teach Writing* and co-edited the award-winning *Poetry After Lunch: Poems to Read Aloud.* In addition to his direct involvement with the writing pedagogy presented in this series, Wilson provided inspiration for the Spotlight on Humanities feature. Wilson's poetry appears in Paul Janeczko's anthology *The Music of What Happens.* Wilson co-directs the New Jersey Writing Project in Texas.

Gary Forlini

Gary Forlini, a nationally known education consultant, developed the grammar, usage, and mechanics instruction and exercises in this series. After teaching in the Pelham, New York, schools for many years, he established Research in Media, an educational research agency that provides information for product developers, school staff developers, media companies, and arts organizations, as well as private-sector corporations and foundations. Mr. Forlini was co-author of the *S.A.T. Home Study* program and has written numerous industry reports on elementary, secondary, and post-secondary education markets.

National Advisory Panel

The teachers and administrators serving on the National Advisory Panel provided ongoing input into the development of *Prentice Hall Writing and Grammar: Communication in Action.* Their valuable insights ensure that the perspectives of teachers and students throughout the country are represented within the instruction in this series.

Dr. Pauline Bigby-Jenkins
Coordinator for Secondary English
  Language Arts
Ann Arbor Public Schools
Ann Arbor, Michigan

Lee Bromberger
English Department Chairperson
Mukwonago High School
Mukwonago, Wisconsin

Mary Chapman
Teacher of English
Free State High School
Lawrence, Kansas

Jim Deatherage
Language Arts Department
  Chairperson
Richland High School
Richland, Washington

Luis Dovalina
Teacher of English
La Joya High School
La Joya, Texas

JoAnn Giardino
Teacher of English
Centennial High School
Columbus, Ohio

Susan Goldberg
Teacher of English
Westlake Middle School
Thornwood, New York

Jean Hicks
Director, Louisville Writing Project
University of Louisville
Louisville, Kentucky

Karen Hurley
Teacher of Language Arts
Perry Meridian Middle School
Indianapolis, Indiana

Karen Lopez
Teacher of English
Hart High School
Newhall, California

Marianne Minshall
Teacher of Reading and Language Arts
Westmore Middle School
Columbus, Ohio

Nancy Monroe
English Department Chairperson
Bolton High School
Alexandria, Louisiana

Ken Spurlock
Assistant Principal
Boone County High School
Florence, Kentucky

Cynthia Katz Tyroff
Staff Development Specialist
  and Teacher of English
Northside Independent School District
San Antonio, Texas

Holly Ward
Teacher of Language Arts
Campbell Middle School
Daytona Beach, Florida

Grammar Review Team

The following teachers reviewed the grammar instruction in this series to ensure accuracy, clarity, and pedagogy.

Kathy Hamilton
Paul Hertzog
Daren Hoisington
Beverly Ladd

Karen Lopez
Dianna Louise Lund
Sean O'Brien

CONTENTS IN BRIEF

Chapters 1–13

Part 1: Writing 1

Resources

Writing

The Writer in You

Writing in Everyday Life

You probably write every day without even thinking about it. You may share e-mail messages with friends or write cards to thank relatives for gifts they've given you. Even something as simple as jotting down a phone message is a form of writing. In addition, you do a variety of forms of writing in school— ranging from taking notes to writing stories to completing research reports. In the chapters that follow, you will learn strategies that will not only help you to become a better writer but will also help you get more enjoyment out of the writing that you do.

▲ Critical Viewing
What two questions would you like to ask this student about her writing? [Speculate]

Why Write?

Like speaking, writing allows you to communicate your thoughts, opinions, and knowledge to others. When you write, however, you can communicate with a wider audience than you can in everyday conversation. Some people might read your work today—and others can read your work next week or next year. By developing strong writing skills, you strengthen your ability to communicate with others.

Developing Your Writing Life

Part of becoming a good writer is finding an approach to writing that works for you. Your approach includes everything from where you write and when you write to how you go about choosing topics and revising your work.

Keep Track of Your Ideas

One of the first habits that you should develop as a writer is keeping track of your ideas. Having a great idea and then forgetting it is one of the worst things that can happen to any writer. Don't let it happen to you. Try these techniques for keeping track of ideas that come to mind.

Writer's Notebook You can come across a writing idea at any time. That's why many writers carry a small notebook wherever they go. Keep a notebook in which you jot down things you observe, comments people make, and quotations from books, advertisements, and television programs.

Journal A journal is a great way to capture ideas and ensure that you write regularly. Get a notebook or a tablet, and write in it at regular intervals—ideally, every day.

Idea Card File Use note cards to collect ideas about specific topics. For example, if you're writing about the Grand Canyon, you might write a note card about each landform. Use the note cards to experiment with different ways of organizing your information.

Writers in
ACTION

Author Jane Yolen bases many of her fanciful stories on her study of folklore. Even her most fantastic stories, however, contain a grain of realism. She says of her writing: "Anything I've experienced can find its way into one of my stories."

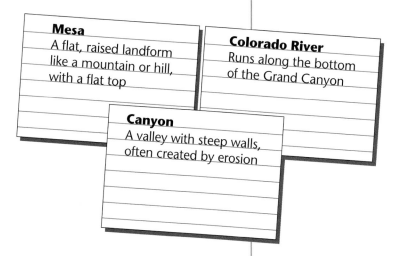

Mesa
A flat, raised landform like a mountain or hill, with a flat top

Colorado River
Runs along the bottom of the Grand Canyon

Canyon
A valley with steep walls, often created by erosion

Keep Track of Your Writing and Reading

Writing Portfolio Every time you complete a writing project, you will learn and grow as a writer. Creating a writing portfolio helps you review your progress. Looking back at what you've done can help you make strong writing choices on your next writing project.

Include a wide range of different types of writing in your portfolio. In addition to final drafts, include notes, graphic organizers, and earlier drafts to capture how the project developed.

Reader's Journal Reading is a good way to provide fuel for your writing. Keeping a reader's journal can also help you keep track of what you read. Make note of the authors and titles of books and articles you enjoy. Include a few quotations that capture each writer's style, too. When you browse through your journal, think of ways you can respond. You might write a review, a sequel, or a letter to the author.

What Works Best for You?

Getting Started There are many different ways to get started on a piece of writing. You may want to plunge in and start typing your ideas on a computer. You may also begin by taking some time to reflect quietly about your topic.

Freewriting Freewriting is another approach to getting started. This involves jotting down any thoughts that come into your mind, with no self-editing. Often, freewriting may provide material for a more formal piece of writing.

Finding Ideas Don't let a blank page intimidate you. Ideas for writing are everywhere! Every day, you can find ideas in newspapers, on television, or in books. If you keep a writer's journal, turn to its pages to find inspiration for your writing.

Improving Your Work One of the great things about writing is that you get a chance to go back and improve what you've done. Take advantage of this opportunity by carefully revising every piece of your writing.

Experiment

As you develop as a writer, experiment with various strategies and techniques. You might try making revisions as you go along. You might also focus on completing a draft in a single sitting. There are many different ways to approach a piece of writing, and one way isn't necessarily better than another. All that really matters is that you find the approach effective.

Technology Tip

If you work on a computer, you can keep an electronic portfolio. Do so by creating a folder for each assignment and storing those folders within other folders. For example, you may want to create a folder for each type of writing.

Spotlight on the Humanities

Analyzing How Meaning Is Communicated Through the Arts

Introducing the Spotlight on the Humanities

In addition to writing, there are many other ways in which you can express yourself. In the Spotlight on the Humanities features, you will discover how all art is connected and how the inspiration that moved the hearts and minds of creative artists in the past continues to touch artists of today. The following art forms provide some of the best opportunities for self-expression.

- **Fine art** includes paintings, sketches, sculpture, and collages. Through the use of color and form, art expresses feelings and conveys ideas about the world in which we live.
- **Photography** allows us to capture people, scenes, and events. Through the choice of subject, composition, and lighting, photography offers the opportunity for the expression of ideas.
- **Theater** is designed to be performed by actors on a stage. Using props, scenery, sound effects, and lighting, drama brings a story to life. In some cases, music and dance are incorporated into the story line.
- **Film** uses sound and motion to capture events and tell a story. Like dramatic theater, most films tell a story. However, filmmakers can also use camera angles, sound techniques, and editing to create special effects.
- **Music** uses sound to create meaning. Whether present-ed as an oboe solo, an operatic aria, or a symphony, music can create moods or present variations on a theme.
- **Dance** creates meaning through organized movement. It can be performed by a single person, a pair, or larger groups.

Writing Activity

Select a work of art from the list above that you consider memor-ble. Write a poem that captures your impressions about that ork of art.

▲ **Critical Viewing**
What mood and what ideas does this sculpture convey?
[Analyze]

Plan to Write

The best way to improve as a writer is to write. Set aside time to write as often as you can. You don't have to wait until you've been given a writing assignment in school. Write on your own. You can write stories, journal entries, letters to your newspaper—any type of writing that interests you. Not only will you improve as a writer, but you'll probably have some fun in the process.

Organize Your Environment

Choose the Right Spot To make yourself more comfortable and efficient when you write, find a special place to do your writing. You might prefer a quiet library or a room with quiet music. Try writing in different places, and decide which environment works best for you. You might even find that you prefer one place for writing poems and another for writing letters.

Be Ready to Write American author Ernest Hemingway once told a friend that he began writing each morning by sharpen-ing twenty pencils! You may not need that many pencils, but it's good to begin with everything you will need. Before you start, make sure that you have pens, paper, and your notes. If you're working on a computer, be sure to use word-processing software with which you feel comfortable and to have access to a printer. Also, have a diction-ary and a thesaurus nearby.

Budget Your Time A long writing assignment may take a few days to finish. Make a schedule to help keep you on track. Divide your project into stages, and give yourself a set amount of time for each stage. If one stage takes longer than expected, adjust the amount of time you spend on later stages.

▲ **Critical Viewing**
Could you write effectively in this environment? Why or why not?
[Apply]

Project To-Do List

Day 1	Begin collecting ideas
Day 2	Continue collecting ideas
Day 3	Decide which ideas to include
Day 4	Write a first draft
Day 5	Revise and proofread piece

1

Working With Others

Runners can run by themselves or as part of a team. Writers can also work independently or with others. However, there are many benefits to working with others.

Group Brainstorming It can be challenging to come up with ideas on your own. Group brainstorming helps many writers develop their ideas. Brainstorming means freely suggesting and building on ideas. Don't stop to think about whether the ideas are any good. Just talk about them with the group. Listening to other people's ideas and responses can help you focus your thoughts.

Collaborative and Cooperative Writing
Writers can collaborate at all stages of the writing process. A team can draft a letter to the editor by dividing the work. One writer might draft the introduction. Another might draft the conclusion. The same team might take turns proofreading the letter. Using more than one proofreader can really help the team catch any mistakes.

Peer Reviewers As a writer, you are very close to your own writing. Another pair of eyes often sees things that you might have missed. Try to work with a peer reviewer as often as possible. Take turns reading each other's work and offering suggestions for improvement. In each chapter that follows, you will find specific strategies and suggestions for working with peer reviewers.

Publishing

When you finish a writing project, consider sharing it with others. Publishing your work can make you feel proud and may even inspire other writers. There are many magazines, contests, and online sites that publish student work. Speak to your teacher or a librarian about possible places to publish, or consult the list on page 743.

Writers in
ACTION

Every writer has unique writing habits. Robert Frost wrote his poems on a writing board. He said, "I've never had a table in my life. And I use all sorts of things. Write on the sole of my shoe."

▼ **Critical Viewing**
Suppose that these students are working together on a school report. How might they share ideas? **[Analyze]**

What Are the Qualities of Good Writing?

Ideas Good writing begins with good ideas. When you come up with ideas to write about, it is important to select those that interest you. The more interested you are in what you write, the better you will write. Consider also whether the ideas will interest the people who read your writing.

Organization The next characteristic of good writing is a clear and consistent organization. Choose a logical way of arranging your information: one that suits the topic and the type of writing that you are doing.

Voice When you speak, you sound different from anyone else. The same is true of your writing. A writer's voice is the unique way every writer has of expressing himself or herself on paper. Voice includes everything from the words you use to the types of sentences you choose to the topics you select.

Word Choice Each word should be selected to convey the exact meaning you intend. In addition, consider the associations that certain words call to mind for readers. If you wish to convey a positive impression of your subject, choose words that support that impression.

Sentence Fluency Be aware of the sound of your writing as well as its meaning. When you read your work aloud, your sentences should flow smoothly from one to another. You can achieve this effect by using transitions to connect your sentences. In addition to using transitions, vary the lengths and types of sentences you use.

Conventions Finally, be careful to follow the conventions of English grammar, usage, mechanics, and spelling. A potentially great piece of writing will have a poor impact if it contains errors. Always proofread your work to eliminate errors.

Reflecting on Your Writing

Asking yourself questions can help you evaluate your opinions about writing. It can also help you focus on your writing goals. Here are just a few questions you might ask:

• What is my favorite kind of writing?

• Where is my favorite place to write?

• Who is my favorite author?

• At what times do I do my best writing?

• What kinds of writing would I like to complete this year?

Take some time to share your responses with a partner, and then jot down your ideas in a writer's journal.

Media and Technology Skills

Making Technology Work for You

Activity: Identify Appropriate Technology

When you do research for a composition or presentation, you choose research tools and sources. Similarly, you have a choice of tools and resources available to share that information with your audience.

Learn About It Choosing the right type of technology for your purpose is the first step in successful communication of your ideas. Learn about the different ways that technology can be used to help you prepare and present information.

- **Writing Tools** Computer *word-processing programs* allow you to store and retrieve text. They also make it very easy to make revisions to your work.

- **Virtual Resources** The *Internet* is an extensive computer network on which individuals get and post information and pictures. Large numbers of individuals and organizations put information on the Internet. Search engines and links between sites allow users to find such information. *E-mail* is a way to send and receive messages nearly instantaneously over the Internet.

- **Audiovisual Tools** Several tools allow you to add sounds and images to your presentations. A *still camera* records still images, which can be displayed on their own or projected in a series with a *slide projector.* A *tape recorder* preserves and plays back sound.

Evaluate It Create a chart with the categories shown below to evaluate which types of technology tools you find most useful and which ones you might want to use in the future.

Uses of Technology

Writing Tools
- Writing software—allows easy revisions; helps you organize the writing process by using some feature prompts

Virtual Resources
- Internet—lets you present your work to a wide audience; permits easy research
- E-mail—allows students to share their work and get fast feedback on it

Audiovisual Tools
- Still camera—can show something that is hard to describe
- Slide projector—adds visual interest to oral presentations
- Tape recorder—helps in taking complete notes; reveals the personality of an interview subject

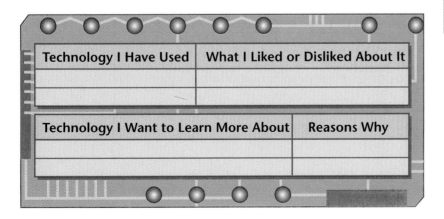

Technology I Have Used	What I Liked or Disliked About It

Technology I Want to Learn More About	Reasons Why

Standardized Test Preparation Workshop

Responding to Writing Prompts

Because writing is such an important skill, standardized tests often include writing sections. In these sections, you will be given a writing prompt and asked to write an essay about it. When your essay is evaluated, scorers will look to see that you have

- responded directly to the prompt and performed all of the tasks called for in the prompt.

- presented your ideas in a clear, well-organized manner.

- backed up your main points with facts, examples, and other types of details.

- followed all of the conventions of grammar, usage, mechanics, and spelling.

When you write for a test, you will often be given a time limit. If this is the case, you have to budget your time wisely. Divide up your time among thinking of ideas, writing your essay, and revising your essay.

Following is an example of one type of writing prompt you might find on a standardized test. Use the suggestions provided to help you respond. The clocks next to each stage show a suggested plan for organizing your time.

Test Tip

In any test question or writing prompt, look for key words that tell you exactly what is required. Words such as *explain, identify, describe,* and *persuade* indicate specific types of responses.

Sample Writing Situation

Writer Jane Yolen comments, "Anything I've experienced can find its way into one of my stories."

Write an essay in which you describe an experience you had that you think would make a good story. Provide the details of the experience, and explain why you think it would make a good story. Identify the types of readers who would like to read your story, and tell why.

Prewriting

Allow about one fourth of your time for prewriting.

Choose an Experience Think about the qualities of a good story. Then, search your memory for an experience that could form the basis for a story that would have those qualities.

Make a Timeline Sketch a timeline on which you outline the key events of the experience. Include such details as the people involved and the setting in which the experience took place.

Drafting

Allow about half of your time for prewriting.

Present Your Main Point Begin with an introduction in which you indicate what makes a good story, and sum up with a sentence or two about why the experience you have selected would make a good story.

Describe the Experience Use your timeline to help you describe the experience in detail. Make sure that you describe it in a way that will support your point that it would make a good story.

Support Your Position After you've described the experience, tell why it would make a good story. Back up your opinion by using details from the experience to illustrate how it fits the qualities of a good story.

Identify the Potential Audience Once you've explained why the experience would make a good story, describe the type of audience who would be most interested in your story.

Revising, Editing, and Proofreading

Allow about one fourth of your time to revise, edit, and proofread.

Check for Missing Details Review your essay to see if you have left out any important details from the experience. If you wish to add details, write them neatly in the margin, and draw an arrow and a line showing where they should be inserted.

Eliminate Errors Check your work carefully to eliminate errors in grammar, usage, mechanics, and spelling. Having these types of errors in your work can hurt your score on a standardized test—even if the content of your essay is good.

A Walk Through the Writing Process

You write every day. The form your writing may take depends on your purpose: You may be working on a school assignment, adding items to a shopping list, writing a post-card while on vacation, or e-mailing a friend. For each different type of writing you do, you may use some or all stages of the writing process, a systematized process for improving your writing.

▲ **Critical Viewing**
How can revising your writing improve it? **[Analyze]**

Types of Writing

To study writing, you can categorize it by **modes,** the forms or shapes that writing can take. The chart at right shows the modes of writing you'll encounter in this book. Writing can also be divided into two broad categories: *reflexive* and *extensive.*

Reflexive writing—such as a postcard to a friend, a note to yourself in your daily planner, or a personal journal essay—is *for* you and *from* you. This kind of writing is tentative and exploratory.

The inspirations for **extensive writing** are *for* others and *from* others. It is usually done for school, and it may be graded and evaluated. The audience for your extensive writing—such as research assignments, persuasive essays, and book reports—is often a general one.

The Modes of Writing

- Narration
- Description
- Persuasion
- Exposition
- Research Writing
- Response to Literature
- Writing for Assessment

The Process of Writing

These are the stages of the writing process:

- **Prewriting** Freely exploring topics, choosing a topic, and gathering and organizing details before you write
- **Drafting** Getting your ideas down on paper in roughly the format you intend
- **Revising** Correcting any major errors and improving the writing's form and content
- **Editing and Proofreading** Polishing the writing by correcting errors in grammar, spelling, and mechanics
- **Publishing and Presenting** Sharing your writing

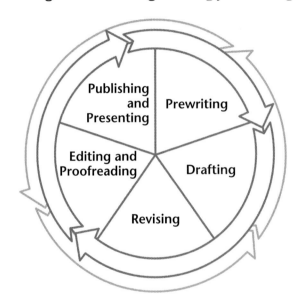

These steps may seem to follow a strict order, but writers often jump back to earlier writing stages as they work. For example, when you are drafting, you may discover that you need to do additional research on your topic. When you are revising, you may decide to include more work from your prewriting stage. You might even put aside work in the prewriting or drafting stage, save it in your portfolio, and go back to it sometime later, when you have thought of different strategies for organizing your writing.

A Guided Tour

Use this chapter as an introduction to the stages of the writing process. Consider the steps of the process presented here. Look at some of the strategies used by effective writers, and experiment with them in your own writing. By applying these strategies when you are engaged in the writing process, you will improve the quality of your final draft.

2.1 *What Is Prewriting?*

All writers can feel challenged when faced with a blank sheet of paper. The prewriting stage acts as a preparation for writing by helping to flex and stretch your creative muscles, just as dancers practice and warm up for a recital or performance. Prewriting consists of activities and strategies for getting started—a "mental warm-up" for writing.

Choosing Your Topic

In order to begin writing, you must first have a topic. Often, you produce your best writing when you are addressing a topic you find interesting. Prewriting strategies allow you to explore issues, ideas, and experiences that are meaningful to you. Prewriting techniques, such as the sample strategy presented here, can help you generate your topic.

SAMPLE STRATEGY

Look Through Photographs or Scrapbooks The photographs of significant events and souvenirs from vacations or local celebrations will help you remember amusing or meaningful events. Look through your scrapbooks and family photo albums. Think about the people, places, and activities that were included, and note those things that were meaningful, unusual, funny, or outrageous. Write notes about your most interesting memories. Then, review your notes to find a topic for an entertaining anecdote.

◀ Learn More

For additional prewriting strategies suited to specific writing tasks, see Chapters 4–13.

◀ Critical Viewing Name two topics that might be inspired by this photo album. **[Apply]**

Narrowing Your Topic

After you choose a topic, make sure it is neither too general nor too broad to write about effectively. While you prepare to write, you can use strategies that will help you narrow your topic and make it manageable.

SAMPLE STRATEGY

Use a Cluster Map Start by writing your broad topic in the center of a sheet of paper. Circle this topic. Then, in the spaces around your topic, jot down and circle related subtopics, connecting ideas to the main topic with linking lines. Then, in the area surrounding each subtopic, repeat the process, circling and linking ideas you have about each subtopic. Review your subtopics and ideas to decide whether any can stand alone as a writing topic. The following model shows a few of the many subtopics of *food*.

CLUSTER MAP

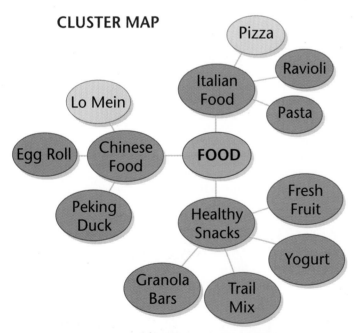

Considering Your Audience and Purpose

Once you have narrowed your topic, think about who will read your work. When you identify your intended audience, you can plan the best way to communicate with it. When you identify your purpose or reason for writing, you can plan what to include or communicate. The suggestions on page 16 will help you consider your audience and purpose.

Consider Your Audience When you think about the people you want to reach, decide who will read your writing and consider what they already know about your subject. An audience profile can help you plan how to address your audience most effectively. Use your answers to the following questions to prepare an audience profile. Then, use your notes to keep you on target as you write.

• What does my audience already know?

• What does my audience need to know?

• What details will interest or influence my audience?

Consider Your Purpose Think about your reasons for writing. Your purpose will influence the kinds of language you include. Consider these specific purposes:

TO PERSUADE: Include language and details to sway your readers.

TO ENTERTAIN: Include elements of humor, such as exaggeration and unexpected turns in the events you describe.

TO INFORM: Use objective language that provides information without taking a persuasive stand.

Gathering Details

To make drafting easier, collect the details and materials that you will need before you write your first draft. This will allow you to concentrate on the form and style of your writing as you draft, instead of trying to locate more information to make your writing clearer. Consider these strategies:

SAMPLE STRATEGY

Use Hexagonal Writing When you are writing about literature, a technique called hexagonal writing can help you gather details on six different aspects of a piece of literature. Complete each segment of the hexagon using the directions and questions shown at right. Then, review your work and add more information to support your ideas. Using this approach, you will be able to write a well-thought-out, thorough analysis.

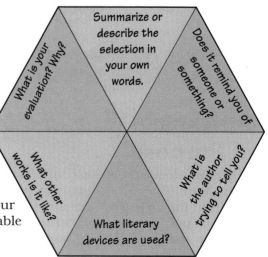

SAMPLE STRATEGY

Make a Sensory Details Chart For many types of writing—both fiction and nonfiction—you'll need to include a variety of details to make your subject clear. If you are describing an object, a place, or an experience, sensory details that tell how your subject looks, smells, tastes, sounds, or feels can improve your draft. Before you start to write, list vivid sensory details that you can use in your description. Create a chart like the one below to help you come up with sensory details.

Topic: New Pizza Restaurant				
Sights	**Sounds**	**Smells**	**Tastes**	**Touch**
checked cloths	chef singing opera	tomato sauce	spicy	gooey
murals from Italy	cheerful hubbub from diners	garlic	fresh	hot
colorful menus		onions	zesty	

▶ APPLYING THE PREWRITING STRATEGIES

1. Look through photo albums or scrapbooks to remember an event, a vacation, or a moment that was meaningful to you. List several ideas and then identify a topic you might choose to write about.
2. Make a cluster map of actions, places, and people you associate with the word *celebration.* To narrow your topic, suggest a more specific topic based on your cluster map.
3. Imagine that you are writing a speech to welcome an audience to a new or renovated school gymnasium. Prepare audience profiles for the following audiences, and then propose a specific purpose for each.
   (a) students
   (b) parents
   (c) members of the committee that raised funds for the renovation
4. Create a sensory details chart for a description of a movie theater.
5. Complete a hexagon for a story you have recently read.

Research Tip

Don't limit detail gathering to your own experiences and knowledge. You may need to conduct library research or interview others to collect the information you need.

Shaping Your Writing

Focus on Form Each form of writing has its own set of objectives: narratives tell a story; editorials and reviews persuade; and how-to writing shows the steps for completing a process. Consider the ideas you'd like to communicate, and match your content to a suitable form. Then, keep the objectives of the particular form in mind as you write.

Pull Readers In With an Enticing Lead To create an impressive opener—opening sentences that grab readers' interest—you might begin with a startling quotation, a surprising bit of dialogue, or a vivid description. Then, complete your introduction by connecting your lead to your main idea.

Providing Elaboration

Make your writing effective by including enough detail and explanation to help readers completely understand your subject. The SEE method is one strategy for developing your ideas and strengthening your writing.

SAMPLE STRATEGY

Use the SEE Method When you follow the steps of the SEE method, you shed more light on your subject. First, write a statement that conveys a main idea. Then, extend the idea by restating or explaining the first sentence. Finally, provide even more details about the main idea, such as examples, descriptions, or facts. Look at this example:

STATEMENT:	Planting bulbs in the fall produces blooms in the spring.
EXTENSION:	With just a little planning and work, you can make a beautiful garden.
ELABORATION:	Choose a variety of flowers, plan a pattern, pull on your gardening gloves, plant the bulbs, and wait for your spring bouquet.

▶ **APPLYING THE DRAFTING STRATEGIES**

1. Write an exciting introduction for an essay about your favorite game.
2. Complete the following sentence, and then use the SEE method to provide elaboration.

   If I could make one change in my town, I would __?__.

Learn More

Chapters 4–13 provide more information about the specific types of writing and the criteria for writing each one effectively.

2.3 *What Is Revising?*

Color-Coding Clues to Revision

When you apply thinking skills to the revision process, you give yourself an opportunity to make educated decisions about improving your writing. For example, the word **ratiocination** (rash´ ē äs ə nā´ shən) describes a method for thinking logically and systematically in order to arrive at a conclusion. When you use ratiocination to revise, you may analyze your draft by coding it in these ways:

• circling verbs

• bracketing sentence beginnings

• highlighting certain language you have used

Once you've coded a specific aspect of your writing, review the marked areas to evaluate and revise your writing. As you work through the revision sections of Chapters 4–13, you'll find strategies for analyzing structure, paragraphs, sentences, and word choice.

Revising Your Overall Structure

Before you begin to look at the finer points of your draft, review the structure and organization of your ideas. To analyze the soundness of the structure, look at the frame of your writing, For example, look for a main idea and the details you've chosen to support it. Consider this helpful strategy:

Writers in ACTION

When she talks about applying a step-by-step approach to revision, researcher Ellen Harkins Wheat acknowledges the value of such a strategy. She encourages writers to devote full attention to the revision process by identifying all the issues they want to address.

"There are lots of checkpoints you have in revising, and you probably need to make a list of all the things you think you need to cover."

SAMPLE STRATEGY

▶ **REVISION STRATEGY**
Color-Coding to Identify Main Ideas

To view the structure of your writing, highlight the main idea of each paragraph. Then, review the highlighted sections to decide whether you have presented your ideas in the best order. (You may want to insert additional information to make your organization more clear to readers.) In the example shown, the writer highlighted main ideas and decided to reorder paragraphs to present ideas more effectively.

IDENTIFYING MAIN IDEAS

Newspaper cartoons add to the joy of childhood. . . .

From a young age, children look forward to reading the comic sections of the paper. . . .

Most of all, Cartoons are something children share with their parents. When children are too young to read. . . .

Sunday comics in color are extra special. . . .

Revising Your Paragraphs

After you have reviewed the overall structure of your draft, study the next level of your writing by looking closely at each paragraph. Whether you are explaining something or narrating a sequence of events, dialogue can draw your readers in to the points you are developing. Consider this strategy:

SAMPLE STRATEGY

▶ **REVISION STRATEGY**
Identifying Places to Add Dialogue

As you read your draft, imagine how dialogue could make your writing more vibrant. Review your writing, placing a check in places where you show a mood, create a character, or build tension through descriptive language or explanation. For each check, draw a dialogue bubble in the margin and jot down notes that reveal a character's thoughts or feelings. Then, consider building some of these quotations into your revision. In this example, the writer deleted some explanation to avoid making a point twice.

ADDING DIALOGUE

We were all waiting on the platform, hoping a train would arrive, but each train that approached roared loudly past the station without stopping. ✓ ~~The wait seemed endless.~~ People shuffled impatiently.

"I've had it," one man said, and sat down with his head in his hands. "How much longer is this going to be?"

Revising Your Sentences

When you examine your writing at the sentence level, review the patterns you have introduced in your writing and introduce variety when you can. Take the time to notice whether you write mostly in short sentences or in long ones. Consider this strategy:

SAMPLE STRATEGY

▶ **REVISION STRATEGY**
Color-Coding to Evaluate Sentence Length

Alternating two different colors, bracket each sentence in your draft. For example, mark the first and third sentences in red and the second and fourth sentences in green. As you do this, pay attention to the length of the sentences in your writing. Then, strive for variety. Introduce a short sentence to break the pattern of long sentences. If you find you have a series of short sentences, combine some of them to improve the flow of ideas.

Revising Your Word Choice

Review your draft to be sure that the language you have used expresses your ideas most effectively. Look for places in your draft where a specific modifier can help to create a more vivid word picture.

SAMPLE STRATEGY

▶ **REVISION STRATEGY**
Circling Vague or Empty Modifiers

Whenever you write, use modifiers that describe exactly how something looks, sounds, feels, tastes, or smells. Avoid vague modifiers, such as *some* or *many*. In addition, revise empty modifiers—such as *nice, really,* or *great*—that don't add to your draft. Using a red pen, circle any vague or empty modifiers in your draft. In the example below, notice how specific modifiers help to bring the scene to life.

REVISING EMPTY AND VAGUE MODIFIERS

Vague, empty modifiers: (Some) (nice) passengers boarded the train for a (great) trip through the western states.

Specific modifiers: *Four smiling passengers boarded the train for a week-long sightseeing trip through the western states.*

Peer Review

As you revise, you'll find it helpful to get someone else's opinion. Each writing chapter offers specific suggestions for inviting peers to review your work.

Get Specific While it may be encouraging to hear your peers say they like your work, challenge your readers to give you specific feedback to help you revise your writing. Avoid questions that can be answered with *yes* or *no*. Consider these focused options:

Focusing Peer Review
• What did you like best?
• What would you like to know more about?

▶ **APPLYING THE REVISION STRATEGIES**

Using a draft you have recently written, apply each revision strategy presented here. When you have finished, review the changes you have made. Then, identify the most effective revision you made to your writing.

⊚ **Technology Tip**

Many word processors have built-in thesauruses to help writers improve their drafts. Highlight a word and use the thesaurus function to preview a list of other words with similar meanings.

What Are Editing and Proofreading?

Once you are satisfied with the ideas your writing expresses, take the time to make sure the form you have used is correct. From correcting errors in grammar, usage, and mechanics to double-checking for neatness, strive to make everything you write error-free.

Focusing on Proofreading

To help you improve your proofreading skills, each writing chapter offers a specific focus and a brief lesson on a related grammar, usage, or mechanics topic. While you can give added attention to each lesson's featured skill, always review your work and correct any errors you see. Here are the general areas you should address as you proofread:

Check Spelling Review the spelling of each word, referring to a dictionary to confirm the spelling of any word about which you are unsure. If no dictionary is available, consider replacing suspect words with synonyms that are easier to spell.

Examine Capitalization and Punctuation At a minimum, check to see that you've begun every sentence with a capital letter and used proper end punctuation. Then, take a close look at the other punctuation you've used.

Follow Grammar and Usage Conventions Check your writing to correct errors in grammar and language. To start, be sure you have corrected sentence fragments and revised agreement errors.

Fact-Check Be sure the ideas you include in your writing are true. Use the accuracy checklist shown here to direct your review.

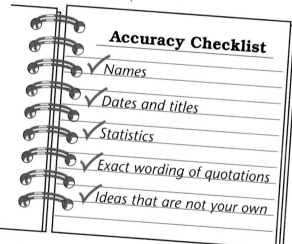

Accuracy Checklist
✓ *Names*
✓ *Dates and titles*
✓ *Statistics*
✓ *Exact wording of quotations*
✓ *Ideas that are not your own*

Confirm Legibility If you are handwriting your final draft, make sure that every word is clear enough to be read. Use a single line to cross out deleted information. Then, rewrite any words that may be hard to decipher.

▶ **APPLYING THE EDITING AND PROOFREADING STRATEGIES**

Using a recent draft you have written, proofread your work according to the categories identified on this page. Identify at least three corrections you have made.

Learn More

Part 2 offers extensive instruction in the conventions of grammar, usage, and mechanics.

2.5 *What Are Publishing and Presenting?*

Moving Forward

This preview of the writing process gives you just a glimpse of the strategies and techniques that you can use in your writing. Chapters 4–13 will teach you specific strategies to apply to a variety of writing situations.

Build Your Portfolio Because they showcase your best work, your finished writing products are valuable. Organize and save them in a portfolio—a folder, file, box, or other safe container. In addition to illustrating your development as a writer, your portfolio can also serve as a resource for future writing. Reserve a section of your portfolio for writing ideas, peer review notes, and photos that inspire you.

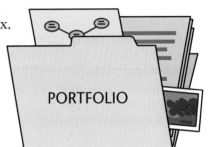

PORTFOLIO

Reflect on Your Writing Every time you complete a piece of writing, you have a chance to learn something about yourself, something about your topic, and something about your writing process. To help you take advantage of this opportunity, review the questions at the end of each writing chapter. Write your responses and save them in your portfolio as evidence of your thoughts and feelings about the writing you have completed this year.

Assess Your Writing At the end of each writing chapter, you will find a rubric, or set of criteria, on which your work may be evaluated. You can refer to the rubric throughout the writing process to be certain that you are addressing the specific conventions for the writing you are creating.

▶ APPLYING THE PUBLISHING AND PRESENTING STRATEGIES

1. Review the prewriting activities you completed in this chapter. Choose one activity to place in your portfolio to be developed at a later time. With a partner, discuss the reasons for your choice.
2. In your notebook or writing journal, reflect on your writing process by answering the following questions:

   - Which strategies in this chapter did you find most worthwhile? Explain.

   - What are your strengths as a writer?

   - What writing goals do you have for the year?

Spotlight on the Humanities

Examining Common Themes in the Arts

Focus on Music: Sergei Prokofiev

Like writers, all artists, dancers, and musicians work to develop inspirations into final performances. Russian composer Sergei Prokofiev (1891–1953) used a well-known fairy tale as the basis for his composition of the music for the ballet *Cinderella*. Whether retelling fairy tales or composing symphonies, Prokofiev was known for taking classical forms and adding satire and playfulness to his compositions.

Theater Connection A theatrical musical adaptation of *Cinderella* was created by American composers Rodgers and Hammerstein in 1964. The musical, which was televised, starred Lesley Ann Warren as Cinderella and Stuart Damon as The Prince. Rodgers and Hammerstein's music and lyrics have made this version of the fairy tale a modern classic.

Literature Connection Over 3,000 versions of the Cinderella story exist, and a version appears in most cultures of the world. The French version, considered one of the earliest, developed among the peasants of seventeenth-century France. Other modern versions of the story include *Just Ella* by Margaret Peterson Haddix and *Ella Enchanted* by Gail Carson Levine, a Newbery Honor Book.

Writing Process Activity: *Cinderella* Inspiration

When underdog teams win championships, announcers often call the unexpected win a "Cinderella story." The expression "if the shoe fits" is a popular cliché. The fairy tale has reached many parts of our culture—and many other cultures. In fact, with over 3,000 versions of the Cinderella story, there must be something universal about this tale. Writing *Cinderella* at the center of a cluster map, work with a group to identify several topics that you could pursue in a writing project. Put your completed map in your portfolio for later development.

▲ **Critical Viewing** Explain the importance of this moment from Walt Disney's version of *Cinderella*. If necessary, conduct research to find the answer. **[Connect]**

Media and Technology Skills

Using Technology to Support Writing

Activity: Building an Electronic Portfolio

Most things get better with practice. The same is true of writing. A good way to track your progress is to save your work in an electronic portfolio, a folder on a computer's hard drive or on a disk.

Learn About It The first step in organizing your writing on a word processor is to make a single folder for all of your work. You might name it "My Writing." For each project you begin, make a subfolder to hold all your files for that project. Then, in each project folder, make files for each stage of the writing process:

- **Prewriting** Put your freewriting notes, topic ideas, and any research work in a word-processing file called "My Notes" or "Ideas," and save it in your writing folder. You can access this file when you are ready to begin drafting.

- **Drafting** When you are ready to write your first draft, open a new file and name it with a working title. Save your work often as you draft. In fact, try to remember to hit the Save key after every paragraph.

- **Revising** After you have finished a first draft, track any revisions you make by choosing the Save As option and making a file with the title of your work and the ending *.1*. Each time you make a new version, increase the number. To avoid confusion, move your old drafts to a folder called "Old Drafts." Look at this example:

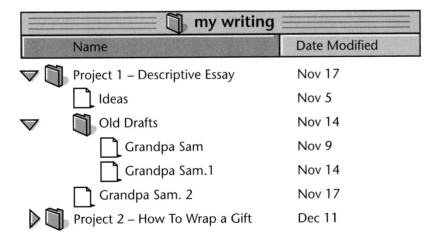

📁 my writing	
Name	Date Modified
▽ 📁 Project 1 – Descriptive Essay	Nov 17
📄 Ideas	Nov 5
▽ 📁 Old Drafts	Nov 14
📄 Grandpa Sam	Nov 9
📄 Grandpa Sam.1	Nov 14
📄 Grandpa Sam. 2	Nov 17
▷ 📁 Project 2 – How To Wrap a Gift	Dec 11

Evaluate It Try the suggested organization for the next writing assignment you complete. Then, get together with a group to discuss the positive and negative aspects of your electronic portfolio.

Standardized Test Preparation Workshop

Using the Writing Process to Respond to Writing Prompts

In order to evaluate the quality of your writing skills, many standardized tests include prompts that offer specific topics for you to address. Use the writing process to generate thoughtful, well-elaborated responses. You will be evaluated on your ability to do the following:

- provide an answer that directly addresses the prompt

- choose an organization suited to your ideas

- elaborate with details appropriate to your specific audience and purpose

- use the conventions of grammar, usage, and mechanics

As this chapter has shown, the writing process can be divided into stages. Even when writing for a test, plan to use a specific amount of time for each stage: prewriting, drafting, revising, and proofreading.

Following is an example of a writing prompt that you might find on a standardized test. Use the suggestions on the following page to help you respond. The clocks next to each stage show a suggested plan for organizing your time.

Test Tips

- While you may feel pressure in a test-taking situation, take the time to prewrite and revise. Each of these steps will help you create a better final draft.
- Use any scrap paper available to jot down your ideas. Then, cross off details as you address them in your writing.

Sample Writing Situation

> While most people expect to spend time at school in classes required for graduation, many students enjoy participating in extracurricular activities such as sports and clubs. In a letter to be included in a new student welcome packet, describe your own experiences in order to encourage others to get involved in such activities.

Prewriting

Allow about one fourth of your time for prewriting.

Consider Your Own Ideas Think about your experience with the subject. Review the activities you have enjoyed, and think about your friends and their involvement. Jot down the clubs you know best. For each, note the possible benefits of participation.

Consider Audience and Purpose As you begin to gather details for your response, keep in mind the audience indicated in the prompt. Many new students may want to know more about the school and how to make friends. Plan to focus on elements that will appeal to this concern.

Draw Up an Outline Organize your ideas to make them easy to follow. For this assignment, you may choose to focus on one activity and all its rewards. Alternatively, you may want to address several activities and discuss a single benefit of each one. Choose the organizational plan best suited to your experiences.

Drafting

Allow about half of your time for drafting.

State Your Position To help your readers understand your ideas, state your main idea in the opening paragraph of your letter. Use the following paragraphs to provide elaboration. Finally, write a conclusion that reminds readers of your key points.

Elaborate With Details An important part of your letter will be the details that you use to prove your points. Include examples or information that encourage students to join school-sponsored activities. Use the SEE method to elaborate ideas in your writing. Review page 18 to see an example of this drafting technique.

Revising, Editing, and Proofreading

Allow about one fourth of your time for revising. Use the few minutes remaining to proofread your work.

Revise to Ensure a Friendly Tone As a student who is thoroughly familiar with your school, take the initiative to make your readers—new students—feel comfortable. Find a level of language somewhere between the formal tone you'd use with adults and the informal slang you'd use with close friends. Revise to achieve this balance.

Make Corrections Review your paper for spelling and punctuation errors. Make all corrections neatly. Cross out text with a single line, and use a caret [^] to indicate insertions precisely.

Sentences, Paragraphs, and Compositions
Structure and Style

Sculpture made from interlocking blocks

What Are Sentences, Paragraphs, and Compositions?

A **sentence** is a group of words with a subject and a predicate. The words in a sentence work together to make a complete thought.

A **paragraph** consists of a group of sentences that work together to support a main idea or to achieve a single effect. Writing in paragraphs helps you focus information logically in separate sections.

A **composition** is a group of related paragraphs. They work together to form a composition in the same way that sentences work together to form a paragraph. Among the compositions you will write are responses to literature, research reports, and various kinds of essays. The chapters that follow will cover specific types of compositions.

▲ **Critical Viewing**
Explain how interlocking blocks could be used in a demonstration of how to construct an effective paragraph. **[Connect]**

3.1 *Sentence Combining*

When writing for young readers, writers use short, direct sentences that are easy to read. For a more experienced reader, this kind of writing can be dull, so it is important to vary your sentences when you write. One way to vary sentences is to combine two shorter sentences into a longer one.

Inserting Words and Phrases

One method of combining sentences is to take key information from one sentence, rewrite it as a phrase, and insert the phrase into another sentence. In some cases, you can combine sentences by adding just one word. You may have to change the form of the words and add punctuation.

EXAMPLE:	Oregon became the thirty-third state in 1859. <u>Oregon is a state in the Pacific Northwest.</u>
COMBINED:	Oregon, **a state in the Pacific Northwest,** became the thirty-third state in 1859.
EXAMPLE:	The name *Oregon* probably comes from the word *Ouragan,* meaning "hurricane." <u>The word *Ouragan* is French.</u>
COMBINED:	The name *Oregon* probably comes from the **French** word *Ouragan,* meaning "hurricane."
EXAMPLE:	Moist Pacific winds blow across Oregon. <u>This gives Oregon a mild climate.</u>
COMBINED:	Moist Pacific winds blow across Oregon, **giving Oregon a mild climate.**

▶ **Exercise 1** Combining With Words and Phrases Combine each pair of sentences by inserting key information from one sentence into the other. Add commas as necessary.

1. Oregon is bordered on the north by Washington. Washington was the forty-second state to join the United States.
2. The Columbia River flows into the Pacific Ocean. It forms most of the border between Oregon and Washington.
3. The world's smallest official park is called Mills End Park. It is 24 inches long and is located on a traffic island in Portland, Oregon.
4. Crater Lake is 1,932 feet deep. It is the deepest lake in the United States.
5. Mt. Hood is the tallest mountain in Oregon. It is an inactive volcano.

Using Compound Subjects, Verbs, and Objects

Two or more short sentences may have elements in common. These sentences may be combined by using a compound subject, a compound verb, or a compound object.

EXAMPLE:	Oklahoma is a southwestern state. New Mexico is a southwestern state, too.
COMPOUND SUBJECT:	**Oklahoma and New Mexico** are southwestern states.
EXAMPLE:	The Red River **forms** part of the border between Texas and Oklahoma. The Red River **flows** toward the Gulf of Mexico.
COMPOUND VERB:	The Red River **forms** part of the border between Texas and Oklahoma **and flows** toward the Gulf of Mexico.
EXAMPLE:	Oklahoma produces wheat. Oklahoma also produces beef.
COMPOUND OBJECT:	Oklahoma produces **wheat and beef.**

▶ **Exercise 2** Using Compound Subjects or Verbs Combine each pair of sentences by creating compound subjects, compound verbs, or compound objects as indicated in parentheses.

1. Natural gas is plentiful in Oklahoma. Petroleum is plentiful, too. (compound subject)
2. In Oklahoma City, you can visit the National Cowboy Hall of Fame. You can also visit the Rodeo Hall of Fame in Oklahoma City. (compound object)
3. Rodeo cowboys rope calves. Rodeo cowboys also ride bulls. (compound verb)
4. We visited Tulsa. We visited Oklahoma City. (compound object)
5. Humorist Will Rogers is a famous Oklahoman. Singer Garth Brooks is a famous Oklahoman, too. (compound subject)
6. The Cherokee Nation, a Native American tribal government, is based in Oklahoma. The Muscogee Nation, another tribal government, is also based there. (compound subject)
7. In the 1930's, Oklahomans endured a major drought. At the same time, they endured falling prices for crops. (compound object)
8. Seen in outline on the map, Oklahoma has a part that sticks out like a handle of a pan. Texas also includes a part that sticks out like the handle of a pan. (compound subject)
9. The Oklahoma Panhandle has rocky mesas, or flat-topped hills. The Oklahoma Panhandle also has much grassland. (compound object)
10. The Ouchita Mountains fall in southeastern Oklahoma. The Ouchita Mountains stretch into Arkansas. (compound verb)

◯ Learn More

For additional information about compound subjects and verbs, see Section 19.3.

Forming Compound Sentences

A **compound sentence** is made up of two or more simple sentences. Simple sentences may be combined to form a compound sentence by using a comma and a **coordinating conjunction** such as *and, but, or,* or *nor* or by using a semicolon.

EXAMPLE:	Ohio is not in the Northwest. It is not in the Southwest either.
COMPOUND SENTENCE:	Ohio is not in the Northwest, **nor** is it in the Southwest.
EXAMPLE:	The Adena people of prehistoric Ohio built Great Serpent Mound. They used the mound for burials.
COMPOUND SENTENCE:	The Adena people of prehistoric Ohio built Great Serpent Mound; they used the mound for burials.

Note that each coordinating conjunction expresses a different relationship between ideas. For example, *and* implies that the two ideas being joined are similar or compatible. *But* implies that the ideas are contrasting or opposed.

▶ **Exercise 3** **Forming Compound Sentences** Combine each pair of sentences using a comma and a coordinating conjunction or a semicolon to form a compound sentence.

1. Ohio is in the Midwest. Its capital is Columbus. (comma and coordinating conjunction)
2. The state bird of Ohio is the cardinal. The state tree of Ohio is the buckeye. (comma and coordinating conjunction)
3. Seven presidents of the United States were born in Ohio. More presidents were born in Virginia. (comma and coordinating conjunction)
4. The Rock and Roll Hall of Fame is in Cleveland. The Pro Football Hall of Fame is in Canton. (comma and coordinating conjunction)
5. My grandfather was from Cleveland. He lived his whole life there. (semicolon)

🔁 **Learn More**

For additional information about compound sentences, see Section 20.2.

▼ **Critical Viewing** Great Serpent Mound is located near Hillsboro, Ohio. Describe Great Serpent Mound using a compound sentence. **[Apply]**

Using Adjective and Adverb Clauses

A **subordinate clause** contains a subject and verb but does not express a complete thought. For example, "who developed an alphabet for his language" has a subject (*who*) and a verb (*developed*), but it does not express a complete thought.

To combine two sentences, you may rewrite one as an **adjective clause**—a subordinate clause that begins with *who, whom, whose, which,* or *that*—and join it to the other.

EXAMPLE: Sequoyah was a Cherokee silversmith from Tennessee. He developed an alphabet for the Cherokee language.

COMBINED: Sequoyah was a Cherokee silversmith from Tennessee **who developed an alphabet for the Cherokee language.**

In some cases, you may rewrite one sentence as an **adverb clause**—a subordinate clause that begins with a subordinating conjunction such as *although, after, because,* or *until.* The following chart lists some subordinating conjunctions.

Learn More

For additional information about clauses, see Section 20.2.

Time	Cause or Reason	Condition
after	as	although
before	because	if
when	so that	unless

EXAMPLE: The Ocoee River has impressive white water. It was chosen as the site for the 1996 Olympic white-water competitions.

COMBINED: *Because* the Ocoee River has impressive white water, it was chosen as the site for the 1996 Olympic white-water competitions.

Exercise 4 Combining by Using Clauses Combine each pair of sentences by rewriting one as the indicated type of clause.

1. Tennessee is bordered on the west by the Mississippi River. The Mississippi River is the longest river in the United States. (adjective clause)
2. Andrew Jackson was a native of Tennessee. Andrew Jackson became the seventh president of the United States. (adjective clause)
3. Tennessee is nicknamed the Volunteer State. Many people from Tennessee volunteered to serve in the War of 1812. (adverb clause)
4. Tennessee became the sixteenth state in 1796. Before that, the region belonged to North Carolina. (adverb clause)
5. Bobcat and coyote live in Great Smoky Mountains National Park. You may not see them because they keep to themselves. (adverb clause)

3.2 *Writing Effective Paragraphs*

Main Idea and Topic Sentence

The main idea of a paragraph is usually stated in the paragraph's **topic sentence.** The remaining sentences support, explain, or illustrate the topic sentence.

A paragraph may also have an **implied main idea.** In this case, the sentences in the paragraph contain related facts and details that together communicate the main idea, which the reader can infer.

WRITING MODELS

from **The Shutout**
Patricia C. McKissack and Fredrick McKissack, Jr.

The history of baseball is difficult to trace because it is embroidered with wonderful anecdotes that are fun but not necessarily supported by fact. There are a lot of myths that persist about baseball—the games, the players, the owners, and the fans—in spite of contemporary research that disproves most of them. For example, the story that West Point cadet Abner Doubleday "invented" baseball in 1839 while at Cooperstown, New York, continues to be widely accepted, even though, according to his diaries, Doubleday never visited Cooperstown. A number of records and documents show that people were playing stick-and-ball games long before the 1839 date.

> In this passage, the stated topic sentence is shown in blue italics. This sentence refers to the many myths surrounding baseball. The rest of the paragraph supports and illustrates the opening sentence.

from **The Sound of Summer Running**
Ray Bradbury

Late that night, going home from the show with his mother and father and his brother Tom, Douglas saw the tennis shoes in the bright store window. He glanced quickly away, but his ankles were seized, his feet suspended, then rushed. The earth spun; the shop awnings slammed their canvas wings overhead with the thrust of his body running. His mother and father and brother walked quietly on both sides of him. Douglas walked backward, watching the tennis shoes in the midnight window left behind.

> In this passage, all the sentences work together to support the implied main idea of the paragraph: A pair of sneakers viewed at the beginning of summer exerts a powerful pull on a boy.

> **Exercise 5** Identifying a Stated Topic Sentence Identify the stated topic sentence of the following paragraph.

Martin Luther King, Jr., was an important figure in the last century. King spent years working to gain equal rights for all people. He organized many boycotts, demonstrations, and marches. In 1964, he won the Nobel Peace Prize. Four years later, he was assassinated.

> **Exercise 6** Identifying an Implied Main Idea Identify the implied main idea of the following paragraph.

When I first moved to Vermont, I didn't know how to ski. I would stay at home most weekends during the winter. Finally, I decided to learn to ski. I rented equipment and signed up for a lesson. At first, I moved slowly down the hill, pointing the tips of my skis inward. Then, I learned how to turn. I got better and better, and now, I ski every weekend.

Writing a Topic Sentence

As you plan or outline the subject of your composition, identify the main points you will cover. You can write each main point as a **topic sentence.** A topic sentence states the main idea of a topical paragraph. You can then build your paragraph around the topic sentence.

A strong topic sentence will let readers know what the paragraph is about as well as the point you are making about the subject matter. Here are three pointers for writing a successful topic sentence:

| Review details. |
| Group related details. |
| Write a statement that pulls the details together. |

> **Exercise 7** Writing Topic Sentences Write a topic sentence for a paragraph on each of the following topics.
> 1. Winter sports you'd like to try or master
> 2. A review of the last movie you saw
> 3. A description of your best friend
> 4. How user-friendly or -unfriendly you find your school's computers to be
> 5. Your favorite foods

Writing Supporting Sentences

The topic sentence, whether stated or implied, contains a paragraph's main idea. The sentences in a paragraph that develop, explain, or illustrate the main idea or topic sentence are called *supporting sentences.* You can use one of the following strategies to support or develop the main idea:

Use Facts Facts are statements that are provable. They support your main idea by offering backup, or proof.

TOPIC SENTENCE:	Our playful kitten, Max, will probably grow up to be a very large cat.
SUPPORTING FACT:	Our veterinarian said that, based on his present size and age, Max would grow quite large.

Use Statistics A statistic is a fact often stated numerically.

TOPIC SENTENCE:	Our playful kitten, Max, will probably grow up to be a very large cat.
SUPPORTING STATISTIC:	He weighed just one pound at six weeks, and now, only four months later, he weighs ten.

Use Examples, Illustrations, or Instances
An example, illustration, or instance is a specific person, thing, or event that demonstrates a point.

TOPIC SENTENCE:	Our playful kitten, Max, will probably grow up to be a very large cat.
ILLUSTRATION:	Max is a big eater: He always seems to be waiting for snacks.

Use Details Details are the specifics that make your main idea or key point clear by showing how all the pieces fit together.

TOPIC SENTENCE:	Our playful kitten, Max, will probably grow up to be a very large cat.
DETAIL:	Everyone who sees him now is amazed at how much he's grown in such a short time.

▲ **Critical Viewing**
What details could be used to support a topic sentence that says this kitten is adventurous? **[Support]**

▶ **Exercise 8** **Writing Supporting Sentences** Write two supporting sentences for each of the following topic sentences.
1. It's important to get enough sleep.
2. Programming a VCR can be a frustrating experience.
3. One should never yell "Fire!" in a crowded room.
4. Babies need lots of care.
5. Team sports are fun to play and watch.

Placing Your Topic Sentence

The topic sentence that presents your main idea usually appears at the beginning of a paragraph. Sometimes, a topic sentence can be found in the middle or at the end of a paragraph. Placed at the beginning of the paragraph, the topic sentence focuses the reader's attention before the supporting details are presented. Placed at the end of the paragraph, the topic sentence summarizes the paragraph's details or draws a conclusion.

Paragraph Patterns You can arrange your paragraph in several different patterns, depending on the placement of your topic sentence. Using a TRI pattern, you would put together a paragraph using the following elements:

TOPIC SENTENCE: State your main idea.

RESTATEMENT: Interpret your main idea; put it into other words.

ILLUSTRATION: Support your main idea with an example.

T **R** **I**	A mosquito is an annoying little insect related to the fly. The three most annoying kinds of mosquitoes are the *Anopheles*, the *Aedes*, and the *Culex*. These three kinds are especially annoying because they can spread serious diseases, such as malaria, yellow fever, and encephalitis, or inflammation of the brain.

After you have identified the basic parts of your paragraph, try variations of the TRI pattern, such as TIR, TII, or ITR, until you are satisfied with the results.

T **I** **I**	Unlike many other insects, ladybugs are charming as well as beneficial. Their nonthreatening small, round shape and their cheerful black-spotted red coloring endear them to children and adults. However, ladybugs are more than just fun to watch. Gardeners love ladybugs because they eat the insects that hurt gardens and crops.

▶ **Exercise 9** Placing a Topic Sentence Arrange the following sentences in a paragraph. First, identify the topic sentence that expresses the main idea. Then, rearrange the sentences, using the TRI pattern or a variation.

The number of inches refers to the diameter of the wheel. Bicycles come in many sizes: 12, 16, 20, 24, 26, and 27 inches. Many people ride bicycles for recreation, but some people ride them to school or to work. A bicycle is a two-wheeled vehicle powered by turning two pedals with the feet.

Maintaining Unity and Coherence

Establishing Unity

A paragraph has **unity** when all of its sentences relate to the main idea. They support, explain, or develop the topic sentence. To be sure that your paragraphs have unity, think about your topic sentence as you draft. Check that each point relates to your topic. When you revise, strengthen the unity of the paragraph by deleting details or sentences that do not support, develop, or explain the main idea.

In the following paragraph, one sentence is marked for deletion because it interferes with the unity of the paragraph.

WRITING MODEL

> Some dogs are pests. They bark at your guests and jump on your furniture. They chew your shoes and they bother you when you're eating. Maybe these dogs were born that way, but that's unlikely. They probably became pests because their owners never trained them. ~~Puppies are especially cute and loveable~~. Dogs need to be taught how to behave. They need to learn the family's rules, such as when it's okay to bark. A good obedience class can provide this education. Every pet dog should be required to attend such a class.

▼ Critical Viewing
Give three sentences to support the main idea that the dogs in this photograph are well cared for. **[Draw Conclusions]**

> ◢ **Exercise 10** Revising for Unity On a separate sheet of paper, copy the following paragraph. Mark for deletion any sentences that interfere with the unity of the paragraph.

Obedience schools train the owner as well as the animal. This training is crucial because the owner must know how to control the dog. Otherwise, the dog will forget its training. Dogs love to gnaw on bones. Owners who learn with their pets are rewarded in several ways. Their families and the pets are happier because everyone is following the same rules. Guests feel more relaxed because they don't have to worry about getting dog hair all over their clothes. Regular exercise is also important for dogs.

Achieving Coherence

For a paragraph to have coherence, the supporting ideas must be logically connected and the reader should be able to see how one idea relates to another. When you draft, order the sentences so that one leads logically to the next. Transitional words and phrases, such as those in the chart below, show connections between ideas and help paragraphs flow.

Time-Order Transitions			
after	during	last week (month, and so on)	previously
ago	earlier	later	simultaneously
already	finally	next	then
at the same time	in the meantime	now	when
before	in the past	once	while
Spatial Transitions			
above	back	east (west, and so on)	middle
across	behind	in	there
around	below	into	under
at	down	left (right)	up
Order-of-Importance Transitions			
as much as best	greatest highest	less main	most (important, unforgettable, and so on)
finally	last	mainly	of all
first	least	more moreover	worst

> **Exercise 11** **Revising for Coherence** Revise the following paragraph, adding transitions to achieve coherence and reordering sentences as necessary.

Our vacation in New Mexico was fascinating. We visited the Puye cliff dwellings, which were built into the side of a mesa. We had to climb to reach them. We traveled along desert roads where we saw signs warning "Stock on Highway." We watched for cows but didn't see any on the road. Santa Fe had many Spanish-style buildings. My parents bought jewelry and crafts made by Native Americans. We also visited the charming town of Taos before we went to Santa Fe. I asked my sister if she remembered to bring the camera. Taos is home to Native Americans of the Taos tribe. It was beautiful.

3.3 *Paragraphs in Essays and Other Compositions*

Understanding the Parts of a Composition

When you write a composition, you *compose*—that is, you put all the parts together. Your reports, essays, and test answers may not be literary. Nevertheless, they are compositions, and to write them effectively, you must understand each of the parts.

Introduction

The **introduction** presents the subject of your composition. The introduction should capture the readers' interest with a strong **lead,** or first sentence. The main points of your composition should follow next in a **thesis statement.** Several sentences may follow, outlining how you will make each main point.

Body

Forming the **body** of a composition are several paragraphs that develop, explain, illustrate, and support the main ideas in your thesis statement. The body should be **unified** and **coherent** and logically organized. The topic sentence of each paragraph should tie directly to the points in your thesis statement.

Conclusion

The final paragraph of a composition is the **conclusion.** In the conclusion, you restate your thesis statement, usually using different words. You also summarize the support for the thesis and, if appropriate, offer a reflection or an observation on your subject. To make your conclusion memorable, you may want to end it with a forceful statement, a call to action, a quotation, or a question that causes your reader to give your subject more thought.

> **Exercise 12** Planning a Composition   Think of a subject that interests you. Then, on a separate sheet of paper, prepare a brief outline of the parts of a composition that you would write on that topic. Next, write a lead for your introduction—something to engage your readers' interest—and a thesis statement that includes the points you wish to cover in the composition. Now, write a topic sentence for each of your body paragraphs. Finally, choose a quotation or write a forceful statement for your conclusion, or write a question that will keep your readers thinking.

Types of Paragraphs

A strategy is a plan. Just as teams rely on strategies to win games, so do writers employ strategies to write effectively. An effective paragraph strategy involves choosing which types of paragraphs to write and which sorts of details to include.

Topical Paragraphs

A topical paragraph consists of a group of sentences containing one main idea sentence and several sentences that support or illustrate that main idea.

Functional Paragraphs

Functional paragraphs are used for specific purposes. Although they may not contain a topic sentence, they have unity and coherence because the sentences are clearly connected and logically ordered. Functional paragraphs can serve the following purposes:

To Arouse or Sustain Interest A few vivid sentences can work together to capture the reader's attention.

WRITING MODEL

from **The Fun They Had**

Isaac Asimov

It was a very old book. Margie's grandfather once said that when he was a little boy, *his* grandfather told him that there was a time when all stories were printed on paper.

> This excerpt comes from a story set in the year 2155. It refers to a book that one of the characters has found. The paragraph arouses interest because it describes books on paper as a feature of the past.

To Create Emphasis A short paragraph of one or two sentences breaks the reader's rhythm and adds importance to what is being said.

To Indicate Dialogue One of the conventions of written dialogue is to begin a new paragraph each time the speaker changes.

To Make a Transition A short paragraph can frequently help readers move between the main ideas in two topical paragraphs.

> **Exercise 13** Identifying Functional Paragraphs Skim a short story you have read recently. Find one example of a functional paragraph that sustains interest and one example of a functional paragraph that either indicates dialogue or makes a transition. Explain to a partner how these paragraphs work in the context of the short story.

Paragraph Blocks

Sometimes, you can have so much information that you cannot include it all in one manageable paragraph. Then, you may develop a single idea over several paragraphs. This "block" contains several paragraphs that support the same main idea or topic sentence.

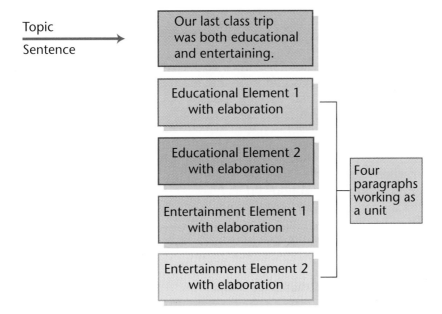

> **Exercise 14** Writing Paragraph Blocks Write a brief account of a class trip or another interesting experience you have had. When you have finished, mark in the margins the paragraph patterns or blocks you've used. Label each paragraph according to the function it performs. Then, mark your paragraph blocks with braces: { }. Study the patterns you have made, and consider whether you should rearrange or add sentences or move sentences from one paragraph to another.

Developing Your Style

You express yourself through your personal style. The way you dress, the videos you like, the music you listen to, how you speak—all are expressions of your personal style. Style also refers to the way you express yourself in writing. Almost every feature of a writer's use of language contributes to that writer's style. Several elements contributing to writing style are highlighted here.

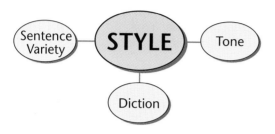

Sentence Variety The different books on your bookshelves indicate some of your literary tastes and styles. You have many options available to contribute to your writing style as well. When you write a paragraph, try to vary your sentence lengths, types, and structures.

Diction The particular words you use add to the style, or overall effect, of a paragraph. Think about your choice of words when planning how to achieve a particular effect. For instance, if you are writing dialogue and want to achieve a realistic conversational tone, you'll probably use informal English. If you intend to convey the seriousness of a certain situation, you will use appropriately formal language. The way words sound can also contribute to a paragraph's style.

Tone Your attitude toward your subject is conveyed in the tone of your writing. You may consider your subject in many ways—for example, with warmth, approval, distance, or admiration. A personal diary entry will probably have a casual tone, while a letter to the editor of your school newspaper will be more serious and formal in tone.

▶ **Exercise 15** **Determining a Writing Style** Read the two Writing Models on page 33. Study the sentence lengths and structures, the word choice, and the tone of each. Then, write a paragraph of your own, modeled on the style of one of the model paragraphs. Show your paragraph to a classmate, and see whether he or she can determine which style you used as a model.

Using Formal and Informal English

Standard English can be either formal or informal. Formal English is appropriate for serious purposes. Informal English is appropriate for casual writing or when you want your writing to have a conversational tone.

Conventions of Formal English

Use formal English for most school assignments and for explanations of processes, reports, essays, speeches, articles, and applications. When writing in formal English, you should follow these conventions:

- Avoid contractions.
- Do not use slang.
- Use standard English and grammar and usage.

Informal English

The English we speak every day is informal English. You can use informal English when you write stories, humorous essays, dialogue, letters to friends, personal notes, and journal entries. When you use informal English, you can

- use contractions.
- use slang and popular expressions.

▲ Critical Viewing Describe this scene using formal English and again using informal English. **[Analyze]**

FORMAL ENGLISH:	This playing field must be rebuilt. It is a hazard to our community. Our children play soccer and baseball on this field, yet it is full of rocks and holes.
INFORMAL ENGLISH:	Hey guys, heads up! This field's a total disaster area. You could break a leg if you're not careful!

▶ **Exercise 16** Using Formal and Informal English Rewrite the following sentences, using formal English for those written informally and informal English for those written formally.

1. I thoroughly enjoyed the soccer season.
2. That last playoff game really rocked!
3. Our new sporting facilities are quite impressive.
4. The stadium cost a bundle and is totally awesome.
5. The best improvement is the Olympic-sized swimming pool.

Spotlight on the Humanities

Examining Musical Compositions

Focus on Music:
Wolfgang Amadeus Mozart

As in a written work, a well-crafted piece of music must have unity, coherence, and other features of good composition. Ranking as one of the great musical geniuses of Western civilization, Wolfgang Amadeus Mozart (1756–1791) was an Austrian composer who could play the clavier (an early keyboard instrument), violin, and organ by the age of six. Also at age six, he composed five short musical pieces, which are still performed today. Mozart came from a musical family and accompanied his father on concert tours throughout Europe. Among Mozart's compositions are sonatas, symphonies, operas, and concertos—music that is technically proficient as well as emotionally stirring. Although Mozart died young, he left us a legacy of astonishing music.

Wolfgang Amadeus Mozart, Barbara Kraft

▲ **Critical Viewing** How do the elements of this portrait work together to convey a strong image of its subject? **[Evaluate]**

Literature Connection When German writer Johann Wolfgang von Goethe (1749–1832) was fourteen years old, he saw Wolfgang Amadeus Mozart perform in Frankfurt, Germany. Goethe was to become one of the most prominent and lasting writers in world literature. Not only was he a poet, dramatist, and novelist, but he was also a scientist. Born the son of a government official, Goethe even obtained a law degree. As a philosopher, Goethe believed in the power of the individual. Probably his best-known work is *Faust* (1832).

Film Connection Winner of eight Academy Awards, including Best Picture, the 1984 film *Amadeus* chronicles the life of Mozart as seen through the eyes of rival composer Antonio Salieri. Directed by Milos Forman and based on the Broadway play of the same name, *Amadeus* depicts Mozart as a strong, precocious, obnoxious character who was also a genius.

Writing Activity: Response to Music

Listen to a work by Mozart—perhaps *Eine Kleine Nachtmusik* ("A Little Night Music") or the overture to *The Magic Flute.* Notice the musical themes that give the work coherence and the surprises that engage your interest. Jot down notes as you listen; then, use your notes to give a short presentation on how the parts of the composition work together. Use the recording in your presentation.

Media and Technology Skills

Evaluating Information Media

Activity: Comparing and Contrasting News Sources

Every day, we have an opportunity to get the news from a number of different sources. Together, these sources are called the **media.** Through print, broadcasts, and—more recently—the Internet, we can learn about local, national, and world events. Many media sources don't just report the news; they provide analyses of it, as well.

Think About It The differences between the various types of media include the depth of coverage, the tone, the method of presentation, and the timeliness of the reports.

- **Print media** include newspapers, which are generally published daily or weekly, and magazines, which appear weekly or monthly. The tone in newspapers and magazines is objective, except on the editorial and opinion pages. News coverage in print media is ongoing, and each new issue updates the information. Magazines provide more in-depth coverage; however, they do not update the information as often. Print media draw readers' attention with headlines and key points in bold typefaces. Articles are commonly accompanied by photographs.

- **Broadcast media** come to their audiences through radio, television, and—increasingly—the Internet. These news sources combine sound, images, and live narration. It is possible to watch television broadcasts of the news around the clock, as well as to see live coverage of many events. Some broadcasts also feature analyses and discussions of the news. Radio conveniently allows the listener to hear the news while engaging in other activities, and, on numerous sites, the Internet provides users the opportunity to access full coverage of an event at any time of the night or day.

Types of Media
Print
• Books
• Magazines
• Newspapers
• Photography
• Print Advertisements
Broadcast
• Television
• Radio
• Film
• Internet Broadcasts

Media Source 1   Media Source 2

Media Sources 1 and 2

Analyze It Compare the coverage of a current news story in two different sources in print and broadcast media. Which source presented the information most fully? Which, most clearly? In what ways were you affected by each of the different sources? Use a Venn diagram like the one above to help you organize the details for your comparison.

Standardized Test Preparation Workshop

Analyzing Strategy, Organization, and Style

Standardized tests often measure your knowledge about writing an effective paragraph. These types of test items consist of a paragraph in which each sentence is numbered and specific questions are based on the passage. These test questions often ask about the writer's strategy, organization, sequence of sentences, choice of words, and overall style of the paragraph. The following are three types of questions that you will need to answer:

- **Strategy questions** ask whether a given revision is appropriate in the context of the essay.

- **Organization questions** ask you to choose the most logical sequence of ideas or to decide whether a sentence should be added, deleted, or moved.

- **Style questions** focus on conveying the writer's point of view and the use of appropriate and effective language for the intended audience.

The sample test item that follows will give you practice in answering questions on writing strategy, organization, and style.

Test Tip

Read each paragraph, and mark with a check any passages that may be out of sequence or that do not make sense. Refer back to your checks as you answer the questions.

Sample Test Item

Directions: Read the paragraph, and then answer the questions that follow.

(1) Later on in the afternoon, we helped groom the horses. (2) Right before lunch, we got a tour of the stables. (3) When we arrived at the ranch in the morning, a cowboy greeted us and showed us to our rooms. (4) At night, we sat around a campfire and sang cowboy songs.

1 Choose the most logical sentence sequence.

  A 2, 4, 3, 1

  B 3, 2, 1, 4

  C 4, 3, 2, 1

  D Correct as is

Answer and Explanation

The correct answer is *B*. In order to arrange the information in the paragraph in a logical sequence, part 3 should begin the paragraph as a topic sentence. Parts 2, 1, and 4 must appear in this sequence to effectively support the topic sentence and conclude the paragraph.

▶ **Practice 1** **Directions:** Read the passage, and then answer the questions that follow. Choose the letter of the best answer.

(1) Yoshi was taken to the emergency medical center at the ski lodge. (2) It was a beautiful January day for skiing. (3) His friend, Maura, drew a cartoon of Yoshi skiing downhill on his cast. (4) Although Yoshi was a pretty good skier, he took a bad spill and broke his leg. (5) Doctors put his whole left leg in a cast. (6) Even Yoshi laughed when he saw the drawing.

1 Which of the following is the most effective topic sentence for the paragraph?

A Yoshi will never ski again.

B Maura is a wonderful cartoonist.

C All skiers have good days and bad days.

D Yoshi's day on the slopes didn't end as he thought it would.

2 Which of the following is the most logical sentence sequence for this paragraph?

F 2, 3, 1, 5, 6, 4

G 2, 4, 1, 5, 3, 6

H 1, 2, 3, 5, 4, 6

J 4, 5, 6, 1, 2 ,3

3 If the writer wanted to add more information about this story, which of the following would be most appropriate?

A Yoshi's favorite hobby was building model airplanes.

B It didn't snow again that year.

C Yoshi's leg was going to take a few months to heal.

D Maura got an "A" in art class.

▶ **Practice 2** **Directions:** Read the passage, and then answer the questions that follow. Choose the letter of the best answer.

(1) The doctor told Yoshi that he would have to wear the cast until May. (2) May is in the spring. (3) He had to use crutches in order to move around. (4) It was slow going at first, but then Yoshi got the hang of using them. (5) He even gave the crutches names: Will and Phil. (6) When the cast came off, Yoshi said: "Now, the weather is perfect for skateboarding!"

1 Which of the following sentences is most irrelevant and could be deleted from the paragraph?

A May is in the spring.

B He had to use crutches in order to move around.

C The doctor told Yoshi that he would have to wear the cast until May.

D It was slow going at first, but then Yoshi got the hang of using them.

2 The tone of this passage can be described as—

F sad

G serious

H humorous

J mysterious

3 Which of the following sentences would best conclude the paragraph?

A It's over.

B With that, he went home and retrieved his skateboard from the garage.

C Skateboarding is for people who can't ski.

D Springtime was Yoshi's favorite time of the year.

Narration
Autobiographical Writing

Autobiography in Everyday Life

Every day, you probably tell other people about events in your life. You might tell a friend about something funny your dog did. You might write a letter to a grandparent about a book you liked. In fact, a big part of life is the stories we tell of it.

When you write autobiographically, you tell a story from your life. Developing strong autobiographical writing skills can help you share your life with others and enrich your own experience.

▲ **Critical Viewing**
What details from an event such as this might you include in a piece of autobiographical writing? Why? **[Analyze]**

What Is Autobiographical Writing?

Autobiographical writing tells the story of an event, period, or person in the writer's life. By writing autobiographically, you can share part of your life with others. You can also learn more about yourself. A well-written autobiographical piece includes

- the writer as a character in the story.
- a lead, or opening paragraph, that catches a reader's interest.
- true events presented in clear, logical order.
- a central conflict, or problem, that the writer or another person has to resolve.

To learn how your work may be graded or judged, see the Rubric for Self-Assessment on page 63.

Types of Autobiographical Writing

These are a few of the types of autobiographical writing:

- **Autobiographical incidents,** which are also called **personal narratives,** tell stories of specific events in your life.
- **Autobiographical narratives,** or **sketches,** tell of periods or groups of events in your life. They include your thoughts and insights about the time.
- **Reflective essays** recount an experience and give your thoughts on its meaning.
- **Memoirs** are true stories of your relationship with a particular person, place, animal, or thing.

Writers in
ACTION

Author Paul Zindel's own experiences appear in almost all his books. Zindel remembers when an editor convinced him to write about teenagers.

She "... brought me into an area that I never explored before, my own confused, funny, aching teenage days."

PREVIEW
Student Work
IN PROGRESS

Coy Walker, a student at Drew Academy in Houston, Texas, wrote an autobiographical essay about a bike accident he once had. In this chapter, you will see how he used the strategies and tips in this lesson to develop his essay. At the end of the chapter, you can read Coy's completed essay.

In her book My Sister Eileen, *Ruth McKenney (1911–1972) tells a few stories about lifesavers, including one starring her sister.*

Reading Strategy: Predict As you read this narrative, **make predictions**—ask yourself, "What will happen next?" Look for hints left by the author. After you make a prediction, read further to see whether or not it comes true.

▲ **Critical Viewing** Does this picture remind you of any event in your own life? Explain whether the event would make a good topic for a story. **[Relate]**

My Sister the "Lifesaver"

Ruth McKenney

. . . Long before I ever had any dealings with professional life-savers my sister nearly drowned me, quite by mistake. My father once took us to a northern Michigan fishing camp, where we found the life very dull. He used to go trolling for bass on our little lake all day long, and at night come home to our lodge, deadbeat and minus any bass. In the meantime Eileen and I, who were nine and ten at the time, used to take an old rowboat out to a shallow section of the lake and, sitting in the hot sun, feed worms to an unexciting variety of small, undernourished fish called gillies. We hated the whole business.

Father, however, loved to fish, even if he didn't catch a single fish in three weeks, which on this trip he didn't. One night, however, he carried his enthusiasm beyond a decent pitch. He decided to go bass fishing after dark, and rather than leave us alone in the lodge and up to [who] knows what, he ordered us to take our boat and row along after him.

Eileen and I were very bored rowing around in the dark, and

McKenney opens with an effective lead sentence. By announcing the startling fact that her sister nearly drowned her, she draws the reader in.

McKenney organizes her story logically. First, she gives background information. Then, she starts at the beginning of the story.

finally, in desperation, we began to stand up and rock the boat, which resulted, at last, in my falling into the lake with a mighty splash.

When I came up, choking and mad as anything, Eileen saw me struggling, and, as she always says with a catch in her voice, she only meant to help me. Good intentions, however, are of little importance in a situation like that. For she grabbed an oar out of the lock, and with an uncertain gesture hit me square on the chin.

I went down with a howl of pain. Eileen, who could not see much in the darkness, was now really frightened. The cold water revived me after the blow and I came to the surface, considerably weakened but still able to swim over to the boat. Whereupon Eileen, in a noble attempt to give me the oar to grab, raised it once again, and socked me square on the top of the head. I went down again, this time without a murmur, and my last thought was a vague wonder that my own sister should want to murder me with a rowboat oar.

As for Eileen, she heard the dull impact of the oar on my head and saw the shadowy figure of her sister disappear. So she jumped in the lake, screeching furiously, and began to flail around in the water, howling for help and looking for me. At this point I came to the surface and swam over to the boat, with the intention of killing Eileen.

Father, rowing hard, arrived just in time to pull us both out of the water and prevent me from attacking Eileen with the rowboat anchor. The worst part about the whole thing, as far as I was concerned, was that Eileen was considered a heroine and Father told everybody in the lake community that she had saved my life. The postmaster put her name in for a medal.

Here, McKenney develops the central conflict or problem of her story: How will she escape from Eileen's "rescue" attempt?

To enrich her story, McKenney adds details about her thoughts at the time.

LITERATURE

To read another example of autobiographical writing, see *The Pigman & Me* by Paul Zindel. You can find an excerpt from this book in *Prentice Hall Literature: Timeless Voices, Timeless Themes,* Copper.

▼ **Critical Viewing** Of what experience in your own life does this oar remind you? Briefly compare your experience with McKenney's. **[Compare and Contrast]**

Reading Writing Connection

Writing Application:

Leave Clues As you write your own autobiographical narrative, build interest by giving your readers clues about what might happen next.

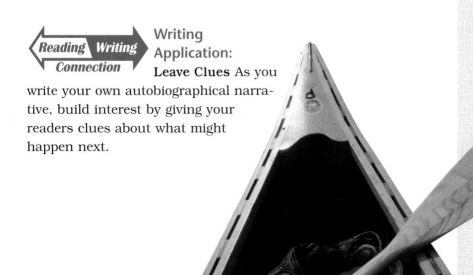

Prewriting

Choosing Your Topic

A lot of things have happened in your life. To find a good topic for autobiographical writing, think of an event that was special for you. Use these strategies to help:

Strategies for Generating a Topic

1. **Freewriting** Write down whatever thoughts occur to you about a general topic such as *holidays*, *adventures*, or *a problem solved*. Focus more on getting your ideas down than on writing correctly. After five minutes, read over your thoughts, and choose a topic from among them.

2. **Quicklist** Divide a sheet of paper into three columns. In the first, list people and places you know and events you've experienced. In the next, write a description of each. In the last, give an example supporting each general description. Choose a memory on your list as your topic.

Text

Try it out! Use the interactive Quicklist in **Section 4.2**, on-line or on CD-ROM.

Student Work
IN PROGRESS

Name: *Coy Walker*
Drew Academy
Houston, TX

Using a Quicklist

Here is how Coy Walker used a Quicklist to generate ideas for a topic. He circled the items connected to his bicycle.

People, Places, and Events	Description	Example
my dad	a smart guy	He warned me about the brakes on my new ten-speed.
Lake Minnetowa	peaceful	We saw deer drinking at the lake last time we were there.
my birthday	a great time!!	I got a bike last time—though I crashed it right afterwards.

My Topic My bike

TOPIC BANK

If you're having trouble finding a topic, consider the following possibilities:

1. **Your Clothes** Clothing can be associated with particular events or circumstances. Maybe you have an outfit you wear at holidays or a baseball cap you wore during a championship game. Identify a piece of clothing you associate with a special event in your life. Use this event as the topic of your narrative.

2. **New Kid on the Block** Have you ever felt like the "new kid on the block"? Recall what it was like being with a group of kids who knew each other well but who didn't know you. Write about the experience and your reactions to it.

Responding to Fine Art

Great Catch, Moses Ros

3. Think of the events leading up to the action in this painting. Think about the mood the colors create—happy, peaceful, or wild. Then, think of a time you did—or tried to do—something special in a game. Write an autobiographical narrative about this time.

Responding to Literature

4. Read "Old Ben" by Jesse Stuart, paying attention to all of the details he includes about his pet snake. Then, write the story of a pet you have had, including similar details. You can find "Old Ben" in *Prentice Hall Literature: Timeless Voices, Timeless Themes,* Copper.

☑ Cooperative Writing Opportunity

5. **Illustrated Record** With a group, discuss the best school event you had last year. After you agree on a topic, write a recollection of the event. Some group members should write recollections of highlights from the event. Others should gather photographs and scrapbook mementos from the event, writing a brief explanation of the significance of each. Assemble the work in an album, and make it available to other students in the school library.

Narrowing Your Topic

Once you've chosen a topic to write about, narrow it by focusing on one significant part: a surprise, a problem, or another interesting experience.

For instance, the story of a trip to the zoo might focus on the tigers. When telling the story, you might include your conversations about tigers, as well as descriptions of the tigers you saw. You might leave out your trip to the snack stand, though. To narrow your topic, you can use a Topic Web.

Use a Topic Web to Narrow a Topic

These are the steps for creating a Topic Web:

1. Write your topic at the center of a piece of paper. Circle it.
2. Write the parts of your topic next to the circle. Circle them.
3. Write down the things each circled topic makes you think of. Circle each new item, and draw an arrow from it to the circled topic that made you think of it.
4. Choose a group of details that belong together to create a narrowed topic.

Student Work IN PROGRESS

Name: *Coy Walker*
Drew Academy
Houston, TX

Using a Topic Web to Narrow a Topic

From his Topic Web, Coy chose details relating to his bike accident. The accident became his narrowed topic.

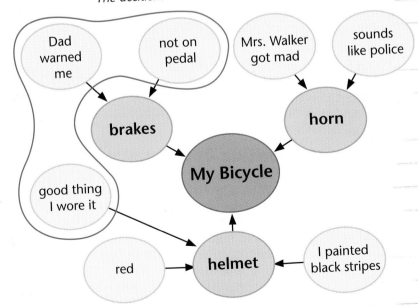

Narrowed Topic: My bike accident

Considering Your Audience and Purpose

As you develop your piece of autobiographical writing, think about your **audience**—those who will read the piece. If you are writing for your little brother, you probably will use simple words. If you are writing for a teacher, you will need to explain details your little brother would already know, such as the name of the family cat.

You also need to consider your **purpose** in writing. Autobiographical writing can be used to entertain, to teach a lesson about life, or to capture the personality of a character from your life.

Analyze Your Purpose

To decide on your purpose, think about your topic and ask yourself these questions:

- Is my topic funny or exciting? Is my purpose to **entertain** the reader?
  If so, focus on interesting details and write about them in a funny or exciting way.

- Does my topic involve a lesson I learned? Is my purpose to **instruct** the reader?
  If so, focus on the details that taught you the lesson and draw conclusions from them.

- Am I writing about a particularly interesting person? Can I **capture that character's personality** in words?
  If so, focus on details that bring the character's personality to life.

Gathering Details

Once you have narrowed your topic and considered your purpose, begin gathering the details. Use the strategy of listing and itemizing.

List and Itemize

List words and phrases connected with your topic. Then, circle the most important or most interesting items on your list. Draw arrows between related circled items, and then write a little more about each. Highlight those details that fit together in a story.

Writers in
ACTION

When Paul Zindel decided that he wanted to write for teens, he used the same strategies that you do.

"I thought I knew what kids would want in a book, and so I made a list and followed it."

▼ **Critical Viewing**
What do you think made this girl smile? Make up a little story about this picture. **[Speculate]**

Drafting

Shaping Your Writing
Present Events in Order

Most stories have a beginning, a middle, and an end. To help your readers understand your story, it's a good idea to retell events in the order in which they happened.

Think about the items you selected to write about. Which one happened first? What happened next? Make a timeline to show the order of events. As you draft, follow your organizer.

Create Tension

Well-told stories create tension—they keep readers wondering how the story will end. Imagine that you and your sister each want the last piece of pie. When telling this story, it's your job to keep the reader wondering: Who will get it?

Using a Conflict Map Writing about a conflict is one important way to create tension. A **conflict** is a struggle between two or more characters or forces, in which one side stops the other from getting what it wants. In the story of the piece of pie, the conflict is between you and your sister. Before you write, focus your thoughts about the conflict. Make a conflict map similar to the one below.

CONFLICT MAP

What Gets In the Way

My Sister

Who? Me

STOP

What the Character Wants

Last slice of pie

There's only one piece left

Providing Elaboration

Picture someone making a sandwich using just bread and nothing else. "That's not really making a *sandwich*," you might say. Similarly, the events you retell in your narrative are just the "bread." To write a finished narrative, you need to add a few other ingredients.

For instance, readers will want to know how the characters in your narrative reacted to events. Use the strategy of Thoughtshots to add such details to your story.

Use Thoughtshots

As you draft, pause for a moment at the end of each paragraph. Then, follow these steps:

1. Scan the paragraph for uses of the word *I*.
2. For each one, ask yourself how you reacted to the events described. For instance, you might have laughed or grown angry or thought, "This is really great!"
3. For each reaction, draw a Thoughtshot in the margin of your draft. (See below for examples.)
4. Inside the Thoughtshot, jot down notes about the reaction.

When it is time to write your final draft, decide which Thoughtshots to include.

Student Work
IN PROGRESS

Name: *Coy Walker*
Drew Academy
Houston, TX

Using Thoughtshots

After he had written this paragraph, Coy looked at sentences containing the word I. He found two places for a Thoughtshot.

Whew! It was hot! It was a quiet Saturday morning, though, and I felt like riding my new ten-speed bike. My parents had just bought it for me. It was a shiny jet black and even had that new-bike smell. Dad warned me that it would feel different from my clunky old two-wheeler. He said I could ride it, but I was restricted from going past the end of the street.

> I was really proud of that bike.

> I thought, "Who cares?" It would be fun just whizzing up and down the street.

Revising

After finishing your first draft, look for ways to improve it. Begin revising by reviewing the overall structure of your story.

Revising Your Overall Structure

Use Logical Order

To improve the organization of your draft, use this strategy:

▶ **REVISION STRATEGY**
Identifying Connections

Draw an arrow from each paragraph to the next. Label each arrow with the relationship between the paragraphs it links:

SEQUENCE: The events in one paragraph lead to the events in the next paragraph.

EXPLANATION: One paragraph gives information the reader needs to understand the next paragraph.

DRAMA: One paragraph makes the reader wonder what will happen next. The next paragraph either heightens the curiosity or satisfies it.

If a paragraph is not clearly related to the one before it and the one after it, rewrite it, or consider moving or deleting it.

Student Work
IN PROGRESS

Name: *Coy Walker*
Drew Academy
Houston, TX

Using Logical Order

When Coy could not determine the connection between two paragraphs, he decided to delete the one that did not add to the action.

...I held the handlebars tight and gained speed. I laughed as I swung wide in order to turn.

explanation

I always loved to do tricks on my bike. I remember watching my cousins popping wheelies. They looked cool.

?

Suddenly, the gate was approaching me fast.... I started to push back on the pedals to lose speed.

drama/sequence

Nothing happened....

Revising Your Paragraphs

Open With an Effective Lead

Writing the first sentences of a narrative—the **lead**—is like opening a door. You need to open the door wide and invite the reader in. Use an interest-grabber like one of the following:

- an engaging **description**
  Model car parts lay in oily heaps all over his workbench.
- a **statement** that hints at a story
  Usually, I try to avoid talking to the Moriarty twins.
- **dialogue** or a character's **thoughts**
  "Come in," said the man at the door. "We've been expecting you."
- an exciting **action**
  Running around the corner carrying several cakes, I nearly collided with Mr. Bernstein.

Use the following strategy to make sure your lead is effective.

▶ **REVISION STRATEGY**
Measuring the Effectiveness of Your Lead

Follow these steps to measure the effectiveness of your lead:
1. Create an index card like the one below.
2. Under "Type of Detail," write in the type of detail your first sentence provides. (Refer to the list above.)
3. Under "Reader's Question," write the question that the sentence will make the reader ask.
4. Under "Connects Back/Forward," fill in the words in the next sentences that connect your first sentence to your story.

If you must leave blanks on the card, consider rewriting the lead until you can fill in all the blanks.

MEASURING A LEAD

Our "search party" moved slowly along the path, looking from one side to the next. I was impatient for a sign of Jiffy, my missing turtle, so time seemed to crawl.

1st Sentence		2nd or 3rd Sentence
Type of Detail	**Reader's Question**	**Connects Back/Forward**
Action: search party searching	"What are they searching for?"	"My missing turtle" connects to first sentence; also shows what story is about

Collaborative Writing Tip

Read the lead sentence at the very beginning of your narrative to a group of students. Discuss any questions the sentence raises. What does the audience hope to find out?

Revising Your Sentences

Vary Sentence Beginnings

Every story has a beat. It can drip along like a leaky faucet, or it can dance about like a butterfly. To give your draft a good rhythm, vary sentence beginnings. Use color-coding to help.

▶ **REVISION STRATEGY**
Color-Coding Sentence Beginnings

Color-code the first word of each sentence, as follows:

Articles include *the*, *a*, and *an*.

Nouns and **pronouns** refer to persons, places, or things. *House*, *Bob*, and *weather* are nouns. *I, you, he, she, it, we,* and *they* are pronouns.

Adjectives tell more about something named by a noun. *Yellow, loud,* and *handsome* are all adjectives.

Adverbs tell more about verbs, adjectives, or other adverbs. *Quickly, brightly,* and *less* are adverbs.

Prepositions show the relationship between things. *In, out, off, on, toward,* and *away* are prepositions.

Find groups of the same colored shape. Rewrite sentences in these groups so that some begin with a different kind of word.

⟳ Learn More

To learn more about the different parts of speech, see Chapters 14–18.

Student Work IN PROGRESS

Name: *Coy Walker*
Drew Academy
Houston, TX

Color-Coding Sentence Beginnings

Coy color-coded his sentence beginnings. When he noticed the number of red rectangles in this paragraph, he rewrote several sentences.

~~I watched the~~ The trees and houses zoomed ~~zoom~~ by in a blur. All I could hear was my own huffing and puffing. The sweat on my back was making my T-shirt cling to me, and it felt sticky and itchy. Then, I was almost home. Moving to the right side of the street, I squinted my eyes tight, ~~and moved to the right side of the street,~~ preparing to do a daredevil stunt as I turned into my narrow driveway. I held the handlebars tight and gained speed. With a laugh, I ~~laughed as~~ I swung wide in order to turn.

Revising Your Word Choice

Use Precise Nouns

Give your reader a clear picture of events by using precise nouns. For example, if you tell about a family dinner, the sentence "We ate some food" will leave your reader hungry for more details. To feed your reader's imagination, use precise nouns like *lamb chops* instead of general nouns like *food*.

▶**REVISION STRATEGY**
Highlighting Nouns for Precision

Highlight the nouns in your draft. Then, circle any general nouns. Consider replacing them with precise nouns.

Grammar in Your Writing
Identifying Nouns

A **noun** names a person, place, or thing (including things you can't see). Here are some examples:

Person	Place	Seeable Thing		Unseeable Thing
friend	Texas	raincoat	walking	warmth
Mrs. Oliver	city	dog	flying	brightness
doctor	theater	truck	resting	joy

Find It in Your Reading Identify three nouns in the first paragraph of "My Sister the 'Lifesaver'" by Ruth McKenney on page 50. For each, explain whether it is precise or general.

Find It in Your Writing Find five general nouns in your draft. For each, explain what picture you wanted to give a reader. If the noun does not give enough information to create that picture, replace it with a precise word.

To learn more about nouns, see Chapter 14.

Peer Review

Process Share

Read your draft to a small group. To start off a discussion, your classmates should ask the following questions:

• How did you come up with the idea for your narrative?

• What problems did you have while writing? What did you do to solve them?

• What are you planning to do next to your draft?

Ask group members for suggestions, and consider using their ideas as you create your final draft.

Editing
and Proofreading

Errors in your autobiographical writing can confuse readers or make them impatient. Before you create your final draft, carefully review your essay. Check for errors in spelling, grammar, punctuation, and usage.

Focusing on Capitalization

Check to make sure that you have capitalized

- the first words of sentences.
- people's names.
- place names.
- the first word and all important words in the titles of books, movies, songs, and other works.

Grammar in Your Writing
Capitalization of Proper Nouns

Capitalize words when they are used as the name by which someone or something is called.

> I rode the bus with **Aunt Ettie**.
> We went to **Lake Michigan** on vacation.

Do not capitalize words that are not used as names (unless they appear at the beginning of a sentence).

> I rode the bus with my **aunt**.
> We went to the **lake** on vacation.

Find It in Your Reading Choose three capitalized words and three uncapitalized words in the first paragraph of "My Sister the 'Lifesaver'" by Ruth McKenney on page 50. For each, explain why it is or is not capitalized.

Find It in Your Writing Review your draft for words you may have capitalized incorrectly. For each, ask yourself: Is this word used as the name of a specific person, place, or thing?

For more on capitalization, see Chapter 27.

4.6 *Publishing and Presenting*

Building Your Portfolio

Consider these ideas for publishing and presenting your work:

1. **Skit** With a group, create a skit from your autobiographical piece. Rehearse what each character will say and what he or she will do, and present your skit to the class.

2. **Magazine Submission** Type your work, and mail it to a magazine that publishes student writing. Include a letter introducing yourself and explaining why your story should be published.

Reflecting on Your Writing

Jot down a few notes for your portfolio about the process of writing an autobiographical piece. Begin by answering the following questions:

- What was the hardest part of writing your piece? What was the easiest? Explain why.

- As you wrote, what did you learn about yourself?

 **Internet Tip**

To see model essays scored with this rubric, go on-line: PHSchool.com
Enter Web Code:
eak-6001

Rubric for Self-Assessment

Use the following criteria to evaluate your autobiographical writing.

	Score 4	Score 3	Score 2	Score 1
Audience and Purpose	Contains an engaging introduction; successfully entertains or presents a theme	Contains a somewhat engaging introduction; entertains or presents a theme	Contains an introduction; attempts to entertain or to present a theme	Begins abruptly or confusingly; leaves purpose unclear
Organization	Creates an interesting, clear narrative; told from a consistent point of view	Presents a clear sequence of events; told from a specific point of view	Presents a mostly clear sequence of events; contains inconsistent points of view	Presents events without logical order; lacks a consistent point of view
Elaboration	Provides insight into and develops a sequence of events	Contains many details that develop a sequence of events	Contains some details that develop a sequence of events	Contains few or no details to develop a sequence of events
Use of Language	Uses word choice and tone to reveal story's theme; contains no errors in grammar, punctuation, or spelling	Uses interesting and fresh word choices; contains few errors in grammar, punctuation, and spelling	Uses some clichés and trite expressions; contains some errors in grammar, punctuation, and spelling	Uses uninspired word choices; has many errors in grammar, punctuation, and spelling

FINAL DRAFT

Those Are the Brakes

Coy Walker
Drew Academy
Houston, Texas

◀ **Critical Viewing**
How might the child in this picture feel about his bicycle? **[Speculate]**

Whew! It was hot! It was a quiet Saturday morning, though, and I felt like riding my new ten-speed bike. My parents had just bought it for me, and I was so proud of it. It was a shiny jet black and even had that new-bike smell. Dad warned me that it would feel different from my clunky old two-wheeler. He said I could ride it, but I was restricted from going past the end of the street. I thought, "Who cares?" It would be fun just whizzing up and down the street.

Coy's lead—his first sentences—brings the reader into his story right away.

As I started my little cruise, Dad called out something. The wind was whipping me in the face, though, and I couldn't really hear. I thought I heard him say something like "Don't break it" and something else about holding the handlebars. But I was having too much fun to stop and ask him to repeat himself. Dad was such a worrywart. Of course, I wouldn't break it. Of course, I would hold the handlebars.

Coy includes details about his own reactions to events. Each detail helps the reader feel a part of the action.

I rode back and forth on the street for about fifteen minutes. The trees and houses zoomed by in a blur. All I could hear was my own huffing and puffing. The sweat on my back was making my T-shirt cling to me, and it felt sticky and itchy. Then, I was almost home. Moving to the right side of the street, I squinted my eyes tight, preparing to do a daredevil stunt as I turned into my narrow driveway. I held the handlebars tight and gained speed. With a laugh, I swung wide in order to turn.

Coy's story is organized logically. He starts at the beginning (getting the bike). Then, he tells what happened next (his first ride).

Suddenly, the gate was approaching me fast. I needed to slow down, so that I could maneuver into the driveway safely. My old bike had pedal brakes, so naturally I started to push back on the pedals to lose speed.

Nothing happened. I pushed harder with my feet, but the pedals just went around and around in the wrong direction. I could feel them spinning like a wheel of fortune.

Uh-oh. The next thing I knew, I was crashing into our four-foot hurricane fence. Seconds later, I went flying across the top. But that's not the worst part. During my flight, the gate caught my arm, scraping across it. I looked like I'd been in a battle.

Mom and Dad heard the noise and came running outside. I was surprised to see that Dad was almost amused. He said that he could remember his own "Fence Incident." Then he told me that now I was a "soldier" and had received my "war wounds." Mom rubbed peroxide and warm water on me, and it stung like a swarm of bees.

"What happened?" Dad asked.

"The pedal brakes didn't work," I said.

"Oh, no," Dad said and laughed. "I called out to you to remind you. The brakes are on the handlebars, the brakes are on the handlebars."

Coy creates a strong conflict: Will he succeed in controlling his bike, or will the bike go out of control?

Coy's main purpose is to entertain. His conclusion shows the amusing side of the events.

◀ **Critical Viewing** What feelings can you associate with the fence in this picture? Do they match the feelings inspired by the fence in Coy's story? Explain. **[Connect]**

Connected Assignment
Firsthand Biography

A biography tells the story of someone's life. A **firsthand biography** tells the story of someone whom the writer knows or knew personally. Because of the writer's perspective, this kind of biography can give readers unique insights into its subject. A short firsthand biography focuses on one event or period in the subject's life.

A firsthand biography includes

- a subject other than the narrator.
- an organized retelling of events from the life of the subject.
- a first-person point of view—the work is narrated using the pronoun *I*.
- an insight into the subject only the writer could provide.

▲ Critical Viewing
What kind of firsthand biography might one of these kids write about the other—serious or entertaining? **[Draw Conclusions]**

Prewriting To find a subject for your firsthand biography, list parts of your life, such as "School," "Sports," "Family," and so on. For each heading, jot down your memories of that part of your life. Choose the person you will write about from among these memories. You might choose a topic in one of the following categories:

- **Firsthand Biography of Someone Who Influenced You**
  Write about a person you know, such as a family member, friend, or teacher, who taught you something important, either in words or by example.

- **Firsthand Biography of a "Character"** Among the people you know, who causes the most trouble? Makes the funniest jokes? Tell the story of such a person.

Once you have selected the person about whom you wish to write, focus on an event involving him or her or on a special characteristic he or she has. To find this focus, list the memories you associate with the person. Choose the most revealing or entertaining memory for your focus.

Then, gather details that reveal your subject's personality and special qualities. Include the following kinds of details:

- things he or she has said
- major accomplishments
- memorable characteristics
- incidents that reveal how he or she has influenced you.

Drafting Once you have focused your topic, organize the events in your story. Retelling events in the order in which they occurred (chronological order) is one of the clearest ways to organize your story. If you select this type of organization, use a timeline like the one below to chart the events of your story.

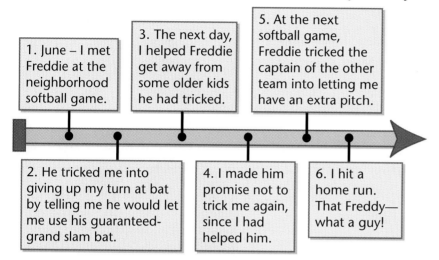

3. The next day, I helped Freddie get away from some older kids he had tricked.

5. At the next softball game, Freddie tricked the captain of the other team into letting me have an extra pitch.

1. June – I met Freddie at the neighborhood softball game.

2. He tricked me into giving up my turn at bat by telling me he would let me use his guaranteed-grand slam bat.

4. I made him promise not to trick me again, since I had helped him.

6. I hit a home run. That Freddy— what a guy!

You might also consider starting with the most important part of your story, and then filling in less important details.

As you draft, make sure that you narrate events in the first person (use the pronoun *I*). Although your focus is on show-ing your subject as he or she is, elaborate on your story by including your own reactions to events.

Revising and Editing After you have finished your draft, review its overall structure. Make the following kinds of revisions:

- **Check Sequence** Make sure that you have presented events and descriptions in a logical sequence.

- **Add Transitions** Use transitional words, such as *afterward*, *before*, *during*, and *as a result*, to show the order and rela-tion of events clearly.

- **Elaborate** Circle places in your draft where the events are most exciting or where you focus on an important part of your subject's character. Add details at these points to give a complete picture of these events or characteristics.

After you have revised your biography, proofread your paper to make sure that there are no errors in spelling, grammar, or punctuation.

Publishing and Presenting Illustrate your firsthand biography with photographs or drawings. Make copies, and place each in a cover or binder. Present a copy to the subject of the piece. Consider presenting copies to your subject's friends or family or to an organization to which he or she belongs.

Spotlight on the Humanities

Interpreting Visual Meaning

Focus on the Visual Arts: Van Gogh's *Starry Night*

Writing an autobiographical narrative is one way to show the world something about yourself. Painting a self-portrait is another. The self-portrait on this page is by Dutch painter Vincent van Gogh (1853–1890).

Van Gogh's life was not a happy one. He was troubled by mental illness. Few people appreciated his work during his lifetime. Of the 1,500 paintings and drawings he produced, he sold only one.

Van Gogh's Art Today, though, van Gogh is considered one of the most important modern artists. People value his powerful, dynamic style.

Van Gogh's self-portrait tells you not only what he looked like. It also tells you something about his personality. You can surmise from the many thick brushstrokes and the vivid colors that van Gogh was a passionate painter. He believed in the power of paint to show us new beauty in the world.

When you look at a painting, notice features such as the brushstrokes and the artist's choice of colors. You may discover for yourself some of the beauty van Gogh found in painting.

Music Connections Van Gogh's life and paintings inspired the songwriter Don McLean. In 1971, McLean wrote a tribute to the painter and his artistic originality, called "Vincent (Starry, Starry Night)."

Literary Connections In 1991, the novelist Alice Walker published a poem praising van Gogh's work, entitled "If There Was Any Justice."

Autobiographical Writing Activity: Imaginary Journal Entry

Using library resources, find a reproduction of van Gogh's painting *Starry Night*. Then, as van Gogh, write an entry in your journal about what inspired you to paint the work. Was it a piece of music? An event? Or an actual starlit evening? Explain the feelings and thoughts that led to your painting the scene as you did.

Self-portrait with Bandaged Ear, Vincent van Gogh, Giraudon

▲ **Critical Viewing** Describe van Gogh's use of space in this self-portrait. Is the painting crowded or spacious? **[Analyze]**

▲ **Critical Viewing** What might a poet such as Alice Walker be interested in van Gogh's life and work? **[Hypothesize]**

Media and Technology Skills

Making Meaning With Visual Images
Activity: Create a Photo Essay

Like van Gogh (see previous page), you can show important things about a person by using images. Learn more about taking photographs, and create a photo essay of someone you know.

Learn About It

Read About It Leaf through an introductory book on taking pictures. Then, read through the owner's manual of your camera to familiarize yourself with its specific features. Get the help of an experienced user of the camera if necessary.

Think About Variables By using different settings on the camera and by taking pictures in different circumstances, you can create different meanings in the photographs you take. For example, a picture taken in a dark room with a flash will look different from a picture of the room with sunlight pouring through the windows.

Experiment Take a few pictures of the same object or scene with different settings or in different conditions. Keep track of the settings and conditions. Look over your developed pictures and take notes on the effects of your choices.

Apply It Take a series of photographs that reveal something about a family member or friend. Choose objects, people, places, and events that tell something about the person, and photograph the person in connection with them. Use a chart like the one below to plan your pictures. Display your results to the class.

Aspect of Person	Type of Photograph	Special Considerations
Mom loves her garden—show her sitting in garden.	Portrait	• Take picture on cheerful, sunny day. • Show some of Mom's favorite roses in the background.

Types of Images

Action Shot
A shot of a person performing a specific action.

Portrait
A close-up of a person or his or her face.

Still Life
A shot of a group of objects. By selecting the right objects, a photographer can use a still life to show something about their owner.

Standardized Test Preparation Workshop

Using Narration to Respond to Writing Prompts

Test Tip

When outlining events for a narrative response to a prompt, place a star next to the most important ones. Focus on these events as you draft.

The writing prompts on standardized tests often measure your ability to tell stories for a specific purpose. The following are the criteria upon which such writing will be evaluated:

- Do you organize details in a logical sequence?

- Do you choose words and write in a style that fits the purpose and audience named in the response? (For example, a letter to a company should be more formal than a letter to a friend.)

- Do you use transitions to create a unified, coherent narrative?

- Do you elaborate on events with the effective use of description, characterization, and other details?

- Do you use correct grammar, spelling, and punctuation?

Following is an example of a writing prompt that requires you to use elements of narrative writing. Use the suggestions on the following page to help you respond. The clocks show the suggested percentage of your test-taking time to devote to each stage.

Sample Writing Situation

Your school is considering cutting back on field trips. Some think that the money spent on these trips would be better spent on books for the library or on computers that will provide Internet access.

In an essay for the school newspaper, argue for or against eliminating school field trips in favor of buying more library books or computers for Internet access. To support your opinion, give your own experiences on field trips and with the school library and computers for research.

Prewriting

Allow close to one fourth of your time for prewriting.

Gather Details Begin by gathering information about your experiences on field trips, on the one hand, and with using school library and computer facilities, on the other.

Take a Stand Review your notes on your experiences. Form an opinion on the issue raised in the prompt—whether school money is better spent on field trips or on extra books and computers.

Focus Your Support Next, use the strategy of listing and itemizing to focus on experiences that show something about the value of field trips. (To learn the steps for listing and itemizing, see page 55.)

Drafting

Allow almost half of your time for drafting.

Organization After you have gathered details, make an outline to organize them. Write a sentence for each of your main points. Underneath each main point, list the experiences that illustrate that point. Each story you tell to support your main idea may be organized in chronological order (the order in which events occurred). For instance, one main point might be that field trips motivate students to learn more.

Introduction, Body, and Conclusion After organizing details, begin drafting. Start off with an introductory paragraph that states your opinion and sums up your major reason for it. Then, discuss each of your main ideas in a paragraph or two. In these paragraphs, retell the experiences that support each point. Finally, conclude by restating your opinion in a memorable way.

Revising, Editing, and Proofreading

Allow almost one fourth of your time to revise and edit. Use the last few minutes to proofread your work.

Strengthen Your Case Review your draft. Make sure that each experience you retell clearly supports the point it should support. Eliminate details that distract from your point. Add transitions, such as *next, then,* and *for this reason,* where necessary to make the relation of events and ideas clear.

Make Corrections Check for errors in spelling, grammar, and punctuation. When making changes, place one line through text that you want to eliminate. Use a caret (^) to indicate the places where you want to add words.

Narration
Short Story

St. George and the Dragon, Paolo Uccello

Short Stories in Everyday Life

People love to tell stories. You might tell your friends stories when you talk on the phone. You might hear family stories when you get together with relatives—like the one about what you did when you were two or the one about how your grandfather survived a tornado!

True stories like these conjure up other times or places. Once you start writing made-up stories, though, there's no telling where you will stop! A short story can take you right out of your own time and place into a world of imagination.

In this chapter, you'll learn strategies for writing a short story that will hook your readers' interest and even open up a new world to them—the unique world of *your* imagination.

▲ **Critical Viewing**
This painting is an illustration for a famous story—can you guess which one? If you don't know the story, explain what story you might make up about the picture. **[Interpret]**

What Is a Short Story?

A **short story** is a brief, made-up narrative—an account of a sequence of events. The events in a short story can take place in a burning desert, in a mountain fortress, or on a street just like yours. From the ordinary to the extraordinary, a short story can show you the world from a different point of view. Most short stories have

- one or more characters (the people involved in the story).

- a conflict or problem that keeps the reader asking, "What will happen next?"

- a beginning that grabs the reader's interest and introduces the characters, setting, and conflict.

- a middle in which the story reaches a climax—its turning point.

- an ending in which the conflict is resolved and loose ends are tied up.

To learn the criteria on which your short story may be judged or graded, see the Rubric for Self-Assessment on page 90.

Writers in
ACTION

Novelist and short-story writer Isaac Bashevis Singer (1904–1991) received the prestigious Nobel Prize for Literature in 1978. Even when he was a child, he knew which kind of story he liked:

"...from my childhood I have always loved tension in a story. I liked that a story should be a story. That there should be a beginning and an end, and there should be some feeling of what will happen at the end."

Types of Short Stories

The following are some of the different kinds of short stories:

- **Realistic stories** take you on a walk through familiar neighborhoods with people much like those you know.

- **Fantasy and science-fiction stories** might whisk you away to strange, new planets or mysterious ancient kingdoms.

- **Adventure stories** tumble you into a world of brave heroes fighting dangerous enemies.

PREVIEW
Student Work
IN PROGRESS

In this chapter, you'll follow the work of John Beamer, a student at David Starr Jordan Middle School in Palo Alto, California, as he developed his story "The Manitoba Monster." You'll see how he used featured strategies to find a topic, develop a conflict, elaborate, and revise. At the end of the chapter, you'll read his finished short story.

Model From Literature

Isaac Bashevis Singer (1904–1991) was born in Poland and moved to New York City in 1935. The author of short stories and novels, Singer wrote in Yiddish, the language of Eastern European Jews. He told many tales of life in the small villages of Eastern Europe. Singer received the Nobel Prize for Literature in 1978.

Reading Strategy: Interpret As you read, **interpret** what you have read by restating its meaning. For example, when you read about an important event, ask yourself: Why did this event happen? When the author mentions a detail that seems to stand out, ask yourself: Why did the writer add this detail?

For example, in "The Snow in Chelm," Singer describes the seven Elders as having "white beards and high foreheads from too much thinking." You might restate the meaning of this detail as follows: "The Elders look the way wise people are supposed to look. Singer says their heads got big from 'too much thinking,' though. He must be poking fun at people who think they are wise."

▲ **Critical Viewing** What features of this man make him look wise? What does the story suggest about judging wisdom on the basis of these features? **[Interpret]**

The Snow in Chelm

Isaac Bashevis Singer

Chelm was a village of fools, fools young and old. One night someone spied the moon reflected in a barrel of water. The people of Chelm imagined it had fallen in. They sealed the barrel so that the moon would not escape. When the barrel was opened in the morning and the moon wasn't there, the villagers decided it had been stolen. They sent for the police, and when the thief couldn't be found, the fools of Chelm cried and moaned.

Of all the fools of Chelm, the most famous were its seven Elders. Because they were the village's oldest and greatest fools, they ruled in Chelm. They had white beards and high foreheads from too much thinking.

Singer begins by introducing his characters with an attention-grabbing statement.

◀ **Critical Viewing**
The villagers once
thought the moon
had fallen into a
barrel. Have you
ever been tricked by
the way something
looked? Explain.
[Relate]

LITERATURE

To read another
humorous short story,
see "Overdoing It" by
Anton Chekhov. You
can find this story in
*Prentice Hall Literature:
Timeless Voices,
Timeless Themes,
Copper.*

Once, on a Hanukkah night, the snow fell all evening. It covered all of Chelm like a silver tablecloth. The moon shone; the
stars twinkled; the snow shimmered like pearls and diamonds.

That evening the seven Elders were sitting and pondering, wrin-
kling their foreheads. The village was in need of money, and they
did not know where to get it. Suddenly the oldest of them all,
Gronam the Great Fool, exclaimed, "The snow is silver!"

"I see pearls in the snow!" another shouted.

"And I see diamonds!" a third called out.

It became clear to the Elders of Chelm that a treasure had fallen
from the sky.

But soon they began to worry. The people of Chelm liked to go
walking, and they would most certainly trample the treasure.
What was to be done? Silly Tudras had an idea.

"Let's send a messenger to knock on all the windows and let the
people know that they must remain in their houses until all the
silver, all the pearls, and all the diamonds are safely gathered up."

For a while the Elders were satisfied. They rubbed their hands in
approval of the clever idea. But then Dopey Lekisch called out in
consternation, "The messenger himself will trample the treasure."

The Elders realized that Lekisch was right, and again they
wrinkled their high foreheads in an effort to solve the problem.

"I've got it!" exclaimed Shmerel the Ox.

"Tell us, tell us," pleaded the Elders.

*Here, Singer sets up
the main conflict of
the story: Will reality
force the foolish
Elders to realize
their mistake?*

*Singer makes the
conflict more inter-
esting by having
characters bring up
"difficulties" with the
plan—all while no
one sees the first
ridiculous mistake!*

"The messenger must not go on foot. He must be carried on a table so that his feet will not tread on the precious snow."

Everybody was delighted with Schmerel the Ox's solution; and the Elders, clapping their hands, admired their own wisdom.

The Elders immediately sent to the kitchen for Gimpel the errand boy and stood him on a table. Now who was going to carry the table? It was lucky that in the kitchen there were Treitle the cook, Berel the potato peeler, Yukel the salad mixer, and Yontel, who was in charge of the community goat. All four were ordered to lift up the table on which Gimpel stood. Each one took hold of a leg. On top stood Gimpel, grasping a wooden hammer with which to tap on the villager's windows. Off they went.

At each window Gimpel knocked with the hammer and called out, "No one leaves the house tonight. A treasure has fallen from the sky, and it is forbidden to step on it."

The people of Chelm obeyed the Elders and remained in their houses all night. Meanwhile the Elders themselves sat up trying to figure out how to make the best use of the treasure once it had been gathered up.

Silly Tudras proposed that they sell it and buy a goose which lays golden eggs. Thus the community would be provided with a steady income.

One of Singer's purposes is to entertain his audience. Another purpose is to show that all the planning in the world is just foolishness if it loses sight of reality. Both purposes are filled by this funny scene: The men carry Gimpel so he will not tread on the snow—while they walk all over it!

Green Violinist, Marc Chagall

▼ **Critical Viewing**
What is the mood of this painting—serious or silly? Compare this mood to the mood of the story. **[Compare and Contrast]**

Winter Night in Vitebsk, Marc Chagall

◀ **Critical Viewing**
Which details of this painting make it seem like a dream? Which make it seem like a real scene? **[Interpret]**

Dopey Lekisch had another idea. Why not buy eyeglasses that make things look bigger for all the inhabitants of Chelm? Then the houses, the streets, the stores would all look bigger, and of course if Chelm *looked* bigger, then it *would be* bigger. It would no longer be a village, but a big city.

There were other, equally clever ideas. But while the Elders were weighing their various plans, morning came and the sun rose. They looked out of the window, and, alas, they saw the snow had been trampled. The heavy boots of the table carriers had destroyed the treasure.

At the climax of the story, the reader wants to know: Will the Elders see the foolishness of their way of thinking?

The Elders of Chelm clutched at their white beards and admitted to one another that they had made a mistake. Perhaps, they reasoned, four others should have carried the four men who had carried the table that held Gimpel the errand boy?

After long deliberations the Elders decided that if next Hanukkah a treasure would again fall down from the sky, that is exactly what they would do.

Right after the climax comes the resolution of the conflict between reality and foolishness. The Elders will continue in their foolishness!

Although the villagers remained without a treasure, they were full of hope for the next year and praised their Elders, who they knew could always be counted on to find a way, no matter how difficult the problem.

Reading Writing Connection

Writing Application: Help Readers Interpret
As you write your short story, emphasize details that will help readers **interpret** a character's personality and actions. You can emphasize a detail by discussing it for one or two sentences. Or, you might make sure it is the only detail of its kind that you include. For instance, Singer mentions little about the looks of the Elders besides their white beards and high foreheads—a sign that these details are meaningful.

5.2 Prewriting

Choosing Your Topic

For some writers, telling a story is easy—the hard part is coming up with a good topic. Here are a few strategies you can use to get your ideas flowing:

Strategies for Generating a Topic

1. **Drawing** Choose a setting in which a story could take place: a house or an apartment where you used to live, a spooky room you wandered into by mistake, a street in a town in which you've just arrived. Draw this setting in detail. Use the ideas suggested by your drawing for your story.

2. **Freewriting** Set a timer for five minutes, and write down as many story ideas as you can. Focus on getting down ideas rather than on spelling, grammar, or punctuation. At the end of five minutes, review your freewriting. Circle ideas to use in your story.

Try it out! Use the interactive Freewriting activity in **Section 5.2** or go to Topic Generators, accessible from the menu bar, on-line or on CD-ROM.

Student Work
IN PROGRESS

Name: John Beamer
David Starr Jordan Middle School
Palo Alto, CA

Freewriting to Generate a Topic

John Beamer freewrote and then circled the phrases that led to his topic: "The Manitoba Monster." Because he was jotting notes only for himself, he used abbreviations and did not correct errors.

mystery story sci-fi something weird in the woods UFO? Loch Ness (monster)? Don't know Scotland change setting 2 where? (nr. Unc. Dave's house—that lake.) Something happens when kids are visiting thr uncle—swimming someone drowns gets sucked into water by monster? or water skiing or fshing. Guy like U Dave sees something. 2 guys, buddies, (ice fishing) cold cold old old guys? (no no just reg joes, argue a lot one of them sees something other guy doesn't believe him)

TOPIC BANK

If you're having trouble coming up with a topic, consider the following possibilities:

1. **Moving Day** Write a story about a person who moves to a new place. (Your story can be based on real life.) Include details about who or what your character misses most and about the surprises he or she finds in the new place.

2. **Be Careful What You Wish For** Many fairy tales feature a character who makes a foolish wish. Think of King Midas, who couldn't eat or drink because everything he touched turned to gold. Write a story about a human or animal character who is granted a wish that turns out to be a disaster.

Responding to Fine Art

3. This painting shows a scene from the story of Noah's ark. Write a story based on the painting. As you write, pretend you are one of the people or animals shown. Your story should answer these questions: Who are you? What events are taking place around you? How do you feel about them? What happens to you?

Noah's Ark, Aaron Douglas, Fisk University Fine Art Galleries, Nashville, Tennessee

Responding to Literature

4. Read the story "Zlateh the Goat" by Isaac Bashevis Singer. Then, write your own story from Zlateh's point of view, telling what she was thinking and feeling—especially when she says "Maaa"! You can find "Zlateh the Goat" in *Prentice Hall Literature: Timeless Voices, Timeless Themes*, Copper.

Cooperative Writing Opportunity

5. **Group Story** Working in a group, create a story. Brainstorm for a topic, and agree on a story plan. Decide on all of the events and characters in the story. Divide the following tasks: writing the story; illustrating the story and writing captions for the illustrations; and performing the story as a dramatic reading or skit.

Developing Narrative Elements

Once you've come up with a topic, set your story in motion. A short story starts out as words lying on a page. In the best stories, though, the words start whisking by, pulling the reader along. Soon, the pages seem to turn themselves! The secret of all this commotion is the story's conflict. To set your story in motion, identify your conflict.

Identify the Conflict

A **conflict** is a struggle between two opposing forces. A race, for instance, is a conflict among runners. An **external conflict** occurs when a character is struggling against an outside force, such as another character or a natural event. An **internal conflict** takes place within a character, as when the character struggles to make a tough decision or to overcome fear.

Using a Conflict Map To identify the conflict in your story, ask yourself:

1. What does my main character want?
2. Who or what is getting in the way?

Create a conflict map like the one below (or one of your own design) to find the answers to these questions.

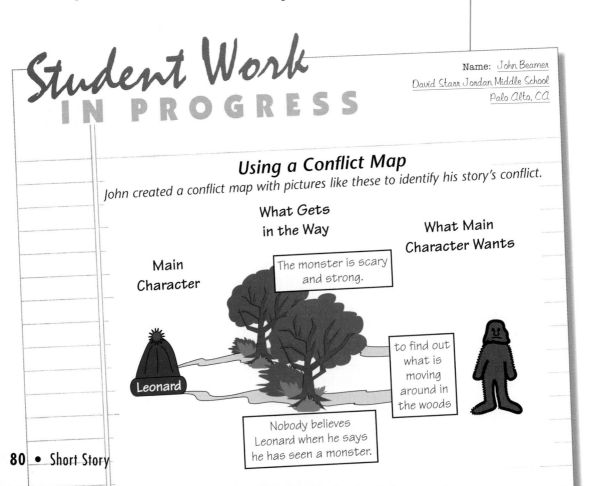

Student Work
IN PROGRESS

Name: John Beamer
David Starr Jordan Middle School
Palo Alto, CA

Using a Conflict Map

John created a conflict map with pictures like these to identify his story's conflict.

What Gets in the Way

What Main Character Wants

Main Character

The monster is scary and strong.

Leonard

to find out what is moving around in the woods

Nobody believes Leonard when he says he has seen a monster.

Considering Your Audience and Purpose

The conflict in your story will keep your readers interested. Before you can start telling your story, though, you must know *who* your readers are—your **audience**—and *what* you want to do for them—your **purpose.** Knowing your audience and purpose will shape your writing, as in these examples:

If your audience is . . .

- **young children,** use simpler words than if you were writing a story for older readers.

- **people who don't go to your school,** remember that if you mention something particular to your school, such as a certain teacher, you must explain who or what you are talking about.

If your purpose is to . . .

- **make readers laugh,** select funny details to include.

- **give readers goosebumps,** include a couple of surprises.

- **present a theme (a question or message about life),** use events that illustrate the question or message.

Gathering Details

Your next step is to gather details to include in your story. Use the strategy of listing and itemizing.

List and Itemize

List ideas about your story topic. Then, circle the most interesting idea. Create another list about that circled item. Review your lists for details to include in your story. If you need more details, repeat the process. Here's an example:

set the story in the future—sci fi
main character is a present-day kid from an average family

kid finds a lamp with a genie who grants her a wish
kid finds a computer that grants her a wish

she wishes she didn't have a little brother
she wishes she could trade places with a wealthy friend
she trades places with her friend
the main character enjoys the limo rides to school and all the clothes
the other kids in school treat her funny, though
at dinner, the wealthy family hardly talks
she wishes she was back with her own family

Text

Get instant help! To find words appropriate to your audience and purpose, use the interactive Word Bins, accessible from the menu bar, on-line or on CD-ROM.

5.3 **Drafting**

Flight of the Thielens, Thomas Hart Benton, © T. H. Benton and R. P. Benton Testamentary Trusts

Shaping Your Writing

Now that you've decided on some of the key elements of your story, it's time to start structuring your ideas into a plot.

Create a Plot

A **plot** is the arrangement of events in the story. It is more than a simple sequence: "This happened, then this happened, then this happened." Instead, a plot is an arrangement of events designed to create interest, even excitement. Plots often follow this pattern:

- The **exposition** introduces the characters and their situation, including the central conflict.

- This **conflict** develops and intensifies during the **rising action,** which leads to the climax.

- The **climax,** or turning point of the story, might take the form of an argument or moment of decision.

- In the story's **falling action,** events start winding down, leading to the resolution.

- At the **resolution,** the conflict is resolved in some way and loose ends are tied up.

Using a Plot Diagram Map out the events in your story using a diagram like the one below. Refer to it as you draft.

▲ **Critical Viewing** Think about the force the people in this painting are struggling against. Then, describe the conflict taking place in the scene. What might happen at the climax? **[Analyze]**

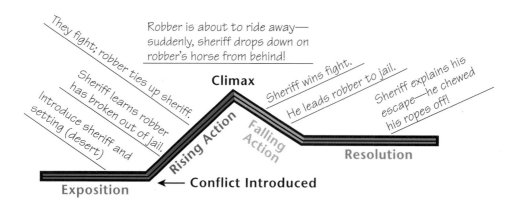

Robber is about to ride away—suddenly, sheriff drops down on robber's horse from behind!

They fight: robber ties up sheriff.

Sheriff learns robber has broken out of jail.

Introduce sheriff and setting (desert)

Climax

Sheriff wins fight.

He leads robber to jail.

Sheriff explains his escape—he chewed his ropes off!

Rising Action

Falling Action

Resolution

Exposition

← **Conflict Introduced**

Providing Elaboration

Use Sensory Details

As you draft your story, make your characters and setting come alive by including sensory details—language that describes how things look, sound, feel, taste, and smell.

Livening Up Descriptions With Sensory Sunbursts

As you write, pause occasionally to find places where you can "burst" open your story, letting in more sights, sounds, textures, smells, and tastes. Circle any spot that could use some sensory pizzazz, and draw a sensory sunburst in the margin next to it. On each of the five rays of the sunburst, jot down details that appeal to a different one of the five senses. Later, review your draft, and add any words that will improve your description of the circled character, place, or thing.

Try it out! Use the interactive Sensory Sunburst activity in **Section 5.3**, on-line or on CD-ROM.

Student Work
IN PROGRESS

Name: John Beamer
David Starr Jordan Middle School
Palo Alto, CA

Using Sensory Sunbursts

Here's an example of how John used sensory sunbursts to enliven his draft.

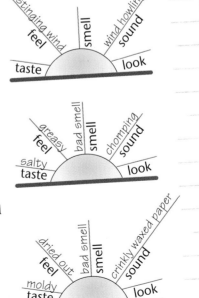

It was a (cold day) in the woods of
Manitoba. *The wind was howling.* Snow covered all the
trees, and the lake was crusted
over with seven inches of ice at
least. Leonard and Troy were out
ice fishing. Leonard, a 60-year-old
insurance salesman, was *chomping on* eating a
greasy chunk
strip of (salami.) Troy, a 48-year-old
daytime gas station manager, was
pulling out his week-old ham
sandwich. *It didn't smell too*
good, but he took
a bite anyway.

Revising

Revising Your Overall Structure

Create Logical Connections Between Events

The first step in revising your story is to make sure that your plot makes sense. Are the events you've included logically connected to one another and to the conflict? Have you left anything out that would explain your characters' actions? Use a bead chart to make sure events are logically connected.

▶ **REVISION STRATEGY**
Using a Bead Chart

Underline each major event in your story. Then, summarize each one in a "bead" on a chart like the one below. Show the connections between events by writing a simple word or phrase, such as *he is curious*, in the connector string. When one event simply happens to occur after another, you might write the word *next* in the connector.

Review your chart. If most of your connectors say *next*, consider adding events in between that explain *why*. If you can't think of a good connection between two events, one of them may not belong in the story. Consider eliminating it or reshaping it to fit better.

Try it out! Use the interactive Bead Chart in **Section 5.4**, on-line or on CD-ROM.

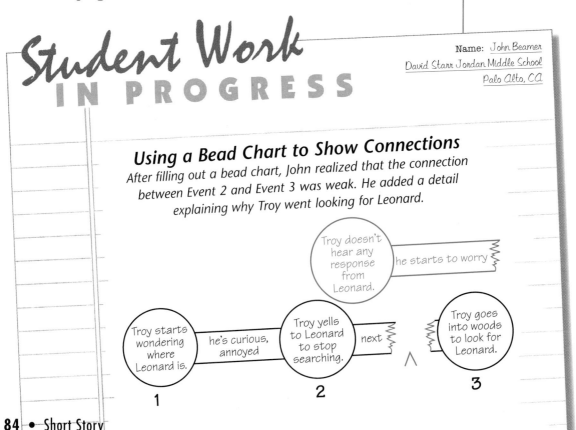

Student Work
IN PROGRESS

Name: *John Beamer*
David Starr Jordan Middle School
Palo Alto, CA

Using a Bead Chart to Show Connections

After filling out a bead chart, John realized that the connection between Event 2 and Event 3 was weak. He added a detail explaining why Troy went looking for Leonard.

Troy doesn't hear any response from Leonard.

he starts to worry

Troy starts wondering where Leonard is.

he's curious, annoyed

Troy yells to Leonard to stop searching.

next

Troy goes into woods to look for Leonard.

1   2   3

Revising Your Paragraphs

Show, Don't Tell

As you revise, look for places where you can *show* instead of *tell*. For example, instead of telling readers "Matty felt afraid," show them her fear by describing the way she walks (quickly), her voice (trembling), and the way she laughs (nervously).

▶ REVISION STRATEGY
Circling Direct Statements

Circle every place in your story where you tell readers directly what a character, setting, or object is like. Then, go back and replace some of these "tellings" with "showings." Here is an example:

TELLING: Sam was an obnoxious know-it-all.

SHOWING: Whenever another kid answered a question, Sam rolled his eyes while frantically waving his hand.

Add Dialogue

To let your characters "show" themselves, add **dialogue**— words you've written as though the characters have said them. Realistic dialogue includes slang, trailing or interrupted speech, and spelling that reflects people's pronunciations.

EXAMPLE: "I dunno if I . . . Hey, wait a minute!" said Sid.

▶ REVISION STRATEGY
Using Dialogue Balloons

Review your draft for places to add dialogue. Using a glue stick, attach a dialogue balloon (a paper circle with a little tail, like those in comic strips) to every spot you find. You can add dialogue showing

1. a character's **answer** or response to another character.
2. **information** one character gives another.
3. an **order,** command, or instruction given by a character.
4. a **question** a character asks.
5. something a character says to express **feelings.**

As you attach a dialogue balloon, label it with reminder words—like *answer, information, order, question,* or *feelings.* After you have finished your draft, go back and add the appropriate kind of dialogue.

▲ **Critical Viewing**
Write one sentence that *tells* what you see in this picture. Now, "translate" your sentence into one that *shows* the same setting. Finally, write a line of dialogue that a parent might say after opening the door and seeing this room. [Describe]

⚙ **Grammar and Style Tip**

When writing dialogue, you may write grammatically incorrect sentences, such as "I ain't got no pencil"—but only if they reflect the way the character would speak.

Revising Your Sentences

Provide Transitions

As you revise, improve the flow of your sentences by adding **transitions**—words that show the connection between ideas.

TRANSITIONAL WORDS AND PHRASES			
Tell when or in what order	Show similarity	Show difference	Show cause and effect
after, during, finally, first, later, next, then, when	also, for example, for instance, similarly	although, despite, however, instead, nevertheless, yet	as a result, because, consequently, if, then, therefore

▶ **REVISION STRATEGY**
Using Transition Boxes

Try this strategy with one paragraph of your story:

1. Draw a box between every two sentences.
2. Place a check in the box if you think that the connection between the sentences is clear.
3. If the connection isn't clear enough, add a transition word or phrase above the line. (See the chart above for ideas.)

Student Work
IN PROGRESS

Name: John Beamer
David Starr Jordan Middle School
Palo Alto, CA

Using Transition Boxes to Show Connections

When John used transition boxes, he realized that he needed to add some transitions to clarify when events occurred.

Troy became pale and yelled, "Leonard—are ya all right?" ☐ *Seconds later, a* ~~A~~ dark shadow fell over him, and everything went black. . . . ☐

A few hours later, some
~~Some~~ campers found the two men wandering in the woods and called the police. ☐ *After* Leonard and Troy told their stories, ~~but~~ the authorities decided that the two terrified men had imagined the whole thing. ☑

Revising Your Word Choice
Use Vivid Verbs

As you revise, replace boring, overused verbs like *said, was, had,* and *went* with colorful verbs that express your meaning more precisely. Review these examples:

OVERUSED: said
VIVID: chuckled, snorted
OVERUSED: was
VIVID: blossomed into, sounded
OVERUSED: went
VIVID: plodded, careened

▶ REVISION STRATEGY
Color-Coding Verbs

Using a green pencil, circle each verb in the first three and the last three paragraphs of your story. Then, go back and draw a red square around any verbs that sound boring or that you've overused (or even used twice in a row). Replace at least half of these weaklings with more exciting, unusual verbs.

💿 Technology Tip

If you think you've used a word too many times, use your word-processing program's Find function to locate each appearance of the word in your draft. Consider replacing it in some cases with another word.

Grammar in Your Writing
Identifying Verbs

A **verb** is a word that shows either an action or a state of being. An **action verb** tells what action the subject of a sentence is doing. This action can be either physical *(run, dance, jump)* or mental *(think, believe, want).* A **linking verb** connects the subject of a sentence with another word that identifies or describes the subject. The most common linking verb is *be* in all its forms. Other linking verbs are *feel, look, appear, become, remain, seem, grow, smell, sound, taste, stay,* and *prove.*

ACTION VERB: Samantha **rides** her bicycle to school.
LINKING VERB: Dan **seems** excited about going to camp.

If you use too many linking verbs, your writing will sound lifeless. If possible, use an action verb instead. (You might need to rewrite your sentence.)

Find It in Your Reading Find three action verbs and three linking verbs in "The Snow in Chelm" by Isaac Bashevis Singer on page 74.

Find It in Your Writing Underline five different action verbs in your story. If you can't find five, consider whether you've overused certain verbs or used too many linking verbs. If so, think of replacements for these verbs.

For more about verbs, see Chapter 15.

Peer Review

Highlighting

Here are the steps for highlighting with a group of peers:

1. Read your revised draft aloud to a small group.
2. Next, ask the group to get ready to note parts they like and parts that need more details.
3. Read your story a second time while the group takes notes.
4. Afterward, ask group members to read back their notes and to explain their reactions.
5. In your draft, highlight the passages peers commented on. Write down specific comments in the margin.

You may use the group's comments to help you revise. Even if you don't accept every suggestion, these comments may help you come up with your own ideas.

Try it out! Use the interactive Highlighting activity in **Section 5.4**, on-line or on CD-ROM.

Student Work IN PROGRESS

Name: John Beamer
David Starr Jordan Middle School
Palo Alto, CA

Highlighting

John highlighted his draft. Then, he wrote down everyone's comments in the margin. He took many of his classmates' suggestions.

After trudging a short way through the woods, he saw Leonard's glove ^and half-eaten chunk of salami^ on the ground. He started to worry. "Come on, Leonard! Let's get out of here!" he called out.

Still silence. Troy jogged about sixty feet into the woods. ^and then^ He saw Leonard lying ^on his back^ in a ditch. Leonard's wool hat was pulled down low over his eyes.

Troy became pale and yelled, "Leonard— are ya all right?" Seconds later, a dark shadow fell over him, and everything went black. . . .

A few hours later, some ^snowmobilers^ campers found the two men. . . .

> "I think it would be funny to say something about the salami."

> "This needs a transition."

> "I want to know what Leonard looked like. Was he hurt?"

> "I like this part. It's spooky."

> "People don't go camping in the winter."

5.5 *Editing and Proofreading*

Proofread your story carefully to catch errors in spelling, punctuation, capitalization, and grammar.

Focusing on Dialogue

Pay particular attention to proofreading your story's **dialogue**—speech that you've quoted exactly. Make sure you've punctuated it correctly.

Grammar in Your Writing
Punctuating and Formatting Dialogue

Dialogue is speech that is presented exactly as a character uttered it. Here are some guidelines that will help you punctuate, capitalize, and in-dent dialogue correctly:

1. Enclose dialogue in quotation marks.

   "I'm moving to California," Maria announced.
2. Don't use quotation marks when you simply report what a character said.

   Maria announced that she was moving to California.
3. If the dialogue comes *after* the "words of saying" in the rest of the sentence, use a comma before the quote.

   Arielle said, "My mom promised we could get a dog."
4. If the dialogue comes *before* the words of saying, use a comma, question mark, or exclamation mark—but not a period—at the end.

   "But now my dad says we have to wait a year," she complained.

   "I'm so annoyed!" she wailed.

   "Have you decided what kind of dog?" asked Abby.
5. Words of saying that interrupt the quote should be set off by punctuation marks and go outside the quotation marks.

   "We all want a poodle," explained Arielle, "except my mom."

Find It in Your Reading Skim "The Snow in Chelm" by Isaac Bashevis Singer on page 74, and find three examples of dialogue. For each, explain why it is punctuated correctly.

Find It in Your Writing Highlight each instance of dialogue in your story, and circle the "words of saying." Correct the punctuation if you find any mistakes.

For more on punctuating with quotation marks, see Chapter 26.

Publishing and Presenting

Building Your Portfolio

Consider these suggestions for sharing your story:

1. **Submit Your Story** Submit your story to your school's literary magazine. You might also submit it to a national magazine, an e-zine, or a contest that publishes student writing. (Ask your teacher, librarian, or media specialist for suggestions.)

2. **Give a Reading** Get together with a group of classmates, and present a literary reading for an audience at your school. Tape your reading, and send copies to friends or family members who couldn't attend.

Reflecting on Your Writing

After you've finished writing your short story, jot down some of your thoughts about your writing experience. You might start by answering the following questions:

• Did you enjoy writing your story? What part of the process did you like most? What was the hardest part for you?

• The next time you write a story, what do you think you might do differently as a result of this experience?

 Internet Tip

To see short stories scored with this rubric, go on-line:
PHSchool.com
Enter Web Code:
eak-6001

Rubric for Self-Assessment

Evaluate your short story using the following criteria:

	Score 4	Score 3	Score 2	Score 1
Audience and Purpose	Contains an engaging introduction; successfully entertains or presents a theme	Contains a somewhat engaging introduction; entertains or presents a theme	Contains an introduction; attempts to entertain or to present a theme	Begins abruptly or confusingly; leaves purpose unclear
Organization	Creates an interesting, clear narrative; told from a consistent point of view	Presents a clear sequence of events; told from a specific point of view	Presents a mostly clear sequence of events; contains inconsistent points of view	Presents events without logical order; lacks a consistent point of view
Elaboration	Provides insight into character; develops plot; contains dialogue	Contains details and dialogue that develop character and plot	Contains details that develop plot; contains some dialogue	Contains few or no details to develop characters or plot
Use of Language	Uses word choice and tone to reveal story's theme; contains no errors in grammar, punctuation, or spelling	Uses interesting and fresh word choices; contains few errors in grammar, punctuation, and spelling	Uses some clichés and trite expressions; contains some errors in grammar, punctuation, and spelling	Uses uninspired word choices; has many errors in grammar, punctuation, and spelling

5.7 Student Work IN PROGRESS

FINAL DRAFT

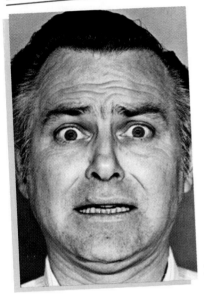

The Manitoba Monster

John Beamer
David Starr Jordan
Middle School
Palo Alto, California

◀ **Critical Viewing**
Pick two or three adjectives to describe the man in this picture. Then, find the part of the story that his expression fits. **[Connect]**

It was a cold day in the woods of Manitoba. The wind was howling, snow covered all the trees, and the lake was crusted over with seven inches of ice at least. Leonard and Troy were out ice fishing. Leonard, a 60-year-old insurance salesman, was chomping on a greasy chunk of salami. Troy, a 48-year-old daytime gas station manager, was pulling out his week-old ham sandwich. It didn't smell too good, but he took a bite anyway.

Leonard and Troy went out ice fishing every January, but this time would be different. The two men were sitting next to their fishing hole. As Leonard chewed on his greasy salami, he occasionally wiped his chin on his jacket sleeve. "I'n it a cold day here in Manitoba?" he said. "You seen the northern pike Joe Hemal caught yesterday? I ain't never seen not'in' like it. So big!"

Troy started to complain, "We've been out here for three hours. I've started thinkin' lately—"

Suddenly looking startled, Leonard shouted, "Hey, did ya see that over to the left? I thought I saw somethin' over by those big trees!"

"It's that bad meat you're eatin', makin' ya see things. Just relax," Troy said with a laugh.

There was silence for two minutes, and then Leonard shouted again, "There it is! I saw it! It looked like a big guy comin' toward us from the trees over there. He was closer this time!"

Troy sighed, "I told you not to eat that garbage! You're seein' things."

John's first sentence uses sensory details to introduce the setting— the woods of Manitoba, Canada.

The spelling of the dialogue shows how these characters actually talk. John also uses interrupted speech, another way to make dialogue sound realistic.

The conflict begins to develop. Leonard thinks he sees something, but Troy doesn't believe him.

"I don't care," Leonard said. "I'm gonna have a look over there!" And with that, he went off. Troy ignored him and continued fishing while eating his week-old ham sandwich.

At the far side of the lake, Leonard called, "Hey you! I know you're here somewhere! What are ya doin', tryin' to scare us?"

Then he heard a rustling in the bushes, and out of the corner of his eye he saw a figure fleeing behind a tree.

"Ah ha!" he said. "I see ya over there! Why 'er you hidin' behind that tree? Ha ha!"

He ran to the tree where he thought he saw the figure. Then, he just stood frozen in shock. About forty feet away from him there was a tall creature. It stood like a man but was covered in wiry brown and black fur, with a long muzzle and small, beady eyes.

Leonard didn't want to show that he was scared, so he sort of joked, "You're a hairy lookin' fella!"

The creature galloped toward him, baring his long, sharp teeth. Leonard was too scared to move. He just stood there, clutching his greasy chunk of salami.

Meanwhile, Troy was starting to wonder about Leonard, and he yelled, "Hey, Leonard! Stop your searching—there's nothin' out there!" When he didn't hear a response, he got up and walked to where he thought he had seen his friend disappear. After trudging a short way through the woods, he saw Leonard's glove and half-eaten chunk of salami on the ground. He started to worry. "Come on, Leonard! Let's get out of here!" he called out. Still silence. Troy jogged about sixty feet into the woods and then saw Leonard lying on his back in a ditch. Leonard's wool hat was pulled down low over his eyes.

Troy became pale and yelled, "Leonard—are ya all right?" Seconds later, a dark shadow fell over him, and everything went black. . . .

A few hours later, some snowmobilers found the two men wandering in the woods and called the police. After Leonard and Troy told their stories, the authorities decided that the two terrified men had imagined the whole thing.

Deputy Dan told them, "You know, you two should take it easy, take a vacation, maybe see a doctor or somethin'."

Finally, Leonard and Troy began to believe that maybe they had just been seeing things. Maybe it was just something they'd eaten!

And the two continued with their lives as if nothing had happened—except that they never went ice fishing again . . . or ate old meat. But reports still come in of men who see large, dark, hairy creatures with long, sharp teeth in the woods of Manitoba—men like Troy and Leonard, who eat a bad diet of greasy salami and old ham sandwiches.

▲ **Critical Viewing**
Compare the monster in the picture to the one in the story. **[Compare]**

Specific sensory details about how the monster looks, and about how his hair might feel to the touch, add color to the story.

This is the story's climax, or turning point. The conflict—will anyone believe Leonard's story?—must be resolved.

At the resolution, the conflict is resolved. Troy now believes Leonard—but no one else believes either of them!

Connected Assignment *Drama*

Writing a short story is not the only way to tell a story. A **drama**, such as a play, uses actors to act out a narrative. Elements of drama include

- **dialogue**—or speech—for one or more characters.
- **stage directions** telling how the characters speak, where they are on stage, and what actions they perform.

MODEL

Grandpa and the Statue
Arthur Miller

Notice how sound effects, stage directions, and the identity of each speaker are set off from the spoken dialogue in this excerpt from a radio play:

[*High wind*]

CHILD MONOGHAN. [*Softly, as though* GRANDPA *is in bed*] Grampa?

MONOGHAN. [*awakened*] Heh? What are you doin' up?

▲ **Critical Viewing** What stage directions might this actor be following? **[Infer]**

Use the following strategies to write a radio script for a dialogue.

Prewriting Imagine two characters talking to each other about a problem. Write down important details about each character and about the problem they face.

Drafting Begin drafting by "listening" to your characters talk. After you write what one character says, imagine how the other character would respond. Then, write down his or her answer. Afterward, add directions that tell a reader how words are said, what characters are doing while they speak, or what sounds are heard in the background.

Revising and Editing Read the draft of your scene out loud. Rewrite lines that do not sound as if they would be said by the characters you have described.

Publishing and Presenting With a classmate, read your dialogue for the class. Have another partner produce the sound effects you need.

Spotlight on the Humanities

Comparing Themes Across the Arts

Focus on Oral Traditions: Dragons

Perhaps the story started with a snake slithering away between two rocks. Perhaps it started with a curl of smoke rising from a mountain where nobody lived. No one is sure how the story of dragons got started. It seems as if the story has always been told.

Images of dragons appear in art as early as 2000 B.C. Dragon stories are familiar in Asia, Europe, and Africa. For the Chinese, the dragon symbolizes good fortune and wisdom. In Chinese mythology, dragons bring the rains from the sea. The ancient Greeks and Romans believed the dragon held great secrets. (The painting shown illustrates the battle between Perseus, a Greek hero, and a dragon-like creature.)

By the time the dragon appears in the tale of St. George, though, he is just an evil, scaly, firebreathing menace. In the legend, St. George saves a princess by battling a dragon who lives in Libya. St. George has appeared in artworks in Ethiopia, Egypt, and Britain.

Dragons make for good stories, in part because they create a strong conflict—they kidnap princesses, steal treasures, and burn towns. Dragon stories also remind us that princesses and treasures are often held captive by an old fear, coiled in a cave. Then, the only way to find the good things is to confront the bad.

Literature Connection The novel *Dragonfly* (1999) by Alice McLerran relates the story of a friendly dragon. Filled with humor and adventure, the novel tells the story of the friendship between a boy named Jason and the dragon "Drag."

Short Story Writing Activity: Story by a Dragon

Write a story from a dragon's point of view. First, decide whether your dragon is nice or nasty. Then, tell the story of his or her confrontation with a hero, with a princess, or with modern times.

Andromeda rescued from the monster by Perseus riding Pegasus, Christine de Pisan, British Library, London

▲ **Critical Viewing** Imagine that one of the three characters shown in this painting was missing. Explain why the story would be less interesting. **[Draw Conclusions]**

Media and Technology Skills

Analyzing Visual Meanings

Activity: Analyze Story Elements in Cartoons

Even the wackiest cartoon includes the same elements as a short story—character, setting, theme, and plot. To appreciate cartoons, learn about the storytelling elements they use.

Think About It Many cartoons feature the following elements:

Distinctive Characters You might remember one cartoon character for his ridiculous looks. You might remember another for her funny way of talking or the special phrases she always uses. For these reasons, viewers recognize cartoon characters easily. The characters quickly become like old friends.

Tricks With Reality Cartoonists often "bend the rules" of reality. Characters' limbs may stretch impossibly, then snap back into shape. People may fall a great distance—then bounce. Cartoonists use these tricks for humor and to show how a lively imagination can always get around reality.

Comic Pacing Think of a cartoon with a goofy hero and his foolish enemy. Each scene in the cartoon will show the hunter trying to capture the hero. Each scene grows more ridiculous than the last. If the hunter used a mousetrap in the first scene, he might use a cannon in the next. By the end of the cartoon, each scene may take place at high speed. In this way, a cartoonist sets up a certain rhythm or pacing, adding to the humor.

Pacing for Suspense In an action cartoon, the action may briefly slow down near the end. For example, just when the villain captures the hero, the cartoon may jump to the hero's friends eating lunch. Here, the pacing of events increases the viewer's suspense.

Analyze It As you watch a cartoon, record the storytelling elements it uses in a chart like the one shown. Referring to the details in your chart, write a paragraph explaining why you enjoyed or did not enjoy the cartoon.

Other Story Elements in Cartoons

- **Conflict** In action cartoons, the conflict concerns the hero's attempt to stop the villain from doing evil. In humorous cartoons, the conflict may be between a zany character and the character he or she is always annoying.
- **Theme** A basic theme of many action cartoons is simple: Good always wins over evil. A basic theme of many comic cartoons is also simple: It is foolish to trust even the best plans, because the world is unpredictable and mischievous.

Character Name	Distinctive Characteristics	Hero or Villain?	My Reaction to the Character

Conflict	My Reaction to the Conflict	Special Effects	My Reaction to the Effects

Standardized Test Preparation Workshop

Responding to Writing Prompts About Narratives

Some standardized tests require you to write a short response to a story you have read. Learning how the elements of a short story work together will help you write about short stories. Before responding to a test prompt on a short story, think about how the following narrative elements shape the story:

- **Plot** is the sequence of events in the story, arranged in a way that will keep readers interested.

- **Characters** are the people, animals, or other beings that take part in the story's action.

- **Setting** is the time and place in which the story unfolds.

- **Theme** is the question or message about life that the story expresses.

As you read the story in a test-taking situation, think about how the writer uses each narrative device to create an effective short story.

To practice for such test questions, respond to the following prompt, using the suggestions on the next page. The clocks show what portion of your test-taking time to devote to each stage of the writing process.

Test Tips

- To get a handle on narrative elements in a story or passage, first jot down the main characters and central events of the story or passage.
- If you are unsure whether you have made a grammar or spelling error in a sentence in your test essay, consider rewriting the sentence to eliminate the need to correct it.

Sample Writing Situation

Read "The Snow in Chelm" by Isaac Bashevis Singer on page 74. Then, answer the following question.

What is the author's opinion of the way the Elders of Chelm make their decisions? Use details and information from the story in your answer.

Prewriting

Allow about one fourth of your time for prewriting.

Gather Details From the Story The prompt asks you to give the author's opinion on the Elders' way of solving problems. Scan the story for specific information about the Elders' decisions and their results. Note any comments the author makes about the Elders and their decisions.

Create a T-Chart As you gather details, enter them in a T-Chart. In one column, list the decisions the Elders make. In the other column, list the reasons they arrive at each decision, the results, and any opinion stated by the author about each.

Analyze Your Chart An author does not have to state his or her opinion on events in the story. Instead, the author can imply an opinion. Review your T-Chart. Evaluate each decision and its results. Ask such questions as the following: Were the results what the Elders intended? Did they look at the matter from a few different angles before deciding? Then, jot down on your chart the author's probable opinion on each decision.

Drafting

Allow approximately half of your time for drafting.

Write an Introduction In your introduction, clearly state what you will be covering in your response. Briefly summarize your conclusions.

Organize Details Outline the main points of your essay. Under each main point, list details from the story or from your own experience that support that point.

Include Story Details If you simply say that the author thinks the Elders are "foolish," you have not conveyed much about the story to your reader. Make sure that you support each statement about the author's opinion or about the Elders and their decisions with specific examples from the story. If you copy the exact words of the story to make a point, place them in quotation marks.

Revising, Editing, and Proofreading

Allow about twenty minutes for revising, editing, and proofreading.

Check Support Read through your response. Neatly draw a line through any details that do not support the main idea of your essay. For any main point you make about the story, be that sure you have supplied an example.

Clean It Up When you are satisfied with your answer, read your draft one last time for problems with spelling. Make all corrections neatly.

Bok Choy and Apples, Pamela Chin Lee

Description in Everyday Life

"What kind of jacket are you looking for?" a sales clerk might inquire. "What does their music sound like?" a friend might ask. To answer these questions, you must describe what you are looking for or what you have heard.

Like your spoken words, a written description can show others what a person, thing, or scene is like. Descriptive writing is much harder than shopping, though! In a store, you can always point to the jacket you want. You can't point in writing. Words alone must do the job of showing what you have in mind.

Tap into the picture-making power of words: Develop your descriptive writing skills.

▲ **Critical Viewing**
Describe this scene, using one word from each of the five senses. **[Apply]**

What Is Descriptive Writing?

Descriptive writing creates a picture of a person, place, thing, or event. Description includes more than just the looks of a thing, however. It lets you hear the "shushing" sound of Grandpa's slippers outside the door. It gives you a sudden whiff of his icy aftershave and a woolly handful of his warm sweater—just like when you give him a hug! The elements of descriptive writing include

- vivid sensory details—details appealing to one or more of the five senses.

- a clear, consistent organization.

- a main impression to which each detail adds specific information.

- the use of figurative language, such as vivid comparisons.

To learn the criteria on which your description may be judged or graded, see the Rubric for Self-Assessment on page 114.

Types of Descriptive Writing

Your description may be one of several types:

- **Descriptions of people or places** portray the physical appearance and personality of a person or place and show readers why the subject is important or special.

- **Observations** describe an event the writer has witnessed.

- **Remembrances** recall a memorable experience in the writer's life; they may describe a specific moment or a longer period of time.

- **Vignettes** capture a single specific moment in the writer's life, painting a picture with words.

Writers in ACTION

Deborah Behler is a zoologist and wildlife writer. She writes about the animals at the Bronx Zoo—more than 4,000 of them! When Behler gathers details for her writing, she relies on her observation of the animals in their exhibits.

"Sensory language in descriptive writing is important because that's how people understand what's going on around them—what you see, what you hear, [what you] touch."

PREVIEW Student Work IN PROGRESS

Leann Goree, a student at Southside Fundamental Middle School in St. Petersburg, Florida, described the sensations and impressions of snow as she remembered them. You can see examples of the prewriting, drafting, and revising techniques she used to create her description. At the end of the chapter, you can read Leann's completed piece, "Snow Dance."

In his novel The Tom Sawyer Fires, *Laurence Yep (1948–   ) recounts the adventures of a fireman named Tom Sawyer. In this excerpt, you can see how effective descriptive writing can create suspense and excitement as well as vivid images.*

Reading Strategy: Infer

A writer does not spell out all the information you need to understand characters or situations. To understand a situation or character fully, **make inferences,** or draw conclusions, based on the details the writer provides. For instance, at the end of the following excerpt, the writer does not tell you that the characters have broken through the roof. You can infer that they have broken through, however, when the narrator sees the sky and says, "You did it."

▲ **Critical Viewing** Write a sentence comparing this fire to a specific kind of living thing. **[Comparison and Contrast]**

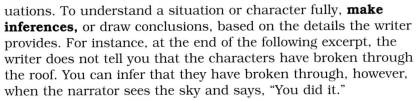

A Narrow Escape

Laurence Yep

Glass began tinkling all around us, and the smell of rotten eggs was overpowering. Flames crackled around the door and walls, small triangles at first, but they shot upward like bright weeds. The shack was already filling with smoke.

We began to swing the chair back and forth in rhythm, so that the legs hammered against the boards. By the sixth or seventh swing, a chair leg broke. And by the twelfth, the chair itself had caught fire.

We dropped it with a crash on the floor, and I got hold of a rag and whipped it against the burning chair leg. Now the boards of the cabin were outlined by fire—it seemed as if we were trapped inside a cell of glowing bars.

The author uses sensory details and a comparison to "bright weeds" to set the scene. The details tell readers what the characters hear, see, and smell.

Vivid sensory details such as "glowing bars" create strong images in the reader's mind.

"Those boards were nailed to stay there till doomsday," Tom said.

"Maybe someone will see the fire," I said, "and get the fire companies."

Mark was doubtful. "Even if they did, how would they know we were in here?"

Once the fire reached the roof, the shack was going to collapse. Tom looked up. "The roof. That's it."

He crouched, pointing his index finger toward a big brown stain in the center of the roof. "See that big patch of tin? Maybe we can knock it off and get out that way."

Tom and Mark had positioned the table underneath the tin patch. "Get Letty's shawl, will you?" Tom ordered. . . . "Come on, Your Grace." Mark got the pot of water and carefully poured it over the shawl.

Then Tom picked up the shawl and draped it over his head and shoulders. Water spattered down the wet fringes. "Stay close to the floor, Your Grace," he said. "More air there."

Tom swung a chair on top of the table and climbed up. "I think heaven is going to have to wait.". . .

Tom thrust the chair against the tin, and there was a hollow, bonging sound. "I think it's giving."

I beat at the flames on the floor, trying to keep them away from the table.

Tom was pounding at the tin, and the metal square boomed and echoed like we were in the middle of a thunderstorm. But by the tenth swing, we heard a crack.

"Was that a roof board?" Mark asked.

"No," Tom sounded grim, "it was a chair leg."

I was hopping around like a crazy frog as I flailed at the fire on the floor.

Tom swung again and I heard another chair leg crack and fall off. He began to batter frantically at the tin. Suddenly he gave a sharp yelp.

I looked up to see a little rectangle of glorious blue sky. "You did it."

Words like then *show that this excerpt is organized chronologically: The author describes events in the order in which they occur.*

Sensory details such as boomed, echoed, *and* crack *let the reader hear what is happening.*

Reading Writing Connection

Writing Application: Help Your Readers Make Inferences As you draft your description, include details that will help readers make inferences about the feelings you have about the person, place, or object that you are describing.

LITERATURE

For another example of vivid descriptive writing, read "The Sound of Summer Running" by Ray Bradbury. You can find this narrative in *Prentice Hall Literature: Timeless Voices, Timeless Themes,* Copper.

6.2 Prewriting

Choosing Your Topic

Almost any person, place, event, or object that you find interesting or that is important to you will make a good topic for descriptive writing. Use these strategies to select a topic:

Strategies for Generating a Topic

1. **Drawing** Think of a place, such as your grandparents' house or a park, that you visit. Draw the people and scenes that come to mind. After five minutes, review your drawings. Select your topic from among the people and events you have drawn or from a memory your drawings bring to mind.

2. **Trigger Words** Think of three general words, such as *night, winter,* and *lunch.* For each word, write whatever pops into your mind. Write about each word for five minutes. Then, review your work, and circle the most interesting words. Select a topic related to these words.

Try it out! Use the interactive Trigger Words activity in **Section 6.2**, on-line or on CD-ROM.

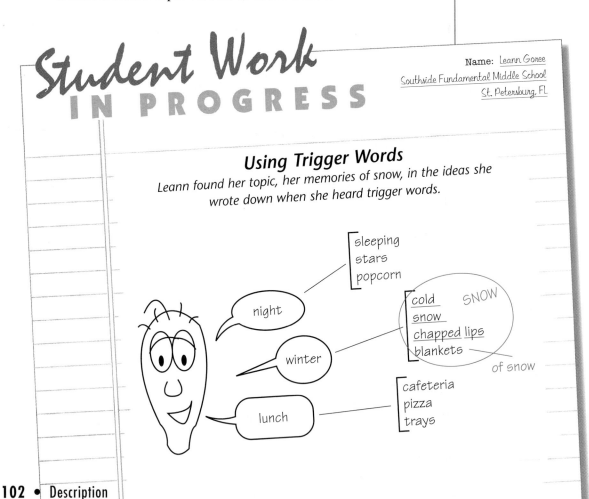

Student Work
IN PROGRESS

Name: Leann Goree
Southside Fundamental Middle School
St. Petersburg, FL

Using Trigger Words
Leann found her topic, her memories of snow, in the ideas she wrote down when she heard trigger words.

night
- sleeping
- stars
- popcorn

winter
- cold
- snow
- chapped lips
- blankets

SNOW
of snow

lunch
- cafeteria
- pizza
- trays

TOPIC BANK

If you're having trouble finding a topic, consider these possibilities:

1. **Description of Weather** Describe weather that is especially noticeable and creates a mood, such as a summer thunderstorm, a sunny day in early spring, a windy fall day, or a dreary, overcast winter afternoon.

2. **Observation of the Animal World** Take your cue from zoologist Deborah Behler, and choose an animal at the zoo or in your home as your topic.

Responding to Fine Art

3. Jot down notes about the scene in this painting. What objects do you see? What details is the painter able to capture? Write a description of the scene in this painting, or of a similar scene in your own life. Be sure to describe the sights, sounds, smells, and textures that belong to the scene.

Farberware Coffeepot, No. VI, Jeanette Pasin Sloan, National Museum of American Art, Washington, DC

Responding to Literature

4. Read "Water" by Helen Keller, paying special attention to the sensory details she uses. Then, write a description of an object. In the first part of your description, use just the senses that Keller uses. Then, describe the object using your other senses. You can find "Water" in *Prentice Hall Literature: Timeless Voices, Timeless Themes*, Copper.

☑ Cooperative Writing Opportunity

5. **Object Observation** With a group of classmates, create a grab bag. Each member should bring a small item from home—an object with an interesting shape, texture, or other sensory quality. Put the items in a bag. Individually, choose an item without looking, and then write a description of it. First, explain what the object felt like in the bag. Then, describe what it turned out to be. Together, organize your descriptions in a booklet.

Narrowing Your Topic

Can you cover your entire topic in a brief description? If not, you must narrow your topic. Maybe your topic can be divided into subtopics. For instance, "the park" is a broad topic, but "the playground" is narrower, and "the swingset at the playground" is even more narrow. Decide which subtopic is most interesting to you. An index-card camera can help you zoom in to narrow your topic.

Zoom in to Narrow Your Topic

Use an index card as a "camera." Follow these steps:

1. Cut a small hole in the index card to make the camera's "lens."
2. Take your camera to the scene, object, or person you will describe. If you want to describe a past event or a place or person that is not nearby, find photographs or make drawings of your subject.
3. Look through the "camera lens" at your subject or at the photographs or drawings you have gathered.
4. Focus first on one part of your subject, and then on another. Look both closely and from a distance.
5. Take notes on the details that are particular to each part, and on the details that are common to the entire image.

Afterward, review your notes, and choose as your topic the most interesting aspect of your subject.

▲ **Critical Viewing** What new details can you see in the "close-up" view of this scene? **[Analyze]**

Considering Your Audience and Purpose

Who will read your description? How much do they know about your subject? If your **audience**—your intended reader—has never seen what you're describing, make sure you describe even the most basic details about your subject. If your readers are already familiar with your subject, focus on details that show how special it is.

Your **purpose** in writing a description is to share what you have experienced with readers. To achieve this purpose, include vivid sensory details in your writing. A **sensory detail** is a word, phrase, or sentence that gives precise information about the look, sound, taste, touch, or smell of something.

Gathering Details

Before you begin writing, gather details about your subject. Make sure you gather details for all of the senses. Sensory details are especially effective for creating a vivid picture for readers, as you can see in this example:

| NO SENSORY DETAILS: | I got into the wagon for a hayride. |
| ADDED SENSORY DETAILS: | The hay crackled when I threw myself down, wrapping me in a cloud of sweet and sour smells and prickling me busily along my arms. |

Use Each of Your Senses

Imagine your subject, along with all the sights, scents, textures, sounds, and tastes linked to it. Then, fill in a chart like the one below to help you gather details for each of the senses. Refer to your chart as you draft, using details from it in your description.

Research Tip

To use each of your senses as you gather details, try to use your senses separately. For instance, you might close your eyes and cover your ears as you taste a strawberry.

Student Work
IN PROGRESS

Name: Leann Goree
Southside Fundamental Middle School
St. Petersburg, FL

Using a Sensory Details Chart

To gather details from her memories of snow, Leann created a chart like the one below. Notice that she found details for each of the senses.

Sensory Details: Snow

sights	sounds	smells	tastes	sensations of touch
drifting	lips smacking	clean smell in the air	like a watery popsicle	chapped lips
flakes—tiny, white, frail	crisp crunch			soft blanket
sparkling and shining				melting from furry to wet
				tingling and cool

Drafting

Shaping Your Writing
Organize to Make Your Ideas Clear

Now that you've gathered details, arrange them in an order that readers can follow. Here are three types of order:

Chronological Order		• Present events in the order in which they occur. • Use for a remembrance or other description of an event.
Spatial Order		• Present details from left to right, top to bottom, or back to front. • Use for descriptions of places or objects.
Order of Importance	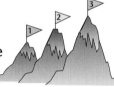	• Present least important details at the beginning and the most important at the end. • Use to lead readers to your main impression.

Create a Main Impression

The descriptions that are most fun to read are those that create a **main impression**—an idea or feeling that ties the details about your subject together. Compare these examples:

NO MAIN IMPRESSION: The box is wrapped in shiny green paper. When I pull the ribbon, it comes free with a soft hissing sound. The top comes off. The object inside sits in light-green tissue paper.

MAIN IMPRESSION: The box keeps calling me. Its wrapping of shiny green paper glints and winks in the light, teasing me to guess what's inside. Finally, it is my turn to open a gift. The ribbon pulls free, sighing "Oh, all right, I'll tell!" The top falls off, revealing a shape nestled in light-green tissue paper.

The second description creates a main impression of suspense by comparing the box to a teasing friend. As you draft, choose details that will create a single main impression.

▼ **Critical Viewing** Give a word from the senses to describe this object. Then, give a word describing a feeling you might associate with it. **[Apply]**

106 • Description

Providing Elaboration
Combine Details From Different Senses

The world offers a feast of sounds, scents, textures, and flavors. If your description tells only what things look like, the reader will feel hungry for more. It is as though you invited the reader to dinner and said, "All you get are potatoes!" Be generous—use "Depth-Charging" to share your sensory feast.

Using Depth-Charging As you draft, pause at the end of each paragraph. Then, follow these steps:
1. Circle an important item about which you can supply information from senses other than sight.
2. Draw an arrow from this circled word to a blank line.
3. Write a new sentence, giving details about the item. Use a sense other than the one you first used to describe it.
4. Circle the most interesting word in your new sentence.
5. Draw an arrow to a new line. Write a sentence using yet another sense.

Then, decide whether to use these sentences in your draft.

Collaborative Writing Tip

Get together with one or two classmates. Without identifying your subject, name details about it, one for each of the senses. Can your partners guess your subject from the details you give? If not, ask for suggestions for more precise details.

Student Work
IN PROGRESS

Name: Leann Goree
Southside Fundamental Middle School
St. Petersburg, FL

Depth-Charging to Use All the Senses
After Leann wrote this paragraph, she realized she had discussed only how the snow made things look. She added a few details from other senses.

The sun is out now! It spreads its cold, golden light along the new white ground. A few flakes still fall from the sky here and there, like they are hurrying to catch up with their friends. Every now and then, they get caught in a sudden gust of chilly wind and are whipped along. My friend Maria and I watch the flakes dancing and sparkling in the sun.

Each gust makes my ears turn to ice! *Touch*

The wind and snow make the world smell new and clean. *Smell*

Revising

After you complete your first draft, review it to make improvements. Start by looking at your overall structure.

Revising Your Overall Structure
Analyze Your Organization

To make sure you have organized your draft consistently, use the following coding strategy.

▶ **REVISION STRATEGY**
Coding for Organization

Highlight each sentence that introduces an aspect of your subject. For instance, you might highlight the sentence "My grandfather likes to rebuild cars." Write a key word next to each highlighted sentence to show its connection to the one before it. Select from these key words:

more important, less important

before, after, during

near, far, up, down, next to, across from

Then, look for out-of-sequence key words. For instance, the words "after . . . before" are out of sequence. Rearrange paragraphs or sentences to create a sensible order.

Student Work
IN PROGRESS

Name: *Leann Goree*
Southside Fundamental Middle School
St. Petersburg, FL

Coding for Organization
Leann rearranged paragraphs when she found that one was out of sequence.

Tiny white snowflakes are drifting slowly toward the ground. . . .   After

Maria and I stick our pink tongues out to catch a few of these late, frail flakes. . . .   After

It's really snowing now! . . . .   Before

The sun is out now! . . . .   After

Revising Your Paragraphs

Use Functional Paragraphs

Mechanics use different tools for different jobs. When you write, you can use different types of paragraphs to get the job done. **Functional paragraphs** perform specific functions. They may

- emphasize an idea.
- make a transition.
- add a special effect, such as dialogue.

A functional paragraph may be one sentence or a series of sentences. Here are a few examples:

▲ **Critical Viewing**
Write a one- or two-sentence functional paragraph introducing this scene.
[Apply]

Arouse or sustain interest:
Not everyone knows what life is like for a hunted man. Not everyone, but Luke Graywolf was an exception.

Present a special effect:
sssSSWOOSH! went the train.

Emphasize a point: Let me put it another way: I would rather move to another country than live in a place with such a law.

Functional Paragraphs

Show a shift from one speaker to another:
Next, Harriet chimed in with, "Oh, not another ice cream cone!"

Provide a transition:
It was only later that night that they got the news.

Add functional paragraphs to your description to get the job done.

▶ REVISION STRATEGY
Adding Functional Paragraphs

Reread your draft. Place brackets around sentences expressing the main idea of each paragraph. Then, evaluate the movement from one main idea to another. Add functional paragraphs where needed to make the movement clear.

Revising Your Sentences
Eliminate Run-on Sentences

When too many details collide in a sentence, the result may be a **run-on sentence**—two or more complete sentences written as though they were a single sentence.

RUN-ON: My grandfather is a tall man, he's strong, he can run three miles a day.

POSSIBLE CORRECTION: My grandfather is a tall man. He's strong, and he can run three miles a day.

Use this strategy to find and eliminate some run-ons.

Try it out! Use the interactive Marking Commas activity in **Section 6.4**, on-line or on CD-ROM.

▶ **REVISION STRATEGY**
Color-Coding for Comma Splices

Mark the first ten commas in your draft with yellow dot stickers. Review your yellow dots. If a yellow dot separates two complete ideas, consider the following changes:

EVALUATE	POSSIBLE REVISION
One idea simply adds to or contrasts with the other.	Add *and* or *but* after the comma. ("Bob is thirsty, and there is no water.")
The two ideas form a cause-and-effect relationship or show that a cause did not have an effect.	Replace the comma with a conjunction such as *because* or *although*. ("Bob is thirsty although I gave him water.")
The two ideas are not closely related.	Replace the comma with a period and capitalize the first letter of the next word.

Student Work
IN PROGRESS

Name: Leann Goree
Southside Fundamental Middle School
St. Petersburg, FL

Marking Commas
Leann marked commas and then made these revisions:

I put my gloves back on, but now the inside of them is wet, too. I turn around and around to see where the snow might end. It is everywhere, it. It covers the roof of the school.

Leann had joined two complete thoughts with a comma. Since the ideas indicated a contrast, she added the conjunction.

Here, Leann turned two complete thoughts into separate sentences by adding a period.

Media and Technology Skills

Analyze Visual Representations

Activity: Analyze Camera Techniques in a Movie

You might describe a hunting cat as "a small, sleek panther" or as "a cruel captor." These two descriptions give very different pictures. Moviemakers can also shape our ideas of a thing. Learn to identify the techniques they use.

Think About It Here are some important camera techniques:

Dramatic Cutting One moment, the movie is showing you a high-speed car chase. The next, it is showing you a quiet scene by the fireplace in someone's living room. Dramatic "cuts" from one scene to another without a break can

- **build suspense.** When the movie interrupts one part of the story and turns to another, you wonder how the first part turns out.
- **create a fast pace for the movie.** One event can follow another quickly. The movie can easily include a few different stories.

Close-Up and Distance Shots When you look at the world, you see more detail in things close by and less detail in those farther away. Watching a movie is not like looking at the world. A camera can change how much detail you see in an instant. In a **close-up** shot,

- the person or thing filmed takes up most of the screen.
- something is emphasized. For example, a movie might use a close-up of the hero's face to emphasize his reaction to bad news.

In a **distance shot,**

- the person or thing filmed takes up little of the screen.
- the "big picture" of how things fit together is clear.

Watch It Watch a movie. Use a chart like this one to note examples of dramatic cutting, close-ups, and distance shots. Write a paragraph describing each.

Other Camera Techniques

"Zoom In" Shots In a zoom in shot, the image of a person or thing moves closer and closer. Like a close-up, a zoom shot tells you that you are looking at something important.

"Zoom Out" Shots In a zoom out shot, the image of a person or thing moves farther and farther away. Like a distance shot, a zoom out lets you see the "big picture."

Movie: _____

Dramatic Cutting		Close-up	Distance Shot
Scene 1: What happened?	**Scene 2:** What happened?	**Scene:** What happened?	**Scene:** What happened?
Who was involved?	Who was involved?	Who was involved?	Who was involved?
When did jump to next scene happen?		What did the close-up focus on?	What did the shot show?

Standardized Test Preparation Workshop

Strategy, Organization, and Style

On standardized tests, some questions require you to read a passage and then choose improvements for it.

- *Strategy* questions ask whether a certain change fits the purpose of the passage.

- *Organization* questions ask you to choose the most logical sequence of ideas or sentences.

- *Style* questions ask you to find the most appropriate and effective language for the intended audience.

Practice for such questions with the following sample items.

Test Tip

Read each answer choice before responding to make sure you choose the best one.

Sample Test Items

Directions Read the passage, and then answer the questions that follow.

(1) It stopped at six. (2) The snow had started around midnight. (3) Eight inches had accumulated on the ground. (4) This morning, we awoke to a world blanketed in white.

1 Choose the most logical sequence.

   A 2, 4, 1, 3

   B 4, 2, 1, 3

   C 1, 2, 4, 3

   D Correct as is

2 Which of the following is the best way to write parts (1), (2), and (3)?

   F It stopped at six after eight inches had accumulated on the ground; the snow started around midnight.

   G It stopped at six but the snow had started at midnight. Eight inches had accumulated on the ground.

   H The snow had started around midnight, and when it stopped at six, eight inches had accumulated.

   J Correct as is

Answers and Explanations

The correct answer is *B*. Part (2) must come before part (1) so events appear in the order they occurred.

The correct answer is *H*. This sentence most clearly expresses the order in which events occurred.

▶ **Practice 1** **Directions:** Read the passage, and then answer the questions that follow. Choose the letter of the best answer.

(1) Each contestant was handed an envelope that contained a monetary gift and free lessons at a well-known cooking school. (2) When the <u>winners</u> were announced, they came up on stage to receive their prizes. (3) Some said a few words, but most just quietly exited the stage and went to <u>lunch</u>!
(4) The International Cooking Contest was a great success. (5) Early Saturday morning, a group of <u>people</u> converted our school cafeteria into an exhibition room. (6) I came extra early to supervise. (7) Every contestant had a small table on which he or she could display the international dish. (8) Judges circled the room trying every sample. (9) Many winners were there. (10) There were three big winners.
(11) First prize went to a hummus dish, a garlicky Middle Eastern chickpea dip. (12) It was accompanied by wedges of pita bread. (13) Second place was won by a man who made spanakopita, a Greek dish consisting of layers of spinach and feta cheese inside buttery phyllo pastry. (14) The recipe that won third place was the Spanish delicacy flan, a delicious caramel <u>custard</u>. (15) It was my favorite.

1 In which part should the underlined word be replaced by a more precise word?

A Part 2

B Part 3

C Part 5

D Part 14

2 Which of the following is the best order for the paragraphs?

F 2, 3, 1

G 1, 3, 2

H 3, 1, 2

J Correct as is

3 Which of the following would be the best way to write parts 9 and 10?

A Many winners were there, but there were only three big winners.

B There were three big winners of many.

C Many winners were there, and there were three big winners.

D Although the contest had many winners, three took top honors.

4 Which of the following sentences could be inserted between parts 8 and 9?

F My aunt was one of the judges.

G They were instructed to choose the best ten dishes.

H Every dish had to be approved and submitted with the application to the contest.

J One judge didn't like kielbasa.

5 Choose the most logical sentence sequence for paragraph 1.

A 3, 2, 1

B 2, 1, 3

C 3, 1, 2

D Correct as is

6 In paragraph 3, which of the following should be deleted as irrelevant?

F First prize went to a hummus recipe, a garlicky Middle Eastern chickpea dip.

G . . . a Greek dish consisting of layers of spinach and feta cheese inside buttery phyllo pastry.

H The recipe that won third place was the Spanish delicacy flan, a delicious caramel custard.

J It was my favorite.

Persuasion
Persuasive Essay

Persuasion in Everyday Life

You've just finished lunch, but you're still hungry. Wait a minute—there's an extra apple on your friend's tray. What might you say to get your friend to share it?

You might use reason: "If you're not going to eat that apple, why not give it to me?" You might appeal to feelings: "Be a pal—share!" These words are examples of **persuasion**—words used to influence people's opinions or actions.

People don't just use persuasion to influence friends. Commercials, editorials, and speeches send persuasive messages. These messages appeal to shared values, such as logic. Learn to write persuasively, and learn more about the values that connect you with others.

▲ **Critical Viewing**
To persuade drivers to use their carwash, these young people might appeal to the value people put on cleanliness. Name another value to which they might appeal.
[Hypothesize]

What Is a Persuasive Essay?

A **persuasive essay** is a brief work that presents the case for or against a particular position. An effective persuasive essay includes

- an issue with two sides.
- a clear statement of the writer's position.
- evidence supporting the writer's position.
- a clear organization, including an introduction, a body, and a strong conclusion.
- powerful images and language.

To learn the criteria on which your persuasive essay may be graded or judged, see the Rubric for Self-Assessment on page 140.

Types of Persuasive Writing

You might write any of the following types of persuasive writing:

- **Persuasive speeches,** such as one persuading students to elect you to the student council
- **Public service announcements,** such as a television commercial persuading people not to abandon their pets
- **Letters to the editor,** such as a letter you submit to your local paper asking people to attend more school games.

Writers in **ACTION**

Doug Raboy writes many forms of advertisements, from television commercials to outdoor ads on billboards.

"The opportunity to influence an incredible number of people is just amazing to me and almost overwhelming."

PREVIEW *Student Work* **IN PROGRESS**

In this chapter, you'll follow the work of Donald Cleary, a student at Maplewood Middle School in Maplewood, New Jersey. You'll see how Donald used prewriting, drafting, and revising strategies to develop a persuasive letter addressed to the members of his town's city council. At the end of the chapter, you can read Donald's completed letter.

Richard Durbin (1944–   ) was first elected to Congress from Illinois in 1982. On July 26, 1989, he gave the following humorous speech in the House of Representatives. In it, he warns against the idea that wooden baseball bats should be replaced by metal ones.

While Durbin is not entirely serious, his speech makes a convincing appeal to the idea of tradition. He also uses real persuasive devices, such as the repetition of words.

Reading **Writing** **Connection**

**Reading Strategy:
Understand a Writer's Purpose** A writer's **purpose**—to inform, to entertain, to argue for a position—affects the facts, arguments, and images he or she uses. When reading, formulate an idea of the writer's purpose. Test whether it is effectively achieved as you read. For instance, Durbin's purpose is both to entertain and to persuade. With this in mind, you can evaluate his question: "What will be next? Teflon balls? Radar-enhanced gloves?"

▲ Critical Viewing
Hank Aaron (1934–   ) was known as the "home run king." What tradition does this 1954 photograph of Aaron bring to mind? [Relate]

In his introduction, Durbin clearly introduces his topic and his position on it.

Preserving a Great American Symbol

Richard Durbin

Mr. Speaker, I rise to condemn the desecration of a great American symbol. No, I am not referring to flag burning; I am referring to the baseball bat.

Several experts tell us that the wooden baseball bat is doomed to extinction, that major league baseball players will soon be standing at home plate with aluminum bats in their hands.

Baseball fans have been forced to endure countless indignities by those who just cannot leave well enough alone: designated hit-ters,[1] plastic grass, uniforms that look like pajamas, chicken clowns dancing on the baselines, and, of course, the most heinous sacrilege, lights in Wrigley Field.[2]

Are we willing to hear the crack of a bat replaced by the dinky ping? Are we ready to see the Louisville Slugger replaced by the aluminum ping dinger? Is nothing sacred?

Please do not tell me that wooden bats are too expensive, when players who cannot hit their weight are being paid more money than the President of the United States.

Please do not try to sell me on the notion that these metal clubs will make better hitters.

What will be next? Teflon baseballs? Radar-enhanced gloves? I ask you.

I do not want to hear about saving trees. Any tree in America would gladly give its life for the glory of a day at home plate.

I do not know if it will take a constitutional amendment to keep our baseball traditions alive, but if we forsake the great Americana of broken-bat singles and pine tar,[3] we will have cer-tainly lost our way as a nation.

Durbin presents humorous "evidence" against metal bats: Other innovations in baseball have been bad, and a metal bat will not make the same satisfying noise as a wooden bat.

Durbin's organiza-tion is simple. He presents his "case" against metal bats. Next, in this para-graph, he dismisses arguments for metal bats. Finally, he con-cludes with a stir-ring call for support.

---

1. designated hitter: player who bats in place of the pitcher and does not play any other position. The position was created in 1973. Some fans argue it has changed the game for the worse.
2. Wrigley Field: historic baseball field in Chicago. It did not have lights for night games until 1988. Some fans regretted the change.
3. broken-bat singles . . . pine tar: When a batter breaks a wooden bat while hitting the ball and makes it to first base, it is a notable event in a baseball game. Pine tar is a substance used to improve the batter's grip on a wooden bat.

Reading ← Writing → Connection

Writing Application: Help Readers Understand Your Purpose To help readers understand the purpose of your essay, begin by introducing your issue and stating your position on it.

LITERATURE

To read a persuasive essay, see Joseph Bruchac's "Restoring the Circle." You can find the essay in *Prentice Hall Literature: Timeless Voices, Timeless Themes,* Copper.

Prewriting

Choosing Your Topic

Your first step in persuasive writing is choosing an appropriate topic. The best topic may be one you feel strongly about. (Remember, the issue on which you write must have more than one side.) Use the following strategies to help you find a suitable topic:

Strategies for Generating a Topic

1. **Media Flip-Through** What's in the news? A blockbuster Hollywood movie has just flopped at the box office. The mayor has ordered all bike riders to wear helmets. You can learn about stories such as these every day in the news. Over the course of two or three days, skim through newspapers and listen to news programs. Write down any topics that interest you, and choose your topic from your list.

2. **Round-Table Discussion** Gather in a group with classmates, and list people, places, and groups that are important to you. Then, think of problems and issues that affect those you have listed. Have one student record on the board the ideas discussed. In your own notebook, jot down any that interest you, and choose a topic from your list.

Get instant help! For further assistance in generating a topic, use the interactive Topic Generators, accessible from the menu bar, on-line or on CD-ROM.

Student Work
IN PROGRESS

Name: *Donald Cleary*
Maplewood Middle School
Maplewood, NJ

Holding a Round-Table Discussion
To come up with topics, Donald and three other classmates held a round-table discussion. Donald selected his topic, a skating park, from his notes on the discussion.

Stray dogs and cats—a problem!

What about new computers for our class?

More choices in cafeteria lunch menu! Yes!

Where can my friends and I skate? A skating park.

TOPIC BANK

If you're having trouble finding a topic, consider the following possibilities:

1. **Editorial on Public Health** Write an editorial expressing your opinion about a problem related to people's health, such as pollution or exercise.

2. **Persuasive Essay on Pets** Take a stand on which kind of animal makes the best pet.

Responding to Fine Art

3. This painting shows the word "silence" in sign language, the language used by deaf people. It reminds us that, even in silence, people can communicate. Write a persuasive essay about a change that might be made to pay phones, at movie theaters, or in some other public place to better accommodate hearing-impaired people. Support your views with reasons.

Silence, collection of Elli Buk

Responding to Literature

4. Read "Jackie Robinson: Justice at Last" by Geoffrey C. Ward and Ken Burns. Then, write a persuasive essay from the point of view of Branch Rickey explaining why Jackie Robinson was the right athlete to integrate major league baseball. Make sure that you back up your viewpoint with facts and reasons. You can read "Jackie Robinson: Justice at Last" in *Prentice Hall Literature: Timeless Voices, Timeless Themes,* Copper.

Cooperative Writing Opportunity

5. **Arts Campaign** In a group, create a brochure on your school's art and music programs. Each member should research a different aspect of the topic: What programs are currently available? What new programs do students want? What programs do other schools have? The group should assemble this research and vote on recommendations to make. Each member should then write or illustrate part of a brochure explaining the group's views.

Narrowing Your Topic

Once you've chosen a topic, trim it down to the right size. For instance, it could take you months to write on "children's rights." This topic includes many issues, such as children at work, children's health, and so on. It is too broad.

If your topic is too broad, narrow it down to the right size. Select one aspect to focus on. For instance, you might narrow "children's rights" to "the 'right' to a summer vacation." One way to narrow a topic is to use a strategy called looping.

Use Looping to Narrow Your Topic

Here's how to use looping to narrow your topic:

1. Write your topic at the top of a sheet of paper.
2. Set a timer for five minutes, and begin writing everything you can think of about your topic.
3. At the end of five minutes, review what you have written. Circle the most interesting idea you find.
4. Draw an arrow from the circle to a new blank line.
5. Write for another couple of minutes on your circled idea.
6. Review your new work. Circle the most interesting idea. If this idea is narrow enough to focus on in your essay, use it as your topic. If not, continue looping until you find a narrow topic.

Considering Your Audience and Purpose

Your purpose in a persuasive essay is to persuade your reader to share your opinion. To do so effectively, you must consider your reader. Ask yourself the following questions:

Are my readers older or younger than I am, or are they the same age? *If they are younger, use simple words. If you are writing for adults, express yourself in a formal way.*

How much does my reader know about the topic? *If the answer is "little," make sure you give enough background information. If the answer is "a lot," discuss your topic in depth.*

About what aspect of my topic are my readers most concerned? *Imagine you are writing about the length of your school's summer vacation. Your principal will care most about whether students will spend enough time learning. Your fellow students may care more about having enough time off. You might use different arguments for each audience!*

Gathering Support

After choosing a topic, gather support. When you present an opinion in an essay, readers will "try it on" to see whether it fits, like a suit of clothing. The reasons you give for your opinion are like buttons and zippers—if you don't use any, the "suit" will fall off as soon as the reader puts it on! Support includes:

🖥 Research Tip

Ask your librarian to help you use guides to periodical literature to find magazine and newspaper articles on your topic.

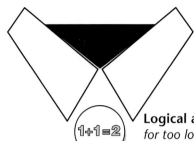

 Logical arguments: *If students are away from school for too long, they forget what they have learned. Therefore, schools should schedule only short breaks.*

 Facts: *Test scores have not gone up in schools that schedule shorter breaks.*

 Expert opinions: *Professor Edmund Havariti argues that a three-month summer vacation refreshes students' minds.*

Personal observations: *When I come back from summer vacation, I feel full of energy, ready to learn!*

Do research on your topic, and gather support using a T-chart.

Complete a T-Chart Fold a piece of paper in two. Jot down support for one side of your issue in one column and support for the other side in the other column. If you don't have an opinion yet, review your T-chart and choose a side.

Drafting

Shaping Your Writing

Develop a Position Statement

The evidence you have gathered will help support your position. To introduce your position to readers, develop a position statement. A **position statement** is a sentence naming the issue on which you are writing and expressing your position.

	POSITION	ISSUE
POSITION STATEMENT:	Schools should keep	a three-month summer vacation.

To develop your position statement, review all of your prewriting notes, and write down one or two sentences summing up your argument.

It is a good idea to follow your position statement with a "directional" statement explaining your main arguments.

	MAIN REASON
DIRECTIONAL STATEMENT:	Shortening the break will hurt students without helping their education.

Include these sentences in the introduction to your essay.

Organize for Clarity

Your essay does not come with a map, but you can still help keep your reader from getting lost. To help your reader follow your argument, organize your ideas clearly.

Introduction Your introduction should tell your readers what to expect in the rest of the essay. Include your position and directional statements in your introduction.

Body In the paragraphs following your introduction, explain each of your main points in turn. For each, provide evidence—facts, statistics, arguments, or expert opinions. Often, a main point and its support will make up one topical paragraph.

Conclusion Finally, write a strong conclusion that summarizes your arguments and restates your viewpoint in a memorable way.

Text

Try it out! Use the interactive Supporting Each Point activity in **Section 7.3**, on-line or on CD-ROM.

Providing Elaboration

As you draft your essay, make sure you explain and support each of your main ideas fully. Elaborate as you draft by providing explanations and evidence, such as statistics, facts, expert opinions, and illustrations.

Support Each Point

To clarify and support your points, use any of the following techniques:

- Compare or contrast your topic with something else.

- Find an example.

- Make a specific observation.

- Use facts or statistics from books, magazines, or other media.

Some evidence comes from researching a topic in the library. Other evidence comes from personal experience and observation. Whatever support you provide must be accurate and clear.

Student Work
IN PROGRESS

Name: *Donald Cleary*
Maplewood Middle School
Maplewood, NJ

Supporting Each Point
Donald supported his proposal for a town skating park with details about its benefits for various groups of townspeople.

The benefits of a skate park are obvious. Kids want to skate, and a skate park is the ideal place for them to do it. The park would give them a place to have fun and practice their skating skills. It would keep kids and pedestrians out of danger because skaters would be in the park instead of on the streets and sidewalks. It would also give owners of private property and the police less to worry about.

In these sentences, Donald states his main idea.

Then, he supports his main idea with a list of examples.

7.4 **Revising**

Once you've written your first draft, find ways to improve it. Start by checking the overall structure of your essay. Then, move to smaller parts, like sentences and words.

Revising Your Overall Structure
Analyze Organization

Sometimes, it is difficult to see problems with structure until your draft is completed. Use the strategy of "Interrogating Paragraphs" to make sure your draft is logically organized.

▶ **REVISION STRATEGY**
"Interrogating Paragraphs" for Logical Order

Every paragraph is innocent until proven guilty—but occasionally one ends up in the wrong place at the wrong time! Draw a box around the main point in each paragraph in your draft. Use the following questions to determine whether your paragraph is in the right place:

PARAGRAPH INTERROGATION	
DESCRIPTION	**PROCEDURE**
Does this paragraph give more details about the main point of the paragraph before it?	Suspect is an upstanding, law-abiding citizen—release it.
Does this paragraph give an opposing argument or an exception to the paragraph before it?	Before releasing this suspect, consider adding a transition such as "in contrast," "however," "some say that," or "still."
Does the main point of this paragraph introduce a new topic?	Before releasing this suspect, make sure it includes a clear statement of the new topic. Consider adding a transition such as "another reason," "in addition," "also," or "next."
Does the main point of this paragraph connect closely with the main point in a paragraph elsewhere in the essay?	Treat this suspect with caution! Consider carefully moving it closer to other, related paragraphs.

Check Your Support

Now that your overall organization makes sense, take a look at the support you provide for each main point. You may have watched courtroom dramas on television. If so, you know that if there is too little evidence, a case can get kicked out of court! Each paragraph in your essay should provide a good amount of evidence for the case you are making. If it does not, evaluate whether you should strengthen it or eliminate it.

▶ **REVISION STRATEGY**
Circling Supporting Evidence

Review each of your main points. Circle the evidence that supports each one. Then, evaluate your circled support.

Strong Support If you find support that is especially strong, consider building on it. For instance, you might draw attention to a well-supported point by adding charged language or a colorful comparison.

No Support If you find a paragraph without circled sentences in it, review your prewriting notes for evidence and add support. If necessary, do extra research to find the support you need.

Technology Tip

If you are using a word-processing program, type in supporting details at the bottom of your document. Split the screen; then, scroll through your document in the top window while supporting details remain on view in the bottom. Find just the right spot to insert each detail.

Student Work
IN PROGRESS

Name: Donald Cleary
Maplewood Middle School
Maplewood, NJ

Circling Supporting Evidence

After circling support, Donald found one paragraph without any circles. He added the missing support.

I know what you're thinking as you read this: cost, cost, and cost. Building a skate park will not be cheap, but it also won't be very expensive. Burlington built its park for only $18,000. And if the jumps are under six feet, the insurance won't be too much.

Donald found no support to circle in this paragraph. He called the Town Hall in Burlington and did a little more research into the cost of building a skate park. Then, he added these two details supporting the idea that a park might not be too expensive.

Revising Your Paragraphs

Check Coherence

Now that you have improved the overall structure of your paper, check each paragraph. Every sentence in a paragraph should connect with the others in one of these ways:

- It should tell more about something in a previous sentence.

- It should contain a transition spelling out its connection with a previous sentence. Transitions include *first, however, next, then, for this reason,* and *by contrast.*

Check sentence connections by "Finding the 'Glue.'"

▶ **REVISION STRATEGY**
Finding the "Glue" Between Sentences

Follow these steps for three paragraphs in your draft:
1. In each sentence except the first, find a word that connects to a previous sentence. Highlight the word.
2. Circle the word or words in the earlier sentence to which the highlighted word connects.
3. Draw an arrow between the circled and the highlighted words.
4. For any sentence without a highlighted word, either
   - add words connecting back to the previous sentence, or
   - eliminate the sentence.

Text

Try it out! Use the interactive Checking Coherence activity in **Section 7.4,** on-line or on CD-ROM.

Student Work
IN PROGRESS

Name: Donald Cleary
Maplewood Middle School
Maplewood, NJ

Checking Coherence by Finding the "Glue"

Donald coded for the "glue" between sentences. He decided to eliminate a sentence that he could not connect back to previous sentences.

Another (problem) is where to put a (skate park.)

Well, I've already thought that through. It could

be built in (one of two places.) The first place is

just inside the South Mountain Reservation.

~~The best place for skateboarding is actually a~~

~~completely man-made environment with ramps,~~

~~like you see on television.~~

> Donald could not connect words in this sentence with other sentences. He also found no transition words in the sentence. He decided the sentence did not belong in this paragraph and deleted it.

Revising Your Sentences

Eliminate Fragments

Sometimes the words explaining an idea drift off on their own—they become a sentence fragment.

FRAGMENT: Because we like him.

To eliminate fragments, use the following strategy:

▶ **REVISION STRATEGY**
Circling Sentence Beginnings to Eliminate Fragments

In your essay, circle sentences beginning with these words:

after	but	until
although	if	when
and	or	whenever
because	since	who
before	that	while

Then, read each circled sentence. Does it make sense on its own? If not, rewrite it, using the tips in the box below.

Grammar in Your Writing
Complete Sentences

A **sentence fragment** is a group of words that does not express a complete thought, even though it is punctuated as a sentence. Use these techniques to correct fragments:

Add a verb.

FRAGMENT: Many different endangered and rare animals at the zoo.
COMPLETE SENTENCE: Many different endangered and rare animals live at the zoo.

Add a subject.

FRAGMENT: Enjoy seeing all the animals there.
COMPLETE SENTENCE: I enjoy seeing all the animals there.

Join the fragment to a sentence that comes before or after it.

FRAGMENT: We visit the zoo. When we have guests from out of town.
COMPLETE SENTENCE: We visit the zoo when we have guests from out of town.

Find It in Your Reading Find two sentences beginning with the word *if* in the Student Model on page 141. Explain why they are not fragments.

Find It in Your Writing Read the last five sentences in your draft aloud. If any does not express a complete idea, rewrite it as a complete sentence.

For more on complete sentences, see Chapter 21.

Revising Your Word Choice
Use Precise, Persuasive Language

To persuade your reader, use words that point in a clear direction. Vague or general words, such as *good* or *bad*, will not give the best directions. Instead, choose precise words—words that give specific information—to let your reader know where you are headed.

For instance, if you say that your friend will make a "good class president," think of what you specifically mean by *good*. You might mean *intelligent*, *responsible*, or *honest*—or all three. You can better direct readers if you use these specific terms instead of the vague word *good*.

▶ **REVISION STRATEGY**
Using "Thoughtshots"

Circle words such as *good, bad, better, worse, nice, stupid, dumb,* and other vague words anywhere they appear in your draft. Next to each, place a sticky note. On each sticky note, write a sentence explaining the exact reasons the vague word applies, as in the following example:

SENTENCE USING GENERAL WORD:	My friend will make a **good** class president.
WHY THE GENERAL WORD APPLIES:	My friend is **responsible**, **intelligent**, and **honest**.

After you have finished marking your draft, review each Thoughtshot. Use specific words on the Thoughtshot to replace the general words you have circled in your draft.

Thoughtshot
responsible
intelligent
honest

Peer Review
"Say Back"

Once you have finished revising your essay on your own, you can still use the help of your classmates.

In a small group of four or five students, read your revised persuasive essay twice. Ask your listeners to listen the first time and respond the second time. To respond, listeners can jot down answers to these questions:

1. What details do I find persuasive?
2. What do I want to know more about?

After hearing from your classmates, consider using their suggestions to improve your essay.

Collaborative Writing Tip

Have a classmate circle vague words in your draft. For each one he or she finds, explain why you used it. Your classmate should take notes from your explanation. Review these notes for specific words you can use to replace the vague ones in your draft.

7.5 Editing and Proofreading

When you have finished revising your persuasive essay, you still have one more step to take. Correct any errors in spelling, punctuation, grammar, and usage. After all, your purpose is to persuade your reader of your opinion—not that you have difficulty spelling.

Focusing on End Marks

In persuasive writing, you use sentences to:

- make statements.
- ask questions.
- exclaim, expressing excitement.

  Use the correct end mark for each kind of sentence.

Grammar and Style Tip

A good persuasive writer may build a case, then pose a question to readers asking what conclusions they draw. This strategy is persuasive because it makes readers feel that the author is asking them to make up their own minds.

Grammar in Your Writing
End Marks

Sentences must end with one of three **end marks**—the period (.), the question mark (?), or the exclamation point (!).

Use a period to end a statement of fact or opinion.

The bald eagle is the national bird of the United States.

Use a question mark to ask a direct question.

What can young people do to save the bald eagle?

Use an exclamation point to express strong feeling.

We must preserve the bald eagle!

Find It in Your Reading Find two different end marks used in "Preserving a Great American Symbol" by Richard Durbin on page 126. For each, explain why it is used correctly.

Find It in Your Writing Read your draft aloud with expression. If your voice rises at the end of a sentence, check whether you need a question mark. If you find your voice growing more excited, think about whether you might use an exclamation point.

To learn more on using end marks correctly, see Chapter 26.

Publishing and Presenting

Building Your Portfolio

Consider these ideas for publishing and presenting your persuasive essay:

1. **Create an Opinion Board** With a teacher's help, post student essays on a bulletin board in your school. Use artwork and color to ensure that titles and topics stand out.

2. **Tell It to the Government** If you wrote about a political issue, send a neat copy of your essay with a cover letter to your mayor, state legislator, congressperson, or senator, or to the President. Share your essay and any response you receive with the class.

Reflecting on Your Writing

Jot down a few notes about your experience writing a persuasive essay. You might start off by answering the following questions:

- Did writing a persuasive essay change your feelings about the issue on which you wrote? How?

- Which writing strategy helped you the most? The least? Explain.

Internet Tip

To see persuasive essays scored with this rubric, go on-line: PHSchool.com
Enter Web Code: eak-6001

Rubric for Self-Assessment

Use the following criteria to evaluate your persuasive essay:

	Score 4	Score 3	Score 2	Score 1
Audience and Purpose	Provides arguments, illustrations, and words that forcefully appeal to the audience and effectively serve persuasive purpose	Provides arguments, illustrations, and words that appeal to the audience and serve the persuasive purpose	Provides some support that appeals to the audience and serves the persuasive purpose	Shows little attention to the audience or persuasive purpose
Organization	Uses clear, consistent organizational strategy	Uses clear organizational strategy with occasional inconsistencies	Uses inconsistent organizational strategy	Shows lack of organizational strategy; writing is confusing
Elaboration	Provides specific, well-elaborated support for the writer's position	Provides some elaborated support for the writer's position	Provides some support, but with little elaboration	Lacks support
Use of Language	Uses transitions to connect ideas smoothly; shows few mechanical errors	Uses some transitions; shows few mechanical errors	Uses few transitions; shows some mechanical errors	Shows little connection between ideas; shows many mechanical errors

▼ Critical Viewing
Give an opinion on
the law represented
by this sign.
[Evaluate]

FINAL DRAFT

Say "Yes!" to Skating!

Donald Cleary
Maplewood Middle School
Maplewood, New Jersey

Dear Council Members:

All through the streets of Maplewood, there are signs that read "No Skateboarding or Rollerblading." My friends and I enjoy freestyle skating. However, we have practically no place to do it. If we skate on the sidewalks, we are dangerous to pedestrians. If we skate on the streets, we could get hurt ourselves. We know that skating on private property, such as grocery store parking lots, is a bad idea, since sometimes the owners call the police to have skaters removed. Signs that say "No Skating" are not the answer to these problems. What this town needs is a skate park, and I am asking the council members to have one built.

The benefits of a skate park are obvious. Kids want to skate, and a skate park is the ideal place for them to do it. The park would give them a place to have fun and practice their skating skills. It would keep kids and pedestrians out of danger because skaters would be in the park instead of on the streets and sidewalks. It would also give owners of private property and the police less to worry about. And by building a skate park in Maplewood, you can and will make many frustrated kids happy.

There might be other advantages to the skate park. The skate park in Burlington gives skating lessons, and our skate park could, too. Our skate park could have competitions and family

Donald's introduction clearly states his topic: The need for a skate park in his town. The last sentence in this paragraph is Donald's thesis statement.

Donald's organization is logical. First, he gives his strongest arguments. He follows them with additional arguments.

◀ **Critical Viewing**
Write a caption for this photo that might help persuade town council members to build a skate park in Donald's town. **[Apply]**

gatherings with snack stands. It would be a place where lots of people in the town could have fun.

I know what you're thinking as you read this: cost, cost, and cost. Building a skate park will not be cheap, but it also won't be very expensive. Burlington built its park for only $18,000. And if the jumps are under six feet, the insurance won't be too much.

Another problem is where to put a skate park. Well, I've already thought that through. It could be built in one of two places. The first place is just inside the South Mountain Reservation. It is very hilly, and it's a natural setting for fun skating. My friends and I really like lots of hills, and there is a lot of room to put just about anything in the Reservation. The other place is next to Waterlands soccer field, where the mulch center is. It would be good to have the skate park near the soccer field since the area is already used for sports. Why not make this a center for outdoor fun?

If you will consider this proposition now and vote to approve it, you could start building the park very soon, and it could be ready for us kids as soon as spring comes. Remember, the longer you

The main point in this paragraph is fully supported by detailed information. Donald is answering the arguments against his idea. In this way, he strengthens his own case.

Donald's conclusion clearly sums up his idea and his arguments for it.

wait, the more frustrated kids, property owners, pedestrians, and other citizens will become. I hope that you take this proposal into consideration and not turn it down. Thank you.

Sincerely,
Donald Cleary

▼ **Critical Viewing** Give a detail from Donald's proposal that might persuade this boy to support a skate park. **[Apply]**

Connected Assignment
Advertisement

You can find persuasive writing all around you. You can read it on a poster in the subway. You can hear it in a commercial on television. "20% less fat . . ." or "Cleans better, faster . . ."—these are the kinds of persuasive words you can find in advertisements.

An **advertisement** presents a persuasive message in print or broadcast form (on television or on radio). It is produced and paid for by an individual or a business to persuade you to do something or to form a certain opinion. Most advertisements try to persuade you to buy a product. Some try to change your opinion about an issue. Advertisements may include the following elements:

- the use of pictures, music, and skits

- a **"concept,"** or central theme (for instance, an advertiser might use the concept of *health* to promote a cereal by showing people working out)

- a **"hook,"** such as a catchy jingle, a memorable slogan, or an attention-grabbing image

Create your own print advertisement, following the strategies outlined here.

Prewriting First, make up a product or service you might sell. You might choose a topic like one of the following:

- **Sell a Product** Advertise a product your classmates might use, such as a pencil that erases words with the push of a button.

- **Advertise a Service** Advertise a service you might provide, such as baby-sitting or lawn-raking.

MODEL

*This advertisement is directed at a young audience. The **concept** is to create a friendly, fun atmosphere around the idea of reading. The **hook** is the cute dinosaur, Theo, and the whimsical slogan, "Read. Avoid Extinction." The ad implies that reading is not a chore. Only silly dinosaurs avoid reading, it seems to say—and look what happened to them!*

Once you have chosen something to advertise, focus your topic by creating a "concept" for your advertisement. You might use any of the following themes:

- **enjoying ease of use** (for example, show students happily working with your self-erasing pencil while others using old-style erasers rub away in frustration)

- **making smart choices** (for example, show students who use your pencil talking confidently about how much time they have saved)

- **fitting in with a trend** (for example, show a group of happy students showing off their self-erasing pencils to each other).

After you have developed a concept, brainstorm for a "hook"—a slogan or image—that will sum up your concept. Your hook should use easily understood, eye-catching images and colorful words so that even distracted readers will understand instantly. Gather ideas for your advertisement, using a chart like the one shown.

Product/Service: _Self-Erasing Pencils_

Concept	Hook	Image	Head
Follow the trend	All the popular kids are using self-erasing pencils: "I can't keep the pace without using my Self-Erase."	On left, kid stands, shrugging, with his pockets turned out, looking worried. On the right, a happy group of kids holding their self-erase pencils high walk by.	"I can't keep the pace without my Self-Erase!"

Drafting As you draft, use heads (words, phrases, or sentences set in large type) to grab the reader's eye. Feature your "hook" in these heads. The rest of the text should be short and to the point. When you have finished drafting, lay out your ad on the computer or by cutting and pasting on paper. Arrange pictures and text to create a neat, balanced effect.

Revising and Editing Review your draft. Circle the place where you present your concept most clearly. If necessary, revise to make your concept more easily understood by a reader. Delete any words or images that do not add to your message. Finally, proofread your work for any errors.

Publishing and Presenting Add a poster of your print advertisement to a class Advertising Gallery.

Spotlight on the Humanities

Analyzing Visual Meanings

Focus on Art: Michelangelo

You can change people's minds with words, but how do you persuade a stone? Michelangelo Buonarroti (1475–1564) knew the secret of persuading rough stone to reveal the forms and figures hidden within. A master sculptor and painter, he is considered one of the world's greatest artists.

Born in Caprese, Italy, Michelangelo started studying painting and sculpture at age twelve. Michelangelo attracted the notice of Lorenzo de' Medici (1449–1492), the ruler of Florence, Italy. The Medici family became Michelangelo's patrons (supporters).

The ceiling of the Sistine Chapel is one of Michelangelo's masterworks. (The chapel is in the Vatican, the Pope's official residence in Vatican City, located within Rome.) Michelangelo filled the chapel's ceilings with thirty-three frescos (paintings on plaster) of subjects from the Bible. In the frescos, Michelangelo portrays human forms in a passionate, dynamic style. Among his other famous works, also noted for their expressive, dynamic figures, are the sculptures *David* and the *Pietà*.

▲ Critical Viewing
Study the way David's head and shoulders are turned in Michelangelo's sculpture. Explain how this pose suggests movement, even though the sculpture is still. **[Analyze]**

Film Connection The film *The Agony and the Ecstacy* tells the story of Michelangelo, his painting of the Sistine Chapel, and his conflict over the project with Pope Julius II. Released in 1965 and starring Charlton Heston and Rex Harrison, the film received five Academy Award nominations.

Music Connection Michelangelo's patron Lorenzo de' Medici was called "Lorenzo the Magnificent" because of his statesmanship and support of the arts. When he died at age 43, Italian poet Angelo Poliziano (1454–1494) and Flemish composer Heinrich Isaac (1450–1517) composed a special funeral ode for him entitled "Lament on the Death of Lorenzo de' Medici." The song claims that music and poetry fell silent in the world due to his death. It reflected the profound influence he had on the culture of Florence.

Persuasive Writing Activity: "Artist for Hire" Poster
Choose a sculpture or painting by Michelangelo. Create a poster around it, advertising Michelangelo's services as an artist. Explain why a patron such as Lorenzo de' Medici or Pope Julius II should be eager to hire Michelangelo.

Media and Technology Skills

Analyzing How the Media Shape Perceptions

Activity: Recognizing Persuasion in Sitcoms

You can recognize the persuasive message of television commercials right away: "Buy this product!" Television entertainment programs may also contain persuasive messages. Instead of "Buy this!" these messages might say, "Act this way." Learn to recognize these persuasive messages in television programs such as sitcoms.

Think About It A television sitcom may send a persuasive message through its characters' words and actions. For instance, at the end of an episode, a sitcom character often makes a decision. Viewers may be persuaded that the decision is the best one. They are persuaded in part because the show presents the characters as likeable. Consider these examples of a sitcom story and its message:

- **Message: "Stick to your true friends."** Lance, a wealthy, popular student, starts making friends with one of the main characters of the show, Didi. When Lance makes fun of Didi's best friend, Gogo, Didi does not stand up for him. When Didi goes to Lance's party, though, she realizes Lance is just a snob. She leaves the party and apologizes to Gogo.

- **Message: "Anybody who acts like a snob deserves to be embarrassed."** When Didi goes to Lance's party, she sees that he is just a snob. Fed up with him, she tells the people at the party about the time Lance locked himself out of his house and was stopped by the police—in his pajamas! The kids laugh wildly as Lance runs from the room in embarrassment!

You may agree with the first message. If you think it is wrong to be mean to people, though, you might disagree with the second message.

Analyze It Watch an episode of a sitcom. Use a chart like the one shown to analyze its persuasive messages. Review your chart, and write a paragraph summarizing the show and explaining its message.

> ### How Persuasion Works in Sitcoms
>
> **Likeable Main Character**
> Because viewers like the main character, they tend to approve of what the main character does.
>
> **Foolish Main Character**
> On some shows, one character plays the fool. Viewers like him or her, but recognize that they are meant to laugh at many of the things the character does.

Title of Sitcom: _____

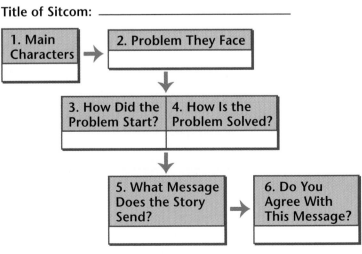

1. Main Characters

2. Problem They Face

3. How Did the Problem Start?

4. How Is the Problem Solved?

5. What Message Does the Story Send?

6. Do You Agree With This Message?

Standardized Test Preparation Workshop

Responding to Persuasive Writing Prompts

Some writing prompts on standardized tests call on you to write persuasively about an issue. Your essay will be evaluated on how well you

- support your position, using examples, facts, and arguments that are appropriate to the purpose and audience named in the prompt.
- organize your points, using a consistent method suited to the topic.
- use correct grammar, spelling, and punctuation.

For practice on such tests, respond to the sample persuasive writing prompt below. The suggestions on the next page will help you to get started. The clocks represent the part of your test-taking time that you should devote to each stage of your writing.

Sample Writing Situation

The faculty and students at your school are being asked to vote on a logo for the school's Web page. The principal as well as many teachers believe that it should represent learning. They are considering an image of a book with the word *Sapientia*, the Latin word for *wisdom*, beneath it. Many students, on the other hand, want something more lively. They think the school mascot, a tiger, should be the logo. Choose one of the following prompts to which to respond.

State your position on the Web page logo in a letter to the editor of your school newspaper. Support your position with arguments, examples, and your own experiences.

State your position on the Web page logo in a letter to your school principal. Support your position with arguments, examples, and your own experiences.

Prewriting

One fourth of your time should be used for prewriting.

Consider Your Audience and Purpose Your purpose is to persuade your audience that your position on the Web page logo is the correct one. Your approach to this task depends on the audience specified in the prompt you have selected. For instance, the school principal cares about what is in the school's best interest. If you choose to write to the principal, focus your arguments on this point. The school newspaper is addressed to students. If you choose to write to the paper, address issues that most concern students, such as school pride or fun.

Gather Support Use a T-Chart to gather logical arguments, facts, and examples on both sides of the issue. Also, list strong images or phrases with which to present your case. Note any weak arguments against your position. You can answer them in your essay. (For instructions on making a T-Chart, see page 131.)

Drafting

Use almost half of your time for drafting.

Write an Introduction Start your letter with an interest-grabbing introduction. You might begin with a strong image or story that illustrates your position. Your introduction should also include a sentence that clearly states your position on the issue.

Develop Your Position In the body of your letter, develop support for your position. Refer to your T-Chart for details as you write. For each main idea, add supporting details. If you have found weak opposing arguments, prove them wrong. You might save your strongest argument for the end of your response.

Write a Conclusion In your conclusion, sum up your main points and restate your position.

Revising, Editing, and Proofreading

Use almost one fourth of your time to revise, edit, and proofread.

Strengthen Support As you revise, revise or eliminate sentences that do not help make your point. Note places in your paper where you have used vague words, such as *better*. Replace them with more precise words by answering the question, "Better in what way?" For example, you might argue that the school mascot is better because it is more colorful than the image of a book. In this case, you could replace *better* with *more eye-catching*.

Correct Errors When you have finished revising, check your work for errors in grammar, spelling, or punctuation. Place one line through any text you are deleting. Use a caret (^) to indicate where to add text.

Exposition
Comparison-and-Contrast Essay

Comparison and Contrast in Everyday Life

Jump into the freezing water of a lake, and you may wish you were swimming in the warm ocean instead. Watch a great movie with your cousin, and later you may find yourself comparing it with the awful movie you saw last week. In both cases, you are comparing and contrasting.

We use comparisons and contrasts all the time. For instance, you might compare two shirts in the morning to decide which one to wear.

It's only the most interesting comparisons that are worth writing down, though. Whether it's a comparison of two vacation spots or of two works of art, a good written comparison shines new light on the things it compares.

▲ **Critical Viewing**
Identical twins look almost exactly alike. Do you know any identical twins? How can you tell them apart? **[Compare and Contrast]**

TOPIC BANK

If you're having trouble finding a topic, consider the following possibilities:

1. **What's Cooking?** Burritos and tacos are two popular Mexican foods. Ravioli and lasagna are famous Italian dishes. Compare any two international food favorites.

2. **Musical Choice** In a large orchestra, there are many different kinds of instruments. To which instrument do you enjoy listening? Which would you like to play? Choose two instruments to compare.

Responding to Fine Art

3. Jot down notes on similarities and differences between the different parts of the landscape in this painting. Use your imagination to describe differences in touch, smell, sound, and even taste, as well as sight. Then, write an essay comparing this landscape to one you know.

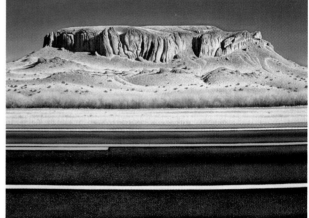

Black Mesa, 1982, Woody Gwyn, Courtesy of the artist

Responding to Literature

4. Compare and contrast the characters of he Lion, Bruh Bear, and Bruh Rabbit in Virginia Hamilton's retelling of the folk tale "He Lion, Bruh Bear, and Bruh Rabbit." Look at similarities and differences in their strength, size, personality, and cleverness. Explain how the differences among them causes the story to end as it does. You can find the story in *Prentice Hall Literature: Timeless Voices, Timeless Themes,* Copper.

☑ **Cooperative Writing Opportunity**

5. **Consumer Guide** Work with your classmates to create a consumer guide on a related group of products. For example, you might write about new computer models or the latest video games. Each student should do a detailed analysis of two specific models, noting key features and their good and bad qualities. Then, work together to assemble the notes into a guide comparing and ranking various items.

Narrowing Your Topic

Make sure your topic isn't too broad to cover thoroughly in a comparison-and-contrast essay. For example, you could write an entire book comparing two countries, such as Mexico and Spain. However, if you were to focus on a Mexican and a Spanish food, you would find that you had a perfect topic for a brief essay. Looping is a good strategy for narrowing your topic.

Looping

Looping is a strategy with several steps. Follow these instructions:

1. Write your topic at the top of a sheet of paper. Then, write for five or ten minutes on your topic. Read what you have written. What is your most important or interesting idea? What "tugs" at you? Circle it.
2. Draw a line connecting the idea you've circled to the next empty line on your paper. Then, write about the circled idea for five or ten minutes. You should find yourself going in a more specific direction. When you finish, circle again what "tugs" at you.
3. Keep repeating this process until you have circled a narrow, focused topic for your essay.

▲ **Critical Viewing**
In what ways are these animals similar? In what ways are they different? **[Distinguish]**

Student Work
IN PROGRESS

Name: *Brendan Barraclough*
Mountain School
Los Alamos, NM

Using Looping

Here is how Brendan used looping to narrow his broad topic, "pets."

Lots of animals can be pets. My dad had a pet goat when he was a kid. I used to have a dog. My mom won't let me get another dog because the big ones are too big, and we didn't want a little dog. (Now I have a cat and a frog.)

I like my cat because she is cuddly. The frogs are fun to watch and take care of. (They are very different animals, but both make good pets.)

Considering Your Audience and Purpose

Next, identify your **audience**—the people who will read your essay—and your **purpose**—what you hope to accomplish. Both your audience and your purpose will affect your choice of words and details, as shown in this chart:

Audience	Purpose	Language	Details
Young children	To instruct	Simple, informal	Basic—assume no knowledge of topic
Adults knowledgeable about topic	To inform, to persuade	Technical language, formal	Leave out the most basic details; offer opinions and back up with examples

Keep your audience and purpose in mind as you gather details, draft, and revise.

Gathering Details

Gather facts, descriptions, and examples that you can use to make comparisons and contrasts between the items about which you are writing. If necessary, consult reference sources. Then, use a Venn diagram to organize your details.

Use a Venn Diagram

Create a diagram like the one shown. Write down details about each item you are comparing in one of the circles. In the two outside sections, write how each is different. Write similarities in the part where the circles overlap.

DIFFERENT KINDS OF VETERINARIANS

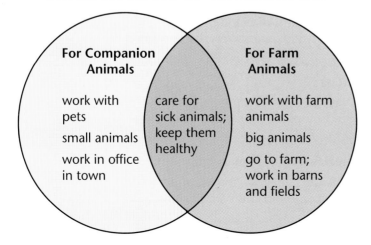

For Companion Animals

work with pets

small animals

work in office in town

care for sick animals; keep them healthy

For Farm Animals

work with farm animals

big animals

go to farm; work in barns and fields

8.3 Drafting

Shaping Your Writing

Before you begin writing your first draft, decide how you want to organize your information.

Select an Appropriate Organization

Following are two methods for organizing your essay:

- **Block Method** To use the block method, present all details about one subject first. Then, present all details about the next. This method works well when you write about more than two things or cover many different types of details.

- **Point-by-Point Method** To use the point-by-point method, discuss each aspect of your subjects in turn. For example, if your topic is bicycling versus skating, you could first discuss the benefits of each, then the disadvantages, and finally the equipment necessary for each.

The following chart shows how each organization might be used for a paper comparing two types of dinosaurs:

1: Introduction

2: *Tyrannosaurus*—its diet, size, and mobility

3: *Velociraptor*—its diet, size, and mobility

1: Introduction

2: Feature—diet (*Tyrannosaurus* versus *Velociraptor*)

3: Feature—size and mobility (*Tyrannosaurus* versus *Velociraptor*)

Shape Your Introduction

Once you have chosen an organizational method, start writing. Begin with an introductory paragraph that

- introduces the subjects you are comparing.

- identifies the features or aspects you are comparing.

- states your conclusion about your subjects—for example, that there are more differences between them than similarities.

Try it out! Use the interactive Using Specific Details activity in **Section 8.3**, on-line or on CD-ROM.

Providing Elaboration

Develop each main point of similarity or difference between your subjects by providing strong examples. For example, if you write that basketball is a faster game than baseball, you might cite the nonstop, end-to-end action in basketball and the long breaks in baseball.

Use Specific Details

Give details that are as specific as possible. The more specific your details are, the easier it will be for readers to see the similarities and differences. Look at the following examples:

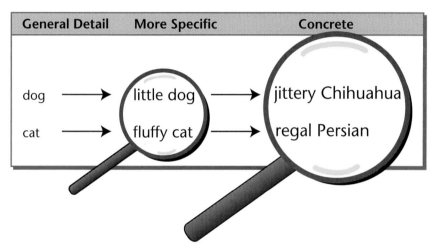

General Detail	More Specific	Concrete
dog ⟶	little dog ⟶	jittery Chihuahua
cat ⟶	fluffy cat ⟶	regal Persian

As you draft, pause now and then to make sure the details you are including are as specific as possible.

Student Work
IN PROGRESS

Name: *Brendan Barraclough*
Mountain School
Los Alamos, NM

Using Specific Details
Notice the specific details that Brendan added to the following paragraph.

the right habitat needs to be provided for both kinds of pets.
To begin with,˄ ~~each pet needs its own home.~~

are easier because they can live in the home you are already in.
You just have to add a litter box, food, and water.
Cats˄ ~~dont need much.~~ As opposed to that,

specially prepared terrarium with dirt for hibernation.
frogs need a˄ ~~special glass box.~~

Revising

When you revise, you strengthen your essay by eliminating unnecessary details and building on important ones.

Revising Your Overall Structure
Check Organization and Balance

Your essay should give equal space to each thing compared. For example, a comparison of baseball and football should give the same number of details about each, not two about baseball and ten about football. Your essay should also be organized consistently. Color-code to check organization and balance.

▶ **REVISION STRATEGY**
Color-Coding Details for Organization and Balance

Reread your essay. Use one color to highlight features of one of the things you're comparing, and another color to highlight features of the other. Review your draft. If you find:

- **more highlights of one color than of the other**—add more details about the subject with fewer highlights.

- **large chunks of a color and places where colors alternate**—reorganize your paper using either the block or the point-by-point method consistently.

Student Work
IN PROGRESS

Name: *Brendan Barraclough*
Mountain School
Los Alamos, NM

Coding for Organization and Balance
Brendan coded each detail about cats in yellow and each detail about frogs in green. He found a spot to create better balance by adding more details.

Cats are easier because they can live in the home you are already in. You just have to add a litter box, food, and water. As opposed to that, frogs need a specially prepared terrarium with dirt for hibernation. ∧
In addition, frogs need the air temperature controlled because they are coldblooded.

> Brendan used point-by-point organization. Here, he included details about the habitats of both cats and frogs. He realized that he had included more than one detail about cats, so he added another detail about frogs.

Revising Your Paragraphs

Check Your Paragraph Structure

A **topical paragraph** explains or illustrates one main idea. Most of the paragraphs in the body of your paper should be topical paragraphs. They should contain the following elements:

T: Topic sentence—a sentence summing up the main idea

R: Restatement—an expanded version of the idea found in the topic sentence

I: Illustration—one or more specific facts, images, anecdotes, or other details supporting or illustrating the main idea.

EXAMPLE:
> **T** I like football better than baseball.
>
> **R** For one thing, football has more action.
>
> **I** Football teams must complete plays in a certain amount of time. Baseball pitchers can take long breaks.

Often, a paragraph with these elements has the structure **T-R-I.** However, in some instances, you might want to lead with the sentence that gives the illustration in order to hook your readers, making your pattern **I-T-R.**

▶ **REVISION STRATEGY**
Marking Paragraph Patterns

Go through your paper, and mark the pattern of each paragraph. Then, revise any paragraphs that are missing one or more of the **T-R-I** elements. For instance, add a topic sentence to any paragraph that is missing one.

🔵 **Learn More**

To learn more about the different kinds of paragraphs, see Chapter 3.

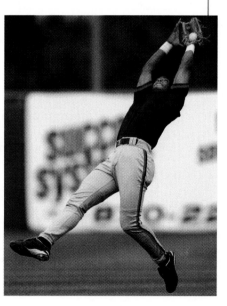

◀ **Critical Viewing**
Write a topic sentence for a paragraph comparing these two pictures.
[Apply]

Revising Your Sentences
Check Subject-Verb Agreement

In sentences comparing two things, pay special attention to the form of the verb you use. Whether you use the plural or singular form depends on how the subjects are joined:

PLURAL: Football and baseball *are* both fast-paced.

SINGULAR: Neither football nor baseball *is* an indoor game.

Check your draft to make sure your subjects and verbs agree.

▶**REVISION STRATEGY**
Coding *and, nor,* and *or*

Review your use of the words *and, nor,* and *or.* Wherever they join two doers of an action or two things sharing a feature, underline the verb in the sentence.

EXAMPLE: Football <u>and</u> baseball <u>are</u> fun to watch.

Then, check your color-coded sentences for errors in agreement.

Grammar in Your Writing
Subject-Verb Agreement

The **subject** of a sentence is the person or thing that performs the action of the sentence. The **verb** is the word expressing the action. Singular subjects take singular verbs. Plural subjects take plural verbs.

SINGULAR SUBJECT: a dog
SINGULAR VERBS: is, barks

PLURAL SUBJECT: dogs
PLURAL VERBS: are, bark

Subjects joined by *and* take a plural verb.
Dogs <u>and</u> cats are common pets.

Subjects joined by *or* or *nor* take a singular verb.
A dog <u>or</u> a cat is a common pet.
Neither a pony <u>nor</u> a pig is considered a good city pet.

Find It in Your Reading Review "More Than a Pinch: Two Salt Lakes" on page 152. Identify three subjects and their verbs. Do they agree?

Find It in Your Writing Identify three subjects and their verbs in your draft. Check to make sure they agree.

To learn more about subject-verb agreement, see Chapter 24.

Revising Your Word Choice
Avoid Repetition

Repeated words or phrases will make your writing dull. Code and replace repeated words.

▶**REVISION STRATEGY**
Highlighting Repeated Words

Reread your essay. Highlight nouns, verbs, adjectives, and phrases that you have used more than once. Then, use a thesaurus to find substitutes for repeated words.

Student Work
IN PROGRESS

Name: *Brendan Barraclough*
Mountain School
Los Alamos, NM

Highlighting Repeated Words
Brendan looked over his first paragraph and eliminated some repeated words.

Cats and frogs make great pets. Even though cats are mammals and frogs are amphibians, they are both lovable pets. Both kinds of pets ⟲ animals require a caretaker, or "parent." The pet needs the caretaker's time, responsibility, and money. There are some similarities and many differences between cats and frogs as pets.

felines
web-footed friends

Peer Review
Pointing

Next, enlist the help of classmates to make additional refinements. Here's a strategy you can use:

1. Read your essay to the group of four or five students.
2. Pause, and ask group members to listen closely a second time, jotting down words, phrases, images—anything that really strikes them. Read your essay again.
3. Afterward, ask listeners to "point" to what they liked. Only positive comments are allowed.

Build on the strengths that classmates have identified. For instance, you might give more details about a point they liked.

Editing and Proofreading

Once you've finished revising, check your essay for errors in spelling, grammar, punctuation, and usage.

Focusing on Pronouns

As you proofread, check pronoun-antecedent agreement, using the chart below and the information that follows.

SINGULAR

PERSONAL	POSSESSIVE
I me	my, mine
you	your, yours
he, she, it him, her, it	his, hers, its

PLURAL

PERSONAL	POSSESSIVE
we us	our, ours
you	your, yours
they them	their, theirs

Grammar in Your Writing
Pronoun-Antecedent Agreement

A pronoun must agree with its antecedent in both person and number. **Person** indicates whether a pronoun refers to the person speaking (first person), the person spoken to (second person), or the person, place, or thing spoken about (third person). **Number** indicates whether a pronoun is singular (referring to one) or plural (referring to more than one).

A pronoun must agree with its antecedent in both person and number.

EXAMPLES: **Esther** is revising **her** essay about Susan B. Anthony. [third person singular]
The women are practicing for **their** debut performance. [third person plural]

Find It in Your Reading Review "More Than a Pinch: Two Salt Lakes" on page 152. Find two pronouns, and identify the antecedent of each.

Find It in Your Writing Circle in red three pronouns in your draft. Then, circle the antecedent of each in green. Revise any pronouns that do not agree with their antecedents.

To learn more about pronoun-antecedent agreement, see Chapter 24.

8.6 *Publishing and Presenting*

Building Your Portfolio

Once you've completed your final draft, consider these ideas for sharing it with a wider audience:

1. **Picture Essay** Find photographs to illustrate your essay. Then, share your illustrated essay with classmates.
2. **Create an Audiotape** Practice reading your essay aloud a few times. Read it slowly and clearly, emphasizing the strong points. Then, record it. You might present your reading to the class and share it with family and friends.

Reflecting on Your Writing

You have taken an idea through many different steps and created an essay. What have you learned? Write a few notes on your writing experience. Start by answering these questions:

- Do you view your topic differently now? If so, why and how?
- Do you think writing a comparison-and-contrast essay is difficult or easy for someone to learn? Why do you think so?

 Internet Tip

To see comparison-and-contrast essays scored with this rubric, go on-line: PHSchool.com Enter Web Code: eak-6001

Rubric for Self-Assessment

Evaluate your comparison-and-contrast essay using the following criteria:

	Score 4	Score 3	Score 2	Score 1
Audience and Purpose	Clearly attracts audience interest in the comparison-contrast analysis	Adequately attracts audience interest in the comparison-contrast analysis	Provides a reason for the comparison-contrast analysis	Does not provide a reason for a comparison-contrast analysis
Organization	Clearly presents information in a consistent organization well suited to the topic	Presents information using an organization suited to the topic	Chooses an organziation not suited to comparison and contrast	Shows a lack of organizational strategy
Elaboration	Elaborates ideas with facts, details, or examples; links all information to comparison and contrast	Elaborates most ideas with facts, details, or examples; links most information to comparison and contrast	Does not elaborate all ideas; does not link some details to comparison and contrast	Does not provide facts or examples to support comparison and contrast
Use of Language	Demonstrates excellent sentence and vocabulary variety; includes very few mechanical errors	Demonstrates adequate sentence and vocabulary variety; includes few mechanical errors	Demonstrates repetitive use of sentence structure and vocabulary; includes many mechanical errors	Demonstrates poor use of language; generates confusion; includes many mechanical errors

FINAL DRAFT

▲ **Critical Viewing**
Are there more
differences or more
similarities between
cats and frogs as
pets? Explain.
[Hypothesize]

Cats and Frogs as Pets

Brendan Barraclough
Mountain School
Los Alamos, New Mexico

Cats and frogs make great pets. Even though cats are
mammals and frogs are amphibians, they are both lovable pets.
Both kinds of animals require a caretaker, or "parent." The pet
needs the caretaker's time, responsibility, and money. There are
some similarities and many differences between felines and
web-footed friends as pets.

To begin with, the right habitat needs to be provided for both
kinds of pets. Cats are easier because they can live in the home you
are already in. You just have to add a litter box, food, and water.
As opposed to that, frogs need a specially prepared terrarium with
dirt for hibernation. In addition, frogs need the air temperature
controlled because they are coldblooded. An advantage of the
terrarium is that frogs can be kept in one place easily.

*By putting his topic
sentence at the end
of the first paragraph,
Brendan makes a
smooth transition to
the next paragraph.*

*Note that Brendan
uses specific examples
with concrete details
to give the readers
precise information.*

A big job as a pet owner is to protect the pets. Some pets, however, are easier to protect than others. It is harder to protect cats when they go outdoors, because in my neighborhood in northern New Mexico there are coyotes, mountain lions, rattlesnakes, owls, and cars that can kill cats. I keep my cat safe in our screened patio. In contrast, frogs just need their terrarium in a closed room protected from the mischievous house cats. This is important, because one time my naughty cat pushed the frog terrarium off my desk. Frogs and crickets were everywhere! My aunt, my mom, and I spent hours searching for the "liberated" frogs. From then on, the cats were banished from my room.

Cats are soft, like my favorite fuzzy blanket, while frogs are like a fragile toy that is fun to watch. Cats can be snuggled anytime. Unlike cats, frogs cannot be held because it will damage their protective mucus, and they might get an infection.

Another difference between cats and frogs as pets is that it is cheaper to take care of frogs. Cats need vaccinations and check-ups by a veterinarian once a year, while frogs never go to a vet. Frog food, which is usually live crickets, costs less than cat food. However, they both need fresh water all the time. In addition, cats require clean litter every few days. In general, neither pet is very expensive to take care of.

A disadvantage of having a cat as a pet is that some people are allergic to cat dander. This can limit the friends who can visit. This is not a problem with frogs.

One happy advantage of having a cat versus a frog is that cats usually live about five times longer than frogs do in captivity. Though I'm very sad when one of my pets dies, I remember all the happy times we had.

Unlike frogs, cats have distinctive personalities. Some cats are aloof, and some are affectionate, but they are all curious. This can be a disadvantage, because a cat's curiosity can result in some accidentally broken objects around the house.

Overall, cats and frogs make excellent pets in spite of their many similarities and differences. If cats are the furry couch potatoes of the pet world, frogs are the lean long-jumpers.

Brendan restates the topic of this paragraph in the second sentence. He gives a number of illustrations of the topic.

Brendan keeps his essay balanced by providing a detail about frogs for every detail he gives about cats.

Notice how Brendan successfully uses point-by-point organization, discussing each aspect of his pets in turn.

▼ **Critical Viewing** Compare this cat to the one on the previous page. **[Compare and Contrast]**

Brendan ends his essay with two memorable figures of speech.

Connected Assignment
Consumer Report

Before people spend money, they often make a comparison and contrast among several products. By comparing different products, they can find the one that will best fit their needs. They can also find the best bargain. A consumer report can help.

A **consumer report** is a comparison of the strengths and weaknesses of different products. It draws conclusions about the advantages of using one over another. Useful consumer reports feature

• a detailed comparison of two or more similar products.

• a rating of the products, backed by facts.

▲ **Critical Viewing**
What might be puzzling the man in this cartoon? **[Infer]**

Prewriting To choose a topic, consider topics such as these:

• **A Recent Purchase** Choose a purchase you or your family has made recently. Then, find a comparable product. Write a report comparing the product your family bought with the second product.

• **Report on a Toy** Choose two similar toys, such as toy cars, dolls or action figures, or board games. Identify the features people want in such a toy. Then, compare the two to find which one would best fulfill people's desires.

Narrow Your Topic After choosing your topic, make sure it is focused. For instance, if your topic is model cars, focus on two in the same price range.

Consider Your Audience Next, think about who will use your report. Will purchasers of the product be

• young people of your age?

• their parents?

• adults in general?

Then, determine the needs of your readers. In the case of model cars, you might ask

• whether they are looking for a car that will be fun to build.

• whether they are looking for a long-term project requiring patience and skill.

• how much money they have to spend.

SOUTHSIDE SALLIE DOLL
• comes with three outfits
• comes in different hair colors
• has many fantasy setups, like the Southside Sallie Moon Walk

• pretty face
• many additional clothes available
• house available separately

MANHATTAN MARY DOLL
• comes with five outfits
• comes in one hair color
• has no fantasy setups

Jot down a description of your audience and its needs on an index card. Refer to this card to make sure you are thinking of your audience as you gather details and draft your report.

Gathering Details To gather the details you need, consult brochures, user's guides, and magazine articles. Record details in a Venn diagram like the one shown.

Drafting After you've gathered information, begin drafting.

- Begin with an introduction clearly stating for whom and about what you are writing your report.
- In the body of your report, compare products point by point.
- Support each point with details about the product.
- Make your recommendation in a conclusion.

Revising and Editing After completing your first draft, check it against your audience description. Ask yourself:

- Is there information I have not included but that my audience needs? (If so, add the missing details.)
- Have I included information my audience doesn't need? (If so, consider deleting those details.)

Then, rearrange sentences to make sure that all those about a given feature appear near each other. Add transitions, such as *in contrast* and *likewise,* to clearly connect ideas.

Publishing and Presenting Create a consumer bulletin board in the school library for students to browse. Post your report on the board.

MODEL

Where to Eat

In this passage, notice that the writer compares the restaurants point by point. The conclusion makes a recommendation specifically meant for the writer's audience.

If you are looking for a lot of food on your plate and don't mind a lot of grease as well, Sloppy Joe's may be the restaurant for you. The cooking at Tartuffe's is a lot better, but the portions are a lot smaller. For prices, Joe's can't be beat. Tartuffe's is the kind of place you probably can afford only on special occasions.

In conclusion, I would recommend Joe's for any student with a little money and a big appetite.

Spotlight on the Humanities

Interpreting Themes in a Variety of Media

Focus on Music: "The Ballad of Tam Lin"

One of the most beautiful comparison-and-contrast pieces is a fairy tale, "Beauty and the Beast." The story includes a strong contrast between a beautiful woman and the beast with whom she lives. The story also contrasts the beast with the handsome prince he turns into.

The fairy tale itself is the subject of comparisons. Many compare "Beauty and the Beast" to a Scottish ballad called "The Ballad of Tam Lin," which dates as far back as 1549. (A *ballad* is a long song or poem that tells a story.)

"Tam Lin" is about a young man who is a captive of the faeries, and about the young woman who rescues him. Like "Beauty and the Beast," the story of "Tam Lin" includes an enchanted forest where sacred roses grow. Trouble starts for both Beauty and Janet, the young woman in "Tam Lin," when they obtain one of these roses. In both stories, the spell on the man is broken only after the young woman expresses devotion to him.

Film Connection French director Jean Cocteau (1889–1963) created a classic film version of "Beauty and the Beast" in 1946. Cocteau was inspired to make this film after studying nineteenth-century artist Gustave Doré's illustrations for the story.

Theater Connection In 1994, a stage version of *Beauty and the Beast* arrived on Broadway. The musical won a Tony Award for Best Costumes in 1995.

Comparison-and-Contrast Writing Activity: Presenting Contrasts in Music

Listen to the songs from the Broadway version of *Beauty and the Beast.* Take notes on how the composer creates a contrast between Beauty and the Beast in music. Write your thoughts in a paragraph or two, and share them with the class. Play examples from the musical to help the class understand the contrast.

Scene from *Beauty and the Beast*, directed by Jean Cocteau.

▲ **Critical Viewing** Compare these two scenes from different versions of "Beauty and the Beast." List at least two similarities and two differences. **[Compare and Contrast]**

Media and Technology Skills

Comparing Stories in Different Media

Activity: Comparing Book and Movie Versions

The world's favorite stories can't stay put. People spread them around by retelling them in a variety of ways. For instance, movie makers often take a favorite book and turn the story into a film. Learn about some of the ways in which movie makers change stories when they film them.

Learn About It Here are some of the changes that take place when a story makes the transition from a book to a film:

- **Actions Versus Thoughts** Movie makers do not often include parts of a book that cannot be shown in actions. Long discussions between characters, or a character's deep thoughts, may not appear in the movie version of a story.

- **Time Limits** You can put a book down, and then pick it up again days later when you have more time to read. Most people, though, get restless if they sit in a movie theater for too long. For this reason, movie makers generally limit the length of movies to under two hours. To hold to this time, they may leave out events that appear in the book. They may even eliminate or combine characters.

- **Adding Image and Sound** Writers use only words to shape their story. In contrast, movie makers tell a story not just with words, but with visual images and sounds. They use actors, scenery, and special effects to create these images. Instead of a vivid description of a character's feelings, a movie maker might use yearning, romantic music, or take a close-up shot of a character's tear-streaked face.

Words, though, can express important subtleties of meaning. By using words skillfully, you can show that a character feels fear and longing at the same time. A movie may show only a character's strongest feelings or only the most striking parts of the events in a story.

Watch It Watch a movie production of a book you have read. Take notes, using a chart like the one shown. Then, write a brief comparison of the two versions, noting the important differences between them.

Other Differences to Consider

Purpose
The purpose of a written story may not be the same as that of the movie version. The story's author might want to teach a lesson; the screenwriter might wish only to entertain.

Changing Times
In a modern version of an old story, a movie maker may appeal to current ideas and trends. For instance, the movie maker might add ideas about the rights of children that were not in the written version.

	Written Version	Movie Version
Events (Different/Similar)	1. Pete's dog gets lost. 2.	1. Pete's dog gets lost. 2.
Characters (Different/Similar)	1. Charlie – helps Pete look for his dog 2.	1. Charlie isn't in the movie. 2.
Words vs. Images (Written Descriptions vs. Acting, Scenery, Music, Camerawork)	1. Pete's reaction to missing dog: "like a chunk of ice in his stomach" 2.	1. Pete's reaction to missing dog: close-up of his shocked face; music sounds full of fear and danger 2.

Standardized Test Preparation Workshop

Comparing and Contrasting in Response to Writing Prompts

The writing prompts of standardized tests often judge your ability to write an expository essay in which you compare and contrast things. Your test essay will be assessed on your ability to

- show the similarities and differences between subjects, following the requirements of the prompt exactly.

- use examples based on what you have read in the passage to support each point.

- use a consistent method of organization suited to the topic, such as the point-by-point method.

- unify your essay through the use of transitions.

Test Tip

Pay special attention to key words in the prompt, such as *not, similarities*, and *differences*.

Although on some tests you will not lose points for errors in spelling and grammar, always try to use correct English.

Some prompts ask you to write a short response. Others call for a long response. If you are given a short-response prompt, you should not go through the prewriting, drafting, and revising stages. The writing skills you have learned so far will be sufficient. However, a long-response prompt requires more attention. You can practice for such tests by responding to the sample expository writing prompt below. Use the suggestions on the next page to help you respond. The clocks represent the portion of your test-taking time that you should devote to each stage of your writing.

Sample Writing Situation

Read "More Than a Pinch: Two Salt Lakes" on page 152, and then answer the prompt below.

In "More Than a Pinch: Two Salt Lakes," the writer compares the Great Salt Lake with the Dead Sea. Describe the ways the lakes are *alike* and *different,* using examples from the article.

Prewriting

Allow close to one fourth of your time for prewriting.

Focus on Your Purpose Before you begin to gather details for your essay, keep in mind your purpose in writing. This is already decided by the prompt. For instance, in responding to the example prompt, you should focus on the similarities and differences between the two lakes, and avoid discussing details that do not lead to a comparison or a contrast.

Use a Venn Diagram Gather details for your essay, using a Venn diagram. Draw two overlapping circles. Write similarities in the section that overlaps, and list differences in the outer sections. (For an example of a Venn diagram, see page 157.)

Drafting

Allow nearly half of your time for drafting.

Organize Details Choose a method of organization. You may want to use the organization used in "More Than a Pinch," which is the point-by-point method. To use this method, discuss each aspect of both subjects in turn. After you have chosen a method, follow it in sketching an outline.

Introduction After organizing details, write an introductory paragraph in which you make a general statement comparing the lakes.

Use Examples Follow your organization in presenting necessary support from the model. For each feature that you write about—the level of salt, for instance—use examples from the text to explain how that feature is similar or different in the two lakes.

Use Transitions As you draft, use transitional words to show the connections between ideas. Words such as *but*, *however*, *yet*, *too*, and *likewise* show compare-and-contrast relationships.

Conclusion In your conclusion, sum up the differences and similarities between the lakes.

Revising, Editing, and Proofreading

Allow almost one fourth of your time for revising and editing. Use the last few minutes to proofread your work.

Review Organization of Ideas Check the organization of your essay against your outline. Rearrange sentences or paragraphs if necessary to put them in the best order. Also, make sure your ideas connect between sentences and paragraphs. If a connection seems to be missing between ideas, add an appropriate transitional word.

Make Corrections Check for spelling, grammar, and punctuation errors. When making changes, put one line through text that you are eliminating. Use a caret (^) to show where added text belongs.

Exposition
Cause-and-Effect Essay

Cause-and-Effect Explanations in Everyday Life

Through history, people have tried to understand why things happen. Why does it get dark at night? Why does it thunder and lightning? What causes the seasons to change?

People have tried to answer these questions in many ways. The ancient Greeks, for example, told stories of Zeus, the king of the gods, who hurled lightning bolts from the sky, and of Apollo, who drove a chariot pulling the sun.

The ancient Greeks used these myths to explain **causes**— the reasons behind events—and **effects**—the results produced by events. Today, we use science to explain many causes and effects. In this chapter, you will learn to explain causes and effects by writing a cause-and-effect essay.

▲ **Critical Viewing**
What will happen if one of these gears starts to turn?
[Hypothesize]

What Is a Cause-and-Effect Essay?

Exposition is writing that informs or explains. A **cause-and-effect essay** is a brief piece of expository writing that explains the circumstances leading to an event or a situation. It may also predict what will happen as a result of a current situation. Features of an effective cause-and-effect essay include

- a clear explanation of one or more causes and one or more effects.

- a thorough presentation of facts, statistics, and other details that support each explanation.

- a clear and consistent organization.

- transitions that clearly indicate the connections among the details.

To learn the criteria on which your essay may be judged or graded, see the Rubric for Self-Assessment on page 189.

Types of Cause-and-Effect Essays

Following are some of the specific types of writing that explain causes and effects:

- **History reports** explain the reasons behind past events.
- **Lab reports** explain the results of an experiment.
- **New reports** explain causes and effects of current events or developments.

Writers in
ACTION

Television news correspondent Gary Matsumoto often uses cause-and-effect explanations in his television news stories. He has only a short time to present information, but he realizes that it is important to give his audience background information:

"You can't cram too much into four minutes or ninety seconds. But you have to . . . have a sufficient amount of background information to make it clear why you're doing the story."

PREVIEW
Student Work
IN PROGRESS

Johnny Guo, a student at First Colony Middle School in Sugar Land, Texas, chose to write about the causes and effects of pollution. In this chapter, you will see how Johnny applied the featured strategies to compose his essay, "Saving Our Air." At the end of the chapter, you can read Johnny's completed essay.

Ross Bankson (1942–   ) is a former editor at National Geographic World. *In this essay, he explains why West Indian manatees, large mammals that live in shallow tropical waters off North and South America, are threatened with extinction. Notice that Bankson outlines a variety of specific reasons that the manatee has become endangered.*

Reading Strategy: Create a Cause-and-Effect Chart When you read a cause-and-effect essay, you may find it helpful to **create a cause-and-effect chart** in which you record each of the causes and effects a writer presents. List the causes along the left side of a sheet of paper. Then, list the effects on the right side. Draw arrows connecting related causes and effects.

Ross Bankson

▼ **Critical Viewing** Manatees are often harmed by speed-boats. What effect might seeing this manatee up close have on a speedboat operator? **[Speculate]**

The writer begins with an interesting "hook" that grabs the reader's interest.

Next, the writer presents the various reasons why the manatee is near extinction.

They have no natural enemies, but they are in trouble anyway. West Indian manatees—large, gentle marine mammals—are in danger because of people. . . .

Some manatee feeding grounds have disappeared, filled in for construction projects. Other feeding grounds have been damaged by pollution, which becomes worse as the number of people grows. Discarded plastic objects floating in waterways can kill a manatee that swallows them.

Boaters create the greatest hazard for West Indian manatees in the shallow water that the animals prefer. The slow-moving manatees often cannot get away from speeding boats. In a collision with a boat, a manatee may be killed or injured by the force of the hit or by cuts from the propeller. Of some 1,500 manatees in Florida today, nearly all adults bear scars from run-ins with propellers.

The good news for the West Indian manatee is this: People can help as well as harm. Many in fact are working to save manatees. Some Florida car owners pay extra money for a "Save the Manatee" license plate. By doing so they help fund the state's manatee protection program and other programs for environmental education. Florida laws regulate boating in areas where manatees live. Other laws protect the animal as an endangered species.

Still, the experts say, even more safeguards are needed. The manatee population is shrinking. "With public support," says Judith Valee, "we can bring the species back from the brink of extinction."

The last paragraphs encourage readers to support a solution— part of the writer's purpose.

Reading ► Writing Connection

Writing Application: Making Clear Connections Between Causes and Effects Make it easy for readers to chart causes and effects. Use transitions such as *because of* and *as a result* to show the relationship between each cause and effect you discuss.

LITERATURE

To read a fantasy involving causes and effects, see "Breaker's Bridge" by Laurence Yep. You can find the story in *Prentice Hall Literature: Timeless Voices, Timeless Themes,* Copper.

▼ Critical Viewing
These animals are in danger of extinction. Name something people might do to help the recovery of one of them. **[Apply]**

Clockwise from upper left: San Francisco rainbow garter snake, Florida panther, American bald eagle, orangutan

Prewriting

Choosing Your Topic

If you have an interest in your topic, you are likely to write a lively and interesting essay on it. Start work on your cause-and-effect essay by choosing an event or a situation that interests you. Use these strategies to stimulate ideas:

Strategies for Generating a Topic

1. **Brainstorming** In a group, discuss possible topics. You may wish to begin with a general idea such as "Historical Events" or a fill-in-the-blank exercise such as "What Causes ___?___" One member of the group should list all the ideas mentioned. Choose an idea from this list as your topic.

2. **Browsing** When you're looking for new clothes, you probably browse through the store. Browsing can also work when you need ideas for a piece of writing. Scan the morning newspaper, or look through magazines or books at the library. Skim for words, phrases, or ideas that concern causes and effects until you find just the right topic.

Try it out! Use the interactive Browsing activity in **Section 9.2**, on-line or on CD-ROM.

Student Work
IN PROGRESS

Name: Johnny Guo
First Colony Middle School
Sugar Land, TX

Browsing

After skimming through a number of magazines and browsing through a CD-ROM encyclopedia, Johnny became interested in writing about the causes and effects of pollution.

Ideas for Cause-and-Effect Essay

Television news story: Decrease in crime

Magazine article on the new dance crazes

Radio: air pollution in American cities

Conversation between Mom and Mr. Wexley: why lots of new people are moving to our town

TOPIC BANK

If you're having trouble finding a topic, consider the following possibilities.

1. **Essay About Nature** Choose a natural event that interests you. It might be the blooming of a flower or the rumbling of thunder. Find out about the causes of this event, and write about them in a cause-and-effect essay.

2. **Essay About a Service** Every day people turn on lights, answer phones, and turn on the water. Each of these services—electricity, telephone service, and water—works only because of a series of causes and effects. Do research into one such service, and write about the causes and effects it involves.

Responding to Fine Art

3. In this painting, the people are creating soap bubbles. Think of what a soap bubble looks like. Then, formulate a question about what makes a soap bubble look or act as it does. Do research to answer your question, and write up the results in an essay.

Blowing Bubbles, John Kane, The Phillips Collection

Responding to Literature

4. Read an account of the space shuttle disaster. Write a cause-and-effect essay in which you examine either the causes behind the space shuttle crash or the effects the crash had on the space program. You can find an eyewitness account of the disaster, "Space Shuttle *Challenger*" by William Harwood, in *Prentice Hall Literature: Timeless Voices, Timeless Themes*, Copper.

☑ Cooperative Writing Opportunity

5. **Booklet of Causes and Effects** With a group of classmates, brainstorm for an event that has many causes and effects, such as a traffic jam, the opening of a new mall, or the passage of a law. Choose one topic. Then, have each student write a report on a single cause or effect related to the topic. Assemble the pieces of writing into a booklet with a cover, a table of contents, and illustrations.

Narrowing Your Topic

Before you begin gathering details about your topic, consider whether it is narrow enough to cover thoroughly. For example, the cause that brought the solar system into existence is too broad a topic. You might focus instead on the causes of Earth's rotation.

Use a Topic Web

Create a topic web to help you evaluate and narrow your topic. Follow these steps:

1. Draw a circle in the center of a blank page.
2. Write your topic inside the circle.
3. Write connected ideas inside new circles around your topic. Draw lines connecting them to your main topic.
4. Write additional ideas related to each one of your subtopics in new circles. Connect each to the appropriate subtopic.

When you've finished, review your completed web. To narrow your topic, focus on a single one of your subtopics.

Student Work
IN PROGRESS

Name: Johnny Guo
First Colony Middle School
Sugar Land, TX

Using a Topic Web to Narrow a Topic

Johnny used a topic web to focus his broad topic, "the causes and effects of pollution." He decided to focus on the effects of air pollution.

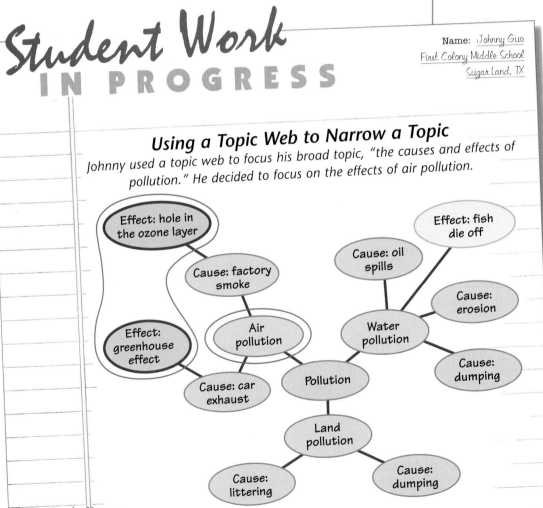

Considering Your Audience and Purpose

Your **audience** is the people for whom you are writing. How much they know and care about your topic will affect how you write your cause-and-effect essay. Jot down information about your audience for each of these categories:

- **Age** Young readers need explanations in simple language with much background; adults want more in-depth details.

- **Interest in Topic** Readers who are very interested will want as many details as you can provide; those who are less interested will feel swamped if you tell them too much.

- **Knowledge of Topic** Readers with little knowledge need background information; experts do not need this background.

Your **purpose**—what you hope to accomplish by writing— will also shape your writing. For instance, in "Gentle Giants in Trouble" on page 176, the writer's purpose is to persuade readers to join him in a cause as well as to explain a topic. To fulfill this purpose, he uses language and chooses details that will help readers see his point of view. Before writing, consider your purpose and how it will shape your writing.

Gathering Details
Research Your Topic

When you write your essay, you must use facts and examples to explain each cause-and-effect relationship you discuss. Gather this information through research in the library or on the Internet.

Using a T-Chart in Research A T-chart is a useful research tool. Use the example below as a model to help you create your own T-chart.

▲ **Critical Viewing** What effects are these people trying to have on life in their city? **[Hypothesize]**

Topic:	The May Flood
What caused the May flood?	**What effects did the May flood have?**
• Hurricane Barbara	• $1.2 million in damages
• 26" of rain	• Schools and businesses closed for 7–10 days.
• Dam broke.	• 35 families left town.
• Ground was already wet from earlier storms.	

Drafting

Shaping Your Writing

Organize Details

Review the information you've gathered, and organize it. Following are two common patterns for cause-and-effect essays. Select a suitable organization from among them, or devise your own, and follow it as you draft.

Many Causes/Single Effect If a number of unrelated events leads to a single result, focus one paragraph on each cause.

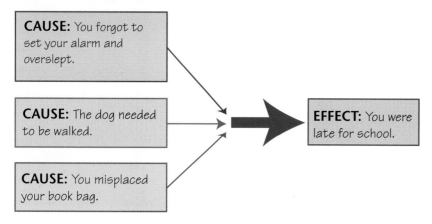

Single Cause/Many Effects If one cause produces several effects, focus one paragraph on each effect.

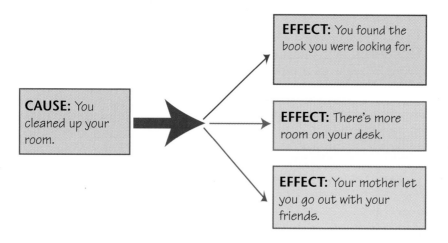

Find Your Focus

Review your information, and identify the main cause or the main effect involved in your topic. As you draft, connect each detail to this main focus.

Providing Elaboration

As you write your first draft, elaborate on each cause and effect by providing a thorough set of facts, statistics, description, and other information. Use the following strategy to help you develop layers of details.

"Explode the Moment"

As you draft, pause at the end of each paragraph. First, circle the most important event mentioned in it. Cut out a few sticky notes in the shape of starbursts. On your sticky notes, jot down notes about the events circled. (To help find details, imagine you are watching the event in slow motion. Note every part of the event as it unfolds.)

Attach each sticky note next to the pertinent paragraph of your draft. Consider adding details from your notes to the paragraph.

Writers in
ACTION

As he writes, reporter Gary Mat-sumoto focuses on his viewer: "You have to grab your viewer right away. Then somewhere around the middle, you've got to think, 'What element of surprise can I offer? [What can] be a nice little kicker line at the end?'"

Student Work
IN PROGRESS

Name: Johnny Guo
First Colony Middle School
Sugar Land, TX

"Exploding the Moment"

When Johnny reread his essay, he realized that he needed to add more information to explain the causes and effects of ozone damage.

You have probably heard about the ozone layer, and how it protects us from harmful UV rays. What you may not know is that driving your car causes the ozone layer to deteriorate at an alarming pace.

plus fluorocarbons, factories, chemical plants

global decrease due to pollution may be 5.5% over 24 years

Revising

Once you've completed your first draft, revise your work carefully. Start by looking at your overall structure.

Revising Your Overall Structure

Analyze Your Sequence of Details

To be effective, your essay should present a clear sequence of causes and effects. If any details are out of order, readers will not be able to follow your explanation. Use the following strategy to check the order of your details.

▶ **REVISION STRATEGY**
Connecting the Steps

As you review your draft, follow these steps:

1. Circle each main cause and each main effect.
2. Use a highlighter to mark each step that leads from a main cause to a main effect.
3. Draw arrows connecting the various steps in the order in which they logically occur.

If there are arrows crisscrossing the draft, consider rearranging details in a more logical order.

If you are drafting in a word-processing program, you can bold-face or highlight main causes and effects. You can then cut and paste to make sure that sentences connecting them appear in the right order.

Student Work
IN PROGRESS

Name: Johnny Guo
First Colony Middle School
Sugar Land, TX

Connecting the Steps
Here is how Johnny marked a paragraph of his essay to check the logic of his cause-and-effect sequences.

CAUSE

An increase in the global temperature would change

CAUSE/EFFECT

climates everywhere. The polar icecaps would begin to melt, leading to a rising sea level. This is dangerous. Many islands such as those in the Caribbean would be submerged if the icecaps melted. The water would cover existing shorelines, causing many coastal cities to be submerged. Millions of

EFFECT

lives would be lost.

Revising Your Paragraphs

Every time you indent a new paragraph, you are signaling your reader, "Here comes a new idea!" This signal helps readers follow your essay. They can still grow confused, however, if you do not tell them what the new idea is. For this reason, many writers begin paragraphs with a topic sentence.

Topic Sentences

A **topical paragraph** is a paragraph that explains or illustrates one main idea. A sentence that states the main idea of a paragraph is called a **topic sentence.** In many cases, it is best to include a topic sentence in the paragraph. Readers will then know exactly what new idea the paragraph discusses.

PARAGRAPH: I didn't waterproof my treehouse. During the summer there were heavy thunderstorms. The rain started the wood rotting. When my cousin Sid climbed into the treehouse, you could feel some of the nails pulling free from the tree branch. One night, the treehouse finally fell to the ground.

TOPIC SENTENCE: There were a few causes leading to my treehouse disaster.

▶ **REVISION STRATEGY**
Finding the "Tug"

Reread each paragraph in your draft. Decide which idea in the paragraph "tugs" at your attention. You can find this "tug" by imagining that someone has asked you, "What is this paragraph about?" Your answer would name the tug.

Summarize this tug in a few words in the margin. Then, check whether your paragraph includes a sentence that expresses this idea clearly. If not, craft a topic sentence explaining the tug.

🔵 Learn More

To learn more about the different kinds of paragraphs and the placement of topic sentences, see Chapter 3.

◀ **Critical Viewing**
Write a short description of this picture. Then, write a topic sentence that identifies the "tug" of the group of sentences. **[Apply]**

Revising Your Sentences
Check Relationships Between Verb Tenses

In a cause-and-effect relationship, one event occurs after another. Changing verb tenses can make this sequence clear:

EVENTS AT
DIFFERENT TIMES: Because I **ran** *(past)* over a nail with my bike,
    I **will not be able** *(future)* to go on the bike trip.

Using different tenses can also lead to errors, however. Use the following strategy to avoid mistakes in tense.

▶**REVISION STRATEGY**
Circling Verbs in Different Tenses

Reread your draft, following these steps:

1. Identify your main tense (the tense of most of your verbs).
2. Circle any verbs in a different tense.
3. Review circled verbs. Are you using them to show a sequence? If not, change them to your main tense.

Grammar in Your Writing
Verb Tense

Verbs are words that express actions or conditions. An action may happen (or a condition may apply) in the past, the present, or the future. To express the time of an action or condition, verbs take different forms, called *tenses*. **Present tense** indicates an action or condition in the present. It may also indicate an action or condition that occurs regularly. **Past tense** shows that an action took place in the past. **Future tense** shows that an action will occur in the future.

PAST: My family and I rode our bikes on a hundred-mile trip this summer.

PRESENT: I am riding my bike right now.
             I ride my bike to school when the weather is good.

FUTURE: We will ride our bikes to the mall this weekend.

Find It in Your Reading Review "Gentle Giants in Trouble" by Ross Bankson on page 176, and identify the tense of the first ten verbs. How many tenses has the writer used? Why has he used these tenses?

Find It in Your Writing Review the first five verbs in your draft. Identify the tense of each verb and explain why you have used that tense. Correct any errors in tense that you find.

To learn more about verb tenses, see Chapter 22.

Revising Your Word Choice
Use Accurate Verbs

Good writers are careful with their selection of verbs because they know that verbs have the power to help readers visualize actions. Use the following strategy to help you choose strong verbs.

▶**REVISION STRATEGY**
Highlighting Verbs

Highlight the verbs in several sentences in your draft. Revise any that are not specific enough to express your meaning clearly. For example, "Sarah went to school this morning" is clear. However, if you picture her moving slowly and dragging her feet as she goes, the verb *went* is not precise enough. Changing the sentence to "Sarah trudged to school this morning" gives readers a clearer sense of Sarah's mood.

Peer Review

Once you've finished revising on your own, enlist the help of classmates in making additional revisions. Use the following strategy:

Summarizing

Form a group of four or five classmates. Read your piece aloud. Pause for one minute. (Keep an eye on the clock—a minute can pass very slowly when you are anxious!) Read aloud again. During this second reading, listeners should focus on what they think is the main idea of your essay. When you have finished reading, each of your listeners should jot down

- the main idea.
- one word that expresses the main idea.
- a synonym for this word.
- a sentence that summarizes the main idea clearly.

Have your peers either give you their notes or read them to you. Check to see that their interpretation of your main idea matches what you had in mind. If not, revise your introduction to state the main idea of your essay more clearly.

▼ **Critical Viewing**
Write a sentence or two describing events that might have led to this scene. Use accurate verbs. **[Hypothesize, Apply]**

Editing and Proofreading

Finally, review your work carefully for errors in grammar, usage, mechanics, and spelling. Focus extra attention on your use of prepositions.

Focusing on Prepositions

Review the prepositions you've used in your essay. Check to see that they express the exact relationship you intended. For example, you might be

- *in the truck* (ready to leave on a trip).
- *on the truck* (checking to see that the load is safely tied).
- *under the truck* (looking for an oil leak).

In each case, the preposition helps readers to picture the relationship between you and the truck. Check your draft to make sure you have used the right prepositions to give readers a good picture. In addition, make sure you have not used two prepositions where one will do.

Grammar in Your Writing
Using Prepositions

A **preposition** is a word that relates a noun or pronoun to another element of the sentence. A number of prepositions are listed below:

about	against	among	before	between	beyond
down	in	inside	inside of	into	off
on	onto	out of	outside	within	

Do not use two prepositions where one will do.

AVOIDABLE: He climbed **up on** the truck.

PREFERRED: He climbed **onto** the truck.

Find It in Your Reading Identify three prepositions in "Gentle Giants in Trouble" by Ross Bankson on page 176. What relationships do they show?

Find It in Your Writing Review your essay, and underline the first ten prepositions. If you have used two where one will do, replace them with a single preposition.

To learn more about prepositions, see Chapter 17.

9.6 Publishing and Presenting

Building Your Portfolio

Here are some ideas for sharing your essay:

1. **Create a Class Anthology** Work with a group of class-mates to create a class anthology of cause-and-effect essays. Work together to create a table of contents, a cover, and illustrations to accompany each essay.

2. **Organize a Group Reading** As a class, read and discuss your essays. Allow time for questions after each reading. Encourage listeners to come up with additional causes and effects related to each topic.

Reflecting on Your Writing

Jot down a few notes about writing your essay. Start by answering these questions:

- What new information did you learn about your topic?

- What was the biggest problem you encountered while writing this essay? How did you resolve it?

 **Internet Tip**

To see cause-and-effect essays scored with this rubric, go on-line:

PHSchool.com

Enter Web Code:
eak-6001

Rubric for Self-Assessment

Evaluate your cause-and-effect essay using the following criteria:

	Score 4	Score 3	Score 2	Score 1
Audience and Purpose	Consistently targets an audience through word choice and details; clearly identifies purpose in introduction	Targets an audience through most word choice and details; identifies purpose in introduction	Misses a target audience by including a wide range of word choice and details; presents purpose unclearly	Addresses no specific audience or purpose
Organization	Uses a clear, consistent organizational strategy to show cause and effect	Uses a clear organizational strategy with occasional inconsistencies to show cause and effect	Uses an inconsistent organizational strategy; creates illogical presentation of causes and effects	Demonstrates a lack of organizational strategy; creates a confusing presentation
Elaboration	Successfully links causes with effects; fully elaborates connections among ideas	Links causes with effects; elaborates connections among most ideas	Links some causes with some effects; elaborates connections among some ideas	Develops and elaborates no links between causes and effects
Use of Language	Chooses clear transitions to convey ideas; presents very few mechanical errors	Uses transitions to convey ideas; presents few mechanical errors	Misses some opportunities for transitions; presents many mechanical errors	Demonstrates poor use of language; presents many mechanical errors

Student Work
IN PROGRESS

FINAL DRAFT

Saving Our Air

Johnny Guo
First Colony Middle School
Sugar Land, Texas

▲ **Critical Viewing**
Solar panels like the ones above generate electricity from sunlight. How might the use of such panels affect scenes like the one on the left? **[Speculate]**

With all the breakthroughs in this century, none has come close to solving the problem of air pollution. It has threatened us for the last 100 years. I believe that it's essential that we act now. To see why, just think about the effects of air pollution.

You have probably heard about the ozone layer, and how it protects us from harmful UV (ultraviolet) rays from the sun. What you may not know, however, is that fluorocarbons (found in aerosol-spray containers), cars, factories, and chemical plants all cause the ozone layer to deteriorate at an alarming pace. Some studies show that pollution may have caused a 5.5 percent decrease in ozone over a 24-year period. That is hazardous to

In his introduction, Johnny identifies his topic, the effects of air pollution, and his purpose—to motivate readers to participate in a solution.

everyone's health and to the planet. Scientists predict that ozone layer damage will cause increases in skin cancer and cataracts (an eye disease) in both humans and animals. In addition, it will hurt certain crops and plankton, both important to the food web.

Air pollution may also lead to dangerous changes in the greenhouse effect. The greenhouse effect prevents Earth from being a frozen planet. Gases such as carbon dioxide, methane, and water vapor absorb energy from the sun and keep the planet warm. However, carbon dioxide has increased because of burning fossil fuels such as oil, gas, and coal. This causes more heat from the atmosphere to be trapped, resulting in global warming.

An increase in the global temperature would change climates everywhere. The polar icecaps would begin to melt, leading to a rising sea level. This is dangerous. Many islands such as those in the Caribbean would be submerged if the icecaps melted. The water would cover existing shorelines, causing many coastal cities to be submerged. Millions of lives would be lost.

These floods would also hurt people and animals in other ways as well. Lost land means less area for growing crops to feed both people and farm animals. In addition, lost land means lost habitats. Take away habitats and animals will die. Loss of habitat can endanger the survival of an entire species.

The disappearance of any species has many effects. The extinction of simple things like insects or worms can hurt the species that feed on insects or worms. To preserve the food chain, we must protect the ozone layer. To protect the ozone, we must start thinking about what we put into the air.

We can all fight air pollution. We can reduce the number of miles our family drives a car. We can walk, take public transportation, or ride our bikes instead of asking our parents to drive us short distances. We can help our parents carpool so they don't drive all over town. We can turn off lights and television sets when they are not in use.

A little help from each of us could add up to a lot. By caring for Earth, we can guarantee the children of tomorrow a safe place to live and a world they can love.

To organize his essay clearly, Johnny addresses each major effect of air pollution in turn. For each major cause, he explains the chain of causes and effects that leads to it.

▼ **Critical Viewing** Explain how this man may be contributing to an improvement in air quality. **[Connect]**

Connected Assignment
Documentary Video Script

You don't just have to read cause-and-effect explanations: You can also watch them on television. Television documentaries feature **cause-and-effect explanations**—explanations showing how one event or situation leads to another. The writing for these shows does not appear on screen. Instead, it exists as a script.

A **documentary video script** outlines the words that are spoken on a television documentary. Some of these words are recorded from interviews. Others are spoken by a reporter or narrator. A video script also includes directions to the narrator, the camera operators, sound and lighting engineers, and the editor who will put the video together.

Write a documentary video script. Use the suggestions that follow to guide you.

Prewriting Watch a television newsmagazine show to see how documentary segments are organized.

Structure The following structure is common:

1. The anchor or host of the show introduces the segment.
2. The reporter who investigated the story gives a more detailed introduction.
3. The segment then alternates among
   - scenes from interviews,
   - scenes of events or places illustrating facts in the story, and
   - more scenes of the reporter giving explanations.
4. At the end, the reporter "wraps it up" with a conclusion.

Choose a Topic After taking notes on a television documentary, choose a topic that interests you—for example, a recent natural disaster.

Gather Details Next, conduct an investigation. Do research using various sources, such as newspapers and the Internet. Focus on the questions: What causes led to the event or situation in my documentary? What effects does it or will it have?

Then, if possible, conduct interviews with experts or eyewitnesses. (If you cannot perform actual interviews, write a fictional one based on what you learn in other sources.) Use an audio or video recorder, if available, to capture interviews and scenes illustrating your story.

▲ **Critical Viewing**
Explain what role news anchors such as these have in presenting a documentary. **[Connect]**

Documentary On: _____

SHOT 1	SHOT 2
Visual: *Host of show at desk.* **Camera Angle/Movement:** *Camera cuts to close-up of her face.* **Narration:** *If you've had "gnawing" doubts about your dog's health, the next story will interest you.* **Other Sound:** *Theme music fades as narration begins.*	**Visual:** _____ **Camera Angle/Movement:** ___ **Narration:** _____ **Other Sound:** _____

Drafting To organize the facts, use a graphic organizer like the one shown. Then, include these elements:

- narration (interviews and the reporter's commentary)
- instruction for the use of visuals, including camera angles
- instructions for the use of sound (sound effects and music)

Revising and Editing Read your script aloud. Mark places where ideas seem disconnected or where transitions are not smooth. Revise to make the script flow better.

Publishing and Presenting If you have access to video equipment, produce your segment and show it to the class.

MODEL

What's the Damage?
News Documentary Segment

In this passage, notice how speakers are identified and how directions for visuals are presented.

[SHOT 10: Reporter standing before ruined house.]

REPORTER: As you can see, this was no small earthquake. Experts estimate that, by Tuesday morning, $10 million dollars worth of property had been damaged. The reason, they say, . . .

[CUT TO SHOT 11: Professor Mendicino in his office, shot from mid-distance.]

REPORTER [voice-over]: . . . was poor planning.

PROF. MENDICINO: . . . those buildings were built right over a major fault line.

[CAMERA MOVES IN ON MENDICINO'S FACE.]

Spotlight on the Humanities

Interpreting Texts Using Varied Means

Focus on Film: *The Gold Rush*

If you were writing a cause-and-effect paper on the Klondike Gold Rushes of 1897 and 1898, you might notice a surprising effect: The people who hurried west to find gold inspired many short stories, poems, and even movies.

Charlie Chaplin, one of the most beloved film personalities of all time, brought the Gold Rush to the screen in 1925. His film *The Gold Rush* tells the hilarious tale of a lone prospector who ventures into Alaska looking for gold. Along the way, he gets mixed up with some tough, burly characters and falls in love with the beautiful Georgia. Chaplin not only wrote and directed the film, but also starred as the charming, zany prospector.

Literature Connection Many authors of the day wrote about the experiences of those who searched for gold. In 1897, author Jack London (1876–1916) joined the rush to the Klondike. He did not turn up much gold, but he made another valuable find—he came to know the people of the Gold Rush. They served as models for his hard-driving heroes. His short stories of the Yukon portray the brutal, vigorous life of the Far North. London was one of the most popular short story writers of his day. He was one of the few writers at the time who were able to support themselves solely through writing.

The Gold Rush continues to inspire writers. In his 1999 novel *Jason's Gold*, author Will Hobbs (1947–   ) tells the story of a 15-year-old boy named Jason who embarks on a 10,000-mile journey to the Klondike to strike it rich. Along the way, he meets the not-yet-famous Jack London, and plenty of life-threatening adventures.

Cause-and-Effect Writing Activity: Gold Rush Journal

At your local library or on the Internet, research the causes and effects of the Klondike Gold Rushes. Then, write three entries from the journal of someone who experienced these events of the time. In one, record the person's decision to move. In the others, record some of the effects of the decision: What happens on the trip out west? Does the person find gold or go bust? Include details showing the thoughts and feelings of your character.

Charlie Chaplin in *The Gold Rush*

Jacket illustration © 1999 by Derek James

▲ **Critical Viewing** Compare the two ideas of life in the Klondike presented in these images. **[Compare and Contrast]**

Media and Technology Skills

Analyzing Images
Focus on Visual Arts: Photographs

One effect of a good photograph is to communicate information. It shows viewers what a person, event, or place looks like. A photograph can also shape your ideas about its subject. Learn about the elements that give an image its special meaning.

Think About It An effective photograph uses these elements:

- **A central point of interest** Most photographs focus on one main action, object, or person. In the photograph shown, the man's predicament, including the water and the telephone booth, is the focus.

- **Composition** The composition of a photograph involves the placement of objects and the use of space and of light. For instance, in the photograph shown:

  ▶ the telephone booth and the man inside are centered in the image.

  ▶ in the background, you can see the floodwaters, which helps you understand what is going on.

  ▶ the lighting is natural, so the photograph shows just what the weather looked like that day.

- **Emotional impact** By choosing the proper central point of interest, and by creating the right composition, a photographer can lead viewers to an emotional response. For instance, you may have laughed at the attempt by the man in this photograph to stay dry. You may also have sympathized with his difficulties.

Apply It Look through a newspaper or magazine for a photograph that catches your eye. Then, using the chart below, take notes on the photograph. Would you have chosen a different image for the story? Explain why or why not.

Source of Photograph: _____

What Is the Central Point of Interest?	Describe the Composition	Describe the Emotional Impact

> **Types of Photographs**
> - Candid—shows natural, unposed behavior
> - Documentary— records an event
> - Portrait—portrays people
> - Abstract—evokes mood
> - Landscape—shows a place

▼ **Critical Viewing** Describe your reaction to this image. **[Relate]**

Standardized Test Preparation Workshop

Using Cause-and-Effect Writing for Expository Writing Prompts

Some writing prompts on standardized tests require you to show the relationships between causes and their effects. You will be evaluated on the ability you show to

- respond directly to the prompt.

- make your writing thoughtful and interesting.

- organize ideas so they are clear and easy to follow.

- develop your ideas thoroughly by using appropriate details and precise language.

- stay focused on your purpose by making sure that each sentence contributes to your composition as a whole.

- use correct spelling, capitalization, punctuation, grammar, usage, and sentence structure.

Following is an example of an expository writing prompt. Respond using the suggestions on the following page. When taking a timed test, you should plan how much time you will devote to each part of the writing process. The clocks on the next page show the suggested percentage of time to devote to prewriting, drafting, revising and editing, and proofreading.

Sample Writing Situation

West Indian manatees are not hunted by other animals, but they have come to be endangered. Read "Gentle Giants in Trouble" by Ross Bankson on page 176, in which he explains the causes of the manatee's problem. Then, respond to the following prompt:

Explain three main causes for the endangerment of manatees. In your response, use details from Ross Bankson's article.

Prewriting

Allow close to one fourth of your time for prewriting.

Review Your Source Read "Gentle Giants in Trouble" by Ross Bankson on page 176. Each time he introduces a main cause for the endangerment of manatees, write it down. When you are done, review his essay to make sure you have correctly identified the three main causes.

Use a Cluster Diagram To create a cluster diagram, circle each cause you have noted. Then, review Bankson's essay. Next to each main cause in your notes, jot down related events and situations. Circle each new item and connect it with a line to the related main cause.

Review your diagram. Number all of the events associated with a main cause in order. If two or more take place at the same time, number each with the same number.

Drafting

Allow almost half of your time for drafting.

Organize Details The prompt asks you to discuss three main causes. Make an outline of these three causes, jotting down related events under each. Use the numbers on your cluster diagram to put events in chronological order—the order in which they occurred.

Elaborate As you write the body of your response, refer to your outline and explain how each main cause contributed to the manatee's problem. Make sure to explain the sequence of events that leads from a main cause to its effect on the manatees. Also, explain what other events added to each main cause.

Revising, Editing, and Proofreading

Allow almost one fourth of your time to revise and edit. Use the last few minutes to proofread your work.

Use Transitions Review your draft. Where needed, add transitional words, such as *as a result, because of, before,* and *after,* to indicate the cause-and-effect relationships between events.

Make Corrections Review your draft for errors in spelling, grammar, and punctuation. When making changes, neatly cross out text that you want eliminated and place it in brackets. Use a caret (^) to indicate the places at which you would like to add words.

Exposition
How-to Essay

How-to Essays in Everyday Life

When you were a young child, you learned how to do an amazing number of things—how to brush your teeth, how to tie your shoes, how to open a door, and so on. It was a very exciting time—especially when you learned to turn on a light! You probably clicked the switch over and over again.

Turning a light on and off gets a little boring after a while. You mastered one skill, however, that can never become dull: You learned to follow instructions. Using this skill, you can learn just about anything—how to program a VCR, play a new computer game, or make a chocolate cake. All you need is the right **how-to**—a user's guide, a manual, or a cookbook.

Now, you can learn a new skill—how to write your own how-to essay! It's even more exciting than turning the lights on.

▲ **Critical Viewing**
Name one mistake in baking that following a recipe can help you avoid. **[Speculate]**

Gathering Details

Now that you have a narrow topic and an audience, you have an idea of the details you need to include in your essay. To help gather your details, try the itemizing strategy.

Itemize to Gather Details

Begin with a simple list of the materials or the steps involved in your topic. Then, itemize each part of the list—break down each major step into the smaller steps it includes, or specify the kind, quantity, or preparation of each material required.

If your itemized list starts getting too long, consider whether your topic is still too broad or whether you are including more details than your audience needs.

Technology Tip

If you have access to a still camera or a video camera, perform the process you are explaining in your how-to essay while a partner takes pictures; then, switch places. Both of you can then review your visual records to identify details for your writing.

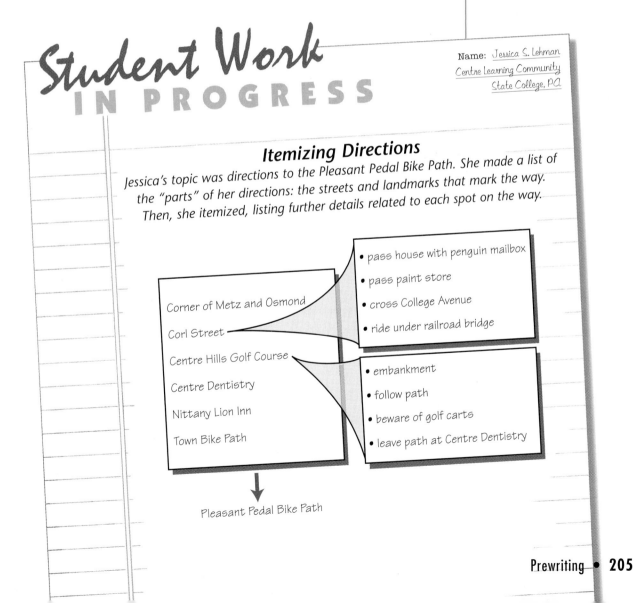

Student Work
IN PROGRESS

Name: Jessica S. Lehman
Centre Learning Community
State College, PA

Itemizing Directions

Jessica's topic was directions to the Pleasant Pedal Bike Path. She made a list of the "parts" of her directions: the streets and landmarks that mark the way. Then, she itemized, listing further details related to each spot on the way.

Corner of Metz and Osmond
Corl Street
Centre Hills Golf Course
Centre Dentistry
Nittany Lion Inn
Town Bike Path

- pass house with penguin mailbox
- pass paint store
- cross College Avenue
- ride under railroad bridge

- embankment
- follow path
- beware of golf carts
- leave path at Centre Dentistry

Pleasant Pedal Bike Path

Drafting

Shaping Your Writing

Once you have gathered your details, you need to put them into some kind of order. The details for your how-to essay are like materials at a construction site. If the workers just start pouring concrete and pounding nails wherever they please, the building will be a disaster! On the other hand, if they follow a blueprint, the building will be sturdy and useful. Before you draft, make a plan in which you organize your details.

Organize Details in Chronological Order

Chronological order is the arrangement of steps in the order in which they take place. Since the reader of a how-to essay usually needs to complete one step before beginning the next, chronological order is the best order for most how-to essays. Organize your how-to steps chronologically by using a timeline.

Using a Timeline Write each step of your how-to topic on its own sticky note or note card. Lay out your notes in order on a table or on the floor. Read through them, and move any notes that are out of order into the right place. Once the steps are in the correct order, number your notes from start to finish.

Research Tip

In slow motion, perform the process you are explaining. Note the individual steps and the exact order in which you complete them. Make sure the steps of your how-to essay are consistent with the way you complete the process yourself.

STICKY NOTE TIMELINE

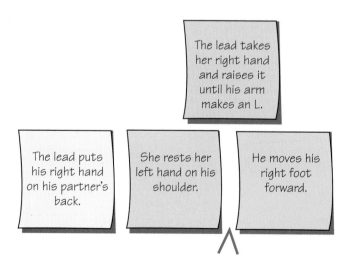

The lead takes her right hand and raises it until his arm makes an L.

The lead puts his right hand on his partner's back.

She rests her left hand on his shoulder.

He moves his right foot forward.

Providing Elaboration

Remember, your reader needs your help! He or she is reading your essay to learn how to do something. Make sure you have sufficiently **elaborated** your explanation—that you have added enough details about *how much, how long,* and *to what extent.* The strategy of "Exploding the Moment" can help.

Add Details by "Exploding the Moment"

Follow these steps to explode the moment:

1. Cut out several "bursts," or "explosions," from colored paper.
2. Begin writing your draft. As you draft, pause at the end of each paragraph or step.
3. Circle words in the paragraph or step that indicate specific things, actions, times, or amounts.
4. For each circled word, think of details that give more specific information, answering *what kind? which one? how many? how much? in what way?* and *to what extent?*
5. Write additional details on the colored-paper explosions, and lightly paste them to your draft.

When you have finished drafting, review your explosions. Decide which details to add to your draft.

Student Work
IN PROGRESS

Name: Jessica S. Lehman
Centre Learning Community
State College, PA

"Exploding the Moment"

Jessica decided that adding measurements and more descriptive details to her directions would help readers find the way to the bike path.

- A short distance past the beginning of the golf course, ride up the embankment on your right and turn onto the path that winds through the golf course. Beware of the golf carts that frequent the path. Follow the path until you get to the parking lot for Centre Dentistry.

About one hundred feet

grassy

gravel

a large building on the left

Revising

You've finished your first draft—but you're just getting started! Now it's time to improve your work. Start by reviewing your essay's structure.

Revising Your Overall Structure

Add an Introduction

Start your essay with a strong introduction. The following strategy will help:

▶ **REVISION STRATEGY**
Writing a Strong Lead

To ensure your introduction is strong enough, ask yourself:

- Does it clearly define the topic?

- Does it make readers want to keep reading?

- Does it make a transition into the steps of the process?

If you answered "no" to any of these questions, think about what your introduction needs before you can answer "yes." Use your ideas to write a stronger lead.

Student Work
IN PROGRESS

Name: Jessica S. Lehman
Centre Learning Community
State College, PA

Writing a Strong Lead
Jessica decided her introduction needed to do more to interest readers.

If you like to bicycle, you may be looking for a good place for a ride. The Pleasant Pedal Bike Path is a scenic route. Here are directions to get to it.

Jessica's first introduction accurately stated her topic. It also made a transition to her directions: "Here are directions to get to it." She decided, though, that it lacked the pizzazz needed to interest a reader.

Attention State College Area Bikers in the Holmes Foster Neighborhood area! Do you like paved paths? Do you like to ride where there is little traffic? Do you like to ride through scenic woodlands just blocks from downtown State College? If your answer to any of these questions is "yes," you'll love the Pleasant Pedal Bike Path. Getting there can be tricky, but if you follow these directions, you'll be pedaling along in no time at all.

Revising Your Paragraphs

Once you've improved your introduction and conclusion, examine the paragraphs in the body of your essay. Identify the purpose of each paragraph, and then add transition words and phrases to make your meaning clearer.

▶ **REVISION STRATEGY**
Identifying Steps, Stacks, Chains, and Balances

Reread each paragraph in your draft. Use the descriptions below to determine whether the paragraph is a "step," a "stack," a "chain," or a "balance." Then, consider adding the transition words listed in the description.

- **Steps** If the paragraph explains one or more steps for which time order is important, the sequence should be indicated. Use words such as *first, next,* and *finally.*

- **Stacks** If the paragraph explains how one part of a process adds to or contributes to another, point out the connection with words such as *and, furthermore,* and *for instance.*

- **Chains** If the paragraph shows the cause-and-effect relationship between steps, use words such as *so, because,* and *consequently.*

- **Balances** If the paragraph shows choice or contrast, use words or phrases such as *but, however, on the other hand,* and *rather.*

▶ **Critical Viewing** Based on details in this picture, what other things do bicyclists need to watch for besides landmarks? Does Jessica mention them in her introduction on the previous page? **[Deduce]**

- As you continue down Corl Street, one of the first landmarks is a railroad bridge you must ride under. You will notice that the landscape is changing from mostly houses to mostly fields. Soon you will see the Centre Hills Golf Course.
- About one hundred feet past the beginning of the golf course, ride up the grassy embankment on your right and turn onto the gravel path that winds through the golf course. Beware of the golf carts that frequent the path. Follow the path until you get to the parking lot for Centre Dentistry, a large building that you will see to your left.
- Ride through the parking lot until you see the sign for the Town Bike Path. Biking on this path, which runs alongside Atherton Street, you will pedal up a hill and past the historic Nittany Lion Inn across the street on your left. You will be riding alongside Atherton Street. Just before you get to the first intersection, there is a small dirt side path. Take this path, which branches out from the Town Bike Path and turns left. You will still be riding with the golf course on your left.
- When the path turns to pavement, you are well on your way. Soon you will see the sign for the Pleasant Pedal Bike Path.

You will be amazed at the beauty and tranquility of the Pleasant Pedal Bike Path. The flowers and trees are breathtaking in all seasons. Furthermore, you will be amused at the antics of the squirrels and birds that make the area surrounding the path their home. And don't forget, it took you only about 15 minutes to get to the bikeway.

Jessica uses the adverb phrase as you continue down Corl Street to make a transition from one step to the next.

At each step, Jessica refers to landmarks and other sights so that someone following her directions will easily know whether they are on track or not.

▶ **Critical Viewing** Find two of the landmarks in Jessica's essay on this map. Explain how this map might help you follow her directions. **[Analyze]**

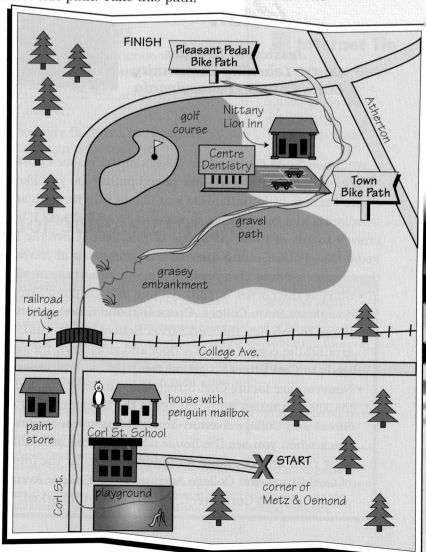

216 • How-to Essay

Connected Assignment
Problem-and-Solution Essay

A **problem-and-solution essay** explains a problem to readers. Then, it offers one or more solutions to the problem. Like a how-to essay, a problem-and-solution essay presents a set of steps to follow in order to achieve a result. An effective problem-and-solution essay

- clearly explains the problem.
- explains and defends the proposed solutions.

Prewriting Choose a topic by interviewing yourself. Ask yourself: What people, places, and organizations in my community are important to me? What problems do they face? If you have trouble finding answers, browse through local news sources for more information. Then, review your answers, and choose a problem that grabs your interest.

To gather details about your problem, use a cluster diagram like the one shown. Do research to find solutions, and collect the facts, expert opinions, and other evidence showing that the solutions will work.

Pay for racks by having bicyclists register.

Install bike racks.

Problem: There's no place to park a bike downtown.

Registered bikes would have stickers.

Drafting After gathering information, begin drafting. In your introduction, clearly state the problem and the solutions you will cover in your essay. In your body paragraphs, explain your solutions in a well-organized, step-by-step manner. Provide evidence to show that your solutions will work.

▼ Critical Viewing
What problem are these students helping to solve? **[Analyze]**

Revising and Editing Review your draft. First, check the sequence of steps: If the order is not clear, rearrange details so readers will be able to follow their sequence. Then, check the connections between ideas. If necessary, add transition words such as *next, then, after,* and *for this reason* to show readers how one step or idea connects with another. Finally, proofread your essay to eliminate errors in spelling, grammar, or punctuation.

Publishing and Presenting Consider submitting your completed essay to a school or local newspaper.

Spotlight on the Humanities

Organizing Information

Focus on Ballet: *Rodeo*

You can write a how-to essay that teaches someone how to find your favorite place. When a choreographer teaches performers dance steps, though, a big part of the how-to is a good piece of music!

Composer Aaron Copland (1900–1990) was asked to write the music for the ballet *Rodeo* in 1942. The choreographer (creator of dance) Agnes de Mille created the plot and the dance steps. Copland's music for *Rodeo* taught many toes how to tap. You can still hear one melody from Rodeo, "Hoedown," which is often played as background music for rodeos on television and in the movies.

Born in Brooklyn, New York, Copland was a landmark influence on American music. Many of his works, like *Rodeo*, incorporate melodies and musical styles from American folk music. He helped Americans take their own musical traditions more seriously.

Film Connection In 1949, Copland won an Academy Award for Best Dramatic Film Score for *The Heiress*. Directed by the legendary William Wyler, the film starred Olivia de Havilland, Montgomery Clift, and Sir Ralph Richardson. Based on a story by the famous author Henry James, *The Heiress* remains a classic American motion picture.

"How-to" Writing Activity: "How to Watch a Dance" Essay

Do some research into ballet or another form of dance performance. Take notes on what choreographers and dancers do to create a dance. Then, explain in a how-to essay what viewers should look for in this kind of dance. Present your essay to the class. If possible, show photographs or video clips to illustrate some of your points.

▲ **Critical Viewing** Judging from these scenes from *Rodeo*, how is this ballet different from other ballets with which you may be familiar? **[Draw Conclusions]**

Media and Technology Skills

Getting "Help" On-line

Activity: Identifying Available Forms of Help

There is a "how-to" built right into most computer programs, a how-to called "Help." When you need to know how to do something as you work in the program, you can call up Help for instructions. By using Help, you can learn as you work.

Learn About It

Balloon Help You can turn Balloon Help on or off through a program's menu bar. With Balloon Help on, a balloon appears whenever you roll your mouse pointer over an active feature on the screen, such as a button or a dialogue box. The balloon contains a brief explanation of the feature on which the pointer is resting.

On-line Manuals When you select Help from the menu bar, you call up an on-line manual for the program. Typically, the manual lists topics by category under Contents. You can also check an alphabetical list by selecting Index. The manual may also have a Search feature that allows you to search for a particular subject.

Other Kinds of Help

Software also comes with a printed manual containing detailed information on using the program.

Explore It Choose an application, such as a word-processing program, to which you have access. Explore the program and the program manual to determine what types of Help the program includes. List these types in a chart like the one shown here.

Computer Help
Built-in Help
• Balloon Help
• On-line manuals
Other Kinds of Help
• Read Me files
• Printed manuals

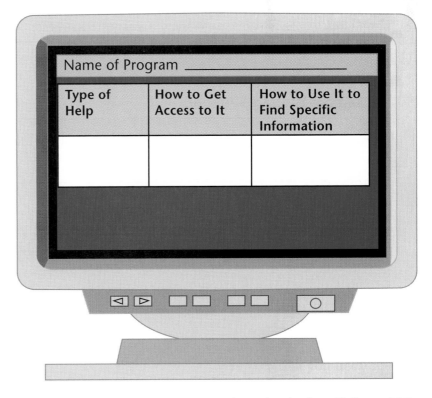

Name of Program _____

Type of Help	How to Get Access to It	How to Use It to Find Specific Information

Standardized Test Preparation Workshop

Responding to Expository Writing Prompts

Some expository writing prompts on standardized tests measure your ability to write a "how-to"—to present clear instructions and explanations in writing. You will be evaluated on your ability to do the following:

- choose a logical, consistent organization
- provide the appropriate amount of detail for your specific audience and purpose
- use complete sentences and follow the rules of grammar
- use correct spelling and punctuation.

The process of writing for a test, or for any other kind of writing, can be divided into stages. Plan to use a specific amount of time for prewriting, drafting, revising, and proofreading.

Following is an example of one type of expository writing prompt you might find on a standardized test. Use the suggestions on the following page to help you respond. The clocks next to each stage show a suggested plan for organizing your time.

Test Tip

When writing a how-to for a test, make sure you include every step necessary for the activity or process you are describing.

Sample Writing Situation

Imagine that you have been asked to help a group of kindergarteners learn how to tie their shoes.

As the basis for the lesson you will give, write a how-to for beginners on tying one's shoes.

Prewriting

Allow one fourth of your time for jotting down the details you want to include.

Whom Are You Instructing? Since you already know how to tie a shoe, you do it automatically. However, that is not the case for a child who is just learning how to do it. Before writing anything, consider how well a young child will understand your instructions.

Take Notes on Tying Your Own Shoe Draw a picture in your mind of how you tie your shoe. As you think about it, consider the many steps that are involved in the process. List these steps.

Drafting

Allow about half of your time for drafting.

Create an Outline Begin your instructional essay by creating a timeline of steps. (See the example on page 206.) Since you are assuming that you are teaching a child who has never tied a shoe before, start by instructing the reader to put his or her shoes on.

Follow Your Outline As you draft, turn your outlined list of steps into sentences. Make sure that each sentence describes only one step. Take care to describe the technique simply, clearly, and completely in language that a child can understand.

Revising, Editing, and Proofreading

Allow almost one fourth of your time for revising. Allow several minutes to give your work one final check for errors in spelling and punctuation.

Put It to the Test Follow your own instructions, step by step. Observe any points where you get confused. Rewrite instructions at these points to make them clearer.

Add Missing Information Review your outline, and fill in any points you may have left out of your draft. Make sure that you connect one step to the next using transition words such as *next*, *then*, and *finally*.

Make Corrections Proofread your draft. Make sure that each sentence is complete, that your words are spelled correctly, and your use of punctuation is correct. If you have made any mistakes, cross them out neatly with a single line.

Research
Research Report

Research in Everyday Life

Think about the facts you know about your friends and family: birthdays, names, ages; how your family first came to this country, or what happened when Grandpa moved North. These facts make up an important part of your picture of the world.

You probably picked up many of these facts here and there, at dinner or at a family gathering. Occasionally, though, you might go out of your way to find more information. Once you start asking questions, looking through photographs, or examining old papers, you are conducting research.

Research takes place when people search for facts on a subject. You can find the results of research in a magazine article about a scientific experiment or on a television program about a movie star. A good research writer helps others expand their picture of the world.

▲ **Critical Viewing**
What does this picture suggest about the difficulties of finding research sources? Name one library resource that can help with these difficulties. **[Infer]**

What Is a Research Report?

A **research report** presents facts about a subject. The writer of a research report gathers these facts from credible **sources,** such as public records, experiments, reference books, and newspapers, and so can verify their truth. By citing these sources, a research writer lets readers check the facts for themselves. A research report includes

- a well-defined topic with an overall focus.
- information gathered from a variety of sources.
- a clear method of organization.
- facts and details supporting each main point.
- accurate, complete citations identifying sources.

To see the criteria on which your research report may be graded or judged, see the Rubric for Self-Assessment on page 237.

Types of Research Reports

The research reports you write might include the following:

- **Biographical sketches** report events in the life of a notable person.
- **Reports of scientific experiments** present the method and results of experiments.
- **Library research reports** present key facts about a topic gathered from library resources.

Writers in **ACTION**

The ancient Greek thinker and scientist Aristotle (384–322 B.C) thought research had its roots in human nature. In one work, he wrote:

"All men desire by nature to know."

In another, he wrote:

"Every science and every inquiry, and similarly every activity and every pursuit, is thought to aim at some good."

For centuries, Aristotle's own works were essential references for scholars.

PREVIEW
Student Work
IN PROGRESS

Christopher Sullivan, a student at Northborough Middle School in Northborough, Massachusetts, wrote a research report about the ancient Roman Colosseum. In this chapter, you will see how he used featured strategies to choose a topic, to gather information, to elaborate, and to revise. You can read his completed report at the end of the chapter.

Model From Literature

Many articles in magazines and newspapers, such as this article by Susan McGrath (1955–), are actually a type of research report: They give facts based on outside research.

Reading Writing Connection

Reading Strategy: Question To get the most out of reading research reports, **ask questions.** For instance, McGrath says that the bad reputation of sharks is based on misunderstandings. As you read further, you might ask, "What ideas about sharks are untrue?" As you read, you will learn the answer.

▼ **Critical Viewing** What features of this shark make it look dangerous? **[Analyze]**

Sharks

Susan McGrath

They're big, they're ugly, they're vicious, and the only good one is a dead one. That's what some people say about sharks. Is their bad reputation based on truth? "No!" say the experts. But is time running out for sharks?

The blue shark looks like any typical shark: streamlined, powerful, bluish gray—more fighter jet than fish. But shark experts are quick to tell you that, among the 370 species of sharks, there simply isn't a "typical" shark (Springer 52–53).

A whale shark is as long as a school bus, while a cigar shark would fit neatly in a pencil case. A frilled shark looks like an eel with a lacy collar. A Pacific angel shark is as flat as a pancake. And the megamouth shark's gums glow in the dark.

Not mindless monsters, sharks are more intelligent than once thought (Allen, *Shadows* 24). They possess highly developed senses, also (Parker 90–91). And a chemical compound that seems to help sharks fight off infections may someday help doctors treat humans (Springer 90).

As for their killer reputation, very few shark species attack humans, and then only under certain conditions (Taylor 50–51). Sharks have more reason to be afraid of people than the reverse. Surprised? Just look at the numbers. Sharks kill between five and

In her introduction, McGrath uses a question-and-answer combination to present the focus of her research: Sharks are more endangered than dangerous.

ten people a year (Allen, *Almanac* 44–46). People kill more than 100 *million* sharks a year (Perrine 17). Placed snout to tail fins, that many sharks would circle the Earth five times. So many sharks have been killed that scientists fear some species may be wiped out.

Why are sharks on the hit list? They are fished for food—shark steak has taken the place of more expensive tuna and swordfish on many menus (*Sharks* 144–148). Also, in a cruel practice called "finning," sharks are hooked; their fins are sliced off; and the animals are tossed back into the sea to die. The sail-shaped fins are used to make shark-fin soup (Allen, *Shadows* 240). Other sharks are killed after being trapped in nets intended for other fish (*Reader's* 133–134).

When you figure that many sharks don't breed until they are more than 12 years old and that only about half of all sharks born survive (Allen, *Shadows* 17–23), you can see how overfishing could eventually threaten sharks with extinction.

The oceans would be a very different place without sharks. As predators at the top of the oceans' food chain, large sharks play an important role in keeping the population of other species in check. Part of their job is to weed out weak and injured animals, leaving the healthiest to reproduce.

Concerned scientists are working with government officials to put reasonable limits on shark fishing (Taylor 35). If they succeed, sharks will survive and maintain a useful place in the oceans of the world.

Works Cited

Allen, Thomas B. *Shadows in the Sea.* New York: Lyons & Burford Publishers, 1999.
———. *The Shark Almanac.* New York: The Lyons Press, 1999.
Parker, Steve and Jane. *The Encyclopedia of Sharks.* Buffalo, NY: Firefly Books, 1999.
Perrine, Doug. *Sharks.* Stillwater, MN: Voyageur Press, Inc., 1995.
Reader's Digest Explores Sharks. Pleasantville, NY: Reader's Digest, 1998.
Sharks, Silent Hunters of the Deep. Pleasantville, NY: Reader's Digest, 1986–1995.
Springer, Victor G., and Joy P. Gold. *Sharks in Question: The Smithsonian Answer Book.* Washington, DC: Smithsonian Institution Press, 1989.
Taylor, Leighton, ed. *Sharks and Rays: The Nature Company Guides.* New York: Time-Life Books, 1997.

Writing Application: Help Readers Answer Questions As you draft your report, answer the questions readers are likely to ask.

McGrath discusses her topics in logical order. First, she shows that the bad reputation of sharks is not deserved. Then, she shows that humans are actually dangerous to sharks!

The writer uses facts and explanations to support her point that people are dangerous to sharks. She gives citations for each source she uses for this information.

McGrath supplies a complete list of the references she cites for her facts.

LITERATURE

To read another example of research writing, read *Lincoln: A Photobiography* by Russell Freedman. You can find "A Backwoods Boy," an excerpt from this book, in *Prentice Hall Literature: Timeless Voices, Timeless Themes,* Copper.

11.2 *Prewriting*

Choosing Your Topic

For a research report, you can choose almost any topic that interests you, as long as you can locate information about it. The following strategies can help you select a topic:

Strategies for Generating a Topic

1. **Browsing** Browse through reference books at the library—for example, a volume from an encyclopedia set, an almanac, or an atlas. Jot down each interesting person, place, object, or event that you come across. Then, scan your notes, and circle any words or phrases that suggest an interesting topic. Do a little more reading on each one, and then choose your topic from among them.

2. **Self-Interview** Create a chart like the one below, and answer the questions shown. Circle words and draw lines to show connections between items on your list. Choose a topic from among these linked items.

Try it out! Use the interactive Self-Interview in **Section 11.2,** on-line or on CD-ROM.

Student Work
IN PROGRESS

Name: *Christopher Sullivan*
Northborough Middle School
Northborough, MA

Conducting a Self-Interview

Christopher conducted a self-interview to identify people, places, and things in which he was interested. He selected the Colosseum when he remembered a video on ancient Rome shown to the class by his history teacher, Mr. Sanchez.

People	Places	Things	Events
• What interesting people do I know or have I heard about?	• What interesting places have I been to or have I heard about?	• What interesting things do I know about or have I seen?	• What interesting events have happened to me or have I heard about?
Randy Mr. Sanchez Ayla Paul	Niagara Falls library playground ancient Rome	soccer dolphins Roman myths aquarium	Thanksgiving Day parade Migraine concert debate in Social Studies

TOPIC BANK

If you're having trouble finding a topic, consider the following possibilities:

1. **Biographical Sketch** Select a person you admire, such as an athlete, a political figure, an artist, an explorer, or an inventor. Focus on one of the person's memorable achievements. Do research, and write a report explaining how the person was able to reach that achievement.

2. **Research Report on an Animal's Habitat** Choose an animal that interests you. Research the animal's characteristics and its habitat: the climate, vegetation, and other species that are present where the animal lives. Write a report explaining how the animal uses its habitat to survive.

Responding to Fine Art

3. Jot down a few notes about the painting on this page. What topics about technology, the environment, or life in the future does the painting suggest to you? Choose a topic from your notes, and write a report on it.

New Man at the New Crossroads, Moses Ros

Responding to Literature

4. Read "The Wounded Wolf," a short story by Jean Craighead George. Think about what the story suggests about the life of a wolf. Then, write a report on the subject, comparing the results of your research with George's story. You can find "The Wounded Wolf" in *Prentice Hall Literature: Timeless Voices, Timeless Themes,* Copper.

☑ Cooperative Writing Opportunity

5. **Effects of Pollution** In a group, do research on the forms of pollution. Then, assign each group member one type of pollution on which to report. Each report should discuss the causes and effects of the pollution and the ways it might be stopped. Members should review one another's work and suggest improvements. Illustrate the reports with charts, graphs, and drawings, and organize them in a binder.

Narrowing Your Topic

Some topics are broader than others. For instance, "The Way Reptiles Live" is a broad topic. It includes everything from how pythons hunt to why lizards lose their tails. It might take years to write a report on this topic! The topic "How Horned Toads Survive in the Desert" is narrow. It covers a clearly limited set of facts.

To make sure that you cover your topic fully in your report, narrow your topic by "questioning" it.

▲ **Critical Viewing**
If you were writing a paper about reptiles for this audience, what subtopics might you include? **[Analyze]**

Question Your Topic

Enter your topic in the top box of a web like the one below. Then, ask yourself the following questions:

- What different kinds of things does my topic include?
- What events are included in my topic?
- What places are included in my topic?
- Who is involved in my topic?

For each answer, enter an item in the second row of boxes in your web. Circle the most interesting of these subtopics. For each, consider whether it is narrow enough to make a good topic. If it isn't, repeat these steps for each subtopic until you reach a narrow topic.

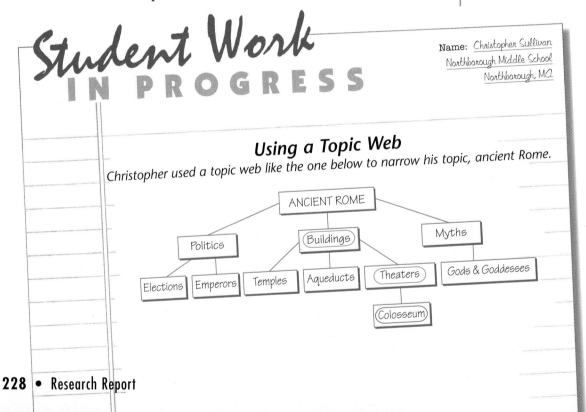

Student Work
IN PROGRESS

Name: *Christopher Sullivan*
Northborough Middle School
Northborough, MA

Using a Topic Web

Christopher used a topic web like the one below to narrow his topic, ancient Rome.

ANCIENT ROME — Politics (Elections, Emperors), Buildings (Temples, Aqueducts, Theaters, Colosseum), Myths (Gods & Goddesses)

Considering Your Audience and Purpose

The **purpose** of any research report is to clearly present facts on a topic. A report may be written for different groups of readers, or **audiences.** Your audience's background and interest in your topic will determine how much you say about each detail, as this chart suggests:

Audience:	Science teacher	A reader's club	Young children
Background in Subject:	Good	Fair	Little
Level of Detail:	Give detailed explanations of specialized facts (for example, the feeding habits of horned toads).	Give the most interesting facts (for example, the fact that horned toads squirt blood) and interesting explanations.	Thoroughly explain basic ideas (for example, the fact that horned toads are reptiles).

Gathering Details

Gather details from several different sources. By doing so, you make sure that your report will be accurate and balanced.

Take Notes

When you find information related to your topic, take notes on index cards. (You can also photocopy pages from sources, as long as you are using them just for research. Highlight the material you use.) Follow these guidelines for note taking:

- Use one card for each note. Give this card a key word.

- Double-check the spelling of names and technical terms.

- Use quotation marks when you copy words from a source.

- For each note, record the title of the book or article and the page number, or the name of the Web site or interviewee.

- Create a source card for each resource, listing the author, the title, the publisher, and the place and date of publication.

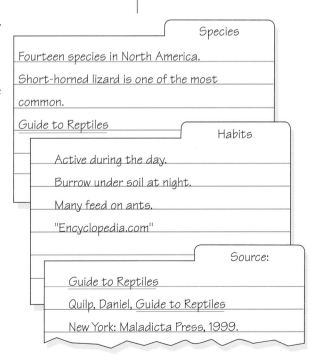

Species

Fourteen species in North America.

Short-horned lizard is one of the most common.

Guide to Reptiles

Habits

Active during the day.

Burrow under soil at night.

Many feed on ants.

"Encyclopedia.com"

Source:

Guide to Reptiles

Quilp, Daniel, Guide to Reptiles

New York: Maladicta Press, 1999.

Drafting

Shaping Your Writing

When you think you have gathered enough information, decide how to organize your report.

Make an Outline

Choosing a Method of Organization Group your note cards by category. For instance, you might put all cards on what horned lizards eat in one group. You might put all cards on their habitats in another group. When you have finished, choose an organization that fits your topic.

- **Chronological order** organizes details according to their sequence in time. You might use chronological order when writing a report on a historical event.

- **Ordering by type** deals with each kind of thing included in your topic, discussing each in turn. It works well when your main ideas are of equal importance. For a report on the different kinds of horned lizards, for example, you might first discuss the desert horned lizard, then the regal horned lizard, and so on.

Next, make an outline following the order you have chosen. You can choose one of two ways of making an outline:

Making a Sentence Outline Jot down a sentence about each main idea in your report. Leave space between sentences. Then, write supporting details under each main idea.

Making a Formal Outline List each major part of your topic. Use Roman numerals (I, II, III) to number your most important points. Under each Roman numeral, list supporting details, labeling them with capital letters (A, B, C).

▼ **Critical Viewing** Using details from this photograph, suggest headings for an outline of a report about the appearance of horned lizards. **[Analyze]**

Horned Toads
- I. Introduction
- II. Horned toads are reptiles
  - A. What is a reptile?
  - B. Differences from other reptiles
- III. Where do horned toads live?

Providing Elaboration

After you have mapped out the organization of your report, you are ready to start drafting. As you write, don't forget about your reader. Clearly explain everything your reader needs to know. Use the strategy below to ensure that you have included enough information.

Write in Layers

As you draft, leave space between sentences. At the end of each paragraph, pause and review your work. Ask yourself:

- Which words name people, things, or events about which I need to give a reader more information?
- Which words might confuse a reader?

Circle words that fit these descriptions. Then, using the space between sentences, add details that will give a more complete picture or that will keep a reader from growing confused.

Research Tip

As you draft, you may discover that you are missing details. Note such spots on your draft with sticky notes. Write your questions about missing information on note cards, do research to answer them, and add the information to your draft.

Student Work IN PROGRESS

Name: *Christopher Sullivan*
Northborough Middle School
Northborough, MA

Using Layers

Christopher wrote about the ancient Roman Colosseum. When he reviewed this paragraph, he realized that he could explain more about how the Colosseum was built. He also saw that unfamiliar names from ancient history could distract readers. He wrote a little bit more about each circled word.

Construction of the Colosseum started around A.D. 75 under the emperor Vespasian. The emperor ordered that a lake located between three of Rome's hills be drained for the project. The theater was named the Flavian Amphitheater, *in honor of Vespasian's family, the Flavians* Later, however, the building acquired its more familiar name, Colosseum, after a colossal statue of Nero, *an earlier emperor,* which stood nearby.

Revising

Revising Your Overall Structure

Analyze Your Organization

Now that you have completed a first draft, look over your report to analyze the organization of details.

▶ **REVISION STRATEGY**
Matching Your Draft to Your Outline

As you read through your report, stop at the end of each paragraph, and refer to your outline. Mark each paragraph with the Roman numeral and capital letter on your outline that designate the subject of the paragraph.

For example, the following might be part of your outline:

I. Horned toads
    A. Different habitats
    B. Different diets

In this case, you should mark a paragraph about the habitat of the desert horned toad "I.A." If your second paragraph explains that desert horned toads eat mainly ants, mark it "I.B." If your third paragraph explains that desert horned toads live in the southwestern United States, mark it "I.A.," and so on.

When you have finished labeling each paragraph, review your labels. Ask yourself the following questions:

- Are all the paragraphs that are labeled with the same Roman numeral-capital letter combination next to one another? If not, would the report make better sense if they were?

- Does the sequence of Roman numerals and capital letters in the report match the sequence on your outline? If not, is the change an improvement? Why or why not?

Reorganize the paragraphs in your draft to achieve the most effective organization.

✐ **Collaborative Writing Tip**

Exchange drafts with a classmate. Check off paragraphs that are placed in a good order. Mark those that seem out of order with a red question mark.

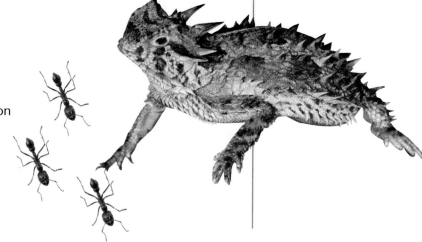

▶ **Critical Viewing** What point on the outline shown on this page does this photograph illustrate? **[Analyze]**

Revising Your Paragraphs

Check Your Paragraph Structure

In a report, most paragraphs should include the following:

- a **topic** sentence **(T)**, stating the main idea
- a **restatement (R)** of the main idea in the topic sentence
- an **illustration (I)**, example, or explanation of the main idea

An effective topical paragraph uses at least one sentence of each kind. The order in which you organize them may vary.

EXAMPLE: **T** Some horned lizards have risky feeding habits.

R While feeding, their body temperature can reach dangerous levels.

I They spend hours under the broiling hot desert sun waiting for or feeding on ants.

Use the following strategy to evaluate paragraph structure.

▶ **REVISION STRATEGY**
Marking Your Paragraph Patterns

Label each of your sentences a *T*, an *R*, or an *I*. Review your draft. If you find a group of *I*'s, make sure there is a *T* they support. If you find a *T* by itself, add an *I* sentence.

Student Work
IN PROGRESS

Name: *Christopher Sullivan*
Northborough Middle School
Northborough, MA

Analyzing Paragraph Patterns
Christopher analyzed paragraph patterns in his paper on the ancient Roman Colosseum. He realized that he needed to revise this paragraph.

The wild animal hunts in the Colosseum were elaborate and often extremely cruel shows. Spectators would occasionally get sick from the bloody sight.

Sometimes, special scenery was built to add to the "realism" of the event. And the animals were not released into the arena any old way; they arrived through hand-operated trapdoors leading from underground cages. The animals either fought each other or were encouraged to attack unarmed slaves or criminals.

T
R

I

I

I

Christopher noticed that his paragraph contained only "illustrations" (I)—details about a main idea—so he added a topic sentence (T) and a restatement (R) of the main idea of the paragraph.

Revising Your Sentences

Vary Your Sentence Structure

"He did this . . . ." "He did that . . . ." No one likes to read one short, choppy sentence after another. Choppy writing often comes from stating each piece of information in its own sentence. Use the following strategy to combine sentences.

▶ **REVISION STRATEGY**
Adding to the Main Action in a Cluster

Select three paragraphs in your draft. In each, circle clusters of short sentences. In each cluster, find a verb that simply adds to the information about a person, a thing, or an event in another sentence. Use this verb to create a participial phrase (see the information in the box below). Add this phrase to the sentence about which it provides more information.

SHORT SENTENCES: The lizard ran away. It *shed* its tail first.

COMBINED: *Shedding* its tail, the lizard ran away.

Get instant help! For feedback on varying sentence structure, use the Sentence Length and Sentence Openers Variety revision checkers, accessible from the menu bar, on-line or on CD-ROM.

Grammar in Your Writing
Participial Phrases

A **participle** is a form of a verb that acts as an adjective. A present participle is the *-ing* form of a verb. A past participle is the past form of the verb, often ending in *-ed* or *-d.* A **participial phrase** combines a present or past participle with other words and phrases. The entire phrase acts as an adjective. It answers the questions *What kind? Which one? How many?* or *How much?* about something in a sentence.

By using participial phrases, you can combine sentences, as in these examples:

SHORT SENTENCES: The lizard crawled slowly. She vanished into her burrow.
COMBINED: Crawling slowly, the lizard vanished into her burrow.

SHORT SENTENCES: He found a reptile egg. It was buried in the desert.
COMBINED: He found a reptile egg buried in the desert.

Find It in Your Reading Find one participial phrase in "Sharks" by Susan McGrath on page 224. Explain what information it adds to the main action or point of the sentence.

Find It in Your Writing Identify two participial phrases that you have used in your research report. If you can't find two examples, find a place where you can combine two short sentences using a participial phrase.

To learn more about combining sentences, see Chapter 21.

Revising Your Word Choice

While writing your research report, you may have found new words, including technical terms such as *reticulated* ("marked with net-like patterns"). Code such terms, and consider adding their definitions to help readers understand their meaning.

▶ **REVISION STRATEGY**
Color-Coding Technical Terms

Highlight technical terms in your report. Check each term in a dictionary and in the source where you found it to make sure that you understand its use. Then, add a definition at the first place each new term appears in your draft.

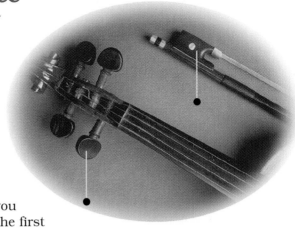

▲ **Critical Viewing**
In what source might you find the name of the parts indicated? **[Apply]**

Student Work
IN PROGRESS

Name: *Christopher Sullivan*
Northborough Middle School
Northborough, MA

Defining Technical Terms

Christopher highlighted a few technical terms. He checked their meanings in his notes and in a dictionary, and then added their definitions.

Gladiators, *the fighters trained for these shows,* were usually either slaves or prisoners.
A gladiator's weapons included tridents *(three-pronged spears, like giant forks)* and swords. The men with tridents were also equipped with nets.

Peer Review
"Say Back"

Join a group of three or four other classmates. Read your report aloud twice to the group. During the second reading, listeners should jot down strong points in your report and points about which they want to know more. Listeners should then "say back" these reactions to you. Consider the group's comments as you make your final revisions.

Focusing on Citations

Cite sources for quotations, facts, and ideas that are not your own.

Internal Citations An internal citation appears in parentheses directly after the information you cited. It includes the author's last name and the page number on which the information appears.

> Although his writing could be savage and sarcastic, Jonathan Swift "was loved throughout Ireland as a defender of the underprivileged" (Sporre 379).

Works Cited List Provide full information about your sources in an alphabetical "Works Cited" list at the end of your report. The following is an example of the correct form:

> Sporre, Dennis J. *The Literary Spirit.* Englewood Cliffs, NJ: Prentice-Hall, 1988.

For each work cited, make sure that you write the author's last name first. Use a period after the author's name, after the title of the work, and at the end of the listing. Use a colon between the place of publication and the publisher. Use a comma between the publisher and the year of publication.

Learn More

For a full explanation of the form for citations, see the section on Citing Sources and Preparing Manuscript, page 724.

Grammar in Your Writing

Quotation Marks and Underlining With Titles of Works

Follow these guidelines for presenting the title of a work in your research report:

Underline (or italicize) the titles of long written works and the titles of periodicals. Also, underline or italicize the titles of movies, television series, and works of music and art.

Use quotation marks around the titles of short written works and Internet sites.

Find It in Your Reading Read the Works Cited list on page 225. Notice how italics are used for the titles of works.

Find It in Your Writing Review your essay to see whether you have used underlining and quotation marks correctly for the titles of works.

To learn more about the form for titles, see Chapters 26 and 27.

11.6 Publishing and Presenting

Building Your Portfolio

Consider the following ways to publish and present your report:

1. **Present a Mini-lesson** Use your report as the basis for a mini-lesson on your topic. Plan a lesson that includes an activity related to the topic. Present your lesson to a group of classmates.

2. **Conduct a Round-Table Discussion** Form a group with others who have researched similar topics—for example, animals, music, or athletes. Each member should present his or her report. After each presentation, other members should ask questions, make comments, and compare the subjects.

Reflecting on Your Writing

Jot down a few notes on your experience writing a research report. To begin, you might answer the following questions:

- What was the most interesting thing you learned about your topic?
- Which strategy for prewriting, drafting, revising, or editing might you recommend to a friend?

 **Internet Tip**

To see research reports scored with this rubric, go on-line: PHSchool.com Enter Web Code: eak-6001

Rubric for Self-Assessment

Use the following criteria to evaluate your research report:

	Score 4	Score 3	Score 2	Score 1
Audience and Purpose	Focuses on a clearly stated topic, starting from a well-framed question; gives complete citations	Focuses on a clearly stated topic; gives citations	Focuses mainly on the chosen topic; gives some citations	Presents information without a clear focus; few or no citations
Organization	Presents information in logical order, emphasizing details of central importance	Presents information in logical order	Presents information logically, but organization is poor in places	Presents information in a scattered, disorganized manner
Elaboration	Draws clear conclusions from information gathered from multiple sources	Draws conclusions from information gathered from multiple sources	Explains and interprets some information	Presents information with little or no interpretation or synthesis
Use of Language	Shows overall clarity and fluency; contains few mechanical errors	Shows good sentence variety; contains some errors in spelling, punctuation, or usage	Uses awkward or overly simple sentence structures; contains many mechanical errors	Contains incomplete thoughts and mechanical errors that make the writing confusing

Student Work
IN PROGRESS

FINAL DRAFT

The Ancient Roman Colosseum

Christopher R. Sullivan
Northborough Middle School
Northborough, Massachusetts

The Colosseum, which may still be seen today in Rome, is one of the most remarkable entertainment centers ever built. Its history, the plan of the building, and the types of shows that were held there are all fascinating subjects.

Construction of the Colosseum started around A.D. 75 under the emperor Vespasian. The emperor ordered that a lake located between three of Rome's hills be drained for the project. The theater was named the Flavian Amphitheater in honor of Vespasian's

▲ **Critical Viewing**
What facts about the ancient Romans make the feat of building the Colosseum especially impressive? **[Evaluate]**

Christopher uses the first paragraph to introduce his research topic. He explains his main idea for the paper. He also gives the subtopics into which his report is organized.

family, the Flavians. Later, however, the building acquired its more familiar name, Colosseum, after a colossal statue of Nero, an earlier emperor, which stood nearby (Nardo 27–29).

Construction of this enormous building lasted for five years. The opening was celebrated with one hundred days of games, in which thousands of animals and numerous fighters were killed. The original spectators must have marveled at the building's dimensions. The outer walls were 157 feet high, and the central arena measured 290 feet by 180 feet (Quennell 36).

The seating plan was like the seating plan of a modern sports stadium. Extending all the way around the building, eighty entrances led to tiers of seats and standing areas. Each entrance was marked with a Roman numeral. The tickets or tokens that spectators needed for admission were probably marked with this section number (Macdonald 28–29).

Although admission to the Colosseum was free, rich, important people got to sit in the best seats. For example, the emperor had a personal entrance that led directly to his seat. Public officials and wealthy people occupied the lower rows of seats. The lower classes had to climb farther up to reach their seats. Finally, at the roof level were all the women. Overall, the Colosseum had a capacity of nearly 50,000 people (Mann 26).

The arena itself was the center of the stadium. It was made of wood and covered with sand. The most popular shows held there were gladiator fights and wild animal hunts (Nardo 38).

Gladiators, the fighters trained for these shows, were usually either slaves or prisoners. A gladiator's weapons included tridents (three-pronged spears, like giant forks) and swords. The men with tridents were also equipped with nets. They tried to cover and knock down the opposition. Fighters with swords wore armor and carried a shield (Connolly 212–215). Some fights ended with one gladiator's death. In cases of injury, however, the emperor, or sometimes the crowd, would decide whether the wounded gladiator would live or die. Some historians say that, contrary to popular belief, the crowd pointed their thumbs at their chests to vote "kill" and used a thumbs-down sign to vote "drop the sword" or "spare" (Nardo 63).

The wild animal hunts in the Colosseum were elaborate and often extremely cruel shows. Spectators would occasionally get sick from the bloody sight. Sometimes, special scenery was built to add to the "realism" of the event. And the animals were not released into

Notice that Christopher uses organization by type in his report, grouping related ideas together.

Christopher supports his point about the size of the Colosseum with precise measurements gathered during research.

Throughout his report, Christopher uses internal citations to refer to the sources of particular facts.

Christopher begins the third main section of the report, in which he discusses the types of shows held in the Colosseum.

Christopher knows readers may doubt his account of "thumbs down" because they have heard another popular but false account. He gives a citation so they can check the facts themselves.

◀ **Critical Viewing** Why might ancient Roman emperors have built buildings and had sculptures made of themselves? **[Hypothesize]**

▲ **Critical Viewing** This photograph shows a section of an ancient Roman mosaic (a picture made from small stone tiles). Judging from the mosaic, how fair were fights between gladiators? **[Evaluate]**

the arena any old way; they arrived through hand-operated trap-doors leading from underground cages. The animals either fought each other or were encouraged to attack unarmed slaves or criminals (Macdonald 31–33).

The Colosseum was used for centuries, but the violent shows staged there became less popular after Rome adopted Christianity as the official religion in the fourth century. For nearly two thousand years, the building has survived many natural disasters, including earthquakes and lightning strikes. The Colosseum still stands today as one of the most dramatic monuments of ancient Roman culture (Quennell 68–69).

In the last paragraph of the report, Christopher concludes with a sentence restating the main idea of the report as a whole.

At the end of his report, Christopher provides a complete list of the works he has cited. He uses the standard format for citing works.

Works Cited

Connolly, Peter, and Hazel Dodge. *The Ancient City*. New York: Oxford University Press, 1998.

Macdonald, Fiona, and Mark Bergin. *The Roman Colosseum*. New York: Peter Bedrick Books, 1996.

Mann, Elizabeth. *The Roman Colosseum*. New York: Mikaya Press, 1998.

Nardo, Don. *The Roman Colosseum*. San Diego: Lucent Books, Inc., 1998.

Quennell, Peter. *The Colosseum*. New York: Newsweek, 1971.

240 • **Research Report**

Connected Assignment *I-Search Report*

An **I-search report** is a personal exploration of a topic that especially interests you. It includes

- a topic you want to know more about, perhaps in order to do something.
- the story of why you are interested in the topic.
- the story of how you researched the topic.
- a report of what you learned.
- the use of the pronoun *I* to tell your story.

An I-search report is *similar* to a research report in that you use outside sources to gather information. It is *different* because it includes your own experiences. Write an I-search report using these suggestions:

Prewriting Choose a topic in which you have a real interest. For instance, you might be interested in building a model car or helping to clean up a local park. After choosing a topic,

- list the questions to which you want answers.
- choose those questions in which your interest is strong and to which you will be able to find answers.

▲ **Critical Viewing** This boy is doing research by phone. Cite details from the picture showing that he is well prepared. **[Analyze]**

- enter your questions in the "W" column of a K-W-L chart like the one shown.
- for each item in this column, list a possible source (a book, magazine, person, and so on) for the answer.
- fill in the chart as you gather details about your topic.

Know	**W**ant to Know	**L**earned
The park is a mess! I can't even play Frisbee there without stepping on broken glass.	Who is supposed to clean it up? (source: I can look in the phonebook for the Parks Department number) Can volunteers help? (source: the Parks Department, or maybe the mayor's office)	The town can only afford two part-time workers to clean up.

Take separate notes on your research experiences.

Drafting Organize your details using an outline. Follow your outline as you draft. For each part of your story, explain exactly what you did and learned.

Revising and Editing Review your draft. Make sure that you present events and ideas in a clear sequence. Add transitions, such as *first, next,* and *for that reason,* to aid readers.

Publishing and Presenting After revising your I-Search report, consider posting it on a school Web site.

Spotlight on the Humanities

Select Visuals to Extend Meaning

Focus on Film: *The African Queen*

You might not guess it, but even an adventure-comedy film may be the result of research. When a film involves historical events, the writers, directors, costume makers, and scenery designers must do research into the period. They use this research to get story ideas and to portray details from the period accurately.

The *African Queen* is one such adventure-comedy. The film is set in Africa at the beginning of World War I. The creators of the film used research into the situation of the time to create a suspenseful story.

Released in 1951 and starring the legendary Humphrey Bogart (1899–1957) and Katharine Hepburn (1909–   ), *The African Queen* is a classic. Bogart won an Academy Award for his portrayal of Charlie Allnut, a tough steamboat captain, who meets the prim and proper Rose Sayer as war is brewing in Central Africa. Directed by John Huston (1906–1987), the exploits of this mismatched pair on the Ulonga-Bora River create a perfect mixture of comedy and adventure.

Literature Connection The British novelist C. S. Forester (1899–1966) wrote the novel *The African Queen*. Born in Africa, Forester grew up in London. He became famous for his eleven-book adventure series featuring Horatio Hornblower, a heroic naval officer.

Theater Connection Director John Huston's father was the stage actor Walter Huston (1884–1950). By 1905, Walter Huston was a successful vaudeville performer. (*Vaudeville* is a form of theater featuring dance, song, and comedy.) In 1924, Walter Huston showed the serious side of his acting ability, starring in Eugene O'Neill's play *Desire Under the Elms*.

Research Writing Activity: Picture Research on Africa

Choose a Central African nation. Imagine that you are doing research for a movie, and select visuals that give an accurate idea of the climate, landscapes, clothing, foods, and the important industries or trades of the country. Show different settings, such as farms and cities.

▲ **Critical Viewing** Using details from this movie still, explain how well the characters of Charlie Allnut and Rose Sayer got along at first in *The African Queen.* **[Draw Conclusions]**

Media and Technology Skills

Using Available Technology for Research

Activity: Finding On-line Sources

When you turn on a computer, you open the door to a world of information. You can use this information as you do research for reports or for your own interests.

Learn About It The **Internet** is a a series of computers linked together across the world. A computer in this network can make information available to any user who logs on to the Internet. To log on and access information, you can use any computer with a Web browser and a connection to the Internet.

Web Sites A **Web site** is a set of connected images, words, and other information stored on a computer. People create Web sites on all sorts of subjects, from tarantulas to tooth decay.

Finding Specific Information You can travel to a particular Web site by typing in its URL (Uniform Resource Locator) address in your Web browser. Many times, though, you will not know of a specific Web site on your topic. To find one, use a search engine (click the "Search" button on your browser to call one up).

Using a Search Engine Enter a search term in the "Search" field of the engine and click "Search." The engine will then list Web pages containing words matching your search term. You are most likely to find the information you need on the pages listed first.

Choosing Good Search Terms A computer will not "know what you mean" if you misspell a term. Spell all search terms correctly. To start, use the most specific terms you can. For instance, *snakes* will bring up too many hits. Use a more specific term, such as *pythons*.

Apply It Come up with three specific questions on different topics. Use three different search engines to answer these questions. Record your results in a chart like the one shown. Then, use your notes to write a brief paragraph describing your Internet experience.

> ### Tips for Using a Search Engine
>
> **Use Quotation Marks**
> If you are searching for information on a certain person or brand name, put quotation marks around your search term. The engine will focus on pages including exactly that name.
>
> **Use the Plus Sign**
> To cut down on the number of irrelevant "hits" in your search results, some search engines let you use the plus sign in your search term. For instance, if you want only information on birds in Africa, use "birds +Africa" as your search term. (Consult Help for more information on the engine you are using.)

Search Engine I Used	My Question	Search Terms I Used	First Five Sites I Found	Sites Answering Question

Standardized Test Preparation Workshop

Revising and Editing

When writing a research report, you must strive to present information clearly. Revising your report to give it a strong, consistent organization is one key to clear writing. On a standardized test, you may be asked questions that test your ability to revise and edit a passage. The sample test item below shows one format for such questions.

Test Tip

When answering revising and editing questions, place each choice in the context of the passage before choosing an answer.

Sample Test Item

Read the passage below. Then, answer the multiple-choice question that follows.

1 The best way to protect against infectious
2 disease is to keep your body healthy. You
3 must eat nutritious food, as well as get
4 plenty of rest, fluids, and exercise. You can
5 also protect yourself by washing your
6 hands often and by not sharing eating
7 utensils or drink containers. You should
8 also make sure that you have all recom-
9 mended vaccinations. Storing food prop-
10 erly, keeping kitchen equipment and
11 surfaces clean, and cooking meats well
12 can prevent food poisoning.

1. Which of these sentences would make the **BEST** topic sentence for this paragraph?

   A   Good health and a little caution are the best defense against disease.

   B   Keeping your body healthy is the only real way to protect yourself from disease.

   C   Food poisoning is a cause of disease.

   D   Cleanliness is important to good health.

Answer and Explanation

The correct answer is *A*. *B* does not make a good topic sentence for the paragraph because the paragraph lists other steps for protecting yourself from disease in addition to keeping your body healthy. *C* does not make a good topic sentence because the main subject of the paragraph is what prevents disease, not what causes it. *D* does not make a good topic sentence because cleanliness is just one way to prevent infectious disease, and the paragraph talks about several preventive measures. *A* is the best choice because each sentence in the paragraph helps build support for this statement.

▶ **Practice** **Directions:** Read the following passage. Then, answer the questions below, choosing the letter of the best answer.

1 Organisms may be composed of only
2 one cell or of many cells. Unicellular,
3 or single-celled, organisms include
4 bacteria, the most numerous organ-
5 isms on Earth. A bacterial cell carried
6 out all of the functions necessary for
7 the organism to stay alive.
8   Multicellular organisms are com-
9 posed of many cells. The cells of many
10 multicellular organisms are specialized
11 to do certain tasks. For example, you
12 are made of trillions of cells.
13 Specialized cells in your body such as
14 muscle and nerve cells work together to
15 keep you functioning. Nerve cells carry
16 messages from your surroundings to
17 your brain. Other nerve cells then
18 carry messages to your muscle cells,
19 making your body move.

1 What is the **BEST** change, if any, to make to the sentence in lines 5–7 (*"A . . . alive."*)?
  A Change *A bacterial cell* to **It**
  B Change *carried* to **carries**
  C Change *carried* to **carry**
  D Make no change.

2 Which of the following sentences would **BEST** fit after the sentence in lines 5–7 (*"A . . . alive."*)?
  F These functions include respiration and excretion.
  G In the twentieth century, scientists began studying bacteria for clues about how life began and maintains itself.
  H Bacteria are also classified by their shape.
  J The word *organism* is used to describe all living things.

3 What is the **BEST** change, if any, to make in the middle of the sentence in lines 8–9 (*"Multicellular . . . cells."*)?
  A Change *are composed of* to **are found in**
  B Change *are composed of* to **are contained in**
  C Delete *are composed of*
  D Make no change.

4 Which of these sentences would **BEST** fit the ideas in lines 9–11 (*"The . . . tasks."*)?
  F Your brain controls muscle movement.
  G Most single-cell organisms are not visible without the aid of a microscope.
  H Humans are considered multicellular organisms.
  J Multicellular organisms are more complex than single-cell organisms.

5 Which is the **BEST** change, if any, that should be made to the sentence in lines 13–15 (*"Specialized . . . functioning"*)?
  A Delete *such as muscle and nerve cells*
  B Change *such as muscle and nerve cells* to *. . .,* **such as muscle and nerve cells,**
  C Change *such as muscle and nerve* cells to **such as muscle-nerve cells**
  D Make no change.

6 Which of the following sentences would **BEST** conclude the passage?
  F From the simplest forms of life to the most complex, cells have many varied roles.
  G Organisms need nerves to survive.
  H Only the most complex organisms can use a large number of cells.
  J Large numbers of specialized cells are the key to life as we understand it.

Response to Literature

Responding to Literature in Everyday Life

You can spend hours by yourself reading a good book. If you enjoyed it, the first thing you want to do is tell someone else about it: "The story was great—full of hair-raising suspense!" When you explain your reaction to a novel, play, short story, or poem, you are giving a **response to literature.** Book reviews and letters to authors are written responses to literature.

Writing down a response to literature takes a little more work than talking with a friend. Once you write about a work, however, more and more of it percolates through your brain. You will see more, and appreciate more, in it than before. To enrich your reading experiences, develop your skills writing a response to literature.

▲ **Critical Viewing**
What might this girl tell someone to encourage him or her to read the book she is enjoying? **[Apply]**

What Is a Response to Literature?

A **response to literature** expresses the writer's feelings and thoughts about a book, short story, essay, article, or poem. Using examples from the work, it explains why the writer reacted to the work as he or she did. The elements of a good response include

- a strong, interesting focus on some aspect of a novel, short story, drama, or poem.
- a clear organization.
- supporting details for each main idea.
- a summary of important features of the work.
- the writer's feelings about or judgment of the work.

To learn the criteria on which your response may be graded or judged, see the Rubric for Self-Assessment on page 264.

Types of Response to Literature

You might write one of the following types of response to literature:

- **Book reviews** give readers an impression of a book, encouraging them either to read it or to avoid reading it.
- **Letters to an author** let a writer know what a reader found enjoyable or disappointing in the writer's work.
- **Comparisons of works** highlight the features of two or more works by comparing them.

Writers in ACTION

Henry Wadsworth Longfellow (1807–1882), one of the most famous American poets of his day, thought that writers wish for a certain kind of response to their work:

"What a writer asks of his reader is not so much to like as to listen."

PREVIEW Student Work IN PROGRESS

Erin Macdonald Roski, a student at Madison Middle School in Oceanside, California, wrote a response to a book retelling the story of the Trojan War. In this chapter, you can follow the strategies she used to choose a topic, draft, and revise her work. The final draft of her essay appears at the end of the chapter.

Revising Your Sentences

Combine Sentences for Variety

In a first draft, you may have used many short sentences in your rush to get your ideas down. Too many short sentences in a row, though, create a monotonous beat. Don't bore your reader. To make your writing flow more smoothly, combine short sentences. The following strategy may help:

▶ **REVISION STRATEGY**
Measuring Sentences

The physical length of your sentences is not the key to good style, but it can help indicate places where you can vary your sentence structure. Using a ruler, measure each sentence in the first three paragraphs of your draft. Circle the two shortest sentences in each paragraph. See whether they can be combined with nearby sentences into longer, more interesting ones. For help combining sentences, see the ideas presented in the box on the next page.

Student Work
IN PROGRESS

Name: Erin Macdonald Roski
Madison Middle School
Oceanside, CA

Measuring Sentences

*After Erin measured the sentences in this paragraph,
she decided to combine the shortest two with other nearby sentences.*

Also, when Epeius builds the horse, he installs a trapdoor. The trapdoor is impossible to open from the outside, *and no* No one can open the lock except Epeius himself. Odysseus and other men squeeze inside with their armor and rations. There is barely room for Epeius. He has *, but he* to be stuffed in somehow, though, for the plan to work! Again, the reader is in suspense until Epeius finally gets in.

Grammar in Your Writing
Compound Sentences

To combine sentences and vary your sentence structure, you can combine clauses. A **clause** is a group of words with its own subject and verb. An **independent clause** is a clause that expresses a complete thought. (An independent clause can stand on its own as a sentence.)

CLAUSES:	when he went to Troy	he stayed in his tent

INDEPENDENT CLAUSES:	the Trojans fought back	he attacked Troy

When a single sentence is made up of two or more independent clauses, it is called a **compound sentence.**

COMPOUND SENTENCE:
┌── ind. clause ──┐ ┌── ind. clause ──────┐
He attacked Troy, but the Trojans fought back.

The clauses in a compound sentence may be connected in one of two ways: with a comma and a coordinating conjunction or with a semicolon.

There are seven coordinating conjunctions: *and, but, for, nor, or, so,* and *yet.* When you join two independent clauses with a coordinating conjunction, use a comma before the conjunction:

COMPOUND SENTENCE:
┌──────── ind. clause ────────┐
The Greeks left a wooden horse by the city, **and**
┌──── ind. clause ────┐
the Trojans took it inside.

You can also form a compound sentence with a semicolon (;).

COMPOUND SENTENCE:
┌──── ind. clause ────┐
The Trojans had been tricked;
┌──────── ind. clause ────────┐
the horse was filled with Greek warriors.

Types of Connections Between Clauses

When you use a coordinating conjunction, you can suggest the relationship between the ideas in the joined clauses. *And,* for instance, suggests that two similar ideas are being added together. *But* suggests that two opposing or contrasting ideas are being joined. A semicolon usually suggests addition or further explanation.

Find It in Your Reading Find one compound sentence in "Introducing Natty Bumppo" by May Lamberton Becker on page 248. Identify the independent clauses.

Find It in Your Writing Find four compound sentences in your response to literature. If you cannot find four, challenge yourself to combine sentences to create new compound sentences.

To learn more about compound sentences, see Chapters 1 and 21.

Revising Your Word Choice
Choose Precise Words for Evaluation

When you write about a literary work, you share your reactions with a reader. It doesn't give a reader much information, however, if all you write is "I didn't like it" or "I thought it was terrific." Use precise words to communicate your opinion clearly.

▶ **REVISION STRATEGY**
Highlighting Value Words

With a colored pencil, highlight words in your paper that express an opinion—words such as *good, bad,* or *exciting.* Rewrite the words to state your meaning clearly and exactly. Here are some examples of general and exact opinion words and expressions:

▲ Critical Viewing
Give three precise words you could use to describe this scene. **[Analyze]**

GENERAL	EXACT
great	well written, fast moving
bad	slow moving, unbelievable
unlikeable (characters)	bland, prim, two-dimensional

Peer Review

After you've finished revising on your own, it's a good idea to share your first draft with some of your classmates. You can learn whether you have clearly described the work and clearly expressed your opinions about it. Use the following strategy to gather comments about your work from classmates.

Pointing

Follow these steps for pointing:

1. Read what you have written to a small group of students.
2. Then, read it a second time.
3. During the second reading, the others in the group should jot down words and phrases that they find effective in some way—interesting, well put, or attention grabbing. No negative comments are allowed.
4. After you have finished reading, have your classmates point out the parts of your work that they liked.

As you write the final version of your paper, use what you learn from the group to build on, or say more about, the points that they liked.

12.5 Editing and Proofreading

After you have improved the organization and expression of your ideas, polish your work. Proofread for errors in spelling, punctuation, or grammar. In a response to literature, pay special attention to punctuating quotations.

Focusing on Punctuating Quotations

Check each quotation against the work quoted to make sure you have copied the words *exactly*. Then, make sure you have followed the rules for punctuating quotations.

Grammar in Your Writing
Rules for Punctuating Quotations

A **quotation** is a word, phrase, sentence, or passage from one work that is cited in another work. Follow these rules for punctuating quotations:

Brief quotations Use quotation marks and commas to separate the quotation from the rest of a sentence. Use single quotation marks for a quotation within the quotation:

> The writer then tells us, "Achilles retreated to his tent, saying, 'Let's see if they can beat the Trojans without me.'"

Long quotations If a quotation runs four lines or more, introduce it with a colon. Skip a line before the quotation and indent it on the left side.

> The author notes the different abilities of the heroes:

> > Achilles was the greatest warrior among them. (His mother had dipped him in the River Styx when he was a baby to make his body nearly invulnerable.) Odysseus, the crafty one, helped the Greeks plan and scheme. Agamemnon was a great leader.

Find It in Your Reading Find an example of a quotation in "Introducing Natty Bumppo" by May Lamberton Becker on page 248. Explain how its length affects its punctuation.

Find It in Your Writing Read over your response to literature, and check each quotation to make sure it is set off or punctuated correctly.

To learn more about punctuating quotations, see Chapter 26.

12.6 Publishing and Presenting

Building Your Portfolio

Consider these suggestions for publishing and presenting your response:

1. **Book Day** Arrange a Book Day on which students read their responses to literature and hold discussions about works they have enjoyed. Announce the day with posters and ads for literary works.
2. **Letter to the Author** If you have written a letter to an author, mail the letter to him or her, care of the publisher. If you have written a review, mail it to the author with a cover letter. Share your letter and any response you receive with the class.

Reflecting on Your Writing

Jot down a few notes on your experience writing a response to literature. Begin by answering the following questions:

- As you took notes, drafted, and revised, what did you learn about the work of literature about which you wrote?
- What aspects of the work did you not write about? Why did you decide to write about the aspect that you chose?

 **Internet Tip**

To see responses to literature scored with this rubric, go on-line: PHSchool.com Enter Web Code: eak-6001

Rubric for Self-Assessment

Evaluate your response to literature using the following rubric:

	Score 4	Score 3	Score 2	Score 1
Audience and Purpose	Presents sufficient background on the work(s); presents the writer's reactions forcefully	Presents background on the work(s); presents the writer's reactions clearly	Presents some background on the work(s); presents the writer's reactions at points	Presents little or no background on the work(s); presents few of the writer's reactions
Organization	Presents points in logical order, smoothly connecting them to the overall focus	Presents points in logical order and connects many to the overall focus	Organizes points poorly in places; connects some points to an overall focus	Presents information in a scattered, disorganized manner
Elaboration	Supports reactions and evaluations with elaborated reasons and well-chosen examples	Supports reactions and evaluations with specific reasons and examples	Supports some reactions and evaluations with reasons and examples	Offers little support for reactions and evaluations
Use of Language	Shows overall clarity and fluency; uses precise, evaluative words; makes few mechanical errors	Shows good sentence variety; uses some precise evaluative terms; makes some mechanical errors	Uses awkward or overly simple sentence structures and vague evaluative terms; makes many mechanical errors	Presents incomplete thoughts; makes mechanical errors that create confusion

12.7 Student Work IN PROGRESS

FINAL DRAFT

A Tale of Troy
by Roger Lancelyn Green

Erin Macdonald Roski
Madison Middle School
Oceanside, California

◀ **Critical Viewing**
This ancient Greek art-work shows a scene from the Trojan War. Draw two conclusions about the way wars were fought at the time. **[Draw Conclusions]**

One of the most famous stories in the world is the ancient Greek tale of the Trojan War. In *A Tale of Troy*, Roger Lancelyn Green retells the tale in a suspenseful, enjoyable style. You can taste the excitement of his book in his retelling of the episode of the Trojan Horse, when the Greeks use trickery and a huge statue of a horse to finally beat the Trojans.

The cause of the Trojan War is mainly the beautiful Helen of Sparta. She is stolen from the Greeks by Paris, a prince in Troy. In a blind fury, her politically powerful husband Menelaus storms the seas, gathering a company of worthy heroes, including brave Odysseus, Agamemnon, and Achilles. Together, they charge their ships across the churning water and surround Troy. Bronze clashes on the windy plains outside the city. Swords ring. The wounded cry out. Despite the might of the Greeks, the war

In her introduction, Erin names the work to which she is responding. She also introduces her focus: the excitement of the episode of the Trojan Horse.

Erin's draft is well organized. First, she gives the reader necessary background information on the story. Then, she summarizes the episode of the Trojan Horse.

stretches on for ten long, draining years.

The Trojan horse wins the war for the Greeks. This victorious plan is concocted by Odysseus: Epeius, the shipbuilder, will build a sturdy, huge horse in which to hide a group of warriors. Once the Trojans bring the horse inside their city, the Greeks inside will leap out and open the gates to the other Greeks!

But one last thing is involved—how will they convince the Trojans to take the wondrous horse into the city? They make it impossible to resist. The author describes the horse in the same poetic, elegant style he uses for the rest of the tale. Epeius

> . . . fitted a neck to it with a purple fringed mane sprinkled with gold. . . . The cunningly fashioned head had blood-red eyes of amethyst surrounded with gems of sea-green beryl. . . . He fitted a flowing tail to it twisted with gold and hung with tassles. . . .

Then, the other Greeks pretend to sail away. A great cry rumbles through the streets of Troy when the Trojans see that the Greek fleet is gone. "We've won!! We've won!!" they cry and rush to the horse outside their city. Most people want to burn the horse or break it apart with their axes.

But a captive Greek named Sinon soon tells a fake story to save his people. And when two serpents crawl out of the sea and kill three of the people in favor of burning the dazzling horse, the Trojans immediately twine garlands of beautiful flowers around it and bring the giant horse into their city. Since it won't fit through the gates, the people take down part of their wall. Once the horse is inside, the Greeks scramble out. That night, great Troy falls. For those of you who are Trojan fans, this was a tragic night. But for friends of the Greeks, like myself, it was a time for rejoicing.

The story is full of suspense. For instance, when the Trojans are talking about burning the horse, you are afraid the Greeks inside will be burned alive! Also, when Epeius builds the horse, he installs a trapdoor. The trapdoor is impossible to open from the outside, and no one can open the lock except Epeius himself. Odysseus and other men squeeze inside with their armor and rations. There is barely room for Epeius, but he has to be stuffed in somehow, though, for the plan to work! Again, the reader is in suspense until Epeius finally gets in.

This book is for anyone who enjoys legends, fairy tales, and myths. I love it for its suspense and frequent cliffhangers. Read this book if you are ready to endure pain, sadness, anger, fear, and happiness under the magnificent pen of Roger Lancelyn Green.

Poetic and elegant are precise evaluative words describing the author's style.

Here, Erin uses a quotation to support two points. First, she supports her point that the book is well written. She also supports her point that the horse is "wondrous."

Erin supports her point that the story is suspenseful with a few examples from the story.

In her conclusion, Erin restates in strong terms her great enjoyment of the book.

Connected Assignment *Movie Review*

When you respond to a story, you explain whether you liked it or not, and why. When you write a movie review, you do the same for a film. A movie review features

- your reactions to the movie.
- details from the movie used to support your opinions.
- a recommendation to moviegoers about whether to see the movie.

Prewriting Choose a movie you have enjoyed. View it again. Write down your opinion of the movie, and collect details explaining your reaction in a Web like the one shown. Include notes on the story, acting, music, and special effects.

Drafting Begin by writing the introduction to your review. Your introduction should

- begin with a funny observation or interesting fact.
- include a sentence explaining your opinion of the film.

    In the body of your review, you should

- give a brief summary of the story.
- explain your reaction to the movie.
- provide examples showing readers why you feel as you do.

    Conclude your review with a recommendation.

Revising and Editing Read over your review. Add any information readers will need to follow your points. Replace vague words, such as *good* or *bad*, with forceful ones, such as *hilarious* or *sappy*.

Publishing and Presenting After revising your movie review, submit it to a school newspaper. Then, compare your review to professionally written reviews of the same movie.

▲ **Critical Viewing**
What kind of movie do you think these people might enjoy seeing? **[Speculate]**

Movie: *Little Cabin in the Big Woods*

Main Opinion: I cared about the characters in this wilderness story.

Special Effect: The fight scene with the grizzly is really scary.

Plot: The Bruder family is trying to survive the winter in their cabin in the woods.

Acting: When Matt Distaff comforts Lucy over her broken doll, he acts just like a real father.

Colors: The shots of the woods in the fall are a little faded.

Spotlight on the Humanities

Understanding Comedy in Film

Focus on Film: *You Can't Take It With You*

There is one response to literature most writers would value—a Pulitzer Prize. This honor is an overwhelmingly positive response to a piece of literature or a theatrical production. In 1937, the Broadway comedy *You Can't Take It With You* won the Pulitzer Prize for Best New American Drama.

The play, considered a classic of American theater, was written by George S. Kaufman (1889–1961) and Moss Hart (1904–1961). It centers around an eccentric family and their funny capers.

The writer James Thurber called Kaufman "the man who was comedy." During his career, Kaufman wrote forty-three plays and had twenty-six hit shows.

A scene from *You Can't Take It With You*

Film Connection In 1935, Kaufman wrote the film *A Night at the Opera* for the Marx Brothers. A comedy team, the Marx Brothers—Groucho (born Julius, 1890–1977), Chico (born Leonard, 1886–1961), and Harpo (born Adolph, 1888–1964)—were masters of the art of slapstick, gags, and wisecracks.

Audiences still find *A Night at the Opera* a hilarious movie. The story is told that one of the lines in Kaufman's script was so funny, it had to be removed. When preview audiences heard the line, they laughed so hard that they could not hear the rest of the movie.

Music Connection In 1931, Kaufman collaborated with composer George Gershwin (1898–1937) on the musical *Of Thee I Sing.* This show was the first Broadway musical ever to win the Pulitzer Prize. Gershwin is perhaps best known for writing the first true American opera, *Porgy and Bess* (1935).

Response to Literature Writing Activity: Comedy Journal Entry

View a Marx Brothers film. In a journal entry, note the three scenes in the movie that you found the funniest— or the dumbest! Explain your reaction to each.

▶ **Critical Viewing** Explain what is comical about each of the scenes on this page. **[Analyze]**

A scene from *A Night at the Opera*

Media and Technology Skills

Using Multimedia to Interpret Literature

Activity: Creating a Multimedia Presentation

You can respond to a story or poem by reading the work to others, accompanied by images, music, and sound effects. To create a multimedia presentation, follow these guidelines:

Learn About It

Plan Your Presentation Carefully Review the piece you have chosen to present. Mark up a photocopy to show which parts might be effectively illustrated with an image or where you might change from one kind of music to another. Referring to your "script," list all of the equipment, images, and music or sound effects you will need.

Learn How to Use Equipment Learn how to use the equipment you have listed—tape recorders, slide projectors, and so on. Read the manuals, and ask questions of experienced users.

Use Audio Elements Your reading of the work is the most important part of your presentation. Practice reading it slowly and with expression.

You may use a piece of music to accompany your reading. Choose pieces appropriate to the mood of the work—happy, sad, or suspenseful. Practice synchronizing your reading with a tape of the music. Consider adding other sound effects, as well.

Use Visual Elements
Consider including visuals in your presentation. You might run a slide show as you read the work. Or, you might videotape others acting out scenes and show the tape as you read. Work with a partner to time your reading with the slides or the video.

Apply It Choose a work of literature, and then plan a multimedia presentation of it using a storyboard organizer like this one.

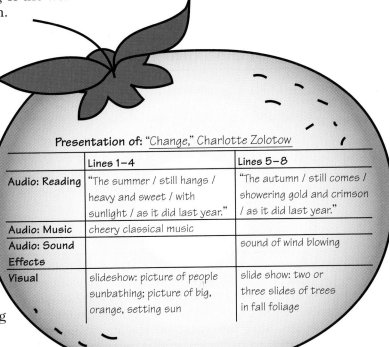

Presentation of: "Change," Charlotte Zolotow

	Lines 1–4	Lines 5–8
Audio: Reading	"The summer / still hangs / heavy and sweet / with sunlight / as it did last year."	"The autumn / still comes / showering gold and crimson / as it did last year."
Audio: Music	cheery classical music	
Audio: Sound Effects		sound of wind blowing
Visual	slideshow: picture of people sunbathing; picture of big, orange, setting sun	slide show: two or three slides of trees in fall foliage

Standardized Test Preparation Workshop

Responding to Prompts About Literature

On standardized tests, you will frequently be asked to write in response to a literary work, or passage. When answering, you will need to comment on the work and support your analysis with examples. You will be evaluated on your ability to do the following:

- develop a clearly stated opinion
- present examples that effectively support your ideas
- organize ideas in a logical manner
- write in a style that flows smoothly
- produce an essay that is free of errors in grammar, usage, and mechanics.

Following is a sample standardized test writing prompt on literature. Use the suggestions on the next page to help you respond to the prompt. Note the clocks next to each stage. They represent suggestions for how much of your test-taking time you should devote to each stage.

Test Tip

When responding to a prompt about a poem, note figurative language in the poem, such as comparisons between unlike things, and repeated imagery. These devices are important effects in poems.

Sample Writing Situation

Read the following poem by Theodore Roethke.

"Child on Top of a Greenhouse"

[1] The wind billowing out the seat of my britches,
[2] My feet crackling splinters of glass and dried putty,
[3] The half-grown chrysanthemums staring up like accusers,
[4] Up through the streaked glass, flashing with sunlight,
[5] A few white clouds all rushing eastward,
[6] A line of elms plunging and tossing like horses,
[7] And everyone, everyone pointing and shouting!

"Child on Top of a Greenhouse" is a good example of the use of perspective, or point of view, in poetry. Write an essay in which you explain the point of view of the speaker in the poem. Answer these questions: Where is the speaker? What can the speaker see from this perspective? Then, explain how the poet uses details to help the reader share in this perspective.

Prewriting

Allow about one fourth of your time for developing your response and noting supporting details.

Create a Thesis Statement The prompt is quite specific about your topic: You must explain the viewpoint of the speaker in the poem. Read the poem twice through. Then, write a thesis statement stating where the speaker is and how this affects what he can see. (A **thesis statement** is a sentence that explains the topic of an essay.)

Write a List After writing your thesis statement, list examples from the poem that support your thesis. Draw a line connecting each example to your thesis. Include in your list special uses of words that help you feel what it is like to be where the speaker is.

Drafting

Allow about half of your time for drafting. Remember to draft neatly and to allow space for revision changes.

Introduce Your Topic Start by writing a strong opening paragraph. This paragraph should include your thesis statement and summarize the details you will discuss.

Use Evidence for Support In the paragraphs following your introduction, discuss one of the examples you have collected in prewriting. Explain how each image shows something the speaker could see only from his point of view. Also, explain how the poet uses special language to convey what it feels like to see the world from that perspective. Include quotations from the poem to illustrate your points.

Conclude With a Summary In your last paragraph, summarize the points you have made.

Revising, Editing, and Proofreading

Allow almost one fourth of your time for revising. Spend any time remaining proofreading your essay.

Check Connections Reread your essay. For each point, ask yourself: What is the connection of this point with my thesis? Consider eliminating or rewording any point that is not well connected to your thesis statement.

Check Quotations Double-check the accuracy of your quotations from the poem. Also, make sure you have put quotation marks around quotations.

Make Corrections Correct errors in spelling, punctuation, and grammar. Neatly cross out mistakes with a single line. Indicate added words using a caret (^).

Writing for Assessment

Assessment in School

By now, you know that tests are an important part of life at school. You probably also know that there are many different types of tests, most of which include sections that call on you to do some writing.

Most people get a little nervous when they have to write in a test situation. Being prepared for this type of writing will help you do your best work even if you are nervous. This chapter provides tips, guidance, and practice to help you feel more confident and prepared when you write on tests.

▲ **Critical Viewing**
Do you think the students in this situation might be nervous? What might they do to make themselves more comfortable? **[Draw Conclusions]**

What Is Writing for Assessment?

Writing for assessment is writing that takes place in a formal testing situation. Teachers use it to measure how much you've learned about a subject or how well your writing skills have progressed. This kind of writing usually involves

- one or more writing prompts that tell you what to write.

- a limited time in which to write.

- no chance to use textbooks or other reference books.

To learn the criteria on which your writing for assessment may be graded or judged, see the Rubric for Self-Assessment on page 282.

Types of Writing for Assessment

The writing prompts on tests may call for the following types of writing:

- **Narrative writing,** with which you tell a story about a personal experience that taught you something.

- **Persuasive writing,** with which you support an opinion or a position.

- **Expository writing,** with which you present information you have learned about a subject. Expository writing may include **cause-and-effect writing,** in which you show how one event or situation leads to others. It may also include **comparison-and-contrast writing,** in which you explore the similarities and differences between two or more things.

- **Response to literature,** normally to a specific passage that is provided on the test.

▲ Critical Viewing
Give an example showing how the object in the picture can help you do well on a test. **[Draw Conclusions]**

PREVIEW
Student Work
IN PROGRESS

In this chapter, you'll follow the work of John Grandy, a student at Holland Woods Middle School in Port Huron, Michigan, as he responds to a writing prompt for an essay test in his literature class. You'll see the strategies he used to narrow his topic, decide his purpose and audience, gather and organize details, draft a response, and revise his work.

Gathering Details

Once you have chosen a writing prompt, focused your topic, and identified your purpose, take a few minutes to collect some ideas by following these steps:

1. Divide your topic into subtopics or categories.
2. Jot down as many facts, quotations, and other types of details as you can for each subtopic.
3. Use a graphic organizer to record these details. If you are writing to classify, you might want to use a Venn diagram to find the similarities and differences between the items you are classifying. If you are writing to persuade, use a T-Chart to identify the pros and cons of the issue. If you are writing a narrative, order events using a timeline. If you are writing to explain, summarize, or inform, use a topic web.

John Grandy was writing to explain, so he used a topic web to organize his ideas.

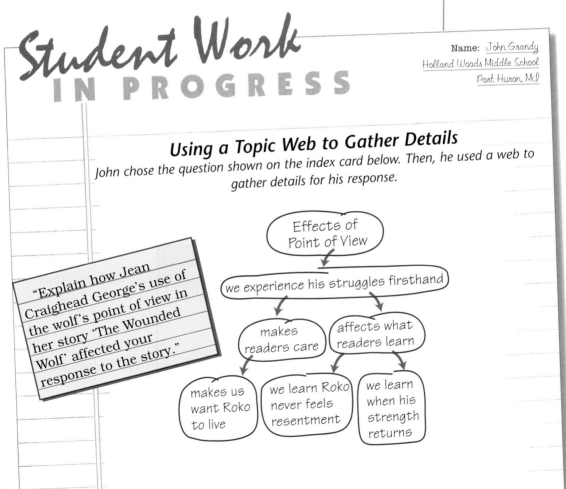

Student Work
IN PROGRESS

Name: John Grandy
Holland Woods Middle School
Port Huron, MI

Using a Topic Web to Gather Details

John chose the question shown on the index card below. Then, he used a web to gather details for his response.

"Explain how Jean Craighead George's use of the wolf's point of view in her story 'The Wounded Wolf' affected your response to the story."

Effects of Point of View

we experience his struggles firsthand

makes readers care

affects what readers learn

makes us want Roko to live

we learn Roko never feels resentment

we learn when his strength returns

13.2 Drafting

Plan to spend half of your testing time writing a first draft of your response to the writing prompt.

Shaping Your Writing

Since you'll have little time to revise, it is important to make your first draft as organized and polished as possible.

Find a Focus

Regardless of the type of essay you're writing, it is essential that you have a main idea that provides a single focus for the entire piece. Review both the prompt and the details you have gathered, and write a single sentence that sums up your main point. For example, if you were describing jobs of the future, you might note: "All of the most important jobs of the future will be related to technology."

Use the focus sentence you've written as the centerpiece of an introductory paragraph. Then, write supporting paragraphs that develop your main point.

Plan Your Organization

Consider the best plan for organizing your details. Generally, each type of essay dictates a specific organization. Consider the following suggestions:

For a **story, summary,** or **explanation,** organize your details in chronological order. Making a timeline is a simple way to do this.

For a **comparison-and-contrast essay,** present details about one subject first, then present details about the other; or, first present similarities, then present differences.

For a **persuasive essay** or a **classification,** organize your points by order of importance. Move from most to least important, or vice versa. In the example below, based on the second writing prompt on page 274, jobs are classified and organized from most to least important.

▲ **Critical Viewing**
What type of organization would be suitable for writing on the subject shown in the photograph? **[Explain, Draw Conclusions]**

JOBS OF THE FUTURE

(most important)	1. Careers in Health
	2. Careers in Computers
(least important)	3. Careers in Recreation

Providing Elaboration

Write your first draft following the organization you've selected. Use the strategy of SEE to develop each paragraph.

Layer Ideas Using SEE

To layer a paragraph, begin with the main idea. Then, create layer after layer to elaborate that idea. Follow these steps:

State the main idea for the paragraph.

Extend the idea. You might give your opinion on the idea, restate it with a new emphasis, or apply it to an example.

Elaborate on the idea in one or more sentences. If your idea explains something, show exactly what details it involves, giving examples and precise descriptions. If you are arguing for or against the idea, give supporting details for your opinion, such as facts and arguments.

Try it out! Use the interactive SEE Technique activity in **Section 13.2**, on-line or on CD-ROM.

Student Work
IN PROGRESS

Name: John Grandy
Holland Woods Middle School
Port Huron, MI

Using the SEE Technique
John wrote this paragraph using the SEE technique.

Statement: This point of view also affects the amount that the reader learns about the wolf's experience. **Extension:** For example, we learn that Roko never feels anger or resentment toward the animals who are trying to eat him. **Elaboration:** In fact, at the end of the story he even shares with them the food that Kiglo brought him.

13.3 Revising

Plan to spend one fourth of your testing time on revising your work. First, consider whether you'll have the time and space to copy a clean final draft, or whether you must make changes neatly in your first draft as you revise.

Revising Your Overall Structure

When teachers evaluate your writing on an essay test, they look for a logically organized piece of writing that clearly follows the directions in the writing prompt. As a result, probably the most important part of revising a test essay is to make sure that your writing presents an organized series of paragraphs that fully develop your topic.

▲ Critical Viewing
What might this student be doing to prepare for a test? [Hypothesize]

▶ **REVISION STRATEGY**
Checking Your Organization

Follow these steps to check your organization and revise it if necessary:

1. Check to see that your opening paragraph clearly states your **main idea.** Try to improve the statement of your main idea to make it stronger and clearer.

2. Also check to see that your introduction presents your **subtopics.** If it does not, add a sentence that previews each subtopic.

3. Review each paragraph to ensure that it focuses on **a single subtopic.** Eliminate or refocus any that do not.

4. Review the **order** of your paragraphs to ensure that you have followed the organization you planned. If necessary, rearrange one or more paragraphs.

Revising Your Paragraphs

Review Paragraph Focus

Teachers will closely examine each paragraph of your response to the writing prompt. They expect to find a strong topic sentence and a focused set of supporting details.

▶ **REVISION STRATEGY**
Crossing Out Unnecessary Sentences

Identify the topic sentence within each paragraph. Review each sentence to see whether it focuses or develops the topic sentence. Cross out any sentences that do not. Then, read the paragraph, omitting the sentences you have crossed out, and consider what details you should add to support the topic sentence more thoroughly.

Revising Your Sentences

Teachers will evaluate how well your writing hangs together and how easy it is to follow the flow of your ideas. They want to see a clear relationship between one sentence and the next.

▶ **REVISION STRATEGY**
Adding Transitions

To make sure your ideas are easy to follow, add transition words and phrases to your sentences. Transitions include words such as *first, for example, because,* and *for this reason.*

Student Work
IN PROGRESS

Name: John Grandy
Holland Woods Middle School
Port Huron, MI

Adding Transitions
John added a few transitions to his essay .

Telling the story from the point of view of the wolf is much more effective than telling it from the point of view of a person.
First of all,
ʌRoko is in big trouble. . . .

This quote also demonstrates the author's use of the present tense. For example, ʌWhen it says in the story, "Roko pulls himself towards the sheltered rock," it gives the reader a sense of actually being there with Roko.

Revising Your Word Choice
Choose Precise and Vivid Words

On a test, you need to use words that say precisely what you mean. Follow this strategy to help revise your word choice:

▶ **REVISION STRATEGY**
Strengthening Word Choice to Achieve Your Purpose

Find general descriptive words, such as *great,* that cover many details. Revise by filling in those details, as in this example:

ORIGINAL SENTENCE: The band was *great.*

REVISED SENTENCE: The band *kept up an energetic groove that kept people dancing all night.*

13.4 Editing and Proofreading

If you want teachers to take your ideas seriously, be sure to express yourself in complete, correctly punctuated sentences. Leave some time before you turn in your work to check that you have corrected any errors you have generated.

Focusing on Complete Sentences

If you have extra time before the test is over, use it to check your sentences. Use these questions to guide your review:

- Does each sentence express a complete thought and contain a subject and a verb?
- Does each sentence begin with a capital letter?
- Does each sentence end with a period, question mark, or exclamation point?
- Are the clauses in compound sentences joined correctly?

Make all corrections neatly.

Get instant help! For practice in the proper uses of commas, complete selected exercises in **Section 26.2**, online or on CD-ROM.

Grammar in Your Writing
Avoiding Comma Splices

One of the most common sentence errors students make is trying to join two clauses with just a comma. This error is called a **comma splice.** Look for comma splices in your writing, and use the following techniques to correct them.

INCORRECT: Nursing is a rewarding career, in the future, we will need more nurses.

CORRECTED:

Add a Conjunction: Nursing is a rewarding career, **and** in the future, we will need more nurses.

Add a Semicolon: Nursing is a rewarding career; in the future, we will need more nurses.

Break Into Two Sentences: Nursing is a rewarding career. **In** the future, we will need more nurses.

To learn more about comma splices and other run-ons, see Chapter 21.

13.5 Publishing and Presenting

Building Your Portfolio

Consider the following suggestions for publishing and presenting your work:

1. **Group Discussion** Compare your work with that of classmates who have responded to the same question. Discuss the difficulties you encountered in answering the question and the solutions you found.

2. **Study for Other Exams** Next time you have a written test coming up, look over past test answers. Recall which strategies for writing worked well for you and which did not.

Reflecting on Your Writing

Note some thoughts on writing for assessment. Start off by answering these questions:

- What do I usually do to prepare for a test? What might I do to prepare more fully?

- What strategy did I find most useful for preparing for a test?

 Internet Tip

To see writing for assessment scored with this rubric, go on-line:
PHSchool.com
Enter Web Code:
eak-6001

Rubric for Self-Assessment

Use the criteria below to evaluate your essay for assessment:

	Score 4	Score 3	Score 2	Score 1
Audience and Purpose	Uses word choices and supporting details appropriate to the specified audience; clearly addresses writing prompt	Mostly uses word choices and supporting details appropriate to the specified audience; adequately addresses prompt	Uses some inappropriate word choices and details; addresses writing prompt	Uses inappropriate word choices and details; does not address writing prompt
Organization	Presents a clear, consistent organizational strategy	Presents a clear organizational strategy with few inconsistencies	Presents an inconsistent organizational strategy	Shows a lack of organizational strategy
Elaboration	Adequately supports the thesis; elaborates each idea; links all details to the thesis	Supports the thesis; elaborates most ideas; links most information to the thesis	Partially supports the thesis; does not elaborate some ideas	Provides no thesis; does not elaborate ideas
Use of Language	Uses excellent sentence variety and vocabulary; includes very few mechanical errors	Uses adequate sentence variety and vocabulary; includes few mechanical errors	Uses repetitive sentence structure and vocabulary; includes some mechanical errors	Demonstrates poor use of language; includes many mechanical errors

13.6 Student Work IN PROGRESS

FINAL DRAFT

◀ **Critical Viewing**
Do you have sympathy for this wolf? Read John's essay, and then explain how your feelings about the wolf have changed. **[Apply]**

LITERATURE

You can find "The Wounded Wolf" by Jean Craighead George in *Prentice Hall Literature: Timeless Voices, Timeless Themes,* Copper.

> John Grandy wrote his essay in response to the following test item: "Explain how Jean Craighead George's use of the wolf's point of view in her story 'The Wounded Wolf' affected your response to the story."

A Wolf's Point of View

John Grandy
Holland Woods Middle School
Port Huron, Michigan

In the story "The Wounded Wolf," a wolf is badly hurt and must find a way to reunite with his pack. His name is Roko, and in his weakened state, he is approached by many animals who want to feed on him. The unique factor of this story is that it is told from the perspective of the wolf.

Telling the story from the point of view of the wolf is much more effective than telling it from the point of view of a person.

The opening paragraph presents John's main idea: Telling the story from the wolf's point of view is more effective than telling it from the point of view of a person.

First of all, Roko is in big trouble. The ravens, the grizzly bear, the fox, and the owl smell death, his death, and approach him. To these animals, Roko is just another meal to sustain them through the winter. This is really bad, but when you think about it, only moments earlier, Roko himself was busy bringing down a caribou, who would have liked to have been spared as well. So why do we even care about Roko? Well, we care because the story is told from his point of view. If the story were told from the point of view of a person, we might be just as likely to care about the caribou. We can imagine what it would be like to be in his place and we want him to survive. "Massive clouds blot out the sun. In their gloom Roko sees the deathwatch move in closer."

This quote also demonstrates the author's use of the present tense. For example, when it says in the story, "Roko pulls himself towards the sheltered rock," it gives the reader a sense of actually being there with Roko.

This point of view also affects the amount that the reader learns about the wolf's experience. For example, we learn that Roko never feels anger or resentment toward the animals who are trying to eat him. In fact, at the end of the story, he even shares with them the food that Kiglo brought him:

> Already Roko's wound feels better. He gulps at the food and feels his strength return. He shatters bone, flesh and gristle and shakes the scraps out on the snow. The hungry ravens swoop upon them. The white fox snatches up a bone. The snowy owl gulps down flesh and fur and Roko wags his tail and watches.

Notice how Roko doesn't hold a grudge for their earlier attempts to eat him. He even wags his tail because he is happy to see them eat! I don't know a lot of people who wouldn't want revenge on their predators.

In conclusion, telling the story in present tense, from Roko's point of view, allows the reader to (1) care about Roko's fate and (2) better understand a wolf's experience. These are reasons why it was very effective telling the story from the wolf's point of view.

John organizes his essay in order of importance, building to his most important point.

▼ **Critical Viewing**
Does this picture capture the mood of Roko's story? Explain your answer.
[Interpret]

Connected Assignment Open-Book Test

When taking most tests, you must work from what you remember of a subject. During an open-book test, you can refer to a textbook or to class notes as well. For such a test, your answer should

- include facts—such as specific names, dates, events, or formulas—from your books or notes.

- sum up your main idea.

- show a clear and logical organization.

Use these strategies to do your best on open-book tests:

Prewriting Organize your time well. Use a little more than one fourth of your time for prewriting.

Begin by outlining your answer to the question, as in the example on this page. Use the information that you remember first. Then, consult your reference materials to add details to each specific point of your outline. Use the index to locate information quickly in books.

▲ Critical Viewing
What advice might you give this student for taking an open-book test? [Analyze]

Drafting Next, allow about one half of your time for drafting. Include the following elements in your draft:

- **Introduction** Include a sentence in your introduction that sums up your answer.

- **Body** In the body of your paper, develop each main point of your outline. Include the specific details you have gathered from your reference materials.

- **Conclusion** In your final paragraph, sum up your answer to the question and the details that support it.

Revising and Editing Allow one fourth of the test-taking time for revising.

Reread your essay. For each point you make, lightly underline details that explain or support the point. Then, look for paragraphs with few underlines. Add additional details from your reference materials to these paragraphs.

Publishing and Presenting Add your graded test to your portfolio.

TOPIC: Ancient Mesopotamia

I. Mesopotamia
  A. Location
    1. In the desert where Iran and
      ? are today   p. 10 – Iraq
    2. Two important rivers: Tigris and ? p. 10 – Euphrates
  B. Reasons for start of civilization
    1. Tigris and Euphrates allow trade
    2. Rivers flood, so farming is possible there

Spotlight on the Humanities

Comparing Themes Across Cultures

Focus on Theater: *Cats*

In school, a teacher assesses your writing. When people write for the theater, their work is assessed by critics. The Broadway musical *Cats* got an "A" from audiences and critics alike. Based upon fourteen poems in T.S. Eliot's *Old Possum's Book of Practical Cats,* the musical *Cats* opened in London in 1981. It became one of the longest-running shows in London and on Broadway. Written by Andrew Lloyd Webber, *Cats* won seven Tony Awards and has played in more than 250 cities all across the world.

▲ **Critical Viewing** What does this photograph from the musical *Cats* suggest about the personality of this particular cat? Explain your answer. **[Speculate]**

Literature Connection Born in St. Louis, Missouri, poet T. S. Eliot (1888–1965) became a citizen of Great Britain. He was one of the most prominent literary figures of the twentieth century. In his poems, Eliot often captured the sound of ordinary spoken language. He also gave poetry the nervous rhythms of the early twentieth century, a time of rapid change. Most of Eliot's work is serious in nature, including "The Wasteland" and "The Hollow Men." In *Old Possum's Book of Practical Cats,* though, he has fun exploring the quirky personalities and mysterious ways of cats.

Art Connection Cats have caught the attention of many artists through the ages. Ancient Egyptian civilization worshiped cats and included feline images in much of its art, especially on jars and urns.

There is a historical reason for the Egyptian celebration of cats. Around 2500 B.C., rats and mice threatened to eat up Egypt's grain. The wild cats of Egypt came from the woods to save the day. The grateful Egyptians welcomed cats into their society and mythology. Killing a cat in ancient Egypt was a serious crime.

◄ **Critical Viewing** How does this sculpture convey the importance of cats in Egyptian culture? **[Evaluate]**

Assessment Writing Application:
Report Card on Cats

Create a set of requirements for an ideal pet. You might include categories such as "Shows Affection." Then, give cats a grade in each of your categories: Do they fulfill the requirement fully, somewhat, or not at all? Write a paragraph explaining the grades you have given.

Media and Technology Skills

Using Available Technology

Activity: Exploring Computer Tests

You can take many kinds of tests on computer. On these tests, you can use many of the same test-taking skills you have developed for printed tests. To do well on a computer-based test, you should get comfortable with the computer test format.

Learn About It

Practice on the Computer If possible, practice using the computer on which the test will be given. For instance, if the test will be given in the school computer room, visit the room before the test. Start up the computer, use the mouse, and open and close applications. This practice will make you more comfortable during the actual test.

Read Instructions Carefully As on a printed test, make sure you read all test instructions carefully before taking a computer-based test. Pay special attention to instructions about using the computer to answer. For instance, you may not be able to change an answer once you have marked it. Or, you may have only a limited time to answer each question.

Take On-line Practice Tests To get comfortable with computer test-taking, practice. Take a few of the practice tests that are available on CD-ROM and on-line. Some of these tests can teach you more about a subject as well as give you practice in test-taking. These tests give you feedback after each answer to let you know why your answer is right or wrong. This feedback will help you learn more about the subject matter covered by the test.

Evaluate It With the help of a teacher or school librarian, locate a computer practice test. Take the test. Then, fill out a graphic organizer like the one shown with your thoughts on the experience. Write a letter to the computer-test maker commenting on the test.

Tips on Computer Test-Taking
• Read directions carefully. They will explain how to answer a question and then move to the next question.
• If you are having trouble with your computer, ask for help right away.

Were the Test Directions Easy to Understand?	Was it Easy to Get Around in the Program? Why?	Was it Easy to Enter Answers? Why?	Did the Program Give Feedback? Was It Helpful?

Standardized Test Preparation Workshop

Proofreading

On writing tests, you may be asked to demonstrate your proofreading skills by producing work that is error-free. Standardized tests also use a multiple-choice format to measure your ability to recognize errors in spelling, capitalization, and punctuation. Use these guidelines to help you answer such questions:

- When checking for punctuation errors, consider whether a mark is missing, unnecessary, or misplaced.
- Look closely at titles and proper nouns for mistakes in capitalization.
- When checking for spelling errors, be alert for homonyms—words that sound like the correct word but are spelled differently.

The following sample test items will help you become familiar with the format of these questions.

Test Tip

Don't assume that a word is spelled correctly because it looks familiar. On an open-book test, look it up in a dictionary or, on a computer-based test, use Spell Check.

Sample Test Items	Answers and Explanations
Read the following passage and decide which type of errors, if any, appear in the underlined sections. Mark the letters for your answer. I beleive that the poem *April Rain Song* (1) (2) was written by Langston Hughes.	

1 A Spelling error
    B Capitalization error
    C Punctuation error
    D No error
	The correct answer for item 1 is *A. Believe* is spelled incorrectly as it appears in the sentence.

2 F Spelling error
    G Capitalization error
    H Punctuation error
    J No error
	The correct answer for item 2 is *H.* The poem's title, "April Rain Song," is incorrectly punctuated as it appears in the sentence. The titles of poems are enclosed in quotation marks, not italicized.

▶ **Practice 1** **Directions:** Read the following passage and decide which type of errors, if any, appear in the underlined sections. Mark the letters for your answer.

Antonio Vivaldi <u>was an italian composer</u>
                             (1)
who wrote one of the <u>worlds most famous</u>
                             (2)
<u>pieces</u> of music about the seasons. It

is called *The four Seasons*. <u>Its a collection</u>
         (3)   (4)
of four violin <u>concertos—one for each</u>
                       (5)
<u>season.</u>

1 A Spelling error
  B Capitalization error
  C Punctuation error
  D No error

2 F Spelling error
  G Capitalization error
  H Punctuation error
  J No error

3 A Spelling error
  B Capitalization error
  C Punctuation error
  D No error

4 F Spelling error
  G Capitalization error
  H Punctuation error
  J No error

5 A Spelling error
  B Capitalization error
  C Punctuation error
  D No error

▶ **Practice 2** **Directions:** Read the following passage and decide which type of errors, if any, appear in the underlined sections. Mark the letters for your answer.

We studied the poem <u>"April Rain Song" in</u>
                            (1)
<u>our Language Arts class.</u> Langston

<u>Hughes, like Vivaldi, was intrested</u> in the
                          (2)
seasons. The poem conveys his wonder at

the rain. It first appeared <u>in a magazine</u>
                             (3)
<u>for African american children</u> in the <u>April,</u>
                                      (4)
<u>1912 issue.</u>

1 A Spelling error
  B Capitalization error
  C Punctuation error
  D No error

2 F Spelling error
  G Capitalization error
  H Punctuation error
  J No error

3 A Spelling error
  B Capitalization error
  C Punctuation error
  D No error

4 F Spelling error
  G Capitalization error
  H Punctuation error
  J No error

Part 2

Grammar, Usage, and Mechanics

Lucky for Us, Sandy Novak

14 *Nouns*
and Pronouns

Runners know how the different parts of their bodies work together to help them move quickly and smoothly. In a similar way, writers know the parts of our language and how they work together to give sentences meaning. Words in English have eight different uses, or parts of speech. These are *nouns, pronouns, verbs, adjectives, adverbs, prepositions, conjunctions,* and *interjections.*

Just as runners stretch their muscles and practice their running technique, writers practice to improve their writing. Both work hard, and both exercise to become better.

This chapter will begin your practice with words. First, you will learn what makes nouns a special category of words and how to identify them. You will also learn about special kinds of nouns. Next, you will learn how pronouns can be used to take the place of nouns in sentences that you write. You will not only learn about nouns and pronouns, but you will also practice using them.

▲ **Critical Viewing**
What nouns and pronouns can you use to describe the people in this picture? **[Identify]**

Diagnostic Test

Directions: Write all answers on a separate sheet of paper.

Skill Check A. Identify each noun in the following sentences.

1. The decathlon includes ten different events.
2. Competition lasts for two days.
3. An athlete must use a variety of skills.
4. Speed and strength are tested in the decathlon.
5. Points are awarded for each event.

Skill Check B. Copy the sentences, underlining compound nouns.

6. The long jump and the shot put are on the first day.
7. The high jump takes place on that day also.
8. One event on the second day is the pole vault.
9. A timekeeper records each athlete's time in the footraces.
10. Finishing all of the events takes great willpower.

Skill Check C. Identify each underlined noun as *common* or *proper*.

11. The final <u>event</u> in the <u>decathlon</u> is the 1,500-meter <u>run</u>.
12. In 1912, <u>Jim Thorpe</u> won a <u>competition</u> in <u>Sweden</u>.
13. <u>Daley Thompson</u> of <u>Great Britain</u> was a two-time <u>winner</u>.
14. Another famous <u>champion</u> was <u>Bob Mathias</u>.
15. He won several gold <u>medals</u> in international <u>competitions</u> for the <u>United States</u>.

Skill Check D. Write each pronoun, and then write its antecedent.

16. The Greeks had the pentathlon in their competitions.
17. There were pentathlons for men and women, but they didn't compete against each other.
18. An athlete's points in each event would be added to his total.
19. Canada added a modern pentathlon to its track meets.
20. The first winner proudly displayed her medal around her neck.

Skill Check E. List the personal pronouns in the following sentences.

21. Do you know what events are in the pentathlon?
22. Two of them are fencing and swimming.
23. I think cross-country running is the most difficult.
24. They also include a horseback-riding event in most pentathlons.
25. We watched the riding on television.

Skill Check F. Write the demonstrative pronouns and the noun to which each refers.

26. The triathlon includes three events. These are very challenging.
27. Those are the participants in this event.
28. That is a distance I cannot run.
29. Many triathlons are held in Hawaii. That is a popular location.
30. This is a very difficult competition.

Nouns

A *noun* is one of the eight parts of speech. It is a word that names something. Some nouns name people, some name places, and some name things. *Wilma Rudolph, Washington,* and *stopwatch,* for example, are all nouns.

> ▶ **KEY CONCEPT** A **noun** is the name of a person, place, or thing. ∎

Nouns name both living and nonliving things. Some nouns name what can be seen, such as *elephant.* Others name ideas, such as *strength.* The nouns in the following chart are grouped under three headings: People, Places, and Things. Notice that the nouns in the third column name things you can see as well as ideas or feelings that you cannot see. Can you think of other nouns to add under each heading in the chart?

Theme: Runners
∙∙∙∙∙∙∙∙∙∙∙∙∙∙∙∙∙∙∙∙∙∙∙∙∙
In this section, you will learn to recognize different types of nouns. The examples and exercises are about running and track stars.
∙∙∙∙∙∙∙∙∙∙∙∙∙∙∙∙∙∙∙∙∙∙∙∙∙
Cross-Curricular Connection: Physical Education

NOUNS		
People	**Places**	**Things**
runner	Ohio	movie
Mrs. Fisher	theater	hunger
Ann	stadium	race
sailor	Rocky Mountains	love

In order to find out whether a word is a noun, look at how it is used in a sentence. If the word names a person, place, or thing, it is a noun. The nouns in the following sentences are underlined.

EXAMPLES: <u>Robert</u> runs every <u>day</u>.
We raced in <u>Canada</u>.
Her <u>breathing</u> was loud.
Many outstanding <u>runners</u> come from <u>Kenya</u>, a <u>country</u> in <u>Africa</u>.

Almost every time you speak, you talk about people, places, or things. When you talk about them, you are using nouns.

Exercise 1 Identifying Nouns List the nouns in each of the following sentences.

EXAMPLE: My favorite sprinter is Carl Lewis.
ANSWER: sprinter, Carl Lewis

1. Meets include many different events.
2. Edward runs the hurdles.
3. First, the runners wait for the signal to start.
4. They place their feet in starting blocks.
5. A loud bang signals the start of the race.
6. All runners race toward the finish line.
7. Ten barriers stand along the track.
8. Runners jump high over the hurdles.
9. Speed, flexibility, and coordination are important for success.
10. Hurdles are more complicated than the sprints.

Exercise 2 More Work With Nouns List the nouns in each sentence. Beside each noun, write whether it names a person, a place, or a thing.

EXAMPLE: The runner captured the gold medal in Seattle.
ANSWER: runner (person), medal (thing), Seattle (place)

1. The dashes are short races.
2. Runners competed in dashes at the Olympics in Atlanta.
3. Some competitors swing their arms and lean their bodies forward.
4. Each racer uses a different strategy.
5. Bursts of speed are combined with periods of coasting.

More Practice

Grammar Exercise Workbook
• pp. 1–2
On-line Exercise Bank
• Section 14.1

Go on-line:
PHSchool.com
Enter Web Code:
eak-6002

Get instant feedback! Exercises 1 and 2 are available on-line or on CD-ROM.

▼ **Critical Viewing** Provide a noun that names something related to each runner in this picture. **[Distinguish]**

Runners get ready for the start of a 50-yard dash.

Recognizing Compound Nouns

Some nouns are made up of two or more words. *Classroom* is a compound noun made up of *class* and *room*. *Homework* is a compound noun made up of the words *home* and *work*.

> **KEY CONCEPT** A **compound noun** is one noun made by joining two or more words. ■

Sometimes, the meaning of a compound noun is more than just the meaning of two or more words put together. Words such as *drumstick, bookworm, boot camp,* and *housecoat* have meanings that are different from those of the individual words that have been combined.

EXAMPLES: Each runner wore a *headband.*
The entire meet ran like *clockwork.*

Check a dictionary when you are not sure of the meaning of a compound noun.

Compound nouns are written in three different ways. Some are written as single words, others as hyphenated words, and still others as two or more separate words.

COMPOUND NOUNS		
Single Words	**Hyphenated Words**	**Separate Words**
crossbar firefighter thunderstorm	shot-put right-hander middle-distance	dinner jacket pole vault pen pal

> **Exercise 3** Finding Compound Nouns Copy each sentence, underlining the compound nouns.

EXAMPLE: The race's <u>endpoint</u> was the <u>Brooklyn Bridge</u>.

1. My sister-in-law wrote a short story about jogging.
2. I hope to follow in her footsteps as a road runner.
3. Her backpack holds a wristwatch and her running shoes.
4. Her mailbox is always full of running newsletters.
5. The doorbell rings when fellow runners stop by.
6. A track circles the football stadium at our high school.
7. On the weekends, she runs in the countryside.
8. Running cross-country provides a great workout for her.
9. Baseball and basketball players also do a lot of running.
10. Her former roommate is a track star.

Spelling Tip

Check your spelling of compound nouns that are single words. For example, in *pastime,* a combination of the words *past* and *time,* there is only one *t* in the compound form.

Get instant feedback! Exercise 3 is available on-line or on CD-ROM.

> **More Practice**

Grammar Exercise Workbook
• pp. 3–4
On-line Exercise Bank
• Section 14.1
Go on-line:
PHSchool.com
Enter Web Code:
eak-6002

Recognizing Common and Proper Nouns

Nouns can be grouped in several different ways. For example, all nouns are either *common nouns* or *proper nouns.* To decide whether a noun is common or proper, you must know whether it names something in a specific way or a general way.

> **KEY CONCEPT** A **common noun** names any one of a group of people, places, or things. ■

It is easy to recognize common nouns. Common nouns are not capitalized (except at the beginning of a sentence or in a title). Words such as *jogger, city,* and *race* are common nouns because they can apply to many different people, places, or things. In addition, a common noun can be a single word, such as *winner* or *track,* or a compound word, such as *muscle strain* or *finish line.*

> **KEY CONCEPT** A **proper noun** names a specific person, place, or thing. ■

Proper nouns, on the other hand, are always capitalized. *Mary Stewart, Chicago,* and *Monday* are proper nouns because they name specific people, places, and things. Proper nouns are often made up of more than one word. When a proper noun, such as *Avenue of the Americas,* contains words such as *a, an, the,* and *of,* these words are not capitalized unless they are the first word in the proper noun.

Jesse Owens competing in the 1936 Olympics in Berlin.

▲ **Critical Viewing** What are some important proper nouns that relate to the life of Jesse Owens? (See Exercise 5 for some ideas.) **[Identify; Support]**

COMMON NOUNS	PROPER NOUNS
scientist	Madam Curie
relative	Aunt Carol
city	Atlanta
state	Kentucky
book	*Julie of the Wolves*
bridge	Golden Gate Bridge
holiday	Columbus Day

GRAMMAR IN
LITERATURE

from **The Sound of Summer Running**
Ray Bradbury

In the following passage, common nouns are shown in blue italics. Proper nouns are shown in red italics.

Well, he felt sorry for *boys* who lived in *California* where they wore *tennis shoes* all *year* and never knew what it was to get *winter* off your *feet*, peel off the iron leather *shoes* all full of *snow* and *rain* and run barefoot for a *day* and then lace on the first new *tennis shoes* of the *season*, which was better than barefoot. The *magic* was always in the new *pair* of *shoes*. The *magic* might die by the *first* of *September*, but now in late *June* there was still plenty of *magic*, and *shoes* like these could jump you over *trees* and *rivers* and *houses*.

> **Exercise 4** Recognizing Common and Proper Nouns On your paper, indicate whether each noun is common or proper.

EXAMPLES: building (*common*)
                     Cole Field House (*proper*)

1. runner
2. Penn Games
3. France
4. relay
5. Nile River
6. university
7. Gail Devers
8. Mercedes Lopez
9. judge
10. stadium

> **Exercise 5** Identifying Common and Proper Nouns Write these sentences on your paper. Circle the common nouns and underline the proper nouns.

1. Jesse Owens was a great track-and-field athlete.
2. In high school, Owens competed all around Ohio.
3. At Ohio State University, the broad jump was his top event.
4. Later, Owens made the United States track team.
5. He captured four gold medals at the Olympics in Berlin.

> **More Practice**

Grammar Exercise Workbook
• pp. 5–6
On-line Exercise Bank
• Section 14.1
  Go on-line:
  PHSchool.com
  Enter Web Code:
  eak-6002

Get instant feedback! Exercises 4 and 5 are available on-line or on CD-ROM.

Section 14.1 **Section Review**

GRAMMAR EXERCISES 6–12

▶ **Exercise 6** Identifying Nouns
Write the nouns in each sentence.

1. The team has practice every afternoon.
2. A whistle signals the start of practice.
3. Runners wear shorts, tank tops, and special shoes.
4. The team runs many short sprints.
5. The coach pays close attention.
6. His stopwatch times all the runners.
7. Some people do the high jump or the hammer throw.
8. The entire team drinks a lot of water.
9. The pulse measures the heartbeat.
10. Stretching is also important at the end of practice.

▶ **Exercise 7** Finding Compound Nouns Copy each sentence, underlining the compound nouns.

1. My family has footraces at the park on the weekends.
2. My brother gives me a head start.
3. Jeff runs track and field for the middle school.
4. I prefer field events like the shot put.
5. Another good exercise for runners is step aerobics.

▶ **Exercise 8** Revising Sentences by Adding Proper Nouns Rewrite the sentences below, replacing the underlined words with proper nouns of your choice.

1. The high school always hosts the county track meet.
2. The race was on a weekday.
3. Our team competed in another state.
4. The mayor made an opening speech.
5. A reporter from the newspaper came.
6. The reporter interviewed the top runner.
7. My friend finished first in one race.
8. A girl cheered the loudest.

9. The award was named for the principal.
10. First prize was dinner at a restaurant.

▶ **Exercise 9** Classifying Nouns
Write the nouns in the following sentences, and label them *compound noun*, *common noun*, or *proper noun*.

1. Florence Griffith Joyner ran her races at high speeds.
2. She placed first at the Jesse Owens National Youth Games.
3. "FloJo" was a gold medalist.
4. She also wrote books and modeled.
5. Her husband starred in the triple jump.

▶ **Exercise 10** Find It in Your Reading List any proper nouns or compound nouns you find in this passage from "The Sound of Summer Running."

Old Mr. Sanderson moved through his shoe store as the proprietor of a pet shop must move through his shop where are kenneled animals from everywhere in the world. . . .

▶ **Exercise 11** Find It in Your Writing Look through your portfolio for a composition about a special person, place, or thing. Circle the proper nouns you used.

▶ **Exercise 12** Writing Application
Write a brief description of a star athlete in your favorite sport. Label all of your nouns *common nouns*, *proper nouns*, or *compound nouns*.

Pronouns

Pronouns are useful words because they can "stand in" for nouns. They prevent people from having to use the same nouns over and over again.

▶ **KEY CONCEPT** A **pronoun** takes the place of a noun. ■

The noun that is replaced by a pronoun is called the *antecedent*. Usually, the antecedent comes before the pronoun. The antecedent is the name of a person, place, or thing.

PRONOUNS AND ANTECEDENTS	
Person	ANTECED PRON Marie said she would watch the news program.
Place	ANTECED PRON Florida is popular because it has a warm climate.
Thing	ANTECED Our old newspapers cannot be recycled PRON until they have been read.

A pronoun and its antecedent will often be in the same sentence, as they are in the examples above. Sometimes, however, a pronoun and its antecedent will be in different sentences.

EXAMPLES: Jane writes well. Many people have enjoyed reading her newspaper articles.
Michael collects magazines. He asks neighbors to save their old magazines for him.

▶ **Exercise 13** Recognizing Pronouns Identify the pronoun or pronouns in each of the following sentences.

EXAMPLE: I bought the newspaper and read it.
ANSWER: I, it

1. The editor read the article and corrected it.
2. The event interested the reporter, so she wrote an article about it.
3. The article was about the mayor and included a recent photo of him.
4. The delivery boys had bikes they could use for their paper routes.
5. I have a subscription to the newspaper. I read my copy every morning as soon as it arrives.

Theme: Media

In this section, you will learn how pronouns can be used to replace nouns in sentences. The examples and exercises are about different news media.

Cross-Curricular Connection: Social Studies

▶ **Exercise 14** Identifying Pronouns and Their Antecedents

Identify the pronouns in each of the following sentences. Then, identify each pronoun's antecedent.

EXAMPLE: The reporter made sure he got his facts right.

ANSWER: he (reporter), his (reporter)

1. Julius Caesar ordered the first news bulletins. They were posted for him every day.
2. Originally, newspapers were one page long, and they were about one event.
3. Johannes Gutenberg invented movable type. His invention made the modern newspaper industry possible.
4. In France, the magazine developed, but it was mainly a collection of literature and not a news source.
5. Each political group had a newspaper in which its leaders expressed their political views.
6. Daniel Defoe and Jonathan Swift were English journalists. They were involved with the struggle for freedom of the press.
7. Benjamin Harris published the first newspaper in the colonies. He was later imprisoned.
8. The publisher John Peter Zenger also got into trouble. A jury found him not guilty in a court trial about the freedom of the press.
9. The Alien and Sedition Acts were passed in 1798. They included laws about censorship.
10. Public education taught more people to read, and they soon demanded newspapers to supply them with the information they wanted to read.

▶ **More Practice**

Grammar Exercise Workbook
• pp. 7–8
On-line Exercise Bank
• Section 14.2
  Go on-line:
  PHSchool.com
  Enter Web Code:
  eak-6002

Get instant feedback! Exercises 13 and 14 are available on-line or on CD-ROM.

Setting up a printing press to produce newsletters

◀ **Critical Viewing** If you were writing about this picture, what pronouns would you use to replace *printer*, *printing press*, and *newsletters*? **[Analyze]**

Recognizing Personal Pronouns

Personal pronouns refer to people who are speaking or the people they are speaking about.

KEY CONCEPT **Personal pronouns** refer to (1) the person speaking or writing, (2) the person listening or reading, or (3) the topic (person, place, or thing) being discussed or written about.■

The first-person pronouns *I, me, my, mine, we, us, our,* and *ours* refer to the person speaking or writing.

EXAMPLE: *I* favor the new layout.
             Give *me* the sports section.

The second-person pronouns *you, your,* and *yours* refer to the person spoken or written to.

EXAMPLE: <u>You</u> will see the photo.

The third-person pronouns *he, him, his, she, her, hers, it, its, they, them, their,* and *theirs* refer to the person, place, or thing being spoken or written about.

EXAMPLES: *He* wants to listen to the radio show.
             They wrote letters to the editor.

Some personal pronouns show possession. Although they can function as adjectives, they are still identified as personal pronouns because they take the place of possessive nouns.

EXAMPLES: *Mary's* town paper comes out weekly.
             Her town paper comes out weekly.
The following chart presents the personal pronouns.

PERSONAL PRONOUNS		
	Singular	**Plural**
First Person	I, me, my, mine	we, us, our, ours
Second Person	you, your, yours	you, your, yours
Third Person	he, him, his she, her, hers it, its	they, them, their, theirs

Grammar and Style Tip

In your writing, try not to use too many pronouns in each sentence. If there is more than one pronoun, your sentence may become confusing.

GRAMMAR IN LITERATURE

from **Hard as Nails**
Russell Baker

Personal pronouns in this passage are printed in blue italics.

My mother started *me* in newspaper work in 1937 right after *my* twelfth birthday. *She* would have started *me* younger, but there was a law against working before age twelve. *She* thought *it* was a silly law, and said so to Deems.

More Practice

Grammar Exercise Workbook
• pp. 9–10
On-line Exercise Bank
• Section 14.2
  Go on-line:
  PHSchool.com
  Enter Web Code:
  eak-6002

iText

Get instant feedback! Exercises 15 and 16 are available on-line or on CD-ROM.

Exercise 15 Recognizing Personal Pronouns Write the personal pronoun in each sentence.
1. Have you ever heard of William Randolph Hearst?
2. He established newspapers in many big cities.
3. *The San Francisco Examiner* was his first newspaper.
4. It featured glaring headlines and stories designed to excite readers.
5. We now consider sensational journalism to be normal.

Exercise 16 Classifying Personal Pronouns Identify whether the underlined pronouns in the sentences below are *first person, second person,* or *third person.*

EXAMPLE: I like to read.
ANSWER: first person

1. <u>I</u> read *The New York Times* every day.
2. Adolph Ochs bought <u>it</u> in 1896.
3. Stories backed by solid facts were <u>his</u> specialty.
4. <u>You</u> probably have seen the paper in the public library.
5 <u>Its</u> circulation is one of the largest in the world.
6. Writers and editors have <u>their</u> names listed in the paper.
7. The staff is much larger than that on <u>our</u> school paper.
8. There are only ten of <u>us</u> on staff here.
9. To <u>me</u>, reporting is the most exciting part.
10. <u>They</u> prefer to sell ads and assist the business manager.

Hundreds of daily and weekly newspapers are published in the United States.

▲ Critical Viewing
Think of a sentence about newspapers that can include pronouns in the first, second, and third person.
[Analyze]

Recognizing Demonstrative Pronouns

Demonstrative pronouns point to people, places, and things, much as you point to them with your finger.

KEY CONCEPT A **demonstrative pronoun** points out a person, place, or thing. ■

There are four demonstrative pronouns. *This* and *that* are singular demonstrative pronouns; *these* and *those* are plural.

EXAMPLES: This is a new invention.

That is newsprint.

I brought some magazines. These are for you.

Those appear to be old papers.

This and *these* point to what is near the speaker or writer. *That* and *those* point to what is more distant.

NEAR: This is the desk where I sit.

Of all the books I own, these are my favorites.

FAR: Is that the computer to use?

Those are well-written articles.

A demonstrative pronoun can point to a noun in the same sentence or in a different one.

SAME SENTENCE: These are the reports I received.

DIFFERENT
SENTENCE: You have a red pencil. That is what I
need.

More Practice

Grammar Exercise Workbook
• pp. 11–12
On-line Exercise Bank
• Section 14.2
  Go on-line:
  PHSchool.com
  Enter Web Code:
  eak-6002

Get instant feedback!
Exercises 17 and 18
are available on-line or
on CD-ROM.

▶ **Exercise 17** Recognizing Demonstrative Pronouns Find the demonstrative pronoun in each sentence. Write both the demonstrative pronoun and the noun to which it refers.

EXAMPLE: This is a new publication.
ANSWER: This (publication)

1. This is a magazine founded by Cyrus Curtis.
2. Isn't that called *Ladies' Home Journal?*
3. That is one of the many magazines that Curtis published.
4. Those were the first popular national magazines.
5. He made several attempts to start a newspaper. Those were not successful.
6. That is the same *Saturday Evening Post* I read today.
7. This is the magazine millions of people bought.
8. Those were record circulation figures in 1897.
9. Curtis printed *Young America* at the age of fifteen. That was his first weekly publication.
10. These are now collectors' items.

▶ **Exercise 18** More Work With Demonstrative Pronouns Identify the demonstrative pronouns in the following sentences. Then, identify each pronoun's antecedent.
1. This is the article I mentioned to you.
2. I was going to show you some others, but those weren't as interesting.
3. Early magazines pushed for social and political changes. These were sometimes adopted.
4. Some in the press helped bring reforms. Those were the journalists called "muckrakers."
5. Horace Greeley founded the *New York Tribune*. That was his outlet for sharing his opinions.

▼ **Critical Viewing**
Think of two sentences to describe this photo, starting one with *"That is . . ."* and the other with *"Those are . . ."*
[Analyze]

The *Saturday Evening Post* has been on newsstands for over 100 years.

Hands-on Grammar

Shape Up Your Pronouns

To practice and remember the first-, second-, and third-person pronouns, do the following activity:

Fold pieces of different-colored construction paper in half. Cut out a large triangle shape, leaving a little space at the point so that when you open the paper you have two connected triangles. Next, cut out a double circle from another piece of construction paper by leaving a little of the circle uncut. Cut out a double square by cutting out a rectangle twice as long as it is wide and folding it in half.

On one triangle, write the first-person singular pronouns. On the other triangle, write the first-person plural pronouns. On the circles, write the second-person pronouns. On the squares, write the third-person pronouns. "Close" each shape and label the front.

Turn over your shapes. On the back side of each one, write a sentence using at least two of the pronoun forms on the reverse side in each of your sentences. Examples: *I gave my dog a bath.* or *We saw our neighbors' new dog.* Compare your sentences to those your classmates create.

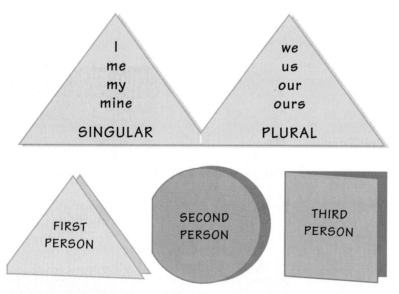

Find It in Your Reading Find sentences in your literature book that contain personal pronouns. Add these examples to your pronoun shapes.

Find It in Your Writing In a piece of autobiographical writing, find sentences that contain personal pronouns. Add them to your pronoun shapes. Look for places where replacing nouns with pronouns would make your writing less repetitive.

Section Review

GRAMMAR EXERCISES 19–25

Exercise 19 Recognizing
Pronouns and Antecedents Copy each
sentence, underlining the pronouns and
their antecedents. Then, draw an arrow
connecting each pronoun and antecedent.

1. The telegraph was the first electric
   medium; it transmitted a message
   along a wire.
2. Several people invented the telegraph,
   and they applied for separate patents.
3. Samuel Morse sent the first message
   when he communicated from
   Washington, D.C., to Baltimore.
4. Morse was aware of the importance of
   his new invention.
5. Alexander Graham Bell invented the
   telephone, and it earned him fame.

Exercise 20 Recognizing
Personal Pronouns Write the personal
pronoun(s) in each sentence. Then, label
the pronouns *first person, second person,*
or *third person.*

1. Have you heard of Guglielmo Marconi?
2. He invented the wireless telegraph.
3. Marconi developed it for military and
   industrial uses.
4. We learned that he also helped invent
   radar.
5. During wartime, our government
   found many uses for his inventions.

Exercise 21 Recognizing
Demonstrative Pronouns List the
demonstrative pronouns that follow and
the noun to which each refers.

1. KDKA and WGY—those were two early
   radio stations.
2. These were stations that attracted
   large audiences.

3. RCA developed home radios. These
   were in 10 million homes by 1929.
4. Broadcasters began selling advertising
   time. This was a new area for growth.
5. American stations had advertising, but
   British stations did not believe in that.

Exercise 22 Identifying All Kinds
of Pronouns List each pronoun below,
and label it *personal* or *demonstrative.*

1. Edward R. Murrow broadcast his
   reports live from London.
2. That was a first for war news.
3. President Roosevelt used the radio to
   broadcast his "fireside chats."
4. This gave his words a personal touch.
5. Leaders of other nations used the
   radio to influence their people.

Exercise 23 Find It in Your
Reading Locate one personal pronoun
and one demonstrative pronoun in this
sentence from "Hard as Nails."

"Get that kick of pride that comes from
knowing you are a newspaper man.
That means something!"

Exercise 24 Find It in Your
Writing Find a paragraph in your portfolio in which you used several pronouns.
Draw arrows linking each pronoun with its
antecedent.

Exercise 25 Writing Application
Write a paragraph about your favorite
radio station. Try to use several personal
and demonstrative pronouns. Underline
the pronouns that you use.

GRAMMAR EXERCISES 26–34

▶ **Exercise 26** Identifying
Compound Nouns Write the compound nouns in each of the following sentences.

1. Local stations transmitted broadcasts over the airwaves.
2. Companies competed for air time for their commercial sales pitches.
3. Many homeowners purchased television sets and placed them in their living rooms.
4. The hours between 8:00 P.M. and 10:00 P.M. were considered prime time for families to watch television.
5. Advertising was featured during station breaks.

▶ **Exercise 27** Identifying Common
and Proper Nouns List the nouns in the following sentences. Identify each noun as *common* or *proper*.

1. After World War II, the government established broadcast regulations.
2. The Federal Communications Commission would not issue licenses to new stations.
3. It made twelve stations available.
4. Three networks dominated television in the United States.
5. After thirty years, Rupert Murdoch started a fourth network.
6. In the following decade, two more networks were established.
7. These stations were funded through advertisements.
8. The Public Broadcasting Act provided money for educational networks.
9. Other independent stations played reruns and movies.
10. Sporting events, such as the World Series, were popular among viewers.

▶ **Exercise 28** Classifying All Kinds
of Nouns List the nouns in each of the following sentences. Tell what kind of noun each one is.

1. After the radio, many inventors turned their attention toward television.
2. As a teenager on a farm in Utah, Philo Farnsworth began work on a television.
3. Later, he was granted the first patent.
4. Companies around the world were working to develop the television.
5. In London, the British Broadcasting Company was moving ahead.
6. In America, networks had development projects.
7. Many people first saw television at the New York World's Fair.
8. There was a live speech by President Roosevelt.
9. Visitors watched on monitors.
10. Experimentation slowed during World War II.

▶ **Exercise 29** Classifying Personal
Pronouns Write the personal pronouns in each sentence. Then, label them *first person, second person,* or *third person.*

1. Do you have a favorite type of show?
2. My brother says his favorites are situation comedies.
3. When our parents get to pick the show we watch, they usually choose a show about family life.
4. I like talk shows more than you or your sister do.
5. The celebrity guests they feature appeal to me.

▶ **Exercise 30** Supplying Personal
Pronouns Rewrite these sentences,

supplying a personal pronoun to fill the blank. Then, circle the pronoun's antecedent.

1. The big networks dominated television so much that ___?___ controlled most programming.
2. Television changed the American way of life wherever ___?___ was watched.
3. Networks brought performers to audiences who hadn't seen ___?___ before.
4. One early star was Milton Berle. ___?___ show was very popular.
5. Cable television provided viewers with shows to match ___?___ interests.

▶ **Exercise 31** Recognizing Demonstrative Pronouns Find the demonstrative pronoun in each sentence. Write both the demonstrative pronoun and the noun to which it refers.

1. Television offered live images. Newspaper readers had never seen these.
2. That is one reason that newspapers changed their role.
3. Live drama and comedy in homes—these were innovations of radio.
4. One television network presented a news program in 1956. This was the first example of the evening news.
5. Presidential candidates participate in debates. Those are broadcast on national television.

▶ **Exercise 32** Classifying Nouns and Pronouns Write all the nouns and pronouns in the following sentences. Label each noun a *common noun* or a *proper noun*. Label each pronoun a *personal pronoun* or a *demonstrative pronoun*.

1. Broadcasting has been regulated since it began.
2. The Wireless Act was the first law to do this.
3. Laws about entertainment came later.
4. First, our legislators set up the Federal Radio Commission.
5. That was then reorganized into the Federal Communications Commission.
6. This was how the government gained its power over broadcasting.
7. The president of the United States names five members to the commission.
8. These are the people responsible for licenses and regulations.
9. Its domain includes all technological media—from radio to the Internet.
10. My report mentions all of this.

▶ **Exercise 33** Revision Practice: Replacing Nouns With Pronouns Rewrite the following paragraph, replacing some repeated nouns with personal or demonstrative pronouns.

(1) Over the years, people have enjoyed watching different types of shows on the people's televisions. (2) Early on, variety shows were very popular. (3) Variety shows featured singers, comedians, dancers, and magicians. (4) One of the most popular variety show hosts was Ed Sullivan. (5) Ed Sullivan was a newspaper columnist; Ed Sullivan was not a performer. (6) Ed Sullivan did not really have any talent. (7) Yet millions of viewers tuned to Ed Sullivan's show every week. (8) Viewers enjoyed the performers Ed Sullivan presented, and viewers liked Ed Sullivan's funny way of introducing Ed Sullivan's guests. (9) Cheryl says Cheryl's grandfather does a great imitation of Ed Sullivan's way of speaking. (10) When Sal and I heard the imitation, Sal and I laughed.

▶ **Exercise 34** Writing Application Write a brief narrative based on a news story you have heard or read about. Include information about *who, what, where, when,* and *how* in your narrative, just as a reporter does. Underline all of the nouns and pronouns that you use.

Standardized Test Preparation Workshop

Completing Analogies

On standardized tests, analogies are test items that measure your understanding of the relationship between word meanings. The relationship between the words in the first pair is similar to the relationship between the words in the second pair.

Look for the following relationships between words in analogies:

synonyms—fondness : affection
antonyms—love : hate
part to whole or whole to part—
  member : club *or* club : member
cause and effect or effect and cause—ice : skid
functional—sewing : thread
degree—warm : sweltering

The following test items will give you practice with analogies. The two different formats used show the most common ways these items appear on tests.

Sample Test Items

Directions: Complete each item by choosing the phrase that best completes the sentence.

Glory is to dishonor as—

(A) power is to energy.
(B) honesty is to trickery.
(C) knowledge is to books.
(D) leader is to troops.
(E) fame is to popularity.

Each question below consists of a related pair of words, followed by five pairs of words labeled A through E. Select the pair that <u>best</u> expresses a relationship similar to that expressed in the original pair.

ROOKIE : NEWCOMER ::

(A) expert : apprentice
(B) professional : amateur
(C) freshman : senior
(D) General : Chief
(E) untrue : false

Answers and Explanations

The correct answer is *B*. The noun *glory* names the condition of being honored or praised, while the noun *dishonor* names the opposite condition—having lost honor or respect. In the same manner, the noun *honesty* names the condition of being truthful, while the noun *trickery* names the practice of being dishonest.

The correct answer is *D*. The noun *rookie* names a person who is just beginning a specific type of training, just as its synonym, *newcomer*, names a person who is new to some place or job. The nouns *General* and *Chief* both name persons in charge. The words in answer choices *A, B,* and *C* express relationships of antonyms or words that have opposite instead of similar meanings. Answer choice *E* presents two synonyms that are adjectives and not nouns, as in the original pair.

Practice 1 **Directions:** Each question below consists of a related pair of words or phrases, followed by five pairs of words or phrases labeled A through E. Select the pair that best expresses a relationship similar to that expressed in the original pair.

1. HERO : VILLAIN ::
   (A) goodness : evil
   (B) guitar : instrument
   (C) teacher : school
   (D) triumph : evil
   (E) slide : toy

2. BEAUTY : ATTRACTIVENESS ::
   (A) pretty : nice
   (B) luck : loser
   (C) happiness : sorrow
   (D) affection : fondness
   (E) honesty : corruption

3. DESERT: SWAMP ::
   (A) jungle : lushness
   (B) forest : trees
   (C) dry : damp
   (D) land : ocean
   (E) humidity : weather

4. TALENT : SKILL ::
   (A) method : way
   (B) style : knowledge
   (C) library : readers
   (D) stylist : hair
   (E) coach : winner

5. WEALTH : POVERTY ::
   (A) television : entertainment
   (B) smart : intelligent
   (C) popularity : loneliness
   (D) store : purchases
   (E) apartment : building

Practice 2 **Directions:** Complete each item by choosing the phrase that best completes the sentence.

1. Expert is to beginner as —
   (A) middle is to outside.
   (B) sickness is to pain.
   (C) paper is to pen.
   (D) experience is to newness.
   (E) pianist is to musician.

2. Calmness is to peace as —
   (A) sorrow is to happiness.
   (B) silence is to a scream.
   (C) sight is to eyes.
   (D) fear is to anger.
   (E) rage is to conflict.

3. Feelings is to emotions as —
   (A) surf is to beach.
   (B) safety is to injury.
   (C) weakness is to power.
   (D) storm is to downpour.
   (E) snow is to sunshine.

4. Darkness is to light as —
   (A) garage is to car.
   (B) winter is to spring.
   (C) sun is to moon.
   (D) train is to transportation.
   (E) night is to day.

5. Vision is to sight as —
   (A) eye is to ear.
   (B) exhaustion is to tiredness.
   (C) train is to tracks.
   (D) airplane is to sky.
   (E) thirst is to water.

15 *Verbs*

When you studied nouns and pronouns, you learned about words that name people, places, and things. To state your ideas, you also need words that express action or condition. Words that let you say what people are doing or what is happening are verbs. Verbs are necessary to tell about the events of the past. Verbs can relate the actions of Greek heroes, for example.

In this chapter, you will learn several things about verbs. First, you will learn how to recognize a verb. Then, you will learn about three different kinds of verbs—verbs that express action, verbs that link the parts of a sentence, and verbs that help other verbs.

▲ **Critical Viewing**
This photograph shows the ruins of a temple honoring the Greek goddess Athena. Describe how the temple looks today, and tell how you think the Greeks might have used the temple thousands of years ago. What verbs did you use and what purpose did they serve? **[Describe]**

Diagnostic Test

Directions: Write all answers on a separate sheet of paper.

Skill Check A. Identify the action verbs in the sentences below.

1. The ancient Greeks wondered about the causes of some events in nature.
2. They saw lightning between rain clouds.
3. They heard thunder soon after the lightning.
4. What caused these frightening occurrences?
5. Other questions also puzzled these early people.
6. As a result, they created myths.
7. The myths explained natural phenomena.
8. They described them as the acts of gods and goddesses.
9. People passed the stories down by word of mouth from one generation to the next.
10. Eventually, someone wrote down the stories.

Skill Check B. Copy the sentences below. Underline each linking verb, and draw a double-headed arrow to connect the words that are linked by the verb.

11. Thunder is an explosive noise.
12. It usually sounds very threatening.
13. A clap of thunder seems longer than a flash of lightning.
14. Thunder becomes evident after a lightning flash.
15. Zeus was the name given to the ruler of all the gods.
16. Perhaps thunder was the voice of this god.
17. Zeus grew angry at times.
18. He appeared more powerful than the other gods.
19. Mount Olympus became his home.
20. Hera was his wife.

Skill Check C. Label each underlined word a *linking verb* or an *action verb*.

21. Before the storm, the air <u>grew</u> quiet.
22. Massive black clouds <u>appeared</u> on the horizon.
23. The thunder <u>sounded</u> frightening.
24. Soon, we <u>felt</u> the first drops of rain.
25. Within minutes, the sky <u>looked</u> clear again.

Skill Check D. Write the verb phrase (main verb plus helping verbs) in each sentence below. Underline the helping verbs, and circle the main verbs.

26. Clouds are divided into four main groups.
27. These groups can be called families.
28. Low clouds might become rain or thunder clouds.
29. They would look thick, dark, and shapeless.
30. Clouds have been blocking the sun.

Action Verbs and Linking Verbs

A verb is an important part of every sentence. No sentence is complete without one. A verb tells what someone or something does or is. In other words, a verb shows action or condition.

▶ **KEY CONCEPT** A **verb** expresses the action or condition of a person, place, or thing. ■

Many verbs express actions or activities that can be completed. In the following examples, the verbs showing action are underlined.

EXAMPLES: The archaeologist <u>digs</u>.
              She <u>found</u> a shard of pottery.

Other verbs express condition, that is, they link a noun or pronoun with words that describe the condition of the noun or pronoun. In the examples below, the verbs expressing condition are underlined.

EXAMPLES: The ruins <u>were</u> spectacular.
              This vase <u>feels</u> smooth.

▶ **Critical Viewing** Describe your impressions of this famous ruin. What verbs did you use in your description? **[Describe]**

The Parthenon in Greece

Using Action Verbs

There are several different kinds of verbs. One kind, *action verbs*, shows what someone or something does or did. *Rise, live, fall,* and *explode* are all action verbs.

▶ **KEY CONCEPT** An **action verb** indicates the action of a person or thing. The action may be visible or mental. ■

Some action verbs show visible action:

EXAMPLES: The Parthenon <u>stands</u> on the Acropolis.
Homer <u>wrote</u> the poem.
Nancy <u>reads</u> history books.

Other verbs indicate mental actions. These actions cannot be seen or heard directly. They are thinking activities, but they are still actions.

EXAMPLES: The students <u>understand</u> the assignment.
Everyone <u>believes</u> you.

▶ **Exercise 1** Identifying Action Verbs Identify the action verb in each sentence below.

EXAMPLE: The audience applauded the performers.
ANSWER: applauded

1. The ancient Greeks called themselves Hellenes.
2. Their small states prized their independence.
3. Invading tribes from the north conquered new territories.
4. Kings replaced the tribal chiefs.
5. Then, noble families in the city-states acquired great wealth and power.
6. The nobility controlled the government completely.
7. They would not share any power.
8. Unhappy commoners disliked the rule of the aristocrats.
9. Tyrants seized political power by force.
10. Eventually, the system changed.

▶ **Exercise 2** Writing Sentences With Action Verbs Write a sentence using each of the following action verbs.

1. discover
2. wish
3. soothe
4. challenge
5. hide
6. announce
7. attempt
8. pursue
9. withdraw
10. scatter

Grammar and Style Tip

Remember that your verbs can add life to your descriptive writing. Choose verbs that add action and energy to your narratives and descriptions.

▶ **More Practice**

Grammar Exercise Workbook
• pp. 13–14
On-line Exercise Bank
• Section 15.1
Go on-line:
PHSchool.com
Enter Web Code:
eak-6002

Get instant feedback! Exercises 1 and 2 are available on-line or on CD-ROM.

GRAMMAR IN
LITERATURE

from **Orpheus**
translated by Alice Low

In the following excerpt from the Greek myth "Orpheus," the action verbs are highlighted in blue italics.

Orpheus *played* his lyre so sweetly that he *charmed* all things on earth. Men and women *forgot* their cares when they *gathered* around him to listen.

Using Linking Verbs

Linking verbs join nouns or pronouns with words that identify or describe them.

▶ **KEY CONCEPT** A **linking verb** connects a noun or pronoun to a word that identifies or describes the noun or pronoun. ■

The most common linking verbs are all forms of the verb *be: am, are, is, was,* and *were.*

EXAMPLES: Laura <u>is</u> the historian. (*Historian* identifies *Laura.*)

Elliot <u>was</u> ready. (*Ready* describes *Elliot.*)

Several other verbs also function as linking verbs. They work to connect the parts of a sentence in the same way as the forms of *be.*

EXAMPLE: The chief <u>remained</u> calm. (*Calm* describes *chief.*)

OTHER LINKING VERBS		
appear	look	sound
become	remain	stay
feel	seem	taste
grow	smell	turn

▶ **Exercise 3** Recognizing Linking Verbs Copy the sentences below onto a piece of paper. Underline each linking verb. Then, draw a double-headed arrow to connect the words that are linked by the verb.

EXAMPLE: The Greek philosophers <u>were</u> thoughtful.

1. The Greek language was understandable throughout the country.
2. All the dialects sounded similar.
3. Within each city-state, customs and religious practices were the same.
4. Four national festivals became traditional.
5. The Olympic Games were the most important.
6. The Greek city-states were very independent.
7. However, some unification seemed possible.
8. States and their weaker neighbors became leagues.
9. Athens and Sparta became the leading city-states.
10. Athens remained the best example of democracy in ancient Greece.
11. Sparta grew more powerful than any other state.
12. Sparta's rules appeared the strictest.
13. Its army was strong.
14. The Greek city-states became united during the Persian Wars.
15. Afterward, Athens was the center of culture in the Greek world.

▶ **Exercise 4** Writing Sentences With Linking Verbs For each pair of words below, write a sentence in which you use a linking verb to connect them.
1. Greek myths/entertaining
2. ruins/old
3. Greek food/delicious
4. tourists/tired
5. music/beautiful
6. weather/outstanding
7. Athens/larger
8. festivals/fun
9. air/cold
10. sculptures/exquisite

▼ **Critical Viewing** What two or three linking verbs might you use in describing this Greek mosaic? **[Describe]**

Distinguishing Between Action Verbs and Linking Verbs

Some verbs can be used as either linking verbs or action verbs.

LINKING: The tyrant *felt* threatened. (*Felt* links *tyrant* and *threatened*.)

ACTION: The tyrant *felt* the sword. (The tyrant performed an action.)

LINKING: The people *grew* unhappy. (*Grew* links *people* and *unhappy*.)

ACTION: The people *grew* poor crops. (The people performed an action.)

To test whether a verb is a linking verb or an action verb, replace the verb with *is, am,* or *are.* If a sentence still makes sense, then the verb is a linking verb.

EXAMPLE: The tyrant *is* threatened.

▲ **Critical Viewing** Think of two sentences to describe this sculpture—one using an action verb, the other using a linking verb. **[Describe]**

▶ **Exercise 5** **Distinguishing Between Action Verbs and Linking Verbs** Identify the verb in each sentence below. Label each one a *linking verb* or an *action verb.*
1. Athens felt most powerful after the Persian Wars.
2. During the war, the city felt great sorrow.
3. Afterward, the situation looked better.
4. Athens considered its former allies as subjects.
5. It seemed the strongest member of the Delian League.
6. The city-state of Athens grew dominant.
7. Pericles, its leader, turned his attention to the city's appearance.
8. He felt pleased with the city's prosperity and cultural accomplishments.
9. Many Greek writers felt the success of their dramas.
10. This period became the Golden Age of Greece.

▶ **Exercise 6** **Identify Action Verbs and Linking Verbs in Literature** Copy this passage from the Greek myth "Orpheus" into your notebook. Then, circle all of the verbs and identify each one as either a *linking verb* or an *action verb.*

Orpheus loved a young woman named Eurydice, and when they were married, they looked forward to many years of happiness together. But soon after, Eurydice stepped on a poisonous snake and died.

Orpheus roamed the earth, singing sad melodies to try to overcome his grief. But it was no use.

Section Review

GRAMMAR EXERCISES 7–12

▶ **Exercise 7** Distinguishing Between Action and Linking Verbs Identify the verb in each sentence below. Then, label each one a *linking verb* or an *action verb.*

1. The city-state of Athens led the Delian League.
2. The citizens of Sparta organized a separate league.
3. Sparta and Athens soon clashed in a war.
4. The conflict turned bitter.
5. Macedonia, to the north, became stronger.
6. With a Greek and Macedonian army, Alexander the Great grew very confident.
7. Later, the Greek world turned its interest to math and philosophy.
8. Many discoveries by Euclid and Archimedes remain correct today.
9. Other people felt the call of poetry.
10. Greek influence grew stronger in Syria and Egypt.

▶ **Exercise 8** Completing Sentences With Linking Verbs Complete each sentence below with an appropriate linking verb.

1. For many years, he ___?___ dominant.
2. His army ___?___ unbeatable.
3. His empire ___?___ enormous.
4. Greek culture ___?___ widely known.
5. The Greek culture and way of life ___?___ still dominant.

▶ **Exercise 9** Completing Sentences With Action and Linking Verbs Complete two of the following sentences with action verbs and three with linking verbs. Label each verb *action* or *linking.*

1. Many city-states ___?___ leagues.
2. They ___?___ helpful for protection.
3. Some ___?___ more powerful than others.
4. Sparta ___?___ independent.
5. More conflicts ___?___.

▶ **Exercise 10** Find It in Your Reading Identify as *action* or *linking* each of the underlined verbs in the following excerpt from the Greek myth "Arachne," translated by Olivia Coolidge.

At last Arachne's fame <u>became</u> so great that people used to come from far and wide to watch her working. Even the graceful nymphs would <u>steal</u> in from stream or forest and <u>peep</u> shyly through the dark doorway, watching in wonder the white arms of Arachne as she <u>stood</u> at the loom and <u>threw</u> the shuttle from hand to hand between the hanging threads, or drew out the long wool, fine as a hair, from the distaff as she <u>sat</u> spinning.

▶ **Exercise 11** Find It in Your Writing Look through your portfolio to find a recent sample of descriptive writing. Go through at least two paragraphs and identify all the action verbs and linking verbs. Then, revise two sentences, replacing linking verbs with action verbs.

▶ **Exercise 12** Writing Application Write a brief summary of something you have learned about ancient Greece. Use at least three action verbs and three linking verbs. Underline the action verbs once and the linking verbs twice.

Helping Verbs

Verbs such as *jump, talk,* and *wait* are called *main verbs.* Sometimes, however, verbs are made up of several words, such as *had jumped, might have talked, would have understood,* and *could have been waiting.* In this case, the verbs that come before the main verb are called *helping verbs.* They help express the meaning of the main verb.

▶ **KEY CONCEPT** A **helping verb** is a verb that comes before the main verb and adds to its meaning. ■

A main verb and one or more helping verbs form a *verb phrase.* In the sentences below, the helping verbs are underlined and the main verbs are boxed. Together, the two kinds of verbs make up verb phrases.

EXAMPLES: He <u>was</u> | *leading* | the Romans.

He <u>had</u> <u>been</u> | *leading* | the Romans.

He <u>should</u> <u>have</u> <u>been</u> | *leading* | the Romans.

The various forms of *be* and *have* are the most common helping verbs. The following chart includes some of the forms of *be* and *have,* as well as other helping verbs.

COMMON HELPING VERBS		
am	have	may
are	has	might
is	had	must
was	can	shall
were	could	should
be	do	will
being	does	would
been	did	

▶ **Exercise 13** Recognizing Verb Phrases Write each sentence below on your paper. Underline the verb phrase.
1. Rome had conquered many territories.
2. The emperors could ignore Greece.
3. Greek states might have worked together.
4. Next year, we will study more about Greece.
5. I have learned about Greece in several classes.

Theme: Ancient
Greece
. . . .
In this section, you
will learn about
helping verbs. The
examples and exer-
cises tell more about
ancient Greece.
. . . .
**Cross-Curricular
Connection:
Social Studies**

❀ **Grammar
and Style Tip**

In your own writing, be careful not to use very long strings of helping verbs. Sometimes they are necessary, but they can also make your sentence confusing. Ask a listener if the verbs in your sentences are clear.

Exercise 14 Identifying Helping Verbs and Main Verbs

Copy the verb phrase in each sentence below. Then, underline the helping verbs and circle the main verbs.

EXAMPLE: Rome was intruding in Greek affairs.
ANSWER: was (intruding)

1. Macedonia had allied itself with Carthage.
2. The Romans were attaining a strong position in the Mediterranean area.
3. Rome had defeated the city-states.
4. All Greek territories would be placed under Roman rule.
5. Athens and Sparta could remain free states.
6. The political role of the city-state had declined.
7. In later years, Greece did experience a rebirth.
8. Trade and intellectual activities were thriving.
9. The emperor Hadrian had appreciated beauty.
10. He would restore the ruins of Athens.

Exercise 15 Writing Sentences With Helping Verbs

Using each of the following verb phrases, write five original sentences.
1. were going
2. must have known
3. should have been studying
4. had been listening
5. might rebound

Exercise 16 Revising Sentences to Include Helping Verbs

Revise each sentence below to include a verb phrase consisting of a helping verb and a main verb.

1. By 700 B.C., Greece organized itself into a loose collection of independent city-states.
2. By 508 B.C., a government formed in Athens that allowed citizens a say in the government.
3. When learning about the ancient Greeks, people study the arts and sciences as well as the government.
4. The story of Orpheus illustrates the Greek belief in the power of music.
5. An interest in Greek culture leads people to read Greek mythology.

More Practice

Grammar Exercise Workbook
• pp. 19–20
On-line Exercise Bank
• Section 15.2
  Go on-line:
  PHSchool.com
  Enter Web Code:
  eak-6002

▼ Critical Viewing This is a photograph of the Roman Colosseum. How do you imagine it was used? What helping verbs did you use in answering this question? [Infer]

Hands-on Grammar

Helping-Verb Expander

To explore how helping verbs expand or change the meaning of a verb, create helping-verb expanders.

First, fan-fold a sheet of paper three times to create four "panels."

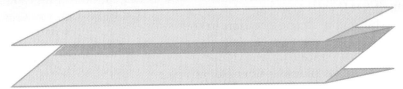

Then, with the paper folded, cut a basic shape, such as a diamond. Do not cut all the way to the folds, because the folds must stay connected, as when you cut a chain of paper dolls.

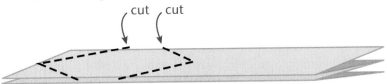

Set the extra paper aside. Unfold the shapes. Fold the outermost left shape inwards. Fold the outermost right shape inwards. The inside points of the end shapes should be next to each other and the middle shapes should be hidden. Write a simple sentence such as *The boat sailed.*

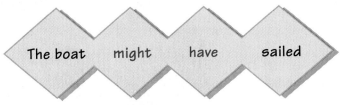

Unfold the helping-verb expander and fill in the blank spaces with helping verbs from the list on page 320. These verbs will "help" you get from the noun at the beginning of the expander to the verb at the end. Read the new sentence and contrast its meaning with the original sentence. Use the leftover paper to make more helping-verb expanders. With a partner, experiment with different numbers of folds and different verbs.

Find It in Your Reading Look in your literature anthology for sentences that contain verb phrases. Create helping-verb expanders for these sentences. Write the sentences with different helping verbs to see how the meaning changes.

Find It in Your Writing Find verb phrases in sentences in your writing. Discuss with a partner how the meaning of each sentence would change if you used different helping verbs.

Section 15.2 Section Review

GRAMMAR EXERCISES 17–22

Exercise 17 Identifying Helping Verbs and Main Verbs Copy the verb phrases in each sentence below. Then, underline the helping verbs and circle the main verbs.

1. Life in ancient Athens was structured differently from life today.
2. Women and men did occupy separate roles.
3. Girls were sheltered within their families.
4. Marriage may have been arranged very early.
5. White dresses would be worn for the ceremony.
6. Also, the girls would wear crowns.
7. Then, their childhood toys were given away.
8. Feasts of celebration could be offered for many days.
9. Both families must have enjoyed the wedding feasts.
10. Then, the bride would move into her new house.

Exercise 18 Completing Verb Phrases Complete each verb phrase below with one of the following: *was, were, would, would have, have been.* (Each will be used only once.)

1. The first Stone Age settlements ___?___ formed around 7000 B.C.
2. In 2500 B.C., the Bronze Age ___?___ just beginning.
3. The Olympic Games ___?___ held since 776 B.C.
4. The first Greek city-states ___?___ appeared between 800–600 B.C.
5. In 336 B.C., Alexander the Great ___?___ become king.

Exercise 19 Revising Sentences to Include Verb Phrases Rewrite each sentence below to include a helping verb and a main verb. Note that you may have to add a verb that changes the meaning of a given sentence.

1. Greek culture glorified the arts.
2. He read the *Iliad* and the *Odyssey*.
3. Hesiod and Alcman were great poets.
4. Lyric poetry achieved great popularity.
5. Thespis was the founder of Greek tragedy.
6. Sculptors and potters became famous.
7. Pythagoras created theories for mathematics.
8. Philosophers wrote many books.
9. Builders designed new buildings.
10. Writers recorded history.

Exercise 20 Find It in Your Reading Find a complete version of the Greek myth "Orpheus." Make a photocopy of it. Then, use a highlighter to identify all of the verb phrases it contains. Circle each helping verb.

Exercise 21 Find It in Your Writing Look through your writing portfolio. Find five sentences in which you have used verb phrases. Make sure that the helping verbs make your meaning clear. Revise any that could be improved.

Exercise 22 Writing Application Write a brief narrative relating an event that might have occurred at the Olympic Games in ancient Greece. Use helping verbs in some of your sentences, and underline all verb phrases.

GRAMMAR EXERCISES 23–31

▶ **Exercise 23** Identifying Action Verbs List the action verb(s) in each sentence below.

1. The Greeks told many stories and legends.
2. We call these stories myths.
3. The stories explained the mysteries of the world.
4. They thought Greek gods and goddesses controlled nature.
5. These characters in the stories exhibited human traits.
6. Like humans, they also had emotions and problems.
7. The mythological gods lived in their own society.
8. Some gods wielded more power than others.
9. They roamed freely around the world.
10. Gods and goddesses possessed immortality.
11. Each Greek god ruled in one part of the world.
12. The twelve chief gods and goddesses spent their time on Mount Olympus.
13. Zeus and Hera, his queen, led the gods in the sky.
14. Poseidon controlled the seas with his wife, Amphitrite.
15. Hades lived in the dark underworld.

▶ **Exercise 24** Recognizing Linking Verbs Copy the sentences below. Underline each linking verb. Then, draw a double-headed arrow to connect the words that are linked by the verb.

1. The influence of mythology was apparent in all areas of Greek life.
2. Certain behavior grew unacceptable.
3. People seemed wary of the gods' punishments.

4. The Greek gods remained well known through the poetry of the Greeks.
5. They were important in the arts.
6. They became the inspiration for beautiful temples.
7. Worship at home was also common for the Greeks.
8. Different places in the home were sacred for different reasons.
9. The hearth became the place of honor for the goddess Hestia.
10. Every person's rituals sounded unique.

▶ **Exercise 25** Distinguishing Between Action Verbs and Linking Verbs Identify the verb in each sentence below, and tell whether it is a *linking verb* or an *action verb*.

1. The temple at Delphi appeared holy to the ancient Greeks.
2. An oracle appeared to visitors.
3. She looked into the future.
4. The site was thought to be holy because of Apollo.
5. He was named the god of the sun.
6. The other gods felt the wrath of Zeus.
7. Zeus' strength appeared the greatest of all the gods.
8. Hermes was a messenger for the other mythological gods.
9. He looked graceful with his winged sandals.
10. A trumpet sounded his arrival.

▶ **Exercise 26** Identifying Helping Verbs and Main Verbs Copy the verb phrase in each sentence below. Underline the helping verbs, and circle the main verbs.

1. Greek mythology did develop from earlier ideas.
2. The Minoan civilization had developed on the island of Crete.

3. The legends of these people would have involved animals and nature.
4. According to their beliefs, all natural objects must have contained individual spirits.
5. These ideas have been included in Greek mythology.
6. Ancient Greeks could have explained events in nature differently.
7. Their heroes had been glorified frequently.
8. The mythological gods might have lived many years before.
9. Most will think them fantastic and unbelievable.
10. Maybe Greek rituals were adapted from Egyptian rituals.

Exercise 27 Writing Sentences With Verbs and Verb Phrases

Write five sentences, each using one of the following verbs.

1. save
2. uncover
3. discover
4. attack
5. defeat

Exercise 28 Revising Sentences With Verbs

Revise each of the following sentences to use an action verb instead of a linking verb. You may make other changes as needed.

EXAMPLE: The Titans were rulers of the Earth.

ANSWER: The Titans ruled the Earth.

1. Zeus was then in control of Mount Olympus.
2. Zeus is the one with lightning bolts for weapons.
3. In some stories, the gods were terrifying to humans.
4. In other stories, the mortal characters are able to trick the gods.
5. Reading mythology is something I like to do.

Exercise 29 Identifying All Types of Verbs

Identify all the verbs and verb phrases in the following sentences. Then, tell whether each verb is an *action verb*, a *linking verb*, a *helping verb*, or a *main verb*.

1. Hercules was the son of Zeus.
2. He became the strongest man on Earth.
3. Single-handedly, he killed a lion.
4. This feat impressed a king.
5. Later, Hercules would marry the daughter of the king of Thebes.
6. For twelve years, Hercules was a servant to King Eurystheus of Tiryns.
7. He performed twelve difficult tasks.
8. He succeeded in killing a nine-headed swamp monster.
9. Then, Hercules was given immortality.
10. Hercules' story is still told today.

Exercise 30 Writing Application

Write a short myth to explain an event in nature, such as lightning or a sunrise. Underline all verbs and verb phrases. Label each one *visible action*, *mental action*, or *linking verb*.

Exercise 31 CUMULATIVE REVIEW Nouns, Pronouns, and Verbs

Identify all the nouns, pronouns, and verbs in this passage. Label each verb an *action verb* or a *linking verb*.

Zeus was the father of the gods. The ancient Greeks understood his strength. His wife, Hera, was often jealous of humans and other gods. Hermes carried messages for the gods. He traveled around the world. The goddess of love was Aphrodite. Many poets and musicians have based their works on myths. An opera retells the story of Orpheus. Shakespeare based some of his works on mythological characters. Myths still capture our imagination.

Standardized Test Preparation Workshop

Standard English Usage: Verbs

Standardized tests of grammar and usage will usually include questions on verb usage. You will be asked to read a passage with numbered blanks. Then, you will have four choices for the best verb or verb phrase to complete each sentence. Often, the choice depends on the time of the action. Sometimes, you will need to evaluate how helping verbs affect the meaning of the completed sentence. The following sample and practice sets will give you practice responding to these types of items in a standardized test format.

Sample Test Item

Read the passage, and choose the letter of the word or group of words that belongs in the space.

The American Red Cross ___(1)___ babysitting certification courses next year.

1 A offers

   B did offer

   C will offer

   D offered

Answer and Explanation

The correct answer is **C.** The helping verb *will* indicates that the action occurs in the future. Since the action occurs next year, *will offer* best completes the sentence.

▶ Practice 1 Directions: Read the passage, and choose the letter of the word or group of words that belongs in each space.

Last spring four rabbits ___(1)___ born in our backyard. When we saw them, we wondered if they ___(2)___ abandoned. The mother, however, ___(3)___ for them. Now, they ___(4)___ around the garden and soon ___(5)___ to climb through the fence.

1 **A** were
  B is
  C will be
  D are being

2 **F** are
  G had been
  H were being
  J will be

3 **A** did care
  B would have cared
  C cared
  D might have been caring

4 **F** were hopping
  G hop
  H must have hopped
  J will hop

5 **A** learned
  B will have learned
  C learns
  D did learn

▶ Practice 2 Directions: Read the passage, and choose the letter of the word or group of words that belongs in each space.

Early in 1874, the small family ___(1)___ their meager belongings into the wagon and set out for their new life in the west. Pa ___(2)___ the wagon while Ma ___(3)___ the family's belongings. The six children ___(4)___ impatiently while the preparations were going on. The whole family ___(5)___ excited about their adventure.

1 **A** loads
  B did load
  C loaded
  D had been loading

2 **F** had prepared
  G did prepare
  H has prepared
  J would have prepared

3 **A** packed
  B will pack
  C might have been packing
  D packs

4 **F** did wait
  G might wait
  H should wait
  J were waiting

5 **A** was being
  B was
  C would be
  D will have been

Some words make language come alive for a reader or listener in the same way that colors and sounds make some video games more exciting. The words that do this are called *modifiers*.

In this chapter, you will learn about *adjectives*. These are the words that help nouns create pictures. You might use adjectives to describe what kind of video game you are playing or how many games you have already played.

You will also learn about *adverbs*. Adverbs are the words that make verbs clear and exact. These words can describe how you are playing the game.

▲ **Critical Viewing**
Identify words to describe the colors and sounds of the raft ride or to describe the way a rafter might feel while speeding down the river. **[Analyze]**

Diagnostic Test

Directions: Write all answers on a separate sheet of paper.

Skill Check A. List the adjectives in the sentences below, and write the noun that each adjective modifies.

1. Bowlers wear special shoes.
2. Players sometimes wear colorful uniforms.
3. A bowling ball has two or three holes.
4. The white pins have narrow necks.
5. A player takes several running steps before releasing the ball.

Skill Check B. Write out each phrase. Replace the blank with the correct indefinite article (*a* or *an*).

6. ___?___ organized sport
7. ___?___ wooden runway
8. ___?___ high score
9. ___?___ unusual bowling style
10. ___?___ pair of strikes

Skill Check C. List the proper adjectives in each sentence. Then, list the noun each modifies.

11. European settlers brought these games to America.
12. Ninepin bowling, known as skittles, is a German game.
13. North American players prefer tenpin bowling.
14. Tenpins was originally a Dutch sport.
15. It quickly caught on among German immigrants in the Midwest.

Skill Check D. Write the possessive adjective in each sentence below. Then, write its antecedent and the noun it modifies.

16. Bowlers have enjoyed their game for hundreds of years.
17. King Edward III discouraged his troops from bowling.
18. Bowling increased its popularity under King Henry VIII.
19. American soldiers based in England during World War II taught British servicemen their version of the game.
20. Floretta McCutcheon gave clinics to teach women her sport.

Skill Check E. Write whether the underlined word is functioning as an *adjective* or a *pronoun*.

21. <u>This</u> was the early development of bowling.
22. Several pins stood at <u>that</u> end of the alley.
23. Variations emerged in <u>those</u> European countries.
24. Andy Varipapa taught me <u>this</u> bowling trick.
25. <u>That</u> is one of my fondest memories.

Skill Check F. Write the adverbs in the following sentences, and then write the word each adverb modifies.

26. Players roll the ball carefully down the alley.
27. They try hard to strike the first pin.
28. It is very difficult to knock down all of the pins.
29. A pinspotter automatically sets up the pins.
30. This invention quickly made bowling more enjoyable.

Adjectives

Adjectives are words that make language more specific. For example, *car* is a general word, but a *red, two-door convertible* is far more specific. Adjectives such as *red* and *two-door* make nouns and pronouns clearer and more vivid.

▶ **KEY CONCEPT** An **adjective** is a word that describes something. ■

Adjectives are often called *modifiers*, because they modify, or change, the meaning of a noun or pronoun. Notice how *game* is modified by each set of adjectives below.

EXAMPLES: *old-fashioned* game
new video game
children's board game

Adjectives answer several questions about nouns and pronouns. They tell *What kind? Which one? How many?* or *How much?*

QUESTIONS ANSWERED BY ADJECTIVES		
What Kind?	*expensive* toys	*colorful* caps
Which One?	*this* man	*these* paddles
How Many? How Much?	*few* cars	*many* people

▶ **Exercise 1** Recognizing Adjectives Identify the adjectives in each sentence. Then, tell which question is answered by each adjective.

EXAMPLE: The amusement park has several rides.
ANSWER: amusement (*What kind* of park?)
several (*How many* rides?)

1. Table tennis is played on green tables.
2. A white stripe runs down the center of the table.
3. Two or four players hit hollow balls over a net.
4. Their wooden racquets have an oval shape.
5. A proper serve bounces once on each side of the net.
6. One player will serve until five points are scored.
7. This game ended when I scored twenty-one points.
8. A shot that tips the table edge is usually a winning shot.
9. After every game, the players switch ends of the table.
10. Doubles games follow most of these rules.

Theme: Sports and Games

In this section, you will learn that adjectives are used to describe nouns and pronouns. The examples and exercises in this section are about sports and games.

Cross-Curricular Connection: Physical Education

▶ **More Practice**

Grammar Exercise Workbook
• pp. 21–22
On-line Exercise Bank
• Section 16.1
Go on-line:
PHSchool.com
Enter Web Code:
eak-6002

Get instant feedback! Exercises 1and 2 are available on-line or on CD-ROM.

▶ **KEY CONCEPT** Adjectives usually come before the nouns they modify. They can come after nouns, but this order is less common. ■

BEFORE: Kevin owns three arcades.

            Large, colorful graphics covered
            the screen.

AFTER: Kevin's arcades are busy.

            Graphics, large and colorful,
            covered the screen.

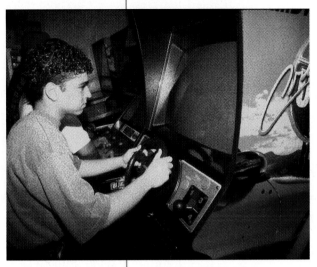

In a similar way, one or more adjectives can come before or after a pronoun.

BEFORE: Intelligent and active, he won the tournament.

AFTER: She is talented.

▲ **Critical Viewing**
Name five adjectives
you would use to
describe your favorite
video game.
[Analyze]

▶ **Exercise 2** Supplying Adjectives Add adjectives to each of the following sentences. Write the new sentences on a separate sheet of paper. You may need to change capitalization. Underline the adjective(s) you add and draw an arrow to the word each modifies.

EXAMPLE: The park has ___?___ rides.

ANSWER: The park has exciting rides.

1. Table tennis is a ___?___ game.
2. ___?___ people enjoy playing the game.
3. The ball is ___?___.
4. Paddles can be ___?___ or ___?___.
5. We had a ___?___ party at the arcade.
6. We each received ___?___ tokens.
7. Maurice was ___?___ at shooting baskets quickly.
8. Kara was ___?___ to play.
9. Everyone had a ___?___ time.
10. We were ___?___ when we had to leave.

Adjectives • **331**

Articles

Three frequently used adjectives are the words *a*, *an*, and *the*. They are called *articles*. Articles can be *definite* or *indefinite*. Both types indicate that a noun will soon follow.

▶ **KEY CONCEPT** *The* is the **definite** article. It points to a specific person, place, or thing. *A* and *an* are **indefinite** articles. They point to any member of a group of similar people, places, or things. ■

DEFINITE: Mr. Ryan is the man to call. (a specific person)

Go into the gym. (a specific place)

INDEFINITE: I want to see a game. (any game)
Please take an apple. (any apple)

A is used before consonant sounds, and *an* is used before vowel sounds. The following chart gives several examples of the indefinite articles used correctly before consonant and vowel sounds.

HOW TO USE *A* AND *AN*	
A Before Consonant Sounds	*An* Before Vowel Sounds
a pineapple *a* useful item (*y* sound) *a* one-way street (*w* sound) *a* taxi *a* lamp	*an* ivory tusk *an* eraser *an* angry look *an* opportunity *an* umbrella

▲ **Critical Viewing**
Find five people or things in the picture. Then, use an adjective to describe each person or thing.
[Identify; Support]

Research Tip

When you are looking up titles in either print or electronic sources, ignore articles at the beginning. Titles are alphabetized by the first word that's not an article.

GRAMMAR IN LITERATURE

from **The Pigman & Me**
Paul Zindel

Notice how the adjectives—awful, one, another, first, gym, and school—make the nouns they modify more specific.

. . . Just when we think something *awful*'s going to happen *one* way, it throws you a curve and the something *awful* happens *another* way. This happened on the *first* Friday, during *gym* period, when we were allowed to play games in the *school* yard.

▶ **More Practice**

Grammar Exercise Workbook
• pp. 23–24
On-line Exercise Bank
• Section 16.1
Go on-line:
PHSchool.com
Enter Web Code:
eak-6002

▼ **Critical Viewing**
Use the articles *a, an,* and *the* with items in this photo. **[Apply]**

▶ **Exercise 3** **Using Indefinite Articles** Copy each phrase. Replace the blank with the correct indefinite article.

EXAMPLE: ___?___ red car
ANSWER: a red car

1. ___?___ amazing track
2. ___?___ driver
3. ___?___ orange sign
4. ___?___ steering wheel
5. ___?___ unusual ride
6. ___?___ international sport
7. ___?___ exciting event
8. ___?___ one-time champion
9. ___?___ innocent mistake
10. ___?___ two-lane track
11. ___?___ original idea
12. ___?___ amateur status
13. ___?___ winning score
14. ___?___ indoor activity
15. ___?___ rubber bumper
16. ___?___ instruction book
17. ___?___ yellow stripe
18. ___?___ successful attempt
19. ___?___ additional invention
20. ___?___ final outcome

Adjectives • **333**

Proper Adjectives

The words *African sunset*, *Siberian climate*, and *Korean Ping-Pong team* all have something in common. An adjective based on a proper noun begins each group of words. Such adjectives are called *proper adjectives.*

▶ **KEY CONCEPT** A **proper adjective** is (1) a proper noun used as an adjective or (2) an adjective formed from a proper noun. ■

When a proper noun is used as an adjective, it answers the question *What kind?* or *Which one?* about the noun it modifies. The chart below lists proper nouns and shows how they can be used as proper adjectives.

Proper Nouns	Proper Nouns Used as Adjectives
Baltimore	Baltimore newspaper
April	April showers
Kennedy	Kennedy family

▶ **Exercise 4** Identifying Proper Adjectives Identify the proper adjective in each sentence. Then, tell which noun it modifies.

EXAMPLE: I went to the foosball arcade Sunday afternoon.
ANSWER: Sunday (afternoon)

1. Table soccer, or foosball, began as a German game.
2. In European countries, it was a popular arcade game.
3. American business people imported the idea.
4. Tables from French companies were shipped to the U.S.
5. Early tournaments were held in Texas towns.
6. Saturday competitions drew large crowds.
7. Canadian trademarks allowed companies to sell across the border.
8. An Oklahoma city hosted one of the first championship matches.
9. A Montana competition was one of the most exciting ever.
10. Now, many American cities host foosball tournaments.

Spelling Tip

Be sure to make spelling changes when turning proper nouns into proper adjectives. However, don't assume that changes are always necessary. Check your dictionary to make the correct adjective form of the noun.

KEY CONCEPT Endings called suffixes are added to many proper nouns to make them into proper adjectives. ∎

Proper Nouns	Proper Adjective Forms
America	<u>American</u> jazz
Inca	<u>Incan</u> empire
Florida	<u>Floridian</u> sunset

Notice that an ending such as *-n* or *-ian* has been added to each of the proper nouns.

The following sentences give additional examples of proper adjectives.

EXAMPLES: <u>Colombian</u> players won the gold medal.
I played with a <u>Korean</u> partner.

Exercise 5 Creating Proper Adjectives Rewrite each sentence to use a proper adjective instead of the underlined proper noun. You may need to rearrange the words.

EXAMPLE: I learned to play a game from <u>Italy</u>.
ANSWER: I learned to play an Italian game.

1. *Croquet* is a word from <u>France</u>.
2. A doctor in <u>Paris</u> chose the name, which means "crooked stick."
3. Nobles in <u>Britain</u> played an earlier form of the game.
4. Golfers in <u>Scotland</u> played it indoors as a way to practice their putting.
5. Players in the <u>United States</u> took up croquet in the 1860's.
6. An office in <u>Florida</u> sets rules for the game in <u>North America.</u>
7. A group in <u>Arizona</u> organized an association for croquet players in the <u>United States</u>.
8. The sport in <u>North America</u> features hard rubber balls, nine narrow wickets, and short mallets.
9. The rules of croquet in <u>England</u> and <u>Egypt</u> call for six wickets and longer mallets.
10. The rules in <u>Australia</u> are the same as in England.

More Practice

Grammar Exercise Workbook
• pp. 25–26
On-line Exercise Bank
• Section 16.1
  Go on-line:
  PHSchool.com
  Enter Web Code:
  eak-6002

Get instant feedback! Exercises 4 and 5 are available on-line or on CD-ROM.

Pronouns as Adjectives

Not only can nouns be used as adjectives, but pronouns can also serve as adjectives. In the word pairs *my computer*, *our class*, and *its cover*, the personal pronouns are working as adjectives.

▶ **KEY CONCEPT** A **personal pronoun** can be used as an adjective if it modifies a noun. ■

The following examples show personal pronouns used as adjectives. Because they show possession, they are called *possessive adjectives.*

EXAMPLES: Eddie played <u>his</u> favorite game.
Jane said, "<u>My</u> team is the Comets."
The students hoped <u>their</u> team would win.

Notice that each underlined pronoun modifies the noun that follows it.

PERSONAL PRONOUNS USED AS POSSESSIVE ADJECTIVES	
Singular	**Plural**
my	our
your	your
his, her, its	their

Each pronoun in the examples above refers back to a noun, its antecedent. The next examples show that personal pronouns (1) work as adjectives and (2) take the place of nouns. The arrows point back to the antecedents and forward to the nouns modified.

EXAMPLES: All students can leave <u>their</u> games here.

Ben predicted <u>his</u> score in the game.

The club wants to increase <u>its</u> membership.

⚙ Grammar and Style Tip

Try not to use too many personal pronouns and possessive adjectives in one sentence. Your readers may have trouble understanding the antecedents, and the meaning of your sentence can become unclear.

Exercise 6 Recognizing Possessive Adjectives Copy each sentence. Underline the possessive adjective. Then, draw one arrow connecting the possessive adjective to its antecedent, if any, and another arrow connecting it to the noun or pronoun it modifies.

EXAMPLE: Eric broke <u>his</u> record at the miniature-golf course.

1. We played miniature golf at our local golf course.
2. I used my club to hit the ball through the windmill.
3. Pam chose a pink ball because pink is her favorite color.
4. Mike says miniature golf is his favorite sport.
5. This course is well known because of its difficulty.
6. You probably don't enjoy competing against your brother.
7. Players must take their time and be patient.
8. Kayla and Serena were the leaders on their team.
9. My best shot ever was a hole-in-one.
10. The last hole on the golf course was its most challenging one.
11. The waterfall near the hole was its biggest obstacle.
12. Cheri hit her third shot right into the water.
13. Martin will show us his final scorecard.
14. Sam and I practiced for hours to improve our scores.
15. Sean promises that next year the championship will be his.

More Practice

Grammar Exercise Workbook
• pp. 27–28
On-line Exercise Bank
• Section 16.1
Go on-line:
PHSchool.com
Enter Web Code:
eak-6002

Get instant feedback! Exercise 6 is available on-line or on CD-ROM.

◀ Critical Viewing Using adjectives, tell how these table-tennis racquets are similar to and different from racquets used in other games. [Compare and Contrast]

Adjectives • 337

Demonstrative Adjectives

The four demonstrative pronouns *this, that, these,* and *those* are often used as adjectives.

PRONOUN: That is difficult.

ADJECTIVE: That game is difficult.

PRONOUN: Try these.

ADJECTIVE: These darts are nicely balanced.

When *this, that, these,* or *those* appears immediately before a noun, that word is functioning as a *demonstrative adjective.*

▶ **Exercise 7** Classifying Demonstrative Pronouns and Adjectives On your paper, indicate whether the underlined word in each sentence is being used as an *adjective* or as a *pronoun.*

1. <u>That</u> game of darts looks like fun.
2. <u>These</u> are the arrows that players have found to be the most accurate.
3. Did you know <u>this</u> rule?
4. I learned that <u>these</u> rules were made more than a hundred years ago.
5. <u>This</u> is a fun game even today.
6. British rules say that <u>this</u> is the correct way to throw.
7. The distance to <u>that</u> target is approximately eight feet.
8. <u>Those</u> champions have great aim.
9. <u>Those</u> are the players who usually win.
10. <u>That</u> is not my best score.
11. Is there a way we can improve <u>these</u> scores?
12. <u>These</u> are the methods we have been taught.
13. When I reached for the dart, I noticed <u>this</u>.
14. I watched as <u>those</u> players practiced new ways to throw their darts.
15. I expect <u>this</u> date to go down in history as the day I won the club championship.

▶ **Exercise 8** Writing Sentences With Demonstrative Pronouns and Adjectives Using each word below, write two sentences. In the first sentence, use the word as an adjective before a noun. In the second sentence, use the word as a pronoun.

1. this   2. that   3. those   4. these

▶ **More Practice**

On-line Exercise Bank
• Section 16.1
  Go on-line:
  PHSchool.com
  Enter Web Code:
  eak-6002

Text

Get instant feedback! Exercises 7 and 8 are available on-line or on CD-ROM.

Section Review

GRAMMAR EXERCISES 9–16

Exercise 9 Identifying Adjectives
Identify the adjectives in each sentence, and tell the questions they answer.

1. Computer games are played in many homes.
2. These games fill store shelves.
3. The first games were simple.
4. Then, game technology advanced.
5. There are learning, adventure, and sports games.
6. A single player competes against the computer.
7. They have realistic sounds and special effects.
8. Modern games have detailed animation.
9. Some games feature virtual reality.
10. Computer games may improve hand-eye coordination.

Exercise 10 Using Indefinite
Articles Write out each phrase. Replace the blank with the correct indefinite article.

1. ___?___ personal computer
2. ___?___ arcade game
3. ___?___ ice hockey competition
4. ___?___ new adventure series
5. ___?___ useful progam

Exercise 11 Identifying Proper
Adjectives List the proper adjectives in these sentences and the nouns they modify.

1. Boccie is an Italian game.
2. Different versions are played in many European countries.
3. English settlers introduced the game in their colonies.
4. It was modified by American players.
5. There are also British and Australian varieties.

Exercise 12 Recognizing
Possessive Adjectives Underline each possessive adjective, and draw arrows to its antecedent and to the word it modifies.

1. Shovel board was developed in England, where its popularity began.
2. The king banned it among his archers.
3. They spent too much of their time on it.
4. Shuffleboard got its name in 1924.
5. Travelers play it often on their cruises.

Exercise 13 Classifying Pronouns
and Adjectives Label the underlined word *adjective* or *pronoun.*

1. These people are playing shuffleboard.
2. Those are the discs they will push.
3. The rules say this shot is your last.
4. That is the stick called a cue.
5. That disc is not a winner.

Exercise 14 Find It in Your
Reading Read the excerpt from *The Pigman & Me* on page 333. Which adjectives answer the question *Which one?*

Exercise 15 Find It in Your
Writing Look through your portfolio for a paragraph that describes a person or thing. Underline the adjectives you used.

Exercise 16 Writing Application
Write a paragraph describing a game you like to play. Use adjectives to add interesting details to your description. Underline the adjectives.

Adverbs

Theme: Wolves
In this section, you will learn that adverbs are used to describe verbs, adjectives, and other adverbs. The examples and exercises in this section are about wolves.
Cross-Curricular Connection: Science

Adverbs are words that modify other words, just as adjectives do. Adverbs most often modify verbs. The first word in each of the following phrases is an adverb: *slowly twisted, skillfully reads, quickly hides.*

Adverbs also modify adjectives and other adverbs. In the sentence *The game was very exciting,* the adverb *very* modifies the adjective *exciting.* In *They played extremely well,* the adverb *extremely* modifies the adverb *well.*

▶ **KEY CONCEPT** An **adverb** is a word that modifies a verb, an adjective, or another adverb. ■

Adverbs answer several questions when they modify verbs.

WHAT ADVERBS TELL ABOUT VERBS	
Where?	He lives <u>nearby</u>. I looked <u>inside</u>.
When?	Janice played <u>yesterday</u>. The message arrived <u>early</u>.
In What Way?	The musician performed <u>perfectly</u>. The dancers moved <u>gracefully</u>.
To What Extent?	Amy <u>fully</u> agrees with me. I am <u>totally</u> opposed to it.

▶ **Exercise 17** Identifying Adverbs Identify the adverb that modifies the underlined word in each sentence.

EXAMPLE: The wolves playfully <u>fought</u> with each other.
ANSWER: playfully

1. Wolves <u>howl</u> loudly to establish their territory.
2. The sounds <u>travel</u> quickly to other wolves.
3. They often <u>communicate</u> in this way.
4. Wolves have very <u>accurate</u> hearing.
5. Howling usually <u>expresses</u> their excitement as well.
6. Howling frequently <u>occurs</u> before a hunt.
7. Howls are one of the most <u>effective</u> ways to attract a mate.
8. Wolves <u>listen</u> closely and follow the howls.
9. Wolf habitats <u>range</u> widely in North America.
10. When wolves <u>awaken</u> early in the morning, they howl to greet the new day.

▼ **Critical Viewing**
Identify three adverbs that could tell in what way a wolf howls.
[Describe]

GRAMMAR IN LITERATURE

from **Mowgli's Brothers**
Rudyard Kipling

Notice in the following sentence that the adverbs down *and* clearly *modify the verb* lays. Down *tells* where, *and* clearly *tells* in what way. Very *modifies* clearly *by telling* to what extent.

. . . The Law of the Jungle lays *down very clearly* that any wolf may, when he marries, withdraw from the Pack. . . .

Grammar and Style Tip

To keep your writing interesting, use adverbs to modify verbs, adjectives, and other adverbs. Just be sure not to overuse them.

▶ **KEY CONCEPT** When adverbs modify adjectives or adverbs, they answer the question *To what extent?* ■

ADVERB MODIFYING A VERB:	The mother <u>tenderly</u> moved the pup.
ADVERB MODIFYING AN ADJECTIVE:	A <u>very</u> kind woman helped me.
ADVERB MODIFYING ANOTHER ADVERB:	The males hunt <u>extremely</u> well.

Text

Get instant feedback! Exercises 17 and 18 are available on-line or on CD-ROM.

▶ **Exercise 18** **Identifying Adverbs and the Words They Modify** On your paper, identify the adverb(s) in each sentence. Then, write the word that each adverb modifies.

EXAMPLE: Wolves live socially in packs.
ANSWER: socially (live)

1. A double layer of fur effectively covers a wolf.
2. The underfur grows very thick in the cold months.
3. An outer layer fully repels snow and water.
4. A wolf often lies near trees or rocks during a storm.
5. This location shelters it very effectively from wind.
6. The wolf curls up tightly into a ball.
7. Its tail completely covers its nose.
8. During the spring, the underfur sheds quickly.
9. That way, the wolf survives the extremely hot months.
10. Wolves can live happily in almost any climate.

▶ **More Practice**

Grammar Exercise Workbook
• pp. 29–30
On-line Exercise Bank
• Section 16.2
Go on-line:
PHSchool.com
Enter Web Code:
eak-6002

Adverb or Adjective?

You may sometimes have to think carefully before identifying a word as an adverb or an adjective. The reason is that some words may be used as an adverb in one sentence and as an adjective in another.

▶ **KEY CONCEPT** If a noun or pronoun is modified by a word, that modifying word is an *adjective.* If a verb, adjective, or adverb is modified by a word, that modifying word is an adverb. ■

The next examples show how the word *right* is used as an adverb in the first sentence and as an adjective in the second.

ADVERB:　　　When the wolves reached the clearing, they turned <u>right</u>.
　　　　　　　(*Right* modifies the verb *turned.*)

ADJECTIVE:　　This is the <u>right</u> spot to view the wolves safely.
　　　　　　　(*Right* modifies the noun *spot.*)

Adjectives and adverbs also answer different questions. Adjectives answer the questions *What kind? Which one? How many?* and *How much?* Adverbs answer the questions *Where? When? In what way?* and *To what extent?*

To decide whether a word is an adjective or an adverb, look at the part of speech of the word it modifies. Then, decide which question it answers about the word it modifies.

ADVERB:　　　The pack stopped <u>short</u> outside the forest. (*Short* modifies the verb *stopped* and tells *in what way* the pack stopped.)

ADJECTIVE:　　The pack made a <u>short</u> stop outside the forest. (*Short* modifies the noun *stop* and tells *what kind* of stop.)

Note also that while many words that end in *-ly* are adverbs, some are not. Several adjectives also end in *-ly.* These adjectives are formed by adding *-ly* to certain nouns, such as *friend, prince,* or *shape.*

EXAMPLES:　　Wolves are not very <u>friendly</u> animals.
　　　　　　　The leader of the pack had a <u>princely</u> attitude.

Spelling Tip

Some adjectives can be changed into adverbs by adding *-ly* to the end of the word. For example, in *I was careful, careful* is an adjective, but in *I looked carefully, carefully* is an adverb.

Exercise 19 Distinguishing Between Adverbs and Adjectives Tell whether each underlined word in the sentences below is an adverb or an adjective.

EXAMPLE: I saw a <u>wild</u> wolf.
ANSWER: adjective

1. Wolves travel <u>far</u> when they hunt.
2. Their prey takes them over the <u>far</u> horizons.
3. When they see prey, they move <u>near</u>.
4. The wolf failed at the hunt, but it was a <u>near</u> miss.
5. Wolves circle their prey and begin a <u>forward</u> movement.
6. As they inch <u>forward</u>, the wolves threaten their prey.
7. They try <u>hard</u> not to miss.
8. Hunting for food is a <u>hard</u> life.
9. Trying to find food is a <u>daily</u> event.
10. However, the wolves do not eat <u>daily</u>.

Exercise 20 Writing Sentences With Adverbs and Adjectives Use each numbered pair of words in a sentence. Write the sentence on a separate sheet of paper. Tell whether the underlined word is an adjective or adverb, and identify the word it modifies.

EXAMPLE: <u>wild</u> wolf
ANSWER: The <u>wild</u> wolf ran free in the woods. (adjective modifying *wolf*)

1. <u>distant</u> howling
2. move <u>close</u>
3. <u>close</u> call
4. <u>fast</u> rabbit
5. run <u>fast</u>

More Practice

Grammar Exercise Workbook
• pp. 31–32
On-line Exercise Bank
• Section 16.2
  Go on-line:
  PHSchool.com
  Enter Web Code:
  eak-6002

Complete the exercises on-line! Exercises 19 and 20 are available on-line or on CD-ROM.

◄ **Critical Viewing** How would you distinguish between the wolf in this picture and the one on page 340? **[Compare and Contrast]**

Hands-on Grammar

Adjective or Adverb Slide

Create a three-window frame for sliding word strips, as in the model below. Then, create three word strips. The first word strip should list nouns, such as *job, decision, side, movement,* and *destination.* The second word strip should list a mix of adjectives and adverbs, including words that can function both as adjectives and as adverbs, such as *daily, hard, far,* and *forward.* The third strip should list verbs, such as *work, play,* and *move.* Leave enough blank space at the end of each strip to allow the strip to remain in the slots as it moves to the right and to the left. Label the front of the windows as shown.

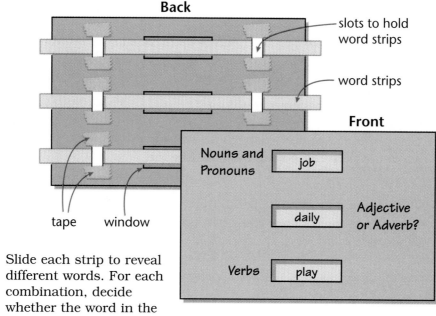

Slide each strip to reveal different words. For each combination, decide whether the word in the center window can modify the word in the upper window, the lower window, or both. Based on the part of speech each word modifies, determine whether it functions as an adverb or an adjective. (Although only verbs are used in the bottom window, remember that adverbs can also modify adjectives and other adverbs.)

Find It in Your Reading In your reading, find examples of words that can function both as adverbs and as adjectives. Create strips to challenge a partner to identify how these words function when they modify different parts of speech.

Find It in Your Writing Look through samples of your own writing to find words that modify other words. Identify the part of speech being modified, and then identify the modifier as an adjective or an adverb.

Section Review

GRAMMAR EXERCISES 21–27

▶ **Exercise 21** Identifying Adverbs
On your paper, write the adverb that modifies each underlined word or phrase.

1. Wolves closely <u>resemble</u> other animals.
2. The coyote is very <u>similar</u> looking.
3. However, the coyote weighs much <u>less</u>.
4. Dogs and wild wolves <u>are</u> somewhat <u>related</u>.
5. No one <u>has tamed</u> wolves successfully.

▶ **Exercise 22** Identifying Adverbs and the Words They Modify Identify the adverb(s) in each sentence. Then, write the word or phrase each adverb modifies.

1. The gray wolf is sometimes called the timber wolf.
2. It was once found in North America, Europe, and Asia.
3. Wolves are equally comfortable in many environments.
4. During the winter, they travel together to find food.
5. In packs, wolves are very cooperative.
6. They live closely with their families.
7. Pups wrestle playfully to practice hunting skills.
8. Wolves usually hunt weak animals.
9. They run easily and rarely tire.
10. For small animals, wolves hunt alone.

▶ **Exercise 23** Distinguishing Between Adverbs and Adjectives Label each underlined word *adverb* or *adjective*.

1. Wolf puppies grow <u>quickly</u>.
2. New wolf mothers can be <u>unfriendly</u>.
3. The small wolves chew <u>hard</u> on bones.
4. Their <u>hard</u> teeth make a loud sound.
5. The pups nearly always stay <u>close</u> to their mother.

▶ **Exercise 24** Understanding Adverbs and Adjectives Copy each sentence. Underline the adverbs, and circle the adjectives, other than articles. Then, draw an arrow from each adjective or adverb to the word it modifies.

1. Each pack has a lead male.
2. Other males willingly obey him.
3. An alpha female firmly leads the others.
4. Every wolf is then ranked accordingly.
5. Leaders are strong and usually quite large.
6. The order often results in fewer fights.
7. A wolf snarls menacingly to show confidence.
8. The back fur rises automatically.
9. The other wolf hangs his head down.
10. He rolls over to avoid a fight.

▶ **Exercise 25** Find It in Your Reading Locate each adverb and the word it modifies in this sentence from "Mowgli's Brothers" by Rudyard Kipling.

Mowgli was still deeply interested in the pebbles, and he did not notice when the wolves came and looked at him. . . .

▶ **Exercise 26** Find It in Your Writing Look through your portfolio for a paragraph that describes how someone did something. Circle any adverbs you used. If you didn't use any adverbs, challenge yourself to add some.

▶ **Exercise 27** Writing Application Write a short description of an animal that you have observed or read about. Use modifiers to help describe how the animal behaves. Underline every adverb you use.

GRAMMAR EXERCISES 28–39

▶ **Exercise 28** Identifying **Adjectives and the Words They Modify**
On your paper, write the adjectives in each sentence and the word each modifies.

1. Coyotes are close relatives of wolves.
2. They have larger ears and shorter muzzles.
3. Their habits are also very different.
4. Coyotes do not live in social groups.
5. Pups leave their parents after they grow.
6. Single coyotes hunt unprotected sheep.
7. They also seek weak, small animals.
8. They live in many North American regions.
9. Their eastern expansion has reached the Atlantic coast.
10. Coyotes are seen in suburban areas.

▶ **Exercise 29** Supplying Adjectives
On your paper, supply an adjective to modify the underlined word. Use the pictures in the preceding section to help you.

1. Wolves are __?__ hunters.
2. They have __?__ fur.
3. A wolf has a __?__ nose and __?__ ears.
4. A wolf's tail is __?__.
5. The teeth are probably __?__.

▶ **Exercise 30** Using Indefinite **Articles** Write out each phrase, replacing the blank with the correct indefinite article.

1. __?__ timber wolf
2. __?__ abundant species
3. __?__ large pack
4. __?__ alpha female
5. __?__ young animal

▶ **Exercise 31** Revision Practice: **Proper Adjectives** Revise each sentence, replacing the underlined phrase with a proper adjective. You may need to rearrange some words in the sentence.

1. Wolves of the Arctic are usually white.
2. Some people call them wolves of Alaska.
3. States in America like Minnesota also have these wolves.
4. The coast of North Carolina is the habitat for red wolves.
5. Wolves of Mexico once had a much wider range than they do now.

▶ **Exercise 32** Supplying Possessive **Adjectives** Copy each sentence. Supply the possessive adjective to fill in the blank. Then, draw an arrow connecting the possessive adjective to the noun it modifies.

1. Coyotes do most of __?__ hunting at night.
2. A female has __?__ pups in the spring.
3. A wolf brings meat to __?__ den to feed the pups.
4. A father coyote helps raise __?__ pups.
5. A coyote stays with __?__ mate for life.

▶ **Exercise 33** Distinguishing **Between Pronouns and Adjectives** Identify whether the underlined word is functioning as an adjective or a pronoun.

1. These are western coyotes.
2. This red color is one of their particular characteristics.
3. We consider those animals to be very similar.

4. <u>This</u> is the bushy tail of a coyote.
5. It is different from <u>this</u> wolf tail.

▶ **Exercise 34** **Recognizing Adverbs**
Write the adverbs in each of the following sentences.

1. Foxes feed mostly on small rodents.
2. They often hunt alone, rather than in packs.
3. Swift runners, foxes are very agile.
4. They bravely defend their territory from intruders.
5. This territory usually measures about three square miles.

▶ **Exercise 35** **Identifying Adverbs and the Words They Modify** Write down each adverb and the word it modifies.

1. The red fox is easily recognized.
2. Its tail often grows a white tip.
3. The black ears and feet are very noticeable.
4. Its reddish-brown coat is quite lovely.
5. Its range stretches widely across North America, Europe, and Asia.
6. Red foxes have even been seen in Africa and the Arctic.
7. They adapt to entirely new environments quickly.
8. The red fox lives easily near humans.
9. It uses its very keen senses to stay quite camouflaged.
10. Its food sources vary greatly.

▶ **Exercise 36** **Distinguishing Between Adverbs and Adjectives** Tell whether each underlined word in the sentences below is an adverb or adjective.

1. Foxes spend the <u>early</u> spring near a den.
2. They fit <u>snugly</u> into enlarged groundhog holes.
3. The young stay in the den for <u>nearly</u> five weeks.
4. They are born with their eyes closed <u>fast</u>.

5. In the fall, the young make a <u>fast</u> trip away from the home territory.

▶ **Exercise 37** **Revision Practice: Adverbs and Adjectives** Add adjectives and adverbs to the following paragraph. You may need to add words other than adjectives and adverbs for the new paragraph to make sense.

Wolves, dogs, foxes, and coyotes are all part of a family. They have habits and instincts. They travel to find food. When they hunt, they move. Eyes help them see prey, but the sense of smell helps them find prey. Fur keeps them warm when they can't be in a den. Wolves hunt as a pack, but foxes hunt alone.

▶ **Exercise 38** **CUMULATIVE REVIEW Nouns, Pronouns, and Verbs** Copy the following paragraph onto your paper. Underline each noun once and each verb twice. Circle each personal or demonstrative pronoun.

(1) Three concerned naturalists formed the organization Wolf Help to help people better understand wolves. (2) They travel around the country, give lectures, and show photographs. (3) If you are worried about the survival of wolves, you might contact Wolf Help. (4) You may also enjoy a video called *Winter Wolf*. (5) This is about a fourteen-year-old Native American girl who learns what wolves meant to her ancestors.

▶ **Exercise 39** **Writing Application**
Write a descriptive paragraph about a pet that you have had or one that you would like. Give your reader a clear picture of the pet—how it looks and how it acts. Use at least one adjective and one adverb in each sentence. Underline the adverbs, and circle the adjectives that you use.

Standardized Test Preparation Workshop

Using Adjectives and Adverbs

A knowledge of how adjectives and adverbs function will help you answer several types of standardized test questions that measure your ability to express yourself effectively. The following test items will give you practice with items that measure your ability to use adjectives and adverbs.

Test Tip

- Read through the answer choices, and eliminate the ones that would change the meaning of the sentence.

Sample Test Items

Directions Read the passage, and choose the letter of the word or group of words that belongs in each space.

Yesterday, the class took a _____ bus ride to the museum.

1 A slowly
  B very
  C hardly
  D long

Directions Read the passage. Some sections are underlined. Choose the best way to write the underlined section.

Last year, we also took a bus trip. <u>We took a bus ride to the zoo. The bus ride was short.</u>

1 A We took a short bus ride to the zoo.
  B We took a short ride on the bus to the zoo.
  C We took a bus ride to the zoo that was short.
  D We took a bus ride. Short was the bus ride.

Answers and Explanations

The correct answer is *D*. Because the word in the blank space is meant to modify *bus ride,* a noun, the only correct choice is an adjective.

The correct answer is *A. We took a short bus ride* is the clearest and most effective way to express the underlined sentences. This choice does not change the meaning of the passage, and it is more to the point than the original.

▶ **Practice 1** **Directions:** Read the passage, and choose the letter of the word or group of words that belongs in each space.

All my relatives gather __(1)__ to celebrate the Fourth of July. We choose a spot that is __(2)__ for everyone, so that each person can get there __(3)__ . __(4)__ we meet in a park. When we get together as a group, my family can be __(5)__ .

1 A year
  B yearly
  C some
  D silly

2 F nearly
  G outside
  H conveniently
  J convenient

3 A fair
  B fairly
  C easy
  D easily

4 F Some
  G Sometimes
  H Frequent
  J Rare

5 A lately
  B soon
  C loud
  D loudly

▶ **Practice 2** **Directions:** Read the passage. Some sections are underlined. Choose the best way to write each underlined section.

The guide told a story. The story
                  (1)
was humorous. We all enjoyed the
                  (2)
tale. The tale was funny. Then he

asked us a question. He asked if anyone was curious about the origins of
                  (3)
the tale. Although nobody raised a

hand, it was obvious that we hoped he

would tell us. He had our attention.
                  (4)
That was certain. We had lunch. We
                  (5)
had lunch later in the cafeteria.

1 A The humorous guide told a story.
  B Humorously, the guide told a story.
  C The guide told a humorous story.
  D The guide told a story humorously.

2 F We all enjoyed the tale that was funny.
  G We all enjoyed the tale.
  H Funny, we all enjoyed the tale.
  J We all enjoyed the funny tale.

3 A He asked if anyone was curious about the tale's origins.
  B He asked, curiously, if anyone wanted to know the origin of the tale.
  C He asked if anyone wanted to know the origin of the curious tale.
  D Curious, he asked if anyone wanted to know the origin of the tale.

4 F Certain he had our attention.
  G He certainly had our attention.
  H He had our certain attention.
  J He had our attention.

5 A We had lunch in the cafeteria.
  B We were late to lunch in the cafeteria.
  C We had a late lunch in the cafeteria.
  D Later, we had lunch in the cafeteria.

A nineteenth-century baseball game in progress

▲ **Critical Viewing**
Describe the setting
and the action in the
field. Use at least
two prepositions in
your description.
[Interpret]

Some words are important simply because they show how other words are related to each other. They may not provide as much meaning as these other words, but they make it possible for them to do their work.

Prepositions are one of the kinds of words that serve this necessary function. Although many prepositions are short words—*at, on, by*—they have a big effect on meaning. For example, would a baseball player rather be *at* the base, *on* the base, or *by* the base?

In this chapter, you will learn how to recognize prepositions. Then, you will learn how to tell whether a word is being used as a preposition or an adverb. Finally, you will practice using prepositions.

Diagnostic Test

Directions: Write all answers on a separate sheet of paper.

Skill Check A. Write the preposition(s) in each of the following sentences.

1. Games like baseball were played in ancient Egypt.
2. They were played for recreation or for ceremonial purposes.
3. By the Middle Ages, these games were played in Europe.
4. Their popularity spread across many countries.
5. Europeans brought these games to the Americas.

Skill Check B. Write the preposition(s) in each of the following sentences.

6. Aristocrats had no interest in regular baseball.
7. They played the game of cricket.
8. A game called *rounders* was more like baseball.
9. Like baseball, it had a system of hits and outs.
10. Runners ran around the bases.

Skill Check C. Copy each sentence below, replacing the blank with a preposition.

11. The rules varied __?__ place to place.
12. Baseball was very unorganized __?__ 1842.
13. The *Knickerbocker Base Ball Club* moved __?__ modern baseball.
14. They set up the field __?__ a home plate and three bases.
15. The Knickerbockers made the rule __?__ foul lines.

Skill Check D. Replace the underlined preposition in the following sentences with a different preposition.

16. The Knickerbockers' style of baseball spread <u>during</u> the 1850's.
17. Its popularity spread <u>beyond</u> New York.
18. People all <u>across</u> the country formed teams.
19. At first, they played other teams <u>inside</u> their own states.
20. Professional baseball started with a team <u>in</u> Ohio, the Cincinnati Red Stockings.

Skill Check E. Identify the underlined word in each sentence below as a *preposition* or an *adverb*.

21. In 1869, baseball teams traveled <u>around</u>, playing outside their own areas.
22. More teams came <u>out</u> following the formation of the National League in 1876.
23. The American League was organized soon <u>after</u>.
24. The leagues fought <u>over</u> the best baseball players.
25. They searched for players <u>around</u> the country.

Using Prepositions

Prepositions help a reader or listener understand the relationship of one word to another.

KEY CONCEPT A **preposition** relates a noun or pronoun to another word in the sentence. ■

In the examples below, notice how changing the preposition also changes the meaning.

EXAMPLES: The ball was hit <u>over</u> the fence.
The ball was hit <u>toward</u> the fence.
The ball was hit <u>through</u> the fence.
The ball was hit <u>into</u> the fence.
The ball was hit <u>around</u> the fence.

Some frequently used prepositions are listed in the following chart.

Theme: Baseball

In this chapter you will learn about prepositions. The examples and exercises are about baseball.

Cross-Curricular Connection: Physical Education

FIFTY PREPOSITIONS				
about	behind	during	off	to
above	below	except	on	toward
across	beneath	for	onto	under
after	beside	from	opposite	underneath
against	besides	in	out	until
along	between	inside	outside	up
among	beyond	into	over	upon
around	but	like	past	with
at	by	near	since	within
before	down	of	through	without

A few prepositions are made up of more than one word.

EXAMPLES: That is the score <u>according to</u> the umpire.
We need good pitching <u>in addition to</u> good hitting.
The fielder's glove is <u>next to</u> the ball.
Today, he bats first <u>instead of</u> batting cleanup.
The game was postponed <u>on account of</u> rain.

Exercise 1 Substituting Prepositions Write at least five prepositions from the preceding chart that could logically replace the underlined preposition in the following sentence.

The stadium is located <u>opposite</u> the school.

▶ **Exercise 2** Identifying Prepositions Copy each sentence below and underline the preposition(s).

EXAMPLE: Let's go to the ball game.
ANSWER: Let's go <u>to</u> the ball game.

1. Lou Gehrig was the son of German immigrants.
2. He grew up in New York City.
3. Gehrig went to Columbia University.
4. He was discovered by scouts while playing baseball in Hartford.
5. Then, he signed with the New York Yankees.

▶ **Exercise 3** Supplying Prepositions Copy each sentence below, replacing the blank with a preposition. Use the chart to help you.

EXAMPLE: I will meet you __?__ the stadium.
ANSWER: I will meet you outside the stadium.

1. Gehrig was a Yankee __?__ 1923 __?__ 1939.
2. __?__ thirteen seasons, he played every game.
3. Gehrig played __?__ eight championship teams.
4. He hit 493 homers __?__ the outfield fence.
5. His batting average was __?__ .300 twelve times.

GRAMMAR IN
LITERATURE

from **Lou Gehrig:
The Iron Horse**
Bob Considine

In the following excerpt, the prepositions are highlighted in blue.

After a game *at* Yankee Stadium he told Shirley Povich *of* the Washington *Post* and me that a frightening thing had happened *to* him while pitching *against* Gehrig. Joe had uncorked his high inside fast ball *with* the expectation that Lou would move back and take it, *as* a ball. Instead, Krakauskas said, Lou—a renowned judge *of* balls and strikes—moved closer *to* the plate.

▶ **More Practice**

Grammar Exercise Workbook
• pp. 33–34
On-line Exercise Bank
• Section 17
  Go on-line:
  PHSchool.com
  Enter Web Code:
  eak-6002

Complete the exercises on-line! Exercises 1, 2, and 3 are available on-line or on CD-ROM.

Distinguishing Between Prepositions and Adverbs

Many words can be used either as prepositions or as adverbs. You must see how a word is being used in a sentence in order to know which part of speech it is.

▶ **KEY CONCEPTS** A *preposition* will always be followed by a noun or pronoun, forming a prepositional phrase. An *adverb* can stand alone. ■

PREPOSITION: The ball rolled <u>outside the infield</u>.

                       prepositional phrase

ADVERB: The game is played <u>outside</u>.

Prepositional phrases always include a preposition followed by a noun or pronoun. They may also include words that modify the noun.

                        prep   noun

EXAMPLES: The "wave" started <u>in the bleachers</u>.

                     prep modifiers noun

          The batter ran <u>along the base path</u>.

The phrases "in the bleachers" and "along the base path" are prepositional phrases. Adverbs, on the other hand, are used alone. They can end a sentence. Also, they answer questions that prepositions do not: *In what way?* and *To what extent?*

The following chart shows more examples of words that can be used as either prepositions or adverbs.

Prepositions	Adverbs
We played <u>before</u> a crowd.	I've played third <u>before</u>.
The ball rolled <u>down</u> the baseline.	The man sat <u>down</u>.
The ball bounced <u>off</u> the wall.	Harry walked <u>off</u>.
The umpire stands <u>behind</u> the catcher.	Barbara stayed <u>behind</u>.

Learn More

To review what you've learned about adverbs, see Chapter 16.

◀ **Critical Viewing**
Use a prepositional phrase in a sentence that tells how or in what direction this ball moves.
[Describe]

▶ **Exercise 4** Revising Sentences With Prepositions Rewrite each sentence below, replacing the preposition with one that makes more sense.

1. Gehrig was good about everything—hitting and base-running.
2. When he stole home, he slid all the way with the plate.
3. On the end of the 1936 season, he had earned the Most Valuable Player award.
4. Lou Gehrig batted fourth, for Babe Ruth.
5. He was inducted after the Hall of Fame in 1939.

▶ **Exercise 5** Distinguishing Between Prepositions and Adverbs Tell whether each underlined word in the following sentences is a *preposition* or an *adverb*.

1. Satchel Paige was tested <u>before</u> joining the Major Leagues.
2. He had already played for many years <u>before</u>.
3. Paige threw the ball <u>over</u> home plate.
4. His time in the Negro Leagues was <u>over</u>.
5. He played <u>past</u> his fifty-ninth birthday.

▶ **More Practice**

Grammar Exercise Workbook
• pp. 35–36
On-line Exercise Bank
• Section 17
   Go on-line:
   PHSchool.com
   Enter Web Code:
   eak-6002

▼ Critical Viewing Use at least two prepositions in sentences that describe the action in this stadium. [Describe]

Hands-on Grammar

Preposition Pop-Up Book

Create a preposition pop-up book to practice using prepositions and prepositional phrases.

Make one pop-up to illustrate *over*, *under*, and *through*. Fold a piece of colored paper in half, as shown below. Cut as shown in the diagram. Unfold the paper and pop out the step that is created. Glue or tape a piece of string to the base of your pop-up. To the other end of the string, attach a figure or shape.

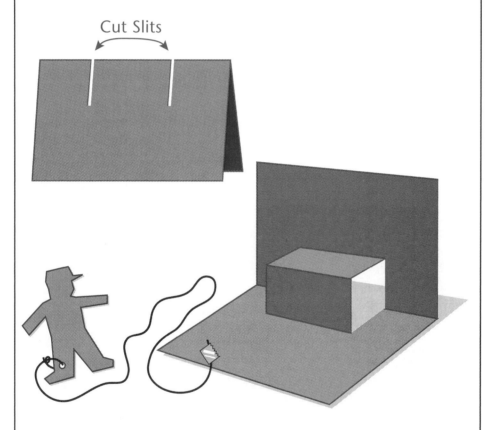

Cut Slits

Move the figure *over, under,* and *through* the step. Use complete sentences to describe how the figure is being moved in relation to the step. Write your sentences on the base of your pop-up. Find ways to demonstrate other prepositions with this pop-up. Use these prepositions in complete sentences that describe how the figure is being moved. Write the new sentences on the base of your pop-up.

Hands-on Grammar (cont.)

Make another pop-up to illustrate *with, after, before, in front of,* and *behind.* Fold a sheet of colored paper in fourths, lengthwise. On each of the three folds, draw four simple shapes, such as cats, snowmen, or geometric shapes, such as triangles. The bottom of each shape should rest on the fold. (Do not draw a row of cats on the outside edge.) Leave a space between the top of each shape and the next fold. Label each shape with a letter or a name. Carefully cut the outline of each shape, but do not separate the shape from the fold. Push each shape up so it stands up.

In complete sentences, use prepositions to describe the space or time relationship of one figure to another. For example, "A is *in front of* B." "I popped up B *after* popping up A." Use the pop-up to demonstrate as many prepositions as you can. Write the sentences that include the prepositions on a separate sheet of paper. Use one staple to attach the paper to the back of your pop-up.

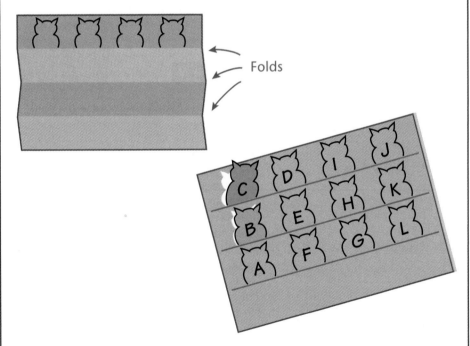

Folds

Find It in Your Reading In a short story or nonfiction work from your literature anthology, locate sentences that contain prepositions. Use one or both of your pop-ups to demonstrate the meaning of the prepositions. Add the sentences that you find to your pop-up list.

Find It in Your Writing Choose a piece of writing from your portfolio. Locate the prepositions you have used. Evaluate whether you have used the best preposition in each case.

Chapter Review

GRAMMAR EXERCISES 6–14

Exercise 6 Recognizing Prepositions Write the prepositions in the following sentences.

1. Baseball is played on a level field.
2. The field is approximately two acres in size.
3. The infield area consists of a diamond shape.
4. There are canvas bases at three of the corners.
5. Home plate is opposite second base.
6. Batters hit the ball from home plate.
7. Then, they run around the bases.
8. The pitcher's mound is near the center of the diamond.
9. It is between home plate and second base.
10. A strip of rubber is nailed to the top of this mound.

Exercise 7 Supplying Prepositions Copy each sentence below, replacing the blank with a preposition.

1. Base lines run __?__ home plate to third and first base.
2. Foul lines run __?__ the edges of the outfield.
3. The lines separate the field __?__ fair and foul areas.
4. Base lines also mark the path __?__ the runner.
5. The region __?__ the infield is the outfield.
6. Dugouts are shelters __?__ each side of the field.
7. Players sit __?__ the cover of the dugouts.
8. __?__ the field markings, there are several chalk boxes.
9. They show people where to stand __?__ a game.
10. Players can walk __?__ the various lines.

Exercise 8 Revising Sentences With Prepositions Replace each underlined preposition with a different preposition.

1. Baseball is played <u>at</u> the stadium.
2. The game begins <u>with</u> the first pitch.
3. The pitcher throws the ball <u>toward</u> home plate.
4. A good pitch is <u>over</u> the knees.
5. Also, it must be <u>below</u> the shoulders.
6. The batter stands <u>beside</u> home plate.
7. He swings the bat <u>at</u> the pitched ball.
8. A good hit is <u>inside</u> the two foul lines.
9. Then, the batter runs <u>around</u> the bases.
10. The team hopes to win <u>by</u> many runs.

Exercise 9 Distinguishing Between Prepositions and Adverbs Tell whether each underlined word below is a *preposition* or an *adverb*.

1. We cheer our favorite team <u>on</u>.
2. I'm rooting <u>for</u> the shortstop.
3. He runs quickly <u>after</u> the ball.
4. Then, he spins <u>around</u> and throws to first base.
5. The ball flies <u>across</u> the infield.
6. The throw beats the runner <u>to</u> the base.
7. He is out <u>by</u> one small step.
8. The runner looks <u>behind</u> to see the call.
9. He returns to the dugout and sits <u>down</u>.
10. <u>Inside</u> the dugout, he talks with the coach.
11. With two more outs, the inning is <u>over</u>.
12. They haven't gotten a hit <u>since</u> the sixth inning.
13. Our team has beaten this team <u>before</u>.
14. <u>After</u> the final play, they congratulate each other.
15. Then, the players take <u>off</u> and head for the showers.

▶ **Exercise 10** Working With Prepositions and Adverbs Identify each underlined word as a *preposition* or an *adverb*. If the word is a preposition, write the entire prepositional phrase.

1. Often, a stadium is built <u>outside</u> a city.
2. Old stadiums are being replaced <u>by</u> new ones.
3. When an old stadium closes, players <u>around</u> the league are sometimes sad.
4. Many new stadiums have been built <u>since</u> the 1980's.
5. Baseball fans are more comfortable than ever <u>before</u>.
6. Usually a stadium is named <u>for</u> its team, but not always.
7. A stadium's upper deck hangs <u>over</u> the lower deck.
8. Many times, players hit the ball <u>into</u> the stands.
9. Some home runs fly <u>to</u> the upper deck.
10. On the outfield wall, the scoreboard hangs <u>down</u>.
11. <u>In</u> one stadium, it was located <u>behind</u> the pitcher.
12. However, <u>in</u> that position, it interfered <u>with</u> the batter; so it was moved.
13. The dugouts are <u>along</u> the foul lines.
14. For the championship games, many fans come <u>out</u>.
15. When fans crowd the exits, guards move them <u>along</u>.

▶ **Exercise 11** Find It in Your Reading Identify the prepositions you find in the following excerpt from *Lou Gehrig: The Iron Horse*. Identify at least one word that is used here as an adverb but can also be used as a preposition.

Joe McCarthy started Gehrig at first base on opening day of the 1939 season, contemptuous of a fan who, a few days before in an exhibition game at Ebbets Field, had bawled, in earshot of both of them, "Hey Lou, why don't you give yourself up?". . .

Lou hobbled as far into the 1939 season as May 2. Then, on the morning of the first game of a series against Detroit, he called McCarthy on the hotel's house phone and asked to see him.

"I'm benching myself, Joe," he said, once in the manager's suite. McCarthy did not speak.

▶ **Exercise 12** Find It in Your Writing Look through your portfolio. Identify examples of prepositions and prepositional phrases in your own writing. Challenge yourself to improve a piece of writing by using prepositions to indicate relationships.

▶ **Exercise 13** Writing Application Write a brief description of a sport or activity that you enjoy. Identify the prepositions that you use.

▶ **Exercise 14** CUMULATIVE REVIEW Nouns, Pronouns, Verbs, Adjectives, Adverbs, and Prepositions Write these labels down the side of your paper, leaving two or three lines between one and the next: *Common Nouns, Proper Nouns, Personal Pronouns, Demonstrative Pronouns, Action Verbs, Linking Verbs, Adjectives, Adverbs, Prepositions*. Then, next to each label, write the appropriate words from the following paragraph.

I follow certain rituals at a baseball game. Do you? I always go to games on Saturday, when the stadium is full of excited fans. I usually buy two souvenirs—a cap for me and a pin for my friend Ellen. I buy a hot dog and a drink, and then I take my seat in the lower deck, near first base. This is the best seat!

Standardized Test Preparation Workshop

Revising and Editing

One way standardized test questions evaluate your knowledge of standard grammar and usage is to test your ability to connect ideas using prepositional phrases. Before you answer this type of question, first read the entire passage. Then, choose the answer that best uses prepositional phrases to connect similar ideas and eliminate unnecessary words.

The following test item will give you practice with questions that measure your ability to use prepositional phrases.

Test Tip

Identify repeated ideas and words in the passages chosen. Combining those ideas with a prepositional phrase and eliminating unnecessary words will provide the best rewrite.

Sample Test Item

Directions Read the passage, and choose the letter of the best way to write the underlined sentences.

The eighteenth century was a time when there were shoemakers. Every town had a shoemaker.

1 A The eighteenth century was a time of shoemakers in every town.

 B During the eighteenth century, every town had a shoemaker.

 C The eighteenth century was a time when there were shoemakers in every town.

 D The eighteenth century was a time for every town to have a shoemaker.

Answer and Explanation

The best answer is *B.* Since both sentences provide information about shoemakers, the best way to rewrite the sentences is to combine similar ideas using the prepositional phrase, *during the eighteenth century.*

Practice 1 **Directions:** Read the passage, and choose the letter of the best way to write the underlined sentences.

During the eighteenth century, men wore
(1)
shoes made of certain materials. Buckskin

or cowhide were those materials. Most
(2)
shoes were not fastened by laces. Buckles

fastened most shoes.

1 A During the eighteenth century, men wore shoes made of certain materials, and buckskin or cowhide were those materials.
 B During the eighteenth century, men wore shoes made of buckskin or cowhide.
 C During the eighteenth century, men wore shoes made of certain materials; buckskin or cowhide were those materials.
 D Buckskin or cowhide were the materials of men's shoes during the eighteenth century when men wore shoes made of certain materials.

2 F Most shoes were not fastened by laces but with buckles.
 G Most shoes were not fastened by laces but with buckles were most shoes fastened.
 H With most shoes, laces were not used but instead buckles fastened most shoes.
 J Most shoes were not fastened by laces or by buckles.

Practice 2 **Directions:** Read the passage, and choose the letter of the best way to write the underlined sentences.

Today, shoes can be fastened. They can be
(1)
 fastened by using laces. Some shoes don't
(2)
need to be fastened because they are made

in materials that stretch.

1 A Today, shoes can be fastened on laces.
 B Today, shoes can be fastened in laces.
 C Today, shoes can be fastened with laces.
 D Today, shoes can be fastened for laces.

2 F Some shoes don't need to be fastened because they are made of materials that stretch.
 G Some shoes don't need to be fastened because they are made around materials that stretch.
 H Some shoes don't need to be fastened because they are made by materials that stretch.
 J Some shoes don't need to be fastened because they are made for materials that stretch.

18 *Conjunctions and Interjections*

In this chapter, you will learn more about two important kinds of words: conjunctions and interjections. *Conjunctions* connect sentence parts and help you add information to your sentences. *Interjections* express feelings.

If you are writing about sea mammals, for example, you might have many interesting details to share. Conjunctions can help you add these pieces of information to your sentences. Interjections might help you express just how you feel.

In the following sections, you will learn how to identify conjunctions and interjections and how to use them properly in your sentences. When used correctly, conjunctions and interjections help hold sentences together and add emotion to your writing.

▲ **Critical Viewing**
How do you feel when you look at the sea otter in this photograph? Express your feelings in a sentence with an interjection.
[Analyze]

Diagnostic Test

Directions: Write all answers on a separate sheet of paper.

Skill Check A. For each sentence, list the coordinating conjunction and the words or word groups it connects. Circle the conjunction.

1. Sea otters and river otters look very much alike.
2. The sea otters have thicker bodies, but they have shorter tails than the river otters.
3. There are four kinds of sea otters, yet most people cannot tell them apart.
4. Many live in the Pacific Ocean near the Americas or Asia.
5. Their front paws have five fingers, so they can hold on to food and seaweed.

Skill Check B. Copy each sentence below. Circle both parts of each correlative conjunction, and underline the words or word groups it connects.

6. Sea otter fur has not only brown but also silver in its coloring.
7. Their teeth are both large and strong.
8. They break open shells either with their teeth or with a rock.
9. Sea otters float on their backs whether they are eating or nursing their babies.
10. They neither swim very fast nor defend themselves very well.

Skill Check C. Write the conjunctions in the following sentences, and label them *coordinating* or *correlative.*

11. Sea otters dive deep under the water, for that is where they find clams and sea urchins.
12. They use both their paws and their forearms to gather food.
13. To keep warm, they not only eat lots of fish, but they also constantly clean their fur.
14. They don't have blubber, so the fur traps air against their skin.
15. This air protects them from the cold and helps them to maintain their warm body temperature.

Skill Check D. Identify the interjection in each sentence.

16. Wow! Can sea otters really stay underwater for four minutes?
17. Well, that is how they gather food.
18. Gosh! That is also how sea otters avoid danger.
19. Alas, they can't swim fast enough to escape.
20. Oh! What about baby sea otters?

Skill Check E. Supply an interjection to fill in the blank in each sentence. Properly punctuate the interjections with a comma or an exclamation mark.

21. _____ Baby sea otters are certainly adorable.
22. _____ they depend on their mothers for a long time.
23. _____ I didn't know they live in such large groups!
24. _____ They float in the same area most of the time.
25. _____ they hold onto the seaweed to keep from drifting away.

Conjunctions

Conjunctions connect. They often join words in pairs, such as *Romeo and Juliet, light but sturdy,* and *swimming or running.* Conjunctions also connect larger word groups, such as phrases and sentences.

▶ **KEY CONCEPT** **Conjunctions** connect words, groups of words, and whole sentences. ■

Using Coordinating Conjunctions

Coordinating conjunctions connect words or groups of words that are similar in form: noun with noun, phrase with phrase, sentence with sentence, and so on.

COORDINATING CONJUNCTIONS	
Conjunction	Function
and	Adds ideas of equal importance
or	Presents options, alternates, or substitutes for ideas of equal importance
but	Indicates a contrast or exception
nor	Presents an alternate negative idea
for	Connects ideas that follow logically
yet	Connects ideas that follow logically and are contrary
so	Shows the consequence of related ideas

In the following chart, each coordinating conjunction is boxed and each set of connected words is underlined.

USING COORDINATING CONJUNCTIONS	
Words Connected	Examples
Nouns	The seals and sea lions live there.
Pronouns	He or I will lead the nature talk.
Verbs	The scientists planned and practiced.
Adjectives	That photo is attractive but expensive.
Adverbs	He works quickly yet carefully.
Prepositional Phrases	The hikers followed the trail over the hill and to the beach.
Sentences	You should come soon, for next week we will be leaving.

Theme: Sea Mammals

In this section, you will learn how conjunctions connect words and phrases. The examples and exercises are about sea mammals.

Cross-Curricular Connection: Science

💡 **Spelling Tip**

When using *for* as a coordinating conjunction, remember that it looks like the preposition but that it is being used differently. Also, remember that the number *four* is spelled differently and has a completely different meaning.

GRAMMAR IN LITERATURE

from **Greyling**
Jane Yolen

The coordinating conjunctions in this excerpt have been highlighted in blue italics.

Now the fisherman was also sad that they had no child. But he kept his sorrow to himself so that his wife would not know his grief *and* thus double her own. Indeed, he would leave the hut each morning with a breath of song *and* return each night with a whistle on his lips. His nets were full *but* his heart was empty, *yet* he never told his wife.

Text

Get instant feedback! Exercise 1 is available on-line or on CD-ROM.

▶ **Exercise 1** **Recognizing Coordinating Conjunctions** For each sentence below, list the coordinating conjunction and the words or word groups it connects. Circle the conjunction.

EXAMPLE: Seals prefer to eat fish or shellfish.
ANSWER: fish (or) shellfish

1. Harbor seals cannot walk or travel on land with their hind flippers.
2. Sea lions and furred seals travel well on land.
3. These two water mammals are similar yet different.
4. Small sea lions are trained for circuses or for zoos.
5. Their fur is rich and silky.
6. The male seals' fur is mostly brown but also a little gray.
7. This large male has fought off its rivals, so it will keep its harem.
8. Immature males play together, for this is good practice for fighting.
9. The seal's fur is very valuable, so seals are hunted frequently.
10. Now, the population is protected and thriving.

More Practice

Grammar Exercise Workbook
• pp. 37–38
On-line Exercise Bank
• Section 18.1
Go on-line:
PHSchool.com
Enter Web Code:
eak-6002

▶ **Critical Viewing** Using coordinating conjunctions in sentences, describe the behavior of this elephant seal. [**Describe**]

3. My, the killer whale will even eat walruses.
4. Boy! The teeth look pretty sharp.
5. Aha, they are in both its upper and lower jaws.
6. Golly! It's smaller than I expected.
7. Well, it is only twenty or thirty feet long.
8. Well, do they live alone or in groups?
9. Oops! I didn't know that they do both.
10. Psst! Those groups are called pods.

▶ **Exercise 24** Choosing Interjections Fill in the blank in each sentence below with an interjection that expresses the emotion indicated in brackets. Add an appropriate punctuation mark.

1. [curiosity] ___?___ What is the big fin called?
2. [hesitation] ___?___ I think that's the dorsal fin.
3. [agreement] ___?___ it can be up to six feet tall.
4. [enthusiasm] ___?___ All of their flippers are oval.
5. [surprise] ___?___ that looks different from the other toothed whales.
6. [happiness] ___?___ Now we will be able to tell them apart.
7. [confusion] ___?___ isn't their coloring also different?
8. [excitement] ___?___ The black-and-white combination is very distinctive.
9. [frustration] ___?___ I knew I had forgotten something.
10. [unhappiness] ___?___ I don't think I can stay any longer.

▶ **Exercise 25** Combining Sentences With Conjunctions Combine each pair of sentences below with the conjunction specified.

1. Many whale species are considered rare. Many are endangered. (and)
2. This includes the blue whale. It also includes many other species. (not only . . . but also)

3. The International Whaling Commission is a group of whaling nations. Non-whaling nations belong, too. (both . . . and)
4. Do they want to conserve whales? Do they want to protect whales? (and)
5. Well, whaling is easier these days. We need stricter regulations. (so)

▶ **Exercise 26** Writing Sentences With Conjunctions and Interjections Write an original sentence using each of the following conjunctions and/or interjections.

1. not only . . . but also
2. gosh
3. either . . . or
4. for
5. neither . . . nor

▶ **Exercise 27** Revising a Passage With Conjunctions and Interjections Revise the following passage, combining sentences where appropriate and inserting interjections to add emotion.

I was in the ocean swimming. I saw a fin in the distance coming toward me. My heart began to beat rapidly. I wanted to swim to shore. I wanted to grow wings and fly out of there. The fin came closer. I screamed. Then, I woke up from the dream.

▶ **Exercise 28** Writing Application Write an account of an experience you had in or near the water. Use at least three interjections, three coordinating conjunctions, and two correlative conjunctions in your sentences. Underline these parts of speech.

Diagnostic Test

Directions: Write all answers on a separate sheet of paper.

Skill Check A. Copy the sentences below. Underline the simple subject once and the simple predicate twice.

1. Scientists invented miniature computer parts.
2. In the 1950's, they used silicon wafers.
3. Strong acids carved patterns into the silicon.
4. These patterns represent many larger parts.
5. Electricity flows through the patterns.

Skill Check B. Copy each sentence. Put a vertical line between the complete subject and the complete predicate. Underline the simple subject once and the simple predicate twice.

6. The pieces of silicon were called "integrated circuits."
7. Integrated circuits contain thousands of electronic parts.
8. These parts include diodes, resistors, and transistors.
9. A memory chip is a type of integrated circuit.
10. Most electronic equipment uses integrated circuits.

Skill Check C. Copy each sentence below, and then underline the subject once and the verb twice. Be sure to underline all the parts of compound subjects and verbs. Circle the conjunctions.

11. Scientists and researchers called the silicon pieces "chips."
12. Many circuits and other devices are on a chip.
13. Transistors either stop electrical current or allow its flow.
14. Scientists experimented and made even smaller chips.
15. Microchips are even tinier and perform many functions.

Skill Check D. Write the simple subject of each sentence.

16. There is another, more advanced computer.
17. Measure that in nanoseconds.
18. When was the first microchip used?
19. Here is a pocket calculator.
20. Use this calculator to find your answer.

Skill Check E. Write all direct objects and indirect objects on your paper, and then label them.

21. Engineers continually improve technology.
22. They offer the public new options all the time.
23. Computers perform both simple and complicated tasks.
24. We give computers essential tasks.
25. They give us more free time.

Skill Check F. Write all predicate nouns and predicate adjectives on your paper, and then label them.

26. The transistor was a new invention in 1947.
27. Three American physicists were responsible for its invention.
28. It was considered revolutionary in its time.
29. Transistors are essential parts of radios and television sets.
30. With transistors, circuits became smaller and more efficient.

The Basic Sentence

Theme: Old and
New Computers
....
In this section, you
will learn how sub-
jects and predicates
are joined to create
simple sentences.
The examples and
exercises are about
old and new types
of computers.
....
Cross-Curricular
Connection: Math

The sentence is a basic unit of speech and writing. By using sentences, particularly in writing, people make themselves understood. If you study the way sentences are put together, you will be able to recognize correct, well-formed sentences and learn which parts of a sentence are necessary and which parts are not.

▶**KEY CONCEPT** Every complete sentence contains a sub-ject and a predicate. The **subject** tells who or what the sen-tence is about. The **predicate** tells something about the subject. ■

The Subject Sentences can be about anything. Any person, place, or thing can be a subject. The *simple subject* of a sen-tence is the main word or words in the subject part of the sen-tence. It answers the question *Who?* or *What?* in relation to the verb.

EXAMPLES: He asked me for help.
China was where the abacus was invented.
Computers are complicated machines.

Usually, the simple subject is a noun or pronoun found at the beginning of a sentence. However, there are some excep-tions. First, there are simple subjects that consist of more than one word. These include titles, names, and compound nouns.

EXAMPLES: Wilhelm Schikard invented an early computer.
Pen pals can now use computers.

Second, subjects sometimes appear at the middle or the end of a sentence. Sometimes the subject can even appear after the verb. Notice the position of the subjects in the following examples:

EXAMPLES: After the debate, Marion sent an e-mail.
On the table sat the brand-new monitor.

Third, a sentence that makes a request or a command can have an unstated but understood subject. The subject *you* is not stated.

EXAMPLE: Type the word.
(The sentence is understood to mean "*You* type the word.")

▶ **Exercise 1** Finding Simple Subjects Write the simple subject in each sentence below. If the subject is understood, write (*you*).

EXAMPLE: The students enjoyed the computer lesson.

ANSWER: students

1. Humans have always used numbers.
2. They counted objects around them.
3. In trading, numbers were important.
4. Two sheep might be traded for one goat.
5. Devices help us make calculations.
6. Use the abacus.
7. Inventors soon made better machines.
8. Eventually came computers.
9. Computers now solve math problems.
10. Imagine our world without computers.

▶ **More Practice**

Grammar Exercise Workbook
• pp. 43–44
On-line Exercise Bank
• Section 19.1
  Go on-line:
  PHSchool.com
  Enter Web Code:
  eak-6002

Get instant feedback! Exercise 1 is available on-line or on CD-ROM.

◀ **Critical Viewing** Write two sentences about this picture. Use *boy* as the simple subject of one sentence and *computer* as the simple subject of the other. [Connect]

GRAMMAR IN
LITERATURE

from **The Fun They Had**
Isaac Asimov

In the following passage, the simple subjects have been highlighted in blue italics.

Margie even wrote about it that night in her diary. On the page headed May 17, 2155, *she* wrote, "Today *Tommy* found a real book."

The Predicate The *simple predicate* is a verb that tells what the subject does, what is done to the subject, or what the condition of the subject is.

EXAMPLES: Connie <u>drew</u> the graphic for the cover.
The programs <u>were changed</u>.
Marvin <u>is</u> ready.

In the sentences shown in the next chart, the simple subjects are underlined once and the simple predicates are underlined twice.

SIMPLE SUBJECTS AND PREDICATES
<u>Donna</u> <u>types</u>.
The <u>plant</u> in the corner <u>blooms</u> every summer.
My new <u>keyboard</u> <u>is sitting</u> in the box.

It is easy to find the simple subject and simple predicate if you ask yourself the following questions:

SIMPLE SUBJECT: What noun or pronoun answers the question *Who?* or *What?* before the verb?

SIMPLE PREDICATE: What verb expresses action done by or to the subject or tells the condition of the subject?

> **Grammar and Style Tip**
>
> Try to avoid sentence fragments in your writing. A fragment is a group of words that is punctuated as if it were a sentence, but it is incomplete. It is missing either a subject or a predicate, or it does not express a complete thought.

> ▶ **Exercise 2** Finding Simple Predicates Identify the simple predicate in each sentence below.

EXAMPLE: The computer program played the music beautifully.

ANSWER: played

1. Primitive people counted with their fingers.
2. This system works with small numbers.
3. Early Romans used pebbles for counting.
4. The pebbles were painted different colors.
5. Each color represented a different amount.
6. Some people tied knots in a cord.
7. Others made marks on wood.
8. Ancient Egyptian mathematics was very advanced.
9. The Egyptians developed formulas for area and volume.
10. They determined the size of their fields with these formulas.

More Practice

Grammar Exercise
Workbook
• pp. 43–44
On-line Exercise Bank
• Section 19.1
  Go on-line:
  PHSchool.com
  Enter Web Code:
  eak-6002

Get instant feedback!
Exercise 2 is available
on-line or on CD-ROM.

◀ **Critical Viewing**
Name four verbs you
could use as simple
predicates in sen-
tences about this
telephone keypad.
[Analyze]

Exercise 3 Finding Simple Subjects and Simple Predicates

Copy the sentences below. Underline each simple subject once and each simple predicate twice. (Remember—the simple subject will be a noun or a pronoun that answers the question *Who?* or *What?* before the verb. The simple predicate will be a verb or verb phrase.)

1. The next system was beads on wires.
2. The wires were stretched across a wooden frame.
3. Each wire held ten movable beads.
4. The beads stood for different quantities.
5. They were pushed from the left side to the right side.
6. This device is called an *abacus*.
7. The Chinese were among the first to use the abacus.
8. The Japanese called their version of the abacus the *soroban*.
9. They solved complex problems very quickly.
10. People utilized these devices until the 1950's.
11. John Napier discovered logarithms.
12. Logarithms make complicated problems much easier.
13. Then, he put the multiplication tables onto rods.
14. Multiplication became much easier.
15. Some people wanted mechanical devices for counting.
16. Blaise Pascal invented the first mechanical calculator.
17. It consisted of several interlocking wheels.
18. The machine made calculations automatically.
19. This invention was the first adding machine.
20. It performed addition and subtraction.

▼ **Critical Viewing**
In two or three sentences, compare the workings and parts (such as these resistors) of a calculator with those of an abacus. [**Compare and Contrast**]

Section 19.1 Section Review

GRAMMAR EXERCISES 4–9

Exercise 4 Finding Simple Subjects and Simple Predicates Write the sentences below on your paper. Underline each simple subject once and each simple predicate twice.

1. Gottfried Leibniz designed a special mathematical system.
2. It made multiplication possible on a mechanical calculator.
3. Leibniz's model computed higher numbers.
4. It still solved only simple problems.
5. His calculator used a hand crank.
6. This device increased the speed of multiplication and division.
7. The science of astronomy required more advanced methods.
8. Astronomers studied orbits of planets.
9. Logarithm tables at that time often contained mistakes.
10. Scientists demanded very precise measurements.

Exercise 5 Supplying Simple Subjects and Simple Predicates Write the sentences below on your paper, filling each blank with a logical simple subject or verb.

1. A French ___?___ made a type of computer.
2. Joseph-Marie Jacquard ___?___ an automated loom.
3. ___?___ programmed the loom for different patterns.
4. The system ___?___ rigid cards with holes in them.
5. The different patterns of holes ___?___ different woven patterns.
6. The ___?___ of France rewarded Jacquard.
7. However, his invention ___?___ the jobs of workers.

8. The angry ___?___ chased him out of Paris.
9. In the city of Lyon, his looms ___?___ very popular.
10. Today, some fabric ___?___ still use this kind of loom.

Exercise 6 Revising to Eliminate Incomplete Sentences Revise this paragraph on your paper, adding missing sentence parts.

   William Oughtred found a way to speed up calculations. Printed numbers on wooden rulers. The numbers were positioned according to their logarithms. Then, the rulers together. Called this device the "slide rule." A slide rule simple to use. Two numbers on the different rulers are lined up. Then, the product from the rulers. Before calculators were invented, many students slide rules.

Exercise 7 Find It in Your Reading
   In the excerpt from "The Fun They Had" on page 382, identify the simple predicate for each highlighted subject.

Exercise 8 Find It in Your Writing
   Choose a paragraph from your own writing. Identify the simple subject and the simple predicate in each sentence.

Exercise 9 Writing Application
   Write a description of some of the programs you use or activities you do on a computer. Underline simple subjects once and simple predicates twice.

Complete Subjects and Predicates

Sentences can be expanded beyond a simple subject and simple predicate. A writer can add to both the subject and the predicate of a sentence.

> ◤ **KEY CONCEPTS** The **complete subject** of a sentence includes the simple subject and the words related to it. The **complete predicate** includes the verb (simple predicate) and the words related to it. ■

A sentence can have just a simple subject and a simple predicate. Such a sentence will usually be quite brief. In the following sentence, the vertical line separates the simple subject *people* from the simple predicate *type*.

EXAMPLE: People | type.

The sentence could be expanded by adding words to the subject and the predicate. The words would be part of the *complete subject* and the *complete predicate.*

EXAMPLE: Many people from different places | type on their computers and typewriters.

The following chart shows the complete subject and the complete predicate of several sentences. Each simple subject is underlined once, and each simple predicate is underlined twice.

| COMPLETE SUBJECTS AND PREDICATES ||
Complete Subjects	Complete Predicates
My old <u>friend</u>	<u>returned</u> my floppy disk
A new <u>model</u> of the computer	<u>sits</u> in the store window.
That strange <u>noise</u>	<u>frightened</u> my brother.
The skilled <u>technician</u>	quickly <u>repaired</u> the machine.

Theme: Computers and Their Inventors

In this section, you will learn to identify complete subjects and predicates in simple sentences. The examples and exercises are about the inventors of early computers.

Cross-Curricular Connection: Math

▶ **Exercise 10** Recognizing Complete Subjects Write the complete subject of each sentence below on your paper, and underline the simple subject.

EXAMPLE: A simple mechanical computer was invented during the 1820's.

ANSWER: A simple mechanical <u>computer</u>

1. A mathematician named Charles Babbage designed an early mechanical computer.
2. He called his invention the "Difference Engine."
3. The small parts were made precisely.
4. A working model was produced in 1822.
5. A steam engine provided power for the machine.
6. Babbage announced plans for a new machine ten years later.
7. This more powerful machine had more versatility.
8. The name for the new machine was the "Analytical Engine."
9. The Analytical Engine was able to solve any sort of mathematical problem.
10. The operator of the machine switched it from one kind of problem to another.

▶ **Exercise 11** Recognizing Complete Predicates
Write the complete predicate of each sentence below on your paper, and underline the simple predicate twice.

EXAMPLE: A simple mechanical computer was invented during the 1820's.

ANSWER: <u>was invented</u> during the 1820's.

1. Charles Babbage built only working models of his calculating machines.
2. His ideas and detailed plans were later put to use by other inventors.
3. The clever Englishman was interested in economics, too.
4. He wrote a guide to the economics of manufacturing.
5. Babbage is still remembered today.

▶ **More Practice**

Grammar Exercise Workbook
• pp. 45–46
On-line Exercise Bank
• Section 19.2
Go on-line:
PHSchool.com
Enter Web Code:
eak-6002

British inventor Charles Babbage was a computer pioneer.

▲ **Critical Viewing**
Write a sentence explaining what this man did or why he is still important today. Underline the complete subject once and the complete predicate twice. **[Analyze]**

GRAMMAR IN LITERATURE

from **The Fun They Had**
Isaac Asimov

In the following excerpt, the complete subject of the sentence in quotation marks is shown in red italics, and the complete predicate is shown in blue italics.

The screen was lit up, and it said: *"Today's arithmetic lesson is on the addition of proper fractions. . . ."*

▶ **Exercise 12** Recognizing Complete Subjects and Predicates Copy each sentence below. Put a vertical line between the complete subject and the complete predicate. Underline the simple subject once and the simple predicate twice.

1. Babbage imagined a printing device for his machine.
2. Then, the machine could print the answers.
3. Cards with punched holes programmed the Analytical Engine.
4. That idea was borrowed from Jacquard's loom.
5. The punched cards stored instructions.
6. Babbage never obtained the funds for his machine.
7. A student of his named Augusta Ada Byron produced detailed notes of Babbage's ideas.
8. This expert mathematician was the daughter of the poet Lord Byron.
9. Augusta Ada Byron also devised several programs for the Analytical Engine.
10. Her key concepts, such as memory and storage, are incorporated in modern computers.

▶ **Exercise 13** Matching Complete Subjects and Complete Predicates On your paper, combine a complete subject from the first column with a complete predicate from the second column to form a complete sentence.

1. Word-processing software
2. With a computer mouse, you
3. Computer games
4. Today's microcomputers
5. With the help of the Internet, I

can click on a menu item.
can require lots of memory.
researched a science topic.
makes writing papers easier.
can handle multiple tasks.

More Practice

Grammar Exercise Workbook
• pp. 45–46
On-line Exercise Bank
• Section 19.2
  Go on-line:
  PHSchool.com
  Enter Web Code:
  eak-6002

Text

Get instant feedback! Exercises 12 and 13 are available on-line or on CD-ROM.

Section
19.2 Section Review

GRAMMAR EXERCISES 14–19

▶ **Exercise 14** **Identifying Complete
Subjects and Complete Predicates**
Copy each of the following sentences onto
your paper. Put a vertical line between
the complete subject and the complete
predicate. Underline the simple subject
once and the simple predicate twice.

1. Herman Hollerith was an American
   inventor and businessman.
2. One of Hollerith's ideas combined
   punched-hole cards with an electric
   power source.
3. The 1890 census used some of
   Hollerith's inventions.
4. An operator of a tabulating machine
   placed cards in a slot of the machine.
5. Many pins pressed against the card.
6. The holes in the card allowed some
   pins through.
7. Those pins picked up an electrical
   current.
8. The current controlled dials on the
   face of the machine.
9. The operator read the dials on the
   machine carefully.
10. Hollerith's tabulator was the first
    electromechanical computing machine.

▶ **Exercise 15** **Supplying Sentence
Parts for Complete Subjects and
Complete Predicates** Copy each sentence
below onto your paper, supplying a word or
phrase to fill the blank. Identify whether the
blank is part of the complete subject or the
complete predicate.

1. My ___?___ writes e-mail messages to
   most of his friends.
2. On most mornings, he ___?___ at least
   a dozen replies.
3. Using e-mail, my brother ___?___ with
   friends all around the world.

4. Last week, a ___?___ from Portugal
   sent him a message.
5. My brother's friends often ___?___ digital photographs with their messages.

▶ **Exercise 16** **Supplying Complete
Subjects and Complete Predicates** Add
a complete subject or a complete predicate
to each item to make a complete sentence.

1. My next project in science
2. looks like my machine at home
3. The newly designed keyboard
4. carried out a research project
5. A very useful Internet site

▶ **Exercise 17** **Find It in Your
Reading** Identify the complete subject
and complete predicate in each of these
sentences from "The Fun They Had."

". . . Those things happen sometimes.
I've slowed it up to an average ten-
year level. Actually, the overall pattern
of her progress is quite satisfactory."
And he patted Margie's head again.

▶ **Exercise 18** **Find It in Your
Writing** Choose a paragraph from your
own writing. Draw a line between the
complete subject and the complete predicate
in each sentence. Underline the simple subjects once and the simple predicates twice.

▶ **Exercise 19** **Writing Application**
Write an explanation of some ways that
computers make life easier for us.
Underline each complete subject once and
each complete predicate twice.

Compound Subjects and Compound Predicates

Section 19.3

A sentence can have more than one simple subject and more than one verb. When there is more than one subject, it is called a *compound subject*. When there is more than one verb related to the subject, it is called a *compound predicate*.

> **KEY CONCEPT** A **compound subject** includes two or more simple subjects that have the same verb. ■

Compound subjects are connected by conjunctions such as *and* or *or*.

EXAMPLES: <u>Bob</u> or <u>Sue</u> will go.
<u>Hockey</u> and <u>football</u> are my favorite sports.
<u>Anna</u>, <u>Steve</u>, and <u>Jane</u> are studying computer science.

> **Exercise 20** Identifying Compound Subjects Identify the compound subjects in each of the following sentences.
> 1. Businesses and schools use computers.
> 2. Neither government nor industry can function without them.
> 3. Words, pictures, and sounds are changed into numbers.
> 4. A memory and a processor are the basic parts.
> 5. Designers or artists may also use computers.

> **KEY CONCEPT** A **compound predicate** includes two or more verbs that relate to the same subject. ■

The following examples contain compound predicates. The verbs that make up each compound predicate are underlined twice.

EXAMPLES: At school, I <u>read</u> books, <u>made</u> friends, and <u>played</u> sports.

My friends <u>play</u> video games, <u>surf</u> the Internet, and <u>do</u> research on the computer.

Occasionally, a sentence may have both a compound subject and a compound predicate.

EXAMPLE: <u>Sandy</u> and <u>Marie</u> <u>called</u> and <u>asked</u> for help.

Theme: Uses of Computers

In this section, you will learn to recognize compound subjects or predicates in sentences. The examples and exercises are about different uses of computers.

Cross-Curricular Connection: Math

More Practice

Grammar Exercise Workbook
• pp. 47–48
On-line Exercise Bank
• Section 19.3

Go on-line:
PHSchool.com
Enter Web Code:
eak-6002

Get instant feedback! Exercises 20 and 21 are available on-line or on CD-ROM.

Exercise 21 Identifying Compound Predicates Identify the compound predicate in each of the following sentences.

1. The memory of a computer receives data and stores it.
2. The processor changes data into useful information and performs calculations.
3. A computer operator uses a keyboard or manipulates a mouse.
4. That person normally inputs data or enters instructions.
5. People can think about problems and solve them with the help of a computer.
6. Computers manage and organize large amounts of information.
7. With their help, we create and display documents quickly.
8. Computers make models and simulate situations.
9. Scientists develop and test theories with the help of computers.
10. People even play games and compose music on computers.

▼ Critical Viewing Write a sentence with a compound predicate describing two or more steps for getting inside a computer. [Connect]

GRAMMAR IN
LITERATURE

from **The Fun They Had**
Isaac Asimov

In the excerpt below, the parts of the compound predicate are highlighted in blue italics.

He was a round little man with a red face and a whole box of tools with dials and wires. He *smiled* at her and *gave* her an apple, then *took* the teacher apart.

▶ **Exercise 22** **Recognizing Compound Subjects and Predicates** Copy the sentences below. Underline the parts of each compound subject once and the parts of each compound predicate twice. Circle the conjunctions.

EXAMPLE: The <u>functions</u> (and) <u>uses</u> of computers seem endless.

1. With word-processing programs, people write and edit various documents.
2. Reports and letters are just two examples of the ways people use word processors.
3. Typing errors and misspellings can be easily corrected on a computer.
4. A writer also adds, moves, or deletes copy easily before printing out a finished copy.
5. Business people, students, and scientists use word processors.
6. Newsletters and other documents can be created conveniently on computers.
7. Some computer programs create pictures or draw diagrams.
8. Engineers and architects may also use these types of programs.
9. They may plan a bridge or design a building with special software.
10. A light pen and a mouse are useful tools for working on a computer.

More Practice

Grammar Exercise Workbook
• pp. 47–48
On-line Exercise Bank
• Section 19.3
Go on-line:
PHSchool.com
Enter Web Code:
eak-6002

Get instant feedback! Exercise 22 is available on-line or on CD-ROM.

Section 19.3 Section Review

GRAMMAR EXERCISES 23–28

Exercise 23 Identifying Compound Subjects or Predicates On your paper, write the parts of the compound subject or predicate in each sentence below.

1. Students and teachers use computers in the classroom.
2. The computer screen displays information and provides choices.
3. The keyboard or a mouse can highlight an item.
4. Maps, charts, graphs, and articles can be viewed on the computer.
5. Students can copy the information and save it or print it out.

Exercise 24 Supplying Parts of Compound Subjects and Compound Predicates Copy the sentences below on your paper, supplying a part of a compound subject or predicate to fill the blank. Underline the parts of each compound subject once and each compound predicate twice.

1. Computers guide students and ___?___ instruction.
2. Students and ___?___ use them on a daily basis.
3. The United States ___?___ and uses more computers than any other country.
4. Both European schools and Japanese ___?___ are also highly computerized.
5. Videos and animation provide information and ___?___ interaction.
6. Spreadsheets and databases organize and ___?___ data.
7. They ___?___ and transmit information.
8. ___?___ and instructors can communicate through a variety of programs.
9. Computer ___?___ and CD-ROMs store large amounts of data.
10. Computer learning is individual and ___?___ immediate answers.

Exercise 25 Revising a Paragraph by Creating Compound Subjects or Compound Predicates Revise the paragraph below by combining information in sentences to form compound subjects or compound predicates.

My family purchased a new computer. We signed up with an Internet provider. The computer has more memory than our old model. It also processes information more quickly than our old model. My brother set up his own password for the computer. I set up my own password for the computer, too. My father has asked me to help him use the computer. My mother has also asked me to help her use the computer.

Exercise 26 Find It in Your Reading Identify the compound verb in this excerpt from "The Fun They Had."

"A man? How could a man be a teacher?"
"Well, he just told the boys and girls things and gave them homework and asked them questions."

Exercise 27 Find It in Your Writing Look through your writing portfolio. Find an example of a compound subject or a compound verb.

Exercise 28 Writing Application Write a narrative about an activity that your entire class performed. Use compound subjects and compound predicates in your account. Underline the compound subjects once and the compound predicates twice.

Hard-to-Find Subjects

This section shows how to identify simple subjects in three different kinds of sentences.

The Subject of a Command or Request When a sentence commands or requests someone to do something, the subject is often unstated.

▶ **KEY CONCEPT** The subject of a command or request is understood to be the word *you*. ■

Sentences	How the Sentences Are Understood
Stop!	<u>You</u> stop!
Begin at once.	<u>You</u> begin at once.
Audrey, make a list.	Audrey, <u>you</u> make a list.
Bob, get the tickets.	Bob, <u>you</u> get the tickets.

Even though a command or request may begin with the name of the person spoken to, the subject is still understood to be *you*.

▶ **Exercise 29** Recognizing Subjects in Commands or Requests List the simple subject of each sentence below. If the subject is understood as part of a command or request, write it in parentheses.

EXAMPLE: Jennifer, look out the window at the stables.
ANSWER: (you)

1. Show me the photo of the horse.
2. Horses live in family groups.
3. Look at the different sizes of the horses.
4. These wild horses have traveled great distances searching for food.
5. Emily, take a picture of the Shetland pony.
6. A pony is a small horse.
7. Listen to the sounds of the horses.
8. The *hand* is a measurement used for horses.
9. Take the measurement from the feet to the shoulders.
10. One hand is equal to four inches.

Theme: Horses

In this section, you will learn to identify hard-to-find subjects in commands, questions, and other sentences. The examples and exercises are about horses and horseback riding.

Cross-Curricular Connection: Science

▶ **More Practice**

Grammar Exercise Workbook
• pp. 49–50
On-line Exercise Bank
• Section 19.4
Go on-line:
PHSchool.com
Enter Web Code:
eak-6002

Get instant feedback! Exercises 29 and 30 are available on-line or on CD-ROM.

The Subject of a Question If a sentence asks a question, the subject usually follows the verb. This is called *inverted order.*

▷ **KEY CONCEPT** In questions, the subject often follows the verb or is located between a helping verb and the main verb. ■

EXAMPLES: How <u>can</u> <u>Claude</u> <u>ride</u> such an energetic horse?
             <u>Is</u> there a good <u>movie</u> <u>playing</u> this evening?

If you are not sure of the subject of a question, turn the question into a statement. It will be easier to find the subject when the words are in normal order.

Questions	Questions Changed to Statements
<u>Has</u> <u>Ruth</u> <u>been practicing</u>?	<u>Ruth</u> <u>has been practicing</u>.
<u>Will</u> <u>David</u> <u>start</u> tomorrow?	<u>David</u> <u>will start</u> tomorrow.
<u>Can</u> this <u>horse</u> <u>hold</u> a mature rider?	This <u>horse</u> <u>can hold</u> a mature rider.

▷ **Exercise 30** **Finding the Subjects of Sentences That Ask Questions** Write the simple subject of each question below. Remember to change the question into a statement if you are not sure of the subject.

EXAMPLE: Why did Laura try the difficult jump?
ANSWER: Laura

1. What is the difference between a zebra and a horse?
2. In what ways do horses differ from donkeys?
3. When did you see the shire horse named King?
4. What was the horse's height?
5. How did you know about measuring horses?
6. Why is the Shetland pony so small?
7. Is it well adapted to its environment?
8. Do children ride that kind of pony?
9. Do horses live in Africa?
10. When did European travelers introduce domesticated horses?

▼ **Critical Viewing** Write three questions you might ask about this horse before you ride it. Identify the subject in each sentence. [**Connect, Identify**]

The Subject of a Sentence Beginning With *There* or *Here* *There* and *here* often begin sentences, but these words are never subjects.

▶ **KEY CONCEPT** The words *there* and *here* are never used as subjects. ■

Sometimes *there* and *here* are used as adverbs that answer the question *Where? There* can also be used as a sentence starter.

ADVERBS: There <u>is</u> my <u>saddle</u>.
            Here <u>are</u> the <u>albums</u>.

SENTENCE   There <u>are</u> fifty <u>states</u> in the United States.
STARTERS: There <u>was</u> a young <u>boy</u> here.

You can see that the order of subject and verb in each sentence above is inverted—that is, the subject follows the verb. If you have trouble finding the subject of sentences like these, rewrite the sentence so that it does not begin with *there* or *here*. When *there* is used as a sentence starter, it can safely be left out—the sentence will still make sense.

Sentences	Rewritten Sentences
Here <u>is</u> your <u>certificate</u>.	Your <u>certificate</u> <u>is</u> here.
There in the window <u>was</u> a tiny <u>monkey</u>.	A tiny <u>monkey</u> <u>was</u> there in the window.
There <u>are</u> two <u>senators</u> <u>elected</u> from every state.	Two <u>senators</u> <u>are elected</u> from every state. (*There* has been left out.)

▶ **Exercise 31** Identifying Hard-to-Find Subjects Write the simple subject of each of the following sentences.
1. When did people start riding horses?
2. Look in the museum.
3. There are statues of early horseback riders.
4. Did soldiers fight battles on horseback?
5. There were many horses in Genghis Khan's army.
6. Here are some carvings from 10,000 years ago.
7. What do historians think about the taming of the horse?
8. Here is an article about horses.
9. Read about their investigations.
10. There are cave drawings of horses.

Text

Get instant feedback! Exercise 31 is available on-line or on CD-ROM.

▶ **More Practice**

Grammar Exercise Workbook
• pp. 49–50
On-line Exercise Bank
• Section 19.4
Go on-line:
PHSchool.com
Enter Web Code:
eak-6002

Section 19.4 *Section Review*

GRAMMAR EXERCISES 32–37

▶ **Exercise 32** Rewriting Questions as Statements to Locate Their Subjects
On your paper, rewrite each question below as a statement. Then, underline each simple subject.

1. Is a bit needed in horseback riding?
2. Should all riders use this type of bridle?
3. Do you prefer an English saddle or a Western saddle?
4. Is the saddle too tight?
5. Was it uncomfortable to ride sidesaddle?

▶ **Exercise 33** Locating Hard-to-Find Subjects On your paper, write the simple subject of each sentence below.

1. Do you ever ride your horse in competitions?
2. Here is your formal riding jacket.
3. Wear a special helmet.
4. Which school teaches riding?
5. Use an English saddle.
6. When and where was the first jockey club founded?
7. There were races in Russia in 1775.
8. Have you ever seen a real racehorse?
9. There are several thoroughbreds near the track.
10. Go ahead and touch one.

▶ **Exercise 34** Supplying Subjects in Questions and Sentences Beginning with *Here* or *There* Rewrite the following sentences on your paper, supplying an appropriate simple subject for each blank. Then, underline the simple subject of your sentence once and the simple predicate twice.

1. Is this ___?___ easy to ride?
2. There are three ___?___ standing near the stables.

3. Have ___?___ ever wanted to gallop through the woods on a horse?
4. Here is my favorite ___?___.
5. Is this ___?___ planning to ride that horse?
6. Where is the ___?___ going?
7. A short distance from here, there is a large ___?___.
8. Can ___?___ see it from here?
9. Here are my ___?___ to help you.
10. Will the horse and ___?___ reach their destination on time?

▶ **Exercise 35** Find It in Your Reading Scan a sports article in a newspaper or magazine. Find at least one question and one sentence beginning with *here* or *there*. Name the subject of each sentence.

▶ **Exercise 36** Find It in Your Writing Look through your writing portfolio. Find a sentence that asks a question and one that begins with *here* or *there*. Write the subjects of those sentences.

▶ **Exercise 37** Writing Application Write a description of the picture on page 395. Include two sentences that begin with *here* or *there* and one question. Underline the simple subject of each sentence in your description.

Direct Objects and Indirect Objects

Identifying Direct Objects

You already know that a sentence must have two parts—a simple subject and a simple predicate. Some sentences need additional words to complete their meaning. These words are called *complements*. In the sentence *Jane gave a speech, speech* is a complement. It completes the meaning of *Jane gave*. It tells *what* Jane gave.

A *direct object* is one type of complement. It is used to complete many sentences that have action verbs.

> ▶ **KEY CONCEPT** A **direct object** is a noun or pronoun that appears with an action verb and receives the action of the verb. ■

A direct object answers the question *Whom?* or *What?* after an action verb.

EXAMPLE: Mrs. Gomez picked $\boxed{\text{us}}^{\text{DO}}$.

QUESTION: Picked *whom?* Answer: *us*

EXAMPLE: Fred asked a $\boxed{\text{question}}^{\text{DO}}$.

QUESTION: Asked *what?* Answer: *question*

EXAMPLE: The detective drove $\boxed{\text{Abe}}^{\text{DO}}$ across the river.

QUESTION: Drove *whom?* Answer: *Abe*

The following chart shows how simple subjects, simple predicates, and direct objects form complete sentences. As you can see, a direct object may be *compound*. That means that one verb can have two or more direct objects.

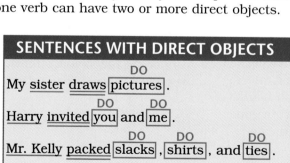

SENTENCES WITH DIRECT OBJECTS
My sister draws $\boxed{\text{pictures}}^{\text{DO}}$.
Harry invited $\boxed{\text{you}}^{\text{DO}}$ and $\boxed{\text{me}}^{\text{DO}}$.
Mr. Kelly packed $\boxed{\text{slacks}}^{\text{DO}}$, $\boxed{\text{shirts}}^{\text{DO}}$, and $\boxed{\text{ties}}^{\text{DO}}$.

Theme: Bridges

In this section, you will learn to recognize two new sentence parts: direct and indirect objects. The examples and exercises are about bridges around the world.

Cross-Curricular Connection: Social Studies

▲ **Critical Viewing**
Write three sentences about this picture using the verbs *rode, crossed,* and *saw*. What is the direct object in each sentence? **[Identify]**

GRAMMAR IN LITERATURE

From **Breaker's Bridge**

Laurence Yep

Notice the highlighted direct object in the following excerpt. What question does it answer?

. . . He could design a *bridge* to cross any obstacle. No canyon was too wide. No river was too deep. Somehow the clever man always found a way to bridge them all.

Exercise 38 **Finding Direct Objects** Copy each sentence below. Then, underline each direct object.

EXAMPLE: Ivan often crosses the Brooklyn Bridge.

1. The Pont Neuf crosses the Seine River in Paris.
2. It connects an island to the mainland.
3. The bridge has two arms.
4. The Pont Neuf replaced the older Pont Notre Dame.
5. Workers spent twenty-nine years building the bridge.
6. Religious wars interrupted the construction.
7. The plans for the bridge included space for shops.
8. Merchants displayed their goods in stalls on the bridge.
9. All levels of society visited the bridge for various reasons.
10. The Pont Neuf has played a big part in Parisian history.
11. Besides streets, Venice has canals.
12. The Rialto Bridge crosses the narrowest point of the Grand Canal.
13. Venetians have built several bridges at that spot.
14. They collected tolls on the Money Bridge.
15. The emperor Frederick III visited Venice.
16. A huge crowd watched him from the bridge.
17. The weight of the crowd caused the collapse of the bridge.
18. Eventually, Venetians built a larger stone bridge.
19. They lined it with shops.
20. Then, the Venetians changed its name to the Rialto Bridge.

More Practice

Grammar Exercise Workbook
• pp. 51–52
On-line Exercise Bank
• Section 19.5
  Go on-line:
  PHSchool.com
  Enter Web Code:
  eak-6002

Get instant feedback! Exercise 38 is available on-line or on CD-ROM.

Identifying Indirect Objects

A sentence that has a direct object can also have an indirect object. An indirect object is another type of complement. It also helps complete the meaning of a sentence.

KEY CONCEPT An **indirect object** is a noun or pronoun usually located between an action verb and a direct object. It tells which person or thing something is being given to or done for. ■

An indirect object answers the question *To or for whom?* or *To or for what?* after an action verb.

EXAMPLE: Yolanda sent [IO Marge] a [DO postcard].
QUESTION: Sent *to whom?* Answer: *Marge*

EXAMPLE: We gave the [IO magazine] a [DO title].
QUESTION: Gave *to what?* Answer: *magazine*

You should not confuse an indirect object with an object of a preposition. An indirect object cannot be part of a prepositional phrase. In the sentence *Yolanda sent a postcard to Marge, Marge* is part of a prepositional phrase. It is the object of the preposition *to* and is not an indirect object.

Indirect objects can be compound. That is, a verb can be followed by two or more indirect objects.

EXAMPLES: Rose sold [IO John] and [IO Eric] the [DO tickets].

Sally sent [IO Stan] and [IO Martin] [DO photos] of the Tower Bridge .

SENTENCES WITH INDIRECT OBJECTS

Mrs. Lawton teaches [IO us] [DO engineering].

The editor gave [IO Molly] and [IO Roy] an [DO assignment].

A salesperson showed [IO Stan] a [DO watch].

Exercise 39 Identifying Indirect Objects Copy each sentence below, and underline each indirect object. If a sentence has no indirect object, write *none*.

EXAMPLE: I owe <u>Martin</u> a letter.

1. The Roman Empire built its citizens many bridges.
2. The Romans gave each bridge several arches.
3. Bridges with several tiers offered Romans many options.
4. The Pont du Gard at Nîmes provided the area with much-needed water.
5. The aqueducts sent water to the cities.
6. They brought the citizens running water.
7. History tells us the benefits of the structure.
8. The Roman examples taught modern engineers much about bridge building.
9. I bought my friends postcards of the bridge.
10. I also sent my mother a photograph of the aqueducts.
11. In the Dark Ages, the monks built bridges for travelers.
12. The bridges saved the travelers a great deal of trouble.
13. Bridges offered them more protection from bandits.
14. Monks paid builders for their work.
15. The work also gave the builders training for other projects.
16. Some people taught themselves the skills to build bridges.
17. A shepherd boy promised the people of Avignon a bridge.
18. They granted him permission to build one.
19. A bishop lent the boy money for the project.
20. This book showed me the remaining four arches of the bridge.

More Practice

Grammar Exercise Workbook
• pp. 53–54
On-line Exercise Bank
• Section 19.5
Go on-line:
PHSchool.com
Enter Web Code:
eak-6002

Get instant feedback! Exercise 39 is available on-line or on CD-ROM.

▼ **Critical Viewing** In what ways can you compare an indirect object in a sentence to a bridge? **[Compare]**

An old stone bridge spans the Tarn Gorge in France.

Hands-on Grammar

Indirect Object Spinner

Sometimes you can use indirect objects instead of prepositional phrases in your sentences to add variety to your writing. To practice using indirect objects or prepositional phrases, try this activity:

Cut an index card in half. Fold each half to form an open rectangular box. You can do this by making a crease in the middle of the card piece and then folding in from the top and the bottom to your crease. (See the diagram below.) On each of the four creased areas of one of your index card halves, write a simple subject and predicate, using one of the following verbs: *sent, gave, made, offered, showed,* or *sent.* Examples: *My aunt gave* or *The teacher offered.* On the four creased areas of the other index card half, write two pairs of related endings for the sentence. One ending in each pair will contain the word *me* as an indirect object followed by a direct object. The other will contain the same direct object and a prepositional phrase ending with *me.* Examples: *me an alligator* and *an alligator to me.* Write the word *me* in one color when it is an indirect object and in another color when it is the object of a preposition.

Tape the edges of each card half together to form a box. Place your two boxes onto a pencil so that you can spin them around. Read each sentence opener with each pair of related endings. You will form sentences such as *My aunt gave me an alligator*

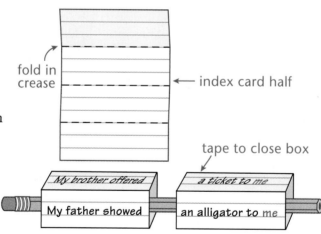

and *My aunt gave an alligator to me.* You can identify in which sentences *me* is functioning as an indirect object by its placement between the verb and the direct object in the sentence. The color coding will help you know whether you are right.

Find It in Your Reading Select a paragraph from a story in your literature book that contains a sentence with an indirect object. Make sure you can identify the indirect object and the direct object.

Find It in Your Writing Look for sentences in your own compositions that contain prepositional phrases beginning with *to* or *for.* Decide whether you should use an indirect object instead.

Section
19.5

Section Review

GRAMMAR EXERCISES 40–45

▶ **Exercise 40** Identifying Direct
Objects Identify the direct object in
each sentence below.

1. The Romans invented special arched
   bridges.
2. These aqueducts carried water from
   reservoirs to towns.
3. Modern builders make arches out of
   steel.
4. Sometimes cables attach the roadway
   to the framework.
5. Suspension bridges span the longest
   distances.

▶ **Exercise 41** Identifying Direct
and Indirect Objects Write each sentence below on your paper. Underline the
indirect object and circle the direct object.
Write *none* after a sentence if it has no
indirect object.

1. My grandparents took me on a tour of
   the Brooklyn Bridge.
2. The guide gave us a lecture on the history of the bridge.
3. The tour guide handed a brochure
   about the bridge to me.
4. We photographed the patterns of the
   cables.
5. Thousands of steel wires give each
   cable its strength.
6. Steel suspenders hold the roadway
   above the water.
7. Streetcars no longer take riders across
   the Brooklyn Bridge.
8. A walkway offers pedestrians a route
   to Brooklyn.
9. The bridge gives drivers a great view of
   the East River.
10. I sent my aunt and uncle postcards
    and photographs of the bridge.

▶ **Exercise 42** Revising Sentences
by Using Indirect Objects Revise the
sentences below by using an indirect
object in place of a prepositional phrase.

1. My brother built a model of the
   Brooklyn Bridge for me.
2. I showed the model to my science
   teacher.
3. She thought that it gave a good idea to
   everyone of the complexity of the
   bridge.
4. My brother offered help to me in building a model of another famous bridge.
5. He gave advice on how to get started
   to me.

▶ **Exercise 43** Find It in Your
Reading In the last sentence of the
excerpt from "Breaker's Bridge" on page
399, find the direct object of the verb
found.

▶ **Exercise 44** Find It in Your
Writing In your own writing, find
three examples of direct objects. Also, see
whether you have used indirect objects
in any of your sentences.

▶ **Exercise 45** Writing Application
Write a postcard telling about a place
you have visited or would like to visit.
Include three direct objects and at least
one indirect object. Circle the direct
objects, and underline the indirect objects.
You might want to use some of these verbs:
gave, made, told, bought, showed, sent.

Predicate Nouns and Predicate Adjectives

In this section, you will learn about two sentence parts often found in a complete predicate. *Predicate nouns* and *predicate adjectives* are called *subject complements.* A predicate noun renames the subject. A predicate adjective describes the subject. Both subject complements add details about the subject.

Identifying Predicate Nouns

A subject and a linking verb will generally be followed by one or more words that are needed to form a complete sentence. Predicate nouns often follow linking verbs.

▶ **KEY CONCEPT** A **predicate noun** is a noun that appears with a subject and a linking verb. It renames or identifies the subject. ■

EXAMPLES:

PN
Robert is the captain.

PN
The bridge was a very old structure.

PN
My dog is a poodle.

All the verbs in the sentences above are linking verbs. They are forms of the verb *be,* the most common linking verb.

A linking verb functions like an equal sign. In the first sentence above, *Robert is the captain* means *Robert = the captain.* The word *is* links *Robert* and *the captain* by saying that the one equals the other.

GRAMMAR IN LITERATURE

from **Breaker's Bridge**
Laurence Yep

In the following excerpt, the predicate noun is shown in blue italics, and the word it identifies is in red italics.

Breaker became uneasy. "*This* is a *place* that doesn't like people very much."

Theme: Bridges

In this section, you will learn to recognize and use predicate nouns and predicate adjectives. The examples and exercises provide more information about bridges around the world.

Cross-Curricular Connection: Social Studies

▶ **KEY CONCEPT** Two or more nouns can be used after a linking verb to form a compound predicate noun. ■

In the example below, two nouns are joined by the conjunction *and* to form a compound predicate noun. Both nouns identify or rename the same subject.

EXAMPLE: The <u>speakers</u> today <u>are</u> Jim and Rebecca.

▶ **KEY CONCEPT** A predicate noun is never part of a prepositional phrase. ■

Predicate nouns, like other complements, can never be part of prepositional phrases.

EXAMPLE: <u>Engineering is</u> an interesting branch of science.

Branch is a predicate noun, but *science* is not. It is part of the prepositional phrase *of science.*

▼ **Critical Viewing** Think of three different predicate nouns to complete this sentence: *This old bridge is a (an) . . . .* **[Connect]**

Built in 1870, this bridge in Waco, Texas, is one of the oldest suspension bridges in the United States.

▶ **Exercise 46** Identifying Predicate Nouns Identify the predicate noun in each sentence below.

EXAMPLE: Jane became a student.
ANSWER: student

1. Tower Bridge is a landmark in London.
2. Its supports are two Gothic-style towers.
3. The middle portion is a central drawbridge.
4. The design was a requirement of the government.
5. The engineer of the bridge was Sir John Wolfe Barry.
6. Sir Horace Jones was the architect.
7. The upper level is a pedestrian walkway.
8. The walkway became a popular tourist spot.
9. Devices in the towers are the machines that lift the draw-bridge.
10. Other devices in the towers are elevators to the upper walkway.

More Practice

Grammar Exercise
Workbook
• pp. 55–56
On-line Exercise Bank
• Section 19.6
    Go on-line:
    PHSchool.com
    Enter Web Code:
    eak-6002

▼ **Critical Viewing**
Think of sentences that include predicate nouns to identify the bridge (named in the exercise above) and the boat passing under it. **[Identify]**

Identifying Predicate Adjectives

An adjective may also follow a linking verb. If it completes the sentence, it is called a *predicate adjective.*

▶ **KEY CONCEPT** A **predicate adjective** is an adjective that follows a subject and a linking verb. It describes or modifies the subject of the sentence. ■

Predicate adjectives always modify the subject of a sentence. The arrows in the examples below connect the boxed predicate adjectives with the subjects they modify.

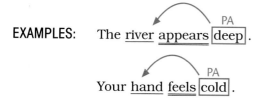

EXAMPLES: The river appears deep.

Your hand feels cold.

Predicate adjectives follow linking verbs such as those in the examples above. Other linking verbs include *be, become, grow, look, smell, sound, stay,* and *turn.*

A sentence may also have a compound predicate adjective—two or more adjectives following a linking verb.

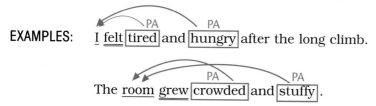

EXAMPLES: I felt tired and hungry after the long climb.

The room grew crowded and stuffy.

The following chart gives more examples of sentences with one or more predicate adjectives. An arrow connects each predicate adjective with the subject it modifies.

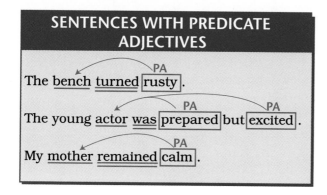

SENTENCES WITH PREDICATE ADJECTIVES

The bench turned rusty.

The young actor was prepared but excited.

My mother remained calm.

Exercise 47 **Identifying Predicate Adjectives** Copy each of the sentences below. Underline each predicate adjective. Then, draw an arrow connecting it to the subject it modifies. Some compound predicate adjectives are included.

EXAMPLE: The bridge grew crowded with traffic.

1. Early bridges in New England were wooden.
2. The supply of lumber was abundant.
3. Covered bridges may be narrow or wide.
4. Even today, they remain very sturdy.
5. The roof was useful for protecting the bridge from the elements.
6. The sun and rain were harmful to the wood.
7. With a roof, the plank floor would stay strong.
8. The speed of horses and carriages seemed very slow.
9. These bridges were vulnerable to fires.
10. The truss system was important in the construction of covered bridges.

More Practice

Grammar Exercise Workbook
• pp. 57–58
On-line Exercise Bank
• Section 19.6
Go on-line:
PHSchool.com
Enter Web Code:
eak-6002

▶ Critical Viewing
Think of several adjectives to describe this bridge. Use your words as predicate adjectives in sentences about the bridge. [Analyze]

Section 19.6 Section Review

GRAMMAR EXERCISES 48–54

Exercise 48 Recognizing
Predicate Nouns Identify the predicate
noun in each sentence below.

1. Charles Crocker was the originator of
   the idea.
2. Joseph Baermann Strauss was a well-
   known designer of bridges.
3. He was a believer in the plan.
4. The waterway in question was the
   Golden Gate Strait.
5. In 1930, the people in the area were
   supporters of the project.

Exercise 49 Identifying Predicate
Adjectives Copy each of the sentences
below. Underline each predicate adjective.
Then, draw an arrow connecting it to the
subject it modifies.

1. The bridge's color is orange.
2. Most modern bridges are black or
   gray.
3. The bridge is well maintained even
   today.
4. The Golden Gate Bridge has become
   irreplaceable.
5. It is useful for drivers and pedestrians.

Exercise 50 Identifying Predicate
Nouns and Adjectives Identify the
predicate nouns and the predicate adjectives in the following sentences. Label each
one PN or PA.

1. The study of bridges is fascinating.
2. Many bridges are wooden.
3. Concrete became a common material
   in combination with iron wire.
4. Ancient castles stayed safe behind
   drawbridges.
5. The movement of drawbridges is simple to understand.

6. The basic principles are the same as in
   other lift bridges.
7. A counterweight looks hard to move.
8. Actually, it becomes very useful in
   raising and lowering heavy bridges.
9. The small motors are powerful tools.
10. Bridges are important structures all
    around the world.

Exercise 51 Supplying Predicate
Nouns or Predicate Adjectives in
Sentences Copy the sentences below on
your paper, supplying an appropriate predicate noun or predicate adjective to fill
each blank. Underline the words you add,
and label them PN or PA.

1. This rope bridge seems ___?___.
2. Is it ___?___ enough to hold my weight?
3. The rope bridge was the only ___?___ to
   get across the ravine.
4. All of us were ___?___ as we crossed
   the bridge.
5. John was an expert ___?___ , so he led
   the way.

Exercise 52 Find It in Your
Reading In the excerpt from "Breaker's
Bridge" on page 404, identify a predicate
adjective and the word it modifies.

Exercise 53 Find It in Your
Writing Look through your writing
portfolio. Find two predicate nouns and
two predicate adjectives in your writing.

Exercise 54 Writing Application
Write a description of a bridge that you
have seen. Use predicate nouns and predicate adjectives to tell more about your
subjects. Label each one PN or PA.

Chapter Review

GRAMMAR EXERCISES 55–62

Exercise 55 Identifying Complete Subjects and Predicates and Simple Subjects and Predicates Copy each sentence below. Put a vertical line between the complete subject and the complete predicate. Underline the simple subject once and the simple predicate twice.

1. The *Mayflower* sailed across the Atlantic Ocean.
2. The ship was headed for Virginia.
3. It carried the Pilgrims to the New World.
4. Thrown off course, the boat reached Massachusetts instead of Virginia.
5. The Pilgrims founded Plymouth Colony.
6. All adult males gathered in the cabin of the *Mayflower*.
7. Forty-one men, including John Alden and Miles Standish, signed the Mayflower Compact.
8. The compact established the rule of the majority.
9. It remained their fundamental principle of government.
10. Plymouth Colony was absorbed by the Massachusetts Bay Colony in 1691.

Exercise 56 Identifying Hard-to-Find Subjects Write the simple subject of each sentence below.

1. There is the *Great Eastern*.
2. When was that steamship launched?
3. Look at the six masts!
4. Here is its route to Australia.
5. Could the ship carry enough coal?
6. There is a paddle wheel with an 18-meter diameter.
7. Start the paddle wheel.
8. Was it famous for its size?
9. Learn about the transatlantic cable.
10. Did the *Great Eastern* lay any other cables across the ocean?

Exercise 57 Revising a Paragraph by Forming Compound Subjects or Predicates Revise the paragraph below by combining information in sentences to form compound subjects or compound predicates.

The *Merrimack* was sunk by Union forces. The *Merrimack* was at first abandoned. Then, Confederate workers raised it. They rebuilt it as the *Virginia*. The *Virginia* destroyed two Union ships. It then engaged the *Monitor* in battle. The two ironclad ships faced off against each other. They opened fire. The *Virginia* sustained some damage. The *Monitor* also sustained some damage. The battle at Hampton Roads was called a draw.

Exercise 58 Identifying Direct and Indirect Objects Write the sentences below on your paper. Underline the indirect objects and circle the direct objects.

1. Our teacher showed the class pictures of caravels.
2. Caravels used the wind for power.
3. Traders sailed caravels on the Mediterranean Sea in the 1300's.
4. The town of Palos in Spain gave Christopher Columbus two caravels.
5. Columbus sailed these caravels and another ship west across the Atlantic.
6. The three ships carried ninety men.
7. Columbus paid the men monthly wages.
8. Cannons on the ships could fire large stones at enemies.
9. Queen Isabella gave the ships several flags to fly.
10. Columbus's journeys brought him fame.

▶ **Exercise 59** **Identifying Predicate Nouns and Adjectives** Write any predicate nouns or predicate adjectives you find in the following sentences. Label them *PN* or *PA*.

1. The *Niña* and the *Pinta* were caravels; the *Santa María* was much larger.
2. Caravels were smaller and lighter than galleons.
3. These ships were tiny compared to modern ships.
4. The *Santa María* was the slowest of the three ships.
5. Food, fuel, candles, and tools were important supplies.
6. "Bombards" were a type of cannon.
7. Other weapons were more accurate.
8. The trip across the Atlantic became very long.
9. The sailors grew tired.
10. Columbus was an experienced sailor.

▶ **Exercise 60** **Identifying Basic Sentence Parts** On your paper, indicate whether the underlined sentence part is a *subject, verb, direct object, indirect object, predicate noun,* or *predicate adjective.*

1. Today's cruise ships are <u>large</u> and luxurious.
2. They offer <u>passengers</u> fine food and accommodations.
3. The *Queen Mary* and *Queen Elizabeth* were early ocean <u>liners</u>.
4. Raging <u>fires</u> destroyed the *Queen Elizabeth* in 1972.
5. The *Andrea Doria* was very large and <u>fast</u>.
6. It <u>was called</u> the "Grande Dame of the Sea."
7. The ship provided swimming <u>pools</u> for all three classes.
8. Captain Calami <u>gave</u> the *Andrea Doria* a heading for New York.
9. The *Stockholm* and the <u>*Andrea Doria*</u> crossed paths.

10. Gunnar Nordensen was <u>captain</u> of the *Stockholm.*
11. How dense the <u>fog</u> was that night!
12. "<u>Pull</u> to the left!" the captain shouted.
13. Both boats maneuvered but still <u>collided</u>.
14. My father told <u>us</u> the story of the sinking of the *Andrea Doria.*
15. Today, most <u>passengers</u> cross the ocean in planes instead of ships.

▶ **Exercise 61** **Revising by Adding Basic Sentence Parts** Revise the following paragraph, adding subjects or predicates to any incomplete sentences as needed, forming compound subjects or predicates, or adding predicate nouns or predicate adjectives to provide details.

I saw a television documentary about the *Titanic.* Was a large luxury liner. Everyone thought it was. Nevertheless, it crashed. Sank quickly. The show included old newsreel films. The show featured interviews with survivors. Quite interesting. Provided many details about the disaster. Described the passengers' fates graphically. Many people lost their lives when sank. Some young, some old. The whole incident seemed so to me. I told my brother the story. He also felt about what happened.

▶ **Exercise 62** **Writing Application** Write a comparison of two means of transportation. Use some compound subjects and compound predicates in your writing. Also include some predicate nouns and predicate adjectives to add descriptive details.

Standardized Test Preparation Workshop

Recognizing Appropriate Sentence Construction

Standardized tests that measure writing and communication skills often test your ability to identify a complete sentence. The following elements must be in place for a sentence to be complete and correct:

- **Subject**—the noun or pronoun that tells *who* or *what* performs the action;

- **Verb**—the action performed by or to the subject, or the condition of the subject.

All complete sentences must express a complete thought. If any of these elements is missing, the sentence is incomplete, a fragment.

When answering these test questions, check the numbered passages for the elements of a complete sentence. Then, choose the group of words that contains all the elements of a complete sentence and best fits in the context of the passage. The following sample test item will give you practice with the format used for testing your knowledge of basic sentence parts.

> ### Test Tip
>
> Remember that not all verbs express action. A form of the verb *be* can be the main verb of a sentence, but it does not express action; instead, it links words together.

Sample Test Item

Choose the letter of the best way to write the underlined section. If the underlined section needs no change, choose *Correct as is*.

After school, several of the children walked home together. <u>Were very careful at the</u> <u>crosswalks.</u>
(1)

1 A Were very careful to look both ways at the crosswalks.

   B Careful at the crosswalks.

   C They were very careful at the crosswalks.

   D Correct as is

Answer and Explanation

The underlined phrase consists of a linking verb, *were*, without a subject. It does not express a complete thought. The correct answer, *C*, adds a subject that is consistent with the rest of the passage, making the phrase a complete sentence.

Practice 1 **Directions:** Choose the letter of the best way to write each underlined section. If the underlined section needs no change, choose "Correct as is."

Seldom seen in modern offices. The ancestor
(1)
of today's wordprocessor. Although the
(2)
typewriter has existed in its current form

only since 1873. In 1714, a patent was

requested for an early version. After over
(3)
150 years of experimentation, the first

standard typewriter was introduced in 1873.

1 **A** Seldom seen in modern offices, the ancestor of today's word processor.
   B The typewriter is seldom seen in modern offices. The ancestor of today's word processor.
   C The typewriter, seldom seen in modern offices, is the ancestor of today's word processor.
   D Correct as is

2 **F** Although the typewriter has existed in its current form only since 1873, a patent was requested for an early version in 1714.
   G In 1714 a patent was requested. It was for an early typewriter.
   H The typewriter has existed in its current form since 1714, when a patent was requested for an early version.
   J Correct as is

3 **A** After over 150 years of experimentation, the first standard typewriter in 1873.
   B In 1873, the first standard typewriter was introduced. After over 150 years of experimentation,
   C After over 150 years of experimentation, the first standard typewriter in 1873.
   D Correct as is

Practice 2 **Directions:** Choose the letter of the best way to write each underlined section. If the underlined section needs no change, choose "Correct as is."

According to scientists, the involuntary
(1)
contraction of fifteen facial muscles.

This is caused by spontaneous laughter.

This involuntary contraction accompanied
(2)
by changed breathing patterns. Both
(3)
physical and mental. Events can cause

spontaneous laughter.

1 **A** According to scientists, the involuntary contraction of fifteen facial muscles produces spontaneous laughter.
   B According to scientists, spontaneous laughter produces the involuntary contraction of fifteen facial muscles.
   C According to scientists, spontaneous laughter contracts fifteen facial muscles.
   D Correct as is

2 **F** This involuntary contraction causes breathing patterns to change.
   G This involuntary contraction with accompanying changed breathing patterns.
   H Changed breathing patterns accompany this involuntary contraction.
   J Correct as is

3 **A** Both physical and mental events can cause. Spontaneous laughter.
   B Physical events can cause spontaneous laughter. Mental events can cause spontaneous laughter.
   C Both physical and mental events can cause spontaneous laughter.
   D Correct as is

Phrases and Clauses

Two African elephants confront each other near a watering hole.

▲ **Critical Viewing**
What distinct difference do you see between these two elephants, and what might it indicate? **[Speculate]**

You have already learned about the parts of speech and the basic parts of a sentence: the simple subject and the simple predicate. This chapter will present two other grammatical structures: the *phrase* and the *clause*.

Phrases and clauses are groups of words that add information or create a complete thought. In sentences, they add details or bring pieces of information together. If you were writing about endangered animals, for example, you might include information about certain species that are protected by laws. The phrases and clauses in your writing might add information about habitats, lifestyles, and appearances of different animals. This information would help readers to understand your ideas better.

Diagnostic Test

Directions: Write all answers on a separate sheet of paper.

Skill Check A. Copy the following sentences. Underline the prepositional phrases used as adjectives, and draw an arrow from each phrase to the word it modifies.

1. Have you read many articles about elephants?
2. The trunk is the most distinctive feature of the elephant.
3. It is a combination of a nose and an upper lip.
4. The fingerlike extensions on the end of the trunk hold objects.
5. Elephants in Africa are larger than those in Asia.

Skill Check B. Copy the following sentences. Underline the prepositional phrases used as adverbs, and draw an arrow from each phrase to the word it modifies.

6. An elephant does not actually drink water with its trunk.
7. Instead, it draws water through its nostrils.
8. Then, it squirts the water into its mouth.
9. Also, elephants smell with their trunks.
10. They can use their trunks as snorkels when they are swimming.

Skill Check C. Copy the following sentences. Underline the appositive phrases, and draw an arrow to the word each phrase identifies or explains.

11. Tusks, their enlarged incisor teeth, can grow up to 10 feet long.
12. Their molars, the grinding teeth, are on each side of both jaws.
13. Coarse plants, an elephant's main food, wear down its teeth.
14. Final molars, the largest ones, come in when the elephant is forty years old.
15. An aged elephant, one over sixty years old, may lose its teeth and be unable to eat.

Skill Check D. Label the following groups of words *independent clause* or *subordinate clause.*

16. the African elephant has larger ears
17. whereas the Asian elephant has only one "finger" on its trunk
18. both male and female African elephants have tusks
19. when the two kinds are side by side
20. the African will be somewhat larger and darker in color

Skill Check E. Identify each sentence below as *simple, compound,* or *complex.*

21. Elephant eyes are very small, and their eyesight is not very good.
22. In the water, elephants can swim for long distances.
23. When a baby cries, other elephants will gather to comfort it.
24. They frequently flap their ears, for this action cools them off.
25. When males reach about the age of fourteen, they leave the herd.

Phrases

All phrases are alike in two ways. First, every phrase is made up of a group of words that do the work of a single part of speech. For example, a phrase can do the work of a single adverb or a single adjective. Second, a phrase never has a subject *and* a verb.

KEY CONCEPT A **phrase** is a group of words that functions in a sentence as a single part of speech. Phrases do *not* contain a subject and a verb. ■

Using Prepositional Phrases

By itself, a *prepositional phrase* is made up of at least two parts: a preposition and a noun or pronoun that is the *object* of the preposition.

EXAMPLE:
    PREP   OBJ
    near *jungles*

The object of the preposition may be modified by one or more adjectives:

EXAMPLE:
    PREP   ADJ   ADJ   OBJ
    near remote Asian *jungles*

The object may also be compound:

EXAMPLE:
    PREP   ADJ   ADJ   OBJ   OBJ
    near remote Asian *grasslands* and *jungles*

No matter how long a prepositional phrase is or how many different parts of speech it contains, a prepositional phrase always acts in a sentence as if it were a one-word adjective or adverb.

Exercise 1 Identifying Prepositional Phrases Copy each sentence below onto your paper. Underline each prepositional phrase, and circle the object of the preposition.

EXAMPLE: See the tiger waiting <u>in the tall (grass)</u>.

1. Tigers are members of the cat family.
2. They are related to lions and jaguars.
3. Bengal tigers are found in Asia.
4. They are well camouflaged by their stripes.
5. Tigers do not survive easily near people.

Theme: Endangered Species

In this section, you will learn how to use phrases to add details to the sentences you write. The examples and exercises are about endangered species of animals.
Cross-Curricular Connection: Science

Get instant feedback! Exercise 1 is available on-line or on CD-ROM.

More Practice

Grammar Exercise Workbook
• pp. 59–60
On-line Exercise Bank
• Section 20.1
Go on-line:
PHSchool.com
Enter Web Code:
eak-6002

Using Phrases That Act as Adjectives

A prepositional phrase that acts as an adjective in a sentence is called an *adjective phrase.*

KEY CONCEPT An **adjective phrase** is a prepositional phrase that modifies a noun or pronoun by telling *what kind* or *which one.* ■

Like a one-word adjective, an adjective phrase answers the question *What kind?* or *Which one?* While one-word adjectives usually come before nouns, adjective phrases usually come after nouns.

Adjectives	Adjective Phrases
The *tiger* story begins now.	The story *about tigers* begins now.
The *striped* tiger faced us.	The tiger *with the stripes* faced us.

▼ Critical Viewing Using adjective phrases, describe some of the differences between a tiger and a house cat. **[Distinguish]**

▶ **Exercise 2** Identifying Adjective Phrases Copy the sentences below onto your paper. Underline each adjective phrase, and draw an arrow pointing from it to the word it modifies.

EXAMPLE: Pollution <u>from aircraft</u> may destroy

habitats <u>near busy urban airports.</u>

1. The tiger was a symbol of power.
2. Now, tigers around the world are endangered species.
3. Three subspecies of tigers have already become extinct.
4. Humans are the greatest threat to the tiger.
5. Tiger hunting was once a sport for rich people.
6. Many thousands of tigers were killed this way.
7. Tiger body parts became ingredients for Chinese medicines.
8. Tiger hunting in India is now forbidden.
9. Groups of conservationists promote laws protecting tigers.
10. Did you help these tigers in danger?

▶ **Exercise 3** Writing Sentences With Adjective Phrases Using the numbered items below, write sentences with prepositional phrases used as adjectives.

EXAMPLE: about giant pandas (news story)

ANSWER: Today, I read a news story about giant pandas.

1. of pandas (home)
2. in the San Diego Zoo (two pandas)
3. from China (gift)
4. around the panda enclosure (visitors)
5. on the increase (endangered species)

▶ **Critical Viewing** Where was the photographer in relation to this giant panda? Answer using an adjective phrase. **[Infer]**

GRAMMAR IN
LITERATURE

from **The Tiger Who Would Be King**
James Thurber

The phrases that act as adjectives are highlighted in the following excerpt.

It was a terrible fight, and it lasted until the setting *of the sun*. All the animals *of the jungle* joined in, some taking the side *of the tiger* and others the side *of the lion*.

▶ **Exercise 4** Supplying Prepositions to Form Adjective **Phrases** Rewrite the sentences below, supplying a preposition to complete each adjective phrase. Then, underline the adjective phrase, and draw an arrow pointing from it to the word it modifies.

1. There are many species ___?___ animals that are endangered and have a need ___?___ protection.
2. The giant panda is the subject ___?___ antihunting laws ___?___ China.
3. The snow leopard is the biggest threat ___?___ the panda's survival.
4. The panda's limited habitat ___?___ western China is very small.
5. Pandas prefer to eat the tender leaves and stems ___?___ only a few types ___?___ bamboo.
6. Researchers ___?___ the world admit that the lifestyle ___?___ the panda is not well known.
7. Valleys ___?___ flowers and bamboo are the panda's favorite areas to roam.
8. Their senses ___?___ smell and hearing are better than their eyesight.
9. Zoos around the world provide protection ___?___ small numbers ___?___ pandas.
10. We have read articles ___?___ pandas and seen television shows ___?___ them.

▶ **More Practice**

Grammar Exercise Workbook
• pp. 59–60
On-line Exercise Bank
• Section 20.1
   Go on-line:
   PHSchool.com
   Enter Web Code:
   eak-6002

Complete the exercises on-line! Exercises 2, 3, and 4 are available on-line or on CD-ROM.

Exercise 6 Identifying Appositive Phrases Rewrite each sentence below, underlining the appositive or appositive phrase and drawing an arrow from it to the noun it renames.

EXAMPLE: Buffalo, "wild cattle" to the early Spanish settlers, were present throughout North America.

1. This animal, the American buffalo, is one of the largest land mammals.
2. Cows, the females, live in small groups with their calves.
3. One-year-old buffalo, the yearlings, practice survival skills by playing.
4. A related group, the European bison, is almost extinct.
5. The American buffalo, a threatened species, now lives in protected areas.
6. The early buffalo population, 30 million animals, had declined to 500 by 1900.
7. The bull of the American buffalo, *Bison bison*, may weigh more than 2,000 pounds.
8. The Plains Indians used buffalo skins and bones for these daily needs: shelter, boots, and tools.
9. The American buffalo, an enduring symbol of power and strength, is rich in western imagery.
10. I'm learning about the buffalo in my social studies class, American History I.

▼ **Critical Viewing** Based on this photograph, where do the buffalo roam? Include an appositive phrase in your response. **[Analyze]**

Exercise 7 Revising to Combine Sentences With Appositive Phrases Combine each pair of sentences below with an appositive phrase. Underline the appositive phrase.

EXAMPLE: Steller's sea eagle can be spotted at dusk. It is one of several eagles in the area.

ANSWER: Steller's sea eagle, one of several eagles in the area, can be spotted at dusk.

1. The North American bald eagle is another threatened species. It is America's national symbol.
2. Acid rain poisons their food supply. Acid rain is a form of pollution.
3. Congress passed the Endangered Species Act. This law has guaranteed protection of the bald eagle.
4. Groups of scientists, conservationists, and volunteers study the eagles. They are eagle recovery teams.
5. Hospitals for wounded eagles restore birds to health, and then set them free. They are raptor rehabilitation centers.

▶ **More Practice**

Grammar Exercise Workbook
• pp. 63–64
On-line Exercise Bank
• Section 20.1
  Go on-line:
  PHSchool.com
  Enter Web Code:
  eak-6002

Get instant feedback! Exercises 6 and 7 are available on-line or on CD-ROM.

Section 20.1 Section Review

GRAMMAR EXERCISES 8–13

Exercise 8 Supplying Prepositions in Adjective Phrases Copy each sentence below, and supply a preposition to complete the adjective phrase. Then, draw an arrow from it to the word it modifies.

1. There are fifty species __?__ monkeys __?__ South America.
2. Now, their habitats __?__ the rain forest are being destroyed.
3. This destruction reduces the sources __?__ food __?__ the monkeys.
4. Marmosets and tamarins eat small animals __?__ frogs and snails.
5. They also drink the gum __?__ trees.

Exercise 9 Supplying Prepositions in Adverb Phrases Copy each sentence below and supply a preposition to complete the adverb phrase. Then, draw an arrow from it to the word it modifies.

1. Spider monkeys swing __?__ the forest __?__ the branches.
2. They can hang __?__ branches __?__ their tails.
3. Sometimes they drop twigs __?__ their enemies.
4. Spider monkeys live __?__ large groups.
5. These groups frequently split __?__ smaller subgroups __?__ the day.

Exercise 10 Combining Sentences With Appositive Phrases Combine each pair of sentences below with an appositive phrase.

1. Uakaris have short tails. They are mid-sized South American monkeys.
2. Uakaris are the best jumpers of all South American monkeys. They spend most of the year in the trees above flooded land.

3. Two species are the bald uakari and the black uakari. They look very different from each other.
4. The bald uakari's distinctive feature is its bright pink face. It is very noticeable.
5. Different shades of color may result from varying amounts of time each monkey spends in the sun. The shades are pale pinks and bright reds.

Exercise 11 Find It in Your Reading Find one adjective phrase and one adverb phrase in this opening sentence from "The Tiger Who Would Be King" by James Thurber.

One morning the tiger woke up in the jungle and told his mate that he was king of beasts.

Exercise 12 Find It in Your Writing Look through your portfolio to find examples of sentences that contain prepositional phrases used as adjectives, adverbs, or appositive phrases. Underline each phrase, and draw an arrow to the word it modifies.

Exercise 13 Writing Application Pick an animal that is endangered, such as the tiger, elephant, bald eagle, grizzly bear, panda, or uakari. Write the copy for an advertisement designed to interest people in helping to save the animal. Include adjective phrases, adverb phrases, and at least one appositive or appositive phrase to explain where the animal lives, how it looks, and why it needs to be protected.

Clauses

This section will deal with another important group of words—*clauses*.

> **KEY CONCEPT** A **clause** is a group of words with its own subject and verb. ■

Using Independent and Subordinate Clauses

There are two basic kinds of clauses, and there is an important difference between them. The first kind is called an *independent clause.*

> **KEY CONCEPT** An **independent clause** has a subject and a verb and can stand by itself as a complete sentence. ■

Independent clauses can be short or long. What is important is that the clause can express a complete thought and can stand by itself as a sentence.

INDEPENDENT CLAUSES:

The ski lift took us up the mountain.

In the morning, we practiced on the beginners' slope.

Lance Armstrong, an American cyclist, won the Tour de France.

Theme: Extreme Sports

In this section, you will learn to recognize different types of clauses and to classify sentences according to their structure. The examples and exercises are about extreme sports.

Cross-Curricular Connection: Physical Education

◀ **Critical Viewing** In a sentence with a single subject and verb, describe the quality of a bike ride on rocky terrain like that in the picture. **[Evaluate]**

GRAMMAR IN LITERATURE

from **Becky and the Wheels-and-Brake Boys**

James Berry

In the following excerpt, notice the two independent clauses joined together by the word but.

It was evening time, but *sunshine was still big patches in yards and on housetops.*

The second type of clause is called a *subordinate clause.* This type of clause also contains a subject and a verb, but it differs from an independent clause in one important way: By itself, it does *not* express a complete thought.

▶ **KEY CONCEPT** A **subordinate clause** has a subject and a verb but cannot stand by itself as a complete sentence. It is only *part* of a sentence. ■

Read the following examples. Do these clauses express complete thoughts, or do you need more information?

SUBORDINATE
CLAUSES:

$\overset{\text{S}}{\text{she}} \overset{\text{V}}{\text{reached}}$

After <u>she</u> <u>reached</u> the top of the cliff

$\overset{\text{S}}{\text{bicycle}} \overset{\text{V}}{\text{had}}$

When the <u>bicycle</u> <u>had</u> a flat tire

As you can see, these subordinate clauses do have a subject and a verb. However, in each case something is missing; more information is needed. Consider the first clause. *After she reached the top of the cliff,* what happened or how did she feel? The thought is not complete, and the reader still has questions.

▶ **Exercise 14** Identifying Independent and Subordinate Clauses Label each group of words below as an independent clause or a subordinate clause.
1. When mountain biking began in California.
2. Although regular bikes did not work very well.
3. Riders made their own bikes for their special needs.
4. Mountain bikes are made of strong, light metals.
5. Cyclists ride.

▶ **More Practice**

Grammar Exercise Workbook
• pp. 65–66
On-line Exercise Bank
• Section 20.2
  Go on-line:
  PHSchool.com
  Enter Web Code:
  eak-6002

 Text

Get instant feedback! Exercise 14 is available on-line or on CD-ROM.

Classifying Sentences by Structure

All sentences can be classified according to the number and kinds of clauses they contain. The three basic types of sentence structures are *simple, compound,* and *complex.*

The Simple Sentence

The *simple sentence* is the most common type of sentence structure.

> **KEY CONCEPT** A **simple sentence** consists of a single independent clause. ■

Simple sentences vary in length. Some are quite short; others can be several lines in length. All simple sentences, however, contain just one subject and one verb.

A simple sentence can have a compound subject, a compound verb, or both. Sometimes it may have other compound elements, such as a compound direct object or a compound phrase. All of the following sentences are simple sentences.

ONE SUBJECT AND VERB:	The <u>bell</u> <u>rang</u>.
COMPOUND SUBJECT:	<u>You</u> and <u>I</u> <u>need</u> some lessons.
COMPOUND VERB:	The <u>skier</u> <u>turned</u> and <u>jumped</u>.
COMPOUND SUBJECT AND VERB:	My <u>mother</u> and <u>father</u> <u>wished</u> me luck and <u>drove</u> me to the race.
COMPOUND DIRECT OBJECT:	I <u>tried</u> ski-jumping and snowboarding.
COMPOUND PREPOSITIONAL PHRASE:	She <u>rode</u> up the path to school.

> **Exercise 15** Recognizing Simple Sentences Copy each simple sentence below onto your paper, and underline the subject once and the verb twice. Notice that some of the subjects and verbs are compound.

EXAMPLE: <u>Jan</u> <u>opened</u> the catalog and <u>read</u> about the bikes.

1. Mountain bikes have fifteen to twenty-one gears.
2. You pedal with your feet and shift gears with your hands.
3. A rider uses high gears to keep the bike at speed during level riding.
4. Low gears allow quick acceleration and help on inclines.
5. Flat levels and smooth surfaces are the right terrains for using the middle and high gears.

Journal Tip

This section focuses on several kinds of outdoor sports. In your journal, note some of the facts that interest you. Then, review them later to find a writing topic—perhaps for a how-to essay.

Text

Get instant feedback! Exercises 15 and 16 are available on-line or on CD-ROM.

More Practice

Grammar Exercise Workbook
• pp. 65–66
On-line Exercise Bank
• Section 20.2
Go on-line:
PHSchool.com
Enter Web Code:
eak-6002

The Compound Sentence

A *compound sentence* is made up of more than one simple sentence.

▶ **KEY CONCEPT** A **compound sentence** consists of two or more independent clauses. ■

In most compound sentences, the independent clauses are joined by a comma and a coordinating conjunction *(and, but, for, nor, or, so,* or *yet).* The comma and conjunction come before the final independent clause. The independent clauses in a compound sentence may also be connected with a semicolon (;) if the clauses are closely related.

EXAMPLES: I planned to go to the hockey game, but I could not get tickets.
Dorothy enjoys white-water rafting; she also likes kayaking.
In the club triathlon, Cara rode her bike for ten miles, she swam for a mile, and then she ran for five miles.

Notice in the preceding examples that there are two or three separate and complete independent clauses. Each of the clauses has its own subject and verb. Like simple sentences, compound sentences never contain subordinate clauses.

▶ **Exercise 16** Recognizing Compound Sentences Copy each compound sentence below onto your paper. Then, underline the subject of each clause once, and the verb twice.

EXAMPLE: Bridget ran the first part, and Tara biked the second part.

1. Rock climbers concentrate on the climb, and they practice as often as possible.
2. Rock-climbing is a recreational sport, but it can be very dangerous.
3. Ropes and harnesses are used for safety, and climbers always wear helmets.
4. Climbers learn special words, and they use them to communicate during the climb.
5. One should always take lessons, for instructors teach many good techniques, and good techniques are necessary for a safe climb.

▼ **Critical Viewing** Of what childhood activity does this picture remind you? Respond using a complex sentence. **[Connect]**

The Complex Sentence

Complex sentences contain both independent and subordinate clauses.

> ▶ **KEY CONCEPT** A **complex sentence** consists of one independent clause and one or more subordinate clauses. ∎

In a complex sentence, the independent clause is often called the *main clause.* The main clause has its own subject and verb, as does each subordinate clause.

               MAIN CLAUSE   SUBORD. CLAUSE

EXAMPLES: This is the event that he describes in the book.

                   SUBORD. CLAUSE

                Because Kayla has so much climbing experience,

                MAIN CLAUSE

                we asked her to lead our group.

The preceding two examples are both complex sentences. Each has a main clause and a subordinate clause. In the first, the subordinate clause is an adjective clause that modifies the noun *event.* In the second, the subordinate clause is an adverb clause that modifies the verb *asked.*

In the next example, the complex sentence is more complicated because the main clause is split by an adjective clause.

           MAIN CLAUSE   MAIN CLAUSE

               ⌐ SUBORD. CLAUSE ¬

EXAMPLE: Andrea, who plays basketball, won a trophy.

> ▶ **Exercise 17** **Recognizing Complex Sentences** Copy each complex sentence below onto your paper. Underline the subject of each clause once and the verb twice. Then, put parentheses around each subordinate clause.

EXAMPLE: Alan is stronger (than we realized).

1. The belayer stands at the bottom of the cliff while the climber moves up the rock face.
2. If the climber slips, the belayer helps prevent falls.
3. After it is anchored at the top of the cliff, the rope is connected to the belayer and the climber.
4. The climb begins when the commands have been exchanged.
5. The phrase "on belay" is spoken when the climber is ready.

Grammar and Style Tip

Many words that introduce subordinate clauses are called **subordinating conjunctions.** They include *after, although, because, before, if, since, than, until, when,* and *while.* Other words that introduce subordinate clauses are called **relative pronouns.** They include *which, that who, whoever, whom,* and *whose.*

▶ **More Practice**

Grammar Exercise Workbook
• pp. 67–68
On-line Exercise Bank
• Section 20.2
  Go on-line:
  PHSchool.com
  Enter Web Code:
  eak-6002

Get instant feedback! Exercises 17, 18, and 19 are available on-line or on CD-ROM.

► **Exercise 18** Distinguishing Between Compound and
Complex Sentences Label each sentence below *compound* or
complex.

1. As busy resorts show, skiing is very popular.
2. Unless a person practices, however, his or her skills won't improve.
3. I took lessons from a pro, and I learned excellent techniques.
4. After I conquered beginners' slopes, I took on the higher slopes.
5. Suddenly, a tree appeared in front of me, and I swerved to avoid it.
6. You can rent equipment, unless you prefer to buy your own.
7. Follow the rules, and stay on the designated trails.
8. Before you travel, you should check the weather.
9. My brother likes cross-country skiing, but I prefer downhill.
10. He won't try downhill skiing, nor will he snowboard.

▲ **Critical Viewing** What is the possible effect of this ski jump into the air? Answer using a complex sentence. [**Analyze; Cause and Effect**]

► **Exercise 19** Writing Simple, Compound, and Complex
Sentences Write sentences on the topics given below, using
the type of sentence structure indicated. Then, underline each
subject once and each verb twice.

EXAMPLE: snow (compound sentence joined by *but*)
ANSWER: My dad likes snow, but he does not like to shovel the driveway.

1. ice skating (compound sentence joined by *and*)
2. sledding (complex sentence with a subordinate clause beginning with *because*)
3. figure skating competitions on television (complex sentence with a subordinate clause beginning with *whenever*)
4. snowcapped mountains (simple sentence)
5. a winter vacation (compound sentence joined by *or*)
6. a parka and warm gloves (complex sentence with a subordinate clause beginning with *before*)
7. snowboarding competitions on television (simple sentence with a compound verb)
8. a snowman (compound sentence joined by *nor*)
9. a head cold (simple sentence with a compound subject)
10. a warm climate (complex sentence with a subordinate clause beginning with *if*)

Clauses • **429**

Hands-on Grammar

Complex Sentence Shifter

Make and use a Complex Sentence Shifter to help you learn ways to use subordinate clauses to vary your sentences. Fold a piece of plain paper (or construction paper) in half lengthwise, and then in half again; now, unfold it. You will have three equally spaced creases down the length of the paper. Then, mark and cut six 1" slits across each crease at equal intervals. Flatten the paper. (See illustration A.)

Next, using colored paper, cut out 12 T-shaped pieces—the top measuring 1-1/2" x 1", and the stem tapering from 1/2" to a point. Cut out 6 more Ts in a contrasting color. (See illustration B.) Now, on each of the original 12 Ts, print a short sentence to pair with another sentence. Examples: HE CAME—SHE WENT / WE SING—THEY SING / THEY WATCH TV—SHE STUDIES / I RIDE MY BIKE—YOU WALK / MY FRIEND WORKS—HE PLAYS / I HIT THE BALL—THEY WAIT.

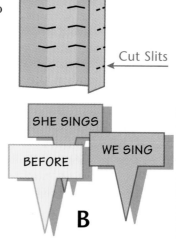

Then, print one of these subordinating conjunctions on each of the other 6 Ts: AFTER, BECAUSE, ALTHOUGH, BEFORE, IF, WHEN.

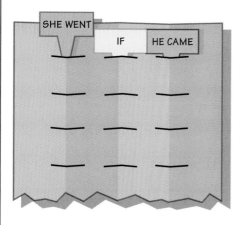

Now, begin making complex sentences by inserting the Ts into the slitted paper. A sentence might read, "Before he came, she went," or "She went because he came," or "After he plays, my friend works." Revise each sentence several different ways, changing the word order and using different subordinating conjunctions. Notice how many variations you can make.

Find It in Your Reading Look through a story or essay for several examples of complex sentences. Notice how the writer varied the position of the subordinate clauses, and the effect.

Find It in Your Writing Review the complex sentences in a piece of your writing. Try changing the position of some subordinate clauses to give your sentences variety.

Section
20.2

Section Review

GRAMMAR EXERCISES 20–26

Exercise 20 Recognizing **Independent and Subordinate Clauses in Sentences** Copy each sentence below. Underline each independent clause twice, and each subordinate clause once.

1. After diving sports became popular, the United States created an underwater national park.
2. Divers can see animals, fishes, and coral while they use the underwater signs to find their way around.
3. Some divers search for treasure, while other divers explore nature.
4. When divers visit shipwrecks, they use modern devices to find artifacts.
5. There is much to explore underwater because the ocean is so vast.

Exercise 21 Recognizing **Compound Sentences** Copy each sentence below. In each independent clause, underline the subject once and the verb twice.

1. Some people have trouble breathing through a snorkel, but it becomes easier with practice.
2. Lessons are given in swimming pools, so the students feel comfortable and safe.
3. Divers enter the water from a boat, and they go in feet first or backward.
4. One should take a deep breath first, for water may get in the snorkel tube.
5. It is easy to swim with the fins on, and the flutter kick helps you go faster.

Exercise 22 Revising to Create **Compound Sentences** Rewrite the simple sentences below as compound sentences by adding a conjunction and another independent clause to each one.

1. Divers and snorkelers must swim well.
2. Rubber fins fit securely on your feet.
3. The mask is rubber with a plastic face.
4. Teeth grip the snorkel's mouthpiece.
5. People often dive in groups for safety.

Exercise 23 Recognizing **Subordinate Clauses in Complex Sentences** Copy each sentence below, and put parentheses around the subordinate clause.

1. While they are under the water, divers are in a new and silent world.
2. Unless divers are careful, motor boats could pose a danger.
3. Boaters have difficulty seeing divers when divers are under the water.
4. Some fish, since they are so curious and unafraid, will follow divers.
5. When a diver wants to surface, she should swim up slowly.

Exercise 24 Find It in Your **Reading** Identify each type of sentence in this excerpt from James Berry's "Becky and the Wheels-and-Brake Boys."

I ride into town with the Wheels-and-Brake Boys now. When she can borrow a bike, Shirnette comes too.

Exercise 25 Find It in Your **Writing** Look through your portfolio to find examples of simple, compound, and complex sentences. Label each type.

Exercise 26 Writing Application Imagine that you are exploring an underwater park. Write a paragraph about the animals and things you see. Use all three types of sentences in your paragraph.

Chapter Review

GRAMMAR EXERCISES 27–34

▶ **Exercise 27** Distinguishing Between Adjective and Adverb Phrases Identify whether the underlined prepositional phrase in each sentence below functions as an *adjective* or as an *adverb.*

1. Skis are strips of wood, metal, or plastic.
2. The front tips of all skis curve upward.
3. Boots with flat soles are attached tightly to the skis by bindings.
4. Ski poles provide skiers with a way to balance themselves.
5. The disk at the bottom of the pole allows a firm hold in the snow.
6. Alpine skiing races vary in distance.
7. Gates mark courses for downhill races.
8. The racer passes through these gates quickly.
9. Slalom skiers zigzag across the slope, moving between flags.
10. A skier's total time is a combination of two runs.

▶ **Exercise 28** Revising to Combine Sentences Using Appositive Phrases Combine each pair of sentences below with an appositive phrase.

1. The results of the super giant slalom are decided after only one run. The super giant slalom is a combination of downhill and giant slalom.
2. Cross-country is another kind of skiing. It is performed on rolling courses.
3. The cross-country stride is a kickoff step and then a glide step. This stride propels the skier.
4. Ski jumping is a part of Nordic competition. This competition is judged for distance and style.
5. Freestyle skiing is an event that includes ballet and aerials. It tests different abilities.

▶ **Exercise 29** Recognizing Phrases and the Words They Modify Copy the sentences below. Underline all the adjective, adverb, and appositive phrases. Then, draw an arrow from each phrase to the word it modifies or explains.

1. A kick turn is a special turn for flat ground.
2. Sidestepping moves a skier successfully up a hill.
3. The herringbone step, another way to move uphill, makes marks like fishbones.
4. The inside edges of the skis dig into the snow.
5. The chairlift carries skiers to the top of the mountain.

▶ **Exercise 30** Classifying Compound and Complex Sentences Copy each sentence below and identify it as *compound* or *complex*. Then, underline each independent clause once and each subordinate clause twice.

1. Stretching exercises warm up your body before you hit the slopes.
2. While you warm up, it is also good to check all your equipment.
3. You should examine the two edges of your snowboard, so you will understand your braking system.
4. If you practice jump turns, you can get a good feel for your board.
5. First, you can maneuver on flat ground, where only one foot needs to be attached to the board.
6. Since you may have to take some steps up the slope, it is good to practice walking uphill.
7. "Skating" is a series of small steps, but it is a good skill to practice.
8. Because everyone falls while snow-

boarding, the ability to fall safely is important.

9. Also, the board can help you get up from the ground, and you should practice falling and rising.

10. Sideslipping helps control the board's movement until you become more experienced.

Exercise 31 **Classifying Phrases and Clauses** Label the following sentences as *simple, complex,* or *compound.* List the adjective phrases, adverb phrases, and appositives or appositive phrases.

1. When you learn tricks, beginning ones form the basis for more advanced skills.
2. A tail slide, a variation of the basic slide, is the first level of tricks.
3. As you gain skill, you can experiment with tricks like nose slides.
4. Ollies, a kind of jump, carry you over small obstacles.
5. Safe jumping is important, so you should check your landing area for rocks or other obstacles.
6. Snowboard racers use special boards, and they wear special boots for extra speed and control.
7. Racing competitions are arranged for all levels.
8. Protective helmets and arm guards provide safety.
9. The board is more controllable with your feet when your boots fit well.
10. After you master turning, slalom races can test your abilities on the slopes.

Exercise 32 **Revising to Expand Simple Sentences** Expand each simple sentence below into a compund sentence—adding another independent clause—or into a complex sentence—adding a subordinate clause.

1. Mountain weather is often very cold and snowy, but . . .

2. Waterproof gloves and pants are good clothing choices because . . .
3. When . . . , a hat will warm your head and keep body heat from escaping.
4. Padding can protect you if . . .
5. Snowboarding boots are bulky but comfortable, and . . .

Exercise 33 **Writing Application**
Write a paragraph giving advice to someone about how to do well in your favorite sport. Underline any adjective or adverb phrases you include in your paragraph. Vary your sentence structure, and put parentheses around subordinate clauses.

Exercise 34 **CUMULATIVE REVIEW Basic Sentence Parts and Phrases and Clauses** On your paper, write whether each underlined word is a *subject, verb, direct object, indirect object, predicate noun,* or *predicate adjective.* Then, identify each sentence as simple, compound, or complex. Circle five prepositional phrases.

(1) Mogul skiing is a difficult sport. (2) You maneuver over and around bumps of snow as you move down a mountain. (3) When you begin mogul skiing, several tips are important. (4) Your speed should remain constant, and you should remember to keep your head up and look down the mountain. (5) Make a plan for yourself. (6) Do not keep your attention just on one turn, but focus on several turns. (7) If one of your knees feels tired, you may be putting too much weight on one side of your body. (8) Lack of good balance can also give you a sore knee. (9) One key to successful skiing is rhythm; another is balance. (10) Follow these tips, and you will improve your skills and have a terrific time.

Standardized Test Preparation Workshop

Revising and Editing

Knowledge of grammar is tested on standardized tests. Questions that measure your ability to use phrases and clauses reveal your understanding of basic sentence construction and style. Remember that a *phrase* is a group of words, without a subject and a verb, that acts as a unit. A *clause* is a group of words that contains a subject and a verb. Use the following strategies when answering these types of questions:

- First, read the entire passage to get an idea of the author's purpose.

- Focus on the underlined groups of words, and note any similarities, or ways they can be combined with a phrase or clause without changing meaning.

- Then, choose a revision that uses a phrase or clause to combine like ideas without changing the meaning.

The following sample test item will give you practice with the format of questions that test standard rules of grammar.

> **Test Tip**
>
> Make sure the answer you've chosen is a complete sentence. Other choices may seem correct, but there is only one correct answer. Read them all carefully.

Sample Test Item	Answer and Explanation

Choose the letter of the best way to write each underlined section. If the underlined section needs no change, choose "Correct as is."
 	
 Bacteria are microorganisms. Bacteria belong (1)
 to the kingdom Monera.
 	
 1 A Bacteria are microorganisms, and they belong to the kingdom Monera.
 	
   B Bacteria are microorganisms belonging to the kingdom Monera.
 	
   C Microorganisms, which belong to the kingdom Monera, are bacteria.
 	
   D Correct as is
	The correct answer is *B*. This is the best rewrite of the two sentences because it combines related ideas and eliminates extra words without changing the meaning. Changing the second sentence into a phrase eliminates the repetition of the word *bacteria*.
	
	 Choice *A* combines the sentences but does not eliminate extra words. Choice *C* changes the original meaning.

Practice 1 **Directions:** Choose the letter of the best way to write each underlined section. If the underlined section needs no change, choose "Correct as is."

Bacteria appear in many shapes and sizes.
(1)
You may not know this. Some bacteria
                              (2)
look like spheres. They are called cocci.

Other bacteria are shaped like corkscrews.
(3)
Bacteria shaped like corkscrews are known

as spirilla.

1 A Bacteria appear in many shapes and sizes, and you may not know this.

B You may not know this: There are many shapes and sizes of bacteria.

C You may not know that bacteria appear in many shapes and sizes.

D Correct as is

2 F Some bacteria with a spherical shape are called cocci.

G There are some sphere bacteria, and they are called cocci.

H Some of the bacteria that are called cocci look like spheres.

J Correct as is

3 A Other bacteria are shaped like corkscrews, which are known as spirilla.

B There are other corkscrew bacteria, which are known as spirilla.

C Other bacteria, which are known as spirilla, are shaped like corkscrews.

D Correct as is

Practice 2 **Directions:** Choose the letter of the best way to write each underlined section. If the underlined section needs no change, choose "Correct as is."

Although some bacteria are dangerous,
(1)
others are quite useful. Good bacteria
                              (2)
digest organic matter, they break down

organic matter. Good bacteria can also be
                              (3)
found in food. Foods such as cheese or

yogurt contain bacteria.

1 A Bacteria are dangerous and also quite useful.

B Some bacteria are dangerous although some others are useful.

C Some bacteria are dangerous; other bacteria are quite useful.

D Correct as is

2 F Good bacteria digest and break down organic matter.

G Good bacteria digest organic matter and then it break it down.

H Good bacteria digest organic matter. Then it break down organic matter.

J Correct as is

3 A Good foods such as cheese or yogurt contain bacteria.

B Good bacteria can also be found in foods such as cheese or yogurt.

C Also found in food, such as cheese and yogurt, are good bacteria.

D Correct as is

Effective Sentences

We use sentences every day. We ask questions, make statements, express emotion, or share information, all of which require sentences. Therefore, we rely on sentences as our basic unit of communication. Without sentences, we would be unable to convey our thoughts and needs effectively.

In writing, putting words together in effective sentences is the first step to clear communication. In this chapter, you will learn basic sentence functions and structures, ways in which you can vary sentence structures to make your writing clearer, and some common pitfalls that hinder clear communication.

▲ **Critical Viewing**
Write an exclamatory sentence describing this photograph. Then, change it into a declarative sentence. **[Describe]**

Diagnostic Test

Directions: Write all answers on a separate sheet of paper.

Skill Check A. Identify each sentence below by its sense as *declarative, interrogative, imperative,* or *exclamatory.*

1. The entire class became interested in comets
2. In what year will Halley's Comet be visible again
3. Ask Carla if she knows the date
4. She has spent nearly two weeks collecting facts
5. That's amazing

Skill Check B. Combine the following sentences, using the construction given in parentheses.

6. (compound verb) From early times, people have been fascinated with the stars. People have wondered about their meaning.
7. (comma and coordinating conjunction *but*) The sun is only a medium-sized star. Its diameter is more than 100 times that of the Earth.
8. (semicolon) Some stars look yellow. Others glow blue or red.
9. (comma and coordinating conjunction *and*) During the day, sunlight brightens the sky. We cannot see the stars.
10. (comma and compound direct objects) Space exploration has aided science. It has aided medicine. It has aided industry.

Skill Check C. Change each of the following items into a complete sentence.

11. So far away.
12. When stars twinkle.
13. We do not see the sun every day I miss it when it does not come out.
14. A microscope is usually smaller than a telescope, we have both at my school.
15. Visiting the planetarium.

Skill Check D. Rewrite the following sentences to eliminate sentence problems such as misplaced modifers and double negatives.

16. I lost the ticket to the planetarium that my uncle bought.
17. I wanted to see the mountains at the planetarium on Mars.
18. Jim, Alex, and I are not going on no trip to the planetarium.
19. We can't find none of the tickets.
20. Nobody doesn't feel as bad as I do about it.

Skill Check E. For each of the following sentences, choose the correct form in parentheses.

21. You should not stare directly into the sun because it can (effect, affect) your vision.
22. It must be (kind of, rather) frightening to travel into space.
23. Do you know where the Milky Way (is at, is)?
24. (Their, There, They're) must be a large telescope at the university.
25. The reason I am interested is (because, that) I would like to become an astronaut.

The Four Functions of a Sentence

Sentences can be classified according to what they do. The four types of sentences in English are *declarative*, *interrogative*, *imperative*, and *exclamatory*.

Declarative sentences are the most common type. They are used to "declare" or state facts.

▶ **KEY CONCEPT** A **declarative sentence** states an idea and ends with a period. ■

DECLARATIVE: Space travel is very exciting.

Interrogative means "asking." An *interrogative sentence* is a question.

▶ **KEY CONCEPT** An **interrogative sentence** asks a question and ends with a question mark. ■

INTERROGATIVE: Which planet is closest to Earth?

The word *imperative* comes from the Latin word *imperare*, which means "to command." Imperative sentences give commands.

▶ **KEY CONCEPT** An **imperative sentence** gives an order or a direction and ends with either a period or an exclamation mark. ■

Most imperative sentences start with a verb. In this type of imperative sentence, the subject is understood to be *you.*

IMPERATIVE: Follow the directions carefully.
               Wait for me!

Notice the punctuation at the end of these examples. In the first sentence, the period suggests that a mild command is being given in an ordinary tone of voice. The exclamation mark at the end of the second sentence suggests a strong command, one given in a loud voice.

To *exclaim* means to "shout out." *Exclamatory sentences* are used to "shout out" emotions such as happiness, fear, delight, and anger.

▶ **KEY CONCEPT** An **exclamatory sentence** conveys strong emotion and ends with an exclamation mark. ■

EXCLAMATORY: She's not telling the truth!
                What an outrage that is!

Theme: The Earth and Moon

In this section, you will learn about the four functions of sentences. The examples and exercises are about the Earth and moon.

Cross-Curricular Connection: Science

> **Exercise 1** Identifying the Four Types of Sentences Read each of the following sentences carefully, and identify it as *declarative*, *interrogative*, *imperative*, or *exclamatory*. Then, write the appropriate end mark.

EXAMPLE: How do you say "moon" in Italian
ANSWER: interrogative (?)

1. The Italian word for "moon" is *luna*
2. Wow, that's how you say it in Spanish, too
3. What words in English do you know with the *luna* root
4. I have heard the words *lunatic* and *lunacy*
5. Tell me what they mean
6. *Lunatic* means "insane" and *lunacy* means "insanity"
7. Does that make sense to you
8. Well, the word *moonstruck* means "crazy" or "insane," so it makes sense to me
9. Oh, look at the time
10. Don't be late

> **Exercise 2** Writing the Four Types of Sentences Rewrite each sentence below to fit the type of sentence specified in parentheses. Be sure to use the correct end mark.

1. The moon travels around the Earth in an elliptical orbit. (interrogative)
2. The moon travels at more than 2,300 miles per hour. (exclamatory)
3. Does the gravitational pull of the Earth keep the moon in orbit? (declarative)
4. We have been studying the moon in science class this year. (imperative)
5. Measure time by the phases of the moon. (interrogative)
6. Does the word *Monday* come from the word *moon*? (declarative)
7. Look at the man in the moon! (interrogative)
8. Some people thought the moon was made out of green cheese. (exclamatory)
9. If you look out this window, you can see the full moon. (imperative)
10. How beautiful that moon is! (declarative)

▲ **Critical Viewing** Write one each of the four types of sentences about this photograph of the moon. **[Describe]**

> **More Practice**

Grammar Exercise Workbook
• pp. 69–70
On-line Exercise Bank
• Section 21.1
Go on-line:
PHSchool.com
Enter Web Code:
eak-6002

Complete the exercises on-line! Exercises 1 and 2 are available on-line or on CD-ROM.

Section Review

GRAMMAR EXERCISES 3–9

Exercise 3 Identifying the Four Types of Sentences Read each of the following sentences carefully, and identify it as *declarative, interrogative, imperative,* or *exclamatory.*

1. Open your books to page 45 and begin reading.
2. How many have finished reading the assignment?
3. Raise your hands.
4. This week's topic is the solar system.
5. I can't wait for class to be over!

Exercise 4 Punctuating the Four Types of Sentences Copy the sentences below onto your paper, adding the appropriate end mark. Then, label each sentence by its type.

1. On July 20, 1969, for the first time in history, humans landed on the moon
2. Who was the first human to walk on the moon
3. Was it Neil Armstrong or was it Edwin E. Aldrin
4. Look it up in your book
5. It was Armstrong, of course

Exercise 5 Revising Sentences to Vary Type Rewrite each sentence below to fit the function indicated in parentheses. Add the appropriate end mark.

1. Galileo Galilei was the first person to look at the moon through a telescope. (interrogative)
2. Did he notice the light areas and dark areas on the surface? (declarative)
3. You should look at the moon on the second or third day after the first-quarter phase. (imperative)

4. At this time, the moon is in a good position in the evening sky and many surface features are clearly visible. (interrogative)
5. Did you know that the length of a day on the moon equals about fourteen Earth days? (exclamatory)

Exercise 6 Writing the Four Types of Sentences For each subject listed below, write a declarative, an interrogative, an imperative, and an exclamatory sentence.

1. the moon
2. the sun
3. the Earth
4. a star
5. an astronaut

Exercise 7 Find It in Your Reading Read the following excerpt from "If I Forget Thee, Oh Earth . . ." by Arthur C. Clarke. Identify the type of each sentence.

Well, *he* knew what the stars were. Whoever asked that question must have been very stupid. And what did they mean by "twinkle"? You could see at a glance that all the stars shone with the same steady, unwavering light.

Exercise 8 Find It in Your Writing Look through your portfolio for examples of all four types of sentences. If you can't find examples of each, challenge yourself to revise a piece of writing to vary your sentence types.

Exercise 9 Writing Application Write a brief description of the sky on the night of a full moon. Use all four types of sentences in your description.

Section 21.2 *Combining Sentences*

Books written for very young readers present information in short, direct sentences. While this method makes the book easy to read, it doesn't make it enjoyable or interesting to older readers. Writing that is to be read by mature readers should include sentences of varying lengths and complexity to create a flow of ideas. One way to achieve sentence variety is to combine sentences.

EXAMPLE: We went to the planetarium. We saw planets.

COMBINED: We went to the planetarium and saw planets. We saw planets at the planetarium.

Sentences can be combined by using a compound subject, a compound verb, or a compound object.

EXAMPLE: Mori enjoyed watching the sky.
Tatiana enjoyed watching the sky.

COMPOUND SUBJECT: *Mori* and *Tatiana* enjoyed watching the sky.

EXAMPLE: Leelee assembled the telescope.
Leelee watched the stars.

COMPOUND VERB: Leelee *assembled* the telescope and *watched* the stars.

EXAMPLE: Martin likes the sun.
Martin likes the moon.

COMPOUND OBJECT: Martin likes the *sun* and the *moon*.

Theme: Planets and Stars

In this section, you will learn about combining sentences to give your writing smoothness and variety. The examples and exercises are about planets and stars.

Cross-Curricular Connection: Science

GRAMMAR IN LITERATURE

from "Space Shuttle *Challenger*"
William Harwood

This sentence uses a compound subject. The simple subjects are highlighted in blue italics.

A veteran shuttle reporter with an encyclopedic memory for space trivia, *Rob* and *I* had covered fourteen straight missions together.

 Critical Viewing
Write a sentence
about Saturn and its
rings using a com-
pound subject and a
compound verb.
[Apply]

▶ **Exercise 10** **Combining Sentences** Combine each pair of
sentences below by using a compound subject, a compound
verb, or a compound object. Identify what you have done to
combine them.

EXAMPLE: Frank stared at the full moon.
             Bertha stared at the full moon.

ANSWER: Frank and Bertha stared at the full moon.
             (compound subject)

1. Elliot went to P.S. 101. Melvin went to P.S. 101.
2. They were in the sixth grade. They liked science class.
3. They studied the planets. They studied the stars.
4. The teacher assigned Melvin a written project. The teacher
   assigned Elliot a written project.
5. Melvin decided to write about Mars. Elliot decided to write
   about Mars.
6. They studied the planet. They studied its moons.
7. They researched separately. They wrote their papers
   separately.
8. The teacher read their papers. The teacher thought they
   had worked together.
9. Melvin said he had liked the subject. Elliot said he had
   liked the subject.
10. The teacher praised them. The teacher gave them good
    grades.

> **KEY CONCEPT** Sentences can be combined by using *and, but, or, nor,* or a semicolon. These combined sentences are called **compound sentences.** ∎

EXAMPLE:	The moon was full. It illuminated the night.
COMPOUND SENTENCE:	The moon was full, **and** it illuminated the night.

EXAMPLE:	The sun shone brightly. Its rays beat down on the pavement.
COMPOUND SENTENCE:	The sun shone brightly**;** its rays beat down on the pavement.

> **Exercise 11** Combining Independent Clauses to Form Compound Sentences Combine the following pairs of sentences, using the method given in parentheses.

EXAMPLE:	The planet Venus is very hot. Lead, tin, and zinc would easily melt on its surface. (semicolon)
ANSWER:	The planet Venus is very hot; lead, tin, and zinc would easily melt on its surface.

1. Mercury is the planet closest to the sun. Consequently, it is the hottest. (semicolon)
2. It is about 36 million miles from the sun. That is close enough for the sun's rays to scorch its surface. (comma and coordinating conjunction)
3. Mercury does not reflect much sunlight. Its surface is rough, dark-colored rock. (semicolon)
4. Its volume is much less than Earth's. Its density is about equal to Earth's. (comma and coordinating conjunction)
5. Temperatures vary wildly on Mercury. They range from 810° Fahrenheit on the sunlit side to –290° Fahrenheit on the dark side. (semicolon)
6. Mercury revolves around the sun in about 88 days. It takes only 59 days for it to rotate on its axis. (comma and coordinating conjunction)
7. Cliffs crisscross Mercury's surface. They may have been created when the planet was formed. (semicolon)
8. The *Mariner 10* spacecraft passed Mercury in 1974 and 1975. It sent pictures of the planet back to Earth. (comma and coordinating conjunction)
9. Vast sheets of ice were discovered in 1991 by powerful telescopes. These areas were not covered by *Mariner 10.* (semicolon)
10. Space exploration has advanced tremendously in the past twenty-five years. What we know about Mercury is limited. [comma and coordinating conjunction]

> **More Practice**
>
> Grammar Exercise Workbook
> • pp. 71–72
> On-line Exercise Bank
> • Section 21.2
>   *Go on-line:*
>   PHSchool.com
>   *Enter Web Code:*
>   eak-6002

Complete the exercises on-line! Exercises 10 and 11 are available on-line or on CD-ROM.

▶ **KEY CONCEPT** Sentences can be combined by changing one of them into a subordinate clause. ■

Use a complex sentence when you are combining sentences to show the relationship between ideas. The subordinating conjunctions will help your readers understand the relationship.

EXAMPLE: We were frightened. We thought an asteroid would hit Earth.

COMBINED WITH A
SUBORDINATE CLAUSE: We were frightened *because* we thought an asteroid would hit Earth.

▶ **Exercise 12** Combining Sentences Using Subordinating Conjunctions and Subordinate Clauses Combine the following sentences, using the conjunction given in parentheses.

EXAMPLE: (although) Neptune's volume is 57.4 times that of Earth. Its mass is only seventeen times Earth's mass.

ANSWER: Although Neptune's volume is 57.4 times that of Earth, its mass is only seventeen times Earth's mass.

1. (because) Venus is known as Earth's twin. The two planets are similar in size.
2. (although) Venus is nearly the same size as Earth. It has a completely different surface.
3. (because) Venus is brighter than any other planet. It is the second planet from the sun.
4. (after) Scientists learned about the surface of Venus. They used radar and radio astronomy equipment.
5. (although) Venus has a bright color. Its surface can never be seen with the unaided eye.

▶ **KEY CONCEPT** Sentences can be combined by changing one of them into a phrase. ■

EXAMPLE: The space shuttle will be launched tomorrow. It will orbit Earth.

COMBINED: The space shuttle will be launched tomorrow *to orbit Earth.*

EXAMPLE: The space shuttle will be launched tomorrow to orbit Earth. The space shuttle is the most advanced vehicle in the world.

COMBINED: The space shuttle, *the most advanced vehicle in the world,* will be launched tomorrow to orbit Earth.

More Practice

Grammar Exercise
Workbook
• pp. 71–72
On-line Exercise Bank
• Section 21.2
  Go on-line:
  PHSchool.com
  Enter Web Code:
  eak-6002

 Text

Complete the exercises on-line! Exercises 12 and 13 are available on-line or on CD-ROM.

▶ **Exercise 13** Combining Sentences Using Phrases

Combine the following pairs of sentences by changing one of them into a phrase.

EXAMPLE: Pluto is the outermost known member of the solar system. Pluto is the ninth planet from the sun.

ANSWER: Pluto, the ninth planet from the sun, is the outermost known member of the solar system.

1. The search for Pluto was begun by Percival Lowell. He was an American astronomer.
2. The search ended in 1930. The search was finished by the members of the Lowell Observatory staff.
3. Clyde William Tombaugh found Pluto where Lowell had predicted. Tombaugh was also an American astronomer.
4. Pluto orbits around the sun once in almost 250 Earth years. It is at a distance of almost 4 billion miles from the sun.
5. Sometimes Pluto is closer to the sun than Neptune. Neptune is Pluto's neighbor.
6. Pluto appears to have a yellowish color. It is visible only through very large telescopes.
7. In 1978, astronomers discovered Pluto's moon. It is named Charon.
8. Pluto was discovered to have a thin atmosphere. The atmosphere is probably methane gas.
9. The Hubble Space Telescope was launched in 1990. It allowed astronomers to learn a great deal about Pluto and Charon.
10. Pluto is made of rockier material than the other planets of the solar system. It has a density twice that of water.

▼ **Critical Viewing**
Write two sentences about this image of the Milky Way galaxy. Then, combine the two sentences by making one of them a phrase. [**Draw Conclusions**]

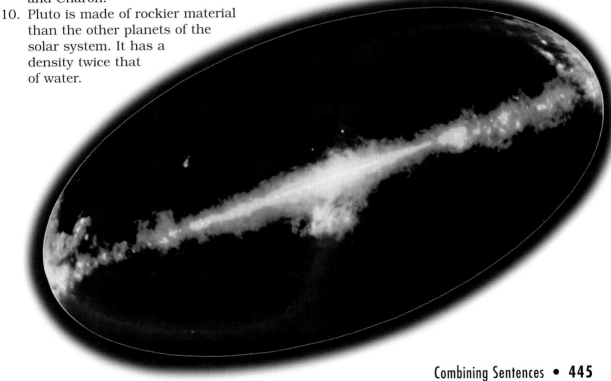

Hands-on Grammar

Conjunction Pop-up

Practice combining sentences with conjunctions.

Fold a piece of paper so that there is a pocket, as shown in the illustration. Write the first sentence of each pair on the left side of the pocket and the second sentence of each pair on the right.

The moon was full.
The sky was bright.

The moon was full.
It lit up the night sky.

The moon was full.
I could see things clearly in the yard.

You might want to write them more than once and join them by using different conjunctions.

In the pocket between each pair of sentences, write a conjunction —such as *and, or, but, so, because,* or *although*—that can be used to join the sentences. When you "pop" the pocket open, you will see a complete sentence joined by the conjunction. On a separate sheet of paper, write the new sentence with the correct punctuation.

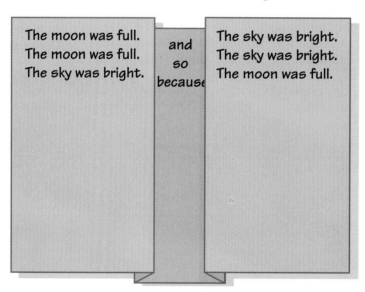

Find It in Your Reading Look through a story or essay for several examples of sentences that have been combined using conjunctions. See if the sentences could be joined in any other way.

Find It in Your Writing Look through your writing portfolio. See if you can smooth out the style of your writing and add interest to it by combining some of the sentences.

Section 21.2 Section Review

GRAMMAR EXERCISES 14–19

Exercise 14 Combining Sentences Combine the following pairs of sentences, using the method given in parentheses.

1. Venus is one of the planets of the solar system. It is second from the sun. (comma and coordinating conjunction)
2. The sun and the moon are the brightest objects in Earth's sky. Venus is almost as bright. (comma and coordinating conjunction)
3. Venus is known as the morning star when it appears in the east at sunrise. It is called the evening star when it is in the western sky at sunset. (semicolon)
4. In ancient times, the evening star was called Hesperus. The morning star was referred to as Phosphorus. (comma and coordinating conjunction)
5. The phases of Venus repeat about every 18 months. Venus is brightest in the crescent phase. (semicolon)

Exercise 15 Combining Sentences Using Subordination Combine the following sentences, using the subordinating conjunction given in parentheses.

1. (although) It may seem strange. Ninety-seven percent of Venus's atmosphere is carbon dioxide.
2. (because) The moon appears to give light. It reflects the light of the sun.
3. (even though) The cloud cover of Venus is very dense. Features can be seen from the cloud tops.
4. (which) Venus is encircled by high-altitude winds. The winds can be gauged by the cloud patterns.
5. (because) The upper-level winds remain above the planet's surface. The atmosphere at ground level is still.

Exercise 16 Combining Sentences Using Phrases Combine the following pairs of sentences by changing one of them into a phrase.

1. Saturn is the sixth planet from the sun. Saturn is the second largest planet in the solar system.
2. Saturn's most noticeable feature is its rings. The rings are a collection of rock, frozen gases, and ice.
3. The rings were first seen in 1610 by the Italian scientist Galileo. He saw them through his primitive telescope.
4. Galileo described them incorrectly. He described them as handles.
5. In 1655, Christian Huygens became the first to describe the rings of Saturn correctly. Huygens was Dutch.

Exercise 17 Find It in Your Reading Read the following sentence from "An Astronaut's Answers" by John Glenn. On a separate sheet of paper, write the two sentences that were combined to make this sentence.

In 1962, I looked down from an orbit high above our planet and saw our beautiful Earth and its curved horizon against the vastness of space.

Exercise 18 Find It in Your Writing Select a piece of your writing. Use a comma and a coordinating conjunction to combine two related sentences.

Exercise 19 Writing Application Write an expository paragraph providing information you know about some part of the solar system. Be sure that some of your sentences use coordination and that others use subordination.

Varying Sentences

Vary your sentences to create a rhythm, to achieve an effect, or to emphasize the connections between ideas. There are several ways you can create variety in your sentences.

Varying Sentence Length

You have already learned that you can combine several short, choppy sentences to create a longer, more fluid, and stylistically mature sentence. However, too many long sentences in a row is as uninteresting as too many short sentences. When you want to emphasize a point, or surprise a reader, insert a short, direct sentence to interrupt the flow of long sentences. Read the following example.

EXAMPLE: Veteran's Day is a holiday that is observed in the United States to honor all those who served in the armed forces in time of war. It is celebrated in most states on November 11 and in some states on the fourth Monday of October. *However, it was first known as Armistice Day.*

Some sentences contain only one idea and can't be broken up. It may be possible, however, to state the idea in a shorter sentence. Other sentences contain two or more ideas and may be shortened by breaking up the ideas.

EXAMPLE: This holiday was proclaimed in 1919 by President Woodrow Wilson to commemorate the ending of World War I, which occurred on November 11, 1918.

SHORTER
SENTENCES: This holiday was proclaimed in 1919 by President Woodrow Wilson. It commemorated the ending of World War I, which was November 11, 1918.

Theme: Festivals

In this section, you will learn about varying the length of your sentences. The examples and exercises are about festivals and holidays.

Cross-Curricular Connection: Social Studies

▶ **Critical Viewing** What do you think is the occasion for this parade? Write two sentences about it—one that is short and choppy, the other long and flowing. **[Infer]**

▶ **Exercise 20** Varying Sentence Length In the following items, break up long sentences into two or more simple sentences, or restate long sentences more simply.

EXAMPLE: Millions of people in the United States celebrate the Fourth of July by gathering together with family and friends for picnics and fireworks and by watching or participating in parades.

ANSWER: Millions of people in the United States celebrate the Fourth of July. Family and friends gather together for picnics and fireworks. Some watch or participate in parades.

1. One important holiday is the Fourth of July, or Independence Day, when people often get together to watch fireworks displays.
2. Some people celebrate the Fourth of July by sharing a simple picnic of hot dogs and hamburgers with family and friends in the backyard.
3. Others look forward to seeing one of the many huge public fireworks displays, often staged in city and town parks, which seem to bring the excitement of the day to life.
4. Leaving fireworks to the experts is a good idea because the private use of fireworks is illegal in many states.
5. Most states have passed laws restricting the private use of fireworks to protect people from the many injuries that can happen when people handle these explosives.

▲ **Critical Viewing** In one long and one short sentence, tell what this photograph of fireworks makes you think of. [**Describe**]

GRAMMAR IN LITERATURE

from **Parade**
Rachel Field

Note how several details (in blue) are combined in this long, fluid, poetic sentence.

This is the day the circus comes / With blare of brass, with beating drums, / And clashing cymbals, and with roar / Of wild beasts never heard before / Within town limits.

Exercise 21 Varying Sentence Length Read the following paragraph. Then, rewrite it, breaking up long sentences into two or more simple sentences or restating long sentences more simply.

Among the most popular festivals in the United States are the state, county, or local fairs, which are usually held in the summer months. Most of these fairs have amusement park rides, game booths, and food courts, but some fairs also have contests. The contests may include beauty pageants, bake-offs, automobile races, horse shows, and 4-H club events, in which boys and girls show off the animals they have raised. Politicians often attend local and state fairs and give speeches and talk to the voters about various issues. If you have never been to a state, county, or local fair, find out if one is being held in your community, and plan to go this summer.

▲ **Critical Viewing** In two or three sentences, tell what makes this clown funny. Use a different part of speech to begin each sentence. **[Deduce]**

Varying Sentence Beginnings

Another way to create sentence variety is to start sentences with different parts of speech.

NOUN:	Carnivals are excellent fund-raisers.
ADVERB:	Often, carnivals are excellent fund-raisers.
PARTICIPIAL PHRASE:	Having helped with many carnivals, I know they are excellent fund-raisers.
PREPOSITIONAL PHRASE:	For large churches or small communities, carnivals are excellent fund-raisers.

▶ **Exercise 22** Writing Sentences With Varied Beginnings
Write sentences following the instructions given below.
1. Begin with the noun *Holidays.*
2. Begin with the adverb *Usually.*
3. Begin with the present participial phrase *Watching the people.*
4. Begin with the past participial phrase *Excited by the events.*
5. Begin with the prepositional phrase *After the celebration.*

▶ **Exercise 23** Revising Sentences by Varying Sentence
Beginnings Follow the instructions in parentheses to revise each sentence below.

EXAMPLE: Clowns are very popular. (Start with an adverb.)
ANSWER: Not surprisingly, clowns are very popular.

1. Clowns wear bright-colored makeup. (Start with an adverb.)
2. The high wire looks very frightening. (Start with a prepositional phrase.)
3. I know that training lions is very difficult. (Start with a participial phrase.)
4. Living on the road can be hard. (Start with a prepositional phrase.)
5. Some circuses no longer have live animals. (Start with an adverb.)
6. Some people are worried that the animals suffer. (Start with a participial phrase.)
7. Animal trainers make sure that the animals are well cared for. (Start with an adverb.)
8. Elephants are used by circus workers to help with heavy lifting. (Start with a prepositional phrase.)
9. I have been to the circus three times this year. (Start with a participial phrase.)
10. The popcorn and peanuts taste good. (Start with an adverb.)

▶ **More Practice**

Grammar Exercise Workbook
• pp. 73–76
On-line Exercise Bank
• Section 21.3
  Go on-line:
  PHSchool.com
  Enter Web Code:
  eak-6002

Text

Complete the exercises on-line! Exercises 21, 22, and 23 are available on-line or on CD-ROM.

Learn More

To learn more about participles, see Chapter 22.

KEY CONCEPT You can also vary sentence beginnings by inverting the traditional subject-verb order. ■

            S   V

EXAMPLE: The clowns are here.

             V   S

INVERTED: Here are the clowns.

             S   V   Prep. Phrase

EXAMPLE: The acrobats soared through the air.

            Prep. Phrase   V   S

INVERTED: Through the air soared the acrobats.

Exercise 24 **Inverting Sentences for Variety** Invert the subject-verb order in the following sentences.

EXAMPLE: The circus is in town.

ANSWER: In town is the circus.

1. The opening procession comes first.
2. The animals and performers parade around the ring.
3. The clowns tumble in the ring.
4. The music plays loudly.
5. The ringmaster is announcing the acts.
6. The lions jump through the hoops.
7. The acrobat falls into the net.
8. The crowd roars with excitement.
9. The jugglers enter after the acrobats.
10. We go home.

▲ Critical Viewing What would you expect to find inside the big tent? Use sentences with inverted word order in your response. **[Infer]**

More Practice

Grammar Exercise Workbook
• pp. 73–76
On-line Exercise Bank
• Section 21.3
Go on-line: PHSchool.com *Enter Web Code:* eak-6002

Complete the exercise on-line! Exercise 24 is available on-line or on CD-ROM.

Section 21.3 Section Review

GRAMMAR EXERCISES 25–30

Exercise 25 Revising Long Sentences Rewrite the following sentences by breaking each into two sentences, or by forming a simpler, more direct sentence.

1. One of the oldest types of clown is the whiteface, which dates back to the eighteenth century; the white color of the face was originally achieved with flour.
2. White lead later replaced flour, but after the 1880's, when lead was discovered to be toxic, safer greasepaints were introduced.
3. The whiteface clown evolved from earlier whiteface entertainers, and one of the most popular whiteface characters in history is Harlequin.
4. English actor John Rich, who performed in the eighteenth century, was the most famous Harlequin of his time.
5. The clown gradually replaced the Harlequin character; English entertainer Joseph Grimaldi is considered the most famous clown.

Exercise 26 Varying Sentence Beginnings Rewrite each sentence below, following the instructions in parentheses.

1. Modern clowns are performers who have turned away from traditional clown acts. (Start with an adverb.)
2. Some wear no makeup. (Start with a participle.)
3. They interact closely with their audiences. (Start with a prepositional phrase.)
4. Some of the new clowns perform with circuses. (Start with an adverb.)
5. Others make their mark in the theater. (Start with a participle.)

Exercise 27 Inverting Subject-Verb Order Invert the subject-verb order in the following sentences.

1. The Ferris wheel spins around and around.
2. We whirl through the darkness.
3. The sticky cotton candy clings to our clothes.
4. The child desired a green stuffed bear.
5. The band is here.

Exercise 28 Find It in Your Reading Reread the excerpt from "Parade" by Rachel Field on page 449. On your paper, write the phrases that appear in the sentence.

Exercise 29 Find It in Your Writing Choose a piece of writing from your portfolio, and make the following changes to three sentences.

1. Start with an adverb.
2. Start with a participle.
3. Start with a prepositional phrase.

Exercise 30 Writing Application On your paper, write a descriptive paragraph of ten sentences about an entertainment event that you have watched. Include details about the location and the performers. Then, on the same paper, rewrite the paragraph by varying the lengths of your sentences. Be sure to vary the beginnings of your sentences as well as the phrases and clauses.

Avoiding Sentence Problems

Being able to recognize the parts of sentences can help you avoid certain errors in your writing.

Avoiding Fragments

Some groups of words, even though they have a capital letter at the beginning and a period at the end, are not complete sentences. They are *fragments*.

▶ **KEY CONCEPT** A fragment is a group of words that does not express a complete thought but is punctuated as a sentence. ■

A fragment is only *part* of a sentence.

FRAGMENTS
In the center ring.
Felt happy and excited.
The man on the trapeze.
The elephants coming into the tent.
When she smiled.

You will usually be able to tell whether a group of words expresses a complete thought. One trick is to read the words aloud. This will help you hear whether or not some part is missing.

In the following chart, words have been added to the preceding fragments to make complete sentences. Read each italicized fragment; then, read the complete sentence. Can you hear the difference?

COMPLETE SENTENCES
The clowns arrived *in the center ring.*
I *felt happy and excited.*
The man on the trapeze is agile.
The elephants are *coming into the tent.*
When she smiled, the clowns were pleased.

Each of the preceding examples needed one or more new parts. The first needed both a subject and a verb. The second needed only a subject. The third became complete when a verb and an adjective were added. The fourth became complete when a helping verb was added. The final example needed a complete main clause to go with the subordinate clause.

Theme: Circuses

In this section, you will learn how to avoid sentence errors, including fragments, run-on sentences, misplaced modifiers, and some common usage errors. The examples and exercises are about circuses.

Cross-Curricular Connection: Social Studies

▶ **Exercise 31** Recognizing Sentence Fragments Each of the following numbered items is either a sentence or a fragment. Write *F* if it is a fragment and *S* if it is a complete sentence.

EXAMPLE: Clowns climbing ladders.
ANSWER: F

1. Lights dimmed.
2. With three rings.
3. Painted beautiful colors.
4. Waiting for her cue.
5. Clowns tumbled.
6. When the horse rode by.
7. The tiger in its cage.
8. Before the clown tripped.
9. The acrobats are here.
10. On the flying trapeze.

Phrase Fragments A phrase by itself is a fragment. It cannot stand alone because it does not have a subject and a verb.

▶ **KEY CONCEPT** A phrase should not be capitalized and punctuated as though it were a sentence. ■

Three types of phrases—prepositional, participial, and infinitive—are often mistaken for sentences. A *phrase fragment* can be changed into a sentence in either of two ways.

FRAGMENT: The circus began this evening. *In the arena.*

You can correct this fragment simply by attaching it to the preceding sentence.

ADDED TO   The circus began this evening *in*
NEARBY SENTENCE: *the arena.*

You can correct other fragments simply by attaching them to the beginning of a sentence.

FRAGMENT: *Arriving in the center ring.* The clowns were greeted by cheers.

ADDED TO   *Arriving in the center ring,* the
NEARBY SENTENCE: clowns were greeted by cheers.

Sometimes, however, you may not be able to correct a phrase fragment by adding it to a nearby sentence. Correct the fragment by adding to the phrase whatever is needed to make it a complete sentence. Often, this method requires adding a subject and a verb.

More Practice

Grammar Exercise Workbook
• pp. 77–80
On-line Exercise Bank
• Section 21.4
  Go on-line:
  PHSchool.com
  Enter Web Code:
  eak-6002

▼ **Critical Viewing** Turn the fragments *with a goose* and *wearing bright clothing* into complete sentences that describe this photograph. **[Describe]**

CHANGING PHRASE FRAGMENTS INTO SENTENCES

Phrase Fragment	Complete Sentence
Near the old clown.	S V The silly puppy flopped down *near the old clown.*
Taking a bow.	S V *Taking a bow,* the ringmaster had tears in his eyes.
To ask nicely.	S V She planned *to ask nicely* to go to the circus.

▶ **Exercise 32** Changing Phrase Fragments Into Sentences
Use each of the following phrase fragments in a sentence. You may use the phrase at the beginning, at the end, or in any other position in the sentence. Check to see that each of your sentences contains a subject and a verb.

EXAMPLE: Before the show started.
ANSWER: Before the show started, the performers got ready.

1. To the circus.
2. In town last weekend.
3. Having a great time.
4. My first time at the circus.
5. Taking in all the colors and sounds.
6. To be over.
7. After the show.
8. To learn to use the flying trapeze.
9. Enjoyed the circus.
10. The cunning lion tamer.

Clause Fragments All clauses have subjects and verbs, but some cannot stand alone as sentences.

Subordinate clauses do not express complete thoughts. Although a subordinate clause has a subject and a verb, it cannot stand by itself as a sentence. (See Chapter 20 for more information about subordinate clauses and the words that begin them.)

▼ **Critical Viewing**
How do you feel looking at the balancing act in this photograph? Change the phrase fragment *on the edge of my seat* into a sentence. **[Respond]**

▶**KEY CONCEPT** A subordinate clause should not be capitalized and punctuated as though it were a sentence. ■

Like phrase fragments, *clause fragments* can usually be corrected in either of two ways: by attaching the fragment to a nearby sentence or by adding whatever words are needed to make the fragment into a sentence.

Notice how the following clause fragments are corrected using the first method.

FRAGMENT: The class enjoyed the poem. *That I recited to them as part of my oral report.*

ADDED TO NEARBY SENTENCE: The class enjoyed the poem *that I recited to them as part of my oral report.*

To change a clause fragment into a sentence by the second method, you must add an independent clause to the fragment.

CHANGING CLAUSE FRAGMENTS INTO SENTENCES	
Clause Fragment	**Complete Sentence**
That you described.	I saw the show *that you described.* The show *that you described* was in town.
After he knocked.	A pie hit him *after he knocked.* *After he knocked,* a pie hit him.

Text

Complete the exercises on-line! Exercises 32 and 33 are available on-line or on CD-ROM.

▶**Exercise 33** Changing Clause Fragments Into Sentences
Use each of the clause fragments below in a sentence. Make sure that each sentence contains an independent clause.

EXAMPLE: That we saw last week.
ANSWER: We enjoyed the circus that we saw last week.

1. That they wear in the show.
2. When it is time to go on.
3. When they are in the ring.
4. Because they make children laugh.
5. While they are on.
6. That they are funny.
7. As long as there is an audience.
8. That they wear.
9. Because they travel often.
10. That I'll be a clown.

More Practice

Grammar Exercise Workbook
• pp. 77–80
On-line Exercise Bank
• Section 21.4
Go on-line:
PHSchool.com
Enter Web Code:
eak-6002

Avoiding Run-ons

A *run-on sentence* contains two or more complete sentences that have been improperly combined.

▶ **KEY CONCEPT** A **run-on** is two or more complete sentences that are not properly joined or separated. ■

Run-ons are usually the result of haste. Learn to check your sentences carefully to see where one sentence ends and the next one begins.

Two Kinds of Run-ons There are two kinds of run-ons: One kind is made up of two or more sentences run together without any punctuation between them; the other consists of two or more sentences separated only by a comma.

RUN-ONS	
With No Punctuation	**With Only a Comma**
I go to the fair often the arts and crafts are my favorite part.	Fireworks and parades mark July 4th in the United States, family picnics are also a feature.

A good way to distinguish between a run-on and a sentence is to read the words aloud. Your ear will tell you whether you have one or two complete thoughts.

Get instant feedback! Exercise 34 is available on-line or on CD-ROM.

▶ **Exercise 34** Recognizing Run-ons On your paper, write *S* if an item below is a sentence and *R-O* if it is a run-on.

EXAMPLE: The clowns are silly and fun to watch they wear colorful suits.

ANSWER: R-O

1. A circus is usually held in a round theater it usually has tiers of seats for the audience.
2. It may be held in the open air, but it is usually under a tent.
3. The first modern circus was staged in London in 1768, a former cavalry rider performed tricks on his horse.
4. Philip Astley, the rider, brought his show to Paris, it soon spread throughout Europe.
5. By the nineteenth century, there were many permanent circuses in Europe; small caravans of traveling performers also gave shows.

More Practice

Grammar Exercise Workbook
• pp. 81–84
On-line Exercise Bank
• Section 21.4
  Go on-line:
  PHSchool.com
  Enter Web Code:
  eak-6002

Correcting Run-ons There are three easy ways to correct a run-on.

Using End Marks *End marks* are periods, question marks, and exclamation marks.

KEY CONCEPT Use an end mark to separate the parts of a run-on into two sentences. ■

Properly used, an end mark splits a run-on into two shorter but complete sentences. Which end mark you use depends on the function of the sentence.

RUN-ON: Every year we celebrate Independence Day with
               fireworks, a circus comes to town, too.

CORRECTED: Every year we celebrate Independence Day with
               fireworks. A circus comes to town, too.

RUN-ON: Have you found my tickets,
               I lost them yesterday.

CORRECTED: Have you found my tickets?
               I lost them yesterday.

▶ **Critical Viewing** Who is this man and what do you think he is saying? Make sure to avoid run-ons in your response. **[Deduce]**

Using Commas and Coordinating Conjunctions Sometimes the two parts of a run-on are related and should stay in the same sentence.

▶ **KEY CONCEPT** Use a comma and a coordinating conjunction to combine two independent clauses into a compound sentence. ■

RUN-ON: The lions and the tigers are roaming around the ring they look scary.

CORRECTED: The lions and the tigers are roaming around the ring, *and* they look scary.

Using Semicolons You can sometimes use a semicolon to punctuate the two parts of a run-on.

▶ **KEY CONCEPT** Use a semicolon to connect two closely related ideas. ■

Do not overuse the semicolon. Remember, semicolons should be used only when the ideas in both parts of the sentence are closely related.

RUN-ON: The circus begins at 7:30, I don't want to be late.
CORRECTED: The circus begins at 7:30; I don't want to be late.

▶ **Exercise 35** Revising to Correct Run-ons Correct each of the following run-on sentences using any of the three methods described in this section. Write the corrected sentences on a separate sheet of paper.

EXAMPLE: My sister hates the circus she is afraid of clowns.
ANSWER: My sister hates the circus. She is afraid of clowns.

1. Traveling shows were quite simple they usually had a fiddler, a juggler, a rope dancer, and an acrobat.
2. These early circuses performed in open spaces the performers took up a collection for pay.
3. Later, the performers used an enclosed area, they began to charge admission.
4. Permanent, indoor European circuses staged elaborate shows, they specialized in horse tricks.
5. The circus was introduced to the United States in 1793 John Bill Ricketts brought his circus to Philadelphia.

▶ **More Practice**

Grammar Exercise Workbook
• pp. 81–84
On-line Exercise Bank
• Section 21.4
  Go on-line:
  PHSchool.com
  Enter Web Code:
  eak-6002

Complete the exercise on-line! Exercise 35 is available on-line or on CD-ROM.

Correcting Misplaced Modifiers

A phrase or clause that acts as an adjective or adverb should be placed close to the word it modifies. Otherwise, the meaning of the sentence may be unclear.

▶ **KEY CONCEPT** A modifier should be placed as close as possible to the word it modifies. ■

Misplaced Modifiers A modifier placed too far away from the word it modifies is called a *misplaced modifier*. Because they are misplaced, such phrases and clauses seem to modify the wrong word in a sentence.

MISPLACED
MODIFIER: The circus featured an acrobat on

the high wire *with an umbrella.*

The misplaced modifier is the phrase *with an umbrella.* In the sentence, it sounds as though the high wire has an umbrella. The sentence needs to be reworded slightly to put the modifier closer to *acrobat.*

CORRECTED: The circus featured an acrobat *with an umbrella* on the high wire.

Below is a somewhat different type of misplaced modifier.

MISPLACED
MODIFIER: *Balancing on her toes,* the net seemed far away.

In this sentence *balancing on her toes* should modify a person. Instead, it incorrectly modifies *net.*

CORRECTED: *Balancing on her toes,* the acrobat thought the net seemed far away.

◀ **Critical Viewing**
Tell what would happen if one of these acrobats were in the wrong position.
[Infer]

Solving Special Problems

Many mistakes in speaking and in writing involve words and expressions that are sometimes used in very informal conversation but are considered nonstandard for most writing and speaking. Other problems involve words that are easily confused because they are spelled almost alike. In the following sections, note those problems that occur in your speaking or writing.

Double Negatives

Negative words, such as *nothing* and *not,* are used to deny or to say *no.* At one time, it was customary to use two or more negative words in one clause to add emphasis. Today, only one negative word is used to give a sentence a negative meaning.

KEY CONCEPT Do not write sentences with two negative words when only one is needed. ■

INCORRECT	My parents *never* take me *nowhere.*
CORRECT:	My parents *never* take me *anywhere.*
	My parents take me *nowhere.*

The sentences on the left in the following chart contain double negatives. Notice on the right how each can be corrected in either of two ways. Usually, either negative word can be changed to a positive to correct the sentence.

Double Negatives	Corrected Sentences
Shelly did*n't* invite *nobody.*	Shelly did*n't* invite anybody. Shelly invited *nobody.*
I have*n't* *no* time now.	I have*n't* any time now. I have *no* time now.
She *never* told us *nothing* about her party.	She *never* told us anything about her party. She told us *nothing* about her party.

More Practice

Grammar Exercise Workbook
• pp. 85–86
On-line Exercise Bank
• Section 21.4
  Go on-line:
  PHSchool.com
  Enter Web Code:
  eak-6002

Text

Complete the exercises on-line! Exercises 38 and 39 are available on-line or on CD-ROM.

▶ **Exercise 38** Correcting Double Negatives
The following sentences contain double negatives, which are underlined. Correct each sentence in *two* ways.

EXAMPLE: I <u>didn't</u> see <u>no</u> clowns.
ANSWER: I didn't see any clowns.
            I saw no clowns.

 1. We <u>couldn't</u> go to <u>no</u> circus.
 2. I <u>haven't</u> <u>no</u> money to buy tickets.
 3. Father <u>wouldn't</u> let me bring <u>nobody</u>.
 4. Stella <u>doesn't</u> like <u>no</u> lions.
 5. The lion tamer <u>didn't</u> get scared by <u>no</u> lions.
 6. The clowns <u>never</u> played with <u>no</u> lions.
 7. We <u>never</u> get to see <u>nothing</u> like the circus.
 8. When the clown opened the fake door, there <u>wasn't</u> <u>no one</u> there.
 9. The trapeze artists <u>weren't</u> scared of <u>no</u> heights.
10. They <u>didn't</u> work with <u>no</u> net.

▶ **Exercise 39** Writing Negative Sentences Write ten negative sentences, following the instructions given below.

EXAMPLE: Use *ever* in a negative sentence about going up in a hot-air balloon.
ANSWER: My sister hasn't ever gone up in a hot-air balloon.

 1. Use *nothing* in a sentence about the contents of a box.
 2. Use *no one* in a sentence about the people who had seen a certain movie.
 3. Use *anything* in a negative sentence about what your friend did wrong.
 4. Use *anyone* in a negative sentence about whom you saw at the movies.
 5. Use *none* in a sentence about cake left over after a birthday party.
 6. Use *never* in a sentence about walking a tightrope.
 7. Use *ever* in a negative sentence about seeing a comet.
 8. Use *nobody* in a sentence about knowing a password.
 9. Use *somebody* in a negative sentence about liking loud noises.
10. Use *everyone* in a negative sentence about voting.

▲ Critical Viewing
Write two negative sentences about something these trapeze artists should never do. [Draw Conclusions]

Avoiding Sentence Problems • **465**

Fifteen Common Usage Problems

This section contains fifteen common usage problems in alphabetical order. Some of the problems are expressions that you should avoid in both your speaking and your writing. Others are words that are often confused because of similar spellings or meanings.

As you read through the list, note the problems that may have caused you difficulty in the past. Then, use the exercises for practice in recognizing and avoiding those problems.

Later, when you write and revise your compositions, this section can help you check your work. If you do not find the explanation of a problem in this section, check for it in the index at the back of the book.

(1) accept, except Do not confuse the spelling of these words. *Accept*, a verb, means "to take (what is offered)" or "to agree to." *Except*, a preposition, means "leaving out" or "other than."

VERB: She willingly *accepted* responsibility for the others.

PREPOSITION: Everyone *except* him will be at the party.

(2) advice, advise Do not confuse the spelling of these related words. *Advice*, a noun, means "an opinion." *Advise*, a verb, means "to give an opinion to."

NOUN: My mother gave me *advice* about how to answer the letter.

VERB: My mother *advised* me to accept the invitation to the dance.

(3) affect, effect *Affect*, almost always a verb, means "to influence" or "to bring about a change in." *Effect*, usually a noun, means "result."

VERB: The rainy weather *affected* the outdoor wedding.

NOUN: What *effect* does the Mardi Gras celebration have on the city of New Orleans?

(4) at Do not use *at* after *where*.

INCORRECT: Do you know *where* the circus is *at*?

CORRECT: Do you know *where* the circus is?

(5) because Do not use *because* after *the reason*. Eliminate one or the other.

INCORRECT: *The reason* I am late is *because* the bus broke down.

CORRECT: *The reason* I am late is *that* the bus broke down.

▶ **Exercise 40** Avoiding Usage Problems For each of the following sentences, choose the correct word or phrase from the choices in parentheses, and write it on your paper.

EXAMPLE: I can't (accept, except) these tickets to the circus.
ANSWER: accept

1. What (effect, affect) will clown college have on my future?
2. My father (advised, adviced) me that I should not be a clown.
3. The reason I want to be a clown is (because, that) it looks like fun.
4. I don't know where the clown college (is at, is).
5. Everyone (accept, except) me thinks clown college is a bad idea.

(6) beside, besides These two prepositions have different meanings and cannot be interchanged. *Beside* means "at the side of " or "close to." *Besides* means "in addition to."

EXAMPLES: The clown sat down *beside* the child.
             No one *besides* us was there.

(7) different from, different than *Different from* is generally preferred over *different than.*

EXAMPLE: The clown's routine was *different from* what I had expected.

(8) farther, further *Farther* is usually used to refer to distance. *Further* means "additional" or "to a greater degree or extent."

EXAMPLES: Haven't we walked much *farther* than a mile?
             I need *further* advice.
             When he began raising his voice, I listened no *further.*

(9) in, into *In* refers to position. *Into* suggests motion.

POSITION: The ringmaster is *in* the big top.
MOTION: The ringmaster stepped *into* the center ring.

(10) kind of, sort of Do not use *kind of* or *sort of* to mean "rather" or "somewhat."

INCORRECT: The new CD that I brought home sounds *sort of* interesting.

CORRECT: The new CD that I brought home sounds *rather* interesting.

▶ **More Practice**

On-line Exercise Bank
• Section 21.4
  Go on-line:
  PHSchool.com
  Enter Web Code:
  eak-6002

Get instant feedback! Exercise 40 is available on-line or on CD-ROM.

▶ **Exercise 41** Avoiding Usage Problems For each of the following sentences, choose the correct word or phrase from the choices in parentheses, and write it on your paper.

1. No one (beside, besides) the acrobat has the courage to go on the trapeze.
2. The circus is very (different from, different than) the opera.
3. There is no one who can tumble (farther, further) than Lucinda.
4. The lion tamer put his head (in, into) the lion's mouth.
5. A ringmaster is (kind of, rather) like an orchestra conductor.

(11) like *Like*, a preposition, means "similar to" or "in the same way as." It should be followed by an object. Do not use *like* before the subject and verb of a clause. Use *as* or *that* instead.

PREPOSITION:	The rubbing alcohol felt *like* ice on my feverish skin. *(Obj. above "ice")*
INCORRECT:	The stew that I ordered doesn't taste *like* it should. *(S above "I", V above "taste")*
CORRECT:	The stew that I ordered doesn't taste *as* it should.

(12) that, which, who *That* can be used to refer to either things or people. *Which* should be used to refer only to things. *Who* should be used to refer only to people.

THINGS:	The dress *that* I designed won first prize.
PEOPLE:	The dancer *that* (or *who*) performed is my brother.

(13) their, there, they're Do not confuse the spelling of these three words. *Their*, a possessive adjective, always modifies a noun. *There* is usually used either as a sentence starter or as an adverb. *They're* is a contraction for *they are*.

POSSESSIVE ADJECTIVE:	The team won all of *their* games.
SENTENCE STARTER:	*There* are no easy answers to the problem of prejudice.
ADVERB:	Move the chair over *there*.
CONTRACTION:	*They're* trying to set new track records.

▶ **More Practice**

On-line Exercise Bank
• Section 21.4
  Go on-line:
  PHSchool.com
  Enter Web Code:
  eak-6002

Text

Get instant feedback! Exercises 41 and 42 are available on-line or on CD-ROM.

(14) to, too, two Do not confuse the spelling of these words. *To*, a preposition, begins a prepositional phrase or an infinitive. *Too*, with two *o*'s, is an adverb and modifies adjectives and other adverbs. *Two* is a number.

PREPOSITION:	*to* the store	*to* Maine
INFINITIVE:	*to* meet	*to* see
ADVERB:	*too* sad	*too* quickly
NUMBER:	*two* buttons	*two* apples

(15) when, where, why Do not use *when, where,* or *why* directly after a linking verb such as *is*. Reword the sentence.

INCORRECT:	In the evening *is when* I do my homework.
	The gym *is where* the acrobats practice.
	To see the circus *is why* we came to New York City.
CORRECT:	I do my homework in the evening.
	The acrobats practice in the gym.
	We came to New York City to see the circus.

Exercise 42 Proofreading to Correct Usage Problems

Rewrite the following sentences, correcting any usage problems.
1. The carnival is coming together like it should.
2. At the carnival is where there will be games.
3. It is almost to exciting at Mardi Gras.
4. Do you know all the people which are coming to the party?
5. They're will be a lot of delicious food at the carnival.

▼ **Critical Viewing**
How does a ride like this affect you? Respond using the word *effect* (not *affect*) correctly. **[Analyze]**

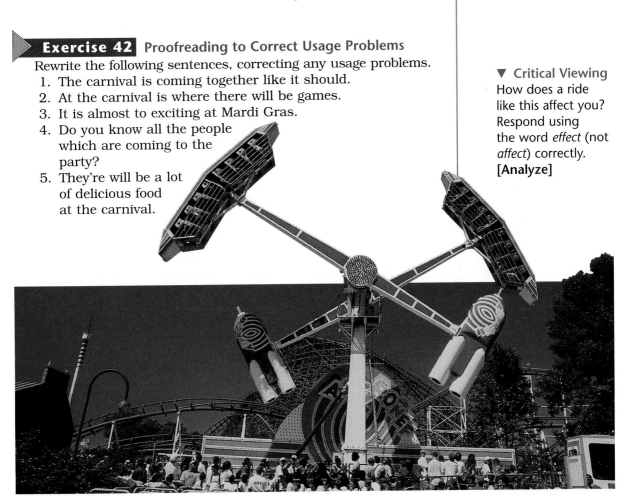

Section Review

GRAMMAR EXERCISES 43–52

Exercise 43 Writing Sentences From Fragments Use each of the following fragments in a sentence.

1. Into the big top.
2. Before the show started.
3. Feeling excited.
4. When the lion roared.
5. In the air.
6. Staring at the fire-eater.
7. Following the bareback rider.
8. Although there was a net.
9. Which were the most fascinating.
10. Have been so tired!

Exercise 44 Avoiding Usage Problems For each of the following sentences, choose the correct word or phrase in parentheses, and write it on your paper.

1. The rainy weather will (effect, affect) the barbecue.
2. (Their, There, They're) picnic will be ruined.
3. This picnic will be a lot (different from, different than) last year's.
4. The man (which, who) runs the barbecue will be late.
5. The reason he is late is (because, that) he has a flat tire.
6. No one showed up on time for the dress rehearsal (accept, except) the trapeze artist.
7. The ringmaster (advised, adviced) the other performers that attendance at rehearsals was important.
8. The reason the lion tamer was late was (because, that) he tripped on a chair.
9. "Do you know where the first aid kit (is at, is)?" he asked.
10. "I put it (in, into) the box in the cupboard," said the ringmaster.

Exercise 45 Revising to Eliminate Run-Ons Correct the following run-ons, using any of the three methods described in this section.

1. George Washington attended a Ricketts circus, he sold the company a horse.
2. The Ricketts circus existed through the early nineteenth century, it changed its name several times.
3. The circus evolved throughout the nineteenth century the programs became more elaborate.
4. Horse tricks dominated circuses at first, clowning, acrobats, juggling, and the like were soon introduced.
5. Tents were not used until the 1820's, the flying trapeze was not invented until 1859.

Exercise 46 Revising to Eliminate Misplaced Modifiers Rewrite the following sentences to eliminate misplaced modifiers.

1. Although usually used as pack animals, circuses often feature camels or dromedaries.
2. Having only one hump, the characteristics of dromedaries are that they are intelligent and easy to train.
3. Making them more gentle, some trainers bottle-feed baby dromedaries.
4. Dromedaries are rewarded with carrots learning to respond to commands.
5. So that its mouth doesn't get irritated, the bit in the bridle must be put in upside down in the dromedary.

▶ **Exercise 47** Revising to Eliminate Double Negatives The following sentences contain double negatives, which are underlined. Correct each sentence in two ways.

1. We <u>won't</u> be going to <u>no</u> carnival.
2. My sister <u>doesn't</u> have <u>no</u> time to take us.
3. I <u>never</u> played <u>none</u> of the games at the carnival.
4. I <u>can't</u> get <u>nobody</u> to take me.
5. My friend <u>won't</u> tell me <u>nothing</u> about the fun he has.
6. The lion tamer <u>won't</u> let <u>none</u> of the audience see his fear.
7. I have <u>never</u> seen <u>no</u> courage like that.
8. We have <u>never</u> seen <u>nobody</u> tame lions.
9. I <u>don't</u> think I can learn to do <u>nothing</u> like that.
10. The lion tamer <u>hardly</u> spent <u>no</u> time training the animals.

▶ **Exercise 48** Revising a Passage to Eliminate Run-ons Rewrite the following paragraph to eliminate the run-on sentences. Use end marks, commas and coordinating conjunctions, and semicolons.

Many circuses feature trained animals they play an important part in the circus. Clowns in funny clothes provide the comedy for the show the circus band adds to the excitement. A colorful parade begins the show animals and circus performers march around the arena the circus band plays music.

▶ **Exercise 49** Revising a Passage to Eliminate Sentence Errors Rewrite the following paragraph to correct sentence fragments, run-ons, misplaced modifiers, double negatives, and usage problems.

In the mid-nineteenth century, the arrival of the circus was a huge event in a small town. Many people lived on farms. Isolated from neighbors with few entertainments. There wasn't no television or movies, or even radio. The circus brought drama and mystery, for example it often featured sword swallowers. Also wild animals such as lions and tigers. Posters advertised the arrival of the circus, people lined the streets to watch the animals and performers parade through town. Local townspeople, serving like circus staff, helped set up the tent. Sideshows entertained people before the show started with unusual sights. Such as a sheep with three heads. No one had never seen such things on the farm.

▶ **Exercise 50** Find It in Your Reading Read the following excerpt from Rachel Field's "Parade," and explain why her use of the word *like* instead of *as* is correct.

. . . There will be floats / in shapes like dragons, thrones and boats. . . .

▶ **Exercise 51** Find It in Your Writing Choose a piece of writing from your portfolio. Find and correct two examples of run-on sentences, using end marks or commas and coordinating conjunctions. If you are unable to find run-on sentences, challenge yourself to add a sentence that uses a comma and a coordinating conjunction to combine two independent clauses into a compound sentence.

▶ **Exercise 52** Writing Application Write a brief narrative about a performance you once gave. (It can be imaginary or real.) In addition to including information about the place and the audience, relate the events as they occurred. Avoid fragments and run-ons in your writing, and include the words *effect*, *they're*, and *further* in your narrative.

Chapter Review

GRAMMAR EXERCISES 53–61

Exercise 53 Identifying Types of Sentences Identify each sentence below as *declarative, interrogative, imperative,* or *exclamatory.* Then, write the end mark for each sentence.

1. Will you take me to the circus
2. Ask Nancy whether she wants to go, too
3. Nancy can go if she saves her allowance
4. What fun it will be
5. The circus will be in town for a month
6. May I have cotton candy and peanuts
7. Tell the clown he is funny
8. The ringmaster is a busy man
9. Do the elephants sleep in the big top
10. Wow—I can't wait to go

Exercise 54 Combining Sentences Combine the following sentences, using the construction given in parentheses.

1. A clown is a performer who plays the fool. He also performs practical jokes. (compound verb)
2. Clowns do tricks to make people laugh. They are also called buffoons, jesters, fools, and harlequins. (subordinate conjunction *because*)
3. We often think all clowns are alike. Each clown develops a unique face, or performance personality. (subordinate conjunction *although*)
4. It takes years for a clown to establish a face. It eventually becomes the clown's unique personal property. (semicolon)
5. Clowning techniques are taught in specialized clown schools. The most famous clown school is in Florida. (comma and conjunction *and*)

Exercise 55 Varying Sentence Beginnings Reorder the words in the following sentences according to the instructions in parentheses.

1. (Start with an adverb.) Canadians celebrate Canada Day annually on July 1.
2. (Start with a prepositional phrase.) The country marks with parades and fireworks the anniversary of the unification of Upper and Lower Canada.
3. (Start with a participle.) The union, created through passage of the British North American Act, took place on July 1, 1867.
4. (Start with an adverb.) The celebration was formerly known as Dominion Day.
5. (Start with a prepositional phrase.) Canada Day, for its display of patriotism, is quite similar to Independence Day in the United States.

Exercise 56 Writing Sentences From Fragments Use each of the following fragments in a sentence.

1. On the Ferris wheel.
2. Above the carnival.
3. Eating cotton candy.
4. Spending money on the games.
5. That I won at the carnival.

Exercise 57 Revising to Eliminate Run-ons Rewrite the following sentences to eliminate run-ons, using any of the three methods described in Section 21.4.

1. The Circus Maximus was an arena of ancient Rome it was located between the Palatine and Aventine hills.
2. It was the main amusement place of the city from 600 B.C. to the early days of the Roman Empire, it was enlarged by Julius Caesar.

3. The Circus Maximus had three tiers of seats it had room for almost 200,000 spectators.
4. It was the scene of athletic contests and chariot races, it was an adaptation of the Greek hippodrome.
5. In the center was a low wall that ran lengthwise, riders or charioteers rode around it.

Exercise 58 **Revising to Eliminate Errors** Rewrite the following sentences to eliminate the misplaced modifiers and double negatives.

1. Balancing on the wire, the audience gasped at the tightrope walker.
2. The ringmaster shouted at the elephants and jugglers above the din.
3. The juggler won't drop none of his pins.
4. I have never seen no pins like that.
5. We have never seen nobody juggle like that!
6. We finally went to the circus that was advertised on the radio with the terrific clowns.
7. The man on the flying trapeze reached for the second swing with a free hand.
8. Circling the ring, we were excited to watch the tigers.
9. I don't think I can learn to do nothing like that.
10. I don't have no time to learn.

Exercise 59 **Writing Sentences Using Difficult Words Correctly** Write a sentence illustrating the correct usage of each word listed below.

1. effect, affect
2. advise, advice
3. because, that
4. farther, further
5. accept, except
6. to, two, too
7. that, which, who
8. they're, their, there
9. like
10. in, into

Exercise 60 **Revision Practice: Writing Effective Sentences** Rewrite the following paragraphs to make the entire piece more effective. Vary the openers and the structures of sentences, vary sentence lengths, and correct fragments, run-ons, and other problems in word usage.

The first modern circus performance. It occurred in 1768 in London, England. It consisted of trick horseback riding by Philip Astley. He was a former cavalry officer he later took his circus to Paris and other cities.

The circus came to America in George Washington's time, introduced in the United States by an English rider, John Ricketts. He opened a show in Philadelphia in 1793. The circus gradually evolved. It evolved throughout the nineteenth century. In the beginning, horse shows and riding. They dominated circuses. Juggling, acrobatic and trapeze acts, and wild animal shows were gradually added, sideshows and parades did not appear until the end of the century.

Exercise 61 **Writing Application** Write a brief persuasive essay to convince your readers to watch your favorite show or a special performance. In addition to including good reasons, use effective sentences to hold your reader's attention. Use a variety of sentence openers and structures, and vary the length of your sentences.

Standardized Test Preparation Workshop

Recognizing Appropriate Sentence Construction

Standardized tests often evaluate your ability to recognize effective sentences. Sometimes, these items require you to identify a problem and choose the best way to rewrite to eliminate the problem. First, read the passage. Some sections are underlined. The underlined sections may be one of the following:

- incomplete sentences
- run-ons
- correctly written sentences that should be combined
- correctly written sentences that do not need to be rewritten

Sample Test Item	Answer and Explanation
Directions: Choose the best way to write the underlined section, and mark the letter for your answer. If the underlined section needs no change, mark "Correct as is." Connie made a silly face. It was by sticking her tongue out.	
1 A Connie made a silly face with her tongue out. B Connie made a silly face by sticking her tongue out. C Connie made a silly face, it was by sticking out her tongue. D Correct as is	The correct answer is *B*. Choice *B* correctly combines the important elements of both sentences to form one complete sentence.

> **Practice 1** **Directions:** Choose the best way to write each underlined section, and mark the letter for your answer. If the underlined section needs no changes, mark "Correct as is."

The parade lasted all morning, the band
(1)
went on. The floats were colorful and
          (2)
the floats were imaginative. The band
                         (3)
played marching music, the music was by

John Philip Sousa.

1 A The parade lasted all morning it went on.

B The parade lasted all morning and then the band went on.

C The parade lasted all morning.

D Correct as is

2 F The floats were colorful, imaginative floats.

G The floats were imaginative and colorful.

H The floats were colorful, and the floats were imaginative.

J Correct as is

3 A The band played marching music by John Philip Sousa.

B The band played John Philip Sousa's marching music.

C The band played music, the marching was by John Philip Sousa.

D Correct as is

> **Practice 2** **Directions:** Choose the best way to write each underlined section, and mark the letter for your answer. If the underlined section needs no changes, mark "Correct as is."

We went to the street fair that took
(1)
place after the parade was over then.

The handicrafts sold there were from
(2)
everywhere all over the world.

My favorite was a marionette, the
(3)
marionette was from Thailand.

1 A We went to the street fair which was after the parade was over then.

B After the parade was over we went to the street fair.

C Then, we went to the street fair that took place after the parade was over then.

D Correct as is

2 F The handicrafts sold there were from everywhere all over.

G The handicrafts sold there were from all over the world.

H Everywhere, the handicrafts sold were from all over the world.

J Correct as is

3 A My favorite was a marionette, and it was from Thailand.

B My favorite was a Thailand marionette.

C My favorite was a marionette from Thailand.

D Correct as is

Cumulative Review

PHRASES, CLAUSES, AND SENTENCES

▶ **Exercise A** Recognizing Basic Sentence Parts Copy the following sentences, underlining each simple subject once and each simple predicate twice. Circle the complements and label each one *direct object*, *indirect object*, *predicate nominative*, or *predicate adjective*. Then, identify each sentence as *declarative*, *imperative*, *interrogative*, or *exclamatory*.

1. Does Matt or Jeremy enjoy figure skating or speed skating?
2. Speed skating is good exercise.
3. There are races against the clock and against other skaters.
4. Speed skaters use skates with long straight edges.
5. Wow! The blades are so long and look so sharp!
6. Try that pair of skates.
7. I gave Danielle figure skating lessons.
8. She and Hannah were eager and attentive.
9. We practiced cross-overs and snow-plow stops.
10. Can you do any jumps?

▶ **Exercise B** Using Basic Sentence Parts Rewrite the following sentences according to the directions in parentheses. In your new sentences, underline each simple subject once and each simple predicate twice. Circle each complement.

1. Ice hockey is a winter sport. It is a rough game. (Combine by creating a compound predicate nominative.)
2. Hockey-playing countries include Canada. Hockey is a big sport in Russia. (Combine by creating a compound direct object.)
3. Defense is an important part of the game, and so is offense. (Rewrite by creating a compound subject.)

4. The players use hockey sticks. They wear protective pads. (Rewrite by creating a compound predicate.)
5. Goaltenders wear face masks. They wear other protective equipment. (Combine by creating a compound direct object.)
6. One area on the ice is the neutral zone. Another is the attacking zone. (Combine by creating a compound predicate nominative.)
7. Substitution of players is frequent. It occurs during the game. (Combine by creating a compound predicate.)
8. Hockey skate blades are thin. They are also short. (Combine by creating a compound predicate adjective.)
9. Teams pass the puck, shooting it with their sticks. (Rewrite by creating a compound predicate.)
10. Ancient Egyptians played games similar to hockey, and so did the Persians. (Rewrite by creating a compound subject.)

▶ **Exercise C** Identifying Phrases and Clauses Label each phrase in the following sentences an *adjective prepositional phrase*, an *adverb prepositional phrase*, or an *appositive phrase*. Identify and label each clause.

1. Skiing is a popular winter sport in many countries.
2. Boots, flexible or rigid, are important pieces of equipment.
3. Ski poles that vary in length are used for balance.
4. There are three kinds of skiing that have been developed.
5. One type, Alpine skiing, involves racing down steep, snow-covered slopes.
6. Skiers descend in the fastest time possible.

7. A course is defined by a series of gates, which are made of poles and flag markers.
8. The racer passes through these gates.
9. This downhill racing includes the slalom, in which the course is made of many turns.
10. The super giant slalom, a combination of downhill and slalom, is decided after one run.

▶ **Exercise D** Using Phrases and Clauses Rewrite the following sentences according to the instructions in parentheses.

1. Cross-country skiing is called Nordic skiing and is practiced in many parts of the world. (Rewrite by creating an appositive phrase.)
2. It is performed on longer courses. These courses are also flatter than downhill courses. (Combine by creating a clause.)
3. Nordic skiing emphasizes two things. Those are endurance and strength. (Combine by creating a clause.)
4. A side-to-side motion is the way cross-country skiers move. (Rewrite by creating an adverb prepositional phrase.)
5. Cross-country skiing developed to fill a need. That need was for transportation. (Combine by creating an adjective prepositional phrase.)

▶ **Exercise E** Revising Sentences to Eliminate Errors and Create Variety Rewrite the following sentences according to the instructions in parentheses.

1. Bobsledding was first developed in Saint Moritz, Switzerland, the first competition was held there. (Correct the run-on sentence.)
2. Teams of two or four people descend an icy run in bobsledding. (Vary the sentence by beginning with a prepositional phrase.)
3. The part of a bobsled run most critical is its start. (Correct the misplaced modifier.)

4. The captain occupies the front position in the sled. This person is also called the driver. (Combine the sentences by creating a phrase.)
5. The crew members lean backward and forward in unison and accelerate the speed of the sled. (Vary the sentence by beginning with a participial phrase.)
6. Bobsledding is different than the luge. (Correct the common usage problem.)
7. Lie on their backs with their feet at the front of the luge sled. (Correct the sentence fragment.)
8. Luge courses aren't constructed for nothing other than this sport. (Correct the double negative.)
9. These courses feature turns. Courses also feature straight stretches. (Combine by creating a compound direct object.)
10. The reason it looks dangerous is because luges travel at high speeds. (Correct the common usage problem.)

▶ **Exercise F** Revision Practice: Sentence Combining Rewrite the following passage, combining sentences where appropriate.

Most children are delighted when it snows. They wake up early. They listen for school cancellations on the radio. If school is cancelled, the children are excited. The parents say "Oh, no!" It means the schedule is off. The day has to be rearranged. They get out the boots and warm clothes. They get out the sleds. An unexpected vacation day.

▶ **Exercise G** Writing Application Write a description of a winter activity that you enjoy. Vary the lengths and beginnings of your sentences. Underline each simple subject once and each simple verb twice. Then, circle at least three phrases and three clauses. Avoid fragments, run-ons, double negatives, misplaced modifiers, and common usage problems.

The Kremlin, a former royal palace, has been the headquarters of Russia's government since 1918.

▲ **Critical Viewing**
Name verbs to describe actions or conditions of the lights, flag, and building in this picture. **[Identify]**

Usage refers to the way a word or expression is used in a sentence. The rules in this and the following chapters are those of standard English. You will apply these rules in most of your writing and speaking.

If you wanted to write an essay about Russia, you would use many different verbs to show actions or conditions of the people, the cities, the landforms, and anything else. Just like a large country, verbs have different parts; you will learn about those parts in this chapter. Also, a country like Russia has a past, a present, and a future, so the verbs you would use in your essay would need to show whether an action takes place in the past, the present, or the future.

In this chapter, you will learn rules about using verbs correctly. Some rules will teach you about the parts of verbs. Other rules will help you use the different tenses. Finally, there are rules that will help you solve verb problems.

Diagnostic Test

Directions: Write all answers on a separate sheet of paper. (The sentences that follow are not intended to be in the same verb tense. Read each sentence as though it stood alone.)

Skill Check A. Label the principal part of each underlined verb *present, present participle, past,* or *past participle.*

1. Yesterday, Katerina <u>saw</u> a Russian film from the 1940's.
2. She has <u>seen</u> many foreign films.
3. Her friends <u>enjoy</u> these films with her.
4. She is <u>planning</u> to study filmmaking.
5. She has <u>heard</u> of a good film school in Moscow.

Skill Check B. Write the present participle, past, and past participle forms of the following verbs.

6. earn
7. laugh
8. drink
9. have
10. ride

Skill Check C. In each sentence below, choose the correct verb in parentheses.

11. My friend Vladimir (grew, growed) up in Russia.
12. He and his family (come, came) to this country last year.
13. They (saw, seen) many new things when they arrived.
14. He has (spoke, spoken) often about his life back in Moscow.
15. Vladimir has (wrote, written) beautiful stories about his grandparents in Moscow.

Skill Check D. Rewrite each sentence below, changing the tense of the underlined verb to the tense indicated in parentheses.

16. I <u>have studied</u> Russian for two years. (future)
17. It <u>is</u> one of the most difficult languages to learn. (past)
18. Earlier, I <u>studied</u> Spanish. (past perfect)
19. Studying the Russian language <u>helped</u> me to appreciate Russian culture better. (present perfect)
20. This summer, my family <u>visited</u> Russia. (present)

Skill Check E. In each sentence below, choose the correct verb in parentheses.

21. We (did, done) several things to prepare for our trip to Russia.
22. First, my father (set, sat) a map of Russia on the kitchen table, and we studied it.
23. We noted that Moscow (lies, lays) in the western part of the country.
24. The Kremlin in Moscow (sits, sets) alongside the Moscow River.
25. The map has (lain, laid) on the table ever since, so we can look at it whenever we pass.

The Four Principal Parts of Verbs

Verbs have different forms to express time. The form of the verb *walk* in the sentence "They *walk* very fast" expresses action in the present. In "They *walked* too far," the form of the verb shows that the action happened in the past. In "They *will walk* home," the verb expresses action in the future. These forms of verbs are known as *tenses*. To use the tenses of a verb correctly, you must know the *principal parts* of the verb.

▶ **KEY CONCEPT** A verb has four **principal parts:** the *present*, the *present participle*, the *past*, and the *past participle*. ■

Here, for example, are the four principal parts of the verb *walk:*

THE FOUR PRINCIPAL PARTS OF *WALK*			
Present	Present Participle	Past	Past Participle
walk	(am) walking	walked	(have) walked

The first principal part, called the *present*, is the form of the verb that is listed in a dictionary. Sometimes, the present tense has an *s* on the end when it is used with a singular subject. Notice also the helping verbs in parentheses before the second and fourth principal parts in the chart. These two principal parts must be combined with helping verbs before they can be used as verbs in sentences. The result will always be a *verb phrase.*

Following are four sentences, each using one of the principal parts of the verb *walk:*

EXAMPLES: He *walks* slowly through the Moscow Zoo.
A large bear *was walking* around in its cage.
My parents *walked* to the Belorussian Station.
We *have walked* all through this part of Moscow.

The way the last two principal parts of a verb—the past and past participle—are formed shows whether the verb is regular or irregular.

▼ Critical Viewing Write a sentence about this bear. Then, rewrite it in the past tense and in the future tense. [Describe]

Using Regular Verbs

Most verbs are *regular*, which means that the past and past participle of these verbs are formed according to a predictable pattern.

KEY CONCEPT With **regular verbs**, the past and past participle are formed by adding *-ed* or *-d* to the present form. ■

To form the past and past participle of a regular verb, such as *talk* or *look*, you simply add *-ed* to the present tense. With regular verbs that already end in *e*—verbs such as *move* and *charge*—you simply add *-d* to the present tense. ■

PRINCIPAL PARTS OF REGULAR VERBS			
Present	**Present Participle**	**Past**	**Past Participle**
talk	(am) talking	talked	(have) talked
look	(am) looking	looked	(have) looked
move	(am) moving	moved	(have) moved
charge	(am) charging	charged	(have) charged

Exercise 1 Recognizing the Principal Parts of Regular Verbs
Identify the principal part used to form each underlined verb or verb phrase in the following sentences.

EXAMPLE: Mia is painting a portrait of the Russian president.

ANSWER: present participle

1. Our class is reading about Russia.
2. Every Friday, we look at videos about Russian cities and culture.
3. The country has served as a bridge between Europe and Asia for many centuries.
4. From the sixteenth century to the early part of the twentieth century, an emperor ruled over Russia.
5. In 1917, a revolution occurred in Russia.
6. A new government was established there.
7. We are studying the Russian Revolution in our social studies class.
8. Our teacher describes it as a major event of the twentieth century.
9. For more than seventy years, Communist leaders controlled the government.
10. Today, elected officials are governing the people of Russia.

More Practice

Grammar Exercise Workbook
• pp. 87–88
On-line Exercise Bank
• Section 22.1
  Go on-line:
  PHSchool.com
  Enter Web Code:
  eak-6002

Get instant feedback! Exercise 1 is available on-line or on CD-ROM.

► **Exercise 2** Supplying the Principal Parts of Regular Verbs
Copy each of the following sentences onto your paper, writing
the correct form of the verb in parentheses.

EXAMPLE: We have (visit) the famous art museum in
             St. Petersburg.

ANSWER: We have visited the famous art museum in
             St. Petersburg.

1. I am (give) an oral report on Peter I of Russia.
2. He has often been (call) Peter the Great.
3. Peter (inherit—past) the throne as czar of Russia in 1682.
4. He (want—past) to make Russia more modern.
5. Peter (disguise—past) himself as a ship's carpenter.
6. He (travel—past) in disguise to England and Holland.
7. Peter actually (labor—past) in shipyards in those countries.
8. He was (impress) with the industrial development he had
   (observe) in Western Europe.
9. He (model—past) changes in his country after things he
   had (learn) during his travels.
10. I am (plan) to show several portraits of Peter during my
    report.

GRAMMAR IN LITERATURE

from **Overdoing It**
Anton Chekhov

The verbs in this excerpt are printed in blue italics.
Stretched, merged, *and* disappeared *are in the past tense.*
Try *and* come *are in the present tense. Was sinking is made
up of the past tense of the verb* be *and the present participle
of the verb* sink.

. . . To the right of the surveyor *stretched* the dark,
frozen plain—broad and endless. *Try* to cross it and you'll
come to the end of the world. On the horizon, where the
plain *merged* with the sky and *disappeared*, the autumn
sun *was* lazily *sinking* in the mist.

Using Irregular Verbs

Many common verbs are *irregular*. These are the verbs that tend to cause the most problems.

KEY CONCEPT With **irregular verbs**, the past and past participle are *not* formed by adding *-ed* or *-d* to the present. ■

The third and fourth principal parts of irregular verbs are formed in various ways. You should memorize them.

IRREGULAR VERBS WITH THE SAME PAST AND PAST PARTICIPLE			
Present	Present Participle	Past	Past Participle
bring	(am) bringing	brought	(have) brought
build	(am) building	built	(have) built
buy	(am) buying	bought	(have) bought
catch	(am) catching	caught	(have) caught
fight	(am) fighting	fought	(have) fought
find	(am) finding	found	(have) found
get	(am) getting	got	(have) got *or* (have) gotten
hold	(am) holding	held	(have) held
lay	(am) laying	laid	(have) laid
lead	(am) leading	led	(have) led
lose	(am) losing	lost	(have) lost
pay	(am) paying	paid	(have) paid
say	(am) saying	said	(have) said
sit	(am) sitting	sat	(have) sat
spin	(am) spinning	spun	(have) spun
stick	(am) sticking	stuck	(have) stuck
swing	(am) swinging	swung	(have) swung
teach	(am) teaching	taught	(have) taught

💡 **Spelling Tip**

Pay particular attention to the word *paid*. Make sure you do not spell it *payed*.

Exercise 3 Using Irregular Verbs Rewrite each sentence below, replacing the underlined verb with the principal part shown in parentheses. Refer to the chart above if you need help.

EXAMPLE: I buy a painting from a gallery in Moscow. (past)
ANSWER: I bought a painting from a gallery in Moscow.

1. Russians <u>fight</u> many wars on the site that is now the city of St. Petersburg. (past participle)
2. In 1240, Russians <u>hold</u> off the Swedes there. (past)
3. In 1703, Peter I <u>lay</u> out plans for his new capital there. (past)
4. He <u>bring</u> in architects to build palaces and factories. (past)
5. We are <u>study</u> Russia in social studies. (present participle)

More Practice

Grammar Exercise Workbook
• pp. 89–94
On-line Exercise Bank
• Section 22.1
Go on-line:
PHSchool.com
Enter Web Code:
eak-6002

IRREGULAR VERBS WITH THE SAME PRESENT, PAST, AND PAST PARTICIPLE

Present	Present Participle	Past	Past Participle
bid	(am) bidding	bid	(have) bid
burst	(am) bursting	burst	(have) burst
cost	(am) costing	cost	(have) cost
hurt	(am) hurting	hurt	(have) hurt
put	(am) putting	put	(have) put
set	(am) setting	set	(have) set

Exercise 4 Revising Sentences With Irregular Verbs Copy each sentence below, replacing the underlined verb with the principal part indicated in parentheses. Refer to the chart above if you need help.

EXAMPLE: I <u>set</u> the delicate Russian doll on the store counter. (past participle)

ANSWER: I have set the delicate Russian doll on the store counter.

EXAMPLE: The clerk <u>put</u> it in a box. (present participle)

ANSWER: The clerk is putting it in a box.

1. Moscow <u>burst</u> forth as a major tourist attraction in recent years. (past participle)
2. The city <u>has set</u> itself apart from other Russian cities with its beautiful architecture. (past)
3. As in most metropolises, things <u>cost</u> more in Moscow than in rural regions of Russia. (past participle)
4. The high prices <u>hurt</u> tourism only slightly. (present participle)
5. Despite the high cost of housing, people <u>have set</u> up homes in all parts of the city. (present)
6. The increase in population <u>has put</u> great strain on the city of Moscow. (past)
7. The population <u>spread</u> out rapidly to the surrounding regions. (present participle)
8. Many of the city's residents <u>have set</u> up new shops and businesses. (present participle)
9. Construction companies <u>have bid</u> on contracts to build new office buildings and factories in the city. (past)
10. Many Russians <u>put</u> their life savings into a new house or business in Moscow. (past participle)

More Practice

Grammar Exercise Workbook
• pp. 89–94
On-line Exercise Bank
• Section 22.1
  Go on-line:
  PHSchool.com
  Enter Web Code:
  eak-6002

Get instant feedback! Exercise 4 is available on-line or on CD-ROM.

◀ **Critical Viewing**
Red Square in Moscow, Russia, does not look very red or very square in this photograph. Imagine that you have just returned from a trip to Moscow, and write three sentences about what you saw in Red Square while you were there. [Infer]

⚙ Grammar and Style Tip

The past participle of *dream* is *dreamed* or *dreamt*. Both are correct, and both are used.

IRREGULAR VERBS THAT CHANGE IN OTHER WAYS			
Present	Present Participle	Past	Past Participle
be	(am) being	was	(have) been
begin	(am) beginning	began	(have) begun
choose	(am) choosing	chose	(have) chosen
come	(am) coming	came	(have) come
do	(am) doing	did	(have) done
draw	(am) drawing	drew	(have) drawn
drink	(am) drinking	drank	(have) drunk
drive	(am) driving	drove	(have) driven
eat	(am) eating	ate	(have) eaten
fly	(am) flying	flew	(have) flown
give	(am) giving	gave	(have) given
go	(am) going	went	(have) gone
know	(am) knowing	knew	(have) known
lie	(am) lying	lay	(have) lain
ring	(am) ringing	rang	(have) rung
rise	(am) rising	rose	(have) risen
see	(am) seeing	saw	(have) seen
sing	(am) singing	sang	(have) sung
speak	(am) speaking	spoke	(have) spoken
swim	(am) swimming	swam	(have) swum
take	(am) taking	took	(have) taken
tear	(am) tearing	tore	(have) torn
throw	(am) throwing	threw	(have) thrown
write	(am) writing	wrote	(have) written

Check a dictionary whenever you are in doubt about the correct form of an irregular verb.

Exercise 5 Revising Sentences With Other Irregular Verbs
Copy each sentence below, replacing the underlined verb with
the principal part indicated in parentheses. Refer to the chart
on the previous page if you need help.

EXAMPLE: We <u>take</u> a tour of the Kremlin. (present participle)
ANSWER: We are taking a tour of the Kremlin.

1. Many Russian novelists <u>have written</u> about their country
and its people. (past)
2. Russia <u>gave</u> the world many memorable writers. (past
participle)
3. One of the most famous Russian writers <u>was</u> Leo Tolstoy.
(present)
4. Tolstoy <u>begins</u> his career in 1852 with the autobiographical novel *Childhood*. (past)
5. We <u>choose</u> a short story to read in class. (present
participle)
6. We <u>begin</u> to study Tolstoy's life. (past participle)
7. Nearly everyone in the world <u>knew</u> Tolstoy's epic novel *War
and Peace* (1865–1869). (present)
8. My brother <u>speaks</u> to me about that book. (past participle)
9. He <u>has done</u> a college paper on *War and Peace*. (past)
10. Numerous students <u>choose</u> to study Tolstoy's novels. (past
participle)

More Practice

Grammar Exercise Workbook
• pp. 89–94
On-line Exercise Bank
• Section 22.1
Go on-line:
PHSchool.com
Enter Web Code:
eak-6002

Get instant feedback!
Exercise 5 is avail-
able on-line or on
CD-ROM.

◄ **Critical Viewing**
What details in this
photograph of Leo
Tolstoy tell you that
he lived in a different
time period? Respond
with sentences using
irregular verbs in
different tenses.
[Analyze]

Section 22.1 Section Review

GRAMMAR EXERCISES 6–12

Exercise 6 Identifying Regular and Irregular Verbs Specify whether the following verbs are *regular* or *irregular*.

1. put
2. drink
3. stop
4. inform
5. lose
6. ring
7. hurt
8. turn
9. do
10. visit

Exercise 7 Recognizing Principal Parts of Regular Verbs Identify the principal part used to form the underlined regular verb(s) in each sentence below.

1. Russians have <u>enjoyed</u> the works of many outstanding native poets.
2. In their writings, the poets <u>are expressing</u> strong emotions.
3. The writings of Aleksandr Pushkin are still <u>cherished</u> today.
4. Pushkin <u>is considered</u> by some to be Russia's greatest poet.
5. Composers <u>combined</u> their music with his dramatic poems to create operas.

Exercise 8 Recognizing Principal Parts of Regular and Irregular Verbs Identify the principal part used to form each underlined verb below. Then, specify whether the verb is *regular* or *irregular*.

1. Many outstanding composers have <u>come</u> from Russia.
2. Most music lovers <u>know</u> the works of Peter Ilich Tchaikovsky.
3. Tchaikovsky <u>created</u> many masterpieces during the nineteenth century.
4. He <u>studied</u> music in St. Petersburg.
5. People around the world are still <u>listening</u> to his music.
6. Have you ever <u>heard</u> *The Nutcracker*?
7. Tchaikovsky <u>began</u> that ballet in 1891 and <u>finished</u> it in 1892.

8. Numerous ballet companies around the world are <u>performing</u> the ballet.
9. Many music lovers have <u>flown</u> to Russia and <u>visited</u> Tchaikovsky's home.
10. They are <u>impressed</u> with his music.

Exercise 9 Revising to Eliminate Errors in Verb Usage Rewrite the following sentences, correcting all misused principal parts of verbs.

1. Russia has did much for the development of motion pictures.
2. Have you ever saw any films by the Russian director Sergei Eisenstein?
3. Eisenstein winned recognition for *The Battleship Potemkin* in 1925.
4. The film becomed an international hit.
5. Critics have gave this film much praise.

Exercise 10 Find It in Your Reading Identify the four principal parts of each underlined verb in this excerpt from Anton Chekhov's "Overdoing It."

It <u>grew</u> dark. The wagon suddenly <u>creaked</u>, <u>squeaked</u>, <u>shook</u>, and, as though against its will, <u>turned</u> left.

Exercise 11 Find It in Your Writing Look through your writing portfolio. Find examples of sentences with regular and irregular verbs. Identify which principal part of each verb you used.

Exercise 12 Writing Application On your paper, write a descriptive paragraph about a foreign city or country. Try to use all four principal parts of verbs in your sentences. Include both regular and irregular verbs.

Verb Tenses

English verbs have six basic tenses: *past, present, future, past perfect, present perfect,* and *future perfect.* The tenses are formed by using the principal parts of verbs along with helping verbs.

▶ **KEY CONCEPT** A **verb tense** tells whether the time of an action or condition is in the past, the present, or the future. ■

Using Present, Past, and Future Tenses

Refer to this chart as you learn how the six basic tenses are formed.

PRINCIPAL PARTS OF FOUR COMMON VERBS			
Base	Present Participle	Past	Past Participle
look	looking	looked	(have/had) looked
eat	eating	ate	(have/had) eaten
speak	speaking	spoke	(have/had) spoken
wait	waiting	waited	(have/had) waited

Present Tense The *present tense* shows actions that happen in the present. This tense is also used to show actions that occur regularly (every day, every week, all the time). The present tense is formed with the base form of the verb.

EXAMPLES: We *help.*
The firefighters *race* to the burning building.

When a present tense verb follows a singular noun or the pronoun *he, she,* or *it,* add *-s* or *-es* to the base of the verb.

EXAMPLES: Amelia *speaks* to the nurses.
She *hopes* to become a nurse someday.

Past Tense The *past tense* shows actions that have already happened. Regular verbs form the past tense by adding *-ed* or *-d* to the present form. Irregular verbs form the past tense in a variety of ways.

EXAMPLES: We *helped.*
The firefighters *raced* to the burning building.
Amelia *spoke* to the nurses.

Theme: Helping Jobs

In this section, you will learn to recognize and use the six tenses of verbs. The examples and exercises are about careers of people who help others.

Cross-Curricular Connection: Social Studies

Future Tense The *future tense* shows actions that will take place in the future. The future tense is formed by using the helping verb *will* with the base of the verb.

EXAMPLES: We *will help.*
              The firefighters *will race* to the burning building.
              Amelia *will speak* to the nurses.

> **Exercise 13** Identifying the Present, Past, and Future Tenses On your paper, write the tense of each underlined verb in the following sentences.

EXAMPLE: The chauffeur <u>raced</u> through the traffic.
ANSWER: past

1. Ambulances <u>bring</u> sick or injured people to hospitals.
2. The first ambulances <u>carried</u> wounded soldiers in wartime.
3. Until the twentieth century, animals <u>pulled</u> ambulances.
4. Sick or injured people usually <u>went</u> to crude hospitals.
5. Today, an engine <u>propels</u> an ambulance.
6. Paramedics <u>ride</u> in ambulances to treat the injured.
7. Fast action by paramedics <u>will save</u> many lives.
8. In the twenty-first century, engineers <u>will make</u> even better ambulances.
9. New equipment <u>offers</u> hope that more lives will be saved.
10. My brother <u>brought</u> his paramedic equipment aboard the ambulance.

> **Exercise 14** Supplying Verbs On your paper, complete each sentence with a verb from the list below. Then, indicate whether the verb is in the *present, past,* or *future tense.* Use each verb only once.

| managed | occur | will be |
| occurred | arrived | walked |

1. Accidents rarely ___?___ in my neighborhood.
2. However, one ___?___ as I ___?___ home from school yesterday.
3. The police ___?___ first and, soon afterward, a rescue helicopter.
4. The helicopter team ___?___ to get the victims to a hospital quickly.
5. The victims ___?___ grateful to the emergency workers for a long time to come.

Text
Get instant feedback! Exercises 13 and 14 are available on-line or on CD-ROM.

More Practice

Grammar Exercise Workbook
• pp. 95–96
On-line Exercise Bank
• Section 22.2
Go on-line:
PHSchool.com
Enter Web Code:
eak-6002

▼ **Critical Viewing** Describe this skateboarder's accident using past tense verbs. Describe the police officer's actions using present tense verbs. **[Analyze]**

Exercise 15 Using the Basic Forms of Verbs Rewrite each sentence below, changing the tense of the underlined verb to the one indicated in parentheses.

EXAMPLE: The nurse checks his temperature. (future)

ANSWER: The nurse will check his temperature.

1. The forest ranger gives us a tour of the state park. (past)
2. The ranger showed us many strange plants. (present)
3. She also teaches us how to recognize poison ivy. (past)
4. Touching poison ivy causes a painful rash. (future)
5. Calamine lotion will take away the itch. (past)
6. Now, we knew how to avoid poison ivy. (future)
7. The ranger carefully tears off a leaf from a tree. (past)
8. She warned us to avoid poison sumac, too. (present)
9. Forest rangers assist travelers to state parks. (future)
10. I will write her a note of thanks for her help. (past)

Using Perfect Tenses

Present Perfect Tense The *present perfect tense* shows actions that began in the past and continue to the present. It also shows actions that began in the past and ended in the past. The present perfect tense is formed by using *have* or *has* with the past participle.

EXAMPLES: We *have helped.*
Amelia *has spoken* to the nurses.

Past Perfect Tense The *past perfect tense* shows a past action or condition that ended before another past action began. The past perfect tense is formed by using *had* with the past participle.

EXAMPLES: We *had helped* her before today.
Amelia *had spoken* to the nurses. Then, she wrote her report.

▲ **Critical Viewing** Use verbs in the present perfect tense to describe what the forest ranger is doing. **[Infer]**

Future Perfect Tense The *future perfect tense* shows a future action or condition that will have ended before another begins. It uses *will have* with the past participle.

EXAMPLES: By the end of this week, we *will have helped* her five times.

Amelia *will have spoken* to the nurses before she begins her report.

> **Exercise 16** Identifying Perfect Verb Tenses Identify the perfect tense of each underlined verb in the following sentences.

EXAMPLE: My brother <u>has</u> already <u>learned</u> how to perform CPR.

ANSWER: present perfect

1. People <u>have written</u> letters for hundreds of years.
2. Postal workers <u>have delivered</u> mail for nearly as long.
3. Before the telephone was invented, people <u>had written</u> more letters to each other.
4. They <u>have had</u> few other means of communication.
5. By the late twenty-first century, people <u>will have turned</u> to other forms of communication.
6. Since last year, we <u>have</u> often <u>corresponded</u> by e-mail.
7. Nevertheless, before the year has ended, mail carriers <u>will have placed</u> millions of letters in people's mailboxes.
8. We <u>have</u> always <u>relied</u> on postal workers to handle our important correspondence.
9. They <u>have been</u> able to meet our needs.
10. <u>Had</u> you ever <u>thought</u> of becoming a postal worker before?

More Practice

Grammar Exercise Workbook
• pp. 95–98
On-line Exercise Bank
• Section 22.2
  Go on-line:
  PHSchool.com
  Enter Web Code:
  eak-6002

Get instant feedback! Exercises 15 and 16 are available on-line or on CD-ROM.

◀ **Critical Viewing** Does it appear that a mail carrier has visited these mailboxes recently? Tell why or why not, using verbs in the present and past perfect tenses in your response. [Speculate]

▶ **Exercise 17** Revising Sentences With Verb Forms
On your paper, rewrite each sentence below, changing
the tense of the underlined verb to the one indicated
in parentheses.

EXAMPLE: That lifeguard <u>rescued</u> three swimmers.
                      (present perfect)

ANSWER: That lifeguard has rescued three swimmers.

1. Firefighters <u>save</u> thousands of lives. (present perfect)
2. There <u>are</u> firefighters in the seventeenth century.
   (past)
3. Until recently, most firefighters <u>were</u> volunteers.
   (past perfect)
4. Salaried firefighters usually <u>worked</u> in large cities.
   (present perfect)
5. Until some time ago, volunteer firefighters <u>served</u>
   small communities. (past perfect)
6. Some things <u>remain</u> the same. (present perfect)
7. Before their first real fire experience, firefighters
   <u>train</u> for six months to learn firefighting and
   lifesaving techniques. (future perfect)
8. They often <u>risk</u> their lives to protect people. (future)
9. Firefighters also <u>teach</u> fire prevention methods.
   (present perfect)
10. Within just a few years, smoke alarms <u>prevent</u> thousands
    of fires and deaths. (past perfect)

▲ **Critical Viewing**
This firefighter
appears to have
been working
hard. Describe
some of his actions
in the past. **[Infer]**

GRAMMAR IN
LITERATURE

from **Count That Day Lost**
George Eliot

*Notice the highlighted verbs in this poem stanza. Present
tense verbs are highlighted in blue, past tense verbs in
green, and present perfect tense verbs in red.*

If you *sit* down at set of sun
And *count* the acts that you *have done*,
   And, counting, *find*
One self-denying deed, one word
That *eased* the heart of him who *heard*,
   One glance most kind
That *fell* like sunshine where it *went*—
Then you *may count* that day well spent.

▶ **More Practice**

**Grammar Exercise
Workbook**
• pp. 95–98
On-line Exercise Bank
• Section 22.2
  Go on-line:
  PHSchool.com
  Enter Web Code:
  eak-6002

Section 22.2 Section Review

GRAMMAR EXERCISES 18–23

Exercise 18 Recognizing Verb Tenses Write the tense of each underlined verb in the sentences below.

1. A flight attendant <u>serves</u> an important role on an airplane flight.
2. Until the 1980's, most airlines <u>had hired</u> only female flight attendants.
3. This trend <u>began</u> to change.
4. Most people <u>have welcomed</u> the change.
5. Male and female flight attendants now <u>work</u> together on many flights.
6. They <u>will help</u> you during a flight.
7. They <u>have made</u> flying safer and more comfortable for passengers.
8. Before the plane <u>takes</u> off, flight attendants <u>will present</u> safety instructions.
9. By the time they <u>have worked</u> for several years, flight attendants <u>will have repeated</u> the instructions many times.
10. By the end of your ride, a flight attendant <u>will have worked</u> hard to assure that your trip <u>has been</u> pleasant.

Exercise 19 Forming Verb Tenses Write the tense indicated for each verb below.

1. go (present)
2. hurt (past)
3. become (future perfect)
4. take (past perfect)
5. teach (future)

Exercise 20 Recognizing Correct Verb Forms Choose the correct verb from each pair in parentheses below. Then, identify the tense of the verb or verb phrase.

1. In the past, many accident victims had (suffer, suffered) because they could not receive medical care in time.
2. The modern EMT, or emergency medical technician, has (did, done) much to change that situation.
3. An EMT has (chose, chosen) to work in emergency situations.
4. EMTs will (arrived, arrive) at the scene of an accident and know exactly what to do.
5. During training, EMTs will have (went, gone) over many first-aid techniques.
6. They will have (became, become) familiar with emergencies by practicing on volunteers and specialized dummies.
7. Hospitals have (put, putted) a lot of responsibility on EMTs.
8. During one recent year, EMTs (gave, gived) emergency medical care to more than 25,000 people in our city.
9. Often, EMTs will (begin, began) treating victims on the way to the hospital.
10. Some EMTs have even (flew, flown) by helicopter to help injured people.

Exercise 21 Find It in Your Reading On your paper, rewrite the first four lines of the stanza from "Count That Day Lost" on page 492. Change each present tense verb to past tense and each present perfect tense verb to past perfect.

Exercise 22 Find It in Your Writing Look through your writing portfolio. Find examples of sentences with verbs in different tenses. Circle each verb or verb phrase, and identify its tense.

Exercise 23 Writing Application Imagine that you are a medical doctor at a busy hospital. On your paper, write five sentences describing a case you had recently. Use the verbs listed below.

1. past perfect of *catch*
2. past of *become*
3. present perfect of *have*
4. future of *be*
5. future perfect of *receive*

Troublesome Verbs

Using *Did* and *Done*

Did and *done* are both forms of the frequently used verb *do*.

> **KEY CONCEPT** *Did* is the past form of *do*. It is used without a helping verb for actions that began and ended in the past. ∎

EXAMPLE: She *did* the drawing of Tom Sawyer, and I *did* the painting of Huck Finn.

> **KEY CONCEPT** *Done* is the past participle of *do*. It is always used with a helping verb, such as *have* or *has*. ∎

EXAMPLES: We *have done* all the research for Mark Twain's biography.
Dylan *has done* all of the illustrations for this book.

The following chart shows the conjugation of two of the tenses of *do:*

| CONJUGATION OF TWO TENSES OF *DO* ||
Past Tense	Present Perfect Tense
I did	I have done
you did	you have done
he, she, it did	he, she, it has done
we did	we have done
you did	you have done
they did	they have done

If a sentence contains the past participle *done* without a helping verb, it is incorrect. To correct it, add a helping verb or change *done* to *did*.

INCORRECT: We *done* the assignment.
CORRECT: We *have done* the assignment.
We *did* the assignment.

Theme: Mark Twain's Mississippi

In this section, you will learn the correct uses of several verbs that sometimes give people trouble. The examples and exercises are about the author Mark Twain and the Mississippi River he loved.

Cross-Curricular Connection: Social Studies

More Practice

Grammar Exercise Workbook
• pp. 101–102
On-line Exercise Bank
• Section 22.3
Go on-line:
PHSchool.com
Enter Web Code:
eak-6002

Get instant feedback! Exercises 24 and 25 are available on-line or on CD-ROM.

> **Exercise 24** Using *Did* and *Done* On your paper, write the
correct verb from the choices in parentheses.

EXAMPLE: We have (did, done) a biography of Mark
            Twain.

ANSWER: done

1. Mark Twain was once asked to name his
   favorite job of all of those he had (did, done).
2. He said he most enjoyed the work he (did,
   done) as a riverboat pilot on the Mississippi
   River.
3. However, he is best known for what he (did,
   done) as a writer.
4. His stories (did, done) much to make him rich
   and famous.
5. People have (did, done) many studies of
   Mark Twain's work.
6. Thanks to this research, we have a better
   appreciation of what Mark Twain (did, done) in
   the nineteenth century.
7. Not many people knew what Twain had
   (did, done) before he became a famous
   writer.
8. Before his writing career, he (did, done)
   many odd jobs.
9. Piloting a riverboat was just one job he
   had (did, done).
10. He also (did, done) stints as a printer
    and prospector.

> **Exercise 25** Supplying the Correct Principal Part of *Do*
Rewrite the following sentences on your paper, filling in the
blank with the correct form of the verb *do*.

EXAMPLE: They have ___?___ what we asked them to do.
ANSWER: done

1. Our class is ___?___ oral reports on Mark Twain.
2. I am going to tell what Twain ___?___ as a riverboat pilot
   on the Mississippi River.
3. I have ___?___ most of my research.
4. Twain's work on the Mississippi was ___?___ before the
   Civil War began.
5. Many of the things Twain ___?___ on the Mississippi are
   described in his novels and stories.

▲ **Critical Viewing**
Write three sen-
tences about some
things you know
Mark Twain did.
Use the verb *do* in
your sentences.
[Connect]

Troublesome Verbs • **495**

Using *Lay* and *Lie*

Lay and *lie* are two different verbs with different meanings.

▶ **KEY CONCEPT** *Lay* means "to put or place something." ■

PRINCIPAL PARTS OF *LAY*			
Present	**Present Participle**	**Past**	**Past Participle**
lay	(am) laying	laid	(have) laid

When the verb *lay* is used in a sentence, it takes a direct object.

EXAMPLES: Sue usually *lays* her bags in the hallway.
$\qquad\qquad$ (DO above *her bags*)

The workers *are laying* the foundation for the house.
$\qquad\qquad$ (DO above *foundation*)

The captain *laid* the navigation map on the table.
$\qquad\qquad$ (DO above *map*)

I *have laid* my glasses on the desk.
$\qquad\qquad$ (DO above *glasses*)

▶ **KEY CONCEPT** *Lie* means "to rest in a reclining position." Another meaning for *lie* is "to be situated." ■

PRINCIPAL PARTS OF *LIE*			
Present	**Present Participle**	**Past**	**Past Participle**
lie	(am) lying	lay	(have) lain

Lie does not take a direct object. It can, however, be followed by an adverb or a prepositional phrase.

EXAMPLES: The city *lies* at the mouth of the Mississippi River.
Your atlas *is lying* on my desk.
I *lay* down on the raft and fell asleep.
This Mark Twain novel *has lain* in the attic for years.

Exercise 26 Using the Correct Form of *Lay* or *Lie*

On your paper, write the correct verb from the choices in parentheses.

EXAMPLE: The riverboat captain is
             (lying, laying) in his cabin.

ANSWER: lying

1. Mississippi (lies, lays) west of Alabama.
2. The beauty of Mississippi has (laid, lain) in its rivers and meadows.
3. Following the hurricane, many tree branches (lay, laid) along the shore of the Gulf of Mexico.
4. Some Mississippi families have (laid, lain) plans for new homes along the state's many rivers.
5. For years, many Mississippians have (laid, lain) under magnolia trees on warm spring days.
6. Jackson, the capital of Mississippi, (lies, lays) on the Pearl River in southwest central Mississippi.
7. Jackson's planners (lay, laid) the city out on the site of an old trading post.
8. The Mississippi River (lies, lays) at the western border of Mississippi.
9. Many residents of Mississippi have (laid, lain) their roots within the state.
10. At this very moment, people are (laying, lying) the foundations for new homes and businesses throughout the state.

▲ **Critical Viewing** Using *lie* or *lay* correctly in a sentence, tell what might be around the bend of the river in this photograph of a riverboat. **[Speculate]**

Exercise 27 Proofreading for Errors With *Lay* and *Lie*

Read the following sentences. If the verb form is correct, write *correct*. If it is incorrect, rewrite the sentence with the correct form.

1. Mark Twain lain type before writing books.
2. The joy of childhood lays at the heart of many of Mark Twain's books.
3. His characters often spend days lying on the banks of the Mississippi River.
4. You may enjoy his books while laying in a quiet place.
5. He laid to rest his dreams of gold.
6. Small towns that laid throughout the West were depicted in Twain's books.
7. Before that time, Twain lay his stories of the West aside while he prospected for gold.
8. His humor lays at the heart of every story.
9. It is clear to modern readers that important messages are lying in his stories.
10. Yesterday, I lay my copy of *Tom Sawyer* on the table, but someone must have borrowed it.

More Practice

Grammar Exercise Workbook
• pp. 103–104
On-line Exercise Bank
• Section 22.3
Go on-line:
PHSchool.com
Enter Web Code:
eak-6002

Get instant feedback! Exercises 26 and 27 are available on-line or on CD-ROM.

Troublesome Verbs • **497**

Using *Set* and *Sit*

Set and *sit* look and sound similar, but their meanings are different.

► **KEY CONCEPT** *Set* means "to put something in a certain place." ■

PRINCIPAL PARTS OF *SET*			
Present	Present Participle	Past	Past Participle
set	(am) setting	set	(have) set

Set is followed by a direct object.

EXAMPLES: DO
           I *set* the book on top of the shelves.

                             DO
           Our class *is setting* all our poems in notebooks.

                   DO
           The boys *set* the raft afloat.

                         DO
           Mark Twain *had set* this novel in Europe.

► **KEY CONCEPT** *Sit* means "to be seated" or "to rest." ■

PRINCIPAL PARTS OF *SIT*			
Present	Present Participle	Past	Past Participle
sit	(am) sitting	sat	(have) sat

Sit does not take a direct object. Instead, it is often followed by an adverb or a prepositional phrase, as in the following sentences.

EXAMPLES: We *sit* at tables in our English class.
              Paul *is sitting* with Tim and Jackie.
              Carmen and Claudia *sat* quietly in the library.
              We *have sat* here for more than three hours.

> ▶ **Exercise 28** Using *Set* and *Sit* In the sentences below, choose the correct verb from the pair in parentheses.

EXAMPLE: Felicia usually (sits, sets) in the first row.
ANSWER: sits

1. I am (sitting, setting) here reading a story by Mark Twain.
2. Soon, I must (set, sit) the book down and do my other homework.
3. Believe it or not, this book (set, sat) in the library for two years before anyone checked it out.
4. I would love to (sit, set) a place at our dinner table for Mark Twain.
5. I could (set, sit) for hours and listen to him talk.
6. Until Mark Twain came along, most American writers had (sat, set) their stories in New England or other eastern states.
7. Unlike them, Twain (sat, set) many of his stories in small towns along the Mississippi River.
8. My small town (sits, sets) in the center of our state.
9. If you wanted, you could probably (sit, set) many of the characters in Twain's stories right in my town.
10. If you had (set, sat) down near Main Street in our town in 1870, you would have met similar people.

▼ **Critical Viewing**
Using *set* or *sat* correctly in a sentence, describe what the frog in this picture is doing. **[Describe]**

> ▶ **Exercise 29** Supplying Forms of *Set* or *Sit* in Sentences

Rewrite the following sentences on your paper, filling in each blank with the proper form of *set* or *sit*.

1. Twain's books have ___?___ a high standard for American literature.
2. Thousands of people are ___?___ and reading these American classics every day.
3. Twain's many novels have ___?___ prominently on library shelves all over the world.
4. Twain ___?___ humor and satire into his stories.
5. Almost everyone who has ___?___ down to read one of his novels has started to laugh.
6. Twain ___?___ *The Adventures of Huckleberry Finn* (1884) along the Mississippi River.
7. During much of the novel, Huck and Jim ___?___ on a raft and discuss life.
8. In the daytime, they ___?___ the raft near the shore and hide from slave catchers.
9. They must ___?___ quietly so that Jim will not be caught.
10. Where should I ___?___ this biography of Mark Twain that I checked out of the library?

▶ **More Practice**

Grammar Exercise Workbook
• pp. 105–106
On-line Exercise Bank
• Section 22.3
Go on-line:
PHSchool.com
Enter Web Code:
eak-6002

Get instant feedback! Exercises 28 and 29 are available on-line or on CD-ROM.

Chapter Review

GRAMMAR EXERCISES 36–44

▶ **Exercise 36** Classifying Regular
and Irregular Verbs List the verbs
below on your paper. Then, label each verb
regular or *irregular*.

1. want
2. travel
3. read
4. lie
5. describe
6. think
7. write
8. begin
9. replace
10. sail

▶ **Exercise 37** Identifying Principal
Parts of Regular and Irregular Verbs
On your paper, write the principal part
used to form each underlined verb below.

1. Mark Twain <u>is</u> only one famous person
from Missouri.
2. President Harry Truman <u>grew</u> up there.
3. He <u>became</u> president in 1945, after
Franklin Roosevelt had <u>died</u>.
4. Inventor George Washington Carver
also <u>spent</u> his early years in Missouri.
5. His parents had <u>been</u> slaves.

▶ **Exercise 38** Supplying the
Correct Verb Form Revise the following
passage by writing the correct form of each
underlined verb. If the correct form of the
verb has been used, write *correct* on your
paper.

The first Europeans <u>arrive</u> in Missouri in
the late 1600's. In 1673 two French explorers, Marquette and Joliet, had <u>travel</u> down
the Mississippi River. They had <u>came</u> to
where the Mississippi and Missouri rivers
met. They <u>drawed</u> a map of the area. Soon,
other French explorers and trappers <u>begin</u>
arriving in the area. They <u>give</u> the area the
name *Missouri*, after a Native American word
that means "canoe owner." In 1764, the city
of St. Louis was <u>established</u> there. When

Thomas Jefferson <u>maked</u> the Louisiana
Purchase in 1803, Missouri was included in
the purchase. Jefferson had <u>buyed</u> millions
of acres of new territory for the United
States. In 1821, Missouri <u>become</u> the
twenty-fourth state to join the Union.

▶ **Exercise 39** Classifying Verb
Tenses On your paper, write the tense
of each underlined verb in the following
sentences.

1. Many people <u>have dreamed</u> of traveling
down a river on a makeshift raft.
2. In the 1800's, steamboats <u>ferried</u> people up and down American rivers.
3. People <u>flocked</u> to the Mississippi River
to ride on steamboats.
4. Many steamboats <u>had</u> luxurious cab-
ins and dining halls.
5. Until the early 1900's, steamboats <u>had
dominated</u> transportation along the
nation's rivers.
6. Today, people <u>travel</u> mostly on airplanes and in automobiles.
7. For the most part, that era of steamboat travel <u>has come</u> to an end.
8. Improvements in transportation and
highways <u>have pushed</u> steamboats out
of existence.
9. Transportation <u>will improve</u> even more
in the near future.
10. By the next century, most people <u>will
have forgotten</u> what it was like to travel
on a steamboat.

▶ **Exercise 40** Supplying the
Correct Verb Form On your paper,
rewrite the following sentences, replacing
the underlined verb with the tense indicated in parentheses.

1. Mark Twain's stories <u>inspire</u> many

readers and writers. (present perfect)

2. This <u>be</u> true even when Mark Twain was alive. (past)

3. By the early 1900's, thousands of Twain's fans <u>see</u> the Mississippi River for themselves. (past perfect)

4. Many admirers of Mark Twain's stories <u>make</u> trips to towns along the Mississippi River. (past perfect)

5. Many <u>do</u> so to see the places that inspired Twain. (past)

6. They <u>continue</u> to do so in the future. (future)

7. Missouri always <u>welcomes</u> its visitors warmly. (present perfect)

8. For many years, cities and towns throughout Missouri <u>hold</u> festivals for visitors. (present perfect)

9. By the end of each year, thousands of visitors <u>take</u> part in these festivals. (future perfect)

10. By the end of next year, even more Mark Twain fans <u>set</u> off on journeys along the Mississippi. (future perfect)

▶ **Exercise 41** **Revising Sentences With Troublesome Verbs** Rewrite the following sentences, correcting the verbs. If a sentence is correct, write *correct*.

1. When the first French explorers came to Missouri, they did not know what riches laid beneath the soil.

2. A rich deposit of lead had lain in Missouri's hills for thousands of years.

3. In the 1770's, adventurous people who were setting in their homes in the East heard about the lead deposits.

4. Many sat all of their belongings into wagons and proceeded west.

5. Some who had done poorly in other parts of the country done quite well for themselves in Missouri.

▶ **Exercise 42** **Revising a Paragraph to Eliminate Errors in Verb Usage** Rewrite the following paragraph, correcting all errors in verb usage.

The Mississippi River has play a key role in United States history. Today, many important cities lay along the river. New Orleans, Memphis, St. Louis, and Minneapolis are just a few of the cities that set along the river's banks. During the 1600's, the Mississippi becomed a vital transportation route for trappers. They sat furs upon rafts and ship them up or down the river. Later, settlers move into these areas. Steamboats make the river an even more important trade route. You may have thunk the Mississippi was a southern river. However, it actually begun in Minnesota and flows southward. If you travel down the entire river, you will have went 2,340 miles.

▶ **Exercise 43** **Writing Sentences With Different Verb Tenses** On your paper, write a sentence using each verb below in the tense specified.

1. notice (present perfect)
2. bring (past)
3. create (past perfect)
4. write (future perfect)
5. begin (past)
6. remember (future)
7. continue (present)
8. get (present perfect)
9. remark (present perfect)
10. set (past perfect)

▶ **Exercise 44** **Writing Application** Write a description of an interesting trip you have taken. Use both regular and irregular verbs in different tenses. Circle the verbs you use. Use each of the following verbs at least once.

1. did
2. set
3. had sat
4. lay
5. had lain

Standardized Test Preparation Workshop

Standard English Usage: Verb Tenses

Your knowledge of verb usage is frequently measured on standardized tests. Your ability to determine the correct tense of a verb—present, present perfect, past, past perfect, future, and future perfect—is tested when you must choose a verb or verb phrase to complete a sentence. When choosing a verb, first read the sentence to yourself and determine when the action is taking place. Then, choose a verb in the tense that indicates the time of the action.

The following sample test items will give you practice with the format of questions that test verb usage.

Test Tip

Read the sentence to yourself several times, substituting each answer choice in place of the blank. Eliminate those choices that sound awkward or change the meaning of the sentence.

Sample Test Items

	Answers and Explanations
Directions Read the passage, and choose the letter of the word or group of words that belongs in each space. Dinosaurs ____(1)____ in an Earth much different from today. In this chapter, you ____(2)____ about the major differences.	

1 A live
  B are living
  C lived
  D had lived
	The correct answer is C. The passage indicates an action that took place in the past. Therefore, the past tense verb form *lived* is the correct choice for completing the sentence.

2 F have learned
  G is learning
  H are learning
  J will learn
	The correct answer is J. The passage indicates an action that will occur in the future. Therefore, the future tense verb *will appear* is the correct choice for completing the sentence.

Practice 1 **Directions:** Read the passage, and choose the letter of the word or group of words that belongs in each space.

Many scientists _____(1)_____ that present-day continents were once a single land mass. During the Mesozoic Era, the continents slowly _____(2)_____ apart. Before this occurred, dinosaurs _____(3)_____ over land connections between the continents. As the continents drifted apart, however, their climates _____(4)_____ more and more. One theory to explain the disappearance of dinosaurs _____(5)_____ this change in climate.

1 A have believed
   B are believing
   C believed
   D believe

2 F is drifting
   G drifted
   H have drifted
   J drift

3 A had wandered
   B wander
   C has wandered
   D are wandering

4 F changed
   G are changing
   H was changing
   J will change

5 A concerns
   B concern
   C concerned
   D was concerned

Practice 2 **Directions:** Read the passage, and choose the letter of the word or group of words that belongs in each space.

Today, in science class, we _____(1)_____ the theories as to why dinosaurs died out. Many scientists _____(2)_____ their theories on a change in climate—from tropical to cold. Other experts believe that plant-eating dinosaurs _____(3)_____ the new plants that developed and starved. Another theory _____(4)_____ that a large asteroid _____(5)_____ into Earth, thus creating billions of tons of dust that blocked out the sun for three to six months.

1 A was investigating
   B are investigating
   C investigate
   D investigated

2 F had based
   G will base
   H base
   J were basing

3 A ate
   B are not eating
   C could not eat
   D cannot have eaten

4 F are suggesting
   G had suggested
   H suggests
   J will suggest

5 A crash
   B are crashing
   C were crashing
   D crashed

Personal pronouns have different forms, such as *he, his,* and *him,* that tell how the pronouns are being used. Personal pronouns can be subjects *(he)*, objects *(him)*, or words showing ownership *(his)*.

You must use different forms of pronouns to make your ideas clear. For instance, without pronouns you might write *Jack caught the football. Jack then ran Jack's fastest to score a touchdown.* Using the correct forms of pronouns, however, you can write this:

Jack caught the football. He then ran his fastest to score a touchdown.

This chapter will tell you more about the three types of personal pronouns. Each type does a different job when used in a sentence. In this chapter, you will learn about each type. Then, you will practice using the pronouns correctly.

▲ **Critical Viewing**
What are the football players and fans doing or about to do? Use the pronouns *they* and *them* in your answer.
[Infer]

Diagnostic Test

Directions: Write all answers on a separate piece of paper.

Skill Check A. Write the correct subject pronoun from the choices in parentheses.

1. The coach and (they, them) decided on the play.
2. The quarterback and (he, him) discussed several options.
3. Either the fullback or (I, me) will run with the ball.
4. (He, Him) and the other linemen will block for us.
5. The fans and (we, us) will hope for a touchdown.

Skill Check B. Select the correct objective pronoun from the pair in parentheses, and tell whether it functions as a *direct object*, an *indirect object*, or an *object of a preposition*.

6. Knute Rockne taught (we, us) many lessons about the game of football.
7. His innovations to the game made (it, its) much more exciting.
8. The forward pass was pioneered by Charles Dorais and (he, him).
9. Football fans regard (they, them) as legends.
10. Rockne's determination inspires my friends and (me, I).

Skill Check C. Select the correct possessive pronoun from the choices in parentheses.

11. Are these tickets to the baseball game (yours, your's)?
12. These seats are (ours, ours').
13. (Hers, Hers') are the ones near first base.
14. Our team is in first place in (it's, its) league.
15. Our second baseman and shortstop are known for (their, there) speed.

Skill Check D. Label each underlined pronoun *nominative*, *objective*, or *possessive*.

16. During the 1950s, the city of Cleveland had <u>its</u> sports hero.
17. Running back Jim Brown was terrific, in <u>our</u> opinion.
18. Opposing players could not stop <u>him</u> from advancing.
19. Brown managed to run past <u>them</u> or through <u>them</u>.
20. <u>He</u> scored 126 touchdowns during <u>his</u> career.

Skill Check E. Select the correct pronoun from the choices in parentheses.

21. Bill Russell is (her, hers) choice for the most valuable professional basketball player ever.
22. The tall, thin center changed how (his', his) position was played.
23. Opponents feared (him, he) and the other players on his team.
24. During his career, (he, him) and his teammates won eleven league titles.
25. (He, him) gave my friends and (I, me) many exciting moments during (he, his) career.

Using Subject Pronouns

Pronouns have different forms to show how they are being used.

▶ **KEY CONCEPT** A *subject pronoun* is used as the subject of a sentence. ■

SUBJECT PRONOUNS	
Singular	Plural
I, you, he, she, it	we, you, they

When a sentence has a single subject, it is easy to select the correct subject pronoun. However, when a sentence has a compound subject, it is more difficult to choose the right pronoun.

EXAMPLES: Fred and *I* [not *me*] agreed to block for Matthew.
The coach and *he* [not *him*] led the parade.

To choose the correct pronoun when the subject is a compound, say the sentence to yourself with only the pronoun as the subject. Omit the other words in the subject. Say the sentence with each pronoun you think might be correct. Choose the one pronoun that sounds correct.

EXAMPLE: Ken and (I, me) organized the pep rally.

Omit the words *Ken and.* Try each of the pronouns with the rest of the sentence. "*Me* organized the pep rally" does not sound correct. "*I* organized the pep rally" does.

▶ **Exercise 1** Identifying the Correct Subject Pronoun On your paper, write the correct subject pronoun from the choices in parentheses.

EXAMPLE: My friends and (I, me) like football.
ANSWER: I

1. The kids down the street and (us, we) often play football.
2. Our team members and (them, they) are the same age.
3. Derrick and (her, she) will be the team captains.
4. Franklin and (him, he) brought their footballs.
5. Julie and (I, me) run faster than anyone else.
6. Terry or (her, she) will receive the kickoff.
7. Bill and (he, him) blocked our opponents.
8. Robert and (she, her) tackled him.
9. John and (I, me) scored a touchdown.
10. (Him, He) and (I, me) celebrated.

Theme: Team Sports
In this chapter, you will learn how to use three different forms of pronouns. The examples and exercises are about team sports and famous players.
Cross-Curricular Connection: Physical Education

More Practice

Grammar Exercise Workbook
• pp. 107–108
On-line Exercise Bank
• Chapter 23
Go on-line:
PHSchool.com
Enter Web Code:
eak-6002

Get instant feedback! Exercises 1 and 2 are available on-line or on CD-ROM.

Using Objective Pronouns

The objective pronouns are *me, you, him, her, it, us, you* (plural), and *them.*

KEY CONCEPT *Objective pronouns* are used as (1) direct objects, (2) indirect objects, and (3) objects of prepositions. ■

Direct Object An objective pronoun used as a direct object appears with an action verb and answers the question *Whom?* or *What?*

EXAMPLE: The referee penalized *her.*

Indirect Object An objective pronoun used as an indirect object appears with an action verb and a direct object. It answers the question *To or for whom?* or *To or for what?*

EXAMPLE: My friend gave *me* highlights of the game.

Object of a Preposition An objective pronoun can also be the object of a preposition.

EXAMPLE: Our team captain voted for *him.*

Sometimes, objective pronouns are part of a compound object. To determine the correct pronoun, use the pronoun by itself without the rest of the compound.

EXAMPLE: The player asked the coach and (he, him) for help.

▼ Critical Viewing
Why might these fans be shouting? Use at least one objective pronoun in your response.
[Speculate]

First, try the pronoun *he* without the words *the coach and.* "The player asked *he* for help" does not sound right. Now, try the pronoun *him.* "The player asked *him* for help" does sound right.

Exercise 2 Identifying Objective Pronouns Choose the correct pronoun(s). Then, tell how each pronoun is being used.

EXAMPLE: The two teams gave (we, us) a great game.
ANSWER: us (indirect object)

1. Tim invited (I, me) to a soccer game.
2. Just above (he and I, him and me) were some rowdy fans.
3. Zoe visited (we, us) before the game started.
4. She brought Tim and (I, me) a game program.
5. Between you and (I, me), it was a fantastic day.

More Practice

Grammar Exercise Workbook
• pp. 109–110
On-line Exercise Bank
• Chapter 23
Go on-line:
PHSchool.com
Enter Web Code:
eak-6002

Using Possessive Pronouns

Possessive pronouns have a special job in sentences.

▶ **KEY CONCEPT** Use the *possessive* forms of personal pronouns to show ownership. ■

Some possessive pronouns come before nouns.

EXAMPLES: I left *my* sneakers at home.
Their team is in first place.

Other possessive pronouns are used by themselves to show ownership. These pronouns do not come before nouns.

EXAMPLES: These sneakers are *mine.*
The trophy will be *theirs.*

Never use an apostrophe when writing a possessive pronoun.

POSSESSIVE PRONOUNS			
Used Before Nouns		**Used by Themselves**	
my	its	mine	its
your	our	yours	ours
his	their	his	theirs
her		hers	

INCORRECT: *Their's* is the best infield in the league.

CORRECT: *Theirs* is the best infield in the league.

INCORRECT: The baseball mitt lying on the chair is *her's.*

CORRECT: The baseball mitt lying on the chair is *hers.*

A common error with possessive pronouns is to use an apostrophe after *it.* The possessive form of *it* is *its. It's* is a contraction that means "it is."

CONTRACTION: I know *it's* an important game, so don't be late.

POSSESSIVE PRONOUN: Be sure to hold the bat with *its* label toward you.

Spelling Tip

Don't confuse the spelling of the possessive pronoun *their* with the adverb *there.* Also, avoid confusing the possessive pronouns *their* and *theirs* with the contractions *they're* (*they are*) and *there's* (*there is*).

▼ **Critical Viewing** How would you personalize a piece of sports equipment, such as a baseball mitt, a hockey stick, or a tennis racquet? Answer using at least one possessive pronoun. **[Connect]**

▶ **Exercise 3** Using Possessive Pronouns Supply a possessive pronoun to fill in each blank correctly.

EXAMPLE: From what I know of Canadian fans, hockey is
                  ___?___ favorite sport.

ANSWER: From what I know of Canadian fans, hockey is
                  their favorite sport.

1. Wayne Gretzky was one of the greatest hockey players of
   ___?___ time.
2. I have several posters of Gretzky on ___?___ wall.
3. I even had a poster with ___?___ autograph.
4. That one is missing from ___?___ frame.
5. If you find it, remember that it is ___?___ and not ___?___.

Using Different Pronoun Cases

The different forms of subject pronouns, objective pronouns, and possessive pronouns are called *cases*. Each case has different uses.

▶ **KEY CONCEPT** Use the *cases* of pronouns correctly. ■

Subject pronouns, which are said to be in the *nominative case*, are used as *subjects* and *predicate pronouns*. Predicate pronouns generally appear after some form of the linking verb *be*. They help identify the subjects of sentences.

PREDICATE
PRONOUNS: The *centers* in the face-off circle are Sue and *she*.

                  The *hero* was *I*.

The chart below summarizes what you have learned so far.

THE THREE CASES OF PERSONAL PRONOUNS AND THEIR USES		
Cases	Pronoun Forms	Uses
Nominative	I, you, he, she, it we, you, they	Subject of a Verb Predicate Pronoun
Objective	me, you, him, her, it us, you, them	Direct Object Indirect Object Object of a Preposition
Possessive	my, mine, you, yours, his, her, hers, its, our, ours, your, yours, their, theirs	To Show Ownership

More Practice

Grammar Exercise Workbook
• pp. 111–112
On-line Exercise Bank
• Chapter 23
  Go on-line:
  PHSchool.com
  Enter Web Code:
  eak-6002

Complete the exercise on-line! Exercise 3 is available on-line or on CD-ROM.

23

GRAMMAR IN
LITERATURE

from **The Shutout**
Patricia C. McKissack and Frederick McKissack, Jr.

In this passage, the pronoun it, *in blue italics, is used as the subject of a clause. The objective pronoun* them, *in red italics, is used as the object of the preposition* of.

The history of baseball is difficult to trace because *it* is embroidered with wonderful anecdotes that are fun but not necessarily supported by fact. There are a lot of myths that persist about baseball—the games, the players, the owners, and the fans—in spite of contemporary research that disproves most of *them.*

More Practice

Grammar Exercise Workbook
• pp. 113–114
On-line Exercise Bank
• Chapter 23
Go on-line:
PHSchool.com
Enter Web Code:
eak-6002

⟩Text⟩

Get instant feedback! Exercise 4 is available on-line or on CD-ROM.

▼ **Critical Viewing** Compare your view from this place in the stands to that of a friend sitting closer to the field. Use possessive pronouns such as *my, our, his, her,* and *their.* [**Compare and Contrast**]

▶ **Exercise 4** **Revising to Correct Pronoun Errors** Revise the following paragraph, correcting the pronouns as necessary. (Not every sentence contains an error.)

Its a fact that Sam Jethroe was one of the fastest men ever to play baseball. However, many baseball fans have never heard of his. My aunt, who loves baseball history, gave my sister and I all the facts about Jethroe. Her friends and her spend a lot of time discussing baseball. Jethroe spent most of his career in the Negro Leagues. He was its leader in batting and base stealing. In 1945, Jackie Robinson and him tried out for a major league team. Despite there talent, the team rejected them. In 1950, Jethroe finally joined a National League team and quickly showed his' skills. As he stole base after base, fans raised they're voices in cheers. Them and the sports writers were impressed by him. My aunt, my sister, and me are very impressed too!

Hands-on Grammar

Nominative and Objective Pronoun People

Use Pronoun People to help you practice the nominative and objective case pronouns. First, cut out your people from construction paper—four single people and three groups of two or three people. Starting with each of the single people, label one side with a nominative pronoun: *I, you, he,* or *she.* On the other side, write the corresponding objective pronoun: *me, you, him, her.* Then, label one side of each group of people *we, you (pl.),* or *they;* label the other side *us, you (pl.),* or *them.* Now, each person or group is labeled with a nominative pronoun on one side and its corresponding objective form on the other.

Next, with a partner, take turns moving and flipping your Pronoun People as you use them in sentences. Build your sentences from the following sentence parts:

- *sat next to*
- *walked between*
- *The next in line is/are*
- *invited*
- *gave some pizza*

Write each sentence as you create it. One partner may not duplicate the other's sentences. Check each other's work to make sure you have used your Pronoun People correctly. When you have finished, you should have used all your people as subjects, predicate pronouns, direct and indirect objects, and objects of prepositions. (See illustration.)

Find It in Your Reading Read an advice column in a newspaper or a magazine. Note the number of pronouns in each of the three cases.

Find It in Your Writing Review a piece of personal writing, and check to make sure that you have used all personal pronouns correctly. Correct those that are in the wrong case.

Chapter Review

GRAMMAR EXERCISES 5–13

▶ **Exercise 5** Identifying Personal Pronouns and Case On your paper, list the personal pronouns in the sentences below. Label each pronoun *nominative*, *objective*, or *possessive*.

1. Have you ever seen a rugby match?
2. It is a sport that requires strength and speed.
3. Two teams try to kick, pass, or carry a ball across their opponent's goal.
4. Players often run into each other as they attempt to advance the ball.
5. They try to tackle their opponents and steal the ball from them.
6. However, you are not allowed to tackle someone if he doesn't have the ball.
7. If you cross the goal line and throw the ball down, your team gets four points.
8. Then, you can place-kick or drop-kick the ball to score two more points.
9. My brother and his friend play on a rugby team.
10. His friend and he have been playing rugby for two years.
11. My mom and I often go to his games.
12. We cheer loudly for him.
13. Today, he looked up and gave us a smile.
14. Then, he turned and grabbed an opponent by his legs.
15. Both of them tumbled to the ground.

▶ **Exercise 6** Revising to Correct Pronoun Errors Revise each of the sentences below, correcting all pronoun errors. If a sentence contains no error, write *correct*.

1. My brother and me read about the history of rugby.
2. Legend says it got it's start at Rugby School in England in 1823.
3. Two teams of students were playing soccer on there school field.
4. One boy picked up the ball and ran with it in his' hands.
5. The opposing team chased after him.
6. Them and his own teammates told him he was breaking the rules.
7. They're warnings didn't bother him.
8. Soon, him and the other boys developed rules for a new game.
9. There new game caught on at other British schools, too.
10. Watching rugby is a lot of fun for my friends and me.

▶ **Exercise 7** Determining the Use of Nominative Pronouns On your paper, identify whether the underlined pronoun is being used as the *subject* of a verb or as a *predicate pronoun*.

1. <u>We</u> often play basketball in gym class.
2. The best shooter in the class is <u>he</u>.
3. Today, <u>he</u> made ten shots in a row.
4. Our teacher was impressed, and <u>she</u> said so.
5. The first players chosen were Jim and <u>I</u>.
6. Sara's next picks were Alan and <u>she</u>.
7. <u>We</u> scored the first six points.
8. Then, <u>they</u> scored the next eight.
9. In the end, the winners were <u>we</u>.
10. Talia hopes that <u>she</u> will play better.

▶ **Exercise 8** Determining the Use of Objective Pronouns On your paper, identify how the underlined objective pronoun is used in each sentence below.

1. The coach showed Eric and <u>them</u> the new play.
2. He worked with <u>us</u> for two hours.
3. The assistant coach encouraged <u>me</u> from the sidelines.
4. She also applauded for Andy and <u>him</u>.

5. Darryl handed <u>her</u> the damaged ball.
6. She threw a new ball to <u>him</u>.
7. The coach instructed Todd and <u>me</u>.
8. The team manager handed Billy and <u>them</u> cups of water.
9. They were grateful to <u>her</u> for the refreshing drinks.
10. The coach rewarded <u>us</u> for our hard work.

Exercise 9 Revising to Correct
Possessive Pronouns Revise the following sentences, correcting possessive pronouns as necessary.

1. The quarterback called his' team into the huddle.
2. The players gathered together to hear there leader's plan.
3. He called a favorite play of there's.
4. The outcome of the game depended on it's success.
5. Fortunately, the element of surprise was our's.

Exercise 10 Supplying Possessive
Pronouns Supply a possessive pronoun to fill in each blank logically.

1. Aunt Pat was on the edge of ___?___ seat.
2. ___?___ whole family was glued to the television screen.
3. My cousin Sean was playing in ___?___ first televised game.
4. ___?___ parents cheered excitedly.
5. The loudest cheers were ___?___.

Exercise 11 Revising Incorrect
Pronoun Usage Rewrite each sentence below, correcting any pronoun errors. If there is no pronoun error, write *correct*.

1. Em's best sport is soccer; my is volleyball.
2. Tim and her are playing on my team.
3. Tim returns almost every shot that is hit toward he.

4. Its not often that he misses the ball.
5. The first player chosen is usually he.
6. When the ball was hit between Connie and I, I got to it first.
7. I lifted the ball up, and she smacked it over the net.
8. The ball sailed untouched on it's flight.
9. The point was our's.
10. Connie and me work well together.

Exercise 12 Writing Application
Imagine that you are a sports announcer. Write a play-by-play description of an event during a game. Use at least three nominative pronouns, three objective pronouns, and four possessive pronouns.

Exercise 13 CUMULATIVE REVIEW
Problems With Verbs and Pronouns
Revise the following paragraph, correcting errors in verb or pronoun usage.

(1) Baseball fans have always went to games to cheer for home-run hitters. (2) In 1927, Babe Ruth wallops sixty home runs. (3) No one ever done that before. (4) The nickname "The Sultan of Swat" was gave to him. (5) The Babe finished his' career with a record 714 homers. (6) Both of Babe's records have since been broke. (7) In 1961, Roger Maris and Mickey Mantle hitted home runs in almost every game. (8) Mantle knowed that either Roger or him would top sixty. (9) On the last day of the season, Maris had drove home run number sixty-one over the fence. (10) Babe's other record laid unbroken for thirteen more years. (11) In 1974, fans in Atlanta cheered for there hero, Henry Aaron, when he hit his 715th homer. (12) That homer sat his name in the record books. (13) Aaron goes on to hit 755 home runs before he retired. (14) By the end of the 1998 season, two players, Mark McGwire and Sammy Sosa, had became the first two players to smash Roger Maris's record. (15) Hitting seventy homers, McGwire showed that the greatest home-run hitter ever may be him.

Standardized Test Preparation Workshop

Standard English Usage: Pronouns

Standardized tests measure your knowledge of the rules of standard grammar, such as correct pronoun usage. Questions test your ability to use the three cases of personal pronouns correctly. When answering these questions, determine what type of pronoun is needed in the sentence—nominative case pronouns are used as subjects or predicate pronouns; objective case pronouns are used as direct objects, indirect objects, or objects of prepositions; and possessive case pronouns are used to show ownership.

The following test items will give you practice with the format of questions that test your knowledge of pronoun usage.

Test Tip

When an object or subject is compound, check to see whether the case is correct by using only the pronoun in the compound construction.

Example: *Karen and I/me went to the bike store.*

Incorrect: *Me went to the bike store.*

Correct: *I went to the bike store.*

Sample Test Items	Answers and Explanations
Read the passage, and choose the letter of the word or group of words that belongs in each space. Ryan and __(1)__ couldn't believe that __(2)__ mom bought new bikes.	

1 A me
  B I
  C my
  D mine
 	
2 F our
  G us
  H we
  J ours
	The correct answer is *B.* Since the sentence calls for a subject, a pronoun in the nominative case is required. Choice *A* is in the objective case, and choices *C* and *D* are in the possessive case.
	
	The correct answer is *F,* since the sentence calls for a pronoun in the possessive case that comes before the noun it modifies. Choice *J* is also in the possessive case, but it stands alone.

Practice 1 **Directions:** Read the passage, and choose the letter of the word or group of words that belongs in each space.

Karen, Ryan, Mike, and ___(1)___ went bike riding on Block Island last summer. Mike's and Ryan's bikes are the smallest, and ___(2)___ have training wheels. Surprisingly, the boys kept up pretty well with Karen and ___(3)___. Karen and Mike forgot to bring ___(4)___ helmets so ___(5)___ rented one for each of them

1 A me
  B I
  C my
  D mine

2 F they
  G they're
  H their
  J there's

3 A mine
  B me
  C I
  D my

4 F they're
  G their
  H there
  J theirs

5 A our
  B us
  C ours
  D we

Practice 2 **Directions:** Read the passage, and choose the letter of the word or group of words that belongs in each space.

All of ___(1)___ rode ahead of me for a few miles. The chain had fallen off ___(2)___ bike. When I finally caught up to them, ___(3)___ and Ryan said it was time for our picnic. Afterward, the boys looked tired, so Karen asked Mike, "Don't ___(4)___ think it's time to head home?"

1 A their
  B them
  C they
  D theirs

2 F me
  G our
  H mine
  J my

3 A him
  B she
  C I
  D me

4 F you and him
  G you and he
  H yours and his
  J you're and he

Chapter 24

Making Words Agree

During a visit to Washington, D.C., you might jot down the following sentences on the back of a postcard of the Lincoln Memorial:

> I love Washington. It is a great city. The Lincoln Memorial is my favorite monument. I like the other monuments, too. All of them are worth visiting.

You probably wouldn't have to think too much about how to word these sentences. However, without even realizing it, you would be following the rules of agreement—both subject-verb agreement and pronoun-antecedent agreement. In this chapter, you'll learn *why* the sentences above are correct, and you will discover how to apply rules of agreement to sentences that are much more complex.

▲ **Critical Viewing**
Write two sentences about this monument, one with *Abraham Lincoln* as the subject and the other with *tourists* as the subject. Which sentence needs a singular verb? Which one needs a plural verb? **[Connect]**

Diagnostic Test

Directions: Write all answers on a separate sheet of paper.

Skill Check A. Choose the verb in parentheses that agrees with the subject of each sentence below.

1. Washington, D.C., (is, are) the capital of the United States.
2. National landmarks (is, are) found throughout the city.
3. The Lincoln Memorial (contain, contains) a 19-foot statue of Abraham Lincoln, the sixteenth president of the United States.
4. In spring, visitors to the Jefferson Memorial (enjoy, enjoys) seeing the cherry trees that surround the monument.
5. When tourists (see, sees) the 555-foot Washington Monument, they wonder whether they will have to climb to the top.
6. Stairs and elevators (is, are) available to those who wish to reach the top of the Washington Monument.
7. Either the Natural History Museum or the Museum of American History (take, takes) hours to tour.
8. Neither my parents nor my brother (want, wants) to miss seeing the Air and Space Museum.
9. The Vietnam Veterans Memorial and the Korean War Veterans Memorial (honor, honors) the men and women who gave their lives during these conflicts.
10. My sister and brother (want, wants) to see as much of Washington, D.C., as possible.
11. Every visitor to Washington, D.C., (is, are) impressed with its national landmarks and museums.
12. None of the national museums (charge, charges) admission.
13. Few people (leave, leaves) the city disappointed.
14. Many visitors (come, comes) back more than once.
15. Most tourists (stay, stays) in hotels.

Skill Check B. Copy each sentence below, filling in the blank with a pronoun that agrees with its antecedent.

16. My parents enjoyed ___?___ trip to Washington, D.C.
17. We girls were excited about ___?___ trip to the nation's capital.
18. Ruth used ___?___ camera to take pictures of the monuments.
19. The Washington Monument had ___?___ exterior walls covered with scaffolding.
20. Either Adam or Keith took ___?___ journal on the trip.
21. The President and the First Lady were having ___?___ breakfast when we toured the White House.
22. When the First Lady stepped out of the door, we waved to ___?___ and she waved back.
23. Rachel and Donald told about ___?___ trip to Washington, D.C.
24. My brother lost ___?___ hat while visiting the Lincoln Memorial.
25. Neither John nor Peter remembered ___?___ camera.

Subject and Verb Agreement

Simple Subjects and Verbs

Subjects are either singular or plural in number. Singular subjects refer to one person, place, or thing; plural subjects refer to more than one. Verbs, too, are either singular or plural. Singular subjects take singular verbs. Plural subjects take plural verbs.

Singular and Plural Subjects

Many subjects are nouns. Most singular nouns can be made plural by adding *s* or *es*. Some nouns, like *woman* and *mouse*, form their plurals differently.

SINGULAR NOUNS: bell, canyon, tax, city, woman, mouse

PLURAL NOUNS: bells, canyons, taxes, cities, women, mice

Singular and Plural Verbs

Present-tense verbs have both singular and plural forms. Third-person singular verbs end in *s*, while plural verbs do not. This is just the opposite of nouns that form their plurals by adding *s*.

The chart below shows how an *s* is added to the third-person singular form of the verb *look*:

PRESENT TENSE VERB FORMS	
Singular	**Plural**
I look	we look
you look	you look
he, she, it looks	they look

Agreement The subject and verb in a sentence must agree in number.

▶ **KEY CONCEPT** Use a **singular** subject with a singular verb. Use a **plural** subject with a plural verb. ■

SINGULAR SUBJECT AND VERB: <u>Terry</u> <u>visits</u> the Statue of Liberty once a year.

PLURAL SUBJECT AND VERB: <u>They</u> <u>visit</u> the Statue of Liberty once a year.

◀ **Critical Viewing**
Use *Statue of Liberty* and *trees* as the subjects of two sentences about this photo. Which subject would agree with the verb *stand*? Which would agree with the verb *stands*?
[Connect]

▶ **Exercise 1** Making Subjects and Verbs Agree For each sentence below, write the verb that agrees with the subject.
1. The Statue of Liberty (is, are) located on Liberty Island, near the southern tip of Manhattan.
2. Ferries (take, takes) passengers to the island.
3. Visitors (is, are) always amazed at the size of the statue.
4. The statue (measure, measures) 151 feet and 1 inch tall.
5. The stone pedestal (add, adds) another 154 feet to the height of the statue.

▶ **Exercise 2** Revising a Paragraph to Correct Errors in Subject-Verb Agreement Rewrite the following paragraph, correcting errors in subject-verb agreement.

The Statue of Liberty is a symbol of freedom. Some visitors weep as they approach the statue. They remembers that the statue was the first thing their great-grandparents saw when they arrived at the United States. In one hand, the Statue of Liberty holds the Tablet of Law bearing the date July 4, 1776. The date is the United States Independence Day. In the other hand, the statue hold a torch. The torch light the way for immigrants to the United States. Many visitors climb the 354 steps to the statue's crown. They gazes out to view the New York City skyline. Others climb just to the top of the pedestal and enjoys the view from there.

More Practice

Grammar Exercise Workbook
• pp. 115–116
On-line Exercise Bank
• Section 24.1
  Go on-line:
  PHSchool.com
  Enter Web Code:
  eak-6002

Get instant feedback! Exercises 1 and 2 are available on-line or on CD-ROM.

Compound Subjects and Verbs

A *compound subject* refers to two or more subjects that share the same verb. They are connected by conjunctions such as *and, or,* or *nor.*

COMPOUND SUBJECTS
<u>Robert</u> and <u>Jennifer</u> enjoy visiting Philadelphia.
The <u>museums</u> or <u>historical sites</u> interest many visitors.
Neither the <u>Liberty Bell</u> nor <u>Independence Hall</u> disappoints tourists.

A number of rules can help you choose the right verb to use with a compound subject.

▶ **KEY CONCEPT** When a compound subject is connected by *and,* the verb that follows is usually plural. ■

EXAMPLE: <u>Washington, D.C.,</u> and <u>Philadelphia</u> <u>are</u> my favorite cities.

There is an exception to this rule: If the parts of a compound subject are thought of as one person or thing, the subject is singular and takes a singular verb.

EXAMPLE: <u>Spaghetti</u> and <u>meatballs</u> <u>is</u> my favorite meal.

▶ **KEY CONCEPT** When two singular subjects are joined by *or* or *nor,* use a singular verb. When two plural subjects are joined by *or* or *nor,* use a plural verb. ■

SINGULAR: A <u>car</u> or a <u>train</u> <u>provides</u> good transportation to Washington, D.C.

PLURAL: Neither <u>children</u> nor <u>adults</u> <u>like</u> to wait in line to enter the White House.

▶ **KEY CONCEPT** When a compound subject is made up of one singular and one plural subject joined by *or* or *nor,* the verb agrees with the subject closer to it. ■

SINGULAR SUBJECT CLOSER: Either the <u>monuments</u> or the <u>White House</u> <u>is</u> interesting to see.

PLURAL SUBJECT CLOSER: Either the <u>White House</u> or the <u>monuments</u> <u>are</u> interesting to see.

✔ Spelling Tip

If you suspect that the plural form of a noun is irregular, use a dictionary to help you find the noun's plural form.

> **Exercise 3** Making Compound Subjects and Verbs Agree

Write the verb that correctly completes each sentence.

1. The White House and the Capitol Building (is, are) sites all visitors to Washington, D.C., should see.
2. Neither my brother nor my sister (has, have) ever visited the White House before.
3. In the White House, the Green Room, the Red Room, and the Blue Room (is, are) open to public touring.
4. The East Room and the State Dining Room (is, are) also open to tours.
5. Neither the President nor the other members of his family (was, were) home when we toured the White House.
6. Uniformed police and plainclothes Secret Service agents (patrol, patrols) the White House.
7. Neither adults nor a child (is, are) permitted to touch anything in the White House.
8. The Senate and the House of Representatives (meet, meets) in the Capitol Building.
9. Either the Senate or the House of Representatives (has, have) its offices in the south wing.
10. Corned beef and cabbage (is, are) a dish the cafeteria in the Capitol Building sometimes serves.

> **Exercise 4** Revising Sentences With Compound Subjects and Verbs Revise the following paragraph, correcting errors in subject-verb agreement.

Either Martha or Irene visit Independence Hall often. The Declaration of Independence and the U.S. Constitution was signed there. Philadelphia's Old City Hall and Congress Hall sit on either side of Independence Hall. Neither Independence Hall nor Philadelphia's museums charges high entrance fees. Macaroni and cheese are the dish Martha and Irene usually order at a restaurant near Independence Hall.

More Practice

Grammar Exercise Workbook
• pp. 117–118
On-line Exercise Bank
• Section 24.1
Go on-line:
PHSchool.com
Enter Web Code:
eak-6002

Get instant feedback! Exercises 3 and 4 are available on-line or on CD-ROM.

Independence Hall in Philadelphia

▶ **Critical Viewing** Write a sentence about this picture, beginning *Neither the dome atop the hall nor the clock. . . .* Does your sentence need a singular verb or a plural one? **[Make a Judgment]**

Pronoun Subjects and Verbs

Indefinite pronouns refer to people, places, or things in a general way.

▶ **KEY CONCEPT** When an indefinite pronoun is the subject of a sentence, the verb must agree in number with the pronoun. ■

INDEFINITE PRONOUNS				
Singular			**Plural**	**Singular or Plural**
anybody	everyone	nothing	both	all
anyone	everything	one	few	any
anything	much	other	many	more
each	neither	somebody	others	most
either	nobody	someone	several	none
everybody	no one	something		some

Indefinite Pronouns That Are Always Singular
Indefinite pronouns that are always singular are used with singular verbs.

EXAMPLE: Everyone <u>is</u> ready.

Indefinite Pronouns That Are Always Plural Indefinite pronouns that are always plural are used with plural verbs.

EXAMPLE: <u>Both</u> of my suitcases <u>are</u> in the closet.

GRAMMAR IN LITERATURE

from **The Phantom Tollbooth**
Based on the book by Norton Juster
Screenplay by Susan Nanus

The singular indefinite pronoun (in red italics) used as a subject in this passage agrees in number with its verb (in blue italics).

CLOCK. . . . Wherever he is, he wants to be somewhere else—and when he gets there, so what. *Everything is* too much trouble or a waste of time. . . . Unless he bothers to notice a very large package that happened to arrive today.

More Practice

Grammar Exercise Workbook
• pp. 119–120
On-line Exercise Bank
• Section 24.1
Go on-line:
PHSchool.com
Enter Web Code:
eak-6002

Get instant feedback! Exercises 5 and 6 are available on-line or on CD-ROM.

Indefinite Pronouns That Are Either Singular or Plural Some indefinite pronouns can be either singular or plural. To decide on the number, look for the noun to which the pronoun refers. If the noun is singular, the pronoun is singular. If the noun is plural, the pronoun is plural.

EXAMPLES: <u>All</u> of my money <u>is</u> gone.
<u>All</u> of these souvenirs <u>are</u> for you.

▶ **Exercise 5** Choosing Verbs That Agree With Indefinite Pronouns Write the form of the verb that agrees with the subject in the following sentences.

1. Everyone who visits the Grand Canyon in Arizona (is, are) impressed.
2. Many (stand, stands) in awe as they gaze into the canyon.
3. Some (is, are) able to hike from the South Rim of the canyon to the North Rim.
4. Either of the rims (offer, offers) visitors spectacular views of the canyon.
5. Much of the day (is, are) spent hiking around the canyon's rim.
6. No one in our group (want, wants) to hike to the bottom of the canyon.
7. All of us (agree, agrees) that the hike back up will be difficult.
8. More of our time (was, were) spent hiking back up the trail than hiking down into the canyon.
9. If someone (wish, wishes) to ride a mule into the canyon, he or she must make a reservation in advance.
10. Others (prefer, prefers) to reach the bottom by foot.

An aerial view of the Grand Canyon

▲ **Critical Viewing**
Write two sentences about this photo. Begin one with *Most of the clouds . . .* and the other with *Most of the day . . . .* Are the verbs in the two sentences the same or different in number? **[Compare]**

▶ **Exercise 6** Revising to Eliminate Errors in Agreement
Look closely at each sentence below. If the subject and verb agree, write *correct.* If a sentence is not correct, revise it to eliminate agreement errors.

1. Many visits the Alamo to learn about its history.
2. Nearly everyone know that the Alamo is in San Antonio, Texas.
3. Anyone in a tour group finds out that Texans defended the fort in 1836 during the Texas War for Independence.
4. Several in our group was not aware that most of the Alamo's defenders died during the battle.
5. Few of the Alamo's original buildings stands today.

Subject and Verb Agreement • 525

Hands-on Grammar

Lining Up Pronouns and Verbs

Make three stacks of index cards. On each card in one stack, draw a diagonal line with a pencil from the lower left corner to the upper right corner. On the left above the line, write a singular indefinite pronoun (Examples: *anybody, each, everyone, either, one*). On the right below the line, write a singular verb (Examples: *arrives, carries, does, has, tries, wants*).

On each card in the second stack, draw a diagonal line from the upper left corner to the lower right corner. This time, write a plural indefinite pronoun (Examples: *all, both, few, some*) on the left below the line and a plural verb on the right above the line (Examples: *arrive, do, have, try, want*).

Use the third stack of cards for pronouns that can be either singular or plural. Draw a diagonal line from the lower left to the upper right on one side. Then, flip the card over and draw a line from the upper left to the lower right. The two lines should match back-to-back. Write a pronoun on the left part of each side of the card. Write a singular verb on the right above the line on one side and a plural verb on the right below the line on the other side. Cut the cards with scissors along the diagonal lines.

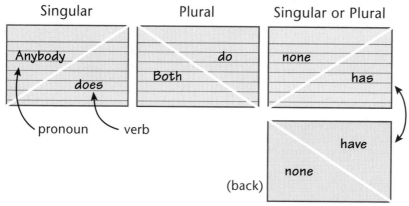

Mix and match pronouns and verbs to create rectangles and two-word sentences. The shape of the card will prevent matching a singular indefinite pronoun with a plural verb.

Find It in Your Reading In your reading, find examples of sentences that contain indefinite pronouns used as subjects. Write the sentences on your paper, and indicate whether the pronouns are singular or plural.

Find It in Your Writing Look through samples of your writing to find sentences in which you have used personal and indefinite pronouns as subjects. Check to see that the pronouns agree in number with their verbs.

Section
24.1

Section Review

GRAMMAR EXERCISES 7–13

▶ **Exercise 7** Making Subjects and Verbs Agree For each sentence below, write the verb that agrees with the subject.

1. The Boston National Historical Park (contain, contains) seven sites that are on Boston's Freedom Trail.
2. These places (include, includes) Bunker Hill Monument, the U.S.S. *Constitution*, and Old North Church.
3. The sites on the trail (is, are) places where historic events occurred.
4. Faneuil Hall (was, were) used as a marketplace and a place for Boston town meetings during the 1700's.
5. The Bunker Hill Monument (commemorate, commemorates) the first major battle in the American Revolution.

▶ **Exercise 8** Supplying Verbs That Agree With Compound Subjects Write each sentence below, filling in the blank with a verb that agrees with the subject.

1. Muir Woods and Golden Gate Park ___?___ located in northern California.
2. Giant redwood and Douglas Firs ___?___ in Muir Woods.
3. Neither redwood nor sequoia roots ___?___ more than six feet underground.
4. Plants and animals ___?___ in Muir Woods.
5. Neither overnight campers nor fire ___?___ permitted in Muir Woods.

▶ **Exercise 9** Making Pronoun Subjects and Verbs Agree Write the verb that agrees with each subject below.

1. Both of my parents (wish, wishes) to visit Utah's Arches National Park.
2. Most of the tourists (visit, visits) the park to see the strange rock formations.
3. All who visit (photograph, photographs) the unusual rock formations.
4. Neither of my brothers (own, owns) a camera.
5. Much of the park's grounds (is, are) filled with natural stone arches, windows, spires, and pinnacles.

▶ **Exercise 10** Revising to Eliminate Errors in Subject-Verb Agreement Revise each sentence below, correcting errors in subject-verb agreement.

1. People enjoys hearing how lanterns hung in the Old North Church's steeple warned colonists that the British soldiers was coming.
2. One of the oldest U.S. ships afloat are the U.S.S. *Constitution*, which sit in Boston Harbor.
3. Either surfers or a bather enjoy the beaches in Golden Gate Park.
4. Often, fog or mist surround the Golden Gate Bridge.
5. Nothing in the world compare to Arches National Park.

▶ **Exercise 11** Find It in Your Reading Identify the four verbs used with the pronoun *he* in the passage on page 524. Are all of the verbs singular, to agree with a singular subject?

▶ **Exercise 12** Find It in Your Writing Review a piece of writing from your portfolio. Identify and correct any errors in subject-verb agreement.

▶ **Exercise 13** Writing Application Write a description of a landmark or site of interest in your area. Include compound subjects and indefinite pronouns.

Section Review • **527**

Pronoun and Antecedent Agreement

An *antecedent* is the word to which a pronoun refers.

▶ **KEY CONCEPT** Use a singular pronoun with a singular antecedent. ■

SINGULAR PRONOUNS AND ANTECEDENTS

The Yukon takes <u>its</u> name from the Native American word Yu-kun-ah.

Melissa planned <u>her</u> trip to Canada's Yukon last month.

Tom will lend Melissa <u>his</u> suitcase.

▶ **KEY CONCEPT** Use a plural pronoun with a plural antecedent. ■

PLURAL PRONOUNS AND ANTECEDENTS

Hikers will have <u>their</u> pick of trails in the Yukon.

The boys have all brought <u>their</u> hiking boots.

The girls knew <u>they</u> had to bring coats and hats.

Two special rules are used for compound antecedents:

▶ **KEY CONCEPT** Use a singular pronoun with two or more singular antecedents joined by *or* or *nor.* ■

EXAMPLE: Andrew or Keith gives <u>his</u> report about the Klondike Gold Rush today.

▶ **KEY CONCEPT** Use a plural pronoun with two or more singular antecedents joined by *and.* ■

EXAMPLE: Joyce and Robert showed <u>their</u> father the drawing of the Yukon River.

Theme: The Yukon

In this section, you will learn how to make pronouns agree in number with their antecedents. The examples and exercises are about the Yukon Territory in Canada.

Cross-Curricular Connection: Social Studies

▶ **Exercise 14** Identifying Pronouns That Agree With Their Antecedents In the sentences below, write the pronoun in parentheses that agrees with its antecedent.

1. The gold prospectors packed up (his, their) supplies and headed toward the Yukon.
2. A man and wife kept a journal of (her, their) travels.
3. Either Claude or his brother hopes to make (his, their) fortune prospecting in the Yukon.
4. Claude's wife and daughter looked sad as (she, they) watched him leave.
5. The Yukon is noted for (its, their) harsh winters.

▶ **Exercise 15** Supplying Pronouns That Agree With Antecedents Copy each sentence below, filling in the blank with a pronoun that agrees with its antecedent.

EXAMPLE: Jake trained ___?___ sled dog to do tricks.
ANSWER: Jake trained his sled dog to do tricks.

1. Fred and Tony are preparing ___?___ report about Canada's Yukon Territory.
2. Neither boy knows what ___?___ will say about the Yukon.
3. Perhaps Tony will ask ___?___ parents to help.
4. Joan has loaned the boys ___?___ book about the Yukon.
5. The book is missing some of ___?___ pages.

More Practice

Grammar Exercise Workbook
• pp. 121–122
On-line Exercise Bank
• Section 24.2
  Go on-line:
  PHSchool.com
  Enter Web Code:
  eak-6002

Text

Get instant feedback! Exercises 14 and 15 are available on-line or on CD-ROM.

◀ Critical Viewing Include a pronoun in a sentence about one of the dogs in this picture. Include a different pronoun in a sentence about both dogs. Make sure your pronouns agree with their antecedents. [Analyze]

▶ **Exercise 16** Revising Sentences to Correct Errors in Pronoun-Antecedent Agreement Revise the following sentences, correcting errors in pronoun-antecedent agreement. If a sentence has no errors, write *correct*.

1. When tourists visit the Yukon, he or she must respect the wilderness.
2. If the Yukon's natural beauty is spoiled, his wilderness areas will be gone forever.
3. Ben and Joe chose to take their vacation in the Yukon last summer.
4. While hiking, Ben slipped and sprained his ankle badly.
5. Rescue workers carried her equipment to the place where Ben had fallen.
6. The rescue workers told Ben that he was lucky that their ankle was not broken.
7. Ben's sister Betsy came to see them at the hospital.
8. Either Betsy or Ben's wife, June, plans to spend their time visiting Ben at the hospital.
9. Despite their accident, Ben decided that they would try to climb Mt. Logan, Canada's highest peak, during his next vacation.
10. Located in the Yukon, Mt. Logan measures 19,524 feet from sea level to their summit.

GRAMMAR IN
LITERATURE

from **The King of Mazy May**
Jack London

In this passage from a story about the Yukon, the personal pronouns, highlighted in blue italics, agree in number with their antecedents, highlighted in red italics.

Walt was born a thousand miles or so down the Yukon, in a trading post below the Ramparts. After *his* mother died, *his father* and *he* came up on the river, step by step, from camp to camp, till now *they* are settled down on the Mazy May Creek in the Klondike country. Last year *they* and several *others* had spent much toil and time on the Mazy May, and endured great hardships; the *creek*, in turn, was just beginning to show up *its* richness and to reward *them* for *their* heavy labor.

More Practice

Grammar Exercise Workbook
• pp. 121–122
On-line Exercise Bank
• Section 24.2
Go on-line:
PHSchool.com
Enter Web Code:
eak-6002

▲ **Critical Viewing** Use the pronouns *their* and *its* in two sentences about this photo. What is the antecedent of each pronoun? [**Analyze, Identify**]

Section Review

GRAMMAR EXERCISES 17–21

▶ **Exercise 17** Supplying Pronouns That Agree With Their Antecedents
Copy each sentence below, filling in the blank with a pronoun that agrees with its antecedent.

1. In the late 1890's, prospectors took ___?___ chances and headed off to the Yukon in search of gold.
2. Men and women hoped to make ___?___ fortunes by finding gold nuggets.
3. Neither men nor women knew what to expect the first time ___?___ decided to journey into the Northwest Territory.
4. One woman, Ethel Bush Berry, went to the Yukon with ___?___ husband.
5. Together, Mr. and Mrs. Berry made ___?___ way along Chilkoot Pass.
6. The second time the Berrys went there, Mrs. Berry's sister went with ___?___.
7. Many gold seekers went to Dawson because ___?___ is located near the Klondike River.
8. When Edith Feero Larson was ten years old, ___?___ family went to the Yukon and the Klondike.
9. Edith's mother and father and ___?___ children left for the Yukon in 1897.
10. Mrs. Larson remembered ___?___ youth in the Klondike with fondness.

▶ **Exercise 18** Revising to Eliminate Errors in Pronoun-Antecedent Agreement Revise the following paragraphs, correcting errors in pronoun-antecedent agreement. If the sentence is correct as is, write *correct*.

Dawson City, located where the Yukon and Klondike rivers meet, is known for its role in the gold rush of the late 1890's. Today, Dawson is a popular place for tourists to go on his or her vacations. Nearly 60,000 people crowd into Dawson each summer, making tourism their biggest industry. Some residents make its living by raising sled dogs. In mid-February, participants in the annual sled-dog race stream through Dawson on her way to Fairbanks, Alaska. The roads into Dawson are known for its scenery. In Dawson, visitors can see how the city has restored its oldest buildings.

When my family visited Dawson during our vacation, the city was lively. Neither my sister nor my mother forgot to bring their camera. My brother and my father wanted us to take his picture near Bonanza Creek, where the first gold nuggets were found. Both my brother and father tried his luck finding gold in the creek.

▶ **Exercise 19** Find It in Your Reading Find the antecedent for each underlined pronoun in this passage from "The King of Mazy May." Indicate whether the antecedent is singular or plural.

Walt has walked all the fourteen years of <u>his</u> life in suntanned, moose-hide moccasins, and <u>he</u> can go to the Indian camps and "talk big" with the men, and trade calico and beads with <u>them</u> for <u>their</u> precious furs.

▶ **Exercise 20** Find It in Your Writing Review a piece of writing from your portfolio. Identify and correct any errors in pronoun-antecedent agreement.

▶ **Exercise 21** Writing Application Write a summary of a short story you have read about a character in conflict with natural forces. Use at least five different pronouns. Draw arrows from each pronoun to its antecedent.

GRAMMAR EXERCISES 22–28

▶ **Exercise 22** Identifying Verbs That Agree With Subjects For each sentence below, write the verb in parentheses that agrees with the subject.

1. The Yukon (is, are) a Canadian territory.
2. It (is, are) located in the northwest corner of Canada.
3. Moose, wolves, and many other animals (live, lives) in the Yukon.
4. Yukon Territory (share, shares) more than 650 miles of border with Alaska.
5. The forests or the mountains (provide, provides) shelter for the Yukon's wildlife.
6. Much of the Yukon (is, are) forest land.
7. Most of the Native Americans in the Yukon (is, are) of the Athabascan language family.
8. Some (is, are) Tlingit-speaking people.
9. Nearly everyone (participate, participates) in the annual Native American festival at Moosehide.
10. No one (care, cares) whether festival goers are Native American or not.
11. Mountains (is, are) a dominant feature of the Yukon's landscape.
12. The Yukon's major mountain range (is, are) the St. Elias in the southwest corner of the territory.
13. Miners and loggers (has, have) left their mark on the land.
14. Each tourist or Yukon resident (look, looks) for signs of wildlife.
15. Either swimming or boating (draw, draws) tourists in the summer.

▶ **Exercise 23** Supplying Verbs That Agree With Subjects Copy each sentence below, supplying the correct form of the verb in parentheses.

1. Because of its harsh climate and terain, very few people (live) in the Yukon.

2. However, thousands of tourists (visit) the region each year.
3. The small city of Whitehorse (serve) as the capital of the Yukon Territory.
4. Most of the Yukon's population (reside) in Whitehorse.
5. If a person anywhere in the Yukon (need) to see a dentist, he or she must go to Whitehorse or Dawson City.
6. Other Yukon communities (include) Watson Lake, Faro, and Ross River.
7. Mining (bring) in much of the Yukon's income.
8. Either tourism or manufacturing (rank) second in economic importance.
9. Salmon, whitefish, and trout (swim) in the Yukon River.
10. A popular museum in Whitehorse (commemorate) the great gold rush in the 1890's.

▶ **Exercise 24** Revising Sentences to Eliminate Errors in Subject-Verb Agreement Revise the following sentences, correcting errors in subject-verb agreement. If a sentence is correct as is, write *correct.*

1. The Yukon River flow through Alaska into the Bering Sea.
2. The Yukon lie in the subarctic climate zone.
3. Bears and some other mammals hibernates when winter comes.
4. Extremely cold temperatures mark the Yukon's climate for much of the year.
5. In summer, however, temperatures has reached as high as 95° F.
6. Eight sled dogs and a driver comes down this road quite often.
7. Either the dogs or the driver makes a great deal of noise.
8. The Yukon's location near the Arctic affect how many daylight hours it receives.

9. Today, more tourists are visiting the Yukon.
10. More of the region's money are coming from "adventure tourism."
11. A trip to the Yukon offer tourists an authentic outdoor experience.
12. In summer in the Yukon, daylight last as long as twenty hours.
13. In winter, the time of daylight is very short.
14. Neither freezing temperatures nor snow keep people from enjoying themselves in the Yukon.
15. Neither bad weather nor icy conditions prevents tourists from exploring the Yukon.

Exercise 25 Supplying Pronouns That Agree With Their Antecedents

Copy each sentence below, filling in the blank with a pronoun that agrees with its antecedent.

1. My brother and ___?___ friend will travel to the Yukon this summer.
2. The two friends are planning to spend much of ___?___ time in Kluane National Park.
3. Kluane is a huge park. ___?___ is Canada's fourth largest park.
4. Visitors to Kluane will get ___?___ fill of the outdoors.
5. It is important that visitors bring all the equipment ___?___ will need.

Exercise 26 Revising a Paragraph to Eliminate All Agreement Errors

Revise the following paragraph, correcting any errors in agreement.

Most of the Yukon's economy is based on mining. Many people in the Yukon mines lead, zinc, copper, or gold. My Aunt Jane moved with their family to the Yukon. Each of my aunt's sons are miners. Either my cousin Theo or his two brothers works in a copper mine. He wrote me about a camping trip he and his mother recently took. During the trip Aunt Jane and Theo was confronted by a bear. The bear stuck their paw out at them. Both Aunt Jane and Theo stood still as she watched the bear lumber away. Each of them feel lucky to have survived that adventure.

Exercise 27 Writing Application

Write a diary entry about a memorable trip that you took with other members of your family. Include compound subjects, and use personal and indefinite pronouns in your writing. Proofread carefully to avoid any agreement errors.

Exercise 28 CUMULATIVE REVIEW Using Verbs and Pronouns Correctly

Rewrite the paragraph below on your paper, correcting any errors in verb or pronoun usage.

In the 1840's, Robert Campbell, a British fur trapper, become the first European to explore the Yukon. He build a trading post near the Pelly River, which laid in the southern part of the region. The Chilkat Indians were distrustful of Campbell, and them burn down their trading post a short time later. For the next fifty years, few other Europeans come into the area. Then, in 1896, three men was prospect on Bonanza Creek, when he spotted flecks of gold setting in the creek bed. Word about them gold strike quickly spread. During the next two years, more than 35,000 people rushed to the Yukon. They was hope to get rich. As the wealth of the region increased, their political importance increased as well. In 1898, the Yukon were named an official Canadian territory.

Standardized Test Preparation Workshop

Standard English Usage: Agreement

Standardized tests frequently test your knowledge of the rules of subject and verb agreement. When checking a sentence for errors, first identify the subject. Next, identify the type of subject: singular, plural, or compound. Then, apply the rules of agreement to make sure that the verb in the sentence agrees with the subject.

The following questions will give you practice with different formats used for items that test knowledge of subject-verb agreement.

Test Tip

Remember, the singular or plural form of the subject in the sentence will dictate which form the verb takes.

Sample Test Items

Identify the underlined word or phrase that contains an error in the following sentence.

Either Simon or the Caseys knows the
  (A)   (B)   (C)

correct answer. No errors.
  (D)   (E)

Choose the revised version of the following sentence that eliminates all errors in grammar, usage, and mechanics.

Either the Caseys or Simon know the correct answer.

A Neither the Caseys nor Simon know the correct answer.

B Either the Caseys or Simon knows the correct answer.

C The Caseys and Simon knows the correct answer.

D The correct answers is known by the Caseys or Simon.

Answers and Explanations

The correct answer is *C*. The compound subject of the sentence is *Either Simon or the Caseys*. When singular and plural subjects are joined by *or* or *nor*, the verb must agree with the subject closer to it. In this case, the closer subject, *the Caseys*, is plural, so the plural verb *know* should be used in the sentence.

The correct answer is *B*. The compound subject of the sentence is *Either the Caseys or Simon*. When singular and plural subjects are joined by *or* or *nor*, the verb must agree with the subject closer to it. In this case, the closer subject, *Simon*, is singular, so the singular verb *knows* should be used in the sentence. Answer choice *C* is incorrect because the two parts of the compound subject are joined by *and*. Therefore, the plural verb *know* should be used. Answer choice *D* introduces a new agreement problem between the plural subject *answers* and the singular verb *is*.

Exercise 2 Identifying Positives, Comparatives, and Superlatives Label each adjective form below *positive*, *comparative*, or *superlative*. Then, write the other two forms of each word.

1. muddy
2. hardiest
3. most
4. cloudy
5. longest
6. grander
7. hardest
8. roomy
9. narrowest
10. shorter

Using Adjectives With *More* and *Most*

Besides adding *-er* and *-est* to adjectives, there is another way to change them to show comparison.

▶**KEY CONCEPT** *More* and *most* can be used to form the comparative and superlative degrees of many adjectives. ■

Although *-er* and *-est* are usually used to change the degree of short adjectives, *more* and *most* may also be used. *More* and *most* should not be used when they sound awkward, as in *He is more tall than I.* With some adjectives, only *more* and *most* are used.

▶**KEY CONCEPT** *More* and *most* can be used with many one- and two-syllable adjectives. ■

EXAMPLE: This dolphin is *more playful* than that one.

When you are unsure about how a modifier forms its degrees of comparison, check a dictionary.

▶**KEY CONCEPT** Use *more* and *most* to form the comparative and superlative degrees of adjectives with three or more syllables. ■

EXAMPLES: Ocean animals are *more interesting* than plants.
Sharks often eat the *most debilitated* fish.

SOME ADJECTIVES REQUIRING *MORE* AND *MOST*		
Positive	**Comparative**	**Superlative**
playful	more playful	most playful
careful	more careful	most careful
devious	more devious	most devious
terrifying	more terrifying	most terrifying

More Practice

Grammar Exercise Workbook
• pp. 123–124
On-line Exercise Bank
• Section 25.1
Go on-line:
PHSchool.com
Enter Web Code:
eak-6002

Get instant feedback! Exercises 1 and 2 are available on-line or on CD-ROM.

Note About *Double Comparisons:* Avoid double comparisons. Never use both *-er* or *-est* and *more* or *most* to form the comparative and superlative degrees in the same sentence.

▶ **Exercise 3** Using Adjectives With *More* and *Most* Use *more* or *most* to form the comparative or superlative form of each adjective shown in parentheses.
1. Because people thought sharks were the (frightening) animals in the ocean, they believed it was all right to kill them.
2. People trapped sharks because the sharks were often (skillful) fishers than humans.
3. Commercial fishers sold the shark meat to some of the (respectable) restaurants in the world.
4. Now, many people think shark is one of the (delicious) meals.
5. Other people, however, feel it is (important) to study the lives and habits of sharks than to eat them.

▶ **Exercise 4** Revising Sentences With Adjectives Read the following sentences. If the modifier in the sentence is correct as written, write *correct.* If the modifier is in the wrong degree or if it is formed incorrectly, rewrite the sentence, correcting it.
1. Of all the underwater animals, sharks have the more fearsome reputation.
2. Some of the most spine-tingling movies involve shark attacks on humans.
3. But many sharks are dociler than their movie counterparts.
4. In fact, sharks are much likeliest to leave humans alone.
5. Some sharks are plain in color than others.

Memorizing Irregular Adjectives and Adverbs

A few adjectives and adverbs are *irregular.* Their comparative and superlative degrees must be memorized.

▶ **KEY CONCEPT** Memorize the irregular comparative and superlative forms of certain adjectives and adverbs. ■

The chart on the next page lists the most common irregular modifiers.

▲ **Critical Viewing** Using one comparative adjective and one superlative adjective in a sentence, describe how you might feel if you were swimming next to this shark. [**Speculate**]

DEGREES OF IRREGULAR ADJECTIVES AND ADVERBS

Positive	Comparative	Superlative
bad	worse	worst
badly	worse	worst
far (distance)	farther	farthest
far (extent)	further	furthest
good	better	best
well	better	best
many	more	most
much	more	most

▶ **Exercise 5** Recognizing the Degree of Irregular Modifiers
On your paper, indicate the degree of the underlined word in each of the following sentences.
1. The bite of a shark is <u>worse</u> than the bite of a dog.
2. Who found the <u>most</u> shells on the beach?
3. I believe that I found <u>more</u> shells than you did.
4. Which do you like <u>better</u>, my drawing or his?
5. This is the <u>worst</u> day of my life!

Using Adverbs to Compare

Adverbs also have three degrees of comparison.

POSITIVE: The fish swims *fast.*
COMPARATIVE: The eel swims *faster* than the fish.
SUPERLATIVE: The shark swims the *fastest* of the three.

The *positive* degree is used to describe only one action. The *comparative* degree is used when two actions are being compared. The *superlative* degree is used when three or more actions are being compared.

▶ **KEY CONCEPTS** To form the comparative of most one-syllable adverbs, add *-er.* To form the superlative, add *-est.* ■

The chart below shows a number of these adverbs.

DEGREES OF COMPARISON FORMED BY ADDING -ER OR -EST

Positive	Comparative	Superlative
hard	harder	hardest
early	earlier	earliest
late	later	latest
far	farther	farthest

▶ **More Practice**

Grammar Exercise
Workbook
• pp. 125–126, 129–130
On-line Exercise Bank
• Section 25.1
  Go on-line:
  PHSchool.com
  Enter Web Code:
  eak-6002

Get instant feedback!
Exercises 3, 4, and 5
are available on-line or
on CD-ROM.

▶ **KEY CONCEPT** With most adverbs of two or more sylla-bles, especially those ending in *-ly*, use *more* to form the com-parative and *most* to form the superlative. ∎

DEGREES OF COMPARISON FORMED BY ADDING *MORE* OR *MOST*		
Positive	Comparative	Superlative
quickly	more quickly	most quickly
constantly	more constantly	most constantly
loudly	more loudly	most loudly

To form the comparative and superlative of some two-syllable adjectives, such as *early*, use *-er* and *-est*. Check a dictionary if you are not sure whether to use these endings or *more* and *most*.

▶ **Exercise 6** Forming the Comparative and Superlative Degrees of Adverbs Make a chart showing the positive, com-parative, and superlative degrees of each adverb listed below. Add *-er* or *-est* to the adverbs whenever possible. When neces-sary, use *more* and *most*.

1. often
2. deep
3. carefully
4. tightly
5. soon
6. fully
7. playfully
8. low
9. frantically
10. smoothly

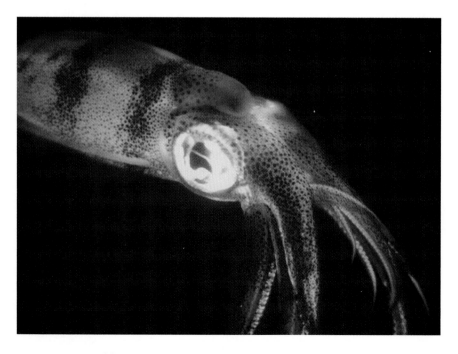

◀ **Critical Viewing**
Compare the way a squid moves with the way a shark moves. Use adverbs in your sentences. **[Compare and Contrast]**

GRAMMAR IN LITERATURE

from **The Loch Ness Monster**
George Laycock

In the following passage, the comparative forms of adjectives are highlighted in blue italics.

. . . The hiding places made the whole story of Nessie *more believable*. Nessie, it was agreed, could cruise about down there among those dark caves without sending a ripple to the surface.

This is also the area in which one *earlier* investigator heard strange underwater sounds the year before, tapping sounds that no biologist has yet been able to successfully identify.

> **Exercise 7** Using the Comparative and Superlative Degrees of Adverbs In the following sentences, use *-er* or *-est* or *more* or *most* to form the comparative or superlative of each adverb in parentheses.
> 1. Some sea creatures behave (playfully) than others.
> 2. Of all the animals that performed in the water show, the dolphins swam the (masterfully).
> 3. Sharks are found in warm waters (commonly) than in cold waters.
> 4. Because of their keen senses, sharks can compete (successfully) for prey than many other fish.
> 5. The shark swims (smoothly) than these fish because of its streamlined shape.

> **Exercise 8** Writing Sentences With Comparative and Superlative Degrees of Adverbs On your paper, write two sentences for each of the following modifiers. One sentence should use the comparative degree; the other should use the superlative degree.
> 1. softly
> 2. hard
> 3. suddenly
> 4. briefly
> 5. badly

> **More Practice**
>
> Grammar Exercise Workbook
> • pp. 127–128
> On-line Exercise Bank
> • Section 25.1
>   *Go on-line:*
>   PHSchool.com
>   *Enter Web Code:*
>   eak-6002
>
>
>
> Get instant feedback! Exercises 6, 7, and 8 are available on-line or on CD-ROM.

Hands-on Grammar

Adjective and Adverb Window Shutters

Practice forming the comparative and superlative degrees with the following activity.

Cut a piece of paper approximately 3" x 7". Fold two sides in (as shown in the illustration), leaving a space in the middle. Cut two slots as shown. Under the left shutter, write *more* and *most.* Under the right shutter, write *-er* and *-est.*

On a strip of paper about 1" wide, list adjectives and adverbs, such as *cold, hard, beautiful, slowly, fast, colorful, muddy, early,* and *quickly.* Feed the strip of paper through the slots, as shown, making sure that a word shows in the window.

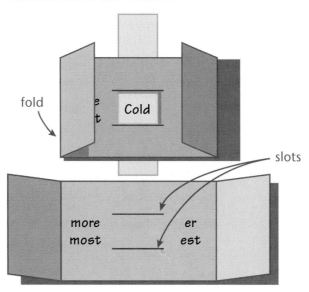

Now, decide whether the modifier forms its comparative and superlative degrees with *more* and *most* or with *-er* and *-est.* First, close the right shutter to cover up *-er* and *-est* and say the word with *more* and *most.* Then, close the left shutter and try the word with *-er* and *-est.* By always closing one shutter, you avoid forming a double comparison. Decide how the comparative and superlative degrees are formed. If you are unsure, consult a dictionary.

Find It in Your Writing Look through your portfolio to find examples of adjectives and adverbs in the positive degree. Write them down on a strip of paper that you can feed through your window shutter. See how they form their comparative and superlative degrees.

Find It in Your Reading In a short story or in a textbook, pick out examples of adjectives and adverbs. Add them to your list of modifiers to test.

Section 25.1 *Section Review*

GRAMMAR EXERCISES 9–14

▶ **Exercise 9** Forming Comparative and Superlative Degrees of Adjectives and Adverbs Make columns for the positive, comparative, and superlative degrees. Write the correct forms of each adjective or adverb below in the appropriate columns.

1. red
2. happy
3. scaly
4. firmly
5. fresh
6. sensible
7. outrageous
8. recently
9. good
10. confidently

▶ **Exercise 10** Using Modifiers Correctly Write the sentences below, using the correct comparative or superlative form of the adjective or adverb in parentheses.

(1) Animals that live in the sea must protect themselves because there is always a (big) animal trying to eat them. (2) Some fish escape their captors by swimming (quickly) than the hunters. (3) Swimming in a school with many other fish can scare away predators who might think that the school is just one animal that is much (large) than itself. (4) Also, the predator might get confused trying to decide which of the fish in the school is the (easy) prey and thus not catch any at all. (5) Other animals protect themselves by hiding in the (dark) places they can find. (6) That way, it doesn't matter if they swim (slowly) than the hunters. (7) Colors can also help animals to protect themselves from the (ferocious) predators. (8) Some fish change color, becoming (dark) or (light) to match their backgrounds. (9) The (bright) the color is, the (poisonous) or distasteful the fish. (10) Although these survival techniques are very helpful, animals still must move (carefully) than their predators.

▶ **Exercise 11** Revising to Eliminate Errors in Comparisons Rewrite the following sentences, correcting any errors in comparisons that you find.

1. That is the most happiest dog that I have ever seen.
2. The situation could not be more worse.
3. She can throw even further than I can.
4. My worse fears have been realized.
5. Jan enjoys writing poetry more better than I do.

▶ **Exercise 12** Find It in Your Reading In addition to the adjectives highlighted in the excerpt from "The Loch Ness Monster" on page 543, the author also used the adjectives *dark* and *strange* and the adverb *successfully*. List the comparative and superlative forms of these modifiers.

▶ **Exercise 13** Find It in Your Writing Look through your writing portfolio. Find one comparative form and one superlative form of an adjective and an adverb. If you cannot find examples, choose an adjective and an adverb in the positive degree and write the comparative and superlative forms.

▶ **Exercise 14** Writing Application Write a brief description of an imaginary sea monster. Include the comparative and the superlative forms of an adjective and an adverb.

Troublesome Modifers

You probably use most adjectives and adverbs with little difficulty. Using modifiers is important, because they add detail
to speaking and writing. They help make communication
clear. For example, if a fish hides in the sea grass, does it hide
well or *badly*? Such modifiers can add important details.

Some frequently used modifiers can be troublesome. For
instance, is it correct to say *It hides bad* or *It hides badly*? (In
this case, the answer is *It hides badly. Badly* is an adverb,
and an adverb is needed to modify the verb *hide*.)

To understand troublesome modifiers, you must learn
which word in each pair is an adjective and which word is an
adverb. Then, when a sentence requires either an adjective or
an adverb, you will know which word to use.

In this section, two pairs of troublesome modifiers are presented. First, the modifiers *bad* and *badly* are explained.
Then, the modifiers *good* and *well* are discussed. The exercises will give you practice in using all of these modifiers.

Using *Bad* and *Badly*

You will not confuse *bad* and *badly* if you remember that
bad is an adjective and *badly* is an adverb.

▶ **KEY CONCEPT** *Bad* is an adjective. It is used with linking
verbs. ■

The two examples that follow show *bad* used correctly.

EXAMPLES: The bite of an alligator is <u>bad</u>.
                             LV
               Your cough sounds <u>bad</u>.

In the sentences above, the adjective *bad* is used following a
linking verb to describe the subject of the sentence. Other
linking verbs that are used with *bad* are *appear, become, feel,
grow, remain, seem, smell, stay, taste,* and *turn.*

▶ **KEY CONCEPT** *Badly* is an adverb. It is used with action
verbs. ■

EXAMPLES: The seal performed <u>badly</u> because it was hurt.
               Jim draws animals <u>badly</u>.

To summarize, if the modifier follows a linking verb and
describes the subject, use *bad.* If the modifier follows an
action verb and describes the action, use *badly.*

Exercise 15 Using *Bad* and *Badly* Choose the correct modifier—*bad* or *badly*—to complete each sentence below.

1. The ocean environment is (bad, badly) for hatching their young, so sea turtles lay their eggs on sandy beaches.
2. Because their flippers are made for swimming, they crawl along the beaches (bad, badly).
3. On the land, they protect themselves (bad, badly), but in the sea, they can rely on their size and strength.
4. Their large flippers ensure that they do not swim (bad, badly).
5. As parents, sea turtles may seem (bad, badly) because they don't return to take care of the eggs.
6. The survival rate of baby sea turtles looks (bad, badly).
7. The number of sea turtles in the world has decreased (bad, badly).
8. They are treated (bad, badly) by humans, who hunt them and their eggs for food.
9. The outlook appears (bad, badly) unless people do more to protect the sea turtles.
10. Turtles are called coldblooded because they are (bad, badly) at regulating their body temperature.

Using *Good* and *Well*

Good and *well* are used differently in sentences. *Good* is always an adjective, but *well* can be either an adjective or an adverb. To decide which word to use, you must think about the meaning of the sentence and how the word is being used.

KEY CONCEPT *Good* is an adjective. It is used with linking verbs. ∎

EXAMPLES: The quality of the water has been <u>good</u>. (LV)

The sea air smells <u>good</u>. (LV)

We felt <u>good</u> after our swim. (LV)

More Practice

Grammar Exercise Workbook
• pp. 131–132
On-line Exercise Bank
• Section 25.2
  Go on-line:
  PHSchool.com
  Enter Web Code:
  eak-6002

iText

Get instant feedback! Exercise 15 is available on-line or on CD-ROM.

▼ **Critical Viewing** Using the words *bad* and *badly* in a sentence, discuss how a sea turtle moves on land. **[Infer]**

> **KEY CONCEPT** *Well* can be an adverb or an adjective. When *well* is an adverb, it is used with an action verb. ∎

WELL AS AN ADVERB:

Many water birds can swim and fly <u>well</u>.
                   AV   AV

Other types of animals also live <u>well</u> both in the water and on land.
  AV

Loons dive <u>well</u> because their feet, which propel them, are set far back on their bodies.
 AV

When *well* is an adjective, it is used with a linking verb and usually refers to a person's health.

WELL AS AN ADJECTIVE:

The fish looked <u>well</u> after the attack by the eel.
  LV

The eel seems <u>well</u>, too, but he looks hungry.
  LV

Are you <u>well</u> enough to travel?
 LV

> **Exercise 16** Using *Good* and *Well* Choose the correct modifier—*good* or *well*—to complete each sentence below.
> 1. Mallard ducks live (good, well) in any type of water—salty, brackish, or fresh.
> 2. They adapt (good, well) to new environments.
> 3. Their webbed feet are (good, well) as paddles.
> 4. It was (good, well) to see the mother protecting the babies.
> 5. I'm afraid that one baby is not (good, well).

> **Exercise 17** Revising Sentences With Troublesome Modifiers Read each of the following sentences. If the modifier is used correctly, write *correct.* If the modifier is used incorrectly, rewrite the sentence, correcting the modifier.
> 1. During his illness, Henry looked badly.
> 2. Tony is very talented; he sings good.
> 3. For a campsite, this spot looks well.
> 4. It was good to hear that song again.
> 5. How good do you know him?
> 6. Paul draws bad.
> 7. This new soap smells good.
> 8. Are you feeling well enough to go?
> 9. Because she was in a hurry, she printed bad.
> 10. I felt badly because I forgot your birthday.

More Practice

Grammar Exercise Workbook
• pp. 133–134
On-line Exercise Bank
• Section 25.2
Go on-line:
PHSchool.com
Enter Web Code:
eak-6002

Get instant feedback! Exercises 16 and 17 are available on-line or on CD-ROM.

Section 25.2 Section Review

GRAMMAR EXERCISES 18–24

Exercise 18 Using *Bad* and *Badly*
Write the correct modifier—*bad* or *badly*—to follow each verb below.

1. sings
2. appears
3. seems
4. limps
5. runs

Exercise 19 Using *Good* and *Well*
Write the correct modifier—*good* or *well*—to follow each verb below. (Assume that none of the verbs refer to a person's health.)

1. dashes
2. sounds
3. skitters
4. floats
5. becomes

Exercise 20 Using Troublesome Modifiers Choose the correct modifier to complete each sentence below.

1. Gulls used to live only near the seashore, but now they can survive (good, well) near inland bodies of water, too.
2. They eat (good, well) off animals that live in the water, although they live on land themselves.
3. Gulls are (good, well) at waiting and will patiently search for locations with many fish.
4. That gull injured its wing (bad, badly) when it flew into the window.
5. The wound looks (bad, badly) enough to prevent it from flying.

Exercise 21 Revising a Passage to Eliminate Problems With Modifiers On a separate sheet of paper, rewrite the passage below, correcting any modifier errors.

The spines along the top of a stingray's tail work good as a form of protection. They protect the stingray well from anything that approaches from above. If you step on a resting stingray, you can cut your foot bad. Not all stingrays behave bad. At "Stingray City" in the Cayman Islands, the relationship between stingrays and scuba divers is well. They play good together. This is good for tourism. People learn that stingrays are not bad. I feel badly that stingrays are misunderstood. It seems good that people are learning more about these animals.

Exercise 22 Find It in Your Reading Skim through a magazine to find examples of *bad, badly, good,* and *well.* Explain why each usage is correct.

Exercise 23 Find It in Your Writing Review the compositions in your portfolio for examples of the troublesome modifiers discussed in this section. Check to make sure that you have used each modifier correctly.

Exercise 24 Writing Application Write a brief description of an animal that has a bad reputation. Explain why you think this reputation is or is not deserved. Use *bad, badly, good,* and *well* in your description.

GRAMMAR EXERCISES 25–32

Exercise 25 **Charting Degrees of Comparison** Make a chart showing the positive, comparative, and superlative forms of each adjective or adverb below.

1. sad
2. eagerly
3. probable
4. unlikely
5. lightly
6. humid
7. wild
8. suddenly
9. cranky
10. powerfully

Exercise 26 **Using Comparative and Superlative Forms of Adjectives and Adverbs** Rewrite the sentences below, using the comparative or superlative form of the adjective or adverb in parentheses.

1. Queen conches can grow (large) than a child's head.
2. Young conches live in sea grass; here, of all places, they can (easily) hide from hungry predators.
3. When they grow (big), they move out of the grass to the sand.
4. Their (common) food is plant matter that they find along the ocean floor.
5. Some people think conch chowder is (delicious) than clam chowder.
6. Those earrings made from conch shells are (beautiful) than these.
7. (Old) civilizations, such as the Mayan, treasured the shells of queen conches.
8. From the shells, people crafted jewelry and spoons, which they considered their (prized) possessions.
9. Overfishing of conches is one of the (serious) problems for Caribbean countries, in whose waters conches live.
10. Governments have made laws to protect the conches from their (fearsome) enemies: humans.

Exercise 27 **Supplying Comparative and Superlative Forms of Adjectives and Adverbs** Use the comparative or superlative form of an adjective or adverb from the list to fill each blank below. Use each word only once.

wet   close   slowly   loud   comfortable
slow   large   strong   similar   tiny

1. The ___?___ instinct of most frogs is to live in a moist area.
2. The frog laid its eggs near the river because it is ___?___ there than in the woods.
3. Some tree frogs lay their eggs on the bottom sides of leaves. They choose the leaves that are the ___?___ to the water.
4. Tadpoles resemble fish ___?___ than they do frogs.
5. They are ___?___ in water than on land.
6. Frogs are carnivorous and will eat animals, insects, worms, and spiders that are ___?___ than themselves.
7. However, they may also eat animals that are ___?___ than they.
8. A tadpole may change into a frog in a few months, but some go through the process ___?___.
9. Snakes and turtles are ___?___ than frogs, but they still feed on them.
10. That frog croaks the ___?___ of all.

Exercise 28 **Using Troublesome Modifiers** Write the correct modifier from those in parentheses when you copy each sentence below.

1. Crabs discard their old shells just as we discard old clothes that fit (bad, badly).
2. A crab's soft, new shell is not (good, well) for protection.

3. Soon, the new shells harden, and they protect the crabs (good, well) once again.
4. This crab looks (good, well) in a shell abandoned by another animal.
5. Crabs are (good, well) scavengers.
6. They also hunt (good, well) for food.
7. Their claws work (good, well) when grabbing worms and tiny animals.
8. The claws of fiddler crabs aren't used for hunting, but they don't function (bad, badly) as warning flags to other fiddler crabs.
9. The porcelain crabs have claws that are (bad, badly) for grabbing food.
10. As a result, they use a method that seems (good, well) for them: They spread a net made of mucus between their two claws to entrap food floating by.

▶ **Exercise 29** Recognizing the Correct Modifier Choose the correct modifier from those in parentheses to complete each sentence.

1. Crocodilians, the word used for both alligators and crocodiles, are (more advanced, most advanced) than the fish, frogs, and salamanders that developed before them.
2. They survive on land (more easily, most easily) than any other animal did before them.
3. They can also breathe (good, well) while they are in the water, as long as their nostrils remain above water.
4. Crocodiles have (narrow, narrower, narrowest) snouts than alligators have.
5. Because they are coldblooded, however, they cannot regulate their body temperatures and do not survive (well, good) in very hot or very cold conditions.

▶ **Exercise 30** Revising a Paragraph With Modifiers Some sentences in the following paragraph contain modifier errors. Rewrite the sentences correctly.

American alligators are found in freshwater lakes, rivers, and swamps most often than crocodiles are. The American alligator is the more famous type of crocodilian. Spanish explorers told stories that portrayed alligators bad. They said alligators were the more ferocious beasts alive. The explorers said that alligators had bulletproof skin and made the loud noises they had ever heard. For the first year or two of their lives, alligators are bad at protecting themselves. Because they are defenseless, they have to rely on most strategic ways to discourage their enemies. Their high-pitched sounds scare away attackers good. The fate of crocodilians does not look good. Crocodilians need humans' help bad to get them off the endangered species list.

▶ **Exercise 31** Writing Sentences With Modifiers Write five sentences, using each of the following modifiers in the degree indicated.

1. slowly (comparative)
2. beautiful (superlative)
3. fast (superlative)
4. tall (comparative)
5. loud (comparative and superlative)

▶ **Exercise 32** Writing Application Write a description of some things you might find during a walk on the beach. Include two comparative forms and two superlative forms of adjectives or adverbs.

Standardized Test Preparation Workshop

Using Modifiers

Standardized test questions often measure your ability to use modifiers correctly. One way this is done is by testing your ability to choose the correct form of comparison to complete a sentence. Use the following strategies to help you determine which form to use in a sentence:

- If no comparison is being made, use the positive form of the modifier.

- If one thing or action is compared with another thing or action, use the comparative form of the modifier—ending in *-er* or preceded by *more*.

- If one thing or action is being compared with more than one other thing or action, use the superlative form of the modifier—ending in *-est* or preceeded by *most*.

The following sample items will give you practice in answering these types of standardized test questions.

Test Tip

Avoid using double comparisons, such as *most happiest,* to complete a sentence. The correct forms are *most happy* or *happiest*.

Sample Test Items

Directions Read the passage, and choose the letter of the word or group of words that belongs in each space.

Today was the ___(1)___ day of the entire year. Although yesterday was uncomfortable, today is even ___(2)___ because it is so windy.

1 A cold
  B colder
  C coldest
  D most coldest

2 F bad
  G badder
  H worse
  J worst

Answers and Explanations

The correct answer for item 1 is *C*. The comparison is being made between today and all the other days of the year, so the superlative form *coldest* should be used to complete the sentence.

The correct answer for item 2 is *H*. The comparison is being made between two days, so the comparative form *worse* should be used to complete the sentence.

► **Practice 1** **Directions:** Read the passage, and choose the letter of the word or group of words that belongs in each space.

During the winter, there is nothing __(1)__ than a big snowstorm. Even the __(2)__ weather can still be enjoyed. A snowstorm can be __(3)__ than a summer thunderstorm. During the storm, we all huddle around the fire, and have a contest to see who can tell the __(4)__ story. After the storm is over, there is no sight __(5)__ than a world covered in a beautiful white blanket.

1 **A** exciting
  B more excited
  C most exciting
  D more exciting

2 **F** bad
  G badder
  H worse
  J worst

3 **A** fun
  B funner
  C more fun
  D funnest

4 **F** good
  G better
  H best
  J more better

5 **A** spectacular
  B spectacularer
  C most spectacular
  D more spectacular

► **Practice 2** **Directions:** Read the passage, and choose the letter of the word or group of words that belongs in each space.

Winter sports are among the __(1)__ challenging. Downhill skiing takes __(2)__ than many sports, and using snowshoes is __(3)__ than hiking in the woods. Walking or gliding on snow or ice requires your body to work its __(4)__ while keeping every muscle moving and maintaining your balance. __(5)__ times, you can push your body too far without even knowing it. Take it easy and have fun!

1 **A** physical
  B more physically
  C physically
  D most physically

2 **F** coordination
  G more coordination
  H most coordination
  J more coordinated

3 **A** exhausted
  B exhausting
  C more exhausting
  D most exhausting

4 **F** harder
  G hardest
  H most hardest
  J more hard

5 **A** Much
  B Many
  C More
  D Most

Cumulative Review

USAGE

Using Verbs Choose the correct verb or verb phrase in parentheses to complete each sentence below. Identify its principal part and tense.

1. Several Native American groups (brung, brought) their culture to what is now Texas.
2. The foundations of early dwellings were found where they were (lain, laid).
3. The Karankawa (did, done) a great deal of fishing in the Gulf of Mexico.
4. The Apache and the Comanche (caught, catched) and (eat, ate) the buffalo.
5. Alonzo Álvarez de Piñeda (set, sat) foot in Texas in 1519.
6. He was (leading, led) a group around the mouth of the Rio Grande.
7. Cabeza de Vaca (began, begun) to explore more of inland Texas.
8. In 1682, the Spanish (built, builded) the first mission in Texas.
9. That was near where present-day El Paso (is, was).
10. Spain (knew, known) that France was claiming the area.

Exercise B **Identifying the Case** of Pronouns Identify the case of each pronoun in the following sentences as *nominative*, *objective*, or *possessive*.

1. One French explorer was La Salle. He built a fort near Matagorda Bay.
2. La Salle named it Fort Saint Louis.
3. France claimed the Mississippi River and its tributaries.
4. In 1716, the Spanish established missions, founding them throughout the territory.
5. They include the city of San Antonio.
6. However, the Spanish found that their hold on the province of Texas was weak.
7. Expeditions of adventurers from the United States had been traveling through it.
8. Philip Nolan led one invasion, but the Spanish captured him.
9. In 1820, Moses Austin, a United States citizen, made his request to settle in Texas.
10. His son, Stephen F. Austin, carried out the plan.

Exercise C **Using Agreement** Fill in each blank below with a pronoun that agrees with its antecedent.

1. In our social studies class, __?__ are studying Texas and __?__ fight for independence.
2. Texans decided that they wanted to make __?__ own laws.
3. The Mexican government wanted settlers in Texas to obey __?__ laws.
4. General Santa Anna gathered __?__ troops together to crush the rebellious Texans.
5. Texans declared __?__ independence from Mexico on March 2, 1836, in Washington-on-the-Brazos.
6. Either Oleg or Sam will give __?__ report on the Alamo today.
7. Fewer than 200 Texans tried to defend __?__ territory against Santa Anna's army there.
8. Jim Bowie, Davey Crockett, and William B. Travis lost __?__ lives at the Alamo.
9. I hope that I will do well on __?__ test about the Alamo.
10. Texans captured Santa Anna and forced __?__ to sign a treaty.

Exercise D — Using Verb Agreement

Write the form of the verb in parentheses that agrees with the subject of each sentence below.

1. All of our reports (be) about the settling of the West.
2. Many students (want) to write about California.
3. No one (know) more about the early days in California than Rudy.
4. Everybody in our class (love) to look at the maps of the trails heading west.
5. Each of the students (have) to pick a trail to report on.
6. Julie and Thomas (ask) to read about the Oregon Trail.
7. Neither Sam nor Randy (have) picked a topic yet.
8. Tanya and I (hope) to do our report on the Santa Fe Trail.
9. Either the Santa Fe Trail or the Oregon Trail (be) interesting.
10. According to the map, each of the trails (appear) to begin in Independence, Missouri.

Exercise E — Using Modifiers

In the sentences below, write the form of the adjective or adverb indicated in parentheses.

1. A Texan army gathered (quickly—comparative) than expected.
2. After taking San Antonio, (many—superlative) soldiers left the city.
3. They believed that Santa Anna, the Mexican dictator, would wait until (late—positive) spring.
4. Santa Anna's army was (large—comparative) than that of the settlers.
5. The (small—superlative) of all Texan forces withdrew to the Alamo.
6. (Brave—comparative) than expected, the Texans fought for thirteen days.
7. (Many—superlative) of the Texan forces were defeated in other battles.
8. Then, a group of Texans declared inde-pendence (cautiously—comparative) than they had earlier.
9. They attacked, (probably—superlative) surprising the Mexican Army.
10. Santa Anna (soon—positive) recognized Texas's independence.

Exercise F — Correcting Usage Mistakes

Rewrite the following sentences, correcting any errors in usage.

1. The Republic of Texas continued their existence for almost ten years.
2. The more prominent of all Texas's problems was finances.
3. There was disputes about the new country's boundaries.
4. More immigrants came to Texas, and the troubles did not prevent they from settling.
5. Sam Houston will be one who wanted the United States to annex the republic.
6. After Sam Houston wins in the battle of San Jacinto, Texas had become independent.
7. These two groups, the Cherokee and the Mexicans, brought its concerns into battle.
8. However, the Cherokee and them were arrested by the Texas army.
9. A new president of Texas, Mirabeau Lamar, were elected in 1838.
10. The Cherokee resist his orders, but they were defeated and moved to what is now Oklahoma.

Exercise G — Writing Application

Write a short description of the state in which you live or one that you have visited. Be sure that the words in your sentences follow the rules of agreement and that your modifiers are used correctly. Then, list the verbs and verb phrases, identifying their tenses. Make a list of pronouns, and identify their case.

Punctuation

How would you punctuate the following string of words? *Please deliver the tomato soup chicken salad corn bread and fruit I ordered.* The sentence needs punctuation to get its meaning across.

Correct punctuation helps make the meaning of a sentence clear. It does this by telling the reader when to pause briefly and when to come to a full stop. It also tells whether a sentence is meant to make a statement, ask a question, give a command, or show surprise or strong emotion.

This chapter tells about five different groupings of punctuation marks: end marks; commas; semicolons and colons; quotation marks and underlining; and hyphens and apostrophes. You should read, study, and practice using all these marks. Notice how they are used in the books, newspapers, and magazines you read.

▲ **Critical Viewing** What physical characteristics help this monkey move successfully through the jungle? How do punctuation marks help readers move successfully through written compositions? **[Connect]**

Diagnostic Test

Directions: Write all answers on a separate sheet of paper.

Skill Check A. Write the correct end mark for each sentence below.

1. What is the difference between a rain forest and a jungle
2. A jungle is like a rain forest but is not as moist or dark
3. Rain forests get more than one hundred inches of rain a year
4. Trees in the rain forest form a canopy over the forest floor
5. Wow That means there's not as much sunlight in a rain forest

Skill Check B. Rewrite the following sentences, adding commas where needed. If a sentence is correct, write *correct.*

6. However due to the heavy forestation all rain forests are jungles.
7. Most of the world's rain forests and jungles are in South and Central America Africa and Southeast Asia.
8. Jamaica is 4244 square miles and it was once mostly rain forest.
9. Many jungles and rain forests are shrinking for the local governments allow the land to be destroyed.
10. The forest can't support life once the trees and plants are gone.

Skill Check C. Rewrite the following sentences, adding colons and semicolons where necessary.

11. Rain forests produce more vegetation than any other land on Earth the tropical sun and heavy rain encourage rapid growth.
12. Trees are the foundation of any jungle they provide shelter for other plants and animals, produce flowers that feed insects and birds, and bear fruits that feed animals and insects.
13. Rain forests shelter three creatures that eat ants the slow loris, the tamandua anteater, and the giant pangolin.
14. It isn't easy to explain rain forests and jungles within each, there is a wide variety of environments.
15. Caitlin posted a sign in her room that read Caution Rain Forests and Jungles Disappearing.

Skill Check D. Add quotation marks to the sentences below.

16. How can the jungles and rain forests be saved? asked my sister.
17. Well, my mother said, we must learn their value to Earth.
18. I read an article last week about Peruvian rain forests.
19. Jim asked, Where can I find out about rain forests and jungles?
20. There's information on the Internet and on television, said Mother.

Skill Check E. Rewrite the following sentences, adding hyphens and apostrophes where necessary.

21. In the 1970s attention began to be focused on saving nature.
22. Many people thought this was somehow anti American.
23. The truth is that conservationists just wanted to defend people, places, and animals that couldnt defend themselves.
24. Without the worlds rain forests, Earth would suffer.
25. Its a problem that is everyones responsibility.

End Marks

Using Periods

A period indicates the end of a sentence or an abbreviation.

▶ **KEY CONCEPT** Use a period to end a declarative sentence—a statement of fact or opinion. ■

DECLARATIVE SENTENCE: Ocean water is always moving.

▶ **KEY CONCEPT** Use a period to end an imperative sentence—a direction or command. ■

IMPERATIVE SENTENCE: Finish reading the chapter.

▶ **KEY CONCEPT** Use a period to end a sentence that contains an indirect question. ■

An *indirect question* reports a question but does not ask it. It does not give the speaker's exact words.

INDIRECT QUESTION: Mae asked me whether I could stay.

▶ **KEY CONCEPT** Use a period after most abbreviations and after initials. ■

ABBREVIATIONS: Gov.   Mrs.   St.   Rd.   in.   Jr.
INITIALS: E. B. White   Robin F. Brancato

WHEN TO USE A PERIOD	
With a Declarative Sentence	Many types of owls live in the desert.
With an Imperative Sentence	Do not carve holes in the cactus.
With an Indirect Question	Carl asked if rattlesnakes can swim.
With an Abbreviation	Mr. Jackson guides tours of the desert.

▶ **Exercise 1** **Using Periods** Copy the following sentences, adding periods where necessary.

1. Coyotes are related to dogs and are smaller than wolves
2. A full-grown coyote measures about 47 in long
3. Coyote babies, called pups, are born in April and May
4. A coyote was once seen near Lester Blvd in our town
5. The tail of a coyote is 11–16 in long

Get instant feedback! Exercise 1 is available on-line or on CD-ROM.

Using Question Marks

A question mark follows a word, phrase, or sentence that asks a question.

▶ **KEY CONCEPT** Use a question mark after an interrogative sentence—one that asks a direct question. ■

INTERROGATIVE
SENTENCES:

Do snakes hatch from eggs?
Are there ever floods in the desert?

Sometimes, a single word or brief phrase is used to ask a direct question. Such a question is punctuated as though it were a complete sentence because the words left out are easily understood.

▶ **KEY CONCEPT** Use a question mark after a word or phrase that asks a question. ■

EXAMPLES:

Many small birds build false nests. Why?
(Understood: Why do small birds build false nests?)
It can be risky to walk alone in the desert. In what way?
(Understood: In what way is it risky to walk alone?)

Do not use a question mark with an *indirect question*—a sentence that is really a statement but relates to a question.

EXAMPLE:

I asked how coyotes raise their young.

▲ **Critical Viewing**
Write a question concerning the ways these coyotes resemble dogs, then write the answer. Make sure that you use the correct end mark with each sentence. **[Compare]**

QUESTIONS AND HOW TO PUNCTUATE THEM	
Direct Question in a Complete Sentence	Use a question mark. (How old is Steven?)
Direct Question in an Incomplete Sentence	Use a question mark. (How tall?)
Indirect Question	Use a period. (I asked Steven where he was born.)

▲ Critical Viewing
Write an indirect
question about the
ability of a cactus to
survive in the dry
desert climate.
Which end mark is
needed for your
sentence? [Analyze]

Exercise 2 **Using Question Marks and Periods** Copy the
sentences below, adding question marks and periods where
necessary.

EXAMPLE: Are all the deserts in the US located between the
Rocky Mts and the Sierra Nevada range

ANSWER: Are all the deserts in the U.S. located between
the Rocky Mts. and the Sierra Nevada range?

1. Where are the four desert areas of the United States located
2. Is a desert defined by the amount of rain it gets each year
3. The Great Basin, a cold desert, is mostly in Nevada and
   Utah
4. People ask whether it can snow in a cold desert
5. In the Mojave Desert lives an animal called a cave myotis
   Does it fly
6. Are the plants, animals, and insects in the Chihuahuan
   Desert different from those at the beach
7. Some of the plants in the desert are cactus and wildflowers
8. The rainbow cactus is found in W Texas and S Arizona
   Can a cactus bloom
9. In the very hot Sonoran Desert, the rabbits sometimes dig
   holes Why
10. One desert reptile, the Texas horned lizard, is also found
    in Oklahoma and Kansas

Using Exclamation Marks

An exclamation mark indicates strong feeling or emotion, including surprise.

▶ **KEY CONCEPT** Use an exclamation mark to end an exclamatory sentence. ■

EXCLAMATORY SENTENCES: Look at that huge vulture!
The sagebrush smells great!
There's a red-tailed hawk!

▶ **KEY CONCEPT** Use an exclamation mark after an imperative sentence that gives a forceful or urgent command. ■

IMPERATIVE SENTENCES: Be careful not to sit on the cactus!
Don't spill the water!

Remember: Only imperative sentences containing *forceful* commands are followed by an exclamation mark. Mild imperatives are followed by a period: Please sit down.

▶ **KEY CONCEPT** Use an exclamation mark after an interjection expressing strong emotion. ■

INTERJECTIONS: Wow! That was a great throw.
Oh! Look what I found.

▶ **Exercise 3**   **Using Exclamation Marks and Periods** Copy the sentences below on your paper, adding the necessary exclamation marks and periods.

1. Giant scorpions can be 5 1/2 in long That's pretty big
2. The great horned owl lives in deserts It really seems to have horns
3. Conservationists work to protect deserts and desert creatures It's a very important job
4. A slider sounds like it should be a snake, but it's a turtle
5. Get too close and the Western diamondback rattlesnake will rattle its tail and bite
6. Desert candles don't really burn They're wildflowers
7. Turkey vultures live in the Sonoran Desert They don't look like turkeys at all
8. The white-winged dove is so beautiful However, it sometimes makes an annoying sound
9. The common nighthawk hunts mainly at night, of course
10. You don't wear the desert inky cap on your head It's a mushroom

▶ **More Practice**

Grammar Exercise Workbook
• pp. 139–140
On-line Exercise Bank
• Section 26.1
  Go on-line:
  PHSchool.com
  Enter Web Code:
  eak-6002

 Text

Get instant feedback! Exercises 2 and 3 are available on-line or on CD-ROM.

Hands-on Grammar

Rounding Up End Marks

The punctuation mark you use at the end of a sentence lets a reader know whether you are making a statement, asking a question, giving an order, or showing strong emotion. Practice using the right end marks for your sentences with the following activity.

Make a spinner out of cardboard or index cards. Cut out two circles, one somewhat smaller than the other. With a pencil, press a hole in the center of each circle. Then, connect the two circles with a paper fastener pushed through the two center holes.

Write the three end marks two times each, evenly spaced around the outside of the larger circle, in an alternating pattern.(See model.) Then, draw three lines across the smaller circle, so that it is divided into six even "pie slices." In each slice, write a simple sentence or question with no end mark. Examples: *Will you open the door / The forest is beautiful / The moon seems very bright tonight / Can you see a rattlesnake over there / The fire did destroy the building / This is exciting /*

Work with a partner. One partner spins the inner circle and lines up the sentences with the end marks. Then, work around the circle, reading each sentence exactly as it is or rewording it slightly so that it fits the end mark. For example, you may need to add an interjection to make the sentence an exclamation, or you may have to invert some words to change a question to a statement or a statement to a question. Spin again to line up the sentences with different end marks, and repeat the exercise.

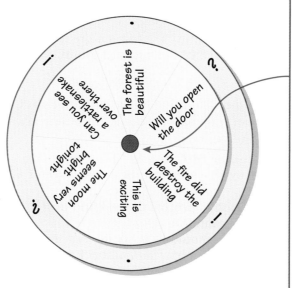

Use a paper fastener to attach wheel

Find It in Your Reading In a story or article, find examples of sentences with all three end marks. Read the sentences aloud to see how the punctuation mark affects the meaning of the sentence.

Find It in Your Writing Look through samples of your own writing to find statements, questions, and exclamations. Check to be sure that you have punctuated them correctly.

Section Review

GRAMMAR EXERCISES 4–9

Exercise 4 **Writing Abbreviations**
Write an abbreviation for each of the following items. Check a dictionary if you need help.

1. Post Office
2. Commander
3. September
4. each
5. yard

Exercise 5 **Supplying Correct End Marks** Copy each sentence or group of sentences below, adding appropriate end marks.

1. Bats fly at night How do they keep from crashing into cactuses
2. Wolves and coyotes don't live together in groups, do they
3. Should desert plants and animals be protected Yes
4. The beavertail cactus has attractive flowers Be careful of its hidden spines
5. I asked where golden eagles nest if there are no trees
6. The Great Basin has fewer cactuses and yuccas than other deserts
7. The elephant tree has beautiful leaves Its flowers are small, but stinky
8. The lowest elevation in the U.S. is in the Mojave Desert What is it called
9. When the zebratail lizard runs, does it hold its tail in the air
10. The Sonoran Desert is home to the tiniest owl on earth Wow The elf owl is only 5–6 in long

Exercise 6 **Identifying Declarative, Imperative, Interrogative, or Exclamatory Sentences** Label each sentence below *declarative, imperative, interrogative,* or *exclamatory.* Then, indicate the appropriate end mark.

1. Is there enough water anywhere in a desert for fish to live

2. The cactus wren lives in the desert
3. Don't bother the badgers
4. The skin of a few North American frogs releases a fluid harmful to humans
5. I know a shrike eats insects, but does it eat anything else
6. Wow A thunderstorm in the desert is very beautiful
7. Don't leave your trash in the desert
8. Be safety conscious Never sit down in the desert without looking first
9. Never go into the desert without water and the proper tools to survive
10. In which three North American deserts does the desert gold plant grow

Exercise 7 **Find It in Your Reading**
Read the following excerpt from "Why Monkeys Live in Trees." Explain why the writer has used three different end marks.

. . . At that exact moment, one of Leopard's children ran up to him. "Daddy! Daddy! Are you going to be in the contest?"

Exercise 8 **Find It in Your Writing**
Look through your portfolio for sentences that you have ended with a period, a question mark, or an exclamation mark. Explain why each end mark is appropriate.

Exercise 9 **Writing Application**
Write five sentences to a friend in which you identify animals you would like to see. Include the following items, and be sure to use the correct end marks.

1. a direct question
2. a forceful imperative sentence
3. a sentence with an interjection
4. an abbreviation
5. an exclamation

Commas

Using Commas to Separate Basic Elements

End marks signal a full stop. Commas signal a brief pause. A comma may be used to separate elements in a sentence or to set off part of a sentence.

Commas in Compound Sentences A comma is used to separate two independent clauses that are joined by a coordinating conjunction to form a *compound sentence*.

▶ **KEY CONCEPT** Use a comma before the conjunction to separate two independent clauses in a compound sentence. ∎

The comma in a compound sentence is followed by one of the following conjunctions: *and, but, for, nor, or, so,* or *yet.*

COMPOUND
SENTENCE: Chimpanzees are grown at age five, but their mothers still take care of them.

Do not use a comma when there is just a word, phrase, or subordinate clause on either side of the conjunction.

WORDS: We saw *chimpanzees* and *gorillas.*

PHRASES: Light was reflected *from the road* and *off the car's hood.*

SUBORDINATE
CLAUSES: Choose someone *who has experience* but *who can also follow directions.*

▶ **Exercise 10** Using Commas in Compound Sentences A comma has been left out of each of the following sentences. On your paper, write the word before the comma, the comma, and the conjunction following the comma.

EXAMPLE: Monkeys are in the animal family called primates and apes and humans are, too.

ANSWER: primates, and

1. Collared brown lemurs are protected as an endangered species but they continue to be killed for food.
2. Olive baboons communicate well with each other for they make more than fifteen different vocal sounds.
3. Geladas live in families of about twenty in Ethiopia yet as many as four hundred may sleep in a group for safety.
4. Orangutans eat soft fruit like figs and mangos or they will eat insects and birds if fruit is not plentiful.
5. Male baboons are larger yet the females carry the young.

Theme: The Jungle

In this section, you will learn how to use commas correctly in your writing. The examples and exercises are about different jungle animals and plants.

Cross-Curricular Connection: Science

▶ **More Practice**

Grammar Exercise Workbook
• pp. 141–142
On-line Exercise Bank
• Section 26.2
  Go on-line:
  PHSchool.com
  Enter Web Code:
  eak-6002

Get instant feedback! Exercises 10 and 11 are available on-line or on CD-ROM.

GRAMMAR IN LITERATURE

from **Why Monkeys Live in Trees**

Julius Lester

In these sentences, the writer has used commas to separate items in a series, making the information easier to read.

Monkey went to the mound, took a tiny bit of pepper on his tongue, swallowed, and went into the tall grasses. A few minutes later, Monkey came out, took a little more, swallowed it, and went into the tall grasses.

▶ **Exercise 11** **Proofreading Sentences for Commas** Copy each of the sentences below, adding commas where needed. If no comma is needed, write *none*.

1. Gorillas and chimpanzees do not have tails but most monkeys do.
2. There are three types of gorillas and mountain gorillas are the rarest.
3. Chimpanzees may use sticks in a humanlike manner to get termites for food but gorillas don't do that.
4. Adult male mountain gorillas weigh four hundred pounds and they stand six feet tall.
5. One would think the mountain gorilla's size would guarantee survival yet in 1997 only six hundred remained in the wild.
6. Leave immediately if a gorilla begins to grunt and beat its chest.
7. A gorilla is too big to live in trees and it cannot swing from branch to branch like a monkey.
8. The fat-tailed dwarf lemur stores fat in its tail so it can hibernate six months each year.
9. The black-capped capuchin monkey lives in trees yet it will hop down to catch frogs for dinner.
10. Primates are generally defenseless against humans and they deserve our help.

Using Commas in Series

Sometimes, a sentence lists a number of items. When three or more items are listed, the list is called a *series*. The items in the series are separated by commas.

KEY CONCEPT Use commas to separate a series of words or a series of phrases. ■

The items in a series may be single words or groups of words.

SERIES OF WORDS: A gorilla's diet includes roots, stems, leaves, and bamboo. Many primates make human-like gestures, sounds, and faces.

SERIES OF PHRASES: All primates have the instincts to have families, to find food, to make safe nests, and to play with one another. When primates play, they may chase one another, hide behind trees, throw things at one another, or wrestle together.

Notice that each of the items except the last one in these series is followed by a comma. The conjunction *and* or *or* is added after the last comma.

If each item in a series is followed by a conjunction, commas are not needed; the conjunctions separate the items.

EXAMPLE: I visited castles and museums and forts.

▲ **Critical Viewing**
Write a sentence listing three different foods this gorilla might find in the jungle. Make sure that you use commas and a conjunction correctly in your sentence. **[Identify]**

Exercise 12 Using Commas With Items in a Series Copy each sentence below, adding commas where they are needed.

EXAMPLE: Redwoods pines and firs are all needleleaf trees.
ANSWER: Redwoods, pines, and firs are all needleleaf trees.

1. Snow monkeys are found in northern Africa India or Southeast Asia.
2. The aye-aye has big ears long fingers and an oversized tail.
3. Pileated gibbons have an eight- to ten-hour day spent sleeping feeding and calling to one another.
4. Uakaris live in the Amazon Basin and have bare red faces bald heads and shaggy white fur.
5. Snow monkeys will eat fruit and insects and small animals.

▶ **Exercise 13** Proofreading Sentences for Commas   Copy each sentence below, adding or removing commas as needed.

1. The Kayapo Indians have lived in the rain forest for centuries, but are losing their land to ranching mining and farming.
2. The tribe depends on the forest to provide food medicine from plants and housing.
3. The Yanomami in the Amazon gather hundreds of plants for food as well as fish fruit and even insects.
4. Native peoples the world over use wild plants as medicine, to heal wounds dull pain and cure fevers.
5. Other uses of plants include fuels dyes and insecticides.
6. The insects eat plants the birds eat insects and other animals eat birds, and plants.
7. The forest's careful balance has sustained the people plants animals and insects for millions of years.
8. We will never know what valuable element might be lost, if these areas are not protected from wasteful, mining logging and farming.
9. Each day a hundred species, including lizards birds snakes and insects are lost forever.
10. We must strive to respect plants, and wildlife.

Using Commas With Introductory Words and Phrases

When a sentence begins with an introductory word or phrase, that word or phrase is generally separated from the rest of the sentence by a comma.

▶ **KEY CONCEPT** Use a comma after an introductory word or phrase. ■

EXAMPLES: Yes, nightjars come out only at night.
Under a full moon, nightjars will sing all night!

The chart below gives additional examples of commas used after introductory words and phrases.

USING COMMAS WITH INTRODUCTORY WORDS AND PHRASES	
Introductory Words	<u>Well</u>, how shall we begin? <u>Jane</u>, please read that page aloud. <u>No</u>, we already have too many magazines.
Introductory Phrase	<u>Besides camping and hiking</u>, Dave also canoes.

▶ **More Practice**

Grammar Exercise Workbook
• pp. 143–144
On-line Exercise Bank
• Section 26.2
   Go on-line:
   PHSchool.com
   Enter Web Code:
   eak-6002

Get instant feedback! Exercises 12 and 13 are available on-line or on CD-ROM.

Exercise 14 Using Commas With Introductory Words and Phrases
Copy the sentences below, placing a comma after the introductory words and phrases.

EXAMPLE: After gathering other birds' feathers the African palm swift builds a nest.

ANSWER: After gathering other birds' feathers, the African palm swift builds a nest.

1. At birth parrots have no feathers and cannot see.
2. A beautiful bird the African gray parrot is a good talker.
3. Like most parrots the African gray nests in tree cavities.
4. Yes gray parrots can be noisy.
5. At 13 inches the African gray is the largest parrot in Africa.

More Practice

Grammar Exercise Workbook
• pp. 145–146
On-line Exercise Bank
• Section 26.2
Go on-line:
PHSchool.com
Enter Web Code:
eak-6002

Get instant feedback! Exercises 14 and 15 are available on-line or on CD-ROM.

Exercise 15 Proofreading a Passage for Commas
Copy the paragraph below on your paper, adding or removing commas as needed.

To protect themselves many plants, in the jungle give off chemicals harmful to insects. This keeps the insects from attacking, devouring and eventually destroying certain types of trees, and smaller plants. Most trees have bad-tasting chemicals in their leaves roots bark, and flowers. Over the centuries a few insects have been able to overcome some of the trees' defenses. For instance some caterpillars are not affected, by the toxic cycad leaf. In fact these caterpillars use the toxin to make their bodies red and yellow to ward off their own predators! Because of these natural chemicals insects are forced to eat a variety of plants. In this way no one plant or tree is wiped out by hungry insects, or animals. Natural characteristics make it possible for all living things to have a chance to survive. Amazingly this is just a tiny portion of what there is to know about the jungles and forests of the world.

▶ **Critical Viewing** Write a sentence with an introductory phrase to explain how this macaw's colors help protect it in the jungle. Make sure that you have used commas correctly in your sentence. **[Infer]**

Using Commas With Interrupting Words and Phrases

Some sentences contain words or phrases that interrupt the flow of the sentence. They should be set off from the rest of the sentence by commas.

KEY CONCEPT Use commas to set off interrupting words and phrases from the rest of the sentence. ■

The commas indicate that these words could be left out, and the sentence would still make sense.

Words That Name a Person Being Addressed

Interrupting words tell who is being spoken to.

EXAMPLES: Look, Nat, at what we did last week.

Well, Sarah, have you cleaned the parrot's cage?

Words That Rename a Noun Words that rename a noun give additional information about it.

EXAMPLES: His present, a camera, is just what he wanted.

My uncle, an expert on chimpanzees, will address the class next week.

Common Expressions Writers often use certain expressions to indicate that they are expressing an opinion, a conclusion, or a summary.

EXAMPLES: The game, I believe, starts at three o'clock.

The answer, in my opinion, lies in the bird's protective coloration.

The following chart presents several more examples of how commas are used to set off interrupting words, phrases, and expressions.

USING COMMAS WITH INTERRUPTING WORDS AND PHRASES	
To Name a Person Being Addressed	Why, Mr. Kane, are you doing that?
To Rename a Noun	Daniel Boone, an American pioneer, helped build the Wilderness Trail.
To Set Off a Common Expression	The forecast, for once, was accurate.

▶ **Exercise 16** Using Commas With Interrupting Words and Phrases Copy each sentence, adding commas where necessary.

1. There are many other ways Kevin for plants, seeds, and pollen to be dispersed in the jungle.
2. Animals and birds for instance may spread seeds or pollen to other areas of the forest.
3. Once deposited, the seeds likely as not will sprout and grow new plants.
4. Not all of the seeds certainly will grow into mature plants.
5. Yet obviously enough do mature to feed future generations.
6. The agouti a large Brazilian rodent sometimes hoards seeds from fruit found on the ground.
7. Later, the seeds long forgotten will sprout.
8. Anything even a raindrop can cause a plant to be pollinated.
9. The puffball a jungle fungus will release spores into the air that can be carried far away.
10. Can you think of other ways Tommy that the jungle has to re-create itself every day?

Using Commas With Addresses and in Letters

Commas are also used in addresses, salutations of friendly letters, and closings of friendly or business letters.

▶ **KEY CONCEPT** Use a comma after each item in an address made up of two or more parts. ■

EXAMPLE: She is writing to her friend Helen Wilson, 1402 Croydon Street, Apt. 2B, Princeton, New Jersey 08540.

Notice, however, that when the same address is written on an envelope, several of the commas are eliminated.

EXAMPLE: Helen Wilson
            1402 Croydon Street, Apt. 2B
            Princeton, NJ 08540

▶ **KEY CONCEPT** Use a comma after the salutation in a friendly letter. ■

SALUTATION: Dear Helen,

▶ **KEY CONCEPT** Use a comma after the closing of every letter. ■

CLOSINGS: Sincerely yours,   With warm regards,

▶ **More Practice**

Grammar Exercise Workbook
• pp. 147–150
On-line Exercise Bank
• Section 26.2
  Go on-line:
  PHSchool.com
  Enter Web Code:
  eak-6002

Get instant feedback! Exercises 16, 17, and 18 are available on-line or on CD-ROM.

Exercise 17 **Supplying Commas With Addresses and in Letters** Copy each address, salutation, and closing below. Add commas where necessary.

1. 1525 Porter Street New Kingston NY 12459
2. Very truly yours
3. Dear Louis
4. Best regards
5. 719 Desert Rim Ave. Apt. 6D Phoenix AZ 85001

Exercise 18 **Revising a Letter by Adding Needed Commas** Copy the following letter, adding commas where necessary.

Ms. Joan Conklin
42 Ralston Beach Road Apartment 5
Chicago Illinois 60660

Dear Ms. Conklin:

    Thank you for sending the slides of your trip to the Kenyan wildlife reserve. Your work I must say is very important and your slides are fascinating to view. You must feel a sense of reward knowing that your photos document progress and that your work has saved human as well as animal lives. Over the next few weeks we will complete our planning for the new book on wildlife preservation. Your photos certainly will be an important part of the book. Thank you for the fine work.

Warm regards

Melissa Smithson
New World Books

▲ **Critical Viewing** Use the phrase *a dense section of rain forest* as an interrupter in a sentence about this photo. Where should commas be used in your sentence? **[Describe]**

Using Commas in Numbers

Numbers of one hundred or less and numbers made up of two words (for example, three thousand) are generally spelled out. Other large numbers (for example, 8,463) are written in numerals. Commas make large numbers easier to read.

KEY CONCEPT Use commas with numbers of more than three digits. ■

To place the comma correctly, count from the right: Commas are placed before every third digit.

EXAMPLES: a population of 247,867
an area of 3,615,122 square miles

Commas are also used with a series of numbers.

KEY CONCEPT Use commas with three or more numbers written in a series. ■

EXAMPLE: Read pages 123, 124, and 125 carefully.

KEY CONCEPT Do not use a comma with ZIP Codes, telephone numbers, page numbers, years, serial numbers, or house numbers. ■

NUMBERS WITHOUT COMMAS

ZIP Code: Jamaica, NY 11432
Telephone number: (617) 532-7593
Page number: page 1002
Year: the year 2010
Serial number: 026 35 7494
House number: 1801 Houston Street

Exercise 19 Using Commas in Numbers Copy each sentence below, adding commas where necessary. If no commas are needed, write *correct*.

1. Information can be found on pages 322 323 and 324.
2. The Amazon River mostly in Brazil is about 4080 miles long.
3. The Amazon has over one thousand tributaries, or secondary streams.
4. The Amazon rain forest has over 1500 species of fish.
5. The population of Brazil was 169806557 in 1998.

Text

Get instant feedback! Exercise 19 is available on-line or on CD-ROM.

More Practice

Grammar Exercise Workbook
• pp. 151–152
On-line Exercise Bank
• Section 26.2
Go on-line:
PHSchool.com
Enter Web Code:
eak-6002

Section 26.2 Section Review

GRAMMAR EXERCISES 20–25

Exercise 20 Supplying Commas in Compound Sentences Write the following sentences on your paper, adding commas where needed.

1. Nature is a partnership so flowers and their pollinators work closely together.
2. This might seem mysterious but birds are attracted to bright colors.
3. The rafflesia is the largest flower in the world and it grows in Southeast Asia.
4. It grows mostly underground so only the bloom is visible.
5. You can read about colorful plants but you should really see them up close.

Exercise 21 Using Commas With Items in a Series Write the following sentences on your paper, inserting commas where needed. If no comma is needed, write *none*.

1. Can only birds or insects pollinate jungle plants?
2. Will snakes monkeys or bats do the job?
3. Frogs, toads and squirrels are also good pollinators.
4. Bats locate trees and flowers using sonar at night.
5. They have long tongues big appetites and furry wings for quick pollen pickup.

Exercise 22 Proofreading Sentences for Commas Copy these sentences, adding or removing commas as needed. If a sentence is correct, write *correct*.

1. Not only plants, Jessie but animals must have special qualities to survive.
2. Without bright feathers of course many male birds would never attract a mate.
3. The dappled coat, of the jaguar, helps it hide in the forest, so it can remain unnoticed, until its prey draws near.

4. The coat may hide the jaguar from other animals, but the cat has not successfully escaped human hunters.
5. Unbeknownst to humans moths butterflies and some other insects give off odors to attract mates.
6. Male baboons yawn oddly enough and toss their heads to show off big teeth to potential rivals.
7. Black howler monkeys shout so loudly that explorers once thought they were jaguars.
8. No matter, how frightening their howl it is meant only to defend their territory.
9. Part of the moth caterpillar its tail looks like a poisonous snake's head.
10. The mandrill a West Central African monkey has inflated blue face markings, that look like a permanent snarl.

Exercise 23 Find It in Your Reading Read a paragraph from your favorite magazine that contains at least three commas. With a friend, explain the use of the commas in the paragraph.

Exercise 24 Find It in Your Writing Look through your portfolio to find a paragraph that includes several commas. Explain the purpose of each comma.

Exercise 25 Writing Application Write a paragraph of at least five sentences describing plants or animals that you might see in a jungle. Include the following items and use commas correctly.

1. a compound sentence
2. a list of items in a sentence
3. an introductory phrase
4. an interrupting word or expression
5. a number of at least four digits

Semicolons and Colons

Using Semicolons

Sometimes two independent clauses are so closely connected in meaning that they make up a single sentence, rather than two separate sentences.

▶ **KEY CONCEPT** Use a semicolon to connect two independent clauses that are closely connected in meaning. ■

If the two independent clauses do not make up a single sentence, they should be punctuated separately, with periods.

EXAMPLES: Bill enjoys exploring jungle areas; Betsy is more interested in deserts. (two independent clauses closely connected in meaning)

Bill and Betsy don't agree. Betsy is working on a paper about newts. (two separate sentences)

The following chart gives more examples of independent clauses so closely connected in meaning that a semicolon should be used between them.

In this section, you will learn when to use semicolons and colons in your writing. The examples and exercises focus on additional jungle animals and plants.

Cross-Curricular Connection: Science

INDEPENDENT CLAUSES PUNCTUATED BY SEMICOLONS
The rain forest has no marked trails; don't forget your compass.
The river has many hazards; it's full of snakes.
Every inch of the forest is valuable; watch where you walk.

▶ **Exercise 26**   **Using Semicolons** Copy the sentences below, adding semicolons where necessary.

1. The green algae growing on sloths are protective they are good camouflage in the trees.
2. The colors of black and yellow insects are a warning they say leave me alone.
3. The poison in poison-arrow frogs has more than one use it contains antibiotics that protect the frogs against infections.
4. The pitohui bird and the poison frog emit the same toxin such a similarity is rare in nature.
5. Glass frogs can cling to leaves their bodies blend in.

▼ **Critical Viewing** Write two independent clauses connected by a semicolon to identify characteristics that help the giant tree frog survive in the rain forest. **[Infer]**

Exercise 27 Using Semicolons Copy each sentence below, adding a semicolon where necessary.

1. The parrot snake bluffs with a wide-open mouth it has no venom.
2. Shield bugs use color to ward off predators they also form large groups for protection.
3. One shield bug may be sampled by a bird the remaining bugs are safe after that.
4. Thorn bugs look like parts of branches from afar up close, their red stripes discourage birds.
5. Chameleons are said to change color to conceal themselves in fact, they are responding to temperature changes.

Using Colons

A colon (:) is a punctuation mark with a number of uses.

KEY CONCEPT Use a colon after an independent clause to introduce a list of items. Use commas to separate three or more items. ■

The independent clause that comes before the colon often includes the words *the following, as follows, these,* or *those.*

EXAMPLES: The rain forest is home to many beautiful birds: scarlet macaws, black-necked red cottingas, and bowerbirds.

Some orchids grow only in the following countries: Costa Rica, Peru, and Brazil.

Olaf's favorite orchids are the ones in these colors: red, pale pink, and purple.

Do not use a colon after a verb or a preposition.

INCORRECT: Veronica always orders: soup, salad, and dessert.
CORRECT: Veronica always orders soup, salad, and dessert.

SOME ADDITIONAL USES OF THE COLON	
To Separate Hours and Minutes	3:15 P.M., 9:45 A.M.
After the Salutation in a Business Letter	Gentlemen: Dear Miss Robinson:
On Warnings and Labels	Warning: The ice is thin. Note: Shake before using. Caution: Children Playing

More Practice

Grammar Exercise Workbook
• pp. 153–154
On-line Exercise Bank
• Section 26.3
Go on-line:
PHSchool.com
Enter Web Code:
eak-6002

Get instant feedback! Exercises 26 and 27 are available on-line or on CD-ROM.

> **Exercise 28** Supplying Colons in Sentences Rewrite each of the sentences below, adding colons where needed. If a sentence is correct, write *correct*.

EXAMPLE: We visited three Canadian cities Calgary, Edmonton, and Winnipeg.

ANSWER: We visited three Canadian cities: Calgary, Edmonton, and Winnipeg.

1. Many types of jungle creatures build nests ants, wasps, and monkeys.
2. Frogs will nurture their eggs in several places under leaves, in plants, or on their backs.
3. Items that could be made from unknown plants include waxes, oils, and perfumes.
4. The river tour leaves three times each day 1100 A.M., 200 P.M., and 400 P.M.
5. Marty fears these jungle animals snakes, jaguars, and poison frogs.

> **Exercise 29** Proofreading for Colons Rewrite the sentences below on your paper, adding colons as needed. If a sentence is correct, write *correct*.

1. Lynn will not eat ants, monkeys, or sloths.
2. "Danger No Swimming Allowed," read the sign by the river.
3. Jungle plants provide medicines to treat several ailments malaria, heart disease, and leukemia.
4. To flourish, termites need darkness, decaying matter, and moisture.
5. The Yanomami succeed in harvesting many crops plantains, sugar cane, and maize.

More Practice

Grammar Exercise Workbook
• pp. 155–156
On-line Exercise Bank
• Section 26.3
  Go on-line:
  PHSchool.com
  Enter Web Code:
  eak-6002

Get instant feedback! Exercises 28 and 29 are available on-line or on CD-ROM.

◀ Critical Viewing Write a sentence with a colon to introduce a list of characteristics that enable a jaguar to survive in the jungle. **[Infer]**

Section 26.3 *Section Review*

GRAMMAR EXERCISES 30–34

Exercise 30 Using Semicolons to Connect Independent Clauses Add a semicolon to connect clauses in each sentence below. On your paper, write the word before each semicolon, the semicolon, and the word following the semicolon.

1. The native people of the rain forest don't want to leave development is driving them out.
2. Industries that produce income from the forest can seem helpful however, they deplete the resources forever.
3. Laws have been made to protect the native people it is very difficult to enforce them.
4. Some African peoples work for timber companies their low wages cannot replace their vanishing forest.
5. Many governments feel that they must exploit their rain forests they owe huge debts to other countries.

Exercise 31 Using Colons Add colons where appropriate in the following sentences. On your paper, write the word before the colon, the colon, and the word following the colon.

1. Much of New Zealand's rain forest has protected species that evolved there the kiwi, a flightless bird; the kakapo, one of the largest parrots in the world; and the saddleback bird.
2. New Zealand's agricultural development sustains itself and allows for exportation lamb and wool provided by sheep, butter and beef from cattle, and fruits and vegetables from farms.
3. The terrain of New Zealand is diverse and beautiful the snow-covered Mt. Cook, the Tasman Glacier, and the flooded valleys of Fiordland.

4. New Zealand has several overseas territories Rarotonga, Tokelau, and Niue Island, among others.
5. The California Monterey pine was introduced to New Zealand and contributes to the export of many products paper, pulp, timber, and woodchips.
6. Dear Captain Cook
7. At 1230 P.M. today, we board the ship.
8. Caution No Alcohol Allowed Inside.
9. To Whom It May Concern
10. Be ready to leave at 600 A.M.

Exercise 32 Find It in Your Reading Read the following excerpt from the Greek myth "Arachne." Explain why the writer used a semicolon in this sentence.

. . . Before the group that was gathered there she [Arachne] would not give in; so pressing her pale lips together in obstinacy and pride, she led the goddess to one of the great looms and set herself before the other.

Exercise 33 Find It in Your Writing Look through your portfolio for passages containing compound sentences or a list of items. Rewrite the passages using semicolons or colons correctly.

Exercise 34 Writing Application Write a brief paragraph explaining the preparation necessary for taking a trip into a forest. Use semicolons at least twice to connect related ideas, and use colons at least three times.

Section 26.4
Quotation Marks and Underlining

Using Quotation Marks With Direct Quotations

A *direct quotation* conveys the exact words that a person wrote, said, or thought.

▶ **KEY CONCEPT** Use quotation marks to enclose a person's exact words. ■

A direct quotation is often accompanied by words such as *he said* or *she replied*. These words, which may fall at the beginning, middle, or end of a quotation, identify the speaker.

Introductory Words When words that identify the speaker come right before a direct quotation, they are followed by a comma.

EXAMPLE: Jennifer said, "The acorn is one of the most important sources of food in the woods."

Interrupting Words When words that identify the speaker come in the middle of a quoted sentence, each part of the interrupted quotation is enclosed in quotation marks. The first part of the quotation ends with a comma followed by quotation marks. The interrupting words are also followed by a comma.

EXAMPLE: "Don't forget the hickory nuts," Mark said, "or the walnuts and pecans."

Concluding Words If the words that identify the speaker are placed at the end of a direct quotation, the quoted material is followed by a comma, a question mark, or an exclamation mark placed inside the final quotation marks.

EXAMPLE: "Did you know that one oak tree can produce 30,000 acorns in a year?" the ranger asked.

▶ **Exercise 35** Using Quotation Marks With Direct Quotations Copy each sentence below, adding commas and quotation marks where necessary.

1. A herbivore said Matt is any animal that eats vegetation.
2. Insects eat plants too said Chuck.
3. Yes insects can be herbivores as well Matt answered.
4. Barry said A scavenger is any creature that eats dead meat or decayed matter.
5. Vultures are scavengers said Chuck.

Theme: North American Animals

In this section, you will learn when to use quotation marks with direct quotations and when to use either quotation marks or underlining with titles. The examples and exercises are about animals native to the United States.

Cross-Curricular Connection: Science

▶ **Exercise 36** Punctuating Quotations With the Speaker
Introduced at Different Locations Use each direct quotation
below in a sentence. Supply a verb and the name of a speaker
in the location indicated in parentheses. Add the necessary
commas and quotation marks.

1. A tree bears a nut, a squirrel eats it, and then a predator
   eats the squirrel. (introductory words)
2. I know what that's called. It's the food chain. (concluding
   words)
3. Correct. (concluding words)
4. When food chains form a network, all connected in the forest, it's a food web. (interrupting words)
5. You are absolutely right. (introductory words)

Using Quotation Marks
With Other Punctuation Marks

Commas, periods, question marks, and exclamation marks
are often used with quotation marks.

▶ **KEY CONCEPT** Place commas and periods inside final
quotation marks. ■

EXAMPLES: "Our class trip is this Tuesday," said Janet.

Matthew added, "We are leaving very early."

Place a question mark or an exclamation mark inside the
final quotation marks if it is part of the quotation.

EXAMPLES: Retha asked, "What animal eats the most leaves?"

Peter said to Andy, "Help me get this raccoon out
of my car!"

Each sentence above is declarative. That is, each makes a
statement by reporting what someone said. Nevertheless, neither ends with a period. Since a sentence cannot have two
final punctuation marks, the punctuation needed for the
direct quotation stands alone, inside the quotation marks.

INCORRECT: Dan asked, "When can I get a pet"?
CORRECT: Dan asked, "When can I get a pet?"

Place a question mark or exclamation mark outside the
final quotation marks if the mark is not part of the quotation.

EXAMPLES: Who said, "We have nothing to fear but fear itself"?

Don't say, "I doubt that it will work"!

More Practice

Grammar Exercise
Workbook
• pp. 157–158
On-line Exercise Bank
• Section 26.4
 Go on-line:
 PHSchool.com
 Enter Web Code:
 eak-6002

Get instant feedback!
Exercises 35 and 36 are
available on-line or on
CD-ROM.

**Grammar
and Style Tip**

Sometimes, for the sake of
clarity, quotation marks
are used to refer to words
that are out of context, as
in these sentences:

Every time he wrote
"dog," he should have
written "cat."

The sign said "Private
Party," so we left.

▶ **Critical Viewing** With a partner, exchange observations about the appearance of this turkey. Write your statements as correctly punctuated dialogue. **[Apply]**

▶ **Exercise 37** Using Quotation Marks With Other Punctuation Marks Copy each sentence below, adding commas, periods, question marks, and exclamation marks where needed.

EXAMPLE: I was annoyed when you yelled I'm staying here
ANSWER: I was annoyed when you yelled, "I'm staying here!"

1. Do you know which bird Benjamin Franklin wanted as our national bird asked Lucy
2. Beth exclaimed I would imagine it was the duck
3. No laughed Lucy Franklin wanted the wild turkey to be the national bird
4. Why asked Beth
5. Because explained Lucy he thought that the bald eagle was the wrong choice because it eats carrion, as do vultures
6. Turkeys are stupid, aren't they asked Beth
7. Some Native American people thought so, too Lucy agreed but they are smart enough to sleep in branches over water so nothing can catch them during the night
8. Are there very many wild turkeys left in the forests asked Chuck
9. Not as many as there used to be Lucy explained but they can still be found across the East and Southeast, down into Florida, and up to New York State
10. Chuck asked Do they gobble like turkeys on a farm

More Practice

Grammar Exercise Workbook
• pp. 159–160
On-line Exercise Bank
• Section 26.4
  Go on-line:
  PHSchool.com
  Enter Web Code:
  eak-6002

Get instant feedback! Exercises 37 and 38 are available on-line or on CD-ROM.

Using Quotation Marks
for Dialogue

A dialogue is talk between two or more people. A new paragraph signals that a different person is speaking.

> **KEY CONCEPT** In dialogue, start a new paragraph to signal a change of speaker. ■

EXAMPLE: "William!" Erica shouted to her brother. "You'd better get up and feed the dog."

"All right," William groaned, "I'm coming."

"And hurry. Champ looks mighty hungry."

"I said all right, Erica," William snapped. "C'mon, Champ, breakfast time."

GUIDELINES FOR WRITING DIALOGUE

1. Follow the general rules for using quotation marks, capital letters, end marks, and other punctuation marks.
2. Start a new paragraph with each change of speaker.
3. When a speaker utters two or more sentences without an interruption, put quotation marks at the beginning of the first sentence and at the end of the last sentence.

Guideline 3 is illustrated in the following examples:

INCORRECT: Martha said, "I think I heard a screech owl."
"Let's go outside and see."

CORRECT: Martha said, "I think I heard a screech owl. Let's go outside and see."

> **Exercise 38** Supplying Quotation Marks in a Dialogue
Rewrite the dialogue below on your paper, adding punctuation and quotation marks where needed.

That, said Corey, sounded like a wolf howling! Let's open the window in case it howls again!

I replied, I don't think we're in the right part of the country to hear a wolf.

Oh, yes, Corey insisted northern Washington has wolves.

Well, I said, open the window, but not too much. I'd like to hear it howl, but I don't want to meet it!

Don't be silly Corey said impatiently. Wolves are really shy.

Really I asked.

Oh, yes, Corey insisted as he opened the window. They stick close to their pack and do not generally attack people.

So wolves are actually peaceful and family oriented. I didn't know, I said softly.

> **Exercise 39** Revising Punctuation and Paragraphing in a **Dialogue** Rewrite the numbered sentences below as a dialogue. Add any missing punctuation marks, and start a new paragraph whenever the speaker changes.

(1) My goodness! What is that creature cried Mother. (2) Do you mean the hump-backed, cat-sized, dinosaurlike thing beside the tree? Josh asked. (3) I certainly do Mother said What is it? Will it bite? (4) No Josh assured her. It's an armadillo. The thing it wants most is to find a full trash can or some baby birds. (5) Then can I pet it? Mother asked. (6) Mother, make up your mind Josh laughed. Are you afraid of it, or do you want to take it home? (7) A little of both Mother replied. It is cute, with its bands of armor and tiny little feet. I like its pointy little face and long tail (8) If you get close to it, it will do one of two things Mother said Josh. (9) And those two things are what asked Mother. (10) That armadillo will either roll up into a ball or tunnel into the ground so quickly you'll hardly be able to see it go!

Underlining and Quotation Marks in Titles

Many titles and names are either underlined or enclosed in quotation marks. Underlining is used only in handwritten or typewritten material. In printed material, italic (slanted) print is used instead of underlining.

> **KEY CONCEPT** Underline the titles of long written works, movies, television and radio series, paintings, and sculptures. Also underline the names of specific vehicles. ■

KINDS OF TITLES THAT ARE UNDERLINED

Written Works	
Books	The Outsiders, The Good Earth
Plays	The Miracle Worker, Pygmalion
Magazines and Newspapers	Newsweek, USA Today
Other Artistic Works	
Movies	Gone With the Wind, Star Wars
Television Series	Hill Street Blues
Paintings and Sculptures	Christina's World, The Thinker
Names of Specific Vehicles	
Aircraft	Spirit of St. Louis
Ships	Queen Mary
Trains	Yankee Clipper
Spacecraft	Discovery

More Practice

Grammar Exercise Workbook
• pp. 161–162
On-line Exercise Bank
• Section 26.4
Go on-line:
PHSchool.com
Enter Web Code:
eak-6002

Complete the exercises on-line! Exercises 39 and 40 are available on-line or on CD-ROM.

◀ **Critical Viewing** Write a sentence noting that this picture is described on pages 48–49 in a book entitled *The Historic Hudson.* What words should be underlined in your sentence? **[Identify]**

▶ **Exercise 40** Underlining Titles and Names On your paper, write the items that should be underlined, and then underline them.

1. Henry Hudson explored the Hudson River in the Half Moon.
2. In 1976, Viking I landed on Mars.
3. J.R.R Tolkien's novel The Hobbit is a classic.
4. The Venus de Milo is in the Louvre Museum in Paris.
5. Cats was the longest-running play on Broadway.

▶ **KEY CONCEPT** Use quotation marks around titles of short written works and other short artistic works. ■

KINDS OF TITLES THAT ARE ENCLOSED IN QUOTATION MARKS

Written Works	
Stories Chapters Articles	"The Most Dangerous Game" "The First Americans" "Meet a Mystery Writer"
Other Artistic Works	
Episodes	"Foreign Territory" (the second episode of <u>To Serve Them All My Days</u>)
Songs	"Memories"

26.4

▶ **Exercise 41** Using Underlining and Quotation Marks

Copy each sentence below, adding underlining, quotation marks, and correct punctuation where necessary.

EXAMPLE: In our English class we are reading the novel Call of the Wild.

ANSWER: In our English class, we are reading the novel <u>Call of the Wild</u>.

1. Her favorite patriotic song was Katharine Lee Bates's America the Beautiful.
2. To Serve Man is one of the episodes in the famous series The Twilight Zone.
3. Misty of Chincoteague is Leah's favorite book from her childhood.
4. Carter is reading Romeo and Juliet this week for the first time.
5. I have always remembered the story The Open Window by Saki.
6. My father's favorite movie is Revenge of the Pink Panther.
7. Did you see the review in the Cleveland Plain Dealer of the play The Miracle Worker?
8. Rick just read The Lottery a short story by Shirley Jackson.
9. Chloe's favorite poem is The Road Not Taken by Robert Frost.
10. My grandmother loves the television series Nova on the Public Broadcasting System station.

▶ **More Practice**

Grammar Exercise Workbook
• pp. 173–174
On-line Exercise Bank
• Section 26.4
  Go on-line:
  PHSchool.com
  Enter Web Code:
  eak-6002

Get instant feedback! Exercise 41 is available on-line or on CD-ROM.

◀ **Critical Viewing** If you were listing the titles of these medical books, which titles would you underline? For which parts of the books would you need to use quotation marks? **[Identify]**

Section Review

GRAMMAR EXERCISES 42–46

▶ **Exercise 42** Supplying Correct Punctuation in Direct Quotations Copy each of the following sentences, inserting the proper quotation marks, commas, and end punctuation. (It may help to read the sentences silently to yourself if you have trouble understanding their meanings.)

1. Go now cried Sheila and get the milk before these baby squirrels starve
2. Don't be so upset, honey, said Sheila's mother You are doing your best
3. Remember the ranger said most wild infants can't live outside their natural habitat said Rick trying to calm Sheila.
4. I once raised a baby jackrabbit Grandma claimed loudly.
5. Then please, Grandma, said Sheila desperately help me do this
6. Grandma said Well, they might be big enough to survive on their own Sheila
7. I know said Sheila but a dog might get them if I leave them under the tree
8. Yes said Grandma gently that might happen But they're big enough to climb a tree
9. It's too risky I can't do that shouted Sheila
10. Mother said calmly All right then, dear. We'll call the veterinarian and ask her what we should feed them.

▶ **Exercise 43** Revising Dialogue for Punctuation and Paragraphing Write the following dialogue on your paper, starting a new paragraph each time a different person speaks. Insert quotation marks, commas, periods, question marks, and exclamation marks where needed. Be sure to capitalize where necessary.

Katie asked what is a lynx and why is Steven so excited about seeing one Roger replied the lynx is a big cat. It's endangered and lives in the forest It stays mostly under ledges said Steven and waits for prey to come by. Then it pounces Kevin read aloud from the encyclopedia: the lynx has big, furry feet that enable it to walk easily in the snow They live in a few states, but only in the extreme northern parts of those states explained Roger. How big are they Katie inquired. Dad says they are about forty inches long when fully grown Kevin replied. The long tufts of fur in their ears are used like antennae to help them hear Kevin continued. bobcats are bigger according to Dad Kevin finished. Where do they live Katie asked Kevin.

▶ **Exercise 44** Find It in Your Reading Look at a dialogue from a short story you have recently read to find examples of a statement, a question, and an exclamation. Notice how the writer uses end punctuation with quotation marks.

▶ **Exercise 45** Find It in Your Writing Look through your portfolio to find a composition that includes at least one direct quotation. Make sure that you used quotation marks correctly with other punctuation marks.

▶ **Exercise 46** Writing Application Write a brief narrative including dialogue in which two people try to identify an animal by its characteristics. You might use one of the photos from this chapter for ideas. Use quotation marks correctly. In your dialogue, mention at least two book or article titles (which you can make up). Proofread to make sure that you have punctuated your narrative correctly.

Hyphens and Apostrophes

Hyphens have many uses with numbers and words.

Using Hyphens in Numbers

▶ **KEY CONCEPT** Use a hyphen when you write two-word numbers from *twenty-one* through *ninety-nine*. ■

EXAMPLES: seventy-eight   thirty-five   forty-six

▶ **KEY CONCEPT** Use a hyphen when you use a fraction as an adjective but not when you use a fraction as a noun. ■

EXAMPLES: This glass is two-thirds full. (adjective)
Two thirds of the members were present. (noun)

Using Hyphens in Words

Hyphens are also used to separate certain words from the prefixes and suffixes attached to them.

▶ **KEY CONCEPT** Use a hyphen after a prefix followed by a proper noun or a proper adjective. ■

EXAMPLES: pre-Columbian   pro-British   mid-August

▶ **KEY CONCEPT** Use a hyphen in words with the prefixes *all-*, *ex-*, and *self-* and the suffix *-elect*. ■

EXAMPLES: all-American   ex-president
self-conscious   mayor-elect

▶ **KEY CONCEPT** Use a hyphen when you write certain compound nouns. ■

Compound nouns are written in three different ways: as single words, as separate words, or as hyphenated words. When in doubt, check a dictionary.

SINGLE WORDS: flashlight   passageway
SEPARATE WORDS: rocking chair   time clock
HYPHENATED WORDS: ten-year-old   mother-in-law

Theme: Forest Life

In this section, you will learn when to use hyphens and apostrophes in your writing. The examples and exercises focus on forest animals and plants.

Cross-Curricular Connection: Science

> **Exercise 47** Using Hyphens in Numbers and Words
Rewrite each of the sentences below, adding hyphens where necessary. If no hyphens are needed, write *correct*.

EXAMPLE: We plan to arrive at the Big Thicket forest in the pre dawn hours.

ANSWER: We plan to arrive at the Big Thicket forest in the pre-dawn hours.

1. Mid January is not the most interesting time to visit the Big Thicket forest in southeastern Texas.
2. Once teeming with a wide variety of plants and animals, the Big Thicket had a pre twentieth century total area of 3,500,000 acres.
3. Hurricanes, fires, and natural plagues have contributed to a ninety percent reduction of the forest.
4. Careful preservation and a current pro forest attitude now protect the thicket's remaining 84,550 acres.
5. Once the most lush forest north of Central America, the thicket takes on a mystical appearance as mist rises from the ground following a midafternoon rain shower.

> **Exercise 48** Proofreading a Passage for Hyphens Rewrite the paragraphs below, adding hyphens as needed.

The Big Thicket forest of southeast Texas was partly consumed by developments after World War II. Even prior to that, during fifty four years from 1876 to 1930, railroads began to crisscross the thicket. The area was the site of a post Depression oil boom. Proud of their state's beauty, most inhabitants would think it un Texan to act in a way that threatens their environment.

As a nine year old, Gwen used to go with her father on photography expeditions to the thicket. The pine trees, dense undergrowth, and faint stirring of unseen creatures intrigued the youngster. Many times, especially at the height of spring in mid May, she would stand quietly and absorb the stillness of the deep forest. She never felt self conscious about her all consuming interest in the forest.

The jaguar, mountain lion, and red wolf are gone, but twenty four different mammals still live in the Big Thicket. One hundred different types of soil lie under the deep carpet of pine needles. Far from being a wasteland, the Big Thicket today has seventy nine types of reptiles and amphibians.

More Practice

Grammar Exercise Workbook
• pp. 163–164
On-line Exercise Bank
• Section 26.5
  Go on-line:
  PHSchool.com
  Enter Web Code:
  eak-6002

▼ Critical Viewing In the middle of which month do you think this photo was taken? Write your answer in a sentence that includes the prefix *mid* and a hyphen. [Make a Judgment]

Using Hyphens at the Ends of Lines

When you cannot avoid dividing a word at the end of a line, the following is the chief rule to follow:

▶ **KEY CONCEPT** Divide a word only between syllables. ■

EXAMPLE: Marcia seems to have
             taken my advice most seri-
             ously.

Check in a dictionary if you are unsure how a word is divided into syllables. Looking up the word *seriously*, for example, you would find that its syllables are *se-ri-ous-ly*.

The following chart presents four other rules for dividing words.

FOUR OTHER RULES FOR WORD DIVISION
1. Never divide a one-syllable word.
2. Never divide a word so that one letter stands alone at the end of a line or at the beginning of the next.
3. Never divide proper nouns or proper adjectives.
4. Divide a hyphenated word only after the hyphen.

If the rules make it impossible for you to fit a word at the end of a line, simply move the word down to the next line.

The following examples illustrate the rules in the chart.

INCORRECT: Karen wanted to take home an orchid fr-
               om the forest.

CORRECT: Karen wanted to take home an orchid
               from the forest.

INCORRECT: Rusty has many photographs of a-
               zaleas in bloom.

CORRECT: Rusty has many photographs of aza-
               leas in bloom.

INCORRECT: The man scared the bear away on Wed-
               nesday.

CORRECT: The man scared the bear away on
               Wednesday.

INCORRECT: Students today are taking an ever-in-
               creasing interest in the environment.

CORRECT: Students today are taking an ever-
               increasing interest in the environment.

▲ **Critical Viewing**
Where should you divide *orchid, blossom,* or *flower* if the word does not fit completely at the end of a line in your writing? **[Identify]**

💡 **Spelling Tip**

In words of two or more syllables that contain double consonants, you can usually place a hyphen between those consonants. Always check in a dictionary if you are unsure. Examples: *col-lar, mil-len-nium,* and *begin-ning.*

Exercise 49 Using Hyphens to Divide Words Hyphenate each word listed below as though it appeared at the end of a line. If a word should not be broken, simply rewrite the word. If you are not sure how to divide a word, look up the word in a dictionary.

1. magnolia	6. white-breasted nuthatch
2. ocelot	7. Antarctica
3. herbaceous	8. acorn
4. lily	9. Mexican
5. snake	10. hurricane

Using Apostrophes to Show Ownership

An apostrophe is used with singular or plural nouns to show ownership or possession.

▶ **KEY CONCEPT** To form the possessive of a singular noun, add an apostrophe and an *s*. ■

EXAMPLES: the doctor's advice   Nat's decision

Some singular nouns already end in *s*. With a few exceptions, add an apostrophe and an *s*.

▶ **KEY CONCEPT** To form the possessive of a singular noun that ends in *s*, add an apostrophe and an *s*. ■

EXAMPLES: James's jacket   his boss's idea

The exceptions are names from classical literature or ancient times. For example, *Ulysses'* and *Moses'*.
Most plural nouns already end in *s*. Form the possessive of these nouns by simply adding an apostrophe.

▶ **KEY CONCEPT** To form the possessive of plural nouns that end in *s*, add an apostrophe. ■

EXAMPLES: the officers' club   the witnesses' testimonies

Some plural nouns do not end in *s*. Form the possessive in the same way as for singular nouns.

▶ **KEY CONCEPT** To form the possessive of a plural noun that does not end in *s*, add an apostrophe and an *s*. ■

EXAMPLES: the men's store   the women's committee

▶ **More Practice**

Grammar Exercise Workbook
• pp. 165–166
On-line Exercise Bank
• Section 26.5
Go on-line:
PHSchool.com
Enter Web Code:
eak-6002

Get instant feedback! Exercise 49 is available on-line or on CD-ROM.

Exercise 54 Avoiding Problems With Apostrophes
Rewrite each sentence below, using the correct word
in parentheses.

EXAMPLE: May I borrow (you're, your) pencil?
ANSWER: May I borrow your pencil?

1. The southern flying squirrel is the smallest squirrel; (it's, its) only ten inches long.
2. They have loose folds of skin between (they're, their) front and hind legs.
3. Bob said, "Is that cat (yours, your's)? It might try to catch the squirrels when they fly by!"
4. Ann answered, "It's (ours, our's), and squirrels don't really fly!"
5. "True," said Bob, "a flying squirrel will leap with (its, it's) legs outstretched and glide up to eighty yards."

Exercise 55 Proofreading for Apostrophes Rewrite the
sentences below to correct problems with the use of apostrophes. If a sentence contains no errors, write *correct.*

1. Who's carrots are these?
2. Ann said that the carrots are her's.
3. Ann brought carrots to tempt the snowshoe hares out of they're warrens.
4. She tracked the hare by following its footprints in the snow.
5. Because snowshoe hares have big, furry feet, you'll always know which footprints are there's.
6. Gary said there's no way to follow the hare unless your able to see the tracks.
7. He said that sometimes the sound and vibration of your footsteps scare them away.
8. Its hard to see the hares against the snow because in winter their white.
9. Ann asked, "Who's going to go with me to photograph the baby rabbits in their warren?"
10. If you dont have a camera, you can borrow our's.

▶ Critical Viewing Write a question and answer about this raccoon, including a contraction and a possessive personal pronoun in each sentence. [Describe]

More Practice

Grammar Exercise
Workbook
• pp. 171–172
On-line Exercise Bank
• Section 26.5
  Go on-line:
  PHSchool.com
  Enter Web Code:
  eak-6002

Text

Get instant feedback!
Exercises 54 and 55
are available on-line
or on CD-ROM.

Section 26.5 Section Review

GRAMMAR EXERCISES 56–62

▶ **Exercise 56** Using Hyphens in Words at the End of a Line Insert hyphens in the proper places to divide the words below. If a word cannot be divided, write the word.

1. knowledge
2. raft
3. closure
4. instinct
5. winner
6. robust
7. extremity
8. overture
9. parliamentarian
10. quote

▶ **Exercise 57** Using Hyphens in Words in Sentences Read each sentence below to find a word that needs a hyphen. On your paper, write that word with a hyphen. If no word in a sentence needs a hyphen, write *correct*.

1. The salt in desert spring water is often eighty eight parts per thousand, more than twice as salty as sea water.
2. In North America, there are thirty one endangered species of fish.
3. Twenty three of the endangered species of fish are found in the south-western American deserts.
4. One threat to the endangered fish has been the appearance of nonnative fish in their habitat.
5. The food supply in the delicate desert springs is threatened by these uninvited guests.

▶ **Exercise 58** Using Apostrophes to Show Ownership Write the possessive form of the underlined singular and plural nouns below, placing the apostrophe correctly.

1. There were no signs we were near the mother <u>bear</u> den.
2. My sister wanted to whisper in the stuffed <u>chipmunk</u> ear.
3. The <u>leaves</u> edges were sharp and scratched our hands.
4. I was wary of the <u>skunk</u> behavior as it rushed toward me.
5. Some kind of sap had fallen on the <u>foxes</u> tails.

▶ **Exercise 59** Using Apostrophes in Contractions On your paper, write the contractions for the following words. Be sure to place the apostrophe correctly.

1. is not
2. did not
3. they are
4. have not
5. we are
6. do not
7. where is
8. should not
9. I will
10. it is

▶ **Exercise 60** Find It in Your Reading Look at an article in a news-magazine. Make a list of words that break at the ends of lines, and show where they have been broken.

▶ **Exercise 61** Find It in Your Writing Look through your portfolio to find a composition that includes possessive nouns and pronouns. Make sure that you used apostrophes correctly.

▶ **Exercise 62** Writing Application Write a narrative about a walk in the woods. Include a hyphenated word and number in your narration, as well as several possessive nouns and pronouns. Proofread carefully to make sure that you have used hyphens and apostrophes correctly.

GRAMMAR EXERCISES 63–71

Exercise 63 Using End Marks
Copy each sentence below, adding end marks where necessary.

1. Deserts can have mountains with snow on them
2. Most of the animals in the desert survive without much water How
3. Wow Don't ask me to go to a desert town called Death Valley
4. Martin asked if we had ever heard of it
5. Is Death Valley the lowest point below sea level in the United States

Exercise 64 Using Commas
Rewrite the sentences below, adding commas where necessary.

1. My favorite gorilla which is named Koko knows human sign language.
2. Koko never stops talking nor is talking her only form of communication.
3. Koko who has never lived in the wild has a daily life a lot like ours.
4. The fully mature gorilla has used painting to express herself for years and she always captures the image of the items she's painting.
5. There are other gorillas who use sign language living with Koko so she is not lonely for animal companionship.
6. Jenny who had never seen a gorilla had a stuffed toy chimpanzee at home.
7. I worried that the apes that were in the zoo were too crowded.
8. Gorillas it is known are quite intelligent.
9. Strict laws armed guards and ground patrols keep endangered species safe.
10. A secure habitat regular observation and emergency food can keep endangered species surviving in the wild.
11. Jane Goodall Dian Fossey and Joy Adamson all added to the study of wild animals by living with their subjects.

12. Yes if you corner a wild animal it will bite you.
13. In the summer of 1960 Jane Goodall went to Tanzania East Africa.
14. The population of Tanzania is 31270820.
15. Jane Goodall was born at 22 Grosvenor Square London England in 1934.

Exercise 65 Using Semicolons and Colons Rewrite each sentence below, adding semicolons and colons where necessary.

1. Some cheeses are made from cow's milk others are made from goat's milk.
2. Mary chose three poets to study Dickinson, Frost, and Sandburg.
3. The trees bear leaves and fruit the leaves and fruit fall on the ground.
4. I saw a sign that said "Caution Guard Dogs on Duty."
5. This glass lens is concave the other is convex.
6. Grate a small amount of cheese over the spaghetti don't smother it.
7. Forest creatures eat the fruit and leaves they eventually die and their bodies feed the fungi.
8. The whistle blew three minutes early it was only 557 P.M.
9. The letter began "Gentlemen I am writing to inform you that your lease has expired."
10. The train leaves at 900 A.M.

Exercise 66 Revising Punctuation and Paragraphing in a Dialogue
Rewrite the following paragraph as a dialogue, adding quotation marks and other punctuation marks where necessary. Make sure that you start a new paragraph for each new speaker.

The river guide said Don't put your hands in the water the fish bite Is the weather always this hot Peter asked Or did we just get lucky The Amazon rain forest temperature is fairly constant said Dr. Franklin I think said Robert that the canopy of trees over the river here is very beautiful The guide was looking ahead down the river There are lots of snakes out today he said because of the rain last night

Exercise 67 Supplying Quotation Marks and Underlining Write the titles in the sentences below, adding quotation marks or underlining as needed.

1. We read A Separate Peace by John Knowles in class last semester.
2. At age seven, Rita performed The Star Spangled Banner at a baseball game, and her mother cried.
3. My grandmother loves to watch the movie Casablanca, but we're tired of seeing it.
4. The Lady or the Tiger is one of my favorite stories.
5. Some people think that reading The Power of Positive Thinking can change their lives.

Exercise 68 Using Hyphens and Apostrophes in Sentences Copy the following sentences, inserting the hyphens and apostrophes where needed.

1. Our ex chairmans daughter studies the biology of the worlds deserts.
2. Often, well receive emails about her midweek observations on a project.
3. Her fathers proud of her self reliance, as shes frequently alone in the desert.
4. When she returns from the desert, theres always a post expedition party.
5. Its interesting to know someone whose all encompassing goal is to assure the deserts survival, in spite of civilizations missteps.

Exercise 69 Supplying Punctuation Marks in Sentences. Copy each sentence below, punctuating as needed.

1. Mother thought the sand dunes were near Yuma Arizona
2. Jason asked Do you know what makes a Mexican jumping bean jump
3. Scorpions arent out much during the day but you'd better watch out at night
4. Some books we have about nature include The Earth and Explore Nature
5. With the proper effort said Kitty many endangered species wont have to die

Exercise 70 Proofreading Sentences for Punctuation Proofread the following sentences to correct any punctuation errors. If a sentence is correct, write *correct*.

1. The baboon called the mandrill has I think a very attractive face?
2. Dear Mr Sartain Well plant the flower seeds the tomato seeds and the bean seeds that you sent us last week!
3. Our ex landlords ranch has 1000 sq miles of desert it must have cactus
4. There are many ducks in our marsh grebes wood ducks and mallards?
5. The Calypso still sails the world, yet its captain, Jacques Cousteau, isn't alive.
6. Dont you wish youd lived in the 1,800's.
7. Dear John the letter began and we knew that shed gone
8. Look George theres a bat in your den?
9. The Broadway Limited leaves Chicago at 900 P.M.
10. Sam my younger brother enjoys skateboarding hockey and baseball!

Exercise 71 Writing Application Write a brief letter to the tourist bureau of a country you would like to visit. (You may invent names and addresses.) Use each of the punctuation marks you have studied.

Standardized Test Preparation Workshop

Proofreading

Some standardized tests ask you to proofread a passage for errors in punctuation. Remember these basic rules to help you identify such errors:

- End marks denote the end of a sentence and identify the type of sentence.

- Commas are used to separate items in a series; after introductory words, phrases, or clauses at the beginning of a sentence; and to set off elements from the rest of the sentence.

- Colons introduce a list of items, and semicolons connect independent clauses that are closely related.

- Review the rules for using quotation marks and underlining, hyphens, and apostrophes.

The following sample test items will give you practice in identifying punctuation errors.

Sample Test Items	Answers and Explanations
Choose the best way to write each underlined section. If the underlined section needs no change, mark the choice "Correct as is." "Hey! Mr Tucker shouted, You can't park (1) (2) there after 700 A.M."	
1 A "Hey"! Mr. Tucker shouted, **B** "Hey!" Mr Tucker shouted, **C** "Hey!" Mr. Tucker shouted, **D** Correct as is	The correct answer for item 1 is *C*. Quotation marks are needed to end the direct quotation, *Hey!*, and they come after the exclamation mark. Also, the title *Mr.* requires a period at the end.
2 F "You can't park there after 7:00 A.M." **G** You can't park, there after 7:00 A.M." **H** "You can't park there after 700 A.M." **J** Correct as is	The correct answer for item 2 is *F*. A colon is needed to separate hours and minutes in expressions of time, and quotation marks are needed before the second part of the quotation.

Practice 1 **Directions:** Choose the best way to write each underlined section. If the underlined section needs no change, mark the choice "Correct as is."

After swim team practice on Tuesday I
(1)
finally received the letter Mom! I shouted.
(2)
It's here! Mom and I opened the letter
(3)
from Blythewood Academy and we

nervously read the brief note inside!

1 A After swim team practice on Tuesday I finally received the letter!

B After swim team practice on Tuesday, I finally received the letter.

C After swim team practice. On Tuesday. I finally received the letter.

D Correct as is

2 F "Mom! I shouted. It's here!".

G "Mom!" I shouted. "Its here!"

H "Mom!" I shouted. "It's here!"

J Correct as is

3 A Mom, and I, opened the letter, from Blythewood Academy, and we nervously read the brief note inside.

B Mom and I opened the letter from: Blythewood Academy and we nervously read the brief note inside!

C Mom and I opened the letter from Blythewood Academy, and we nervously read the brief note inside.

D Correct as is

Practice 2 **Directions:** Choose the best way to write each underlined section. If the underlined section needs no change, mark the choice "Correct as is."

When Mom and Dad took Wesley to the train
(1)
Sara and her sisters were left alone for the

first time They lived on a farm near
(2)
Lincoln, and raised cows chickens, and

sheep. The farm couldn't be left unattended,
(3)
even for a few days, so the four girls were

left to run it themselves.

1 A When Mom and Dad took Wesley to the train, Sara and her sisters were left alone for the first time.

B When Mom and Dad took Wesley to the train; Sara and her sisters were left alone for the first time.

C When Mom and Dad took Wesley to the train Sara and her sisters were left alone for the first time?

D Correct as is

2 F They lived on a farm near Lincoln and raised cows chickens, and sheep.

G They lived on a farm near Lincoln and raised: cows, chickens, and sheep.

H They lived on a farm near Lincoln and raised cows, chickens, and sheep.

J Correct as is

3 A The farm couldn't be left unattended, even for a few days; so the four girls were left to run it themselves.

B The farm couldnt be left unattended, even for a few days, so the four girls were left to run it themselves.

C The farm couldn't be left unattended even for a few days so the four girls were left to run it themselves.

D Correct as is

Capitalization

Zion National Park in Southern Utah

▲ Critical Viewing
Name three things
in this picture that
should be spelled
with a capital letter.
Explain your reason-
ing. [Support]

Several words are capitalized in the following sentence:
*During the winter, Nancy, Marie, Hal, and I skate on Lake Placid
and Lake Champlain.* Some of these words name specific people.
Other words name specific places. The capital letters indicate
that these are important words in the sentence.

Another use of capital letters is to signal the beginning of
a sentence. When several sentences follow one another in a
paragraph, capital letters can help to separate them. Capital
letters indicate when you can pause in your thinking and reading to sort out ideas.

Capital letters have a number of different uses. Besides indicating the beginning of sentences and the names of specific
people and places, capital letters are used to point out specific
things, such as a holiday—Mother's Day—or a document—the
Constitution. Capital letters are also used to show the specific
titles of people, such as President Roosevelt, or of things, such
as the book *My Side of the Mountain.*

In addition, capital letters are used in parts of letters. This
chapter gives information about each of these uses of capital
letters.

Diagnostic Test

Directions: Write all answers on a separate sheet of paper.

Skill Check A. Rewrite each sentence below, using capital letters where necessary.

1. i have never traveled very far from home.
2. hundreds of years ago, travel was difficult.
3. two americans led an expedition to the west.
4. do you know the names of those two men?
5. tell me if you know.

Skill Check B. In the following sentences, list the names of people and places, and capitalize them as needed.

6. meriwether lewis and william clark traveled northwest.
7. Commissioned by president thomas jefferson, they made the first exploration of the louisiana territory.
8. They traveled from st. louis, missouri, to the pacific ocean.
9. They crossed montana to reach the snake river.
10. The interpreter toussaint charbonneau and his wife, sacajawea, joined the party.

Skill Check C. List each specific thing that should be capitalized in the sentences below, adding the necessary capital letters.

11. The traveling group was officially called the corps of discovery.
12. Sacajawea, a native american woman, helped as a peacemaker.
13. She was a shoshone.
14. spanish officials felt threatened by american ambitions.
15. Since the american revolution, they feared, correctly, that the americans would spread across the continent.

Skill Check D. Copy the following items, adding capital letters as needed for titles of people and things and for parts of a letter.

16. This american expedition was president jefferson's idea.
17. He was influenced by the journeys of captain james cook and captain george vancouver.
18. captain meriwether lewis selected his friend, lieutenant william clark, to serve as co-commander.
19. history of the expedition . . . of captains lewis and clark
20. "appalachian spring"
21. the pioneers
22. "oh, susanna"
23. "song of the open road"
24. 86 kirkland street / portland, oregon 97223 / june 15, 1987
25. my dear meriwether,

Using Capitals for Sentences and the Word *I*

Theme: American History

In this chapter, you will learn about many different uses of capitalization. The examples and exercises are about people in American history and the exploration of the American wilderness.

Cross-Curricular Connection: Social Studies

One important use of capital letters is to indicate the beginning of a sentence.

KEY CONCEPT Always capitalize the first word of a sentence. ■

EXAMPLE: He visited the historical landmark.

Some sentences include a person's exact words. These words are called a *direct quotation.*

KEY CONCEPT Capitalize the first word of a direct quotation when it is used as part of a larger sentence. ■

EXAMPLES: He said, "Here is the road map."
"Hawaii," she said, "is made up of islands."

When a quotation is interrupted, the last part of the quotation is not capitalized. In the second example above, the words *she said* interrupt the direct quotation "Hawaii is made up of islands." Notice that the word *is,* in the second part of this quotation, is not capitalized.

When a quotation continues with a new sentence, however, a capital is required.

EXAMPLES: "Look at the road map," he said. "We have about 120 miles to go."
"Hawaii is made up of lush volcanic islands," she sighed dreamily. "They are so beautiful!"

KEY CONCEPT The word *I* is always capitalized. ■

EXAMPLE: The librarian knows I am interested in geology.

EXAMPLES OF CAPITALS FOR SENTENCES AND *I*

Nancy enjoys Western adventure novels and stories. (Capitalize the first word of a sentence.)

Ed asked, "Who brought the shovels?" (Capitalize the first word of a direct quotation within a larger sentence.)

I know I can learn to ski well if I practice enough. (*I* is always capitalized.)

▷ **Exercise 1** Supplying Capital Letters Rewrite each sentence below, using capital letters where necessary.

EXAMPLE: the two rival groups were in the election.
ANSWER: The two rival groups were in the election.

1. all parts of the country have unique landforms.
2. in some places, rivers have shaped the ground.
3. glaciers have carved ravines and scattered rocks.
4. "have you ever seen a desert?" i asked.
5. "yes! I saw one," he replied, "when i traveled across the country."
6. i exclaimed, "that must have been so exciting!"
7. then i asked, "what was your favorite sight?"
8. "the snowcapped mountains were very dramatic," he replied.
9. he continued, "there was great skiing and snowboarding."
10. "i can't wait to travel to other parts of our country," i said.

▷ **Exercise 2** Writing Sentences With Capital Letters Write sentences on the topics listed below. Make sure to capitalize the first word of each sentence and the word *I*.

EXAMPLE: a friend: quotation
ANSWER: My friend Milly shouted, "Don't be late for the party!"

1. a favorite activity
2. a recent news event
3. the season of the year
4. something you know how to build or fix
5. direction from a teacher: interrupted quotation

▷ **More Practice**

Grammar Exercise Workbook
• pp. 175–176
On-line Exercise Bank
• Chapter 27
   Go on-line:
   PHSchool.com
   Enter Web Code:
   eak-6002

Get instant feedback! Exercises 1 and 2 are available on-line or on CD-ROM.

▶ **Critical Viewing** What song could you compare with this picture? Correctly capitalize your response. **[Connect]**

Yosemite National Park

Exercise 3 Proofreading for Capitalization of Sentences

Proofread the following dialogue, adding capital letters where necessary. Copy the dialogue, with corrections, into your notebook.

i had a conversation with my history teacher about the early pioneers who traveled west.

"the pioneers discovered new land formations," he told me. "the hunters and trappers followed paths in the mountains."

he continued, "wagon trails crossed rivers and circled around buttes and plateaus."

"how long were these trips?" i asked.

"the pioneers traveled on foot and by horse," he replied. "it was very slow. they spent months traveling to their new homes."

"i bet they stayed close to rivers," i guessed, "because water is scarce in some western areas."

"you're right," he said.

then he went on, "sometimes, people surveyed the land by climbing rocks and outcroppings."

"i don't know if i would have the courage to make that trip," i said.

then i said, "it must have been a great relief to cross the mountains and start a new home."

More Practice

Grammar Exercise Workbook
• pp. 175–176
On-line Exercise Bank
• Chapter 27
  Go on-line:
  PHSchool.com
  Enter Web Code:
  eak-6002

Get instant feedback! Exercises 3 and 4 are available on-line or on CD-ROM.

◄ **Critical Viewing** Coming upon this sight for the first time, how might a person react? Answer with a quotation, correctly capitalized. **[Infer]**

Bryce Canyon National Park

Using Capitals for Names of People and Places

A capital letter indicates the name of a specific person—John Muir—or a specific place—Denver.

▶ **KEY CONCEPT** Capitalize the name of a specific person. ■

EXAMPLES: John L. Lewis, Clara Barton

Notice that a person's initials are also capitalized.

The names of specific places also begin with capital letters.

▶ **KEY CONCEPT** Capitalize the name of a specific place. ■

The chart below shows some of the kinds of specific places that are capitalized.

EXAMPLES OF CAPITALS FOR SPECIFIC PLACES	
Streets	Warren Street, Carlton Avenue, Interstate 10
Cities	Baltimore, London, Memphis, Tokyo
States	Arizona, Florida, Hawaii, Idaho
Nations	Italy, Canada, Kenya, France, Peru, Korea
Continents	North America, Asia, Africa, Antarctica
Deserts	Sahara, Negev, Mojave
Mountains	Mount Everest, Rocky Mountains
Regions	Great Plains, Appalachian Highlands
Islands	Canary Islands, Fiji Islands
Rivers	Mississippi River, Amazon River
Lakes	Lake Michigan, Great Salt Lake, Lake Erie
Bays	Hudson Bay, Baffin Bay, Biscayne Bay
Seas	Black Sea, Mediterranean Sea, North Sea
Oceans	Atlantic Ocean, Arctic Ocean

▶ **Exercise 4** Using Capital Letters in Sentences About Places Write sentences on the topics given below, using capitals where needed.

EXAMPLE: amusement park and location
ANSWER: Disney World is located in Orlando, Florida.

1. your street or the street on which your school is located
2. your city or town and state
3. your neighbors
4. a body of water in or near your town or city
5. directions from one place in town to another, using street names

▶ **Exercise 5** Proofreading for Capitals for Names of People and Places Proofread each sentence below, copying it into your notebook and adding capital letters where needed.

EXAMPLE: francisco de coronado was born in salamanca, spain.

ANSWER: Francisco de Coronado was born in Salamanca, Spain.

1. In 1535, francisco de coronado arrived in new spain, the old name for mexico.
2. Four years later, he became governor of nueva galicia.
3. That territory included the modern mexican states of aguascalientes, jalisco, and zacatecas.
4. He listened to stories about the spanish explorer cabeza de vaca and the seven golden cities of cibola.
5. coronado set out to conquer these regions for spain.
6. He traveled with spanish soldiers and native americans.
7. They followed the sierra madre to what is now arizona.
8. Members of his group were the first europeans to see the grand canyon and the colorado river.
9. They were also the first europeans to see and describe the american buffalo.
10. They spent the winter near what is now santa fe, new mexico.
11. Heading eastward, they crossed the rio grande and the great plains of northern texas.
12. In 1541, they crossed the canadian and arkansas rivers into kansas.
13. Then, in 1869, the american geologist john wesley powell led the first passage through the grand canyon.
14. He and his party observed the northern rim, the kaibab plateau, and the southern rim, the coconino plateau.
15. The colorado river carved a canyon through the colorado plateau.
16. The glen canyon dam in arizona was built on the colorado river in 1963.
17. powell, born in new york, later moved to illinois.
18. His interest in geography and geology drew him to the ohio river.
19. After the grand canyon, he studied the green river canyon.
20. Between 1870 and 1871, he surveyed much of the rocky mountain region.

▶ **More Practice**

Grammar Exercise Workbook
• pp. 177–178
On-line Exercise Bank
• Chapter 27
  Go on-line:
  PHSchool.com
  Enter Web Code:
  eak-6002

Get instant feedback! Exercise 5 is available on-line or on CD-ROM.

▼ **Critical Viewing**
Why might photographers enjoy visiting this park? **[Infer]**

Powell Memorial Point, Grand Canyon National Park

Using Capitals for Names of Specific Things

In addition to capitalizing the names of specific persons and places, you should also capitalize the names of specific things.

▶ **KEY CONCEPT** Capitalize the names of specific things. ■

The chart below lists a number of categories of specific things that should be capitalized.

CAPITALS FOR SPECIFIC THINGS	
Historical Periods and Events	Renaissance, Battle of Lexington
Historical Documents	Constitution
Days and Months	Monday, December
Holidays	Memorial Day, Arbor Day
Organizations and Schools	Antique Airplane Club, Central High School
Government Bodies	Senate, Congress
Political Parties	Democratic Party
Ethnic Groups	Latinos, African Americans
Nationalities and Languages	Colombian, Spanish
Monuments and Memorials	Washington Monument, Lincoln Memorial
Buildings	Empire State Building
Religious Faiths	Christianity, Judaism, Islam, Hinduism
Awards	Nobel Prize
Air and Sea Craft	*China Clipper, Old Ironsides*
Space and Land Craft	*Apollo 2*, Metroliner

Unlike special holidays, such as Thanksgiving Day, the names of the seasons of the year are not capitalized. Write *spring, summer, fall* (or *autumn*), and *winter* when you are discussing those times of year. When a season is part of a title, however, it should be capitalized.

EXAMPLES: If <u>winter</u>'s here, can <u>spring</u> be far behind?

We always look forward to seeing the scarecrows and the pumpkins at the <u>F</u>all Fun Fair and the ice sculptures at the <u>W</u>inter Carnival.

> **Exercise 6** Proofreading for Capitals for Names of
Specific Things In your notebook, copy the sentences below,
adding capital letters where they are needed.

EXAMPLE: Lucretia Coffin Mott was educated at nine part-
             ners, a quaker boarding school.

ANSWER: Nine Partners, Quaker

1. Lucretia Coffin Mott was born on january 3, 1793, in
   nantucket, massachusetts.
2. After 1817, she became active in the society of friends.
3. Lucretia and her husband, James Mott, helped to organize
   the american anti-slavery society.
4. In july of 1848, she and Elizabeth Cady Stanton organized
   the women's rights convention in seneca falls, new york.
5. Stanton wrote the declaration of sentiments, similar to the declaration of independence.
6. The fugitive slave act was passed in 1850.
7. Then, the Motts made their house a
   stop on the underground railroad.
8. After the american civil war, Carrie
   Chapman Catt formed the national
   woman suffrage association.
9. In november of 1869, other suffra-
   gists formed the american woman
   suffrage association.
10. The territory of wyoming gave
    women the right to vote in 1869.
11. The fifteenth amendment to the
    constitution gave african american
    men the vote.
12. After world war I, on august 18,
    1920, the nineteenth amendment gave
    women the right to vote.
13. There are statues of Susan B. Anthony,
    Lucretia Mott, and Elizabeth Cady Stanton
    at the women's rights national historic park.
14. Jeannette Rankin of montana was the first woman
    elected to congress.
15. For all american citizens, election day is the first tuesday
    after the first monday in november.

More Practice

Grammar Exercise
Workbook
• pp. 179–182
On-line Exercise Bank
• Chapter 27
  Go on-line:
  PHSchool.com
  Enter Web Code:
  eak-6002

▲ Critical Viewing
Name an organiza-
tion that sometimes
marches for a cause
today, and tell how
its marches differ
from this suffragist
march. [**Compare
and Contrast**]

Using Capitals for Titles of People

Whether or not a title of a person is capitalized often depends on how it is used in a sentence.

> **KEY CONCEPT** Capitalize a social or professional title before a person's name or in direct address, but not at other times. ■

BEFORE A NAME: <u>G</u>overnor Brown spoke about taxes.
DIRECT ADDRESS: Tell us, <u>G</u>overnor, about the new program.

SOME OTHER SOCIAL AND PROFESSIONAL TITLES	
Social	Sir, Mister, Miss, Madame, Mesdames
Professional	Congresswoman, Senator, Governor, Mayor, Secretary of the Treasury, Attorney General, Professor, Doctor, Attorney, Judge, Reverend, Father, Rabbi, Bishop, Sister, Private, Lieutenant, Sergeant, Corporal

> **KEY CONCEPT** Capitalize a title showing a family relationship when used before a person's name or in direct address. ■

BEFORE A NAME: I sent a postcard to <u>A</u>unt Alexandra.
DIRECT ADDRESS: I mailed you an invitation, <u>G</u>randpa.

> **KEY CONCEPT** Capitalize a title showing a family relationship when it refers to a specific person, except when it follows a possessive noun or a possessive pronoun. ■

A SPECIFIC PERSON: Ask <u>G</u>randmother her opinion.
AFTER A POSSESSIVE: I'll ask my <u>g</u>randmother.

> **Exercise 7** Using Capitals for Titles of People Copy the following sentences, adding capital letters where necessary.

EXAMPLE: Last summer, doctor Martin traveled to Florida.
ANSWER: Last summer, Doctor Martin traveled to Florida.

1. A school visitor, professor Travis, taught us about Florida.
2. Florida was discovered by explorer juan ponce de León.
3. We learned about chief Osceola.
4. He fought against general Andrew Jackson.
5. "Many Seminoles hid in the Everglades," said mrs. Everett.

Technology Tip

When your spell-check tool identifies a name as unrecognized, choose the "ignore all" option. If the name is one that you use often—such as your town—add it to your customized dictionary.

Using Capitals for Titles of Things

Capitals are used for the titles of things.

KEY CONCEPT Capitalize the first word and all other key words in the titles of books, newspapers, magazines, short stories, poems, plays, movies, songs, and artworks. ■

Do not capitalize articles *(a, an, the)* or prepositions and conjunctions that are only two or three letters long unless they begin a title.

TITLES OF WRITTEN WORKS AND WORKS OF ART	
Books	*O! Pioneers*
Newspapers	Fort Worth *Star-Telegram*
Magazines	*National Geographic*
Short Stories	"The Bet"
Poems	"Birches"
Plays	*Death of a Salesman*
Movies	*The Sting*
Songs	"Singin' in the Rain"
Paintings	*Three Musicians*
Sculptures	*Bird in Space*

Note that in titles, verbs and personal pronouns, no matter how short, are always capitalized.

EXAMPLES: "Why the Tortoise's Shell Is Not Smooth" by Chinua Achebe

"Overdoing It" by Anton Chekhov

KEY CONCEPT Capitalize the title of a school course when it is followed by a number or it refers to a language. Otherwise, do not capitalize school subjects. ■

EXAMPLES: French; History 420; Algebra II

I have social studies and music this morning.

Exercise 8 **Using Capitals for Titles of Things** Rewrite each title, adding capital letters where necessary. Keep the underlining and quotation marks as shown.

1. life on the mississippi
2. "sweet home alabama"
3. "I hear america singing"
4. american history 102
5. the ox-bow incident

Text

Get instant feedback! Exercises 8, 9, and 10 are available on-line or on CD-ROM.

More Practice

Grammar Exercise Workbook
• pp. 183–184
On-line Exercise Bank
• Chapter 27
Go on-line:
PHSchool.com
Enter Web Code:
eak-6002

► **Exercise 9** Proofreading for Capitalization of Titles of **Things** Copy the titles in these sentences, adding capital letters as necessary. Keep the underlining and quotation marks as shown.

EXAMPLE: I like to read the
              <u>rocky mountain
              news</u>.

ANSWER: I like to read the
              <u>Rocky Mountain
              News</u>.

1. Laura Ingalls Wilder wrote about many parts of the country in books such as <u>little house in the big woods</u>.
2. Some of her books, such as <u>farmer boy</u> and <u>by the shores of silver lake</u>, are set in Wisconsin, Kansas, and Iowa.
3. The television show <u>little house on the prairie</u> takes place in Walnut Grove, Minnesota.
4. In the second episode, "country girls," Laura and Mary go to their first day of school.
5. We learned about this historic episode in social studies II.

▲ **Critical Viewing**
Name a book or movie in which a rustic cottage like this one might appear. Capitalize the title correctly. **[Connect]**

► **Exercise 10** Proofreading for Capitalization of Titles of **People and Things** Proofread each sentence below, rewriting it in your notebook and adding capital letters where necessary. Write *correct* if no additional capital letters are needed.

1. The monroe doctrine was written by secretary of state John Quincy Adams.
2. It encouraged foreign leaders, emperors, presidents, and dictators to leave their former colonies alone.
3. When Santa Anna, the Mexican dictator, tried to crush the Texas government, he faced the settlers at the Alamo.
4. Young colonel William Travis commanded the Texas troops.
5. Former congressman Davy Crockett and Jim Bowie were two of the 189 men who defended the Alamo.

Using Capitals in Letters

Several parts of personal letters are capitalized.

> **KEY CONCEPT** In the heading, capitalize the street, city, and state, as well as the month of the year. ∎

HEADING: 17 Vanderburg Street
              Newton, Massachusetts 02162
              May 29, 20––

> **KEY CONCEPT** In the salutation, capitalize the first word, any title, and the name of the person or group mentioned. ∎

SALUTATIONS: My dear Susan,   Dear Uncle Steve,

> **KEY CONCEPT** In the closing, capitalize the first word. ∎

CLOSINGS: Your friend,   Yours truly,   Love,

> **Exercise 11** Proofreading for Capitalization in Letters
Proofread the parts of letters shown below, copying them into your notebook and adding capital letters as needed.

EXAMPLE: dear arnold
ANSWER: Dear Arnold

1. 25 lakeside avenue / somerville, missouri 63344 / october 28, 20––
2. dear sarah and edward,
3. fondly,
4. 5112 brady green / san antonio, texas 78200 / september 4, 20––
5. sincerely,

> **Exercise 12** More Practice Proofreading for Capitalization in Letters Proofread the parts of letters shown below, copying them into your notebook with capital letters as needed.

1. 15 webster avenue / hanover, new hampshire 03755 / december 5, 20––
2. my dear therese,
3. 245 indian trail road / chapel hill, north carolina 27514 / october 13, 20––
4. dear aunt ricki,
5. your friend,

> **More Practice**
>
> **Grammar Exercise Workbook**
> • pp. 185–186
> **On-line Exercise Bank**
> • Chapter 27
> *Go on-line:*
> PHSchool.com
> *Enter Web Code:*
> eak-6002

Get instant feedback! Exercises 11 and 12 are available on-line or on CD-ROM.

Hands-on Grammar

Capitalization Car

Take a ride in a Capitalization Car to help you remember the categories of words that need to be capitalized. To begin, cut out a simple car about 6" long and 3" high. Draw the doors, windows, headlights, trunk, passengers, and so on. Next, draw a road lengthwise across a piece of construction paper. Then, glue or tape down the car in the middle of the road. Around the car and on the road, print these questions:

What are the make and model of the car? **W**ho is the driver? **W**ho is the front-seat passenger? **W**hat is he or she reading? **W**ho are in the back seat? **W**hat are the brands of things in the trunk? **W**hat song is playing? **W**hat is the name of the street or highway? **W**here are they going? **F**rom where are they coming? **On** what date did they leave? **On** what date will they arrive? **W**hat landmarks will they pass along the way?

Under each question, use a ruler to draw an appropriate number of short lines for answers to the questions. (See illustration.)

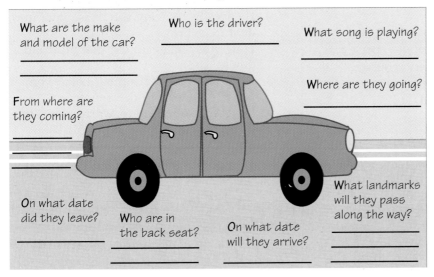

Finally, on the lines, print an answer to each of the questions, using names of specific people, things, and places. Capitalize all the words correctly, and review the categories when you need to know what kinds of words to capitalize.

Find It in Your Reading Read a few paragraphs of a travel article in a magazine or newspaper. Use some of the place names on your Capitalization Car.

Find It in Your Reading Review a piece of writing in your portfolio. Check to see that you have begun each sentence with a capital letter, and that you have capitalized names of specific people, places, and things. Insert capital letters where they are needed.

Chapter Review

GRAMMAR EXERCISES 13–19

Exercise 13 Supplying Capital Letters in Sentences Rewrite each sentence below, using capital letters where necessary.

1. i traveled north through the mountains and saw thousands of lakes.
2. in the fall, all of the leaves were orange and red.
3. he asked, "have you visited this part of the country before?"
4. "i have never seen a waterfall that size before," i replied.
5. "everywhere i go," i replied, "there are new sights to see."

Exercise 14 Proofreading for Capitals for Names of People and Places Proofread each sentence below, copying it into your notebook and adding capital letters where needed.

1. In 1607, henry hudson sailed to greenland and the svalbard islands.
2. hudson sailed past nova scotia and down the coast of north america.
3. He believed that the pacific ocean was connected to the atlantic ocean.
4. Then, in 1609, he explored what was later named the hudson river.
5. He sailed from new york bay to the present site of albany.
6. The river flows past the catskill mountains and the hudson highlands.
7. Near its mouth, it forms the border between new york and new jersey.
8. Several canals link the hudson to lake champlain, the great lakes, and the saint lawrence river.
9. giovanni da verrazzano, from italy, had been the first to explore the river.
10. robert fulton launched one of his first steamboats on the hudson river in 1807.

Exercise 15 Proofreading for Capitals for Names of Specific Things Proofread each sentence below, copying it into your notebook and adding capital letters where needed.

1. Huey Long was educated at the university of oklahoma and tulane university.
2. In 1928, he won the nomination of the democratic party and ran for governor of louisiana.
3. During the great depression, the american people supported him.
4. He won a seat in the senate in 1932.
5. From his seat in the capitol building, Long fought President Roosevelt.
6. He sought to delay the passage of new deal measures.
7. Long was assassinated just after labor day in 1935.
8. His wife, Rose McConnell Long, completed his term in the senate.
9. In 1947, Robert Penn Warren won the pulitzer prize for his novel <u>All The King's Men</u>.
10. The book is about a southern governor resembling Huey Long.

Exercise 16 Proofreading for Capitals for Titles of People and Things Proofread each sentence below, copying it into your notebook and adding capital letters where needed.

1. The mountain now called Pikes Peak was discovered by lieutenant Zebulon Pike.
2. It is located near Colorado Springs, which was founded as a resort by general William Palmer.
3. "Is it true, mr. O'Brien," I asked, "that the pony express was operated by the Pikes Peak Express Company?"

4. "Yes," he replied, "the pony express helped spread the news of president Lincoln's election."

5. Then, in 1863, postmaster general Montgomery Blair established free mail delivery.

6. The expeditions of zebulon mont-gomery pike is a fascinating book, edited by Elliot Coues from Pike's diaries.

7. Pikes Peak eventually became a mining area; Robert L. Brown brings this era to life in his book the great pikes peak gold rush

8. colorado geographic's travel brochure entitled "pikes peak or bust" describes the area's attractions for hikers and campers.

9. Present-day hikers can purchase Kent Schulte's "colorado springs & pikes peak trail map."

10. There's even a video available: vacationing in pikes peak country.

Exercise 17 Proofreading to Follow All the Rules of Capitalization

Proofread the following passage, looking for errors in capitalization. On your paper, rewrite the passage, adding or eliminating capitals as necessary.

in the last of the mohicans, james fenimore cooper describes the hurons, a tribe of native americans. the hurons allied themselves with the french against the british during the american revolution. living near lake ontario and in the st. lawrence river valley, the hurons first met the french explorer jacques cartier in 1534. the meeting was the beginning of a long-lasting friendship between the hurons and the french. You can learn more about this tribe in a book from the junior library of american indians: huron indians by martin and martha schwabacher.

Exercise 18 Proofreading Letters

Practice Rewrite the following friendly letter, adding capital letters as needed.

> 10773 mckenzie avenue
> victoria, british columbia
> canada
> december 5, 20––

dear dominic,

i am so excited to write to you about my new favorite author. i just finished reading some books by the american author john steinbeck. he was from salinas, california, and was educated at stanford university. his first novel, cup of gold, is about the infamous welsh pirate sir henry morgan. many of steinbeck's other novels are about farmers and workers in california. his book the grapes of wrath is about the joad family as they migrate from the oklahoma dust bowl to california during the great depression. steinbeck won a pulitzer prize for that book, and it was made into a successful movie. do you remember when we drove across the country? steinbeck wrote a book, travels with charley, about his drive across the united states with his pet poodle.

also, i found an interesting article by steinbeck in the new york times from 1943. the article, "the making of a new yorker," is about the first time he moved to new york city. although steinbeck had lived in san francisco, mexico city, and paris, he felt that new york city was unique. he said many of the things you had told me about living in the city. i am enclosing a copy of the article and a list of steinbeck's novels.

i miss you very much. please write back soon.

> love,
> maggie

Exercise 19 Writing Application

Write a letter to a friend. Include a heading, salutation, and closing. Describe an interesting place in the United States. Try to include the names of people and places. Use proper capitalization throughout your letter.

Standardized Test Preparation Workshop

Proofreading

Standardized tests often measure your understanding of the rules of capitalization, spelling, and punctuation. You may be expected to recognize errors within the context of a written passage. You will be asked to identify the type of error, if any, in the passage. The following sample test items will give you practice in responding to these types of questions.

Test Tip

Some tests count more points off for wrong answers than they do for unanswered items. Find out how the test you are taking is scored.

Sample Test Items

Read the passage, and decide which type of error, if any, appears in each underlined section.

Excitedly, the class race-walked down the
(1)
school corridor to the gymnazium.

Today was the first day of the mini-course,
(2)
and dr. Cooke would be presenting the

program.

1 A Spelling error

   B Capitalization error

   C Punctuation error

   D No error

2 F Spelling error

   G Capitalization error

   H Punctuation error

   J No error

Answers and Explanations

The correct answer is A. The word *gymnasium* is spelled incorrectly with a *z* instead of an *s.*

The correct answer is G. *Dr.,* the abbreviation for *doctor,* should be capitalized because it is a professional title used with a person's name.

Practice 1 **Directions:** Read the passage, and decide which type of error, if any, appears in each underlined section.

With a large bucket of fresh flowers in
(1)
hand, Ms. Casella entered the clasroom.

The members of the Eastlake middle
(2)
school service club had assembled to

make nosegays—small floral bouquets—

for their monthly project. In Elizabethan
(3)
England, nosegays had been used to ward

off disease but these nosegays would

bring color and cheer to the Residents of
(4)
the Golden Glen Retirement Center.

1 **A** Spelling error
   B Capitalization error
   C Punctuation error
   D No error

2 **F** Spelling error
   G Capitalization error
   H Punctuation error
   J No error

3 **A** Spelling error
   B Capitalization error
   C Punctuation error
   D No error

4 **F** Spelling error
   G Capitalization error
   H Punctuation error
   J No error

Practice 2 **Directions:** Read the passage, and decide which type of error, if any, appears in each underlined section.

Colonists clashed with British soldiers
(1)
in Lexington Massachusetts on April 19,

1775. From 1775 to 1783, the Continental
(2)
Army waged the American Revolution

agianst Great Britain. The leader of the
(3)
Continental Army was general George

Washington. A few years later in 1789, he
(4)
became President George Washington.

1 **A** Spelling error
   B Capitalization error
   C Punctuation error
   D No error

2 **F** Spelling error
   G Capitalization error
   H Punctuation error
   J No error

3 **A** Spelling error
   B Capitalization error
   C Punctuation error
   D No error

4 **F** Spelling error
   G Capitalization error
   H Punctuation error
   J No error

Cumulative Review

MECHANICS

Exercise A Using End Marks Copy the following sentences, inserting the appropriate end marks.

1. What was your favorite toy when you were young
2. My little brother has a rattle and a teething ring
3. Hey, I *really* miss my baby toys
4. Do you still sleep with a favorite stuffed animal
5. Maybe they will be collectible items one day

Exercise B Using Commas, Semicolons, and Colons Copy the following sentences, inserting the appropriate commas, semicolons, and colons.

1. Every summer at the beach we make sand castles using sand seashells and water.
2. I play catch with my cousins who visit us for several weeks each year.
3. Last summer I learned a new sport volleyball.
4. When we first started playing the net seemed so high.
5. Then I learned how to hit the ball it wasn't very difficult.
6. I enjoyed volleyball in fact we played from noon until about 530 p.m.
7. Some people don't play sports at the beach They read listen to music or just lie in the sun.
8. After a full enjoyable day we like to have a barbecue.
9. We cook many of my favorite foods hamburgers hot dogs and corn on the cob.
10. When the sun sets the temperature drops but we still stay outside.

Exercise C Using All the Rules of Punctuation Copy the following sentences, inserting the appropriate end marks, commas, semicolons, colons, quotation marks, underlining, hyphens, and apostrophes.

1. Did you know that there are three types of kites
2. The most well known type is the diamond shaped kite
3. There are also box kites delta kites and bowed kites
4. Paper or cloth is used for the kite however the frame can be wood or metal
5. During the 1800s kites served an important purpose weather forecasting
6. When Benjamin Franklin flew a kite he proved his theory about electricity
7. Alexander Graham Bell the inventor of the telephone also created kites
8. Let's Go Fly a Kite is a great song
9. Remember the line Lets go fly a kite up to the highest height
10. Its from a famous movie Mary Poppins

Exercise D Using All the Rules of Capitalization Copy the following sentences, inserting the appropriate capital letters.

1. people throughout north america, south america, and europe ride bicycles.
2. around 1790, count divrac of france invented a wooden scooter.
3. a german inventor, baron drais, improved upon that model.
4. his version had a steering bar attached to the front wheel.
5. then, a scottish blacksmith, kirkpatrick macmillan, added foot pedals.

6. in 1866, pierre lallement, a french carriage maker, took out the first u.s. patent on a pedal bicycle.
7. mr. j.k. starley of england produced the first commercially successful bicycle.
8. by 1897, more than four million americans were riding bikes.
9. there are many road races like the tour de france.
10. other races, called bmx, are held on bumpy dirt tracks.

Exercise E Proofreading Dialogue for Punctuation and Capitalization

Copy the following dialogue, adding the proper punctuation and capitalization.

1. isnt that a new yo-yo asked pam i've never seen it before
2. no ive had it awhile replied joe i found it underneath my bed
3. i bet you dont know how yo-yos were invented
4. joe answered sure i do arent they toys for children
5. no pam said they originated in the philippines
6. right as toys joe insisted
7. they were weapons and toys pam corrected
8. ok well i know what the word yo-yo means
9. pam said so do i tell me and ill see if you're correct
10. well joe said im pretty sure it means come back
11. thats right pam said
12. its a toy that has been around for more than 3,000 years joe continued
13. it wasnt until the 1920s pam added that they were developed in the united states
14. who was donald duncan asked joe
15. he was the man who improved upon the design of the yo-yo and made it a popular toy in the united states

Exercise F Writing Sentences With Correct Punctuation and Capitalization

Write five sentences following the instructions given below. Be sure to punctuate and capitalize correctly.

1. Write a sentence about your favorite board game or video game.
2. Describe what you like about it.
3. Write a sentence about a favorite outdoor game.
4. Tell what time of year you play it, and name some of the friends who join in.
5. Write an exclamatory sentence about a great play in a game.

Exercise G Proofreading Paragraphs for Punctuation and Capitalization

Proofread the following paragraphs, copying them into your notebook and adding punctuation and capitalization as needed.

Do children still play board games I wonder. perhaps tv and video games have begun to replace checkers and chess.

There was a time you know when i excitedly hoped for board games as gifts on certain special occasions birthdays and holidays. one birthday when my twin sister, lily, and i received our first checkers set we were thrilled we couldn't wait to begin playing i think we played for hours. when aunt dotti and uncle larry came over with our cousins joanie and mark we all took turns playing. wow what a great time we had.

Exercise H Writing Application

Write a brief dialogue between you and a friend about your favorite toy from childhood. Be sure to include proper punctuation, capitalization, and indentation.

Sentence Diagraming Workshop

When you study sentences, it is often helpful to draw diagrams of them.

▶ **KEY CONCEPT** A diagram shows how the parts of a sentence are related. ∎

Sentence diagrams begin with two lines—one horizontal and one vertical. The horizontal line is called a base line and the vertical line is called a bar.

FORM OF A DIAGRAM:

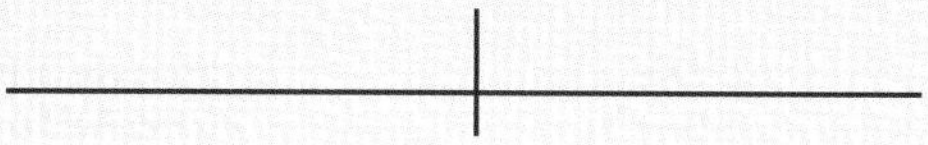

Diagraming Simple Subjects and Simple Verbs

The simple subject of a sentence is written to the left of the bar. The simple verb is written to the right. No punctuation is used in diagrams.

DECLARATIVE SENTENCE: Dogs bark.

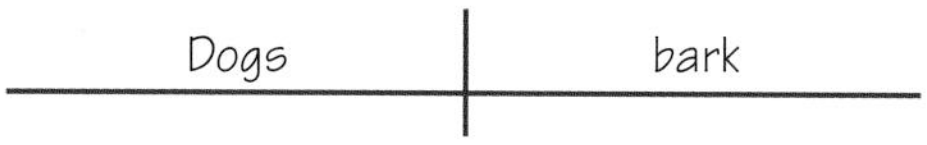

Dogs	bark

Put the subject on the left—even when the sentence begins with a verb.

INTERROGATIVE SENTENCE: Did he remember?

he	Did remember

To diagram an imperative sentence, you must remember that the subject *you* is understood. Put it on the base line in parentheses.

IMPERATIVE SENTENCE: Wait!

(you)	Wait

DIAGRAMING A SENTENCE

1. Draw two lines, the base line and the bar.
2. Write the simple subject on the left and the verb on the right.
3. Capitalize the first word of the sentence.
4. If the sentence is imperative, write the subject as (*you*).

▷ **Exercise 1** **Making Sentence Diagrams** Diagram each of the sentences below, following the explanation on the preceding page.

EXAMPLE: Aunt Deborah called.

ANSWER:

Aunt Deborah	called

1. Iron rusts.
2. Jeffrey will be coming.
3. Is it moving?
4. Cyclones move.
5. Begin.
6. Will language change?
7. Must we leave?
8. Congress has been meeting.
9. Decide!
10. Crickets jump.

▷ **Exercise 2** **More Practice Diagraming Sentences** Diagram each of the following sentences.
1. Karen has been waiting.
2. Did he understand?
3. Opportunities come.
4. Try!
5. Robert was pretending.
6. Concentrate.
7. Shall we try?
8. Mrs. Young hesitated.
9. Has Shelly decided?
10. Finish.

Diagraming Compound Subjects

When there is more than one subject in a sentence, split the base line on the left, or the subject side, so that each subject has its own line. The conjunction joining the subjects goes on a vertical dotted line between the subject lines.

EXAMPLE: She and I ate.

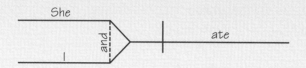

If the subjects have modifiers, put them beneath each noun on slanted lines.

EXAMPLE: The black dog and the gray cat ate.

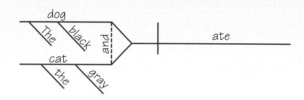

Exercise 3 **Diagraming Compound Subjects** Diagram each of the sentences below,

EXAMPLE: Mike and Ralph were fighting.

ANSWER:

1. Joe and I went.
2. Martha and Joe danced.
3. My mother and I argued.
4. The small child and her big sister laughed.
5. Gloria and I should go.
6. Jonathan, Brandon, and Molly swam.
7. My older brother and his friend came.
8. The small blue vase and the red plate broke.
9. Those two sisters and their boyfriends danced.
10. Three children and two adults are walking.

Diagraming Compound Verbs

When there is more than one verb in a sentence, split the base line on the right, or the verb side, so that each verb has its own line. The conjunction joining the verbs goes on a vertical dotted line between the verb lines.

EXAMPLE:　　Martha dances and sings.

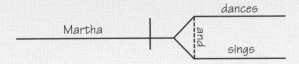

If there is a modifier in the sentence and it modifies both verbs, it goes on a diagonal line beneath the main base line. This shows that it applies to both verbs.

EXAMPLE:　　Martha dances and sings well.

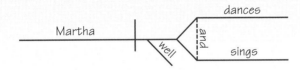

If each verb has its own modifier, each modifier goes on a diagonal line beneath the verb it modifies.

EXAMPLE:　　Nancy dances well but sings poorly.

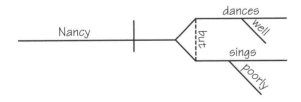

▶ **Exercise 4** **Diagraming Compound Verbs** Diagram each of the sentences below.
1. We swam and canoed.
2. Gerald speaks quietly but sings loudly.
3. My mother ate and drank slowly.
4. Sam walks and runs fast.
5. Katie talks fast but walks slowly.

Diagraming Sentences
With Direct and Indirect Objects

Because objects complete the meaning of a verb, they are diagramed on the verb side of the sentence. Direct objects sit on the same line as the subject and the verb and are separated from the verb by a short vertical line. Indirect objects are placed on a horizontal line extending from a slanted line directly beneath the verb.

EXAMPLES:

The dog ate its dinner.

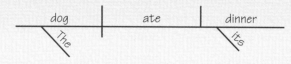

My friend sent me a letter.

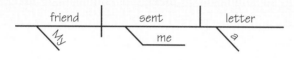

The boy gave the girl a ring.

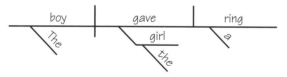

▶ **Exercise 5** Diagraming Sentences With Direct and Indirect Objects Diagram each of the sentences below.

EXAMPLE: I sent Charles a message.

ANSWER:

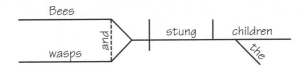

1. We will row the boat.
2. Randy gave me a book.
3. The large dog licked the little kitten.
4. John sent his friend a picture.
5. Aunt Nancy gave my brother a toy train.

▶ **Exercise 6** Diagraming Sentences Diagram each of the following sentences. There are compound subjects, compound verbs, and/or complements in the sentences.

EXAMPLE: Bees and wasps stung the children.

ANSWER:

1. Jack and Joan ate ice cream.
2. My brother and my sister laughed and ran.
3. My younger brother and my older sister laughed loudly and ran quickly.
4. Jeri and David sent their friend a present.
5. Thomas and his brother argued.
6. Molly ate cookies and drank lemonade.
7. Jonathan and Brandon rode their bicycles.
8. The yellow dog chased the black cat.
9. My mother and father gave me a new coat.
10. The student wrote a wonderful paper.

Diagraming Phrases

Prepositional Phrases To diagram a prepositional phrase, draw a slanted line for the preposition and a horizontal line for the noun. Put modifiers on slanted lines beneath the noun.

EXAMPLES: PREP   NOUN
near the red barn

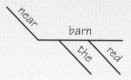

PREP   NOUN
under the old oak tree

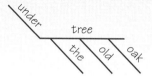

Adjective Phrases A prepositional phrase that acts as an adjective is placed beneath the noun or pronoun it modifies.

EXAMPLES: Our neighbor *down the road* jogs often.

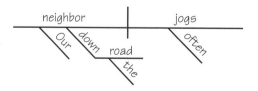

The bridge *over the fast river* collapsed.

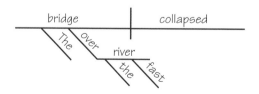

Adverb Phrases A prepositional phrase that acts as an adverb is placed beneath the verb, adjective, or adverb it modifies.

EXAMPLES: The plane flew *over the runway.*

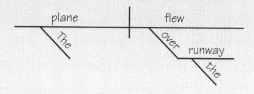

He finished the book *after dinner.*

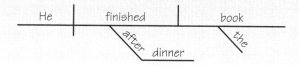

Appositive Phrases To diagram an appositive phrase, put the most important noun in the phrase in parentheses, and place it next to the noun it renames, identifies, or explains. Place the modifiers beneath the noun.

EXAMPLES: Sam, *the manager of a store,* works hard.

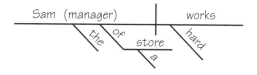

Molly, *my niece,* plays basketball.

Exercise 7 Diagraming Phrases Diagram the sentences below. Each one contains at least one prepositional or appositive phrase.

EXAMPLE: Poe, the author of the story, was born in Boston.

ANSWER:

1. The flowers outside my window are blooming.
2. Mrs. Winters, the new principal, speaks clearly.
3. The restaurant around the corner is expanding.
4. The conversation during dinner was interrupted.
5. Our dog ran past the house.
6. The runner beside me had stopped.
7. A child strolled beyond the gate.
8. Directions with many examples explain clearly.
9. Our vacation, a week in Hawaii, begins tomorrow.
10. The president spoke before a large audience.

Exercise 8 More Practice Diagraming Phrases Diagram the following sentences. Each one contains a prepositional or appositive phrase.

EXAMPLE: Our president, Georgia Smith, will speak now.

ANSWER:

1. These one-act plays, two amusing comedies, are staged frequently.
2. Your bicycle belongs inside the garage.
3. Wendy scurried up the stairs.
4. The woman, an experienced nurse, worked rapidly.
5. The camera on the table loads easily.

Diagraming Compound Sentences

The clauses of a compound sentence are diagramed separately, one under the other. They are connected by a dotted line that looks like a step. The coordinating conjunction or semicolon that connects them is written on the "step."

EXAMPLES:
S   V   DO   S   V   DO
Bob plays the piano, and Sarah plays the violin.

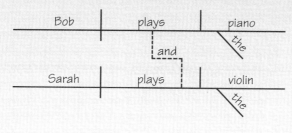

S   V   DO   S V DO
Simon wrote the story, but Ted read it aloud.

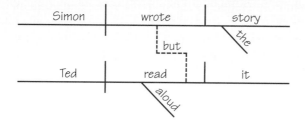

▶ **Exercise 9** **Diagraming Compound Sentences** Diagram each of the following compound sentences.

1. The buildings trembled, and the land shook.
2. We picked fresh strawberries, and they gathered beans.
3. Texas has mountains, and it has sandy beaches.
4. This model changes often, but that model stays the same.
5. We measured the pool in feet; they measured it in meters.
6. We can spend our money, or we can save it.
7. The player leaped up; he made the shot.
8. Some members came by plane, but others arrived by bus.
9. The blizzard could hit the city, or it could move east.
10. She told a story, and I listened attentively.
11. Michael received the message, but his older brother wrote a reply.
12. Amy can plant her seeds now, or she can wait until June.
13. The children arrived early, and they stayed late.
14. Mark hit a home run, but the visiting team still lost the game.
15. I tried hard, but some questions stumped me.

Academic and *Workplace* Skills

Concept, Charlie Hill

Speaking, Listening, Viewing, and Representing

▲ Critical Viewing
What visual medium is this girl using in her presentation? What other options would she have for presenting visual aids? **[Analyze; Extend]**

How much of your day do you spend talking to friends? Listening to the radio? Watching movies or television? Presenting your ideas through pictures, videos, and other visual media? In today's world, speaking, listening, and viewing are a vital part of everyday life, and the ability to communicate through the visual media is becoming more important than ever. In this chapter, you'll learn all of the skills you need to be an effective communicator in the multimedia age.

Speaking *and* Listening Skills

In school, you use speaking and listening skills every day. You listen to your teachers and friends. You give reports and presentations to your classmates. These *formal* activities involve special skills. You also use *informal* skills in your everyday life, in conversations with friends and family members and when you meet new people.

Using Informal Speaking Skills

You use informal speaking skills without thinking about it—on the phone with a friend or talking to a family member. This section will help you apply these skills to other situations, such as class discussions and introductions.

Participate in Class Discussions Participating in class discussions will help you become a successful student. It not only enables you to ask questions that will help you better understand material, but also allows you to contribute your own ideas.

▶ **KEY CONCEPT** By preparing thoroughly for class discussions and practicing your discussion skills, you will develop the confidence and the comfort level you need to be a strong contributor to class discussions. ■

TIPS FOR PARTICIPATING IN CLASS DISCUSSIONS

- Establish a goal for class participation. For example, you might aim to make a minimum of one contribution to every discussion.
- Do whatever studying and homework is required, so that you come to class prepared to participate.
- Listen attentively, not only to your teacher but also to the questions and answers of your classmates.
- Ask questions when you are unclear about something, or when you want to learn more about something.
- When your teacher asks a question that you can answer, raise your hand and, if called on, give your answer.

▶ **Exercise 1** Improving Class Participation Skills Set a goal of answering or asking a question in each subject every day. Keep a record in your notebook of each question you ask or contribution you make. Take notes about which questions were most helpful and which comments were most effective.

▶ **More Practice**

Academic and Workplace Skills Activity Book
- p. 1

Give Directions You have probably given people directions for how to get to your house or apartment. You may also have given someone directions on how to complete an activity. In either case, you probably found that the more specific and accurate details you were able to provide, the easier your directions were to follow.

TIPS FOR GIVING DIRECTIONS

- Think through your directions before you share them. You may even find it helpful to write them down.
- Provide as much detail as possible. Make sure that all of your details are accurate. Just one inaccurate detail can send someone off track.
- Speak slowly and clearly. Pause after each key detail to make sure that your listener comprehends it.
- When you have finished, ask your listener if he or she has been able to understand everything. Answer any questions.

Greet New People and Make Introductions Throughout your life, you will meet many people, and you will often be asked to introduce people you already know to each other.

TIPS FOR GREETING NEW PEOPLE AND MAKING INTRODUCTIONS

- Say the person's name when you greet him or her for the first time. You'll find that it will help you to remember it.
- Ask the person questions about himself or herself, and try to make frequent eye contact.
- Repeat the person's name when your first meeting ends.
- When making introductions, pronounce the person's full name clearly and correctly.
- Add something of interest about the person you're introducing. For example, you might describe that person's hobby.

▶ **Exercise 2** Giving Directions Write a set of accurate directions to a place you like to visit. Then, share these directions with someone who has never been there. Have your listener evaluate whether you have provided enough detail.

▶ **Exercise 3** Greeting People and Making an Introduction Introduce two people you know who have never met one another. Greet each person properly, and follow the checklist for making introductions.

Using Formal Speaking Skills

Formal speaking refers to speeches and presentations delivered to an audience. At this point in your life, most of the formal speaking you do will be at school. As you grow older, however, you may very well find yourself in other situations in which you are called on to deliver a speech or presentation. Following are some of the situations outside school in which you may deliver speeches and presentations:

Occasions for Formal Speeches

- Speeches at weddings and formal parties
- Presentations in the workplace
- Speeches at town meetings, board of education meetings, and other public forums
- Speeches to clubs or sports teams

Understand Different Kinds of Speeches Following are the three main kinds of speeches:

- An **explanatory** speech explains a situation or event. It presents facts without attempting to sway the audience.
- A **persuasive** speech attempts to convince an audience to agree with a point of view or to take some course of action. It may use techniques such as repetition of key points to capture the attention of an audience.
- An **entertaining** speech is given to amuse the audience and may be included in other kinds of speeches. Often, a good speaker will use informal language (such as humor) to relax the audience.

The kind of speech you give will depend on your audience, your purpose, and the occasion on which you are delivering your speech. For example, if you are giving a speech to friends to add to the enjoyment of a party, it will most likely be an entertaining speech.

> **Exercise 4** Listing Kinds of Speeches Give two topic examples for each kind of speech described above. Then, identify appropriate audiences for each.

> **More Practice**
>
> Academic and Workplace Skills Activity Book
> • p. 2

▼ **Critical Viewing** Tiger Woods is a popular and extremely successful professional golfer. What nonverbal communication skills is Woods displaying in this photograph? **[Analyze]**

Prepare and Deliver a Speech After deciding on your topic and type of speech, plan your speech carefully.

▶ **KEY CONCEPT** Use an organized plan to prepare and present your speech. ■

Gather Information Research the subject for reliable information by using the library and other sources. Take careful notes, quoting the author's exact words where helpful. Record the source of each piece of information.

Outline Main Points and Supporting Details Create an outline using the information you have gathered. Group your information into main points or subtopics and provide supporting details for each. Look at this sample outline.

The Land and Climate of California

A. Landscape
   1. two mountain ranges
      a. coast ranges—along coast
      b. Sierra Nevada—borders
         Nevada and Arizona
   2. fertile central valley

B. Climate
   1. lots of rain in the north
   2. desert in the south
   3. mild temperature except
      in mountains

Prepare Note Cards Jot down each main point with its accompanying details on a separate index card. You can glance at your cards while speaking to help you remember each point. Use few words and write them in large letters.

Practice Your Speech Practice your speech using *verbal* and *nonverbal language* to emphasize your points. V*erbal* techniques include altering the loudness of your voice and the rate at which you speak. *Nonverbal* techniques include your use of movements, posture, facial expressions, and gestures to reinforce your meaning.

Deliver Your Speech Use your note cards to guide you as you speak. Use your examples to illustrate each point. Conclude your speech with a restatement of your main idea.

▶ **Exercise 5** Preparing and Presenting a Speech Prepare and deliver a brief speech on a topic that interests you.

Learn More

For tips on writing a persuasive speech, review the elements of persuasive writing in Chapter 7. For help writing an explanatory speech, review the guidelines for writing a how-to essay in Chapter 10.

Technology Tip

Practice your speech by recording it on tape. Play it back to hear how you sound.

Listening Effectively

To become a good listener, you must get involved in what you are hearing. Concentrate on the speaker's words. Listen for his or her main points, and evaluate what he or she is saying. You will understand more, and you will better enjoy the time you spend listening.

KEY CONCEPT Listening is a two-step process consisting of identifying and then evaluating a speaker's message. ■

Active Listening Active listening means getting involved in what you hear—the more involved you become, the more you will learn.

Determine Your Purpose for Listening The way you listen depends upon what you are listening for. There are three main purposes for listening:

- **To gain information:** Listen for main ideas and major details.
- **To solve problems:** Listen and ask questions to clarify problems so a solution can be found.
- **To enjoy and appreciate:** Listen for artistic elements, such as rhyme, imagery, and descriptive language.

Eliminate Barriers Prepare to listen by putting away all distracting material (books, magazines, homework). Block out all disruptive noises, inside and outside the classroom, so you can concentrate on the speaker and his or her message.

Summarize Main Ideas and Supporting Details

Summarizing a speaker's message forces you to listen attentively and to make decisions about what is important. Use the suggestions below to summarize a speaker's message:

- In your own words, write only main ideas and supporting details—the information you want to remember.
- Underline main ideas so they are easy to locate when you want to refer back to them.
- Write notes in short phrases, not complete sentences.

Exercise 6 Becoming an Active Listener For one week, practice active listening techniques in one of your classes. Remember to decide on your purpose, block out all distractions, and take notes on important information. Track your progress after each class by reviewing how well you listened. Analyze whether or not you accomplished your purpose for listening.

▶ **More Practice**

Academic and Workplace Skills Activity Book
• p. 4

Listening Critically

KEY CONCEPT Do not accept all that you hear at face value. Analyze and evaluate as you listen to draw your own conclusions about a speaker's message. ■

Use these techniques to become a critical listener:

Analyze Persuasive Techniques Speakers often use techniques like these to persuade you to think a certain way:

- **Emotional Appeals** The speaker uses emotional words to persuade you to agree with a certain point of view.

- **Propaganda** The speaker presents selected information to promote a particular set of ideas.

Interpret Verbal and Nonverbal Gestures Paying attention to verbal and nonverbal gestures can enhance your comprehension of a speaker's message.

- **Verbal Gestures** Pay attention to when speakers choose to raise or lower, or slow down or speed up, their voices.

- **Nonverbal Gestures** Notice a speaker's movements, such as arm-waving or head-nodding.

Evaluate Your Listening To find ways to improve your listening skills, take time to evaluate yourself.

- **Monitor Your Understanding** You can test your understanding of the speaker's message by restating parts of it to the speaker. Does the speaker agree with your restatement?

- **Compare and Contrast Interpretations** Write your interpretation of a speaker's message, and use a chart such as a Venn diagram to compare and contrast it with a peer's interpretation.

Exercise 7 Listening Critically Listen to a political speech. Note each of the speaking techniques the speaker uses. Analyze and interpret the content of the message, and then compare your view with a peer's.

Exercise 8 Evaluating Your Listening Skills Listen to a political speech and take note of the speaker's use of persuasive techniques and gestures. Report your findings to the class.

More Practice

Academic and Workplace Skills Activity Book
- p. 5

Viewing and Representing Skills

You are surrounded by visual images: A fire truck screaming across the television screen, a painting pouring out colors on a museum wall, a page bristling with buttons on a Web site—these are all visual images. In this section, you will learn how to interpret and create images.

Interpreting Maps, Graphs, and Photographs

Maps, graphs, and photographs can convey as much information as written texts—sometimes more.

KEY CONCEPT Learn the key features of maps, graphs, and photographs to learn how to interpret them properly. ■

When you interpret any type of visual aid, follow these steps:

1. **Determine your purpose** for viewing. What information do you hope to gain?
2. **Study the title, caption, and labels**. What information do they add?
3. **Examine all symbols.** Use a key if one is provided.
4. **Connect the visuals to the written text** they accompany.

Read Maps

Different kinds of maps give different information. **Political** maps show boundaries, cities, towns, and capital cities of a particular place. **Physical** maps show the different land and water forms, such as mountains, deserts, farmland, rivers, lakes, and oceans. **Climate** maps and **population** maps give information on these topics for a particular region.

Use these steps to help you interpret maps:

1. Determine the type and purpose of the map.
2. Examine the map's distance scale and any symbols.
3. Relate the map's information to any accompanying written information.

▼ **Critical Viewing**
This map shows the territorial extent of an ancient culture. What information does the map convey? What do the symbols on the map represent? **[Analyze, Extend]**

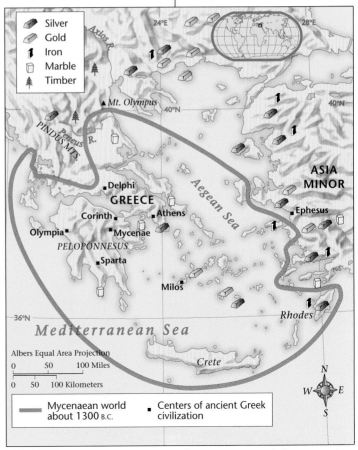

Silver
Gold
Iron
Marble
Timber

Mycenaean world about 1300 B.C.

Centers of ancient Greek civilization

Albers Equal Area Projection

0   50   100 Miles

0   50   100 Kilometers

Read Graphs

Graphs provide a visual comparison of related information.

Line Graph A line graph shows change over a period of time. It features a line that connects points. The points represent numbers. To interpret a line graph: (1) Read the labels on the outermost horizontal and vertical lines (called axes) to determine what information is shown. (2) Match each point on the line to the point straight across and the point straight down from it on each axis. (3) Combine the information for these two points to determine what was happening at a given time.

WORLD POPULATION GROWTH, A.D. 1200–2000

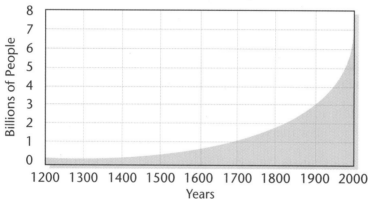

Bar Graph A bar graph compares and contrasts amounts. To interpret a bar graph: (1) Look at the lengths of the bars. (2) Match the subject that goes with the bar to the number the bar reaches. (3) Compare and contrast the size of the bars.

LIFE EXPECTANCY, 1995

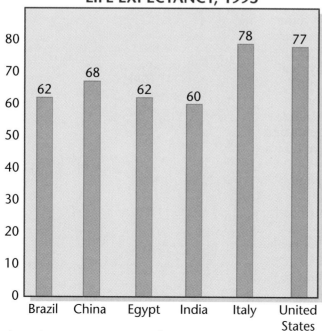

◀ **Critical Viewing**
The numbers on the vertical axis represent the population in billions; the numbers on the horizontal axis represent years. What conclusion can you draw about the world's population based on this graph? [**Analyze, Draw Conclusions**]

◀ **Critical Viewing**
Based on the title of this graph, what do the numbers on the vertical axis represent? [**Analyze, Draw Conclusions**]

Pie Graph A pie graph is shaped like a circle divided into parts. The graph shows how each part is related to the whole circle. The circle stands for 100 percent of something. Each part stands for a certain portion, or percentage, of the whole. To interpret a pie graph: (1) Look at the numbers that go with the individual parts. (2) Match the parts to the key. (3) Use the numbers and parts to make comparisons.

POPULATION DIVIDED BY AGE GROUP

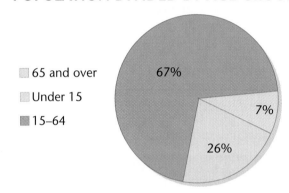

- 65 and over
- Under 15
- 15–64

67%

7%

26%

◀ **Critical Viewing** According to this pie graph, which age group makes up the largest proportion of the population? The smallest? Why would this information be useful for a social scientist? [**Analyze, Draw Conclusions, Speculate**]

▶ **Exercise 9** **Working With Others to Interpret Maps and Graphs** Working with three other classmates, find a map, a line graph, a bar graph, and a pie graph. Assign one group member to find each map or graph. After you find your assigned map or graph, use the appropriate steps mentioned above to acquire information. Then, share the information and how you found it with the other members of the group. Ask them whether they can find any additional information you may have overlooked.

▶ **More Practice**

Academic and Workplace Skills Activity Book
• pp. 6–7

Analyze Photographs

Photographs can also contribute to your understanding of books, magazines, and Web sites. Follow these steps to help you get the most out of photographs:
1. Look carefully at the details to make sure that you are viewing the picture correctly. Sometimes, when you take a quick glance at a picture, you may be misled.
2. Carefully read any accompanying captions.
3. Connect the photograph to the accompanying text.

▶ **Critical Viewing** If this photograph appeared in a school brochure, what would it imply about interaction in classrooms? [**Interpret**]

Viewing and Representing Skills • **641**

Viewing Information Media Critically

You view some form of information every day—television programs, newspaper or magazine articles, and Internet Web sites. Learn to evaluate the information you are viewing for content, quality, and importance.

▶ **KEY CONCEPT** Become a critical viewer by learning to identify and evaluate different types of visual media and images. ■

Kinds of Information Media Technology provides different kinds of information media. Knowing how to tell them apart will help you to understand the information and points of view conveyed by each.

This chart shows several forms of information media.

TYPES OF INFORMATION MEDIA	
Television News Program	**Television Newsmagazine**
• Covers current news events • Gives information objectively	• Covers variety of topics • Entertains and informs
Editorial	**Commercial**
• Covers current issues • Expresses an opinion	• Presents products, people, or ideas • Persuades people to buy or take action

Research Tip

Many television news organizations have Web sites with in-depth coverage of current events.

▶ **Exercise 10** Classifying Information Media Identify at least three examples of each of the following:

1. Television newsmagazines
2. Internet news sources
3. Nightly news programs

For what types of information would you use each of these sources? Why?

More Practice

Academic and Workplace Skills Activity Book
• p. 8

Evaluate Information From the Media Once you understand the different types of media, become a critical viewer. Do this by carefully analyzing and evaluating everything you see and hear.

- **Distinguish facts and opinions**. A *fact* is a statement that can be proved to be true. An *opinion* is what someone believes and may not have been proven to be true. Avoid mistaking opinions for facts.

- **Look for emotional words (also known as *loaded language*) and pictures.** By appealing to our emotions through words and images, programs can persuade us to see things in a certain way without giving us real reasons for that viewpoint. Rely on evidence, such as facts and expert opinions, when making up your mind about an issue.

- **Identify bias.** Bias occurs when a subject is looked at from only one viewpoint. To be fair, all viewpoints should be presented.

Learn More

For more information about methods of persuasion, see Chapter 7, Persuasion.

TIPS FOR EVALUATING INFORMATION MEDIA

- Be aware of the kind of program you are watching, its purpose, and its limitations.
- Sort out facts from opinions.
- Be aware of any loaded language or sensationalist images that might cause you to react in a certain way.
- Listen for bias and note any points of view not discussed.
- Check surprising or questionable information in other sources.
- View the complete program before reaching a conclusion.
- Develop your own views on the issues, people, and information.

Exercise 11 Analyzing Information Media Watch a television program that provides information, such as a news program, a documentary, or an interview. Pay attention to the commercials as well. Then, write a few paragraphs in which you identify the type of program and describe the topics covered. In addition, comment on what the commercials were selling. Finally, evaluate the information on each topic in the program and in the commercials, using the strategies listed above.

Viewing Fine Art Critically

Fine art, such as painting and sculpture, can show you fascinating scenes and beautiful objects. A painting is not just a picture of a thing, though. It is a creation of colors, lines, and shapes that express a mood, idea, or energy all its own. Using these elements, an artist shares what he or she sees or feels.

KEY CONCEPT It is important to learn about some of the basic elements of art so that you can understand what the artist is trying to express. ■

Following are some of the elements of painting:

1. **Color** Artists choose specific colors to convey a mood or atmosphere.
2. **Perspective** The same scene or object can be viewed from different angles or perspectives. Why did the artist choose the one he or she used?
3. **Style** Some works are painted in a realistic style; others look far different from a photograph. What is the artist trying to convey through choice of style?

Parkville, Main Street (Missouri), 1933, Gale Stockwell, National Museum of American Art, Washington, D.C.

Exercise 12 Interpreting Fine Art Have a class discussion about the painting above, *Parkville Main Street* by Gale Stockwell. How has the artist used color, perspective, and style? Remember that some students will likely have differing ideas. Respect everyone's opinion.

⊙ **Technology Tip**

There are many art museums to visit online. For example, you can take a tour of The National Gallery of Art in Washington, D.C., by visiting their Web site: **www.nga.gov**

🔲 **Research Tip**

Browse in the library for books of fine art. Spend some time looking at paintings, sculptures, and photographs in these books to discover your favorites.

▶ **More Practice**

Academic and Workplace Skills Activity Book
• p. 9

Creating Graphic Organizers

Graphic organizers are an excellent tool for breaking down the main ideas in what you read and see and for understanding how those ideas are related.

 **KEY CONCEPT** Putting information into visual form makes ideas easy to identify and comprehend. ■

Follow these steps to help you use graphic organizers:

- **Identify Your Purpose** Are you making the graphic organizer to help you study and remember ideas? Will you present your graphic organizer to other people in a report or presentation?

- **Use Organizing Elements in the Text** Textbooks and other information sources, such as encyclopedias, usually have information organized under headings and subheadings. Use these headings and subheadings to identify main points for your graphic organizer.

- **Decide on the Type of Graphic Organizer** The type of graphic organizer you create depends on how the information is organized in the text you use.

  1. If the text compares and contrasts two or more things, you might want to make a T-chart or a Venn diagram. Both of these graphic organizers can be used to show similarities and differences.
  2. If you want to show cause-and-effect relationships, a flowchart might be the best way to illustrate them.
  3. For main ideas and details, you might make an outline.
  4. A timeline is a good way to show events over a period of time.
  5. A drawing can show what a thing or place looks like.
  6. A diagram can show how a process works.

Use graphic organizers and other visual aids, like those described on the pages that follow, to enhance oral and written presentations.

Learn More

For more information about comparing and contrasting, see Chapter 8, Exposition: Comparison-and-Contrast Essay. For more information on cause-and-effect relationships, see Chapter 9, Exposition: Cause-and-Effect Essay.

 **Technology Tip**

Use the computer to make charts, graphs, and tables. Look in the computer manual or use the Help function to find out how you can draw diagrams and illustrations on screen.

Charts, Graphs, and Tables Charts can show numbers, words, or pictures. An example of a picture chart is a seating plan for a classroom. A graph can be a bar, line, or circle graph. Graphs show how things change over time. Tables help you organize information so that facts can be found quickly and easily. An example of a table is a bus or train schedule.

Diagrams and Illustrations Diagrams are simple line drawings. They may show what something looks like, such as the parts of a computer. A set of diagrams might show how to put together the computer. Illustrations may show an object in more detail than a diagram. Both diagrams and illustrations use labels to identify objects and their parts.

Maps It is useful to make a map when you are giving someone directions to get to a place. You might also make a map for a report, showing the geographical area you are writing about. A map can show many kinds of information besides location. It can also show population, climate, and so on.

MAP OF MY MIDDLE SCHOOL CAMPUS

Research Tip

The reference section of your library has encyclopedias and almanacs that provide a variety of information presented in graph, map, diagram, and chart form.

◄ **Critical Viewing** For what purpose might a student have created this map? What information might he or she wish to convey? **[Analyze, Draw Conclusions]**

▶ **Exercise 13** Creating a Visual Representation To present some information from your science or social studies textbook, create a graphic organizer. Choose a chart, graph, table, diagram, or map. Share your graphic organizer with the class, and explain why you chose that form to present your information.

More Practice

Academic and Workplace Skills Activity Book
• pp. 10–11

Formatting to Create an Effect

Use basic word-processing formatting features to enhance written work. Following are some formatting features and tips for creating effective visual enhancements to your text:

- **Capitals** Use capital letters in headings for key ideas.
- **Boldface** Use boldface to highlight ideas.
- **Italics** To give words special emphasis, use italics.
- **Numbered Lists** Use numbered lists to show a sequence.
- **Bulleted Lists** Items that can be presented in any order can go in a bulleted list.

Icy Sunshine in a Cup

Fresh homemade lemonade

12 oz. cup for only $1
Two glasses for $1.50

- Freshly squeezed lemons
- Bottled spring water
- Sweetened and chilled to perfection
- Refreshment guaranteed!!!

*Every Saturday in July
From noon to 2 P.M.
227 Grove Ave.
Between Chestnut
and Oak Streets*

Stop by and cool off!

Technology Tip

Find out how to use these formatting techniques on your computer. Experiment with other formatting options, such as page borders and shading, colors, different fonts (type styles), and special effects on type, such as outlines and shadows. Use software to add pictures.

▶ **Exercise 14** Using Formatting to Create a Timeline
Create a timeline using formatting to clarify your work. First, choose an author, artist, or historical figure you would like to research. Next, gather data about your subject. Organize your material into chronological order and create your timeline. Use the tips on formatting to create an easy-to-follow timeline.

▶ **More Practice**

Academic and Workplace Skills Activity Book
- p. 12

Developing a Multimedia Presentation

An oral report can be made more effective with the use of slides, videos, and audiotapes, as well as charts, maps, and graphs. These forms of media can help illustrate the main points of your report and make them more understandable to your listeners.

KEY CONCEPT Multimedia presentations supply information through a variety of media, including text, slides, videos, music, maps, charts, and artwork. ■

Tips for Preparing a Multimedia Presentation

- First, make an outline of your report. Look for parts you would like to illustrate through the use of media.

- Choose a form of media that fits your topic. For example, if your report is about another country, you might show slides of important sites and play a tape of that country's music. If you report on becoming a veterinarian, or animal doctor, you might videotape your veterinarian examining your pet.

- Don't put all your media presentations at the beginning or end of your report. Space them out.

- Make your posters, maps, or slides big enough for the audience to see.

- Check all your equipment before you give your presentation. Make sure the cassette player, overhead projector, or slide projector is working properly. It's a good idea to ask a friend to be your media helper. He or she can run the equipment while you speak.

- Always have a backup plan in case something goes wrong with the equipment. For example, you might have photographs to pass around in case the slide projector doesn't work.

- Rehearse with the equipment (and your helper) before the day of your presentation.

Exercise 15 Preparing a Multimedia Presentation Look through your writing portfolio. Choose a piece of writing that you could make into a multimedia presentation. Make a list of some ideas for media you might use to illustrate the topic.

🎧 Research Tip

Your school or public library may have slides, videos, and audiocassettes you can use in your multimedia presentation.

More Practice

Academic and Workplace Skills Activity Book
• pp. 13–14

Creating a Video

Telling a story or reporting on a topic by using images, sound, and dialogue is a powerful way to communicate. Video allows your viewers to see a particular subject matter, event, or story just as *you* see it. Videos can be informative, humorous, or dramatic.

▶ **KEY CONCEPT** Create a video to communicate information, to entertain, or to do both. ■

Organization is the component most essential to making a video. Follow these basic steps when making your video:

Step-by-Step Guide to Video Production

1. Create a shooting script that contains
   • any lines of spoken dialogue.
   • directions about camera angles.
   • descriptions of settings, costumes or wardrobe, and props.
2. Use your shooting script to map out a storyboard, a cartoonlike map of the key events in your video.
3. Choose the locations in which you'll shoot your video.
4. Get permission to use these locations and identify when you'll use them.
5. Choose crew members and assign tasks.
6. Cast the roles and rehearse.
7. Write out a shooting schedule (listing each scene and who is in it) and distribute it.
8. Film the scenes.
9. Review your scenes and edit them together to make a completed video.

Tips for Filming

• Hold the camera steady.

• Avoid quick actions, such as zooming in or out too fast.

• Shoot as much footage as possible. It is easier to edit out footage than to add it later.

• Make sure you have good lighting at your locations.

▶ **Exercise 16** **Creating a Video Report** Choose a place in your town that interests you or a local event that you have always enjoyed. Capture this place or event in a video. Work with a team of classmates, with each of you assuming different roles. Follow the step-by-step tips above.

Standardized Test Preparation Workshop

Interpreting Graphic Aids

Some standardized tests contain questions measuring your ability to gather details and draw conclusions from maps, charts, graphs, and other graphic aids. The following sample item will help you become familiar with these types of questions.

Test Tip

As you examine each graphic aid, ask yourself what each part of the graphic means or represents in relation to the whole.

Sample Test Item

Directions: Read the passage and answer the question that follows.

Feudalism was a system of rule by local lords who were bound to a king by ties of loyalty. Under feudalism in Europe, everyone had a well-defined place in society. The king granted estates to powerful lords. These lords owed military service to the king. The lords divided their estates among vassals (lesser lords). The estates were then subdivided among knights, or mounted warriors. Finally, there were the common people, or serfs. Although they were not slaves, serfs were not free to leave the land. They lived on lands owned by lords and worked the land in return for protection.

1 Which class of the population had more power than the lords?

   A   Peasants

   B   Lesser lords

   C   King

   D   Knights

Answer and Explanation

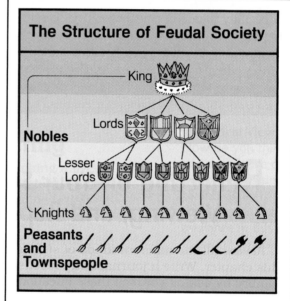

The Structure of Feudal Society

The correct answer is C. The chart indicates that the lords are second in rank according to the feudal system.

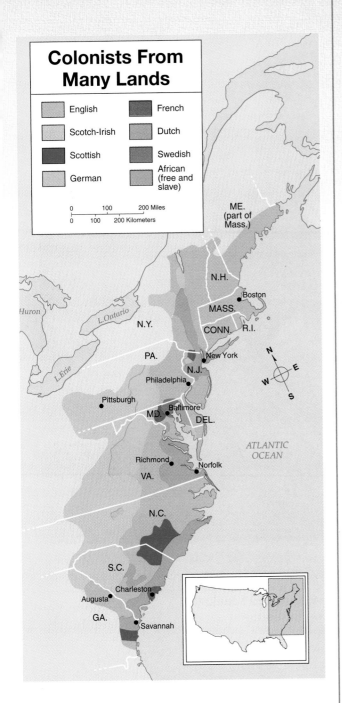

Colonists From Many Lands

- English
- Scotch-Irish
- Scottish
- German
- French
- Dutch
- Swedish
- African (free and slave)

0   100   200 Miles
0   100   200 Kilometers

ME. (part of Mass.)

N.H.

Boston
MASS.
CONN. R.I.

L. Ontario

N.Y.

PA.
New York
N.J.
Philadelphia

Pittsburgh

MD. Baltimore
DEL.

Huron

L. Erie

ATLANTIC OCEAN

Richmond
Norfolk
VA.

N.C.

S.C.

Charleston
Augusta

GA.
Savannah

N
W   E
S

▶ **Practice**   **Directions:** Read the passage and answer the questions that follow.

Colonists from all over the new world came to the American colonies. From the beginning, the United States has been a melting pot of cultures. The English were strongly represented in the original thirteen colonies, while many other groups settled outside of the English areas.

1 Which group settled in all the colonies?
   A Scotch-Irish
   B German
   C African
   D English

2 Which group was represented the least?
   F French
   G Swedish
   H Dutch
   J Scottish

3 Why might certain groups of people decide to live outside of predominately English areas?
   A This would enable them to preserve their own culture.
   B They were battling with the English.
   C The English enforced harsh rules and regulations.
   D The English were unfair business associates.

Vocabulary and Spelling

Still Life: Shelf with books, Master of the Aix Annunciation (15th century, French)

One of the most useful parts of your education is the development of good vocabulary and spelling. By learning new words, you will improve your reading, writing, and speaking—and even your thinking. Not only will you be better at these activities, you will also enjoy them more.

Expanding your vocabulary and your knowledge of spelling will help you in many ways. Vocabulary and spelling mistakes, for example, will lower your grades. A narrow vocabulary will limit what you are trying to say or write. However, with a little effort, you can greatly improve your vocabulary and spelling skills.

▲ **Critical Viewing**
What kind of vocabulary might the reader of books like these have? **[Infer]**

Section 29.1

Developing Vocabulary

Developing Vocabulary Through Listening

Taking part in conversations, listening to works read aloud, and reading many types of works are three of the most common ways to increase your vocabulary.

Conversation

From the time you were born, you have been listening to the words of others. In these conversations, you learned—and continue to learn—the meanings and pronunciations of new words. You can improve your vocabulary even more if you take note of unfamiliar words in your conversations, especially those with people whose life experiences and ideas are different from your own. Learn the meanings of unfamiliar words by asking or by looking them up in a dictionary.

Works Read Aloud

Listening to works of literature read aloud is another important way to build your vocabulary. Nearly all types of literature —including plays, poems, and short stories—are available on audiocassette or compact disc. By listening to these works, you will learn the pronunciations of unfamiliar words. You will also hear the context—the words and sentences around the unfamiliar word that help give it meaning. Read along as you listen so you can see unfamiliar words as you hear them.

Wide Reading

Among the many benefits of reading is developing your vocabulary. As you read, you encounter new words and their meanings. The more you read, the more familiar many of these new words will become. Wide reading—reading a variety of books, newspapers, magazines, Internet articles, and so on—will expose you to many new words and their different uses.

> **More Practice**
>
> Academic and Workplace Skills Activity Book
> • p. 17

Using Context Clues

Every word you hear or see has a context. The context goes a long way toward giving meaning to a word.

▶ **KEY CONCEPT** The **context** of a word means the group of words—the sentence or passage—that surrounds it. ■

In the example below, you can figure out two different meanings of *bear* by looking at the surrounding words.

EXAMPLES: I could no longer <u>bear</u> the pain. ("endure")
The shelf cannot <u>bear</u> a huge
number of books. ("support")

USING CONTEXT CLUES

1. Read the sentence carefully and focus on the overall meaning.

2. Look for clues in nearby words.

3. Guess the meaning of the unfamiliar word.

4. Reread the sentence and see whether your guess seems to fit.

5. Check your guess in a dictionary.

Figurative Language Figurative language is language used to mean something different from its ordinary meaning. It often involves unusual comparisons or familiar words in unfamiliar ways. For instance, consider this sentence: "The suffering engine groaned as the train climbed the steep hill." Engines cannot literally suffer or groan. You can tell from context that *suffering* and *groaned* are used figuratively to show that the engine was straining to pull the train.

Idioms Idioms are common expressions that are not meant literally. For example, in the sentence "David went home early, explaining that he was feeling under the weather," there is no literal meaning for *feeling under the weather*. The context of this sentence, however, makes it clear that David was not feeling well.

Research Tip

Look in a geography book or an atlas, and find three unfamiliar words. Check their meanings in a dictionary.

Use Context Clues in All of Your Reading Very often, you can figure out the meaning of a word from its context, whether you are reading literature or articles, or even instructions or directions for making or fixing something.

Use "Possible Sentences" This strategy can help you to increase your vocabulary and your understanding of words in context. Try using this method to learn and reinforce the meanings of unfamiliar words.

STEPS FOR USING "POSSIBLE SENTENCES"

1. Find an unfamiliar word in your reading, and use context clues to try to figure out its meaning.

2. Write a sentence for the unfamiliar word in your vocabulary notebook.

3. Check the actual meaning of the word in a dictionary.

4. Evaluate your sentence to see whether you have used the word correctly.

5. Revise your sentence to make it correct.

Exercise 1 Using Context Clues Explain how context clues help determine the meanings of the underlined words below.
1. Fencing is a sport that requires speed and agility.
2. Dad bought some fencing for our vegetable garden.
3. My mother will book a hotel room with an ocean view.
4. You will need a book of matches to light this campfire.
5. The book I read last night kept me awake for hours.

Exercise 2 Using the "Possible Sentences" Strategy With Words in Context Find a story or an article of interest to you. Read through it, and identify five words that are unfamiliar to you. Then, use the "Possible Sentences" strategy to try to determine the definitions of the words. Enter the words and their correct meanings in a vocabulary notebook.

More Practice

Academic and Workplace Skills Activity Book
• p. 18

Studying Meanings in the Content Areas

Use a Notebook and a Glossary

During your school studies, you will encounter many unfamiliar words related to specific subjects. While context can help you determine the meanings of some of them, you should record and study any unfamiliar words related to the topic you are learning in class. For each subject area, write the meanings and pronunciations of new words in a special section of your notebook. Use the glossary at the back of your textbook to find the subject-specific meanings of unfamiliar words.

Social Studies Words that you are likely to encounter in social studies deal with types of government, political activity, history, society, and geography. To aid your studying, group new words under these categories.

Science Many terms in science textbooks have Latin or Greek origins. Categorize new science words by their prefixes, suffixes, or roots. For example, you could group *atmosphere* with *biosphere* because they both end with *-sphere*. Once you have learned that *-sphere* means "something resembling a sphere, or globe" you will more easily remember the meanings of both words.

Current Events Whenever you listen to the news or read a newspaper, it is likely that you will encounter words you have learned in science and social studies. Remember—the more times you hear or see a word used, the greater your command of the word. Use current event topics as a source of vocabulary reinforcement.

 **Internet Tip**

Find a short entry about any history or science topic in an on-line encyclopedia. Find an unfamiliar word, look it up in a dictionary, and add it to your notebook.

> **Exercise 3** **Studying Words in the Content Areas** Compile a list of unfamiliar words from a chapter of your social studies or science book. Then, read newspaper or newsmagazine articles over a period of a week, identifying passages in which these words appear. In your notebook, write the sentence or paragraph from the article in which the word appears. Compare the word's meaning in the article with its meaning in your textbook.

More Practice

Academic and Workplace Skills Activity Book
• pp. 19–20

Section
29.2

Studying Words Systematically

Keeping a Vocabulary Notebook

Use a vocabulary notebook to help you learn new words from textbook reading or from reading for pleasure.

▶ **KEY CONCEPT** Study and review new words in your vocabulary notebook a few times each week. ■

Create a Vocabulary Notebook Keep a notebook to list new words. On the page, write the source of the word. Then, list the word, its definition, and examples of how to use it.

VOCABULARY NOTEBOOK		
Chapter 3: Europeans Explore America		
Words	Definitions	Examples
navigate	1. to steer or direct a ship	The Prince used the instruments
	2. to travel through or over water	to navigate the ship into safe waters.

▶ **Exercise 4** Using a Vocabulary Notebook
Look up the following words, and add them, their definitions, and an example of your own to your vocabulary notebook.

1. bleach
2. hangar
3. germinate
4. indigent
5. literate
6. patriot
7. parched
8. manipulate
9. acceleration
10. instill

▶ **Critical Viewing** What kinds of words would you expect to be defined in the glossary of a geography book? **[Relate]**

Studying New Words

It is important to set a regular time to review new vocabulary words, such as just before you begin your daily homework assignments. Use one or more of the following methods to review new words.

Use Your Notebook

To help you remember the meaning of each new word in your notebook, cover its definition with your hand. Then, look at the word and the example sentence and define the word. Check your definition against the definition in your notebook. Finally, write a sentence using the new word.

Write Sentences With Vocabulary Words When you write a sentence using a new vocabulary word, include the word's definition in the sentence. This will help you remember the word by reinforcing its meaning.

EXAMPLE: He *acquired* a college loan, *getting* it by working out a deal with the bank.

Use Flashcards

Make a flashcard for each new word from your notebook. Write the word on the front of an index card. On the back, write the word's definition and, if necessary, the subject to which it relates. Consider including the word's pronunciation and a sentence using the word. Working with a partner, test your knowledge of the new words.

Use a Tape Recorder

Record a vocabulary word, pronouncing it carefully. Then, after a pause, record its definition. To review, play the tape. During the pause, recall the word's definition. Listen to the recorded definition to check yourself and to reinforce the word's meaning.

Exercise 5 Making Flashcards or Tapes Make a set of flashcards or tapes to study the following words. Add words from your own reading or from assigned vocabulary lists.
1. prodigy
2. conspired
3. uncanny
4. intrigue
5. eminent

Research Tip

Find a science book in the library. Locate a few sentences in the book that suggest the meaning of a word through context clues. Add the new word to your notebook.

More Practice

Academic and Workplace Skills Activity Book
• pp. 21–22

Using a Dictionary

When you want to find the exact meaning of a word, consult a dictionary. Besides giving the definition of a word, a dictionary will also tell you the word's pronunciation, part of speech, and history. Words in a dictionary are listed alphabetically.

KEY CONCEPT Use a **dictionary** to find meanings of words you do not know. ■

Using Other Reference Aids

Thesaurus Use a thesaurus to find synonyms (words with similar meanings) and sometimes antonyms (words with opposite meanings) to a given word. A thesaurus is useful for finding more precise words for your writing.

Synonym Finder If you are drafting with a word-processing program, check to see whether it includes a synonym finder in one of the pull-down menus. If so, highlight a word for which you want to find a synonym, and the synonym finder will check for alternative words.

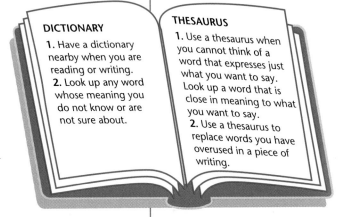

DICTIONARY
1. Have a dictionary nearby when you are reading or writing.
2. Look up any word whose meaning you do not know or are not sure about.

THESAURUS
1. Use a thesaurus when you cannot think of a word that expresses just what you want to say. Look up a word that is close in meaning to what you want to say.
2. Use a thesaurus to replace words you have overused in a piece of writing.

Glossary Many textbooks include a glossary of terms and definitions. The terms are specific to the field of study covered in the textbook. The glossary lists the words you need to learn and know in the subject area.

Software In addition to being available in book form, most references, including dictionaries and thesauruses, are available as software. You can purchase some of these programs, while others are available for free on the Internet.

 **Learn More**

To find more detailed information about reference aids, and to see an annotated dictionary entry, turn to Chapter 31.

KEY CONCEPT Use **references**, such as thesauruses, synonym finders, or glossaries, to find the exact words you need when writing. ■

Exercise 6 Using Vocabulary Reference Aids Look up the words below in the references indicated. Compare and contrast the information found in each source. Then, look up each word in a thesaurus, and write down three similar words.
1. cerebral (science textbook glossary, dictionary)
2. patriot (dictionary, social studies textbook glossary)
3. eccentric (dictionary, synonym finder)
4. synthesis (science text book, on-line dictionary)
5. cabinet (social studies textbook glossary, dictionary)

Studying Word Parts and Origins

Using Word Roots

The root of a word is the word part containing the word's basic meaning. The chart below contains ten common roots whose meanings you should know.

▶ **KEY CONCEPT** A **root** is the base of a word. ■

Roots have come into the English language from many sources. In the first column below, additional spellings for each word root are in parentheses. The origins of the roots are indicated by the abbreviations *L.*, *Gr.*, and *A.S.* (Latin, Greek, and Anglo-Saxon).

TEN COMMON ROOTS		
Root and Origin	**Meaning**	**Example**
-cap- (-capt-) [L.]	to take, seize	*cap*tivate (to take hold of)
-dic- (-dict-) [L.]	to say in words	pre*dict* (to say before)
-dyna- [Gr.]	to be strong	*dyna*sty (a state of strength)
-mov- (-mot-) [L.]	to move	*mov*able (able to be moved)
-nym- [Gr.]	to name	anto*nym* (to name as an opposite)
-pon- (-pos-) [L.]	to put, place	com*pose* (to put together)
-spec- (-spect-) [L.]	to see	*spect*ator (one who sees)
-ten (-tain-) [L.]	to hold	de*tain* (to hold back)
-vert- (-vers-) [L.]	to turn	in*vert* (to turn upside down)
-vid- (-vis-) [L.]	to see	*vis*ible (able to be seen)
-heal- [A.S.]	sound, whole	*heal*th (physical and mental well-being)

▶ **Exercise 7** Using Roots to Define Words Match the words in the first column below with their definitions in the second column.

1. prospect
2. inversion
3. diction
4. mobility
5. homophonic
6. transpose
7. dynamite
8. supervise
9. attain
10. captive

a. way of using words
b. sounding alike
c. a strong explosive
d. a turning upside down
e. oversee
f. future outlook
g. someone taken as a prisoner
h. reach
i. change places
j. ease of movement

▶ **More Practice**

Academic and Workplace Skills Activity Book
• pp. 23–24

Using Prefixes

Knowing only a small number of prefixes can help you understand thousands of words.

KEY CONCEPT A **prefix** is one or more syllables added to the beginning of a word to form a new word. ■

Learn the prefixes in the chart below to create new words and to enlarge your vocabulary. The origins of the roots are indicated by the abbreviations *L.*, *Gr.*, and *A.S.* (Latin, Greek, and Anglo-Saxon).

TEN COMMON PREFIXES		
Prefix and Origin	**Meaning**	**Example**
anti- [Gr.]	against	*anti*social (against society)
dis- [L.]	away, apart	*dis*grace (to lose favor)
ex- [L.]	from, out	*ex*port (to send out)
mis- [A.S.]	wrong	*mis*lead (to lead in a wrong direction)
mono- [Gr.]	one, alone	*mono*rail (a single rail)
non- [L.]	not	*non*profit (not trying to earn a profit)
pre- [L.]	before	*pre*view (to view beforehand)
re- [L.]	back, again	*re*view (to view again)
trans- [L.]	over, across	*trans*mit (to send across)
un- [A.S.]	not	*un*known (unable to be determined)

▼ **Critical Viewing** If he is studying *before* a test, what will this boy be? If he studies well, what will he avoid? Use words with the prefixes *pre-* and *mis-* in your answer. [**Draw Conclusions**]

Exercise 8 Working With Prefixes On a piece of paper, combine the prefix in parentheses with each word below to create a new word. In your notebook, write the definition next to each word. Use a dictionary to check your answers.

1. appear (dis-)
2. historic (pre-)
3. behave (mis-)
4. aircraft (anti-)
5. available (un-)
6. vocal (non-)
7. syllable (mono-)
8. form (trans-)
9. claim (re-)
10. act (ex-)

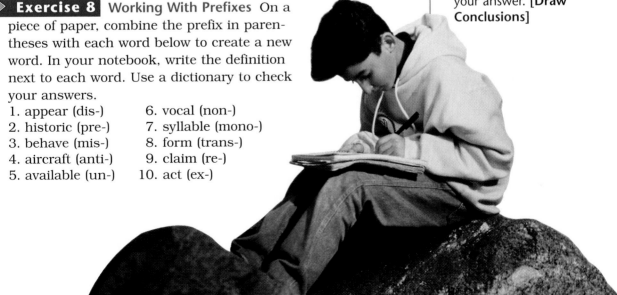

Using Suffixes

> **KEY CONCEPT** A **suffix** is one or more syllables added to the end of a word to form a new word. ■

Suffixes can change both the meaning and the part of speech of a word. For instance, the noun *color* becomes the adjective *colorless* when the suffix *-less* is added. In the following chart, five common suffixes are listed. Alternative spellings are in parentheses. The abbreviations *L.*, *Gr.*, and *A.S.* mean Latin, Greek, and Anglo-Saxon, the origins of the suffixes.

TEN COMMON SUFFIXES		
Suffix and Origin	**Meaning**	**Example**
-able (-ible) [L.]	capable of being	laugh*able* (capable of being laughed at)
-cy (-acy) [Gr.]	quality of	democra*cy* (quality of being democratic)
-ful [A.S.]	full of	hope*ful* (full of hope)
-ism [Gr.]	idea, belief, act	national*ism* (belief in a nation)
-ist [Gr.]	believer, doer	violin*ist* (player of the violin)
-ity [L.]	state of being	char*ity* (state of being charitable)
-less [A.S.]	without, lacking	sound*less* (without sound)
-ly [Gr.]	in a certain way	local*ly* (in a local way)
-ment [L.]	result or act of	state*ment* (result of stating)
-tion (-ion, -sion) [L.]	act of, state of being	crea*tion* (act of creating)

> **Exercise 9** **Working With Suffixes** Divide a piece of paper into two columns. In the first column, write two new examples for each suffix listed above. In the second column, write their definitions. Check your answers in a dictionary.

> **Exercise 10** **Changing Suffixes to Make New Words** Define each word below; then, change the suffix as indicated, and define the new word. Write a sentence for every word. Check the meanings in a dictionary if necessary.
> 1. helpful (change *-ful* to *-less*)
> 2. prediction (change *-tion* to *-[t]able*)
> 3. realism (change *-ism* to *-ity*)
> 4. consistency (change *-cy* to *-[t]ly*)
> 5. purity (change *-ity* to *-ist*)

More Practice

Academic and Workplace Skills Activity Book
• pp. 25–26

Examining Word Origins

You may not ever have thought about it, but English is one of a family of languages with a very long history. English is part of the Indo-European family of languages. Its closest relatives are other Germanic languages, such as Dutch and German. English is the most widely spoken language in the Western world. It has also borrowed words from more languages than any other. In fact, more than 70 percent of the words we call English are borrowed from other languages.

Understanding Historical Influences

Throughout its history, English has been exposed to many other languages. Events and circumstances—such as wars and trade with other nations, new inventions, and emerging technologies—have contributed to the growth and change of the language.

INFLUENCES ON THE GROWTH OF ENGLISH		
Conquest	Throughout history, invasion and conquests of Great Britain added many words to English.	earth (Anglo-Saxon) secure (Latin) avenue (French)
Travelers	Travelers, including merchants, explorers, and soldiers, added words to English from languages and cultures they encountered around the world.	moose (North America) banjo (Africa) calico (India) boondocks (Malayan) tea (China)
New Words	New words were coined to describe new inventions and technologies.	automobile photography movie Internet suburb

▶ **Exercise 11** Analyzing Word Origins Write the words below on a separate sheet of paper, and look them up in a print or electronic dictionary. Then, write the language from which each word comes.
  1. balcony
  2. piano
  3. mustard
  4. encyclopedia
  5. nickel

💻 **Internet Tip**

To find Internet sites containing information about how English developed with influences from other languages, type "origins of English" in the query field of your search engine.

Improving Your Spelling

Whether you are writing for a teacher, a friend, or someone you haven't met, your writing makes an impression on the reader. You want that impression to be positive. Anyone can learn to eliminate nearly all spelling errors by using a dictionary, keeping a spelling list, and observing some basic rules.

Using a Spelling List

KEY CONCEPT When selecting the words for your spelling list, focus on words you frequently misspell. Enter the spelling and pronunciation of each word in your notebook, and study your list regularly. ■

SPELLING NOTEBOOK	
Words	Definitions
necessary	essential
Mississippi	
accessible	can be approached or entered
spaghetti	

Internet Tip

On the Internet, you can find lists of words that are frequently misspelled. To access them, type "commonly misspelled words" in the query field of your search engine.

Exercise 12 **Developing a Spelling List** Look carefully at each word below. On a piece of paper, write *correct* if the word is spelled correctly, or change the spelling if it is incorrect. Check each word in a dictionary. Add any words that give you trouble to your personal spelling list.

1. avenue
2. compleet
3. encouragment
4. expense
5. ninteenth
6. defeat
7. riligion
8. science
9. ninty
10. season
11. potatoe
12. sincerely
13. tomatoe
14. weapon
15. width
16. excape
17. medecine
18. cafeteria
19. punctuation
20. Wensday

Studying Your Spelling Words

It is important to study the words on your spelling list regularly. To make this task more manageable, divide your list into groups of five or ten words. Study each group separately for about a week. As you master more and more words, test yourself on larger groups from your list.

▶ **KEY CONCEPT** Review your spelling words each week, several times a week. ■

A METHOD FOR STUDYING YOUR SPELLING WORDS

1. *Look* at each word. Notice any unusual features about the spelling of the word. For example, in the word *argument*, the *e* in *argue* is dropped before the ending is added. Concentrate on the part of the word that gives you the most trouble. Then, cover the word and try to picture it in your mind.

2. *Say* the word aloud. Then, sound the word out slowly, syllable by syllable.

3. *Spell* the word by writing it on a sheet of paper. Say each syllable aloud as you write it down.

4. *Compare* the word that you wrote on the paper with the word in your notebook. If you spelled the word correctly, put a small check in front of the word in your notebook. If you misspelled the word, circle the letter or letters on your paper that are incorrect. Then, start over again with the first step.

▶ **Exercise 13** Checking Spelling Skills Fill in the missing letter in each word below. Add any words you misspelled to your personal spelling list.

1. element __?__ ry
2. nurs __?__ ry
3. courage __?__ us
4. import __?__ nce
5. experi __?__ nce
6. confu __?__ ion
7. competi __?__ ion
8. accept __?__ ble
9. terr __?__ ble
10. comfort __?__ ble

▶ **More Practice**

Academic and Workplace Skills Activity Book
• pp. 27–28

▶ **Exercise 14** Identifying Commonly Misspelled Words
Record in your notebook any words you have misspelled in your work. Check your writing portfolio, corrected tests, essays, and homework to find these words. After you have studied the words, have a partner test you on them.

Applying Spelling Rules

Choosing Between *ie* and *ei*

Follow basic rules when you spell a word containing the letters *ie* or *ei*. Exceptions to these rules should be memorized.

- When a word has a long *e* sound, use *ie*.
- When a word has a long *a* sound, use *ei*.
- When a word has a long *e* sound preceded by the letter *c*, use *ei*.

COMMON *ie* AND *ei* WORDS

Long *e* Sound: Use *ie*	Long *a* Sound: Use *ei*	Long *e* Sound preceded by *c*: Use *ei*
brief	eight	ceiling
chief	freight	deceive
niece	reign	perceive
piece	sleigh	receipt
relieve	vein	receive
shield	weight	
yield		

EXCEPTIONS: either, neither, seize

KEY CONCEPT Remember the rule: *i* before *e* except after *c* and when sounded like *ay* as in *neighbor* and *weigh*. ■

Try to Think of Additional Words If you can add more words to the chart above, it will help you to remember the basic rules. Add any words you find difficult to your spelling list.

Exercise 15 Spelling *ie* and *ei* Words Fill in the blanks below with either *ie* or *ei*. Check the spellings in a dictionary. Add difficult words to your personal spelling list.

1. br __?__ f
2. fr __?__ ght
3. rec __?__ ver
4. th __?__ f
5. b __?__ ge
6. w __?__ gh
7. dec __?__ ve
8. p __?__ rce
9. p __?__ r
10. r __?__ ndeer

More Practice

Academic and
Workplace Skills
Activity Book
• p. 29

Adding Prefixes and Suffixes

A prefix is one or more syllables added at the beginning of a word to form a new word. A suffix is one or more syllables added to the end of a word.

KEY CONCEPT Adding a *prefix* to a word does not affect the spelling of the original word. Adding a *suffix* often involves a spelling change in the word. ■

Prefixes When a prefix is added to a word, the spelling of the root word remains the same.

EXAMPLES:
    mis- + spell = misspell
    un- + finished = unfinished
    re- + act = react
    dis- + service = disservice
    co- + exist = coexist
    im- + movable = immovable
    de- + press = depress
    in- + accurate = inaccurate

Investigate Long Words The way in which the words in the above list are divided may help you to remember something important to spelling success. Long words (*circumnavigate*) are often made up of small words (*navigate*) and word parts (*circum-*). When you have to spell a long word, try to spell the small words within it.

▼ Critical Viewing How might focusing on correct spelling, as well as on the content of his report, be likely to improve this student's chances of receiving a good grade? [**Connect**]

Exercise 16 Spelling Words With **Prefixes** Make new words by combining the words and prefixes in parentheses below. Check each word in a dictionary to make sure that it is spelled correctly. Add any difficult words to your spelling list.

1. operate (co-)
2. compression (de-)
3. satisfaction (dis-)
4. polite (im-)
5. offensive (in-)
6. fortune (mis-)
7. elect (re-)
8. natural (un-)
9. author (co-)
10. fault (de-)

Standardized Test Preparation Workshop

Using Context to Determine Word Meaning

Standardized tests often contain vocabulary questions. These types of questions require you to find the meaning of a word using the context of a passage. Use the context to help you determine the meanings of idioms, expressions, words with multiple meanings, figurative language, and specialized and technical terms.

The following strategies will help you answer vocabulary questions on standardized tests:

- Read the sentence; carefully focus on the underlined word.
- Determine the overall meaning of the passage.
- Look for clues in the surrounding words.
- Use these clues to guess which answer choice best defines the meaning of the new word.

Test Tip

Before making a final selection, read your choice in place of the underlined word. Evaluate whether it makes sense.

Sample Test Items

Answers and Explanations

Sample Test Items	Answers and Explanations
Directions: Read the passage. Then, read each question that follows the passage. Decide which is the best answer to each question. The <u>counter</u> indicated a <u>record</u> number of visitors to the Web site. **1** In this passage, the word <u>counter</u> means— **A** a place for preparing food **B** a person who counts things **C** a computer hardware device **D** software designed to collect specific data electronically	The correct answer for item 1 is *D*. Although both *A* and *B* are correct definitions of the word, the only meaning that applies in the context of the passage is *D*.
2 The word <u>record</u> in this passage means— **F** evidence of **G** greatest **H** keep details **J** a recording	The correct answer for item 2 is *G*. The adjective *record* is used in this sentence to indicate the highest number of visitors to the Web site.

Practice 1 **Directions:** Read the passage. Then, read each question that follows the passage. Decide which is the best answer to each question.

Collecting antiques is a fast-growing <u>craze</u>. Everything from old furniture to tin toys is showing up in antique stores and flea markets and even on the Internet. Sometimes, <u>individual</u> items gain much greater meaning and value when added to other like items. For example, a signed picture of the <u>late</u> President Eisenhower, although valuable on its own, may triple in value when paired with an <u>original</u> letter from the President.

1 In this passage, the word <u>craze</u> means—
   A fad
   B insanity
   C cult
   D whim

2 In this passage, the word <u>individual</u> means—
   F human being
   G unusual
   H exclusive
   J single

3 The word <u>late</u> in this passage means—
   A behind schedule
   B postponed
   C recent
   D deceased

4 In this passage, the word <u>original</u> means—
   F unique
   G not copied
   H sincere
   J creative

Practice 2 **Directions:** Read the passage. Then, read each question that follows the passage. Decide which is the best answer to each question.

Toward the end of winter, a gardener's <u>fancy</u> turns to spring. Seed <u>catalogs</u> begin to arrive in the mail. Periodically, a warm day will allow the gardener to spend some time pulling weeds and turning the soil in preparation for <u>sowing</u>. If you have a <u>green thumb</u>, all you need is the hope of an early growing season!

1 In this passage, the expression <u>fancy</u> means—
   A decorative
   B to be inclined to
   C imagination
   D ornamental

2 The word <u>catalogs</u> in this passage means—
   F lists
   G classifies
   H sales brochures
   J categories of garden tools

3 The word <u>sowing</u> in this passage means—
   A spreading seed in the ground
   B attaching two pieces of fabric with thread and needle
   C harvesting crops
   D preparing the garden

4 In this passage, the expression <u>green thumb</u> means—
   F a fungal infection of the thumb
   G skill at gardening
   H little experience with gardening
   J a gardening club recognized by its members with green thumbs

Reading Skills

▲ **Critical Viewing**
Point out details from the picture that help you determine whether this girl is reading a textbook or a book for pleasure. **[Draw Conclusions]**

Good readers use different reading skills for different kinds of reading. You probably use different skills when you read a comic book or magazine than when you read a textbook or a novel. No matter what you read, however, it is important to be able to focus on the most important information, understand the ideas being presented, and determine whether the information makes good sense. These skills are especially important when you are reading textbooks and research materials for school.

In this chapter, you will explore new ways to develop your reading skills. The topics discussed in the following pages will teach you how to locate information in your textbooks more easily, how to organize the information you read, and how to apply reading strategies to understand both nonfiction and fiction materials more successfully.

Reading Methods and Tools

In order to better understand the materials you read, become an active reader. Don't just follow the author's words. Build your own meaning by determining the organization of the text, asking questions as you read, and identifying experiences of your own that fit with the ideas in the text.

Using Sections in Textbooks

Most textbooks have special sections in the front and back of the book and at the beginning and end of each chapter to help you find and understand the information each chapter contains. Pick up one of your textbooks, and locate each of the sections discussed below.

▶ **KEY CONCEPT** Use the special sections of your textbook to become familiar with its contents. ■

Table of Contents The table of contents is at the front of your textbook. It lists the units and chapters of the book in the order in which they appear, and the pages on which each begins.

Chapter Introduction and Summaries A chapter introduction describes main ideas you will find in the chapter. The chapter summary, at the end, reviews the main points covered. These parts help you focus on information and remember it.

Glossary The glossary is usually located at the back of the textbook, just before the index. It lists and defines, in alphabetical order, special subject-related terms.

Appendix The appendices at the back of a textbook contain additional information. The appendix often includes charts, maps, formulas, timelines, essays, and biographical or historical information.

Index Found at the back of a textbook, the index lists alphabetically all the subjects covered in the book and tells the specific pages on which each subject is discussed. The index provides more details than the table of contents. Index topics beginning with *a* or *the* are listed alphabetically by the first main word.

GLOSSARY

fraction: petroleum part with its own boiling point
freezing: change of a liquid into a solid
freezing point: temperature at which a substance changes from liquid to solid
frequency (FREE-kwuhn-see): number of waves that pass a certain point in a given amount of time
friction: force that acts in the opposite direction of motion

fulcrum: fixed pivot point of a lever
fundamental tone: note produced at the lowest frequency at which a standing wave occurs
fuse: thin strip of metal used for safety because when the current flowing through it becomes too high, it melts and breaks the flow of electricity

galvanometer: device that uses an electromagnet to detect small amounts of current
gamma (GAM-uh) **ray:** high-frequency electromagnetic wave released during gamma decay; strongest type of nuclear radiation
gas: phase in which matter has no definite shape or volume
Geiger counter: device that can be used to detect radioactivity because it produces an electric current in the presence of a radioactive substance
generator: device that uses electromagnets to convert mechanical energy to electrical energy
gram: one thousandth of a kilogram
gravitational potential energy: potential energy that is dependent on height above the Earth's surface
gravity: force of attraction that depends on the mass of two objects and the distance between them; responsible for accelerating an object toward the Earth
group: column of elements in the periodic table; family

action: petroleum part with its own boiling point
freezing: change of a liquid into a solid
freezing point: temperature at which a substance changes from liquid to solid
frequency (FREE-kwuhn-see): number of waves that pass a certain point in a given amount of time
friction: force that acts in the opposite direction of motion

um: fixed pivot point of a lever
ental tone: note produced at the to be the at which a standing
holography: that uses lasers to produce three-dimensional photographs
homogeneous (hoh-moh-JEE-nee-uhs) **mixture:** mixture that appears the same throughout
hot-water system: heating system in which hot water is pumped through pipes to a convector that heats a room by means of convection currents
hydraulic device: machine that takes advantage of the fact that pressure is transmitted equally in all directions in a liquid; obtains a large force on a large piston by applying a small force with a small piston
hydrocarbon: organic compound that contains only hydrogen and carbon
hypothesis (high-PAHTH-uh-sihs): proposed solution to a scientific problem

illuminated object: object that can be seen because it is lit up
incandescent light: light produced from heat
inclined plane: flat slanted surface that tiplies force
index of refraction: compar light in air with sp materi

Using Features of Textbooks

Within each chapter of a textbook are a number of special features that will help you to read and study the material the chapter contains.

> **KEY CONCEPT** Use the special features of your textbook to aid your reading and studying. ■

Chapter Titles, Headings, and Subheadings These are printed in large, heavy type and help you focus on what the material is about. They also divide the material into sections, so you can learn it more easily.

Questions and Exercises These are located at the end of the chapter to help you retain the information you have read. You might want to preview the questions and exercises before reading the chapter to help you focus on the main ideas.

Pictures and Captions A picture can make a confusing idea clearer. Often, next to a picture there is a printed caption that describes the picture and explains its significance.

> **Exercise 1** Examining the Sections in a Textbook Look at one of your textbooks, and answer the following questions.

- Read the table of contents. How many units and chapters does the textbook contain?
- Does your textbook have a glossary? If so, write the definitions of three words you didn't already know.
- If there is an appendix, tell what types of materials it contains.
- Using the index, find a subject that is discussed on at least four different pages in the book. Locate the subject on each of those pages.

> **Exercise 2** Examining the Features of a Textbook Look at one of your textbooks, and answer the following questions.

1. How many headings and subheadings does the first chapter contain? Describe how the publisher has used size and color to make these headings stand out.
2. Which of these features—introduction, summary, exercises, questions—does each chapter contain? What information can be learned from each?
3. Find three pictures in the textbook that have captions. Describe how the captions explain the pictures. What information in the text does each picture help to explain?

> **More Practice**
>
> Academic and Workplace Skills Activity Book
> • pp. 35–36

Using Reading Strategies

You can use special reading strategies to improve your reading of textbooks. Three helpful reading strategies are varying your reading style, learning *Question-Answer Relationships* (QARs), and using the SQ4R method.

▶ **KEY CONCEPT** Use a combination of reading strategies to help you better understand the material you read. ■

Vary Your Reading Style Three types of reading styles are *skimming, scanning,* and *close reading.* You use each style for a different purpose. Before you start to read, consider your purpose, and use the reading style that best fits that purpose.

Skimming a text means looking it over quickly to get a general idea of its contents. When you skim, look for highlighted or bold type, headings, topic sentences, and photo captions.

Scanning involves looking over material to find a specific word or idea and ignoring other information. You scan, for example, when you use a telephone book.

Close Reading is reading the material carefully to understand and remember information, to link ideas, and to draw conclusions about what you read.

Use Question-Answer Relationships (QARs) You can better understand your reading if you ask questions about it. Get into the habit of asking and answering these four types of questions as you read:

🔋 Research Tip

Try using these same skills when you conduct research using library reference sources. *Skim* to discover the kinds of information available. *Scan* to locate specific pieces of information. Finally, *read closely* to obtain the facts and ideas you need for your report.

RIGHT THERE
The answer is right there in the text, usually in one or two sentences. To answer this question, scan the text to locate specific information.

THINK AND SEARCH
The answer is in the text, but you need to think about the question's answer and then search the text for the evidence to support it.

AUTHOR AND YOU
The answer is not only in the text. Answer this question by thinking about what the author has said, what you already know, and how these fit together.

ON YOUR OWN
The answer is, for the most part, not in the text. To answer this question, you need to draw from your own experiences. You can, however, revise or expand your answer based on your reading.

Use the SQ4R Method Once you have examined your textbook's special sections and features, you can use this knowledge to help you read it more effectively. A good reading plan to follow is called SQ4R, which stands for *Survey, Question, Read, Record, Recite,* and *Review.* Use this method to help you focus on your reading and to assist you in recalling information.

SQ4R METHOD

Survey → Look over the material you are going to read for these features: chapter titles, headings, subheadings, introduction, summary, and questions or exercises.

Question → Ask questions about what information might be covered under each heading. Ask the questions *who, what, when, where,* and *why* about it.

Read → Search for the answers to the questions you thought of in the previous step.

Record → Take notes to remember information better. List the main ideas and major details.

Recite → Aloud or silently, recall the questions and their related answers.

Review → Review the material on a regular basis, using some or all of the steps above.

▶ **Exercise 3** Creating Your Own QAR Questions, and Using Reading Styles to Answer Them Using the description of Question-Answer Relationships on the previous page, create and answer questions of the four general types for your next reading assignment. Use the various reading styles to answer your questions. *Scan* the text to answer a Right-There question. *Skim* the text to answer a Think-and-Search Question, and *closely read* the text to answer an Author-and-You question.

▶ **Exercise 4** Using the SQ4R Method Use the SQ4R method to study a chapter or section of a textbook that has been assigned to you. Then, write a brief account of how the method helped you learn and remember the information.

Using Graphic Organizers

A graphic organizer is a diagram that shows how ideas fit together in the materials you read. You can use a graphic organizer to arrange reading information in an organized way to help you better understand the ideas and to prepare for writing assignments on the material.

KEY CONCEPT Use graphic organizers to help you understand relationships among ideas in a text. ■

Following is a description of three different types of organizers you can use to help you understand what you are reading. Before you make a graphic organizer, think about how the parts of your subject are related. Then, you can choose a format that best fits your needs.

Timeline A timeline shows the order of related events and the amount of time between each. It is a good way to organize historical information, arrange events in the plot of a story, or present data from science experiments.

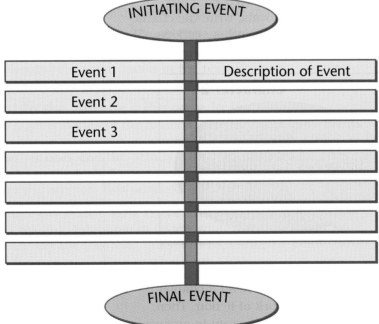

TIMELINE

INITIATING EVENT

Event 1	Description of Event
Event 2	
Event 3	

FINAL EVENT

⊙ Technology Tip

Some computer applications will create graphic organizers for you. Simply enter your data, select a type of chart or graph, and press Enter or Return. You will then have an opportunity to edit the results.

More Practice

Academic and Workplace Skills Activity Book
• p. 37

Distinguishing Fact From Opinion

Part of being a critical reader is learning to tell the difference between statements that express facts and those that contain opinions.

Fact Statements A statement of fact is one that can be proved true (or found to be false) in one of the following four ways: by measurement, by observation, by consulting a reliable source, or by experiment.

FACT STATEMENT:	Joe's brother is five feet ten inches tall.
FACT STATEMENT:	It is raining now.
FACT STATEMENT:	Plants need water and sunlight to survive.

You could test the first statement by measuring Joe's brother's height. You could test the second statement by looking out the window. You could test the third statement by doing an experiment, consulting a textbook, or talking to an expert.

Opinion Statements A statement of opinion, unlike a statement of fact, cannot be completely proved. An opinion may simply express a person's feeling or attitude. Before you trust an opinion statement, you should feel confident that the writer has supported it with evidence, such as related facts or a reliable authority.

OPINION STATEMENT:	Basketball is an exciting sport.
OPINION STATEMENT WITH SUPPORT:	Basketball is an exciting sport; turnovers are frequent, and points are scored nearly every minute of play.

The first example is purely opinion, unsupported by any facts. The second opinion is more reliable than the first one because it is based on facts.

Exercise 7 Evaluating Fact and Opinion Statements
Identify each statement below as *fact* or *opinion*. If the statement expresses an opinion, tell whether it is supported or unsupported by facts. Consult a reference book if necessary.
1. Mount Everest is the tallest mountain on Earth's surface.
2. I have heard that Mount Everest is not as difficult to climb as K2, which is located in the same range.
3. According to this biography, the teddy bear was named for Theodore Roosevelt.
4. Ty Cobb was a great baseball player; his lifetime batting average is the highest of all time.
5. Dogs make better pets than cats do.

Learn More

For more about doing research, see Chapter 11.

More Practice

Academic and Workplace Skills Activity Book
• pp. 40–41

Identifying the Author's Purpose

One important critical reading skill involves examining an author's purpose—why he or she is writing. As you read, remember to look for clues to help you identify the author's purpose. When you think you know the author's purpose, confirm your choice by linking it to details in the text.

KEY CONCEPT Learn to identify the author's purpose by using clues found in the text. ■

The list below describes several common purposes, along with clues to recognize each purpose. Use the clues to help you identify the author's purpose in books or articles you read.

1. **To Inform**—presents a series of factual statements.
2. **To Instruct**—includes a step-by-step explanation of an idea or process.
3. **To Offer an Opinion**—presents a topic from a certain point of view or with a certain intention in mind.
4. **To Sell**—uses persuasive techniques designed to sell a product.
5. **To Entertain**—narrates an event in a humorous manner, sometimes to lighten a serious topic.

Exercise 8 Determining the Author's Purpose Read the following sentences, and determine the author's purpose. Explain your answers.

1. This guide, in four easy steps, tells you how to hook up and operate your stereo system.
2. For the most refreshment possible, try an ice-cold *Lemon Zest Cola.*
3. Mark Twain was born in Hannibal, Missouri, in 1835.
4. I am going to tell you why we should all be using public transportation instead of driving cars.
5. If the dinosaurs could make a comeback, would they enjoy breathing the air or drinking the water on modern Earth?

▼ Critical Viewing Describe how a writer might write about this photograph for each of the five purposes. **[Relate]**

Applying Forms of Reasoning

Once you have learned how to examine and evaluate reading material, you are ready to start drawing your own conclusions about the work's *central idea*—the overall message of the work.

▶ **KEY CONCEPT** Examine the details of the text you read to help you draw conclusions about the work's *central idea*. ■

Draw Conclusions Often, an author does not state a central idea directly. As you read, you must look for clues to the central idea in the way information is organized and presented. Then, draw your own conclusions based on the clues.

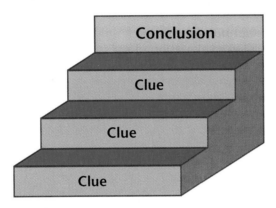

Make Generalizations Another way to draw conclusions is to make generalizations. A **generalization** is a general statement based on a number of facts or examples. A *valid generalization* is an accurate conclusion supported by many examples. A *hasty generalization* may be inaccurate because it is based on too few examples. Ask yourself:

• What facts or cases are presented to make the generalization?

• Will the generalization hold true for all or most cases? Are there exceptions to the statement?

• Are enough examples given to make the generalization valid?

▶ **Exercise 9** Evaluating Conclusions and Generalizations
Identify each sentence below as a *conclusion* or a *generalization*. Then, explain whether it is supported by evidence or not.
1. All PG-rated movies are boring.
2. Ann attends one of the best ballet schools in the country, so she must be a good dancer.
3. Matt failed his last math test; he knows nothing about math.
4. Children have often been known to mistake medicine for candy, so all medicine bottles should have childproof caps.
5. I got lost in the park. Nobody can get around that park.

▶ **More Practice**

Academic and Workplace Skills Activity Book
• pp. 42–43

Analyzing the Text

When you analyze the text of your reading material, you study the language the writer uses and the way the material is put together—its structure. This analysis can help you better understand the author's purpose and the key information presented in the material.

▶ **KEY CONCEPT** Learn to identify different uses of language and how the text is structured. ■

Examine the Author's Words Authors can sometimes present information in a direct way, or they can "load" their words to create certain feelings in readers about the information being presented. *Word choice* and *tone* are two ways that authors use language to influence readers' thinking.

Word Choice can affect meaning. The words an author uses can affect how a reader feels about a subject. Some words are neutral and do not influence a reader's feelings. Other words may create either positive or negative feelings in a reader.

NEUTRAL WORDS: The convertible was long with a large engine.
POSITIVE WORDS: The convertible was sleek and supercharged.
NEGATIVE WORDS: The convertible was slick and overpowered.

Tone Sometimes an author's attitude about a subject comes across both in the words used and by the way they are put together in sentences. Like word choice, tone can be neutral, positive, or negative.

NEUTRAL TONE: The heat and humidity in our community in the summer often keep visitors away.

NEGATIVE TONE: If you hate heat and humidity, you will be like other visitors and avoid our community in the summer.

▶ **Speaking and Listening Tip**

Get together with two or three of your classmates, and practice neutral, positive, and negative tones orally. For each word in Exercise 10, write a sentence. Then take turns reading the sentences in a way that conveys the tone of the word used. Pay attention to how word choice affects tone.

▶ **Exercise 10** Analyzing Word Choices For each set of words below, tell which has a neutral meaning, which is positive, and which is negative. Use a dictionary if you need help.
1. gobble, dine, eat
2. stingy, economical, thrifty
3. talk, babble, communicate
4. gawk, observe, see
5. handwriting, scribbling, calligraphy
6. house, palace, shack
7. mature, old, haggard
8. hard, impossible, challenging
9. brisk, freezing, cold
10. well-dressed, elegant, showy

Identify Text Structure The structure of the text refers to how ideas are arranged and how they relate to one another. Authors arrange their writing so they can communicate their ideas in a clear and effective way.

▶ **KEY CONCEPT** Learn how authors arrange ideas in a text so you can locate and understand information more easily. ■

Chronological Order An author uses chronological order when he or she wants to show events or details in the order in which they occur. Word clues identifying chronological order are shown in the illustration below.

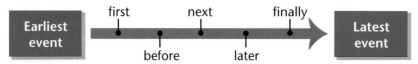

Cause and Effect A cause is an event that makes another event happen. An effect is the event that happens because of a cause. A cause-and-effect structure shows a series of events. Also, note that most effects can also become causes for subsequent events. Some word clues identifying cause and effect are listed in the following illustration.

Order of Importance When an author uses this text structure, he or she arranges events or details from the least to the most significant, or from the most significant to the least. The illustration below contains some of the word clues you can use to identify order of importance.

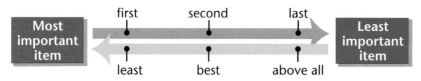

▶ **Exercise 11** Analyzing Text Structure Go back to the cause-and-effect professional and student models in Chapter 9, and identify a cause and effect in the essays. Show the details that support your answer. For chronological order, turn to Chapter 10, and list in order the events of the essay.

Reading Literary Writing

When you read literary works—short stories, novels, poems, or plays—you need to use some special strategies to understand what is happening, who the characters are, what the words mean, and what ideas the writer wants to get across to you. You may need to use different strategies for different types of literary works.

▶ **KEY CONCEPT** Practice a variety of reading strategies that fit the type of literary work you are reading and help you to understand it better. ■

Strategies for Reading Fiction

Fiction is filled with made-up characters and events. Two familiar kinds of fiction are short stories and novels. As you read fiction, you explore a new world. The author's words and your imagination create a map of this world. The strategies that follow can help you find your way:

Identify With a Character or a Situation Imagine that you are the character you're reading about in a story. Put yourself in that character's place. Imagine that you are saying and doing the same things. If you've been in a similar situation or had similar friends or family members, you may find it easier to identify with the character.

Predict As you read, make predictions about what will happen next. Base your predictions on your experience or on information in the story. As you read, new information may lead you to predict new and different outcomes.

Envision the Action and Setting As you read, create mental pictures of the action, setting, and characters. Look for the following kinds of words to help you create these pictures:

- **Action words**—interesting or unusual verbs and nouns
- **Adverbs**—words that tell how an action is performed
- **Sensory words**—descriptive adjectives that tell how things look, feel, taste, smell, and sound

▶ **Exercise 12** Reading Short Stories Read a few pages of a short story, and then begin to list experiences or qualities you share with the main character. Find at least three similarities. Make a prediction about what might happen to the character. You can check your prediction when you finish the story. Find at least two action words, two adverbs, and two sensory words. Use them to describe the action taking place.

▲ **Critical Viewing**
What kinds of places make good settings for reading a novel or short story? Why would you choose them? **[Evaluate]**

▶ **More Practice**

Academic and Workplace Skills Activity Book
- pp. 44–45

Reading Literary Writings • **691**

Strategies for Reading Drama

When you read a play, you focus mainly on the words spoken by the characters, and on the characters themselves. A written play also contains stage directions to tell actors how to move or to speak their lines. Stage directions also describe sets, costumes, and any special lighting or sound effects. To imagine how the play would be performed on stage, use the following strategies:

Preview the Characters   Read the list of characters at the beginning of the play. This will help you to know the different characters and how they relate to one another.

Envision the Setting and the Action   Form a picture in your mind of what is happening and where. If the play does not take place in the present, consider what you already know about the time in history during which it does take place.

Predict   After you have read the first act or scene, try to predict what will happen in the next act or scene. Look for hints in what the characters say or in the action. Using an organizer like the one below, write the reasons for your predictions. Afterward, write the reasons for the actual events.

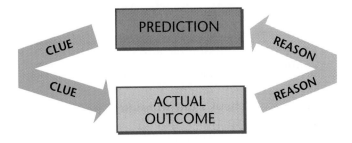

Question   As you read, ask yourself questions like these:

- Why did the character do or say that?
- What does the character mean by that?
- What caused this to happen?

Summarize   Dramas are usually divided into parts called acts. Acts are divided into scenes. At the end of a scene or an act, stop and think about what has happened to that point.

▶ **Exercise 13**   Reading Drama   Read the first few scenes of a drama. List three characters, and explain how they relate to one another. Describe three things you learned about the setting from stage directions. Based on dialogue, make a prediction about what might happen later in the play. After you finish the play, check how accurate your prediction was.

🖥 **Internet Tip**

Try looking up famous characters from literature on the Internet. You may find descriptions that help you get involved in the story.

▶ **More Practice**

Academic and Workplace Skills Activity Book
- pp. 46–49

Strategies for Reading Poetry

When you are reading poetry, you need to focus on how the words sound, what the words mean, and what emotions the poet causes you to feel. In a poem, even everyday words take on new and special meaning. When you read a poem, you should give every word the attention it deserves. Here are some strategies to use:

Read Lines According to Punctuation Even though poems are divided into lines, thoughts and images may continue from one line to the next. Read poems without pausing unnecessarily. Follow these suggestions:

- Don't stop at the ends of lines where there is no punctuation.
- Pause slightly when you come to a comma and a bit longer for semicolons or dashes.
- Make the longest stops for end marks.

Read aloud these lines from "February Twilight" by Sara Teasdale. Pause at the comma and period, and continue to read where there is no punctuation:

EXAMPLE:
> I stood beside a hill
>   Smooth with new-laid snow,
> A single star looked out
>   From the cold evening glow.

Identify the Speaker The poet is not always the speaker in the poem. The speaker is the voice that "says" the words. He or she can be a character in an imaginary situation. Look for clues to who the speaker is. What clues do you have about the speaker in the lines of poetry above?

ANALYZING THE SPEAKER

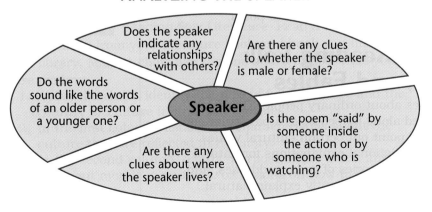

> **Speaking and Listening Tip**
>
> Reading a poem aloud will enable you to hear the sounds and feel the rhythm of the words. Hearing yourself or someone else read a poem will give you a deeper understanding and appreciation of the work.

Reading From Varied Sources

Many different kinds of reading materials are available for you to choose for different purposes. For example, you may read articles and ads in a newspaper or magazine to find current information or to learn about styles and products. You might focus on Internet Web pages for specialized information or up-to-the-minute sports scores. You might read a textbook to study for school, a pamphlet to find data for a research paper, or a manual to get "how-to" details. What you read depends on why you are reading.

Reading Newspapers

Reading daily and weekly newspapers is one of the best ways to find out what is happening in your community, in the state, in the country, or in the world. Suppose that you are looking for local news. If you live in a small community, is there a local newspaper? If you live in or near a large city, are there parts of the big-city or regional daily newspaper that deal with local news items? Make a quick inventory of the newspaper you get regularly at home or that comes to the school or public library. Find its table of contents or index. Note how the news is laid out in sections for local, state, national, or international news. Are there special sections for news, editorials, style, sports, and features such as comics, puzzles, and advice columns? If you have several newspapers from which to choose, evaluate which paper you think best covers the information you want and is the best organized. Decide which paper you should read on a regular basis.

Reading Magazines

Reading magazines is a good way to find information about a specific interest, such as a hobby, sports, fashions, or celebrities. Some magazines deal with news and current events and provide more analysis than newspapers. Other magazines aim at a specialized audience, such as teenagers, cooks, runners, or model train hobbyists. Unlike newspapers, magazines usually offer an opinion or a point of view on a topic they present. Try to recognize where a magazine article reports facts and where it presents opinions.

Reading Manuals

If you want to learn how to do something or how to use a product you have bought, you should read a manual carefully. Look first for the table of contents, main headings, and diagrams. Follow the steps, one-by-one, without rushing ahead.

More Practice

Academic and
Workplace Skills
Activity Book
• p. 51

Reading Electronic Texts

Internet Web pages and electronic texts on disk or CD-ROM provide detailed, specific information on a wide variety of subjects. When you read a Web page, think about who posted the page and whether the information can be trusted as factual or should be considered biased, based upon your opinion of the author. You need to make your own evaluation of how reliable the information is before you use it for a paper or report. You might want to use a search engine to find several pages on a subject, and compare the information you find. Some electronic texts are provided by retailers—companies that want to sell you something. Think of these texts as ads rather than as factual information. Try to recognize which parts seem true and which are sales pitches.

▲ **Critical Viewing** While doing research on the Internet, what kinds of publications might these students find? **[Relate]**

Reading Anthologies

An anthology is a collection of literature. Some anthologies contain a specific kind of literature, such as poems or short stories. Some are organized around one theme; others, around several different themes. Most present works of a variety of writers. Some focus on a specific period of time, such as early American literature or modern short stories. You might choose an anthology if you find a specific kind of literature that interests you. Anthologies are also good references for reports or good ways to get introduced to an interesting or unusual writer or topic.

Reflecting on Your Reading Skills

After a week of practicing your reading skills, write a paragraph about your progress. Use the following questions to get you started:

• Which sections of my textbooks do I use on a regular basis?

• How does varying my reading style help me to find information and to study?

• Which reading strategies do I find most useful?

• How can I become a more careful and reflective reader?

• What different types of materials do I most often read? Why do I read each type?

Standardized Test Preparation Workshop

Make Inferences and Predictions

Standardized tests usually include reading questions that measure your ability to make inferences, or to draw logical conclusions about what you have read. You can make inferences about characters and stories, or you can make them about the author's purpose or point of view. Some questions require you to make a prediction or anticipate what may happen in the future, based on the clues in the reading material. These questions are typically multiple choice. In addition, some tests will ask you to read a passage, then answer, in writing, a specific question about that passage. The following sample test items will help you prepare for answering these types of questions on standardized tests.

Sample Test Items	Answers and Explanations
Read each passage. Then, answer the questions that follow the passage. from "The Outcasts of Poker Flat," Bret Harte Two or three men, conversing earnestly together, ceased as he [Mr. Oakhurst] approached, and exchanged significant glances. There was a Sabbath lull in the air which, in a settlement unused to Sabbath influences, looked ominous.	
1 When the men see Mr. Oakhurst, they— **A** are glad to see their friend **B** are afraid he will hurt them **C** are curious because he is a stranger **D** stop talking so he will not hear them	The answer for item 1 is **D.** By using the information provided in the passage, you conclude that the men are conversing about Mr. Oakhurst, and do not want him to hear what they are saying.
Answer the following question. Base your answer on "The Outcasts of Poker Flat." What is Poker Flat usually like? Support your answer with details from the story.	Your answer should consist of a paragraph that includes a topic sentence and details from the passage that support it. The following is part of a possible response: *The town is a place that is usually full of activity, much of it related to gambling and the saloon. By referring to the Sabbath, a holy day, Harte gives the impression that Poker Flat is not a "clean-living" town.*

▶ **Practice 1** **Directions:** Read the passage. Then, answer the questions that follow the passage.

From "Everyday Use," Alice Walker

I will wait for her in the yard that Maggie and I made so clean and wavy yesterday afternoon. A yard like this is more comfortable than most people know. It is not just a yard. It is like an extended living room. When the hard clay is swept clean as a floor and the fine sand around the edges lined with tiny, irregular grooves, anyone can come and sit and look up into the elm tree and wait for the breezes that never come inside the house.

Maggie will be nervous until after her sister goes: she will stand hopelessly in corners, homely and ashamed of the burn scars down her arms and legs, eyeing her sister with a mixture of envy and awe. She thinks her sister has held life always in the palm of one hand, that "no" is a word the world never learned to say to her.

1 The author writes in first person to—
  A share the character's personal thoughts and feelings
  B use a traditional story form
  C keep the reader guessing
  D create suspense

2 Maggie and her sister are—
  F close friends and confidantes
  G strangers who are about to meet for the first time
  H sisters who spend little time together, and have little in common
  J vicious enemies

3 Maggie's home is—
  A a wealthy plantation
  B a run-down, ill-kept shack
  C a clean, small, rural home
  D a small suburban ranch house

4 The narrator is probably—
  F Maggie's mother
  G Maggie's best friend
  H a stranger to Maggie and her sister
  J Maggie's daughter

5 Why will Maggie be nervous until after her sister goes?
  A She wants to make a good impression on her sister.
  B She is afraid her sister will make fun of her scars.
  C She hopes her sister will move home.
  D She is intimidated by—yet wishes she were more like—her sister.

6 How does the narrator feel about the impending visit?
  F She is tired from the work, and wishing the visit were over already.
  G She is well prepared and ready for the company.
  H She is afraid her visitor will be disappointed.
  J She is so excited she is unable to concentrate.

▶ **Practice 2** **Directions:** Read the following question. Base your answer on "Everyday Use."

READ, THINK, EXPLAIN Describe Maggie's self-image and her relationship with her family. Use details from the story to explain your answer.

Chapter 31

Study, Reference, and Test-Taking Skills

This chapter will help you to improve your skills in studying, researching, and taking tests. If you know how to study and where to look for information, your school experience will be more rewarding. These skills will also come in handy throughout your life. In this chapter, you will learn how to make the most out of your study time, as well as how to research information using printed and electronic reference sources. You will even find useful ideas to help you improve your test scores.

▲ **Critical Viewing**
In what ways does this boy benefit from having a special place to study? **[Infer]**

Section 31.1 *Basic Study Skills*

Study skills—the patterns or habits that you set up to help you study—allow you to get the most out of the time you spend studying. You should have a specific study area, a scheduled study time, an assignment book, and an organized notebook in which you can take useful notes.

Setting Up a Study Area and Study Schedule

You should have a place where you can study and plan for study time. Use these suggestions to improve your study area:

- Your study area should be in the same place every day.
- It should be comfortable and free of interruptions.
- It should have a desk or table, a chair, and good lighting.
- It should have all of the supplies you may need: pens and pencils, paper, erasers, tape, stapler, paper clips, scissors, ruler, felt-tip markers, index cards, and a dictionary.

▶ **KEY CONCEPT** Make a study schedule that allows time for daily assignments and long-term projects. ■

Use the sample study schedule below as a model. Each day, allow some time for the review of difficult subjects, extra study for upcoming tests, and work on long-term projects.

SAMPLE STUDY SCHEDULE	
Time	Activity
3:30–4:00	after-school activity
4:00–4:30	after-school activity
4:30–5:00	homework
5:00–5:30	homework
5:30–6:00	dinner
6:00–6:30	homework
6:30–7:00	homework
7:00–7:30	television
7:30–8:00	television
8:00–8:30	pleasure reading

▶ **More Practice**

Academic and Workplace Skills Activity Book
• p. 52

▶ **Exercise 1** **Rating Your Study Area** List the features and supplies that are available in your study area, then compare them with the ones listed above. Write down the improvements you could make to your study area.

▶ **Exercise 2** Making a Study Schedule Using the model on page 701, make a study schedule of your own. Follow the schedule for two weeks. Notice where you need to spend more time or less time, and make adjustments accordingly. At the end of two weeks, evaluate your schedule, and make any final changes. Keep a copy of your schedule in your notebook.

Keeping an Assignment Book

Keep an assignment book to record tasks you must complete every day for each class. Use your assignment book to keep track of the dates of tests and due dates of long-term projects, as well. Write down each assignment as you receive it. This will help you plan what to work on in your scheduled time. Keeping an assignment book will help you to complete each assignment on time and to be prepared for class discussions and tests.

▶ **KEY CONCEPT** Use an assignment book to record homework assignments and due dates. ■

Date	Subject	Assignment	Due	Completed
11/19	English	Read pages 126-136	11/20	✓
11/19	Math	Study for test on decimals	11/20	
11/20	Science	Report on fruit flies	11/30	
		—Research	(11/23)	
		—Drafting	(11/25)	
		—Revising	(11/27)	
		—Final draft	(11/30)	

▶ **Exercise 3** Organizing an Assignment Book Organize an assignment book page like the one shown in the model. Use this format for one week's assignments. Notice whether you have left enough space to write your assignments and whether you have written your assignments down in enough detail. At the end of a week, discuss with a partner any additional information you might add to an assignment book page.

More Practice

Academic and Workplace Skills Activity Book
• p. 52

Taking Notes

The ability to take notes is important to achieving success in school. To take good notes, listen and read carefully. Record only main ideas and significant details. Use your notes as a framework for studying.

▶ **KEY CONCEPT** Use a modified outline to take notes while listening or reading. ■

Make a Modified Outline A modified outline breaks down information so that you can remember it. It also helps you organize ideas and information for a composition.

Crazy Horse)————————————————— *heading*
1. Chief of Oglala Sioux
2. One of the greatest Native Americans }—— *details*
3. Led Battle of Little Big Horn

▶ **KEY CONCEPT** Write summaries of chapters or lectures to review what you have learned. ■

▶ **Exercise 4** Taking Notes in Outline Form Choose a section in your science or social studies textbook, and take notes on the important information. Use the modified outline form.

◉ **Technology Tip**

Most word-processing programs have an outline feature. When preparing an outline on a computer, choose Outline from the appropriate menu on the toolbar. If you are unsure about how to proceed, select "Creating outlines" from the Help index.

◀ Critical Viewing How would you write an outline detailing the various features of this bear? **[Analyze]**

Reference Skills

As technology becomes more sophisticated, information is easier to find. Many references that used to be available only in print can now be accessed with a computer. You can get information on CD-ROMs or on-line.

Using the Library

Libraries contain many different kinds of resources. The key to finding the information you need is to understand how the books and other materials are organized.

Use the Library Catalog When you are looking for a book, start with the *library catalog.*

▶ **KEY CONCEPT** Use the library catalog to find valuable information about the books in a library. ■

The library catalog will be in one of these three forms:

Card Catalog This index system lists books on cards, with each book having a separate *author card* and *title card.* If the book is nonfiction, it also has at least one *subject card.* Cards are filed alphabetically in small drawers, with author cards alphabetized by last names and title cards alphabetized by the first words of the titles, excluding *A, An,* and *The.*

CARD CATALOG (AUTHOR CARD)

737.4	**Hendin, David**	call number / <u>author</u>
He	**Collecting Coins**	part of call number; <u>title</u>
New York:		city of publication,
Signet,	**1978**	publisher, / <u>publication date</u>
170 p; illus;	**25 cm**	number of pages / <u>size of book</u>
Coins		subject illustrated

Printed Catalog This catalog lists books in printed booklets, with each book listed alphabetically by author, by title, and—if nonfiction—by subject. Often, there are separate booklets for author, title, and subject listings.

🖰 **Research Tip**

Use the subject catalog in your library when you need to locate information on a specific topic but don't have the name of a particular book or author.

Electronic Catalog This catalog lists books on a CD-ROM or in an on-line database that you can access from special computer terminals in the library. Usually, you can find a book's catalog entry by typing in the title, key words in the title, the author's name, or, for nonfiction, the appropriate subject.

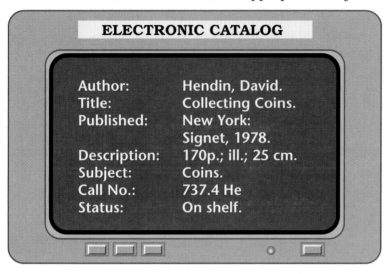

ELECTRONIC CATALOG

Author:	Hendin, David.
Title:	Collecting Coins.
Published:	New York:
	Signet, 1978.
Description:	170p.; ill.; 25 cm.
Subject:	Coins.
Call No.:	737.4 He
Status:	On shelf.

▶ **Exercise 5** **Working With Catalog Entries** Answer the following questions, using either of the two catalog listings shown.
  1. How can you tell that this is an author card?
  2. What is the title of the book?
  3. When was the book published?
  4. How many pages does the book have?
  5. What is the subject of this book?

Finding the Book You Want Libraries organize books so that people can find them. Most books are classified as either *fiction* (novels and stories) or *nonfiction* (factual information).

▶ **KEY CONCEPT** Fiction books are arranged in alphabetical order, using the author's last name. If an author has written several books, they are arranged alphabetically according to the first words of the titles. ∎

Fiction Books If you are looking for the novel *Charlotte's Web*, you can locate it without the card catalog if you know the author's name (E. B. White) and where the fiction section is located.

First, go to the fiction section. Find the books by authors whose names begin with *W*, and find E. B. White. Then. find *Charlotte's Web*. (If you do not know the author of a book, you can locate the book under its title in the card, printed, or electronic catalog.)

▶ **More Practice**

Academic and Workplace Skills Activity Book
• pp. 53–54

▶ **KEY CONCEPT** To find a nonfiction book, look it up in the catalog, and make a note of its *call number*. ■

Nonfiction Books The *call number* is a combination of a number and one or more letters. It is found on the upper left corner of a catalog card and on the spine of the book.

Libraries usually display a range of call numbers for each stack of shelves. Most libraries use the **Dewey Decimal System** to classify nonfiction books.

This illustration shows the number ranges of the main content areas, or classes, of the Dewey Decimal System.

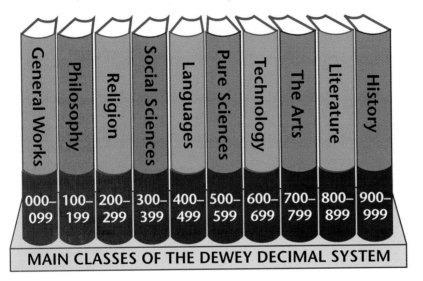

MAIN CLASSES OF THE DEWEY DECIMAL SYSTEM

Biographies These stories about the lives of real people are listed under 921 in the Dewey Decimal System. However, they are often shelved in a special Biography section that is alphabetized by the last name of the person about whom a book is written.

Reference Books Dictionaries, atlases, encyclopedias, and so on may be shelved in a special section. If a book has *R* or *REF* before its call number, go to the library's reference section, and then use the call number to locate the book.

▶ **Exercise 6** **Finding Fiction** Arrange the following listings according to the way you would find these books on a library shelf.
1. *Julie of the Wolves* by Jean Craighead George
2. *The Lion, the Witch, and the Wardrobe* by C. S. Lewis
3. *Alice's Adventures in Wonderland* by Lewis Carroll
4. *The Last Battle* by C. S. Lewis
5. *Across Five Aprils* by Irene Hunt

Challenge

With one or two partners, choose a single topic, and then see in how many Dewey Decimal classes you can find information related to the topic. Using *China*, for example, you would find Chinese *philosophy, religion* in China, Chinese *language*, Chinese *literature*, and so on.

▶ **More Practice**

Academic and Workplace Skills Activity Book
• p. 55

Exercise 7 Working With the Dewey Decimal System
Write the correct call numbers of the group (the range) to which each title below would belong.
1. *A History of Ancient Greece*
2. *The New Columbia Encyclopedia*
3. *Making Masks*
4. *The Plays of Shakespeare*
5. *Snakes, Lizards, and Other Reptiles*

Using Encyclopedias

With the exception of dictionaries, encyclopedias are the most frequently used reference books because they contain concisely presented information on almost any subject.

KEY CONCEPT Use an encyclopedia for three purposes:
1. to get background information on a subject
2. to learn basic facts about a subject
3. to find out where else to go for information. ■

Alphabetical Listings Each encyclopedia is made up of volumes, which are arranged in alphabetical order. Inside each volume, the articles are also in alphabetical order.

Index Most encyclopedias will have an *index,* which is usually in a separate volume. The index shows the volume and page on which you can find the article you need.
   Use these tips when using an encyclopedia:

• Look up the subject under its most common name.

• If there is no article for your subject, you may find "*See* ___?___ " instead.

• At the end of an article, you may sometimes find "*See also* ___?___."

• Some articles list additional readings for further study.

• You can find more sources of information in the index.

▲ **Critical Viewing** What suggests that this student is still trying to locate information on his subject? **[Deduce]**

Exercise 8 Finding Information in Encyclopedias Look up and read the article about your state in an encyclopedia. Follow up on any *See also* directions. Then, check the index. Write a short paragraph that describes the information you found in addition to what was written in the main article.

Periodicals and Periodical Indexes

When you need current information on a subject, you will usually find it in a **periodical**—a newspaper, magazine, or other printed matter that is published at regular intervals.

Using Periodical Indexes The most frequently used periodical index is the *Readers' Guide to Periodical Literature.* In its many volumes, you will find information telling where and when articles on a particular subject were published. Each volume covers a certain time span, and the entries within it are in alphabetical order by subject. You will find some indexes that focus on a particular subject. On-line indexes provide the full text of an article. Check with a librarian if you need help using a periodical index or finding a particular periodical.

Using Dictionaries

A **dictionary** is a collection of words and their meanings, along with other information about the words. A dictionary also tells how words are pronounced, how they are used in a sentence, and their *etymology*—how they came into the language.

▶ **KEY CONCEPT** Dictionaries contain a wealth of useful information. ■

Types of Dictionaries Some dictionaries are for scholars. Others are for general readers. Still others are for people studying a special area of knowledge. *Unabridged* dictionaries have a greater number of words, including more detailed information, than *abridged* dictionaries.

🕐 Learn More

To learn more about how dictionaries can help expand your vocabulary, see Chapter 29.

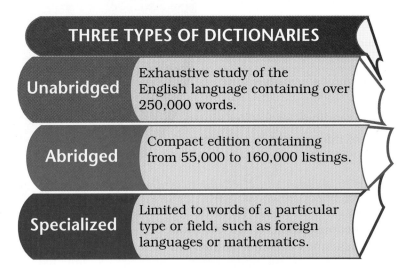

THREE TYPES OF DICTIONARIES	
Unabridged	Exhaustive study of the English language containing over 250,000 words.
Abridged	Compact edition containing from 55,000 to 160,000 listings.
Specialized	Limited to words of a particular type or field, such as foreign languages or mathematics.

Finding a Word Dictionaries can be large, cumbersome books, but they are arranged to help you find a word quickly. In printed dictionaries, all the items are listed in strict **alphabetical order.** To speed your search, use these features:

Thumb Index Some dictionaries have a thumb index— indentations along the side of the book printed with letters. Words that begin with those letters are listed in that section of the book.

Guide Words At the top of each page are *guide words.* The guide word on the left tells you the first word on the page. The guide word on the right tells you the last word on the page.

If you use an *electronic dictionary,* you type a word and the computer searches the dictionary database.

▶ **Exercise 9** Finding Words in a Dictionary Find the following words in a dictionary. Then, list the guide words that appear at the top of each page.

Word	Guide Words	
1. leaf	?	?
2. evening	?	?
3. roadrunner	?	?
4. Arizona	?	?
5. snack	?	?

▶ **More Practice**

Academic and Workplace Skills Activity Book
• pp. 56–57

◀ **Critical Viewing** Name three kinds of information about a particular word that this student might be looking up in the dictionary. **[Speculate]**

Understanding Dictionary Entries

The words listed in a dictionary are called *entry words.* An entry word with all of the information about that word is called a *main entry.*

MAIN ENTRY IN A DICTIONARY

① ② ③ ④ ④ ⑤

pret·ty (prit´ē) *adj.* **-ti·er, -ti·est** [ME. *prati* < OE.

prættig, crafty < *prætt,* a craft, trick] **1.** Pleasing or

attractive in a dainty, delicate, or graceful way rather

than through striking beauty, elegance, grandeur, or

stateliness **2.** *a)* fine; good; nice: often used ironically

[a *pretty* fix] *b)* adroit; skillful [a *pretty* move] **3.** [Archaic]

⑦

elegant **4.** [Archaic or Scot.] brave; bold; gallant

⑦ ③

5. [Colloq.] considerable; quite large [a *pretty* price] —**adv.**

1. fairly; somewhat [*pretty* sure]: sometimes, by hyperbole,

⑦

quite or very [*pretty* angry] **2.** [Colloq.] prettily [to talk

pretty] —**n.,** *pl.* **-ties** a pretty person or thing —**vt. -tied,**

-ty·ing to make pretty (usually with *up*) —**SYN.**

⑧ ⑦

BEAUTIFUL —☆**sitting pretty** [Slang] in a favorable position

⑧ ⑧

—**pret´ti·ly** *adv.* —**pret´ti·ness** *n.* —**pret´ty·ish** *adj.*

⑥ (brackets to the right)

---

1. **Entry Words** This may be a single word, a compound word (two or more words acting as a single word), an abbreviation, a prefix or suffix, or the name of a person or place. Dots, spaces, or slashes in an entry word indicate the syllables. Note that words of one syllable are never divided.

2. **Pronunciations** Appearing immediately after the entry word, the pronunciation uses symbols to show how to say the word and which syllable to stress. The syllable that gets the most emphasis has a *primary stress,* usually shown by a heavy mark after the syllable (´). Words of more than one syllable may also have a *secondary stress,* usually shown by a shorter, lighter mark (ˈ).

3. **Parts-of-Speech Labels** Labels that tell whether the word functions as a noun, a verb, or some other part of speech are given as abbreviations, usually immediately following the pronunciation.

Learn More

To learn more about parts of speech, see Chapters 14–18.

4. **Plurals and Inflected Forms** After the part-of-speech label, the dictionary may also show the plural forms of nouns, as well as inflected forms—past tense and participle forms of verbs—if there is anything irregular about their spelling.

5. **Etymology** The word's etymology, or origin, usually appears in brackets, parentheses, or slashes near the start or end of the entry. Abbreviations used for languages are explained in the dictionary's key to abbreviations.

6. **Definition** A definition is the meaning of a word. Definitions are numbered if there are several meanings, and often will include an example illustrating that meaning.

7. **Usage Labels** These labels show how the word is generally used. Words labeled *Archaic (Arch.), Obsolete (Obs.), Poetic,* or *Rare* are not widely used today. Those labeled *Informal (Inf.), Colloquial (Colloq.),* or *Slang* are not considered part of formal English. Those labeled *Brit.* are used mainly in Great Britain, not the United States.

8. **Idioms and Derived Words** The end of an entry may list and define idioms or expressions that contain the entry word. It may also list derived words (words formed from the entry word) along with a part-of-speech label.

   Field labels show whether a word is used in a special way by people in a certain occupation or activity, such as *History (Hist.)* or *Mathematics (Math.).* Not all entries have field labels.

> **Exercise 10** **Working With Main Entries** Use a dictionary to answer the following questions.
>   1. In what order would these entry words appear?
>   *toast—sadness—field—Arkansas—northwest*
>   2. Which of these entry words would appear on a page with the guide words *nose* and *note?*
>   *north—not—Norway—notch—notify*
>   3. What two guide words appear on the page with *raspberry?*
>   4. What is the origin of the word *paper?*
>   5. Give the definition of the verb *clasp* and the noun *clasp.*
>   6. Give two field labels and definitions for the word *pocket.*
>   7. What is the origin of the word *kindergarten?*
>   8. Which word is not spelled correctly?
>   *spaghetti—mispell—athletic—scissors*
>   9. Which word is spelled correctly?
>   *aniversary—permanant—cematery—calendar*
> 10. Write one idiom using the word *chip.*

Using Other Reference Works

In addition to encyclopedias and dictionaries, there are many other reference tools in school and public libraries. Three important resources are *almanacs*, *atlases*, and *biographical reference books*.

Almanacs An almanac is a book of facts and statistics about subjects of interest to many people, such as government, history, geography, weather, science, technology, industry, sports, and entertainment. It is made up mostly of lists, tables, and charts. Most almanacs are updated every year. With an *electronic almanac*, you can find information by typing in a subject or key word.

> **KEY CONCEPT** Use an almanac to get a brief answer to a question involving facts or statistics. ■

EXAMPLES: What is the distance between Mercury and the sun? (3 million miles)
Who won the 100-meter dash for women in the 1960 Olympics? (Wilma Rudolph, USA)

Facts and statistics are grouped under subject headings. You must look in the index under an appropriate subject heading. For example, if you wanted to know the population of a particular city, you could look it up under either *Cities* or *Population*.

Atlases and Electronic Map Collections Atlases contain maps and geographical information based on them, such as cities, bodies of water, mountains, and landmarks. In *printed atlases*, use an index to locate information. In *electronic atlases*, type the name of a place, and the computer will search the database to find the appropriate map.

> **KEY CONCEPT** Use an atlas for information on the geography of a region. ■

Biographical References These books provide brief life histories of famous or important people.

> **KEY CONCEPT** Use biographical reference books to learn important facts about a person's life. ■

Useful Information Biographical reference books are useful for facts such as the correct pronunciation of a person's name; dates of birth and death; main dates and events of a person's life; and a person's main accomplishments.

Technology Tip

You can use atlases to plan the route for a trip, get local directions, or learn about the rise and fall of empires and changes in countries' borders throughout world history.

Exercise 11 Using Almanacs, Atlases, and Biographical Reference Books For each item below, find the information requested. Indicate the type of reference book you used.
1. chief crops of Cuba
2. rainfall in Brazil
3. year Columbus died
4. length of Cleopatra's rule
5. who discovered uranium
6. number of hijacked planes in a particular year
7. China's natural resources
8. Paul McCartney's age
9. state tree of Georgia
10. baseball players in the Hall of Fame

More Practice
Academic and Workplace Skills Activity Book
• p. 58

Printed and Electronic Thesauruses

A thesaurus is a specialized reference that lists *synonyms*, or words with similar meanings. It may also list *antonyms*, or words with opposite meanings. *Printed* thesauruses usually arrange words alphabetically, although some are arranged according to subject. In *electronic* thesauruses, you type in or highlight a word, and the computer searches a database to provide one or more synonyms.

Electronic Databases

Available on CD-ROM and the Internet, electronic databases let you access large collections of data on particular topics. These databases have search features that allow you to access related information in a variety of ways.

Exercise 12 Using Reference Works Use printed or electronic reference works to answer the following questions. Indicate the type of reference you used.
1. What are three kinds of poisonous snakes, and what is their habitat?
2. What are the latitude and longitude of Anchorage, Alaska?
3. What are five synonyms for the word *good*?
4. Who won the Academy Award for Best Supporting Actor in 1967?
5. What is the average temperature in Morocco in the month of February?
6. What teams won the last four soccer World Cups?
7. Who was the twenty-fourth president of the United States?
8. What word is the opposite of *mercenary*?
9. What countries border the African country of Botswana?
10. What languages are spoken in Switzerland?

Using the Internet

The *Internet* is a worldwide network of computers connected over phone and cable lines. The World Wide Web is the part of the Internet that offers text, graphics, sound, and video over the Internet. When you go *on-line*, you have access to an almost unlimited number of Web sites, where an amazing amount of information can be found. Each Web site has its own address, or URL (Universal Resource Locator). If you don't have the address, you can type a key word or words into a *search engine*, which finds related Web sites for you.

▼ **Critical Viewing**
These students have found a Web page on the solar system. What kinds of links to other Web sites do you think they will be able to access from this page? **[Relate]**

▶ **KEY CONCEPT** Use the Internet for all kinds of information, but judge Web sites for reliability. ■

Here are some guidelines for finding reliable information on the Internet:

- If you know a reliable Web site and its address (URL), simply type the address into your Web browser. Often, television programs, commercials, magazines, newspapers, and radio stations provide Web site addresses where you can find more information about a show, product, company, and so on.

- Consult Internet coverage in library journals (like *Booklist* and *Library Journal*) to learn addresses of Web sites that provide useful and reliable information.

- If you don't know particular Web sites, you can do a general search for a key term on a search engine.

- Remember to bookmark, or save as a favorite, the interesting and reliable sites you find while searching the Web.

▶ **Exercise 13** Using the Internet On a library, school, or home computer, use the Internet to answer the following questions.
1. Find the postal ZIP Code for your town or city.
2. Find the top-five popular songs for the current year.
3. Choose a current-events topic. Do a search on it, and list four Web sites that have information on the subject.
4. Find the five children's movies that have made the most money at the box office to date.
5. Choose a science topic related to the outdoors. Do a search, and list two Web sites that have information on the subject.

▶ **More Practice**
Academic and Workplace Skills Activity Book
• p. 59

Section 31.3 *Test-Taking Skills*

This section provides strategies that will help you to improve the way in which you prepare for and take a test, so you can feel more confident and perform more effectively.

Preparing for a Test Doing well on a test depends a lot on how much preparation you have done.

▶ **KEY CONCEPT** Follow these strategies to prepare for a test:

- Review your notes right after you take them, a few days later, and again before the test.
- Test yourself, or ask someone to quiz you.
- Use memory tricks (rhymes, sentences, related words).
- Do not wait until the last minute to begin! ▪

Taking a Test In addition to test preparation, you can use strategies to help you relax and concentrate during the test.

▶ **KEY CONCEPT** Budget your time as you preview the test, answer the questions, and proofread your answers. ▪

PREVIEW THE TEST

1. Put your name on your paper.
2. Skim the test to see the different kinds of questions.
3. Decide how much time you will spend on each section.
4. Allow time for difficult or high-point questions.

ANSWER THE QUESTIONS

1. Answer easy questions first.
2. If you can, use scratch paper to jot down your ideas.
3. Read each question at least twice before you answer.
4. Give one answer unless the instructions say otherwise.
5. Answer all questions unless you are told not to guess.
6. Do not change your first answer without a good reason.

PROOFREAD YOUR ANSWERS

1. Check that you have followed directions.
2. Reread test questions and answers.
3. Make sure that you have answered all of the questions.

🖥 **Internet Tip**

If you are interested in learning more about preparing for and taking tests, find one or more Internet sites on the subject. Type "test-taking strategies" in the query field of your search engine.

Answering Objective Questions

▶ **KEY CONCEPT** Know the different kinds of objective questions and the strategies for answering them. ∎

Multiple-Choice Questions This kind of question asks you to choose from several possible responses.

EXAMPLE: The opposite of *fierce* is ___?___ .
a. angry   b. gentle   c. ready   d. funny

In the preceding example, the answer is *b*. Follow these strategies to answer multiple-choice questions:

• Try answering the question before looking at the choices. If your answer is one of the choices, select that choice.

• Eliminate the obviously incorrect answers, crossing them out if you are allowed to write on the test paper.

• Read all the choices before answering. There are often two *possible* answers, but only one *best* answer.

Matching Questions Matching questions require that you match items in one group with items in another.

EXAMPLE: ___?___ 1. menace   a. plentiful
___?___ 2. colossal   b. threat
___?___ 3. abundant   c. huge

In the preceding example, the answers are 1. *b*, 2. *c*, and 3. *a*. Follow these strategies to answer matching questions:

• Count each group to see whether items will be left over. Check the directions to see whether items can be used more than once.

• Read all the items before you start matching.

• Match the items you know first, crossing them out if you are allowed to write on the test paper.

• Match remaining items about which you are less certain.

Fill-in Questions A fill-in question asks you to supply an answer in your own words. The answer may complete a statement or may simply answer a question.

EXAMPLE: An ___?___ is a word's opposite.

In the preceding example, the answer is *antonym*.

• Read the question or incomplete statement carefully.

• If you are answering a question, change it into a statement by inserting your answer and seeing whether it makes sense.

Technology Tip

If you are taking a test on CD-ROM, be careful not to answer too quickly. Some electronic tests will not allow you to go back and change your answer if you change your mind.

True/False Questions True/false questions require you to identify whether a statement is accurate.

EXAMPLE: __?__ All citizens vote on Election Day.
            __?__ High-school students always take three math courses.
            __?__ Some schools have a foreign language requirement.

  In the preceding example, the answers are *F, F,* and *T.* Follow these strategies to answer true/false questions:

- If a statement seems true, be sure that the entire statement is true.

- Pay special attention to the word *not,* which often changes the entire meaning of a statement.

- Pay special attention to the words *all, always, never, no, none,* and *only.* They often make a statement false.

▶ **Exercise 14** **Answering Objective Questions** Answer the following questions.

Multiple Choice

1. The word *wealthy* means __?__ .
   a. happy   b. rich   c. worldly   d. successful
2. The opposite of *return* is __?__ .
   a. pay   b. keep   c. remain   d. resound

Matching

3. __?__ heathen   a. hungry
4. __?__ dispute   b. famous
5. __?__ renowned   c. argument
6. __?__ ravenous   d. uncivilized

Fill-in

7. __?__ is the opposite of *generous.*
8. __?__ is the opposite of *rude.*

True/False

9. __?__ All cats have long tails.
10. __?__ Most birds have feathers, lay eggs, and can fly.

▶**Critical Viewing** What suggestions would you make to help this student improve her test performance? [**Apply**]

▶ **More Practice**

Academic and Workplace Skills Activity Book
• p. 60

Analogies An analogy asks you to find pairs of words that express a similar relationship.

EXAMPLE: ELM : TREE :: WHALE :
            a. mammal   b. horse   c. fish

In the preceding example, the answer is *a*. The relationship between the pairs of words is *kind*. An elm is a *kind* of tree, and a whale is a *kind* of mammal.

Exercise 15 **Answering Analogies** Fill in each blank below, choosing the word that best expresses the relationship in the given pair.

1. WAGES : EARNINGS :: FEE : ___?___
   a. debt   b. cost   c. coins

2. MUSICIANS : BAND :: FLOWERS : ___?___
   a. aroma   b. bouquet   c. vase

3. TEACHER : INSTRUCTS :: MECHANIC : ___?___
   a. engines   b. cars   c. repairs

4. INVADE : RETREAT :: INTRIGUE : ___?___
   a. trick   b. interest   c. bore

5. LOYAL : FAITHFUL :: CONSTANT : ___?___
   a. happy   b. consistent   c. changing

More Practice

Academic and Workplace Skills Activity Book
• p. 60

COMMON ANALOGY RELATIONSHIPS	
Relationship	**Example**
synonyms (same meaning)	enrage : anger
antonyms (opposite meaning)	love : hate
an item and its function	ruler : measurement
a part to a whole	page : book

Answering Short-Answer and Essay Questions

Some test questions require you to supply an answer, rather than simply select a correct answer. Identify these questions when you preview the test. Allow time to write complete, accurate answers.

KEY CONCEPT Allow time and space to answer short-answer and essay questions. ■

Identify Key Words Whether you are responding to a short-answer question or an essay prompt, identify the key words in the test item. Look for words like *discuss, explain, identify,* and any numbers or restrictions. If the question asks for three causes, make sure you supply three.

Check Your Space On some tests, you will be given a certain number of lines on which to write your answer. Make sure that you understand whether you are limited to that space or whether you can ask for more paper. If you are limited to a certain amount of space, use it for the most significant and relevant information.

Stick to the Point Do not put down everything you know about a topic. If the question asks you to identify three steps Jefferson took to limit government power, you will not get extra credit for including information about Jefferson's childhood. In fact, including unrelated information may cause you to lose points.

Reflecting on Your Study, Reference, and Test-Taking Skills

Think about what you have learned about the way to study, use reference tools, and take tests. Ask yourself these questions:

- What strategies do I already use for test preparation, and how can I become better prepared?

- Which types of test questions do I find easiest to answer? Which are most difficult?

- Which reference tools do I use most frequently? With which ones should I become more familiar?

Use your answers to identify ways in which you can improve your study, reference, and test-taking skills.

Standardized Test Preparation Workshop

Constructing Meaning From Informational Texts

Standardized tests usually include reading questions. These questions test your ability to construct meaning from the information provided in the passage. The following types of questions will test your ability to read informational texts:

- Identify the main idea, stated or implied, of the passage.
- Identify the best summary—a concise restating of the key points of the passage.
- Distinguish between facts and nonfacts—opinions and untrue, or unprovable, statements.

The following sample test item will give you practice answering these types of questions.

Test Tip

As you read the passage, remember to look for the main idea and the key points.

Sample Test Item

Answer and Explanation

Directions: Read the passage. Then, read the question that follows the passage. Decide which is the best answer to the question.

Sidney Lanier was a talented musician as well as a gifted poet. Lanier was born in Macon, Georgia, in 1842. Lanier believed that poetry should have the natural rhythm and fluidity of music.

1 Which of the following is an OPINION of the writer expressed in the passage?

   A Sidney Lanier was a talented musician as well as a gifted poet.

   B Lanier believed that poetry should have the natural rhythm and fluidity of music.

   C Lanier was born in Macon, Georgia.

   D Lanier was born in 1842.

The correct answer is *A*. The writer of the passage states that Lanier was "talented" and "gifted." The statement is a supportable opinion, but not necessarily a fact. Choice *B* does reflect an opinion, but not the opinion of the writer.

▶ **Practice 1** **Directions:** Read the passage. Then, read each question that follows the passage. Decide which is the best answer to each question.

World War I began in 1914 and was one of the bloodiest and most tragic conflicts ever to occur. Although President Wilson wanted the United States to remain neutral, that proved impossible. In 1915, a German submarine sank the *Lusitania*, the pride of the British merchant fleet. After the sinking, most Americans favored the British and their allies. It soon became impossible for the United States to remain neutral.

1 What is the main idea of this passage?

  A President Wilson wanted the United States to remain neutral.

  B In 1915, a German submarine sank the *Lusitania.*

  C It was impossible for the United States to remain neutral.

  D World War I was one of the bloodiest and most tragic conflicts ever to occur.

2 Which of the following is an OPINION expressed in the passage?

  F World War I began in 1914.

  G In 1915, a German submarine sank the *Lusitania.*

  H After the sinking of the *Lusitania*, most Americans favored the British and their allies.

  J World War I . . . was one of the bloodiest and most tragic conflicts ever to occur.

▶ **Practice 2** **Directions:** Read the passage. Then, read each question that follows the passage. Decide which is the best answer to each question.

When Christopher Columbus reached North America in 1492, several hundred Native American tribes already populated the continent. Although the history of these earliest Americans is shrouded in mystery, we do know that the Native Americans usually greeted the early European settlers as friends. The settlers were pleased to be greeted by the knowledgeable natives. Native Americans instructed the newcomers in New World agriculture and woodcraft and introduced them to maize, beans, and squash.

1 Which of the following is an OPINION expressed in the passage?

  A When Christopher Columbus reached North America in 1492, several hundred Native American tribes already populated the continent.

  B Native Americans instructed the newcomers in New World agriculture and woodcraft.

  C The settlers were pleased to be greeted by the knowledgeable natives.

  D The history of these earliest Americans is shrouded in mystery.

2 Which of the following is the best summary of this passage?

  F Native Americans introduced the settlers to maize, beans, and squash.

  G Native Americans who lived in North America before Christopher Columbus arrived were friendly and helpful to early European settlers.

  H The settlers were pleased to be greeted by the knowledgeable natives.

  J Christopher Columbus made friends with Native Americans in 1492.

Styles for Business and Friendly Letters

Business Letters

From a letter requesting information about a product to a letter asking for charitable donations, business letters are a common form of formal writing, writing intended for readers with whom the writer is not personally acquainted. Whatever the subject, an effective business letter

- includes six parts: the heading, the inside address, the salutation or greeting, the body, the closing, and the signature.
- follows one of several acceptable forms: In *block format,* each part of the letter begins at the left margin; in *modified block format,* the heading, the closing, and the signature are indented to the center of the page.
- uses formal language to communicate respectfully, regardless of the letter's content.

Model Business Letter

In this letter, Yolanda Dodson uses modified block format to request information.

The **heading** indicates the address and business affiliation of the writer. It also includes the date the letter was sent.

The **inside address** indicates where the letter will be sent.

A **salutation** is punctuated by a colon. When the specific addressee is not known, use a general greeting such as "To whom it may concern:"

The **body** of the letter states the writer's purpose. In this case, the writer is requesting information.

The **closing** "Sincerely" is common, but "Yours truly" and "Respectfully yours" are also acceptable. To end the letter, the writer types her name and provides a **signature**.

Students for a Cleaner Planet
c/o Memorial High School
333 Veterans' Drive
Denver, Colorado 80211

January 25, 20 – –

Steven Wilson, Director
Resource Recovery Really Works
300 Oak Street
Denver, Colorado 80216

Dear Mr. Wilson:

Memorial High School would like to start a branch of your successful recycling program. We share your commitment to reclaiming as much reusable material as we can. Because your program has been successful in other neighborhoods, we're sure that it can work in our community. Our school includes grades 9–12 and has about 800 students.

Would you send us some information about your community recycling program? For example, we need to know what materials can be recycled and how we can implement the program.

At least fifty students have already expressed an interest in getting involved, so I know we'll have the people power to make the program work. Please help us get started.

Thank you in advance for your time and consideration.

Sincerely,

Yolanda Dodson

Yolanda Dodson

Friendly Letters and Social Notes

When you write a letter telling news to a friend or thanking a relative for a gift, you are writing a friendly letter or a social note. A friendly letter is any informal letter based on a personal relationship with the reader. A social note includes a thank-you note written to someone you do not know quite well. Friendly letters and social notes feature the following elements:

- a heading, a salutation or greeting, a body, a closing, and a signature; they generally do not include an inside address
- a comma after the greeting
- paragraphs with indented first lines
- the use of a version of semiblock style, in which the heading, closing, and signature align to the right of center
- informal or semiformal language, often featuring the lively expression of feelings or amusement

How careful you need to be in following this format depends on your relationship with the reader: The less well you know the person, the more careful you should be to follow the correct format. Consult the model below for proper formatting.

> The **heading, closing,** and **signature** are aligned, semiblock style, to the right of the center of the page. (In very informal letters, writers may choose to omit their own address in the heading.)

Model Social Note

In this letter, Mayra Gonzalez thanks her aunt for a gift.

> A comma is used after the **greeting;** Mayra addresses her reader semiformally.

> The first line of each paragraph in the **body** is indented. The writer uses informal language and gives details that are of personal interest.

> A friendly letter may use or adapt a **closing** such as "Love," "Yours," and "Best," followed by a comma. As is customary when writer and reader know each other well, Mayra signs her first name only and does not add her name written out.

1111 Main St.
Mayfair, OH
November 11, 20 - -

Dear Aunt Margie,

Well, as you predicted, the trip to the amusement park was a lot of fun. I had a great time! The rides were more thrilling than any I've ever been on before. Even the twins were impressed—I don't think they had a single fight during the entire trip, and you know that's saying a lot!

The only part I wouldn't visit again was the spooky House of Chills. Ugh! I didn't mind the visuals: skeletons, scary pirates, and that sort of thing. But there's one part of the ride that takes place in complete darkness, with very quiet sound effects, and while you sit there wondering what will happen next, a cold, clammy THING runs slithering across your back or your hand! I nearly jumped out of my skin. I wasn't that frightened even when we told scary stories the night the lights went out at your house.

Thanks very much for the tickets and the fun day. We all loved the trip. I hope you'll come to visit again soon.

Your tallest niece,
Mayra

Citing Sources and Preparing Manuscript

The presentation of your written work is important. Your work should be neat, clean, and easy to read. Follow your teacher's directions for placing your name and class, along with the title and date of your work, on the paper.

For handwritten work:

- Use cursive handwriting or manuscript printing, according to the style your teacher prefers. The penmanship reference below shows the accepted formation of letters in cursive writing.
- Write or print neatly.
- Write on one side of lined 8 $\frac{1}{2}$" x 11" paper with a clean edge. (Do not use pages torn from a spiral notebook.)
- Indent the first line of each paragraph.

- Leave a margin, as indicated by the guidelines on the lined paper. Write in a size appropriate for the lines provided. Do not write so large that the letters from one line bump into the ones above and below. Do not write so small that the writing is difficult to read.
- Write in blue or black ink.
- Number the pages in the upper right corner.
- You should not cross out words on your final draft. Recopy instead. If your paper is long, your teacher may allow you to make one or two small changes by neatly crossing out the text to be deleted and using a caret [^] to indicate replacement text. Alternatively, you might make one or two corrections neatly with correction fluid. If you find yourself making more than three corrections, consider recopying the work.

PENMANSHIP REFERENCE

Aa Bb Cc Dd Ee Ff
Gg Hh Ii Jj Kk Ll
Mm Nn Oo Pp Qq
Rr Ss Tt Uu Vv Ww
Xx Yy Zz 1 2 3 4 5 6 7 8 9 0

For word-processed or typed documents:

- Choose a standard, easy-to-read font.
- Type or print on one side of unlined 8 1/2" x 11" paper.
- Set the margins for the side, top, and bottom of your paper at approximately one inch. Most word-processing programs have a default setting that is appropriate.
- Double-space the document.
- Indent the first line of each paragraph.
- Number the pages in the upper right corner. Many word-processing programs have a header feature that will do this for you automatically.

- If you discover one or two errors after you have typed or printed, use correction fluid if your teacher allows such corrections. If you have more than three errors in an electronic file, consider making the corrections to the file and reprinting the document. If you have typed a long document, your teacher may allow you to make a few corrections by hand. If you have several errors, however, consider retyping the document.

For research papers:

Follow your teacher's directions for formatting formal research papers. Most papers will have the following features:

- Title page
- Table of Contents or Outline
- Works-Cited List

Incorporating Ideas From Research

Below are three common methods of incorporating the ideas of other writers into your work. Choose the most appropriate style by analyzing your needs in each case. In all cases, you must credit your source.

- **Direct Quotation:** Use quotation marks to indicate the exact words.
- **Paraphrase:** To share ideas without a direct quotation, state the ideas in your own words. While you haven't copied word-for-word, you still need to credit your source.
- **Summary:** To provide information about a large body of work—such as a speech, an editorial, or a chapter of a book—identify the writer's main idea.

Avoiding Plagiarism

Whether you are presenting a formal research paper or an opinion paper on a current event, you must be careful to give credit for any ideas or opinions that are not your own. Presenting someone else's ideas, research, or opinion as your own—even if you have rephrased it in different words—is *plagiarism*, the equivalent of academic stealing, or fraud.

You can avoid plagiarism by synthesizing what you learn: Read from several sources and let the ideas of experts help you draw your own conclusions and form your own opinions. Ultimately, however, note your own reactions to the ideas presented.

When you choose to use someone else's ideas or work to support your view, credit the source of the material. Give bibliographic information to cite your sources of the following information:

- Statistics
- Direct quotations
- Indirectly quoted statements of opinions
- Conclusions presented by an expert
- Facts available in only one or two sources

Crediting Sources

When you credit a source, you acknowledge where you found your information and you give your readers the details necessary for locating the source themselves. Within the body of the paper, you provide a short citation, a footnote number linked to a footnote, or an endnote number linked to an endnote reference. These brief references show the page numbers on which you found the information. To make your paper more formal, prepare a reference list at the end of the paper to provide full bibliographic information on your sources. These are two common types of reference lists:

- A **bibliography** provides a listing of all the resources you consulted during your research.
- A **works-cited list** indicates the works you have referenced in your paper.

Choosing a Format for Documentation

The type of information you provide and the format in which you provide it depend on what your teacher prefers. These are the most commonly used styles:

- **Modern Language Association (MLA) Style** This is the style used for most papers at the middle-school and high-school levels and for most language arts papers.
- **American Psychological Association (APA) Style** This is used for most papers in the social sciences and for most college-level papers.
- ***Chicago Manual of Style* (CMS) Style** This is preferred by some teachers.

On the following pages, you'll find sample MLA documentation and citation formats for the most commonly cited materials.

MLA Style for Listing Sources

Book with one author	Pyles, Thomas. *The Origins and Development of the English Language.* 2nd ed. New York: Harcourt Brace Jovanovich, Inc., 1971.
Book with two or three authors	McCrum, Robert, William Cran, and Robert MacNeil. *The Story of English.* New York: Penguin Books, 1987.
Book with an editor	Truth, Sojourner. *Narrative of Sojourner Truth.* Ed. Margaret Washington. New York: Vintage Books, 1993.
Book with more than three authors or editors	Donald, Robert B., et al. *Writing Clear Essays.* Upper Saddle River, NJ: Prentice-Hall, Inc., 1996.
A single work from an anthology	Hawthorne, Nathaniel. "Young Goodman Brown." *Literature: An Introduction to Reading and Writing.* Ed. Edgar V. Roberts and Henry E. Jacobs. Upper Saddle River, NJ: Prentice-Hall, Inc., 1998. 376–385. [Indicate pages for the entire selection.]
Introduction in a published edition	Washington, Margaret. Introduction. *Narrative of Sojourner Truth.* By Sojourner Truth. Ed. Washington. New York: Vintage Books, 1993. v–xi.
Signed article in a weekly magazine	Wallace, Charles. "A Vodacious Deal." *Time* 14 Feb. 2000: 63.
Signed article in a monthly magazine	Gustaitis, Joseph. "The Sticky History of Chewing Gum." *American History* Oct. 1998: 30–38.
Unsigned editorial or story	"Selective Silence." Editorial. *Wall Street Journal* 11 Feb. 2000: A14. [If the editorial or story is signed, begin with the author's name.]
Signed pamphlet	[Treat the pamphlet as though it were a book.]
Pamphlet with no author, publisher, or date	*Are You at Risk of Heart Attack?* n.p. n.d. [n.p. n.d. indicates that there is no known publisher or date]
Filmstrips, slide programs, videocassettes, DVDs, and other audiovisual media	*The Diary of Anne Frank.* Dir. George Stevens. Perf. Millie Perkins, Shelley Winters, Joseph Schildkraut, Lou Jacobi, and Richard Beymer. 1959. DVD. Twentieth Century Fox, 2004.
Radio or television program transcript	"Washington's Crossing of the Delaware." Host Liane Hansen. Guest David Hackett Fischer. *Weekend Edition Sunday.* Natl. Public Radio. WNYC, New York City. 23 Dec. 2003. Transcript.
Internet	"Fun Facts About Gum." NACGM site. National Association of Chewing Gum Manufacturers. 19 Dec. 1999. <http://www.nacgm.org/consumer/funfacts.html>. [Indicate the date of last update if known and the date you accessed the information. Content and addresses at Web sites change frequently.]
Newspaper	Thurow, Roger. "South Africans Who Fought for Sanctions Now Scrap for Investors." *Wall Street Journal* 11 Feb. 2000: A1+ [For a multipage article that does not appear on consecutive pages, write only the first page number on which it appears, followed by a plus sign.]
Personal interview	Smith, Jane. Personal interview. 10 Feb. 2000.
CD (with multiple publishers)	Simms, James, ed. *Romeo and Juliet.* By William Shakespeare. CD-ROM. Oxford: Attica Cybernetics Ltd.; London: BBC Education; London: HarperCollins Publishers, 1995.
Article from an encyclopedia	Askeland, Donald R. "Welding." *World Book Encyclopedia.* 1991 ed.

Sample Works-Cited List (MLA)

Carwardine, Mark, Erich Hoyt, R. Ewan Fordyce, and
    Peter Gill. *The Nature Company Guides: Whales,
    Dolphins, and Porpoises.* New York: Time-Life
    Books, 1998.

Ellis, Richard. *Men and Whales.* New York: Knopf,
    1991.

Whales in Danger. "Discovering Whales." 18 Oct. 1999.
    <http://whales.magna.com.au/DISCOVER>

Sample Internal Citations (MLA)

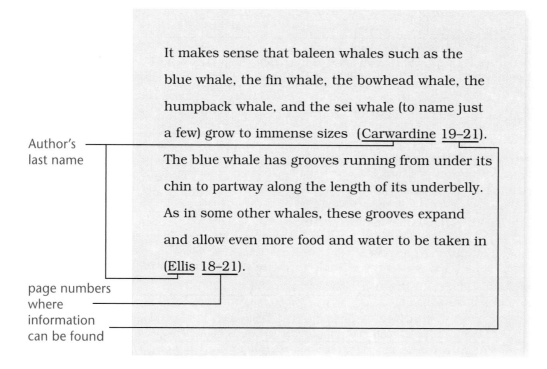

It makes sense that baleen whales such as the
blue whale, the fin whale, the bowhead whale, the
humpback whale, and the sei whale (to name just
a few) grow to immense sizes (Carwardine 19–21).
The blue whale has grooves running from under its
chin to partway along the length of its underbelly.
As in some other whales, these grooves expand
and allow even more food and water to be taken in
(Ellis 18–21).

Author's last name

page numbers where information can be found

Internet Research Handbook

Introduction to the Internet

The Internet is a series of networks that are interconnected all over the world. The Internet allows users to have almost unlimited access to information stored on the networks. Dr. Berners-Lee, a physicist, created the Internet in the 1980's by writing a small computer program that allowed pages to be linked together using key words. The Internet was mostly text-based until 1992, when a computer program called the NCSA Mosaic (National Center for Supercomputing Applications at the University of Illinois) was created. This program was the first Web browser. The development of Web browsers greatly eased the ability of the user to navigate through all the pages stored on the Web. Very soon, the appearance of the Web was altered as well. More appealing visuals were added, and sound was also implemented. This change made the Web more user-friendly and more appealing to the general public.

Using the Internet for Research

Key Word Search

Before you begin a search, you should identify your specific topic. To make searching easier, narrow your subject to a key word or a group of key words. These are your search terms, and they should be as specific as possible. For example, if you are looking for the latest concert dates for your favorite musical group, you might use the band's name as a key word. However, if you were to enter the name of the group in the query box of the search engine, you might be presented with thousands of links to information about the group that is unrelated to your needs. You might locate such information as band member biographies, the group's history, fan reviews of concerts, and hundreds of sites with related names containing information that is irrelevant to your search. Because you used such a broad key word, you might need to navigate through all that information before you find a link or subheading for concert dates. In contrast, if you were to type in "Duplex Arena and [band name]" you would have a better chance of locating pages that contain this information.

How to Narrow Your Search

If you have a large group of key words and still don't know which ones to use, write out a list of all the words you are considering. Once you have completed the list, scrutinize it. Then, delete the words that are least important to your search, and highlight those that are most important.

These **key search connectors** can help you fine-tune your search:

AND: narrows a search by retrieving documents that include both terms. For example: *baseball AND playoffs*

OR: broadens a search by retrieving documents including any of the terms. For example: *playoffs OR championships*

NOT: narrows a search by excluding documents containing certain words. For example: *baseball NOT history of*

Tips for an Effective Search

1. Keep in mind that search engines can be case-sensitive. If your first attempt at searching fails, check your search terms for misspellings and try again.

2. If you are entering a group of key words, present them in order, from the most important to the least important key word.

3. Avoid opening the link to every single page in your results list. Search engines present pages in descending order of relevancy. The most useful pages will be located at the top of the list. However, read the description of each link before you open the page.

4. When you use some search engines, you can find helpful tips for specializing your search. Take the opportunity to learn more about effective searching.

Other Ways to Search

Using On-line Reference Sites

How you search should be tailored to *what* you are hoping to find. If you are looking for data and facts, use reference sites before you jump onto a simple search engine. For example, you can find reference sites to provide definitions of words, statistics about almost any subject, biographies, maps, and concise information on many topics. Some useful on-line reference sites:

- On-line libraries
- On-line periodicals
- Almanacs
- Encyclopedias

You can find these sources using subject searches.

Conducting Subject Searches

As you prepare to go on-line, consider your subject and the best way to find information to suit your needs. If you are looking for general information on a topic and you want your search results to be extensive, consider the subject search indexes on most search engines. These indexes, in the form of category and subject lists, often appear on the first page of a search engine. When you click on a specific highlighted word, you will be presented with a new screen containing subcategories of the topic you chose. In the screen shots below, the category *Sports & Recreation* provided a second index for users to focus a search even further.

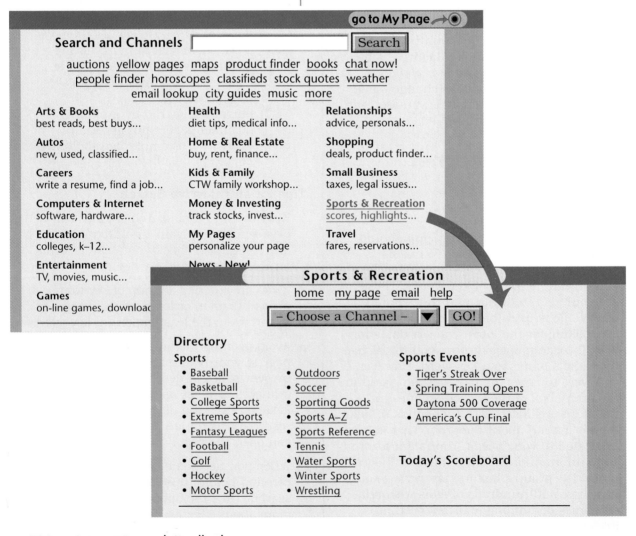

Evaluating the Reliability of Internet Resources

Just as you would evaluate the quality, bias, and validity of any other research material you locate, check the source of information you find on-line. Compare these two sites containing information on the poet and writer Langston Hughes:

Site A is a personal Web site constructed by a college student. It contains no bibliographic information or links to sites that he used. Included on the site are several poems by Langston Hughes and a student essay about the poet's use of symbolism. It has not been updated in more than six months.

Site B is a Web site constructed and maintained by the English Department of a major university. Information on Hughes is presented in a scholarly format, with a bibliography and credits for the writer. The site includes links to other sites and indicates new features that are added weekly.

For your own research, consider the information you find on Site B to be more reliable and accurate than that on Site A. Because it is maintained by experts in their field who are held accountable for their work, the university site will be a better research tool than the student-generated one.

Tips for Evaluating Internet Sources

1. Consider who constructed and who now maintains the Web page. Determine whether this author is a reputable source. Often, the URL endings indicate a source.

   - Sites ending in *.edu* are maintained by educational institutions.
   - Sites ending in *.gov* are maintained by government agencies (federal, state, or local).
   - Sites ending in *.org* are normally maintained by nonprofit organizations and agencies.
   - Sites with a *.com* ending are commercially or personally maintained.

2. Skim the official and trademarked Web pages first. It is safe to assume that the information you draw from Web pages of reputable institutions, on-line encyclopedias, on-line versions of major daily newspapers, or government-owned sites produce information as reliable as the material you would find in print. In contrast, unbranded sites or those generated by individuals tend to borrow information from other sources without providing documentation. As information travels from one source to another, the information has likely been muddled, misinterpreted, edited, or revised.

3. You can still find valuable information in the less "official" sites. Check for the writer's credentials and then consider these factors:

   - Don't let official-looking graphics or presentations fool you.
   - Make sure the information is updated enough to suit your needs. Many Web pages will indicate how recently they have been updated.
   - If the information is borrowed, see whether you can trace it back to its original source.

Respecting Copyrighted Material

Because the Internet is a relatively new and quickly growing medium, issues of copyright and ownership arise almost daily. As laws begin to govern the use and reuse of material posted on-line, they may change the way that people can access or reprint material.

Text, photographs, music, and fine art printed on-line may not be reproduced without acknowledged permission of the copyright owner.

Glossary of Internet Terms

attached file: a file containing information, such as a text document or GIF image, that is attached to an e-mail message; reports, pictures, spreadsheets, and so on transmitted to others by attaching these to messages as files

bandwidth: the amount of information, mainly compressed in bits per second (bps), that can be sent through a connection within a specific amount of time; depending on how fast your modem is, 15,000 bits (roughly one page of text) can be transferred per second

bit: a binary digit of computerized data, represented by a single digit that is either a 1 or a 0; a group of bits constitutes a byte

bookmark: a feature of your Web browser that allows you to place a "bookmark" on a Web page to which you wish to return at a later time

browser: software designed to present material accessed on the Web

bulletin-board system: a computer system that members access in order to join on-line discussion groups or to post announcements

case-sensitivity: the quality of a search engine that causes it to respond to upper- or lowercase letters in different ways

chat room: informal on-line gathering sites where people share conversations, experiences, or information on a specific topic; many chat rooms do not require users to provide their identity, so the reliability or safety of these sites is uncertain

cookie: a digitized piece of information that is sent to a Web browser by a Web server, intended to be saved on a computer; cookies gather information about the user, such as user preferences, or recent on-line purchases; a Web browser can be set to either accept or reject cookies

cyberspace: a term referring to the electronic environment connecting all computer network information with the people who use it

database: a large collection of data that have been formatted to fit a certain user-defined standard

digerati: a slang term to describe Internet experts; an offshoot of the term *literati*

download: to copy files from the Internet onto your computer

e-mail: electronic mail, or the exchange of messages via the Internet; because it is speedier than traditional mail and offers easier global access, e-mail has grown in popularity; e-mail messages can be sent to a single person or in bulk to a group of people

error message: a displayed communication or printout that reports a problem with a program or Web page

FTP site (file transfer protocol): a password-protected server on the Internet that allows the transfer of information from one computer to another

GIF (Graphic Interchange Format): a form of graphics used on the Web

graphics: information displayed as pictures or images instead of text

hits: items retrieved by a key word search; the number tracking the volume of visits to a Web site

home page: the main Web page for an individual or an organization, containing links to subpages within

HTML (HyperText Markup Language): the coding text that is the foundation for creating Web pages

interactivity: a quality of some Web pages that encourages the frequent exchange of information between user and computer

Internet: a worldwide computer network that supports services such as the World Wide Web, e-mail, and file transfer

JPEG (Joint Photo Experts Group, the developers): a file format for graphics especially suited to photographs

K: a measurement of file size or memory; short for "Kilobyte," 1,000 bytes of information (see *bit*)

key word: search term entered into the query box of a search engine to direct the results of the search

link: an icon or word on a Web page that, when clicked, transfers the user to another Web page or to a different document within the same page

login: the procedure by which users gain access to a server or a secure Web site; usually, the user must enter a specific user name and password

modem: a device that transfers data to a computer through a phone line. A computer's modem connects to a server, which then sends information in the form of digital signals. The modem converts these signals into waves, for the purpose of information reception. The speed of a modem affects how quickly a computer can receive and download information

newbie: jargon used to describe Internet novices

newsgroup: an on-line discussion group, where users can post and respond to messages; the most prevalent collection of newsgroups is found on USENET

query box: the blank box in a search engine where your search terms are input

relevance ranking: the act of displaying the results of a search in the order of their relevance to the search terms

search engines: tools that help you navigate databases to locate information; search engines respond to a key word search by providing the user with a directory of multiple Web pages about the key word or containing the key word

server: a principal computer that provides services, such as storing files and providing access to the Internet, to another computer

signature: a preprogrammed section of text that is automatically added to an e-mail message

surfing: the process of reading Web pages and of moving from one Web site to another

URL (Uniform Resource Locator): a Web page's address; a URL can look like this:

http://www.phwg.phschool.com or
*http://www.senate.gov/~appropriations/
labor/testimony*

usenet: a worldwide system of discussion groups, or newsgroups

vanity pages: Web sites placed on-line by people to tell about themselves or their interests; vanity pages do not have any commercial or informational value

virus: a set of instructions, hidden in a computer system or transferred via e-mail or electronic files, that can cause problems with a computer's ability to perform normally

Web page: a set of information, including graphics, text, sound, and video, presented in a browser window; a Web page can be found by its URL once it is posted on the World Wide Web

Web site: a collection of Web pages that are linked together for posting on the World Wide Web

W3: a group of Internet experts, including networking professionals, academics, scientists, and corporate interests, who maintain and develop technologies and standards for the Internet

WWW (World Wide Web): a term referring to the multitude of information systems found on the Internet; this includes FTP, Gopher, telnet, and http sites

zip: the minimizing of files through compression; this function makes for easier transmittal over networks; a receiver can then open the file by "unzipping" it

Commonly Overused Words

When you write, use the most precise word for your meaning, not the word that comes to mind first. Consult this thesaurus to find alternatives for some commonly overused words. Consult a full-length thesaurus to find alternatives to words that do not appear here. Keep in mind that the choices offered in a thesaurus do not all mean exactly the same thing. Review all the options, and choose the one that best expresses your meaning.

about approximately, nearly, almost, approaching, close to

absolutely unconditionally, perfectly, completely, ideally, purely

activity action, movement, operation, labor, exertion, enterprise, project, pursuit, endeavor, job, assignment, pastime, scheme, task

add attach, affix, join, unite, append, increase, amplify

affect adjust, influence, transform, moderate, incline, motivate, prompt

amazing overwhelming, astonishing, startling, unexpected, stunning, dazzling, remarkable

awesome impressive, stupendous, fabulous, astonishing, outstanding

bad defective, inadequate, poor, unsatisfactory, disagreeable, offensive, repulsive, corrupt, wicked, naughty, harmful, injurious, unfavorable

basic essential, necessary, indispensable, vital, fundamental, elementary

beautiful attractive, appealing, alluring, exqui-
site, gorgeous, handsome, stunning

begin commence, found, initiate, introduce, launch, originate

better preferable, superior, worthier

big enormous, extensive, huge, immense, massive

boring commonplace, monotonous, tedious, tiresome

bring accompany, cause, convey, create, conduct, deliver, produce

cause origin, stimulus, inspiration, motive

certain unquestionable, incontrovertible, unmistakable, indubitable, assured, confident

change alter, transform, vary, replace, diversify

choose select, elect, nominate, prefer, identify

decent respectable, adequate, fair, suitable

definitely unquestionably, clearly, precisely, positively, inescapably

easy effortless, natural, comfortable, undemanding, pleasant, relaxed

effective powerful, successful

emphasize underscore, feature, accentuate

end limit, boundary, finish, conclusion, finale, resolution

energy vitality, vigor, force, dynamism

enjoy savor, relish, revel, benefit

entire complete, inclusive, unbroken, integral

excellent superior, remarkable, splendid, unsurpassed, superb, magnificent

exciting thrilling, stirring, rousing, dramatic

far distant, remote

fast swift, quick, fleet, hasty, instant, accelerated

fill occupy, suffuse, pervade, saturate, inflate, stock

finish complete, conclude, cease, achieve, exhaust, deplete, consume

funny comical, ludicrous, amusing, droll, entertaining, bizarre, unusual, uncommon

get obtain, receive, acquire, procure, achieve

give bestow, donate, supply, deliver, distribute, impart

go proceed, progress, advance, move

good satisfactory, serviceable, functional, competent, virtuous, striking

great tremendous, superior, remarkable, eminent, proficient, expert

happy pleased, joyous, elated, jubilant, cheerful, delighted

hard arduous, formidable, complex, complicated, rigorous, harsh

help assist, aid, support, sustain, serve

hurt injure, harm, damage, wound, impair

important significant, substantial, weighty, meaningful, critical, vital, notable

interesting absorbing, appealing, entertaining, fascinating, thought-provoking

job task, work, business, undertaking, occupation, vocation, chore, duty, assignment

keep retain, control, possess

kind type, variety, sort, form

know comprehend, understand, realize, perceive, discern

like (adj) similar, equivalent, parallel

like (verb) enjoy, relish, appreciate

main primary, foremost, dominant

make build, construct, produce, assemble, fashion, manufacture

mean plan, intend, suggest, propose, indicate

more supplementary, additional, replenishment

new recent, modern, current, novel

next subsequently, thereafter, successively

nice pleasant, satisfying, gracious, charming

old aged, mature, experienced, used, worn, former, previous

open unobstructed, accessible

part section, portion, segment, detail, element, component

perfect flawless, faultless, ideal, consummate

plan scheme, design, system, plot

pleasant agreeable, gratifying, refreshing, welcome

prove demonstrate, confirm, validate, verify, corroborate

quick brisk, prompt, responsive, rapid, nimble, hasty

really truly, genuinely, extremely, undeniably

regular standard, routine, customary, habitual

see regard, behold, witness, gaze, realize, notice

small diminutive, miniature, minor, insignificant, slight, trivial

sometimes occasionally, intermittently, sporadically, periodically

take grasp, capture, choose, select, tolerate, endure

terrific extraordinary, magnificent, marvelous

think conceive, imagine, ponder, reflect, contemplate

try attempt, endeavor, venture, test

use employ, operate, utilize

very unusually, extremely, deeply, exceedingly, profoundly

want desire, crave, yearn, long

Commonly Misspelled Words

The list on these pages presents words that cause problems for many people. Some of these words are spelled according to set rules, but others follow no specific rules. As you review this list, check to see how many of the words give you trouble in your own writing. Then, read the instruction in the "Vocabulary and Spelling" chapter in the book for strategies and suggestions for improving your own spelling habits.

abbreviate	athletic	catastrophe	curious
absence	attendance	category	cylinder
absolutely	auxiliary	ceiling	deceive
abundance	awkward	cemetery	decision
accelerate	bandage	census	deductible
accidentally	banquet	certain	defendant
accumulate	bargain	changeable	deficient
accurate	barrel	characteristic	definitely
ache	battery	chauffeur	delinquent
achievement	beautiful	chief	dependent
acquaintance	beggar	clothes	descendant
adequate	beginning	coincidence	description
admittance	behavior	colonel	desert
advertisement	believe	column	desirable
aerial	benefit	commercial	dessert
affect	bicycle	commission	deteriorate
aggravate	biscuit	commitment	dining
aggressive	bookkeeper	committee	disappointed
agreeable	bought	competitor	disastrous
aisle	boulevard	concede	discipline
all right	brief	condemn	dissatisfied
allowance	brilliant	congratulate	distinguish
aluminum	bruise	connoisseur	effect
amateur	bulletin	conscience	eighth
analysis	buoyant	conscientious	eligible
analyze	bureau	conscious	embarrass
ancient	bury	contemporary	enthusiastic
anecdote	buses	continuous	entrepreneur
anniversary	business	controversy	envelope
anonymous	cafeteria	convenience	environment
answer	calendar	coolly	equipped
anticipate	campaign	cooperate	equivalent
anxiety	canceled	cordially	especially
apologize	candidate	correspondence	exaggerate
appall	capacity	counterfeit	exceed
appearance	capital	courageous	excellent
appreciate	capitol	courteous	exercise
appropriate	captain	courtesy	exhibition
architecture	career	criticism	existence
argument	carriage	criticize	experience
associate	cashier	curiosity	explanation

extension
extraordinary
familiar
fascinating
February
fiery
financial
fluorescent
foreign
forfeit
fourth
fragile
gauge
generally
genius
genuine
government
grammar
grievance
guarantee
guard
guidance
handkerchief
harass
height
humorous
hygiene
ignorant
illegible
immediately
immigrant
independence
independent
indispensable
individual
inflammable
intelligence
interfere
irrelevant
irritable
jewelry
judgment
knowledge
laboratory
lawyer
legible
legislature
leisure
liable

library
license
lieutenant
lightning
likable
liquefy
literature
loneliness
magnificent
maintenance
marriage
mathematics
maximum
meanness
mediocre
mileage
millionaire
minimum
minuscule
miscellaneous
mischievous
misspell
mortgage
naturally
necessary
negotiate
neighbor
neutral
nickel
niece
ninety
noticeable
nuclear
nuisance
obstacle
occasion
occasionally
occur
occurred
occurrence
omitted
opinion
opportunity
optimistic
outrageous
pamphlet
parallel
paralyze
parentheses

particularly
patience
permanent
permissible
perseverance
persistent
personally
perspiration
persuade
phenomenal
phenomenon
physician
pleasant
pneumonia
possess
possession
possibility
prairie
precede
preferable
prejudice
preparation
prerogative
previous
primitive
privilege
probably
procedure
proceed
prominent
pronunciation
psychology
publicly
pursue
questionnaire
realize
really
recede
receipt
receive
recognize
recommend
reference
referred
rehearse
relevant
reminiscence
renowned
repetition

restaurant
rhythm
ridiculous
sandwich
satellite
schedule
scissors
secretary
siege
solely
sponsor
subtle
subtlety
superintendent
supersede
surveillance
susceptible
tariff
temperamental
theater
threshold
truly
unmanageable
unwieldy
usage
usually
valuable
various
vegetable
voluntary
weight
weird
whale
wield
yield

Abbreviations Guide

Abbreviations, shortened versions of words or phrases, can be valuable tools in writing if you know when and how to use them. They can be very helpful in informal writing situations, such as taking notes or writing lists. However, only a few abbreviations can be used in formal writing. They are: *Mr., Mrs., Miss, Ms., Dr., A.M., P.M., A.D., B.C., M.A, B.A., Ph.D.,* and *M.D.*

The following pages provide the conventional abbreviations for a variety of words.

Abbreviations of Common Titles

Ambassador	Amb.	Lieutenant	Lt.
Attorney	Atty.	Major	Maj.
Brigadier-General	Brig. Gen.	President	Pres.
Brother	Br.	Professor	Prof.
Captain	Capt.	Representative	Rep.
Colonel	Col.	Reverend	Rev.
Commander	Cmdr.	Secretary	Sec.
Commissioner	Com.	Senator	Sen.
Corporal	Cpl.	Sergeant	Sgt.
Doctor	Dr.	Sister	Sr.
Father	Fr.	Superintendent	Supt.
Governor	Gov.	Treasurer	Treas.
Honorable	Hon.	Vice Admiral	Vice Adm.

Abbreviations of Academic Degrees

Bachelor of Arts	B.A. (or A.B.)	Esquire (lawyer)	Esq.
Bachelor of Science	B.S. (or S.B.)	Master of Arts	M.A. (or A.M.)
Doctor of Dental Surgery	D.D.S.	Master of Business Administration	M.B.A.
Doctor of Divinity	D.D.		
Doctor of Education	Ed.D.	Master of Fine Arts	M.F.A.
Doctor of Laws	LL.D.	Master of Science	M.S. (or S.M.)
Doctor of Medicine	M.D.	Registered Nurse	R.N.
Doctor of Philosophy	Ph.D.		

Abbreviations of States

State	Traditional	Postal Service	State	Traditional	Postal Service
Alabama	Ala.	AL	Montana	Mont.	MT
Alaska	Alaska	AK	Nebraska	Nebr.	NE
Arizona	Ariz.	AZ	Nevada	Nev.	NV
Arkansas	Ark.	AR	New Hampshire	N.H.	NH
California	Calif.	CA	New Jersey	N.J.	NJ
Colorado	Colo.	CO	New Mexico	N.M.	NM
Connecticut	Conn.	CT	New York	N.Y.	NY
Delaware	Del.	DE	North Carolina	N.C.	NC
Florida	Fla.	FL	North Dakota	N.Dak.	ND
Georgia	Ga.	GA	Ohio	O.	OH
Hawaii	Hawaii	HI	Oklahoma	Okla.	OK
Idaho	Ida.	ID	Oregon	Ore.	OR
Illinois	Ill.	IL	Pennsylvania	Pa.	PA
Indiana	Ind.	IN	Rhode Island	R.I.	RI
Iowa	Iowa	IA	South Carolina	S.C.	SC
Kansas	Kans.	KS	South Dakota	S.Dak.	SD
Kentucky	Ky.	KY	Tennessee	Tenn.	TN
Louisiana	La.	LA	Texas	Tex.	TX
Maine	Me.	ME	Utah	Utah	UT
Maryland	Md.	MD	Vermont	Vt.	VT
Massachusetts	Mass.	MA	Virginia	Va.	VA
Michigan	Mich.	MI	Washington	Wash.	WA
Minnesota	Minn.	MN	West Virginia	W. Va	WV
Mississippi	Miss.	MS	Wisconsin	Wis.	WI
Missouri	Mo.	MO	Wyoming	Wyo.	WY

Common Geographical Abbreviations

Apartment	Apt.	National	Natl.
Avenue	Ave.	Park, Peak	Pk.
Block	Blk.	Peninsula	Pen.
Boulevard	Blvd.	Point	Pt.
Building	Bldg.	Province	Prov.
County	Co.	Road	Rd.
District	Dist.	Route	Rte.
Drive	Dr.	Square	Sq.
Fort	Ft.	Street	St.
Island	Is.	Territory	Terr.
Mountain	Mt.		

Abbreviations of Traditional Measurements

inch(es)	in.	ounce(s)	oz.
foot, feet	ft.	pound(s)	lb.
yard(s)	yd.	pint(s)	pt.
mile(s)	mi.	quart(s)	qt.
teaspoon(s)	tsp.	gallon(s)	gal.
tablespoon(s)	tbsp.	Fahrenheit	F.

Abbreviations of Metric Measurements

millimeter(s)	mm	liter(s)	L
centimeter(s)	cm	kiloliter(s)	kL
meter(s)	m	milligram(s)	mg
kilometer(s)	km	centigram(s)	cg
milliliter(s)	mL	gram(s)	g
centiliter(s)	cL	Celsius	C

Other Commonly Used Abbreviations

about (used with dates)	c., ca., circ.	manager	mgr.
and others	et al.	manufacturing	mfg.
anonymous	anon.	market	mkt.
approximately	approx.	measure	meas.
associate, association	assoc., assn.	merchandise	mdse.
auxiliary	aux., auxil.	miles per hour	mph
bibliography	bibliog.	miscellaneous	misc.
boxes	bx(s).	money order	M.O.
bucket	bkt.	note well; take notice	N.B.
bulletin	bull.	number	no.
bushel	bu.	package	pkg.
capital letter	cap.	page	p., pg.
cash on delivery	C.O.D.	pages	pp.
department	dept.	pair(s)	pr(s).
discount	disc.	parenthesis	paren.
dozen(s)	doz.	Patent Office	pat. off.
each	ea.	piece(s)	pc(s).
edition, editor	ed.	poetical, poetry	poet.
equivalent	equiv.	private	pvt.
established	est.	proprietor	prop.
fiction	fict.	pseudonym	pseud.
for example	e.g.	published, publisher	pub.
free of charge	grat., gratis	received	recd.
General Post Office	G.P.O.	reference, referee	ref.
government	gov., govt.	revolutions per minute	rpm
graduate, graduated	grad.	rhetorical, rhetoric	rhet.
Greek, Grecian	Gr.	right	R.
headquarters	hdqrs.	scene	sc.
height	ht.	special, specific	spec.
hospital	hosp.	spelling, species	sp.
illustrated	ill., illus.	that is	i.e.
including, inclusive	incl.	treasury, treasurer	treas.
introduction, introductory	intro.	volume	vol.
italics	ital.	weekly	wkly
karat, carat	k., kt.	weight	wt.
left	L.		

Proofreading
Symbols Reference

Proofreading symbols make it easier to show where changes are needed in a paper. When proofreading your own or a classmate's work, use these standard proofreading symbols.

insert	I proofred.
delete	Ip proofread.
close up space	I proof read.
delete and close up space	I proofreade.
begin new paragraph	¶ I proofread.
spell out	I proofread (10) papers.
lowercase	I Proofread. (lc)
capitalize	i proofread. (cap)
transpose letters	I proofraed. (tr)
transpose words	I only proofread her paper. (tr)
period	I will proofread⊙
comma	I will proofread and she will help.
colon	We will proofread for the following errors
semicolon	I will proofread she will help.
single quotation marks	She said, "I enjoyed the story The Invalid."
double quotation marks	She said, I enjoyed the story.
apostrophe	Did you borrow Sylvias book?
question mark	Did you borrow Sylvia's book ?/
exclamation point	You're kidding !/
hyphen	online /=/
parentheses	William Shakespeare 1564–1616

Student Publications

To share your writing with a wider audience, consider submitting it to a local, state, or national publication for student writing. Following are several magazines and Web sites that accept and publish student work.

Periodicals

Creative Kids P.O. Box 8813, Waco TX 76714-8813

Merlyn's Pen merlynspen.org

Skipping Stones P.O. Box 3939, Eugene, OR 97403
http://www.skippingstones.org

Teen Ink Box 30, Newton, MA 02461
teenink.com

On-line Publications

Kid Pub http://www.kidpub.org

MidLink Magazine http://www.ncsu.edu/midlink

Stone Soup http://www.stonesoup.com

Contests

Annual Poetry Contest National Federation of State Poetry Societies, Contest Chair, Kathleen Pederzani, 121 Grande Boulevard, Reading, PA 19608-9680. http://www.nfsps.com

Paul A. Witty Outstanding Literature Award International Reading Association, Special Interest Group for Reading for Gifted and Creative Students, c/o Texas Christian University, P.O. Box 297900, Fort Worth, TX 76129

Seventeen Magazine Fiction Contest Seventeen Magazine, 1440 Broadway 13th Floor, New York, NY 10018

The Young Playwrights Festival National Playwriting Competition Young Playwrights Inc. Dept WEB, 306 West 38th Street #300, New York, NY 10018 or webmaster@youngplaywrights.org

Glossary

A

accent: the emphasis on a syllable, usually in poetry

action verb: a word that tells what action someone or something is performing (*See* linking verb.)

active voice: the voice of a verb whose subject performs an action (*See* passive voice.)

adjective: a word that modifies a noun or pronoun by telling *what kind* or *which one*

adjective clause: a subordinate clause that modifies a noun or pronoun

adjective phrase: a prepositional phrase that modifies a noun or pronoun

adverb: a word that modifies a verb, an adjective, or another adverb

adverb clause: a subordinate clause that modifies a verb, an adjective, an adverb, or a verbal by telling *where, when, in what way, to what extent, under what condition,* or *why*

adverb phrase: a prepositional phrase that modifies a verb, an adjective, or an adverb

allegory: an indirect literary work with two or more levels of meaning—a literal level and one or more symbolic levels

alliteration: the repetition of initial consonant sounds in accented syllables

allusion: an indirect reference to a well-known person, place, event, literary work, or work of art

annotated bibliography: a research writing product that provides a list of materials on a given topic, along with publication information, summaries, or evaluations

apostrophe: a punctuation mark used to form possessive nouns and contractions

appositive: a noun or pronoun placed after another noun or pronoun to identify, rename, or explain the preceding word

appositive phrase: a noun or pronoun with its modifiers, placed next to a noun or pronoun to identify, rename, or explain the preceding word

article: one of three commonly used adjectives: *a, an,* and *the*

assonance: the repetition of vowel sounds in stressed syllables containing dissimilar consonant sounds

audience: the reader(s) a writer intends to reach

autobiographical writing: narrative writing that tells a true story about an important period, experience, or relationship in the writer's life

B

ballad: a song that tells a story (often dealing with adventure or romance) or a poem imitating such a song

bias: the attitudes or beliefs that affect a writer's ability to present a subject objectively

bibliography: a list of the sources of a research paper, including full bibliographic references for each source the writer consulted while conducting research (*See* works-cited list.)

biography: narrative writing that tells the story of an important period, experience, or relationship in a person's life, as reported by another

blueprinting: a prewriting technique in which a writer sketches a map of a home, school, neighborhood, or other meaningful place in order to spark memories or associations for further development

body paragraph: a paragraph in an essay that develops, explains, or supports the key ideas of the writing

brainstorming: a prewriting technique in which a group jots down as many ideas as possible about a given topic

C

case: the form of a noun or pronoun that indicates how it functions in a sentence

cause-and-effect writing: expository writing that examines the relationship between events, explaining how one event or situation causes another

character: a person (though not necessarily a human being) who takes part in the action of a literary work

characterization: the act of creating and developing a character through narration, description, and dialogue

citation: in formal research papers, the acknowledgment of ideas found in outside sources

classical invention: a prewriting technique in which writers gather details about a topic by analyzing the category and subcategories to which the topic belongs

clause: a group of words that has a subject and a verb

climax: the high point of interest or suspense in a literary work

coherence: a quality of written work in which all the parts flow logically from one idea to the next

colon: a punctuation mark used before an extended quotation, explanation, example, or series and after the salutation in a formal letter

comma: a punctuation mark used to separate words or groups of words

comparison-and-contrast writing: expository writing that describes the similarities and differences between two or more subjects in order to achieve a specific purpose

complement: a word or group of words that completes the meaning of a verb

compound sentence: a sentence that contains two or more independent clauses with no subordinate clauses

conclusion: the final paragraph(s) of a work of writing in which the writer may restate a main idea, summarize the points of the writing, or provide a closing remark to end the work effectively (*See* introduction, body paragraph, topical paragraph, functional paragraph.)

conflict: a struggle between opposing forces

conjugation: a list of the singular and plural forms of a verb in a particular tense

conjunction: a word used to connect other words or groups of words

connotation: the emotional associations that a word calls to mind (*See* denotation.)

consonance: the repetition of final consonant sounds in stressed syllables containing dissimilar vowel sounds

contraction: a shortened form of a word or phrase that includes an apostrophe to indicate the position of the missing letter(s)

coordinating conjunctions: words such as *and, but, nor,* and *yet* that connect similar words or groups of words

correlative conjunctions: word pairs such as *neither . . . nor, both . . . and,* and *whether . . . or* used to connect similar words or groups of words

couplet: a pair of rhyming lines written in the same meter

cubing: a prewriting technique in which a writer analyzes a subject from six specified angles: description; association; application; analysis; comparison and contrast; and evaluation

D

declarative sentence: a statement punctuated with a period

demonstrative pronouns: words such as *this, that, these,* and *those* used to single out specific people, places, or things

denotation: the objective meaning of a word; its definition independent of other associations the word calls to mind (*See* connotation.)

depth-charging: a drafting technique in which a writer elaborates on a sentence by developing a key word or idea

description: language or writing that uses sensory details to capture a subject

dialect: the form of a language spoken by people in a particular region or group

dialogue: a direct conversation between characters or people

diary: a personal record of daily events, usually written in prose

diction: a writer's word choice

direct object: a noun or a pronoun that receives the action of a transitive verb

direct quotation: a drafting technique in which writers indicate the exact words of another by enclosing them in quotation marks

documentary: nonfiction film that analyzes news events or another focused subject by combining interviews, film footage, narration, and other audio/visual components

documented essay: research writing that includes a limited number of research sources, providing full documentation parenthetically within the text

drafting: a stage of the writing process that follows prewriting and precedes revising in which a writer gets ideas on paper in a rough format

drama: a story written to be performed by actors and actresses

E

elaboration: a drafting technique in which a writer extends his or her ideas through the use of facts, examples, descriptions, details, or quotations

epic: a long narrative poem about the adventures of a god or a hero

essay: a short nonfiction work about a particular subject

etymology: the history of a word, showing where it came from and how it has evolved into its present spelling and meaning

exclamation mark: a punctuation mark used to indicate strong emotion

exclamatory sentence: a statement that conveys strong emotion and ends with an exclamation mark

exposition: writing to inform, addressing analytic purposes such as problem and solution, comparison and contrast, how-to, and cause and effect

extensive writing: writing products generated for others and from others, meant to be shared with an audience and often done for school assignments (*See* reflexive writing.)

F

fact: a statement that can be proved true (*See* opinion.)

fiction: prose writing about imaginary characters and events

figurative language: writing or speech not meant to be interpreted literally

firsthand biography: narrative writing that tells the story of an important period, experience, or relationship in a person's life, reported by a writer who knows the subject personally

five W's: a prewriting technique in which writers gather details about a topic by generating answers to the following questions: *Who? What? Where? When?* and *Why?*

fragment: an incomplete idea punctuated as a complete sentence

freewriting: a prewriting technique in which a writer quickly jots down as many ideas on a topic as possible

functional paragraph: a paragraph that performs a specific role in composition, such as to arouse or sustain interest, to indicate dialogue, to make a transition (*See* topical paragraph.)

G

generalization: a statement that presents a rule or idea based on particular facts

gerund: a noun formed from the present participle of a verb (ending in -*ing*)

gerund phrase: a group of words containing a gerund and its modifiers or complements that function as a noun

grammar: the study of the forms of words and the way they are arranged in phrases, clauses, and sentences

H

helping verb: a verb added to another verb to make a single verb phrase that indicates the time at which an action takes place or whether it actually happens, could happen, or should happen

hexagonal writing: a prewriting technique in which a

writer analyzes a subject from six angles: literal level, personal allusions, theme, literary devices, literary allusions, and evaluation

homophones: pairs of words that sound the same as each other yet have different meanings and different spellings, such as *hear/here*

how-to writing: expository writing that explains a process by providing step-by-step directions

humanities: forms of artistic expression including, but not limited to, fine art, photography, theater, film, music, and dance

hyperbole: a deliberate exaggeration or overstatement

hyphen: a punctuation mark used to combine numbers and word parts, to join certain compound words, and to show that a word has been broken between syllables at the end of a line

I

I-Search report: a research paper in which the writer addresses the research experience in addition to presenting the information gathered

image: a word or phrase that appeals to one or more of the senses—sight, hearing, touch, taste, or smell

imagery: the descriptive language used to re-create sensory experiences, set a tone, suggest emotions, and guide readers' reactions

imperative sentence: a statement that gives an order or a direction and ends with either a period or an exclamation mark

indefinite pronoun: a word such as *anyone, each,* or *many* that refers to a person, place, or thing, without specifying which one

independent clause: a group of words that contains both a subject and a verb and that can stand by itself as a complete sentence

indirect quotation: reporting only the general meaning of what a person said or thought; quotation marks are not needed

infinitive: the form of a verb that comes after the word *to* and acts as a noun, adjective, or adverb

infinitive phrase: a phrase introduced by an infinitive that may be used as a noun, an adjective, or an adverb

interjection: a word or phrase that expresses feeling or emotion and functions independently of a sentence

interrogative pronoun: a word such as *which* and *who* that introduces a question

interrogative sentence: a question that is punctuated with a question mark

interview: an information-gathering technique in which one or more people pose questions to one or more other people who provide opinions or facts on a topic

intransitive verb: an action verb that does not take a direct object (*See* transitive verb.)

introduction: the opening paragraphs of a work of writing in which the writer may capture the readers' attention and present a thesis statement to be developed in the writing (*See* body paragraph, topical paragraph, functional paragraph, conclusion.)

invisible writing: a prewriting technique in which a writer freewrites without looking at the product until the exercise is complete; this can be accomplished at a word processor with the monitor turned off or with carbon paper and an empty ballpoint pen

irony: the general name given to literary techniques that involve surprising, interesting, or amusing contradictions

itemizing: a prewriting technique in which a writer creates a second, more focused, set of ideas based on an original listing activity. (*See* listing.)

J

jargon: the specialized words and phrases unique to a specific field

journal: a notebook or other organized writing system in which daily events and personal impressions are recorded

K

key word: the word or phrase that directs an Internet or database search

L

layering: a drafting technique in which a writer elaborates on a statement by identifying and then expanding upon a central idea or word

lead: the opening sentences of a work of writing meant to grab the reader's interest, accomplished through a variety of methods, including providing an intriguing quotation, a surprising or provocative question or fact, an anecdote, or a description

learning log: a record-keeping system in which a student notes information about new ideas

legend: a widely told story about the past that may or may not be based in fact

legibility: the neatness and readability of words

linking verb: a word that expresses its subject's state of being or condition (See action verb.)

listing: a prewriting technique in which a writer prepares a list of ideas related to a specific topic. (See itemizing.)

looping: a prewriting activity in which a writer generates follow-up freewriting based on the identification of a key word or central idea in an original freewriting exercise

lyric poem: a poem expressing the observations and feelings of a single speaker

M

main clause: a group of words that has a subject and a verb and can stand alone as a complete sentence

memoir: autobiographical writing that provides an account of a writer's relationship with a person, event, or place

metaphor: a figure of speech in which one thing is spoken of as though it were something else

meter: the rhythmic pattern of a poem

monologue: a speech or performance given entirely by one person or by one character

mood: the feeling created in the reader by a literary work or passage

multimedia presentation: a technique for sharing information with an audience by enhancing narration and explanation with media, including video images, slides, audiotape recordings, music, and fine art

N

narration: writing that tells a story

narrative poem: a poem that tells a story in verse

nominative case: the form of a noun or pronoun used as the subject of a verb, as a predicate nominative, or as the pronoun in a nominative absolute (See objective case, possessive case.)

noun: a word that names a person, place, or thing

noun clause: a subordinate clause that acts as a noun

novel: an extended work of fiction that often has a complicated plot, many major and minor characters, a unifying theme, and several settings

O

objective case: the form of a noun or pronoun used as the object of any verb, verbal, or preposition, or as the subject of an infinitive (See nominative case, possessive case.)

observation: a prewriting technique involving close visual study of an object; a writing product that reports such a study

ode: a long formal lyric poem with a serious theme

onomatopoeia: words such as *buzz* and *plop* that suggest the sounds they name

open-book test: a form of assessment in which students are permitted to use books and class notes to respond to test questions

opinion: beliefs that can be supported but not proved to be true (See fact.)

oral tradition: the body of songs, stories, and poems preserved by being passed from generation to generation by word of mouth

outline: a prewriting or study technique that allows writers or readers to organize the presentation and order of information

oxymoron: a figure of speech that fuses two contradictory or opposing ideas, such as "freezing fire" or "happy grief"

P

parable: a short, simple story from which a moral or religious lesson can be drawn

paradox: a statement that seems to be contradictory but that actually presents a truth

paragraph: a group of sentences that share a common topic or purpose and that focus on a single main idea or thought

parallelism: the placement of equal ideas in words, phrases, or clauses of similar types

paraphrase: restating an author's idea in different words, often to share information by making the meaning clear to readers

parentheses: punctuation marks used to set off asides and explanations when the material is not essential

participial phrase: a group of words made up of a participle and its modifiers and complements that acts as an adjective

participle: a form of a verb that can act as an adjective

passive voice: the voice of a verb whose subject receives an action (*See* active voice.)

peer review: a revising technique in which writers meet with other writers to share focused feedback on a draft

pentad: a prewriting technique in which a writer analyzes a subject from five specified points: actors, acts, scenes, agencies, and purposes

period: a punctuation mark used to end a declarative sentence, an indirect question, and most abbreviations

personal pronoun: a word such as *I, me, you, we, us, he, him, she, her, they,* and *them* that refers to the person speaking; the person spoken to; or the person, place, or thing spoken about

personification a figure of speech in which a nonhuman subject is given human characteristics

persuasion: writing or speaking that attempts to convince others to accept a position on an issue of concern to the writer

phrase: a group of words without a subject and verb that functions as one part of speech

plot: the sequence of events in narrative writing

plural: the form of a word that indicates more than one item is being mentioned

poetry: a category of writing in which the final product may make deliberate use of rhythm, rhyme, and figurative language in order to express deeper feelings than those conveyed in ordinary speech (*See* prose, drama.)

point of view: the perspective, or vantage point, from which a story is told

portfolio: an organized collection of writing projects, including writing ideas, works in progress, final drafts, and the writer's reflections on the work

possessive case: the form of a noun or pronoun used to show ownership (*See* objective case, nominative case.)

prefix: one or more syllables added to the beginning of a word root (*See* root, suffix.)

preposition: a word that relates a noun or pronoun that appears with it to another word in the sentence to indicate relations of time, place, causality, responsibility, and motivation

prepositional phrase: a group of words that includes a preposition and a noun or pronoun

presenting: a stage of the writing process in which a writer shares a final draft with an audience through speaking, listening, or representing activities

prewriting: a stage of the writing process in which writers explore, choose, and narrow a topic and then gather necessary details for drafting

problem-and-solution writing: expository writing that examines a problem and provides a realistic solution

pronoun: a word that stands for a noun or for another word that takes the place of a noun

prose: a category of written language in which the end product is developed through sentences and paragraphs (*See* poetry, drama.)

publishing: a stage of the writing process in which a writer shares the written version of a final draft with an audience

punctuation: the set of symbols used to convey specific directions to the reader

purpose: the specific goal or reason a writer chooses for a writing task

Q

question mark: a punctuation mark used to end an interrogative sentence or an incomplete question

quicklist: a prewriting technique in which a writer creates an impromptu, unresearched list of ideas related to a specific topic

quotation mark: a punctuation mark used to indicate the beginning and end of a person's exact speech or thoughts

R

ratiocination: a systematic approach to the revision process that involves color-coding elements of writing for evaluation

reflective essay: autobiographical writing in which a writer shares a personal experience and then provides insight about the event

reflexive pronoun: a word that ends in -*self* or -*selves* and names the person or thing receiving an action when that person or thing is the same as the one performing the action

reflexive writing: writing generated for oneself and from oneself, not necessarily meant to be shared, in which the writer makes all decisions regarding form and purpose (*See* extensive writing.)

refrain: a regularly repeated line or group of lines in a poem or song

relative pronoun: a pronoun such as *that, which, who, whom,* or *whose* that begins a

subordinate clause and connects it to another idea in the sentence

reporter's formula: a prewriting technique in which writers gather details about a topic by generating answers to the following questions: *Who? What? Where? When?* and *Why?*

research: a prewriting technique in which writers gather information from outside sources such as library reference materials, interviews, and the Internet

research writing: expository writing that presents and interprets information gathered through an extensive study of a subject

response to literature writing: persuasive, expository, or narrative writing that presents a writer's analysis of or reactions to a published work

revising: a stage of the writing process in which a writer reworks a rough draft to improve both form and content

rhyme: the repetition of sounds at the ends of words

rhyme scheme: the regular pattern of rhyming words in a poem or stanza

rhythm: the form or pattern of words or music in which accents or beats come at certain fixed intervals

root: the base of a word (*See* prefix, suffix.)

rubric: an assessment tool, generally organized in a grid, to indicate the range of success or failure according to specific criteria

run-on sentence: two or more complete sentences punctuated incorrectly as one

S

salutation: the greeting in a formal letter

satire: writing that ridicules or holds up to contempt the faults of individuals or of groups

SEE method: an elaboration technique in which a writer presents a statement, an extension, and an elaboration to develop an idea

semicolon: a punctuation mark used to join independent clauses that are not already joined by a conjunction

sentence: a group of words with a subject and a predicate that expresses a complete thought

setting: the time and place of the action of a piece of narrative writing

short story: a brief fictional narrative told in prose

simile: a figure of speech in which *like* or *as* is used to make a comparison between two basically unrelated ideas

sonnet: a fourteen-line lyric poem with a single theme

speaker: the imaginary voice assumed by the writer of a poem

stanza: a group of lines in a poem, seen as a unit

statistics: facts presented in numerical form, such as ratios, percentages, or summaries

subject: the word or group of words in a sentence that tells whom or what the sentence is about

subordinate clause: a group of words containing both a subject and a verb that cannot stand by itself as a complete sentence

subordinating conjunction: a word used to join two complete ideas by making one of the ideas dependent on the other

suffix: one or more syllables added to the end of a word root (*See* prefix, root.)

summary: a brief statement of the main ideas and supporting details presented in a piece of writing

symbol: something that is itself and also stands for something else

T

theme: the central idea, concern, or purpose in a piece of narrative writing, poetry, or drama

thesis statement: a statement of an essay's main idea; all information in the essay supports or elaborates this idea

tone: a writer's attitude toward the readers and toward the subject

topic sentence: a sentence that states the main idea of a paragraph

topic web: a prewriting technique in which a writer generates a graphic organizer to identify categories and subcategories of a topic

topical paragraph: a paragraph that develops, explains, and supports the topic sentence related to an essay's thesis statement

transition: words, phrases, or sentences that smooth writing by indicating the relationship among ideas

transitive verb: an action verb that takes a direct object (*See* intransitive verb.)

U

unity: a quality of written work in which all the parts fit together in a complete, self-contained whole

V

verb: a word or group of words that expresses an action, a condition, or the fact that something exists while indicating the time of the action, condition, or fact

verbal: a word derived from the verb but used as a noun, adjective, or adverb (*See* gerund, infinitive, participle.)

vignette: a brief narrative characterized by precise detail

voice: the distinctive qualities of a writer's style, including diction, attitude, sentence style, and ideas

W

works-cited list: a list of the sources of a research paper, including full bibliographic references for each source named in the body of the paper (*See* bibliography.)

Index

Note: **Bold numbers** show pages on which basic definitions or rules appear.

A

a, an, the, **332**
Abbreviations, 738–741
-able, 664
Accent, **744**
accept, except, 466
Action, **82**, 691, 692
Action Verbs, **87**, **315**–316, 318–319, **744**
Active Voice, **744**
-acy, 664
Addresses, Punctuating, 570–571
Adjective Clauses, 32, **744**
Adjective Phrases, **417**–419, **744**
Adjectives, 328–339, 342–349
  adverbs modifying, **340**–341
  articles used as, **332**–333
  color-coding, 60
  commas with, 113
  comparative form of, 162
  conjunctions, connecting, 364, 366
  defined, **330**, **744**
  degrees of comparison for, **538**–541, 543, 544–545
  demonstrative, **338**
  distinguishing, 342–343
  irregular forms for, **540**–541
  possessive, **336**–337
  predicate, **407**–408
  pronouns used as, **336**–337
  proper, **334**–335
  test items for, 348–349
  underlining, 111
  See also Modifiers; Using Modifiers
Adventure Stories, 73
Adverb Clauses, 32, **211**, **744**
Adverb Phrases, **211**, **420**, **744**
Adverbs, 328–329, **340**–349
  color-coding, 60
  conjunctions connecting, 364, 366
  defined, **340**, **744**
  degrees of comparison for, **541**–545

distinguishing, **342**–343, **354**–355
in fiction, 691
here and *there* used as, 396
irregular forms for, **540**–541
starting sentences with, 451
test items for, 348–349
usage of, **340**–341
  See also Modifiers; Using Modifiers
Advertisements, 144–145
advice, advise, 466
affect, effect, 466
Agreement, 518–535
  pronoun-antecedent, 164, **528**–531, 533
  subject-verb, 162, **520**–527, 532–535
ain't, 85
Allegories, **744**
Alliteration, **744**
Allusions, **744**
Almanacs, 646, 712, 730
American Psychological Association (APA) Style, 726
Analogies, 310–311, 718
Analysis, Text, 689
and, 162, 261, **364**, 368, **522**, **528**
and, both, 366
Annotated Bibliographies, **744**
Antecedents
  compound, **528**
  possessive adjectives and, 336
  pronouns and, **300**, 301, **528**–533
  See also Pronoun-Antecedent Agreement
Anthologies, 189, 697
anti-, 663
Antonyms, 310–311
APA Style. *See* American Psychological Association (APA) Style
Apostrophes, 510, **589**–594, **744**
Appendixes, Textbook, 679
Appositive Phrases, **421**–422, **744**
Appositives, **421**, **744**
Arguments, Logical, 131
  See also Persuasion

Art, Fine
  basic elements of, **644**
  capitalizing titles of, **610**
  citing titles of, 582–583
  explained, 8
  visual, 195
  See also Humanities; Responding to Fine Art and Literature; Spotlight on the Humanities
Art Museums, 644
Articles, Definite and Indefinite, 60, **332**–333, **744**
Articles, Published, 583, 682
Assessment, 23
  See also Rubrics for Self-Assessment; Writing for Assessment
Assignment Book, 702
Assonance, **744**
at, 466
Atlases, 712
Attached Files, Electronic, **732**
Audiences
  for autobiographical writing, 55
  background and interest of, 229
  categorizing, 181
  for comparison-and-contrast essays, 157
  creating profile for, 16
  defined, **744**
  familiarity to topic of, 253
  for how-to essays, 204
  identifying, 16–17
  persuading, 130
  providing descriptions to, 104
  for short stories, 81
Audiotapes, 165
Audiovisual Tools, 9
Authors
  letters to, 247, 264
  strategies of professional, 19, 49, 73, 99, 125, 151, 175, 199, 223, 247
Autobiographical Writing, 48–71
  defined, **49**, **744**
  drafting, 56–57
  editing and proofreading, 62
  prewriting, 52–55
  publishing and presenting, 63
  revising, 58–61

Invisible Writing, **747**
-ion, 664
Irony, **747**
Irregular Verbs, **483**–487
-ism, -ist, 664
Itemizing, 55, 81, 205, **747**
its, it's, **593**
-ity, 664

J

Jargon, **747**
Journals, 3, 4, **747**
JPEG, Electronic, **733**

K

K Capacity, Electronic, **733**
K-W-L Chart, 684
Key Words, Electronic, 733, **748**
 identifying, 275
 searching with, 682, 729
kind of, sort of, 467

L

Lab Reports, 175
Labels, Field, Dictionary, 711
Language
 charged, 131
 figurative, **99**, 255, 656, 694,
  746
 influence of, 671
 loaded, 643
 nonverbal, 636, 638
 precise and persuasive, 138
 See also English Language
lay, lie, 496–497
Layering, 231, 278, **748**
Leads, **748**
 in compositions, 39
 effective, **59**
 enticing, 18
 strong, 208
Learning Logs, **748**
Legends, **748**
Legibility, 22, **748**
 cursive *vs.* print, 724
 manuscript preparation, 724
-less, 664
Letters
 to authors, 247, 264

commas with, 570–571
 to editors, 125
 personal, 612, 723
 style for, 570, 575, 722–723
Libraries, 704–707
 on-line, 730
 research reports and, **223**
Library Reference Sources, 681
lie, lay, **496**–497
like, 468
Line Graphs, 640
Linking Verbs, **87**, **316**–319, **748**
 examples of, 407
 function of, 404
Links, Electronic, **733**
Listening, Barriers to, 637
Listening Skills
 comparing and contrasting
  news sources, 9, 45
 comparing different media, 9,
  45, 642–643
 comparing personal interpretations with that of others, 638
 critical, **638**
 distinguish between fact and
  opinion, 643
 effective listening, 637
 eliminating barriers to listening,
  637
 evaluating objectivity, 45, 643
 evaluating speeches, 45, 147
 generating criteria for evaluations, 637–638
 identifying main idea and details,
  674
 monitoring listening, 637–638
 peer review and, 61, 112, 138,
  163, 187, 235, 262
 preparing to listen, 673
 set a purpose for, 673
 taking notes, summarizing, and
  organizing, 637
 vocabulary development
  through, 691, 693
 See also Speaking Skills
Listing, 55, 81, **748**
Literary Works
 capitalizing titles of, **610**
 comparisons of, **151**, 247
 readings from, 90

Literature
 grammar in. *See* Grammar in
  Literature
 interpreting, 269
 models for. *See* Models From
  Literature
 prompts for, 270–271
 responding to. *See* Responding
  to Fine Art and Literature
Logical Order, 58
Login, Electronic, **733**
Looping, 130, 156, **748**
-ly, 342, 664
Lyric Poems, **748**

M

Magazines
 capitalizing titles of, **610**
 reading, 696
 submitting work to, 63
 See also Written Works, Titles of
Main Action, 234
Main Clauses, 428, **748**
 See also Independent Clauses
Main Ideas
 clearly stating, 279
 identifying, 19
 implied, 33–34
 supporting, 35
 topic sentences and, 33–34
 See also Ideas
Main Impressions, 106
Main Points
 identifying, 152, 153
 outlining, 636
 summarizing, 637
Main Verbs, **320**–323
Making Words Agree. *See*
 Agreement
Manuals, 696
Manuscripts, Preparing, 724–728
Many Causes/Single Effect, 182
Maps
 cluster, 15, 234
 for conflict, 56, 80
 creating, 646
 types of, 639
 using electronic, 712
Meaning
 analyzing visual, 95

connecting with transition
boxes, 86
measuring and combining,
29–32, 260
varying sentence beginnings,
60, 210
See also Basic Sentence Parts;
Effective Sentences;
Sentences; Topic Sentences
Revising Word Choice, Strategies
for
circling vague modifiers, 21
color-coding technical terms,
235
color-coding verbs, 87
highlighting nouns, 61
highlighting repeated words,
163, 212
highlighting value words, 262
highlighting verbs, 187
underlining adjectives, 111
using precise and vivid words,
280
using thoughtshots, 138
Rhyme/Rhyme Schemes, **118**,
750
right, *write*, 674
Roots, Word, **662**, **750**
Round-Table Discussions, 128,
237, 250
Rubrics for Self-Assessment, **750**
in assessment writing, 282
in autobiographical writing, 63
in cause-and-effect essays, 189
in comparison-and-contrast
essays, 165
in description, 114
in how-to essays, 214
in persuasive essays, 140
in research reports, 237
in response to literature, 264
in short stories, 90
in writing process, 23
Run-on Sentences, 110, **458**–460,
750

S

Salutations, **750**
Satire, **750**

"Say-Back" Strategy, 112, 138,
235
Scanning
on standardized tests, 598
textbooks, 681
Schedules, Study, 701
Science-Fiction Stories, 73
Science, Vocabulary for, 658
Scientific Experiments, **223**
Sculptures, Titles of, 582, **610**
Search Engines, Internet, 243,
729–731, **733**
Second-Person Pronouns, **164**,
302–303
See also Personal Pronouns;
Pronouns
SEE Method. *See* Statement,
Extension, Elaboration Method
Self-Interviews, 226
Semicolons, **574**–575, **750**
in compound sentences, 31,
261
correcting run-ons with, **460**
Sensory Details, 99
adding to stories, 83
charting, 17, 105
defined, **104**
depth-charging for, 107
See also Details; Gathering Details
Sentence Combining, 29–32,
441–445
Sentence Diagraming, 620–629
compound sentences, 629
compound subjects, 622
compound verbs, 623
direct and indirect objects,
624–625
format for, 621
phrases, 626–628
simple subjects and verbs, 620
Sentences, **750**
capitalizing, **602**–604
combining, 29–32, 260, 441–447
complete, 137, 281, 412–413
complex, **428**–430
construction of, 412–413, 474–
475
declarative, **438**–440, **745**
deleting unnecessary, 279
developing style for, 42
double negatives in, **464**–465
evaluating length of, 20

exclamatory, **438**–440, **746**
fluency in, 7
fragments of, 137, **454**–457,
746
functions of, 438–440
grammatically incorrect, 85
imperative, **438**–440, **747**
interrogative, **438**–440, **747**
inverting, 396, **452**
measuring, 260
misplaced modifiers in, **461**–463
new vocabulary in, 660
outlining, 230, 256
punctuating compound, **564**–
565
run-on, **458**–460, **750**
simple, **426**, 429
starters for, 396
supporting, 35
types of, 426–429
usage problems with, 466–471
varying beginnings of, 60, 210,
451–452
varying length of, 29–32,
448–450
varying structure of, 234
See also Basic Sentence Parts;
Compound Sentences;
Effective Sentences; Revising
Sentences, Strategies for;
Topic Sentences
Sequence, for Details, 184
Serial Commas, **566**–567
Servers, Internet, **733**
set, *sit*, **498**–499
Setting
in drama, 692
in fiction, 691
Settings, for Stories, **96**, **751**
Shaping Your Writing
block method for, 158
creating main impressions for,
106
enticing leads for, 18
focusing for, 277
identifying causes and effects
for, 182
objectives for, 18
ordering events for, 56
organization plans for, 277
organizing ideas for, 106, 132
outlines for, 230, 256

graphic aids, 652–653
literature prompts, 270–271
making inferences and predictions, 698–699
modifiers, 552–553
narrative prompts, 70–71, 96–97
persuasive writing prompts, 148–149
pronouns, 516–517
proofreading, 288–289, 598–599, 616–617
revising and editing, 244–245, 360–361, 375, 434–435
sentence construction, 412–413, 474–475
strategy, organization and style, 46–47, 122–123
subject-verb agreement, 534–535
verb tenses, 504–505
verbs, 326–327
writing prompts, 10–11, 26–27
Stanzas, **751**
Statement, Extension, Elaboration (SEE) Method, 18, 278, **750**
Statements
changing questions to, 395
direct, 85
position, 132
thesis, 39, **751**
using in SEE method, 18, 278, **750**
States, Abbreviations for, 739
Statistics, 35, **751**
Steps (sequence), 184, 209
Sticky Notes, 138, 206
Still Cameras, 9
Stories
comparing, in different media, 171
organizing, 277
submitting, 90
See also Short Stories
Strategies
possible-sentence, 657
"say-back", 113, 138, 235
studying, 282
test items for, 46–47, 122–123
Structure, Revising Overall. *See* Revising Overall Structure, Strategies for

Structure, Text, 690
Student Publications, 730, 743
Student Work in Progress, Drafting
depth-charging, 107
"exploding the moment," 183, 207
layering, 231
providing support, 257
sensory sunbursts, 83
specific details, 159
supporting points, 133
thoughtshots, 57
using SEE technique, 278
Student Work in Progress, Final Drafts of
for assessment writing, 283–284
for autobiographical writing, 64–65
for cause-and-effect essays, 190–191
for comparison-and-contrast essays, 166–167
for description, 115–117
for how-to essays, 215–216
for persuasive essays, 141–143
for research reports, 238–240
for response to literature, 265–266
for short stories, 91–92
Student Work in Progress, Prewriting
blueprinting, 202
browsing, 178
conflict maps, 80
freewriting, 78
hexagons, 254–255
itemizing, 205
looping, 156
media flip-throughs, 154
pentads, 252
quicklists, 52
round-table discussions, 128, 250
self-interviews, 226
sensory details charts, 105
topic webs, 54, 180, 228, 276
trigger words, 102
See also Choosing Your Topic
Student Work in Progress, Revising
adding transitions, 280
analyzing paragraph patterns, 233

checking paragraph coherence, 136
circling supporting evidence, 135
coding for organization, 108
color-coding details, 160
color-coding sentence beginnings, 60
connecting steps, 184
creating bead charts, 84
defining technical terms, 235
highlighting drafts, 88
highlighting repeated words, 163
illuminating points, 259
logical order, 58
marking commas, 110
measuring sentences, 260
transition boxes, 86
varying sentence beginnings, 210
writing strong leads, 208
Study Skills, 700–703
Style
elements of, 42
in paintings, 644
test items for, 46–47, 122–123
See also Audiences; Purpose for Writing; Voice; Word Choice
Subject Complements, **404**–409
Subject Pronouns, **508**, 511
Subject-Verb Agreement
checking sentences for, 162
compound forms for, **522**–523
pronouns and, **524**–526, 527
simple form for, **520**–521
test items for, 534–535
Subject-Verb Order, 396, **452**
Subjects, **162**, **380**, **751**
adding, to fragments, 137
of commands or requests, **394**
complete, **386**–389
in complete sentences, 412–413
compound, 30, **390**–393, 441–442, **522**–523
forming plurals for, 520
indefinite pronouns as, **524**–526
Internet searches for, 730
of questions, **395**
simple, **380**–382, 384–385, **520**–521
with *there* or *here*, **396**

Acknowledgments

Staff Credits

The people who made up the *Prentice Hall Writing and Grammar: Communication in Action* team—representing design services, editorial, editorial services, electronic publishing technology, manufacturing and inventory planning, marketing, marketing services, market research, on-line services and multimedia development, product planning, production services, project office, and publishing processes—are listed below. Bold type denotes the core team members.

Ellen Backstrom, Betsy Bostwick, Evonne Burgess, **Louise B. Capuano**, **Sarah Carroll**, **Megan Chill**, Katherine Clarke, Rhett Conklin, Martha Conway, Harold Crudup, **Harold Delmonte**, Libby Forsyth, Ellen Goldblatt, Elaine Goldman, Jonathan Goldson, **Rebecca Graziano**, **Diana Hahn**, Rick Hickox, Kristan Hoskins, Raegan Keida, Carol Lavis, **George Lychock**, **Gregory Lynch**, William McAllister, Loretta Moser, Margaret Plotkin, Maureen Raymond, Gerry Schrenk, **Melissa Shustyk**, Annette Simmons, Robin Sullivan, Julie Tomasella, **Elizabeth Torjussen**, **Doug Utigard**

Additional Credits

Ernie Albanese, Diane Alimena, Susan Andariese, Michele Angelucci, Penny Baker, Susan Barnes, John Carle, Angelo Foccacia, Kathy Gavilanes, Beth Geschwind, Michael Goodman, Jennifer Harper, Evan Holstrom, Leanne Korszoloski, Sue Langan, Rebecca Lauth, Dave Liston, Maria Keogh, Vicki Menanteaux, Gail Meyer, Artur Mkrtchyan, LaShonda Morris, Karyl Murray, Omni-Photo Communications, Kim Ortell, Brenda Sanabria, Carolyn Sapontzis, Mildred Schulte, Slip Jig Image Research Services, Sunnyside, NY, Debi Taffet

Photo Credits

Cover: Stamp design ©United States Postal Service, All Rights Reserved; Luis Casteneda/The Image Bank; **iii:** Getty Images, Inc.; **vi:** (top) Corel Professional Photos CD-ROM™; (bottom) Corel Professional Photos CD-ROM™; **vii:** Corel Professional Photos CD-ROM™; **ix:** CORBIS/Annie Griffiths Belt; **x:** *Flight of the Thielens,* Thomas Hart Benton, ©T.H. Benton and R.P. Benton Testamentary Trusts/Licensed by VAGA, New York, NY; **xi:** Robert Holmes/CORBIS; **xii:** AP/Wide World Photos; **xiii:** Carl Purcell/Photo Researchers, Inc.; **xiv:** *Blowing Bubbles,* John Kane, The Phillips Collection; **xv:** Photofest; **xvi:** ©James Watt/Animals Animals; **xvii:** The Granger Collection, New York; **xviii:** ©1999 VCG/FPG International Corp.; **xix:** (top) Courtesy National Archives, photo no. 306-NT-111998; (bottom) Italian Government Tourist Board; **xxi:** (top) Corel Professional Photos CD-ROM™; (bottom) Corel Professional Photos CD-ROM™; **xx:** Corel Professional Photos CD-ROM™; **xxii:** (top) Corel Professional Photos CD-ROM™; (bottom) Corel Professional Photos CD-ROM™; **xxiii:** (top) Corel Professional Photos CD-ROM™; (bottom) Corel Professional Photos CD-ROM™; **xxiv:** ©The Stock Market/Jose L. Pelaez; **xxv:** (top) Lynn Saville; (bottom) Corel Professional Photos CD-ROM™; **1:** *Am Kaffeetisch (At the Coffee Table),* Carl Schmitz-Pleis, ©Christie's Images, Ltd. 1999; **2:** Myrleen Ferguson Cate/PhotoEdit; **5:** ©The Stock Market/Tom & DeeAnn McCarthy; **6:** ©The Stock Market/LWA-Dann Tardiff; **8:** Archaeological Museum, Istanbul, Turkey, ©Photograph by Erich Lessing, Art Resource, NY; **12:** Will Hart; **24:** ©Walt Disney Productions/Photofest; **28:** Dave G. Houser/CORBIS; **31:** Tony Linck/SuperStock; **35:** GK and Vikki Hart/The Image Bank; **37:** Shelley Gazin/The Image Works; **43:** David Young-Wolff/PhotoEdit; **44:** Erich Lessing/Art Resource, NY; **48:** ©The Stock Market/Rob Lewine; **50:** David Young-Wolff/PhotoEdit; **51:** The Purcell Team/CORBIS; **53:** *Great Catch,* Moses Ros/Omni-Photo Communications, Inc.; **55:** CORBIS/Annie Griffiths Belt; **64:** ©The Stock Market/Paul Barton; **65:** Craig Aurness/CORBIS; **66:** Kathy Ferguson/PhotoEdit; **68:** (top) *Self-portrait with Bandaged Ear,* Vincent van Gogh, Giraudon/Art Resource, NY; (bottom) ©Frank Capri/Saga/Archive Photos; **72:** *St. George and the Dragon,* Paolo Uccello, Art Resource, NY; **74:** Earl & Nazima Kowall/CORBIS; **75:** ©The Stock Market/Rob Matheson; **76:** *Green Violinist,* Marc Chagall, Photo by Francis G. Mayer/CORBIS, ©2001 Artist Rights Society (ARS), New York/ADAGP, Paris; **77:** *Winter Night in Vitebsk,* Marc Chagall/SuperStock, ©2001 Artist Rights Society (ARS), New York/ADAGP, Paris; **79:** *Noah's Ark,* Aaron Douglas, Fisk University Fine Art Galleries, Nashville, Tennessee; **82:** *Flight of the Thielens,* Thomas Hart Benton, ©T.H. Benton and R.P. Benton Testamentary Trusts/Licensed by VAGA, New York, NY; **85:** David Young-Wolff/PhotoEdit; **91:** Paul Ekman, Ph.D., Professor of Psychology; **92:** Russell L. Ciochon, University of Iowa; **93:** Will Hart; **94:** *Andromeda rescued from the monster by Perseus riding Pegasus,* Parisian copy, c. 1410–15 Works of Christine de Pisan (c. 1364–1430), British Library, London/The Bridgeman Art Library, London/New York; **98:** *Bok Choy and Apples,* Pamela Chin Lee/Omni-Photo Communications, Inc.; **100:** ©The Stock Market/Bill Stormont; **103:** *Farberware Coffeepot,* No. VI, Jeanette Pasin Sloan, National Museum of American Art, Washington, DC/Art Resource, NY; **104:** Robert Holmes/CORBIS; **106:** Corel Professional Photos CD-ROM™; **109:** George Lepp/CORBIS; **112:** Mary Kate Denny/PhotoEdit; **115:** Alan Oddie/PhotoEdit; **116:** Robert Brenner/PhotoEdit; **117:** Sid Greenberg/Photo Researchers, Inc.; **120:** (top) *Canyon de Chelly,* Ansel Adams; (bottom) *Among the Sierra Nevada Mountains, California,* 1868, Albert Bierstadt, National Museum of American Art, Washington, DC/Art Resource, NY; **124:** Michael Newman/PhotoEdit; **126:** AP/Wide World Photos; **129:** *Silence, Voices, Money, Danger,* Martin Wong, Courtesy of the artist; **141:** Tom Prettyman/PhotoEdit; **142:** ©The Stock Market/Paul Barton; **143:** David Young-Wolff/PhotoEdit; **144:** Artwork copyright 2000 by Phil Yeh www.ideaship.com; **146:** Scala/Art Resource, NY; **150:** ©1999 Steven M. Jones/FPG International Corp.; **152:** Carl Purcell/Photo Researchers, Inc.; **153:** Dave G. Houser/CORBIS; **155:** *Highway and Mesa,* 1982, Woody Gwyn, Courtesy of the artist; **156:** ©1999 Richard Embery/FPG International Corp.; **161:** (left) Rick Doyle/CORBIS; (right) AP/Wide World Photos/Matt York; **166:** (left) Robert Clay/Monkmeyer; (right) CORBIS/Lowell Georgia; **167:** Brendan Barraclough/Courtesy of Megan Chill; **168:** Randy Verougstraete; **170:** (top) The Metropolitan Museum of Art, The Elisha Whittelsey Collection, The Elisha Whittelsey Fund, 1972. (1972.655.1), Photograph ©1977 The Metropolitan Museum of Art (bottom) Photofest; **174:** ©Telegraph Colour Library/FPG International Corp.; **176:** ©The Stock Market/Kennan Ward;

177: (top left) CORBIS/Robert Garvey; (top right) CORBIS/Ralph A. Clevenger; (bottom left) CORBIS/Joe McDonald; (bottom center) Myrleen Ferguson/Photo-Edit; (bottom right) CORBIS/Stuart Westmorland; 179: *Blowing Bubbles,* John Kane, The Phillips Collection; 181: Jonathan Nourok/PhotoEdit; 185: Corel Professional Photos CD-ROM™; 187: PhotoDisc/ Getty Images, Inc.; 190: (left) Tony Freeman/ PhotoEdit; (right) Jeremy Walker/ Tony Stone Images; 191: PhotoDisc/Getty Images, Inc.; 192: Spencer Grant/PhotoEdit; 194: The Kobal Collection; 195: Joel Librizzi; 198: Pat Olear/ PhotoEdit; 200: Wolfgang Kaehler/ CORBIS; 203: *Practice Session,* Phoebe Beaseley, From the collection of Mr. and Mrs. E.C. Hanes, Winston-Salem, N.C.; 204: (left) Michael Newman/PhotoEdit; (right) Gary Cralle/The Image Bank; 209: David Young-Wolff/ PhotoEdit; 211: Jonathan Nourok/ PhotoEdit; 215: David Young-Wolff/PhotoEdit; 217: Pearson Education/PH College; 218: (top) (bottom) Photofest; 222: ©The Stock Market/Tom Stewart; 224: ©James Watt/Animals Animals; 227: Moses Ros/Omni-Photo Communications, Inc.; 228: Tony Arruza/CORBIS; 230: David A. Northcott/CORBIS; 232: Horned Lizard Conservation Society, Texas Chapter, P.O. Box 122, Austin, TX 78767, photo by Melanie Typaldos; 235: Corel Professional Photos CD-ROM™; 238: Louis A. Goldman/Photo Researchers, Inc.; 239: Museo Archeologico Nazionale, Naples, Italy/The Bridgeman Art Library, London/ New York; 240: Roger Wood/ CORBIS; 241: PhotoEdit; 242: Photofest; 246: ©The Stock Market/Shotgun; 248–249: Photofest; 251: *Children's Round,* Hans Thoma, Corel Professional Photos CD-ROM™; 253: Myrleen Ferguson/PhotoEdit; 255: Photo Researchers, Inc.; 256: Layne Kennedy/CORBIS; 258: ©National Gallery Collection; By kind permission of the Trustees of the National Gallery, London/CORBIS; 262: Bob Krist/CORBIS; 265: National Museums Of Scotland; 267: David Young-Wolff/ PhotoEdit; 268: (top) Photofest; (bottom) The Granger Collection, New York; 272: ©1999 VCG/FPG International Corp.; 273: Andy Whale/Tony Stone Images; 275: ©1999 Telegraph Colour Library/ FPG International Corp.; 277: David Young-Wolff/PhotoEdit; 279: Esbin/Anderson/Omni-Photo Communications, Inc.; 283: Jeff Vanuga/CORBIS; 284: Aaron Horowitz/CORBIS; 285: Mary Kate Denny/PhotoEdit/PictureQuest; 286: (top) UPI/CORBIS-BETTMANN; (bottom) Ashmolean Museum, Oxford, RK/ The Bridgeman Art Library; 291: Sandy Novak/Omni-Photo Communications, Inc.; 292–295: Corel Professional Photos CD-ROM™; 297: Courtesy National Archives, photo no. 306-NT-111998; 303: Corel Professional Photos CD-ROM™; 312: Silver Burdett Ginn; 314–317: Corel Professional Photos CD-ROM™; 318: Courtesy of the Library of Congress; 321: Italian Government Tourist Board; 328: Corel Professional Photos CD-ROM™; 331: Pearson Education Corporate Digital Archive; 332–343: Corel Professional Photos CD-ROM™; 350: Courtesy of the Library of Congress; 354–384: Corel Professional Photos CD-ROM™; 387: Courtesy of the Library of Congress; 391–436: Corel Professional Photos CD-ROM™; 439–445: NASA; 448–461: Corel Professional Photos CD-ROM™; 463: Courtesy of the Library of Congress; 465–478: Corel Professional Photos CD-ROM™; 480: CORBIS; 485: Corel Professional Photos CD-ROM™; 486: Courtesy of the Library of Congress; 490: U.S. Forestry Service; 491–492: Corel Professional Photos CD-ROM™; 495: Courtesy of the Library of Congress; 497: Missouri Division of Tourism; 499: Corel Professional Photos CD-ROM™; 506: PH College; 509–580: Corel Professional Photos CD-ROM™; 583: Joel Greenstein/Omni-Photo Communications, Inc.; 587–606: Corel Professional Photos CD-ROM™; 608: Courtesy of the Library of Congress; 611: Corel Professional Photos CD-ROM™; 631: *Concept,* Charlie Hill, SuperStock; 632: Jonathan Nourok/PhotoEdit; 635: Denis Poroy/AP/Wide World Photos; 641: Corel Professional Photos CD-ROM™; 644: *Parkville, Main Street (Missouri),* 1933, Gale Stockwell, National Museum of American Art, Washington, DC/Art Resource, NY; 650: Frank Siteman/PhotoEdit; 654: SuperStock; 659: ©The Stock Market/Jose L. Pelaez; 663: David Young-Wolff/PhotoEdit; 669–678: Peter Cade/Tony Stone Images; 687: Lynn Saville; 691: David Young-Wolff/PhotoEdit; 697: Tony Stone Images; 700: Michael Newman/PhotoEdit; 703: Corel Professional Photos CD-ROM™; 707: Mary Kate Denny/PhotoEdit; 709: CORBIS; 714: ©The Stock Market/Charles Gupton; 717: Tony Freeman/PhotoEdit